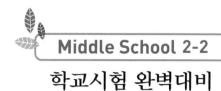
Middle School 2-2

학교시험 완벽대비

2학기 전과정

적중100plus

영어 기출문제집

중2

시사 | 박준언

Best Collection

KB086907

구성과 특징

교과서의 주요 학습 내용을 중심으로 학습 영역별 특성에 맞춰 단계별로 다양한 학습 기회를 제공하여 단원별 학습능력 평가는 물론 중간 및 기말고사 시험 등에 완벽하게 대비할 수 있도록 내용을 구성

Words & Expressions

Step1 Key Words 단원별 핵심 단어 설명 및 풀이
Key Expression 단원별 핵심 숙어 및 관용어 설명
Word Power 반대 또는 비슷한 뜻 단어 배우기
English Dictionary 영어로 배우는 영어 단어

Step2 실력평가 단원별 수시평가 대비 주관식, 객관식 문제풀이

Step3 서술형 대비 학업성취도 및 수행능력평가 대비 서술형 문제풀이

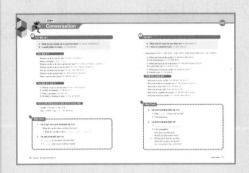

Conversation

Step1 핵심 의사소통 의사소통에 필요한 주요 표현 방법 요약
핵심 Check 기본적인 표현 방법 및 활용능력 확인

Step2 대화문 익히기 상황에 따른 대화문 활용 및 연습

Step3 기본평가 시험대비 기초 학습 능력 평가

Step4 실력평가 단원별 수시평가 대비 주관식, 객관식 문제풀이

Step5 서술형 대비 학업성취도 및 수행능력평가 대비 서술형 문제풀이

Grammar

Step1 주요 문법 단원별 주요 문법 사항과 예문을 알기 쉽게 설명
핵심 Check 기본 문법사항에 대한 이해 여부 확인

Step2 기본평가 시험대비 기초 학습 능력 평가

Step3 실력평가 단원별 수시평가 대비 주관식, 객관식 문제풀이

Step4 서술형 대비 학업성취도 및 수행능력평가 대비 서술형 문제풀이

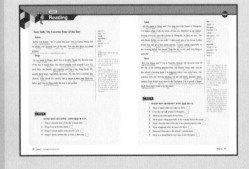

Reading

Step1 구문 분석 단원별로 제시된 문장에 대한 구문별 분석과 내용 설명
확인문제 문장에 대한 기본적인 이해와 인지능력 확인

Step2 확인학습A 빈칸 채우기를 통한 문장 완성 능력 확인

Step3 확인학습B 제시된 우리말을 영어로 완성하여 작문 능력 키우기

Step4 실력평가 단원별 수시평가 대비 주관식, 객관식 문제풀이

Step5 서술형 대비 학업성취도 및 수행능력평가 대비 서술형 문제풀이
교과서 구석구석 교과서에 나오는 기타 문장까지 완벽 학습

Composition

|영역별 핵심문제|
단어 및 어휘, 대화문, 문법, 독해 등 각 영역별 기출문제의 출제 유형을 분석하여 실전에 대비하고 연습할
수 있도록 문제를 배열

|서술형 실전 및 창의사고력 문제|
학교 시험에서 점차 늘어나는 서술형 시험에 집중 대비하고 고득점을 취득하는데 만전을 기하기 위한
학습 코너

|단원별 예상문제|
기출문제를 분석한 후 새로운 시험 출제 경향을 더하여 새롭게 출제될 수 있는 문제를 포함하여 시험에 완벽
하게 대비할 수 있도록 준비

|단원별 모의고사|
영역별, 단계별 학습을 모두 마친 후 실전 연습을 위한 모의고사

INSIGHT on the textbook .... 교과서 파헤치기

- **단어Test1~2** 영어 단어 우리말 쓰기와 우리말을 영어 단어로 쓰기
- **대화문Test1~2** 대화문 빈칸 완성 및 전체 대화문 쓰기
- **본문Test1~5** 빈칸 완성, 우리말 쓰기, 문장 배열연습, 영어 작문하기 복습 등 단계별 반복 학습을
  통해 교과서 지문에 대한 완벽한 습득
- **구석구석지문Test1~2** 지문 빈칸 완성 및 전문 영어로 쓰기

Contents

Lesson 5

Different Countries, Different Cultures

 의사소통 기능

- 길 알려 주기
  Go straight one block and turn right. It's on your left.

- 선호 묻기
  Which do you prefer, the London Eye or the Sky Garden?

 언어 형식

- 수동태
  Spain **is loved by** lots of tourists.

- so ~ that ... 구문
  It was **so** delicious **that** we all enjoyed it.

Words & Expressions

Key Words

- **abroad**[əbrɔ́ːd] 부 외국으로, 외국에서
- **artist**[áːrtist] 명 화가, 예술가
- **capital**[kǽpətl] 명 수도
- **care**[kɛər] 명 돌봄, 보살핌
- **careful**[kɛ́ərfəl] 형 조심하는, 주의 깊은
- **ceiling**[síːliŋ] 명 천장
- **cheer**[tʃiər] 동 환호하다, 갈채하다 명 환호
- **coaster**[kóustər] 명 (롤러) 코스터
- **column**[káləm] 명 기둥
- **curry**[kə́ːri] 명 카레
- **design**[dizáin] 동 설계하다, 디자인하다
- **dish**[diʃ] 명 음식, 접시
- **excuse**[ikskjúːz] 동 ~을 용서하다, 너그러이 봐주다
- **experience**[ikspíəriəns] 명 경험 동 경험하다
- **fan**[fæn] 명 팬, 부채
- **Ferris wheel** 대관람차
- **flamenco**[flɑːméŋkou] 명 플라멩코 (스페인 남부 **Andalusia** 지방 집시의 춤)
- **hamburger**[hǽmbəːrgər] 명 햄버거
- **helpful**[hélpfəl] 형 도움이 되는
- **historic**[histɔ́ːrik] 형 역사적인, 역사상 중요한
- **island**[áilənd] 명 섬
- **language**[lǽŋgwidʒ] 명 언어
- **lizard**[lízərd] 명 도마뱀
- **match**[mætʃ] 명 경기, 시합 동 어울리다

- **movement**[múːvmənt] 명 동작
- **near**[niər] 부 근처에
- **paella**[pɑːéijilə] 명 파에야
- **prefer**[prifə́ːr] 동 선호하다
- **purple**[pə́ːrpl] 명 보라색
- **right**[rait] 형 옳은, 오른쪽의
- **roll**[roul] 동 구르다, 굴리다
- **shine**[ʃain] 동 빛나다
- **slide**[slaid] 동 미끄러지다, 활주하다
- **Spain**[spein] 명 스페인
- **Spanish**[spǽniʃ] 형 스페인의 명 스페인어
- **stadium**[stéidiəm] 명 경기장
- **stop**[stɑp] 명 정거장 동 멈추다, 정지하다
- **tea**[tiː] 명 차
- **theater**[θíːətər] 명 극장
- **title**[táitl] 명 제목
- **tour**[tuər] 명 여행 동 관광하다
- **tourist**[túərist] 명 여행객
- **traditional**[trədíʃənl] 형 전통적인
- **unique**[juːníːk] 형 독특한
- **Vietnamese**[viètnəmíːz] 명 베트남어 형 베트남의
- **view**[vjuː] 명 전망, 경치
- **wave**[weiv] 동 흔들다 명 파도
- **work**[wəːrk] 동 일하다 명 작품

Key Expressions

- **across from**: ~의 맞은편에
- **be famous for**: ~로 유명하다
- **be full of**: ~으로 가득 차다
- **be known for**: ~로 알려져 있다
- **by+교통수단**: 교통수단으로 → **by bus**: 버스로, **by subway**: 지하철로, **by taxi**: 택시로
- **cheer for**: ~을 응원하다
- **far from**: ~로부터 멀리
- **get on**: ~에 타다
- **get to** 장소 명사, **get** 장소 부사: ~에 도착하다
- **go on**: (어떤 일이) 계속되다

- **How can I get there?**: 그곳에 어떻게 가니?
- **on foot**: 걸어서
- **on top of**: ~의 위에, ~의 꼭대기에
- **put off**: (시간, 날짜를) 미루다, 연기하다
- **so** 형용사/부사 **that** 주어 동사: 너무 ~해서 그 결과 …하다
- **take a tour**: 관광하다, 여행을 가다
- **try on**: 입어 보다
- **turn off**: (전기, 가스, 수도 등을) 끄다
- **turn on**: 켜다
- **Which do you prefer, A or B?**: A와 B 중 어느 것을 선호하니?

Word Power

※ 접미사 '-ful'이 붙어서 형용사가 되는 명사
- **pain**(고통) → **painful**(고통스러운)
- **color**(색깔) → **colorful**(다채로운)
- **hope**(희망, 기대) → **hopeful**(희망에 찬, 기대하는)
- **wonder**(놀라움) → **wonderful**(놀랄 만한, 멋진)

- **use**(사용) → **useful**(유용한)
- **peace**(평화) → **peaceful**(평화로운)
- **help**(도움) → **helpful**(도움이 되는)
- **care**(조심) → **careful**(조심하는)

※ 'take'를 사용한 다양한 표현들
- **take a rest**(쉬다)
- **take a walk**(산책하다)
- **take a seat**(자리에 앉다)
- **take a class**(수업을 받다)
- **take a shower**(샤워를 하다)

- **take a look** (**at**)((~을) (한 번) 보다)
- **take a chance**((모험삼아) 해 보다)
- **take a tour**(여행하다)
- **take a picture**(사진을 찍다)

English Dictionary

- **abroad**: 외국으로[에서]
  → in or to a foreign country
  외국에서 또는 외국으로

- **capital**: 수도
  → the main city of a country where its government is
  정부가 있는 한 나라의 주요 도시

- **ceiling**: 천장
  → the upper inside surface of a room
  방의 위쪽 내부 표면

- **cheer**: 환호하다, 갈채하다
  → to give a shout out of pleasure, praise, or support
  기쁨, 칭찬 또는 지지를 위해 소리를 지르다

- **curry**: 카레
  → a spicy Indian food with meat and vegetables in sauce
  소스 안에 고기와 야채가 있는 매운 인도 음식

- **excuse**: ~을 용서하다, 너그러이 봐주다
  → to forgive someone for something bad that they have done, especially something that is not very serious
  어떤 나쁜 일, 특히 매우 심각하지 않은 어떤 일을 한 사람을 용서하다

- **flamenco**: 플라멩코
  → a vigorous rhythmic dance style of the Andalusian Gypsies
  안달루시아 집시의 격렬한 리듬을 가진 춤

- **lizard**: 도마뱀
  → a reptile that has a rough skin and a long tail
  거친 피부와 긴 꼬리를 가진 파충류

- **prefer**: 선호하다
  → to like something or someone better than another
  다른 것보다 어떤 것이나 어떤 사람을 더 좋아하다

- **purple**: 보라색
  → a mixture of blue and red color
  파란색과 빨간색을 섞은 색

- **shine**: 빛나다
  → to produce bright light
  밝은 빛을 만들어 내다

- **slide**: 미끄러지다, 활주하다
  → to move along smoothly
  부드럽게 움직이다

- **Spanish**: 스페인의
  → relating to the language, people or culture of Spain
  스페인의 언어, 사람 또는 문화와 관련된

- **theater**: 극장
  → a building with a big screen or stage where many people watch movies or plays
  많은 사람들이 영화나 연극을 보는 큰 스크린이나 무대를 가진 건물

- **tour**: 여행
  → a journey for pleasure during which various places of interest are visited
  흥미 있는 다양한 장소를 방문하는 즐거움을 위한 여행

- **Vietnamese**: 베트남의
  → relating to the language, people or culture of Vietnam
  베트남의 언어, 사람 또는 문화와 관련된

- **view**: 전망, 경치
  → an outlook onto, or picture of a scene
  어떤 경치의 전망이나 풍경

01 다음 밑줄 친 부분과 의미가 가장 가까운 것을 고르시오.

> Each character has a <u>unique</u> personality.

① various ② only ③ unusual
④ common ⑤ useful

02 중요 다음 빈칸에 들어갈 말로 적절한 것은?

> _____ me, which way is the closest subway station?

① Forgive ② Accuse
③ Watch ④ Exercise
⑤ Excuse

[03~04] 다음 영영 풀이에 해당하는 단어를 고르시오.

03

> the upper inside surface of a room

① wall ② floor ③ roof
④ closet ⑤ ceiling

04

> to produce bright light

① shine ② shut ③ rise
④ tear ⑤ shake

05 서답형 다음 주어진 우리말에 맞게 빈칸을 채우시오.

(1) 파리는 프랑스의 수도이다.
➡ Paris is the _____ of France.
(2) 그녀는 스페인 친구가 있다.
➡ She has a _____ friend.

06 다음 제시된 단어를 사용하여 자연스러운 문장을 만들 수 없는 것은?

> ┌─ 보기 ─┐
> coaster column curry lizard

① The man is riding a roller _____.
② A _____ has four legs and a long tail.
③ The _____ is too spicy for me.
④ I'd like to have a room with a great _____.
⑤ The _____ was made of white marble.

07 서답형 다음 밑줄 친 부분과 의미가 가장 가까운 것을 주어진 철자로 시작하여 쓰시오.

> (1) What do you think the most typical Korean <u>food</u> is?
> (2) Rachel loves the <u>distinctive</u> smell of a rose.

➡ (1) d_____, (2) u_____

08 중요 주어진 단어 뒤에 –ful을 붙여 형용사로 만들 수 없는 것을 고르시오.

① help ② care
③ wonder ④ friend
⑤ peace

01 다음 〈보기〉처럼 짝지어진 두 단어의 관계와 같도록 빈칸에 알맞은 단어를 쓰시오.

┌─ 보기 ─┐
use – useful
└─────┘

(1) tradition : _____
(2) history : _____

02 〈보기〉에서 두 문장에 공통으로 들어갈 수 있는 단어를 찾아 쓰시오.

┌─ 보기 ─┐
cheers match experience waves
works
└─────┘

(1)
- My mom always _____ me up when I am about to give up.
- The _____ of the fans filled the stadium.

(2)
- If you like tennis, let's go to watch a tennis _____.
- Her pants _____ the blouse perfectly.

(3)
- He _____ for the company which sells smartphones.
- His paintings are beautiful _____ of art.

(4)
- Surfers are riding the huge _____.
- She _____ her hands to him when she leaves home.

(5)
- We can learn from _____.
- I can _____ different cultures when I travel to other countries.

03 다음 우리말에 맞게 주어진 단어를 바르게 배열하시오.

(1) 너는 매일 얼마나 많은 여행객들이 Boston을 방문하는지 아니?
(tourists, every, do, know, how, visit, day, Boston, you, many, ?)
➡ _____

(2) 태양은 빛나고 나무는 자란다.
(grows, the, the, tree, and, shines, sun)
➡ _____

(3) 군중은 그 희소식을 듣고 기운이 났다.
(the, news, the, cheered, at, crowd, good, up)
➡ _____

(4) 나는 외국에서 공부하고 싶다.
(study, I, abroad, to, want)
➡ _____

04 다음 빈칸에 알맞은 단어를 〈보기〉에서 골라 쓰시오. (한 단어는 한 번 밖에 사용할 수 없음)

┌─ 보기 ─┐
put take try turn
└─────┘

(1) Do you want to _____ a tour?
(2) Please _____ off the TV. It's past your bedtime.
(3) Is it possible to _____ off my trip until the 25th?
(4) Can I _____ on this jacket?

Conversation

 교과서

① 길 알려 주기

> **Go straight one block and turn right. It's on your left.** 한 블록 직진한 후 우회전하세요. 왼편에 있어요.

■ 'Where is ~?'는 '~가 어디에 있나요?'라는 의미로 길이나 위치를 물어볼 때 사용하는 표현이다. 같은 의미를 가진 표현으로 'How can I get to ~?', 'How do I get to ~?', 또는 'Is there ~ around here?' 등이 있다. 이에 대한 대답으로 'Go straight.', 'Turn left.', 'It's on your right.' 등의 표현을 이용해서 길을 알려줄 수 있다.

길 묻기

- Where is ~? (~가 어디에 있나요?)
- How can/do I get to ~? (~에 어떻게 가나요?)
- Is there ~ around here? (근처에 ~가 있나요?)
- Do you know how to get to ~? (~에 어떻게 가는지 아나요?)
- Can/Could you tell me where ~ is? (어디에 ~가 있는지 말해 줄 수 있나요?)
- Can/Could you tell me how to get to ~? (~에 어떻게 가는지 말해 줄 수 있나요?)

길 알려 주기

- Go straight. (직진하세요.)
- Turn left/right. (좌회전/우회전 하세요.)
- It is across from ~. (~ 맞은편에 있어요.)
- It is on your left/right. (왼편/오른편에 있어요.)
- You'll see ~ on your left/right. (왼편에/오른편에 ~이 보일 거예요.)
- It is around the corner. (모퉁이 지나서 있어요.)
- Walk to the end of this block. (이 블록 끝까지 가세요.)
- Go straight until you see ~. (~가 보일 때까지 직진하세요.)
- It takes ten minutes on foot. (걸어서 10분 걸려요.)
- You can't miss it. (꼭 찾을 거예요.)

장소나 위치를 나타내는 표현

- around(~ 근처에)
- across from(~ 맞은편에)
- before(~ 전에)
- in front of(~ 앞에)
- near(근처에)
- next to(~ 옆에)
- on the corner(모퉁이에)
- around the corner(모퉁이를 돌아서)

핵심 Check

1. 다음 우리말과 일치하도록 빈칸에 알맞은 말을 쓰시오.

   A: Excuse me. _____ is the _____? (실례합니다. 은행이 어디에 있나요?)

   B: _____ until you see a crosswalk. (횡단보도가 보일 때까지 직진하세요.)

   A: And then? Should I cross the street? (그 다음엔? 길을 건너야 해요?)

   B: Yes. Then, you'll see the bank. It is _____ the school.
   (네. 그러면 은행이 보일 거예요. 학교 옆에 있어요.)

② 선호 묻기

> **Which do you prefer, the London Eye or the Sky Garden?** 런던 아이와 스카이 가든 중 어느 곳을 선호하나요?

■ A와 B 둘 중에 어느 것을 더 좋아하는지 물을 때 'Which do you prefer, A or B?'라는 표현을 사용한다. prefer는 like better[more]로도 바꾸어 쓸 수 있으므로 'Which do you like better[more], A or B?'라고도 할 수 있다. which가 뒤에 나오는 명사를 수식하는 의문형용사로도 쓰일 수 있으므로 'Which place do you prefer, the London Eye or the Sky Garden?'이라고도 할 수 있다.

선호 묻기

- Which do you prefer, A or B? (A와 B 중 어느 것을 선호하니?)
- Do you prefer A to B? (너는 B보다 A를 더 좋아하니?)

■ 두 가지 중에서 어느 것을 더 선호하는지 말할 때 'I prefer A to B.', 'I think A is better than B.'로 말할 수 있다. 이때 비교 대상이 되는 than B나 to B는 생략할 수 있다. prefer A to B에서 to가 전치사이므로 뒤에 명사나 동명사가 오는 것에 유의해야 한다.

선호 표현하기

- I prefer A (to B). (나는 A를 (B보다) 선호한다.)
- I like A more than B.
- I think A is better than B.
- I think A is preferable to B.

핵심 Check

2. 다음 우리말과 일치하도록 빈칸에 알맞은 말을 쓰시오. (철자가 주어진 것도 있음)

(1) **A:** _____ do you p_____, baseball or tennis? (야구와 테니스 중에 어느 것을 더 좋아하니?)

   B: I _____ baseball _____ tennis. (나는 테니스보다 야구가 더 좋아.)

(2) **A:** Which do you _____ _____, meat or fish?

   (너는 고기와 생선 중에 어느 것을 더 좋아하니?)

   B: I _____ meat to fish. (나는 생선보다 고기를 더 좋아해.)

 Listen & Speak 1 A-1

B: Excuse me. Is the Picasso Museum ❶near here?

G: Yes. It's not ❷far from here.

B: ❸How can I get there?

G: ❹Go straight one block and turn left. It's on your right.

B: 실례할게. 이 근처에 피카소 박물관이 있니?

G: 응, 여기서 멀지 않아.

B: 그곳에 어떻게 가니?

G: 한 블록 직진한 후 좌회전해. 오른편에 있어.

❶ near: ~ 근처에

❷ far from: ~에서 먼

❸ 'How can I get to 장소 ~?'는 '~에 어떻게 가니?'란 의미로 길을 물어보는 표현이다. 여기서 there는 위에서 언급된 the Picasso Museum을 의미한다. How can I get there? (= Do you know how to get there?)

❹ Go straight.: 직진하세요. Turn left/righ.t: 좌회전/우회전 하세요. It is on your left/right.: 왼편/오른편에 있어요.

Check(√) True or False

(1) The Picasso Museum is near here.　　T ☐ F ☐

(2) The girl knows how to get to the Picasso Museum.　　T ☐ F ☐

(3) The Picasso Museum is far from here.　　T ☐ F ☐

Listen & Speak 2 A-1

B: ❶It's really hot here in Thailand. ❷Let's go to the night market and have some fresh fruit juice.

G: ❸Sounds good. ❹How do we get there?

B: ❺We can go on foot or by bus. ❻Which do you prefer?

G: I ❼prefer the bus.

B: 태국은 정말 더워. 야시장에 가서 신선한 과일 주스를 마시자.

G: 좋아. 우리는 그곳에 어떻게 가지?

B: 우리는 걸어가거나 버스를 탈 수 있어. 어느 것을 선호하니?

G: 나는 버스를 선호해.

❶ 특정한 주어가 없이 날씨, 계절, 시간 등을 나타내는 문장에서는 주어의 자리에 It을 쓸 수 있다. Thailand: 태국

❷ '~하자'라는 제안을 하고자 할 때 'Let's ~'의 표현을 쓸 수 있다. have(먹다, 마시다)는 접속사 and로 go와 연결되어 있다. night market: 야시장

❸ sound+형용사: ~하게 들리다

❹ get to 장소 명사, get 장소 부사: ~에 도착하다

❺ on foot: 걸어서, by+교통수단: 교통수단으로 → by bus: 버스로, by subway: 지하철로, by taxi: 택시로

❻ 'Which do you prefer'의 뒤에 'on foot or by bus'가 생략되어 있다. A와 B 둘 중에 어느 것을 더 좋아하는지 물을 때 'Which do you prefer, A or B?'라는 표현을 사용한다.

❼ prefer: 선호하다

Check(√) True or False

(4) They are going to walk to the night market.　　T ☐ F ☐

(5) They are in Thailand.　　T ☐ F ☐

(6) They are going to the night market to have fruit juice.　　T ☐ F ☐

Listen & Speak 1 A-2

B: Sally, I ❶need to buy some candies for Halloween. Where can I buy ❷them?

G: You ❸can buy them at Wendy's Candy Shop.

B: ❹Where is it?

G: ❺Go straight two blocks and turn right. It's across from the library.

❶ need: ~이 필요하다. need는 뒤에 to부정사(to+동사원형)를 목적어로 취할 수 있다.

❷ them = some candies

❸ can+동사원형: ~할 수 있다. at+장소: ~에서

❹ Where is ~?'는 '~가 어디에 있나요?'라는 의미로 길이나 위치를 물어볼 때 사용하는 표현이다.

❺ Go straight: 직진하세요. Turn left/right: 좌회전/우회전 하세요. across from: ~ 맞은편에

Listen & Speak 2 A-2

G: ❶What is this long dress called?

M: ❷It is an Ao dai, a type of traditional clothing from Vietnam.

G: Can I ❸try one on?

M: Sure. ❹Which do you prefer, the purple one or the yellow one?

G: The purple one, please.

❶ 이름을 모르는 물건에 대해 어떻게 말하는지 물어볼 때 'How do you say ~?', 'What is ~ called?', 'What do you call ~?' 등으로 질문할 수 있다.

❷ an Ao dai와 a type of traditional clothing from Vietnam은 동격 관계이다. traditional: 전통적인 clothing: 옷, 의복

❸ try on: 입어 보다

❹ Which do you prefer, A or B?: A와 B 중 어느 것을 선호하니? one은 an Ao dai를 의미한다.

Conversation A

M: Welcome to London City Tour. ❶Today, we'll visit famous places in London. Can you see the London Eye? ❷It's on your right. ❸It's a Ferris wheel near the River Thames. ❹The view from the London Eye is amazing. Many people visit it every year.

❶ we'll = we will (우리는 ~할 것이다) famous: 유명한 place: 장소

❷ It is on your left/right: 왼편/오른편에 있어요.

❸ Ferris wheel: 대관람차 near: ~ 근처에

❹ view: 전망, 경치 amazing: 놀라운

Conversation B

Staff: ❶How may I help you?

Hana's mom: We ❷want to enjoy a good view of London.

Hana: Where is the best place ❸to go to?

Staff: We have two great places. ❹The London Eye is a Ferris wheel and the Sky Garden is a glass garden on top of a tall building. ❺ Which do you prefer?

Hana's mom: Hmm... I ❻prefer the London Eye.

Hana: Me, too.

Staff: Good choice. You can ❼get there by bus.

Hana's mom: ❽Where is the nearest stop?

Staff: Go straight one block and turn right. It's on your left. ❾Have a good trip!

Hana: Wow, I can see all of London. Look! There is a big clock.

Hana's mom: I think that's Big Ben. ❿Why don't we go and visit it later?

Hana: That sounds great.

❶ 'May I help you?(도와드릴까요?)'에 의문사 How를 붙인 'How may I help you?'는 '무엇을 도와드릴까요?' 또는 '어떻게 도와드릴까요?'의 의미를 지닌다.

❷ want는 뒤에 to부정사(to+동사원형)를 목적어로 취할 수 있지만 동명사는 목적어로 취할 수 없다. view: 전망, 경치

❸ to부정사의 형용사적 용법으로 앞의 the best place를 수식하고 있다. the best place to go to: 가기에 가장 좋은 장소

❹ Ferris wheel: 대관람차 glass: 유리 on top of: ~의 위에, ~의 꼭대기에

❺ 문장 뒤에 'the London Eye or the Sky Garden'이 생략되어 있다. Which do you prefer, A or B?: A와 B 중 어느 것을 선호하니?

❻ prefer: 선호하다

❼ get 장소 부사: ~에 도착하다 by+교통수단: 교통수단으로 → by bus: 버스로

❽ Where is ~?: ~가 어디에 있나요? nearest: near(가까운)의 최상급, 가장 가까운 stop: 정거장

❾ Have a good trip!: 좋은 여행 하세요!

❿ 상대방에게 '함께 ~하자'는 표현으로 'Why don't we ~?'를 사용할 수 있다.

● 다음 우리말과 일치하도록 빈칸에 알맞은 말을 쓰시오.

Listen & Speak 1 A

1. **B:** Excuse me. _____ the Picasso Museum _____ here?

   G: Yes. It's not _____ _____ here.

   B: _____ can I get there?

   G: _____ _____ one block and turn _____. It's _____ your right.

2. **B:** Sally, I need _____ _____ some candies for Halloween. _____ _____ I buy them?

   G: You can buy _____ _____ Wendy's Candy Shop.

   B: _____ _____ _____ _____?

   G: _____ _____ two _____ and turn right. It's _____ _____ the library.

Listen & Speak 1 B

1. **A:** Excuse me. _____ _____ the park?

   B: _____ _____ _____ _____ _____ and turn left. It's _____ your right.

2. **A:** Excuse me. _____ _____ the school?

   B: Go _____ one block and turn left. _____ _____ your right. _____ _____ _____ the restaurant.

Listen & Talk 2 A

1. **B:** _____ really hot here in Thailand. _____ _____ to the night market and have some fresh fruit juice.

   G: Sounds _____. _____ do we _____ _____?

   B: We can go _____ _____ _____ _____ _____ _____. _____ _____ _____ _____ _____?

   G: I _____ the bus.

2. **G:** _____ _____ this long dress _____?

   M: It is an Ao dai, a _____ of _____ _____ from Vietnam.

   G: Can I _____ _____ _____?

   M: Sure. _____ _____ _____ _____, the purple one or the yellow one?

   G: The purple one, please.

해석

1. **B:** 실례할게. 이 근처에 피카소 박물관이 있니?
   G: 응, 여기서 멀지 않아.
   B: 그곳에 어떻게 가니?
   G: 한 블록 직진한 후 좌회전해. 오른편에 있어.

2. **B:** Sally야, 나는 할로윈에 필요한 사탕을 사야 해. 그것들을 어디서 살 수 있니?
   G: 넌 그것들을 Wendy's 사탕 가게에서 살 수 있어.
   B: 그곳은 어디에 있니?
   G: 두 블록 직진한 후 우회전해. 도서관 맞은편에 있어.

1. **A:** 실례합니다. 공원이 어디에 있나요?
   B: 두 블록 직진한 후 좌회전하세요. 오른편에 있어요.

2. **A:** 실례합니다. 학교가 어디에 있나요?
   B: 한 블록 직진한 후 좌회전하세요. 오른편에 있어요. 식당 맞은편이에요.

1. **B:** 태국은 정말 더워. 야시장에 가서 신선한 과일 주스를 마시자.
   G: 좋아. 우리는 그곳에 어떻게 가지?
   B: 우리는 걸어가거나 버스를 탈 수 있어. 어떤 것을 선호하니?
   G: 나는 버스를 선호해.

2. **G:** 이 긴 드레스를 뭐라고 부르나요?
   M: 그것은 베트남 전통 의상의 한 종류인 아오자이야.
   G: 제가 한 번 입어볼 수 있나요?
   M: 물론이지. 너는 보라색과 노란색 중 어떤 것을 선호하니?
   G: 보라색이요.

Listen & Talk 2 B

1. **A:** _____ _____ _____ _____, hamburgers or spaghetti?

   B: I prefer hamburgers.

2. **A:** _____ _____ _____ _____, curry _____ paella?

   B: I prefer paella.

Conversation A

M: Welcome to London City Tour. Today, _____ _____ famous places in London. Can you _____ the London Eye? It's _____ _____ _____. It's a Ferris wheel near the River Thames. The _____ _____ the London Eye is amazing. Many people visit it every year.

Conversation B

Staff: _____ may I _____ you?

Hana's mom: We _____ _____ _____ a good view of London.

Hana: Where is the best place _____ _____ _____?

Staff: We have two great places. The London Eye is a Ferris wheel and the Sky Garden is a glass garden _____ _____ _____ a tall building. _____ do you prefer?

Hana's mom: Hmm... I _____ the London Eye.

Hana: Me, too.

Staff: Good choice. You can _____ there _____ _____.

Hana's mom: _____ is the _____ _____?

Staff: Go _____ one block and _____ _____. It's on your left. Have a good trip!

Hana: Wow, I can see all of London. Look! _____ _____ a big clock.

Hana's mom: I think that's Big Ben. _____ _____ _____ go and visit it later?

Hana: That sounds great.

1. **A:** 햄버거와 스파게티 중 어느 것을 선호하니?
   B: 나는 햄버거를 선호해.

2. **A:** 카레와 파에야 중 어느 것을 선호하니?
   B: 나는 파에야를 선호해.

M: 런던 시티 투어에 오신 걸 환영합니다. 오늘 우리는 런던에서 유명한 장소들을 방문할 거예요. 런던 아이가 보이죠? 오른편에 있어요. 그것은 템스강 근처에 있는 대관람차예요. 런던 아이에서의 전망은 놀라워요. 매년 많은 사람들이 그곳을 방문해요.

직원: 무엇을 도와드릴까요?
엄마: 우리는 런던의 멋진 경치를 즐기고 싶어요.
하나: 가기에 가장 좋은 장소는 어디인가요?
직원: 두 곳이 있습니다. 런던 아이는 대관람차이고 스카이 가든은 높은 건물 꼭대기에 있는 유리 정원이에요. 어느 것을 선호하시나요?
엄마: 흠... 저는 런던 아이가 좋아요.
하나: 저도요.
직원: 좋은 선택이에요. 그곳에 버스로 갈 수 있답니다.
엄마: 가장 가까운 버스 정거장은 어디 있나요?
직원: 여기서 한 블록 직진한 후 오른쪽으로 도세요. 왼편에 있어요. 좋은 여행하세요!
하나: 와, 런던 전체를 다 볼 수 있어요. 보세요! 커다란 시계가 있어요.
엄마: 내 생각에 저것은 빅벤 같아. 우리 나중에 가서 그곳을 방문해 볼래?
하나: 좋아요.

01 다음 대화의 빈칸에 알맞은 말은?

> A: Excuse me. _____ is the park?
> B: Go straight two blocks and turn left. It's on your right.

① When ② Where ③ Who
④ What ⑤ How

02 다음 대화의 밑줄 친 부분과 바꾸어 쓸 수 <u>없는</u> 것을 고르시오.

> A: Which do you prefer, hamburgers or spaghetti?
> B: <u>I like hamburgers more than spaghetti.</u>

① I prefer hamburgers.
② I prefer hamburgers to spaghetti.
③ I think hamburgers are better than spaghetti.
④ I think I prefer hamburgers to spaghetti.
⑤ I think hamburgers are less preferable to spaghetti.

03 다음 대화의 밑줄 친 부분과 바꾸어 쓸 수 있는 것을 <u>모두</u> 고르시오.

> A: Excuse me. <u>Where is the school?</u>
> B: Go straight one block and turn left. It's on your right. It's across from the restaurant.

① How can I get to the school?
② Do you know when to go to the school?
③ How do I get to the school?
④ Could I tell you where the school is?
⑤ Is there the school around here?

04 자연스러운 대화가 되도록 순서대로 배열하시오.

> (A) How can I get there?
> (B) Go straight one block and turn left. It's on your right.
> (C) Excuse me. Is the Picasso Museum near here?
> (D) Yes. It's not far from here.

➡ _____

Conversation 시험대비 실력평가

[01~02] 다음 대화를 읽고 물음에 답하시오.

B: Excuse me. Is the Picasso Museum near here?
G: Yes. It's not far (A)_____ here.
B: (B)_____ can I get there?
G: Go straight one block and turn left. It's on your right.

01 빈칸 (A)에 알맞은 말을 고르시오.

① for ② from ③ to
④ in ⑤ into

02 빈칸 (B)에 알맞은 의문사를 고르시오.

① Where ② How ③ What
④ When ⑤ Who

[03~05] 다음 대화를 읽고 물음에 답하시오.

B: ⓐIt's really hot here in Thailand. (①) ⓑ Let's go to the night market and have some fresh fruit juice. (②)
G: Sounds good. (③)
B: ⓒWe can go on foot or by bus. (④) ⓓ What do you prefer?
G: ⓔI prefer the bus. (⑤)

03 위 대화의 ①~⑤ 중 다음 주어진 말이 들어갈 알맞은 곳은?

How do we get there?

① ② ③ ④ ⑤

04 ⓐ~ⓔ 중 어법상 어색한 것을 고르시오.

① ⓐ ② ⓑ ③ ⓒ ④ ⓓ ⑤ ⓔ

05 위 대화의 내용과 일치하지 않는 것을 고르시오.

① The boy wants to drink some fresh fruit juice.
② They are going to go to the night market.
③ They are in Thailand.
④ They are going to take a bus to go to the night market.
⑤ The girl knows how they get to the night market.

06 다음 중 짝지어진 대화가 어색한 것은?

① A: Which do you like better, Korean movies or foreign movies?
   B: I think Korean movies are better than foreign movies.
② A: Can you tell me how to get to the hospital?
   B: Of course. Go straight and turn left.
③ A: I prefer the park to the beach.
   B: OK. Let's go to the park.
④ A: Do you know how to get to the library?
   B: I'm a stranger, too. Go straight and turn left. It's next to the bookstore.
⑤ A: Which shirt do you prefer, the red one or the yellow one?
   B: I'd prefer the red one.

[07~09] 다음 대화를 읽고 물음에 답하시오.

B: Jisu, (A)[why / how] don't we watch the movie *Best Friends* on Saturday? (①)

G: Sounds good. (②)

B: (③) On Saturday there are two showings, one at five and the other at seven. Which do you prefer?

G: I prefer the seven showing. (④)

B: Okay. Then (B)[how about / let's] meet at six. (⑤)

G: Sounds good.

07 위 대화의 ①~⑤ 중 다음 주어진 말이 들어갈 알맞은 곳은?

> What time does it begin?

①   ②   ③   ④   ⑤

서답형

08 괄호 (A)와 (B)에서 알맞은 말을 골라 쓰시오.

➡ (A) _____ , (B) _____

09 위 대화를 읽고 대답할 수 없는 질문을 고르시오.

① What time does the movie *Best Friends* begin on Saturday?

② Where are they going to meet on Saturday?

③ What time does the girl prefer, five or seven?

④ What time are they going to meet on Saturday?

⑤ What movie are they going to watch on Saturday?

[10~12] 그림을 참고하여 다음 대화를 읽고 물음에 답하시오.

B: Sally, I need to buy some candies for Halloween. (A)_____ can I buy them?

G: You can buy them at Wendy's Candy Shop.

B: (B)_____ is it?

G: (C)_____ It's (D)_____ the library.

서답형

10 (A)와 (B)에 공통으로 들어갈 의문사를 쓰시오.

➡ _____

11 그림에 표시가 되어 있는 곳을 찾아 갈 때 빈칸 (C)에 알맞을 말을 고르시오.

① Go straight one block and turn left.

② Go straight one block and turn right. It's on your right.

③ Go straight two blocks and turn right.

④ Go straight two blocks and turn right. It's on your left.

⑤ Go straight two blocks and turn left.

서답형

12 그림을 참고하여 (D)에 들어갈 단어를 쓰시오. (2 단어)

➡ _____

01 다음 대화에서 어색한 부분을 찾아 고치시오.

> A: Which do you prefer, cookies or pie?
> B: Yes, I do. I prefer cookies

➡ _____

[02~03] 그림을 참고하여 다음 대화를 읽고 물음에 답하시오.

Hot Dog Stand ② Market ④
① Shoe Store ③ Community Center

> B: Excuse me. 나에게 아프리카 박물관에 가는 방법을 말해 줄 수 있니? (how, to, to, African, the, can, me, Museum, you, tell, get, ?)
> G: Sure. Go straight two blocks and turn (A)_____.
> B: Go straight and turn (A)_____. And then?
> G: It's on your (B)_____. It's (C)_____ the shoe store.
> B: I got it. Thank you very much.

02 밑줄 친 우리말에 맞게 괄호 안에 주어진 단어를 배열하여 영작하시오.

➡ _____

03 그림에 표시된 아프리카 박물관(③번)에 갈 때 (A)~(C)에 알맞은 말을 쓰시오.

➡ (A) _____, (B) _____, (C) _____

[04~05] 다음 대화를 읽고 물음에 답하시오.

> B: It's really hot here in Thailand. Let's go to the night market and have some fresh fruit juice.
> G: Sounds good. (a)How do we get there?
> B: We can go (A)____ foot or (B)____ bus. Which do you prefer?
> G: I prefer the bus.

04 빈칸 (A)와 (B)에 알맞은 전치사를 쓰시오.

➡ (A) _____, (B) _____

05 밑줄 친 (a)와 같은 의미가 되도록 주어진 단어를 이용해서 문장을 만드시오.

➡ _____ (can, how)

_____
(how, know)

_____
(how, tell, can)

[06~07] 다음 대화를 읽고 물음에 답하시오.

> A: Which do you prefer, curry (A)_____ paella?
> B: (B)I prefer paella.

06 빈칸 (A)에 알맞은 접속사를 쓰시오.

➡ _____

07 위 대화의 밑줄 친 (B)에서 생략된 것을 쓰시오.

➡ _____

Grammar

① 수동태

> Leonardo da Vinci **painted** *Mona Lisa*. 〈능동태〉 Leonardo da Vinci는 모나리자를 그렸다.
> *Mona Lisa* **was painted** by Leonardo da Vinci. 〈수동태〉 모나리자는 Leonardo da Vinci에 의해 그려졌다.

■ **수동태는 '주어+be동사+동사의 과거분사+by+행위자'**의 형식을 가지며 '…에 의해 ~되다[당하다, 받다]'라는 뜻이며, 주어가 동사가 나타내는 행위를 당하거나 행동의 영향을 받는 것을 나타낸다. 수동태 문장의 주어 자리에는 능동태 문장의 목적어가 오고, by 다음에는 능동태 문장의 주어를 쓴다. 이때 능동태 문장의 주어가 일반인이면 'by + 행위자'는 생략할 수 있다. 누가 그 동작을 했는지 중요하지 않거나 잘 모를 때, 수동태 문장으로 표현한다. 수동태는 현재, 과거, 미래 시제로 쓸 수 있고, 'be동사+동사의 과거분사'에서 be동사로 시제를 표현한다.

• This place **was used** for cooking. 이곳은 요리를 위해 사용되었다.

■ 4형식 문장의 수동태는 간접목적어와 직접목적어 각각을 주어로 하는 수동태가 가능하며 직접목적어를 주어로 한 수동태에서는 간접목적어 앞에 특정한 전치사를 써야 한다. 전치사 to를 쓰는 동사에는 'give, send, tell, teach, show, bring' 등이 있고, 전치사 for를 쓰는 동사에는 'buy, make, choose, cook, get' 등이 있으며, 전치사 of를 쓰는 동사는 'ask' 등이 있다. 또한 make, buy, read, write 등은 직접목적어를 주어로 하는 수동태만 가능하다.

• A book **was given** to Sam by Harry. 책 한 권이 Harry에 의해 Sam에게 주어졌다.

■ 조동사가 있는 문장의 수동태는 '조동사+be+p.p.' 형식을 갖는다.

• A dress **will be bought** for Jennifer by her mom. 옷이 그녀의 엄마에 의해 Jennifer에게 사주어질 것이다.

■ 목적격보어가 원형부정사인 경우, 수동태 문장에서는 to부정사로 바뀐다.

• Jack **was made** to wash the dishes by his mom. Jack은 그의 엄마에 의해 설거지하도록 시켜졌다.

■ by 이외의 전치사를 사용하는 수동태에 유의한다.

• be interested in: ~에 흥미가 있다	• be filled with: ~로 가득 차다
• be covered with: ~로 덮여 있다	• be surprised at: ~에 놀라다
• be made of: ~로 만들어지다(물리적 변화)	• be made from: ~로 만들어지다(화학적 변화)
• be satisfied with: ~에 만족하다	• be pleased with: ~에 기뻐하다

핵심 Check

1. 다음 괄호 안에서 알맞은 말을 고르시오.

(1) The building was (build / built) last year.

(2) The book (will / will be) written by Andy.

② so ~ that ... 구문

> It was **so** delicious **that** we all enjoyed it. 너무 맛있어서 우리 모두는 그것을 즐겼다.
> The movie was **so** funny **that** I laughed a lot. 그 영화는 너무 재밌어서 나는 많이 웃었다.

- **'so+형용사[부사]+that+주어+동사'** 구문은 '너무 ~해서 …하다'라는 뜻으로 원인과 결과를 나타낸다. so 뒤에 나오는 내용이 원인을 뜻하고, that 이하가 결과를 나타낸다. 이때 so는 뒤에 나오는 형용사나 부사를 강조한다.
  - I was **so** tired **that** I couldn't go out. 나는 너무 피곤해서 나갈 수 없었다.

- 'so ... that' 구문에서 that 앞에 형용사나 부사 대신 명사가 오면 so 대신 such를 쓴다.
  - There was **such** a crowd **that** we could hardly move. 사람이 아주 많아서 우리는 거의 움직이지 못했다.

- 'so that+주어+동사'는 목적을 나타내어 '~하기 위해서' 혹은 '~하도록'이라는 의미로 쓰인다. 'so ~ that ...'과 혼동하지 않도록 유의한다.
  - Record this meeting **so that** people can replay it later. 이 회의를 기록하여 나중에 재생할 수 있도록 하십시오.

- 'so+형용사[부사]+that+주어+can ~'은 '형용사[부사]+enough+to 동사원형'으로 바꿔 쓸 수 있으며, 'so+형용사[부사]+that+주어+can't ~'는 'too+형용사[부사]+to 동사원형'으로 바꿔 쓸 수 있다.
  - She was **so** kind **that** she invited me.
    = She was kind **enough to** invite me. 그녀는 너무 친절해서 나를 초대했다.
  - Emma was **so** sick **that** she couldn't lift a finger.
    = Emma was **too** sick **to** lift a finger. Emma는 너무 아파서 손가락도 까딱할 수 없었다.

핵심 Check

2. 다음 우리말에 맞게 괄호 안의 어구를 바르게 배열하시오.

(1) 물이 맑아서 밑바닥까지 보였다.

(you, the water, the bottom, could, was, see, clear, so, that)

➡ _____

(2) 그는 매우 열심히 공부해서 변호사가 되었다.

(he, he, a lawyer, became, worked, hard, that, so)

➡ _____

(3) 당신이 그곳에 제시간에 도착할 수 있게 빨리 몰겠습니다.

(you, I'll, there, time, get, drive, can, so, in, fast, that)

➡ _____

01 다음 문장에서 어법상 어색한 부분을 바르게 고쳐 쓰시오.

(1) The room cleans by him every day.

_____ ➡ _____

(2) *The Kiss* is painted by Gustav Klimt in 1908.

_____ ➡ _____

(3) Mike felt very happy that he danced.

_____ ➡ _____

(4) She exercises hard so that may stay healthy.

_____ ➡ _____

02 다음 중 어법상 바르지 <u>않은</u> 것은?

① The pictures were taken by my sister.
② The bridge was built about 50 years ago.
③ Jessica is loved by everybody.
④ The letter is sent tomorrow.
⑤ *Harry Potter* was written by J.K. Rowling.

03 다음 문장의 밑줄 친 부분 중에서 어법상 잘못된 곳을 고르시오.

①It was ②<u>too</u> ③<u>delicious</u> ④<u>that we</u> ⑤<u>all</u> enjoyed it.

04 다음 우리말에 맞게 주어진 어구를 바르게 배열하시오. (필요하면 어형을 바꿀 것)

(1) 그 물은 너무 깨끗해서 우리는 그것을 마실 수 있었다. (we, the water, was, drink, could, that, it, clean, so)

➡ _____

(2) 그는 축구 시합 중에 부상을 입었다. (he, injure, during, the soccer match)

➡ _____

01 다음 빈칸에 알맞은 것은?

> English _____ all around the world.

① speaks ② spoke
③ spoken ④ is spoken
⑤ to speak

02 다음 빈칸에 알맞은 말이 순서대로 바르게 짝지어진 것은?

> • The car _____ by him every Sunday.
> • The cap was _____ small that I couldn't wear it.

① washes – so
② is washed – too
③ is washed – so
④ was washed – too
⑤ was washed – very

03 다음 중 수동태로의 전환이 <u>어색한</u> 것은?

① Soccer fans filled the stadium.
→ The stadium was filled with soccer fans.
② They make a lot of cars in Korea.
→ A lot of cars are made in Korea.
③ Mom made me a delicious spaghetti last night.
→ A delicious spaghetti was made for me by Mom last night.
④ King Sejong invented Hangeul.
→ Hangeul was invented by King Sejong.
⑤ Jenny sent me the pictures drawn in France.
→ The pictures sent to me were drawn in France by Jenny.

서답형
04 다음 문장에서 어법상 <u>틀린</u> 부분을 찾아 바르게 고치시오.

> He is weak so that he can't swim across the river.

_____ ➡ _____

05 다음 괄호 안에서 알맞은 것을 고르시오.

(1) I was (excited / exciting) because we could watch some of the world's most famous soccer players.
(2) We (consider / are considered) blue whales to be the biggest animals.
(3) English was taught (to / for) us by Ms Green.
(4) Some interesting books were chosen (to / for) me by her.
(5) The way to the station was asked (to / of) me by the old lady.
(6) Angelina is (so / very) shy that she can't speak in front of many people.
(7) Clark was so hungry (that / what) he ate all the food.

06 다음 빈칸에 알맞은 말이 바르게 짝지어진 것을 고르시오.

> • I worked _____ hard _____ I passed the test.

① so – that ② that – so
③ too – that ④ that – too
⑤ too – to

07 다음 빈칸에 공통으로 들어갈 말로 가장 적절한 것은?

> • Does that mean that you're pleased
> _____ it?
> • I am not satisfied _____ the service.

① with   ② for   ③ in
④ at   ⑤ of

중요
08 다음 우리말에 맞게 영작한 것을 고르시오.

> • 그녀는 너무 화가 나서 얼굴이 빨개졌다.

① She was too angry to turn red.
② She was enough angry to turn red.
③ She was angry so that her face turned red.
④ She was so angry that her face turned red.
⑤ She was angry in order that her face turned red.

09 다음 우리말을 영어로 바르게 옮기지 <u>않은</u> 것은?

> Steve는 충분한 수면을 취하려고 어제 일찍 잤다.

① Steve went to bed early yesterday so that he could get plenty of sleep.
② Steve went to bed so early yesterday that he could get plenty of sleep.
③ Steve went to bed early yesterday to get plenty of sleep.
④ Steve went to bed early yesterday in order to get plenty of sleep.
⑤ Steve went to bed early yesterday so as to get plenty of sleep.

10 다음 문장을 수동태로 바르게 바꾼 것은?

> Jenny turned off the TV.

① The TV turned off Jenny.
② The TV turned off by Jenny.
③ The TV was turned off Jenny.
④ The TV was turned by Jenny.
⑤ The TV was turned off by Jenny.

고난이도
11 다음 문장을 수동태는 능동태로, 능동태는 수동태로 고치시오.

(1) Both were designed by Antoni Gaudi.
  ➡ _____
(2) This photo was taken by James.
  ➡ _____
(3) Her mom made her a beautiful dress.
  ➡ _____
(4) The book fair will be held in Seoul.
  ➡ _____
(5) By whom is it considered to be dangerous?
  ➡ _____

서답형
12 다음 괄호 안에서 알맞은 말을 고르시오.

(1) Vietnam is (so / such) beautiful that you should come someday.
(2) I was in (so / such) a hurry that I could not pay you a visit.
(3) The park was so noisy that I (shouldn't / couldn't) rest.
➡ (1) _____ (2) _____ (3) _____

13 다음 중 두 문장을 서로 바꿔 쓸 수 없는 것은?

① *Romeo and Juliet* was written by Shakespeare.

→ Shakespeare wrote *Romeo and Juliet*.

② Morris bought his son a new suit last week.

→ A new suit was bought for his son by Morris last week.

③ They showed the public the photos taken by him.

→ The photos taken by him were shown to the public.

④ The thief forced Judy to hand over the money.

→ Judy was forced to hand over the money by the thief.

⑤ Our teacher made us do our homework.

→ We were made do our homework by our teacher.

14 다음 중 어법상 올바른 문장을 모두 고르시오.

① He was seen put the bag on the table by Ann.

② He was read the storybook every night by his mom.

③ Melbourne is well known for its beautiful ocean roads.

④ It was so a nice day that we went for a walk.

⑤ Julie is so kind that everybody likes her.

서답형

15 다음 문장에서 어법상 어색한 부분을 바르게 고쳐 다시 쓰시오.

(1) The World Wide Web(www) invented by Tim Berners-Lee in 1989.

_____ ➡ _____

(2) The car accident was happened last night.

_____ ➡ _____

(3) I was too careless to trust such a man.

_____ ➡ _____

[16~18] 다음 두 문장이 같은 의미가 되도록 빈칸에 알맞은 말을 고르시오.

16

> Harry chose Christine some books.
> = Some books _____ Christine by Harry.

① chose
② were choosing
③ were chosen
④ were chosen to
⑤ were chosen for

17 중요

> I heard him sing.
> = He _____ by me.

① heard singing
② was singing
③ was heard sing
④ heard sing
⑤ was heard to sing

18

> Because she is very sick, she can't move.
> = She is _____ she can't move.

① too sick that
② to sick too
③ so sick that
④ sick so that
⑤ very sick that

01 다음 문장을 수동태는 능동태로, 능동태는 수동태로 고치시오.

(1) The painting was stolen by someone last week.

➡ _____

(2) Its size and unique design impressed me.

➡ _____

(3) Eva heard Peter open the window.

➡ _____

(4) Angie will give me a present on my birthday.

➡ _____

(5) Cathy took care of the baby.

➡ _____

02 주어진 두 문장을 한 문장으로 만들 때, 빈칸에 알맞은 말을 3단어로 쓰시오.

(1) • I was very stupid.

　• I made the mistake.

➡ I was _____ I made the mistake.

(2) • He is very tall.

　• He can touch the ceiling.

➡ He is _____ touch the ceiling.

(3) • Alice was really shocked.

　• She couldn't say even a word.

➡ Alice was _____ say even a word.

03 다음 우리말을 so와 that을 이용하여 영어로 쓸 때 빈칸에 알맞은 말을 쓰시오.

(1) Robert는 시험에 합격하기 위해서 열심히 공부했다.

➡ Robert studied _____ he could pass the exam.

(2) Robert는 열심히 공부해서 시험에 합격할 수 있었다.

➡ Robert studied _____ he could pass the exam.

04 다음 문장에서 어법상 어색한 부분을 바르게 고쳐 다시 쓰시오.

(1) Cake is made of flour, milk, eggs and sugar.

➡ _____

(2) The shirts are ironed by John tomorrow morning.

➡ _____

(3) Mike was seen be hit by a car by Ms. Brown.

➡ _____

(4) Our dog was ran over by a truck.

➡ _____

(5) The matter will discussed by us tomorrow.

➡ _____

05 다음 문장을 같은 뜻을 갖는 문장으로 바꿔 쓸 때 빈칸을 알맞게 채우시오.

(1) The test was so easy that I could pass it.
→ The test was _____ pass.

(2) Andrew speaks _____ I can't understand him.
→ Andrew speaks too fast for me to understand.

06 다음 우리말을 괄호 안에 주어진 어휘를 이용하여 영작하시오.

(1) 그 소설은 Ernest Hemingway에 의해 씌여졌다. (novel, write)
➡ _____

(2) 최초의 월드컵은 1930년 우루과이에서 열렸다. (Uruguay, the first World Cup, take place)
➡ _____

(3) Laura는 그녀의 딸에게 동화책을 읽어 주었다. (read, a fairy tale book) (수동태로 쓸 것.)
➡ _____

(4) Kimberly는 그 소식을 듣고 낙담했다. (disappointed, the news)
➡ _____

(5) 너는 Allie가 노래하는 것을 들었니? (hear, sing) (수동태로 쓸 것.)
➡ _____

(6) 너무나도 추워서 그는 감기에 걸렸다. (cold, catch a cold)
➡ _____

07 괄호 안의 어휘를 사용하여 주어진 문장을 같은 의미가 되도록 다시 쓰시오.

(1) Claire got up so late that she couldn't get on the train. (too)
➡ _____

(2) Chuck spoke too low for me to hear. (so, can)
➡ _____

(3) Bill was so smart that he could solve the difficult math problems. (enough)
➡ _____

(4) Juliet is rich enough to buy the house. (so, can)
➡ _____

08 다음 문장을 주어진 어휘로 시작하여 다시 쓰시오.

(1) My grandmother made the sweater for me. (the sweater)
➡ _____

(2) Does she clean these rooms every day? (are)
➡ _____

(3) Mariel made Dan prepare dinner. (Dan)
➡ _____

(4) Your recent success pleased Joakim a lot. (Joakim)
➡ _____

Reading

교과서

My Happy Days in Spain

by Park Jinwoo

My family traveled to Spain this summer. Spain is loved by lots of
tourists. We visited many interesting places.

Our trip started in Madrid. Madrid is the capital and is famous for
soccer. We went to a stadium to watch a soccer match. My sister and I
were excited because we could watch some of the world's most famous
soccer players.

The stadium was full of soccer fans. As we watched the match, we
cheered by singing songs, waving our hands, and shouting with the
other fans.

After we toured Madrid, we went to Seville. While we walked around
the city, we saw many historic buildings. We visited a flamenco
museum and watched a flamenco dance. A woman in a red dress was
dancing the flamenco with wonderful movements.

travel 여행하다
tourist 여행객, 관광객
capital 수도
stadium 경기장
match 경기, 시합
be famous for ~으로 유명하다
be full of ~으로 가득 차다
cheer 응원하다
historic 역사적인
flamenco 플라멩코(격정적인 스페인 춤)
movement 동작

 확인문제

● 다음 문장이 본문의 내용과 일치하면 T, 일치하지 않으면 F를 쓰시오.

1 Jinwoo's family traveled to Spain last summer. ☐

2 Jinwoo's family trip started in Madrid. ☐

3 Jinwoo's family went to a stadium to watch a soccer match. ☐

4 The stadium was full of the world's most famous soccer players. ☐

5 Jinwoo's family went to Seville after they toured Madrid. ☐

6 Jinwoo's family watched a flamenco dance on the street. ☐

For dinner, we ate paella. It is a traditional Spanish dish with rice,
vegetables, meat, and seafood. It tasted like fried rice in Korea. It was
so delicious that we all enjoyed it.

In Barcelona, we took a tour of Park Guell and Sagrada Familia.
Both were designed by Antoni Gaudi. In Park Guell, we saw some of
Gaudi's creative works like a colorful lizard.

After Park Guell, we visited Sagrada Familia. Work on the building
started in 1883 and is still going on today. I was impressed by its size
and unique design. The ceiling inside Sagrada Familia shone like the
night sky with bright stars. Its stone columns stood like big trees. At
Park Guell and Sagrada Familia I could feel Gaudi's creativity and his
love of nature.

Traveling in Spain was a wonderful experience. While I was there, I
learned a lot about Spain. I want to visit the country again.

traditional 전통적인
paella 파에야
Spanish 스페인의
lizard 도마뱀
take a tour 여행하다, 관광하다
still 여전히
unique 특별한
ceiling 천장
shine 빛나다
column 기둥
go on 계속하다
impress 감명을 주다
experience 경험

확인문제

● 다음 문장이 본문의 내용과 일치하면 T, 일치하지 않으면 F를 쓰시오.

1   For dinner, Jinwoo's family ate paella. ☐

2   Paella tasted like kimchi pancake in Korea. ☐

3   Park Guell and Sagrada Familia were designed by Antoni Gaudi. ☐

4   Jinwoo's family visited Park Guell after Sagrada Familia. ☐

5   Jinwoo was impressed by the size and unique design of Sagrada Familia. ☐

6   The ceiling inside Sagrada Familia stood like big trees. ☐

● 우리말을 참고하여 빈칸에 알맞은 말을 쓰시오.

1 My _____ _____ in Spain – _____ Park Jinwoo

2 My family _____ _____ Spain this summer.

3 Spain _____ _____ _____ lots of tourists.

4 We _____ many _____ places.

5 _____ _____ started in Madrid.

6 Madrid is the capital and _____ _____ _____ soccer.

7 We went to a stadium _____ _____ a soccer match.

8 My sister and I _____ _____ because we could watch some of _____ _____ _____ _____ _____ _____.

9 The stadium _____ _____ _____ soccer fans.

10 As we watched the match, we cheered _____ _____ songs, waving our hands, and _____ with the other fans.

11 _____ we toured Madrid, we went to Seville.

12 _____ we _____ _____ the city, we saw many historic buildings.

13 We _____ a flamenco museum and _____ a flamenco dance.

14 A woman _____ _____ _____ was dancing the flamenco _____ _____ _____.

1 스페인에서의 행복한 날들 – 박진우

2 나의 가족은 이번 여름에 스페인을 여행했다.

3 스페인은 수많은 관광객들에게 사랑받는다.

4 우리는 여러 흥미로운 장소를 방문했다.

5 우리의 여행은 마드리드에서 시작했다.

6 마드리드는 수도이며 축구로 유명하다.

7 우리는 축구 경기를 보기 위해서 경기장으로 갔다.

8 나의 여동생과 나는 세계에서 가장 유명한 축구 선수 몇몇을 볼 수 있었기 때문에 신이 났다.

9 경기장은 축구 팬들로 가득 차 있었다.

10 우리는 경기를 보는 동안 노래를 부르고, 손을 흔들고, 다른 팬들과 함께 소리를 치며 응원을 했다.

11 마드리드를 여행하고 난 후, 우리는 세비야로 갔다.

12 우리는 도시를 걸어다니는 동안, 역사상 중요한 많은 건물들을 보았다.

13 우리는 플라멩코 박물관을 방문해서 플라멩코 춤을 보았다.

14 빨간 드레스를 입은 여자가 멋진 동작으로 플라멩코를 추고 있었다.

15 _____ dinner, we ate paella.

16 It is a _____ _____ _____ _____ rice, vegetables, meat, and seafood.

17 It _____ _____ fried rice in Korea.

18 It was _____ delicious _____ we all enjoyed it.

19 In Barcelona, we _____ _____ _____ _____ Park Guell and Sagrada Familia.

20 Both _____ _____ _____ Antoni Gaudi.

21 In Park Guell, we saw some of Gaudi's _____ _____ _____ a colorful lizard.

22 _____ Park Guell, we visited Sagrada Familia.

23 Work on the building started in 1883 and _____ _____ _____ _____ today.

24 I _____ _____ _____ its size and unique design.

25 The ceiling inside Sagrada Familia _____ _____ the night sky with bright stars.

26 Its stone columns _____ _____ big trees.

27 At Park Guell and Sagrada Familia I could feel Gaudi's _____ and _____ _____ _____ _____.

28 _____ in Spain was _____ _____ _____.

29 _____ I was there, I learned _____ _____ about Spain.

30 I want _____ _____ the country again.

---

15 저녁 식사로 우리는 파에야를 먹었다.

16 그것은 쌀과 채소, 고기, 해산물이 들어간 전통적인 스페인 요리이다.

17 그것은 한국의 볶음밥과 같은 맛이 났다.

18 너무 맛있어서 우리 모두는 그것을 즐겼다.

19 바르셀로나에서 우리는 구엘 공원과 사그라다 파밀리아를 둘러보았다.

20 두 곳 모두 Antoni Gaudi에 의해 설계되었다.

21 구엘 공원에서 우리는 형형색색의 도마뱀과 같은 몇몇 Gaudi의 창의적인 작품들을 보았다.

22 구엘 공원을 본 다음, 우리는 사그라다 파밀리아를 방문했다.

23 건물 공사는 1883년에 시작되었고 오늘날까지도 여전히 진행 중이다.

24 나는 건물의 크기와 독특한 디자인에 감명 받았다.

25 사그라다 파밀라아 안의 천장은 밝은 별이 있는 밤하늘처럼 빛났다.

26 돌기둥은 큰 나무처럼 서 있었다.

27 구엘 공원과 사그라다 파밀리아에서 나는 Gaudi의 창의성과 자연에 대한 사랑을 느낄 수 있었다.

28 스페인 여행은 훌륭한 경험이었다.

29 나는 그곳에서 스페인에 대해 많은 것을 배웠다.

30 나는 그 나라를 다시 방문하고 싶다.

● 우리말을 참고하여 본문을 영작하시오.

1 ▶ 스페인에서의 행복한 날들 – 박진우
➡ _____

2 ▶ 나의 가족은 이번 여름에 스페인을 여행했다.
➡ _____

3 ▶ 스페인은 수많은 관광객들에게 사랑받는다.
➡ _____

4 ▶ 우리는 여러 흥미로운 장소를 방문했다.
➡ _____

5 ▶ 우리의 여행은 마드리드에서 시작했다.
➡ _____

6 ▶ 마드리드는 수도이며 축구로 유명하다.
➡ _____

7 ▶ 우리는 축구 경기를 보기 위해서 경기장으로 갔다.
➡ _____

8 ▶ 나의 여동생과 나는 세계에서 가장 유명한 축구 선수 몇몇을 볼 수 있었기 때문에 신이 났다.
➡ _____

9 ▶ 경기장은 축구 팬들로 가득 차 있었다.
➡ _____

10 ▶ 우리는 경기를 보는 동안 노래를 부르고, 손을 흔들고, 다른 팬들과 함께 소리를 치며 응원을 했다.
➡ _____

11 ▶ 마드리드를 여행하고 난 후, 우리는 세비야로 갔다.
➡ _____

12 ▶ 우리는 도시를 걸어다니는 동안, 역사상 중요한 많은 건물들을 보았다.
➡ _____

13 ▶ 우리는 플라멩코 박물관을 방문해서 플라멩코 춤을 보았다.
➡ _____

14 ▶ 빨간 드레스를 입은 여자가 멋진 동작으로 플라멩코를 추고 있었다.
➡ _____

15 ▶ 저녁 식사로 우리는 파에야를 먹었다.
➡ _____

16 ▶ 그것은 쌀과 채소, 고기, 해산물이 들어간 전통적인 스페인 요리이다.
➡ _____

17 그것은 한국의 볶음밥과 같은 맛이 났다.

➡ _____

18 너무 맛있어서 우리 모두는 그것을 즐겼다.

➡ _____

19 바르셀로나에서 우리는 구엘 공원과 사그라다 파밀리아를 둘러보았다.

➡ _____

20 두 곳 모두 Antoni Gaudi에 의해 설계되었다.

➡ _____

21 구엘 공원에서 우리는 형형색색의 도마뱀과 같은 몇몇 Gaudi의 창의적인 작품들을 보았다.

➡ _____

22 구엘 공원을 본 다음, 우리는 사그라다 파밀리아를 방문했다.

➡ _____

23 건물 공사는 1883년에 시작되었고 오늘날까지도 여전히 진행 중이다.

➡ _____

24 나는 건물의 크기와 독특한 디자인에 감명 받았다.

➡ _____

25 사그라다 파밀라아 안의 천장은 밝은 별이 있는 밤하늘처럼 빛났다.

➡ _____

26 돌기둥은 큰 나무처럼 서 있었다.

➡ _____

27 구엘 공원과 사그라다 파밀리아에서 나는 Gaudi의 창의성과 자연에 대한 사랑을 느낄 수 있었다.

➡ _____

28 스페인 여행은 훌륭한 경험이었다.

➡ _____

29 나는 그곳에서 스페인에 대해 많은 것을 배웠다.

➡ _____

30 나는 그 나라를 다시 방문하고 싶다.

➡ _____

[01~03] 다음 글을 읽고 물음에 답하시오.

My family traveled to Spain this summer. Spain is loved by ⓐlots of tourists. We visited many interesting places.

Our trip started in Madrid. Madrid is the capital and is famous for soccer. We went to a stadium to watch a soccer match. My sister and I were excited because we could watch some of the world's most famous soccer players.   <I = Park Jinwoo>

01 위 글의 종류로 알맞은 것을 고르시오.

① review   ② essay
③ traveler's journal   ④ biography
⑤ article

02 위 글의 밑줄 친 ⓐlots of와 바꿔 쓸 수 없는 말을 모두 고르시오.

① a few   ② many
③ plenty of   ④ a number of
⑤ much

03 위 글의 내용과 일치하지 않는 것은?

① 진우의 가족은 이번 여름에 스페인을 여행했다.
② 수많은 관광객들이 스페인을 사랑한다.
③ 진우의 가족 여행은 마드리드에서 끝났다.
④ 마드리드는 스페인의 수도이다.
⑤ 진우와 여동생은 세계에서 가장 유명한 축구 선수 몇몇을 볼 수 있었다.

[04~06] 다음 글을 읽고 물음에 답하시오.

After we toured Madrid, we went to Seville. ⓐWhile we walked around the city, we saw many historic buildings. We visited a flamenco museum and watched a flamenco dance. A woman in a red dress was ⓑdancing the flamenco with wonderful movements.
            <we = Jinwoo's family>

서답형
04 Where did Jinwoo's family see many historic buildings? Fill in the blanks with the suitable words.

➡ They _____.

05 위 글의 밑줄 친 ⓐWhile과 같은 의미로 쓰인 것을 고르시오.

① While Tom is very good at science, his brother is hopeless.
② While I was waiting at the bus stop, three buses went by.
③ I've read fifty pages, while he's read only twenty.
④ They chatted for a while.
⑤ The walls are green, while the ceiling is white.

06 아래 <보기>에서 위 글의 밑줄 친 ⓑdancing과 문법적 쓰임이 같은 것의 개수를 고르시오.

┌─── 보기 ├───
① His hobby is collecting stamps.
② They aren't playing tennis.
③ She heard someone calling her name.
④ I like baking cookies.
⑤ The girl standing at the door is my sister.
└─────────────────

① 1개   ② 2개   ③ 3개   ④ 4개   ⑤ 5개

[07~10] 다음 글을 읽고 물음에 답하시오.

For dinner, we ate paella. It is a traditional Spanish dish with rice, vegetables, meat, and seafood. It tasted like fried rice in Korea. ⓐ 너무 맛있어서 우리 모두는 그것을 즐겼다.

In Barcelona, we took a tour of Park Guell and Sagrada Familia. Both were designed by Antoni Gaudi. In Park Guell, we saw some of Gaudi's creative ⓑworks like a colorful lizard. <we = Jinwoo's family>

서답형

07 위 글의 밑줄 친 ⓐ의 우리말에 맞게 주어진 어휘를 이용하여 9단어로 영작하시오.

It, so, delicious

➡ _____

08 위 글의 밑줄 친 ⓑworks와 같은 의미로 쓰인 것을 고르시오.

① He works at a small shop.
② She collected Beethoven's piano works.
③ They started engineering works there.
④ This pill works on me.
⑤ The machine works 24 hours a day.

중요

09 위 글의 주제로 알맞은 것을 고르시오.

① how to make a traditional Spanish dish
② the difference of paella and fried rice
③ the introduction of the dish and places Jinwoo's family enjoyed
④ the historical importance of Park Guell and Sagrada Familia
⑤ the reason why Gaudi designed Park Guell and Sagrada Familia

서답형

10 다음 빈칸 (A)와 (B)에 알맞은 단어를 넣어 구엘 공원에 대한 소개를 완성하시오.

It is in (A)_____ and was designed by Antoni Gaudi. Jinwoo's family saw some of Gaudi's creative works such as (B)_____ _____ _____ there.

[11~13] 다음 인터뷰를 읽고 물음에 답하시오.

How much do you know about Vietnam?

The capital of Vietnam is Hanoi. ⓐ Vietnamese is spoken there. Pho and banh mi are popular dishes in Vietnam. Every year lots of tourists visit Halong Bay and Nha Trang. Halong Bay has 1,969 islands and Nha Trang is well known ⓑ its beautiful beaches. Vietnam is so beautiful that you should come someday.

서답형

11 위 글의 밑줄 친 ⓐ를 능동태로 바꾸시오.

➡ _____

12 위 글의 빈칸 ⓑ에 들어갈 알맞은 전치사를 고르시오.

① to   ② for   ③ by
④ as   ⑤ in

중요

13 위 글의 내용과 일치하지 <u>않는</u> 것은?

① 베트남의 수도는 하노이이다.
② 베트남에서는 주로 영어를 사용한다.
③ pho와 banh mi가 인기 있는 요리이다.
④ 하롱베이는 1,969개의 섬을 가지고 있다.
⑤ 나트랑은 아름다운 해변으로 잘 알려져 있다.

[14~17] 다음 글을 읽고 물음에 답하시오.

After Park Guell, we visited Sagrada Familia. Work on the building started in 1883 and is still going on today. I was impressed by its size and unique design. The (A)[ceiling / sealing] inside Sagrada Familia shone like the night sky with bright stars. Its stone columns stood like big trees. At Park Guell and Sagrada Familia I could feel Gaudi's creativity and his love of nature. ⓐTraveling in Spain was a wonderful experience. While I was (B)[there / in there], I learned a lot (C)[about / of] Spain. I want to visit the country again.   <I = Park Jinwoo>

서답형

14 위 글의 괄호 (A)~(C)에서 문맥이나 어법상 알맞은 낱말을 골라 쓰시오.

➡ (A)_____ (B)_____ (C)_____

15 위 글의 밑줄 친 ⓐ와 바꿔 쓸 수 있는 문장을 모두 고르시오.

① It was a wonderful experience to travel in Spain.
② That was a wonderful experience to travel in Spain.
③ To traveling in Spain was a wonderful experience.
④ To travel in Spain was a wonderful experience.
⑤ That was a wonderful experience traveling in Spain.

서답형

16 본문의 내용과 일치하도록 다음 빈칸 Ⓐ와 Ⓑ에 알맞은 단어를 쓰시오.

To Jinwoo, the Ⓐ_____ and Ⓑ_____ _____ of Sagrada Familia were impressive.

17 위 글을 읽고 답할 수 없는 질문은?

① Where did Jinwoo's family visit before they visited Sagrada Familia?
② When did work on Sagrada Familia start?
③ Why is work on Sagrada Familia still going on today?
④ What were the columns of Sagrada Familia made of?
⑤ Where could Jinwoo feel Gaudi's creativity and his love of nature?

[18~19] 다음 글을 읽고 물음에 답하시오.

For dinner, we ate paella. It is a traditional Spanish dish with rice, vegetables, meat, and seafood. (①) It tasted like fried rice in Korea. (②) It was so delicious that we all enjoyed it. (③) In Barcelona, we took a tour of Park Guell and Sagrada Familia. (④) In Park Guell, we saw some of Gaudi's creative works like a colorful lizard. (⑤)   <we = Jinwoo's family>

중요

18 위 글의 흐름으로 보아, 주어진 문장이 들어가기에 가장 적절한 곳은?

Both were designed by Antoni Gaudi.

①   ②   ③   ④   ⑤

19 위 글을 읽고 대답할 수 없는 질문은?

① What are the ingredients of paella?
② What's the recipe of paella?
③ In Barcelona, what did Jinwoo's family do?
④ By whom were Park Guell and Sagrada Familia designed?
⑤ In Park Guell, what did Jinwoo's family see?

[20~23] 다음 글을 읽고 물음에 답하시오.

After Park Guell, we visited Sagrada Familia. Work on the building started in 1883 and is still ⓐ<u>going on</u> today. I was impressed by its size and unique design. The ceiling inside Sagrada Familia shone like the night sky with bright stars. Its stone columns stood like big trees. At Park Guell and Sagrada Familia I could feel Gaudi's ___ⓑ___ and his love of nature.

Traveling in Spain was a wonderful experience. While I was there, I learned a lot about Spain. I want to visit the country again.

<I = Park Jinwoo>

20 위 글의 밑줄 친 ⓐgoing on과 바꿔 쓸 수 있는 말을 고르시오.

① stopping   ② remaining
③ increasing   ④ continuing
⑤ staying

서답형

21 위 글의 빈칸 ⓑ에 create를 알맞은 형태로 쓰시오.

➡ _____

22 위 글의 마지막 부분에서 알 수 있는 진우의 심경으로 가장 알맞은 것을 고르시오.

① satisfied   ② frightened
③ bored   ④ ashamed
⑤ disappointed

중요

23 위 글의 내용과 일치하지 <u>않는</u> 것은?

① 진우의 가족은 사그라다 파밀리아 보다 구엘 공원을 먼저 보았다.
② 사그라다 파밀리아의 건물 공사는 1883년에 시작되었다.

③ 사그라다 파밀리아 안의 천장은 밝은 별이 있는 밤하늘처럼 빛났다.
④ 진우는 구엘 공원에서 Gaudi의 창의성과 자연에 대한 사랑을 느낄 수 있었다.
⑤ 진우는 스페인 여행 중에 스페인에 대해 많은 것을 배웠다.

[24~26] 다음 글을 읽고 물음에 답하시오.

How much do you know about Australia?

The capital of Australia is Canberra. English ___ⓐ___ there. Meat pie and lamington are popular dishes in Australia. Every year lots of tourists visit Sydney and Melbourne. Sydney has the Sydney Opera House and Melbourne is well known for its beautiful ocean roads. ⓑ<u>오스트레일리아는 너무 멋져서 당신은 언젠가 그곳을 꼭 방문해야 합니다.</u>

서답형

24 위 글의 빈칸 ⓐ에 speak를 알맞은 형태로 쓰시오.

➡ _____

서답형

25 위 글의 밑줄 친 ⓑ의 우리말에 맞게 한 단어를 보충하여, 주어진 어휘를 알맞게 배열하시오.

is / you / that / visit / Australia / someday / wonderful / it / should

➡ _____

서답형

26 위 글을 참조하여 다음 빈칸 (A)와 (B)에 들어갈 알맞은 말을 쓰시오.

The tourist attraction of Sydney is (A)____ ____ ____ ____ and Melbourne is famous for its beautiful (B)____ ____ .

*tourist attraction: 관광명소

[01~03] 다음 글을 읽고 물음에 답하시오.

My family traveled to Spain this summer. ⓐ Spain is loved by lots of tourists. We (A)[visited / visited to] many interesting places.

Our trip started in Madrid. ⓑMadrid is the capital and is famous for soccer. We went to a stadium (B)[watching / to watch] a soccer match. My sister and I (C)[was / were] excited because we could watch some of the world's most famous soccer players.

01 위 글의 밑줄 친 ⓐ를 능동태로 고치시오.

➡ _____

02 위 글의 괄호 (A)~(C)에서 어법상 알맞은 낱말을 골라 쓰시오.

➡ (A)_____ (B)_____ (C)_____

03 위 글의 밑줄 친 ⓑ를 다음과 같이 바꿔 쓸 때 빈칸에 들어갈 알맞은 말을 쓰시오.

➡ Madrid is the capital and is _____ _____ for soccer.

[04~06] 다음 글을 읽고 물음에 답하시오.

The stadium was full of soccer fans. As we watched the match, we cheered by ⓐsing songs, ⓑwave our hands, and ⓒshout with the other fans.

⎽ⓓ we toured Madrid, we went to Seville. While we walked around ⓔthe city, we saw many historic buildings. We visited a flamenco museum and watched a flamenco dance. A woman in a red dress was dancing the flamenco with wonderful movements.

<we = Jinwoo's family>

04 위 글의 밑줄 친 ⓐ~ⓒ를 각각 알맞은 형태로 쓰시오.

➡ ⓐ_____ ⓑ_____ ⓒ_____

05 다음과 같은 뜻이 되도록 위 글의 빈칸 ⓓ에 들어갈 알맞은 말을 쓰시오.

We toured Madrid before we went to Seville.

➡ _____

06 위 글의 밑줄 친 ⓔthe city가 가리키는 것을 본문에서 찾아 쓰시오.

➡ _____

[07~09] 다음 글을 읽고 물음에 답하시오.

For dinner, we ate paella. It is a traditional ⎽ⓐ dish with rice, vegetables, meat, and seafood. ⓑIt felt like fried rice in Korea. It was so delicious that we all enjoyed it.

In Barcelona, we ⓒtook a tour of Park Guell and Sagrada Familia. Both were designed by Antoni Gaudi. In Park Guell, we saw some of Gaudi's creative works like a colorful lizard.

<we = Jinwoo's family>

07 위 글의 빈칸 ⓐ에 Spain을 알맞은 형태로 쓰시오.

➡ _____

08 위 글의 밑줄 친 ⓑ에서 흐름상 어색한 부분을 찾아 고치시오.

➡ _____

09 위 글의 밑줄 친 ⓒtook a tour of를 한 단어로 고치시오.

➡ _____

[10~12] 다음 글을 읽고 물음에 답하시오.

For dinner, we ate paella. It is a traditional Spanish dish with rice, vegetables, meat, and seafood. ⓐ한국의 볶음밥과 같은 맛이 났다. ⓑIt was so delicious that we all enjoyed it.

In Barcelona, we took a tour of Park Guell and Sagrada Familia. Both were designed by Antoni Gaudi. In Park Guell, we saw some of Gaudi's creative works ⓒlike a colorful lizard.

10 위 글의 밑줄 친 ⓐ의 우리말에 맞게 한 단어를 보충하여, 주어진 어휘를 알맞게 배열하시오.

Korea / rice / it / fried / in / tasted

➡ _____

11 위 글의 밑줄 친 ⓑIt이 가리키는 것을 본문에서 찾아 쓰시오.

➡ _____

12 위 글의 밑줄 친 ⓒlike를 두 단어로 바꿔 쓰시오.

➡ _____

[13~14] 다음 글을 읽고 물음에 답하시오.

ⓐAfter Park Guell, we visited Sagrada Familia. Work on the building started in 1883 and is still going on today. I was (A)[impressing / impressed] by its size and unique design. The ceiling inside Sagrada Familia (B)[shone / shined] like the night sky with bright stars. Its stone columns (C)[were stood / stood] like big trees. At Park Guell and Sagrada Familia I could feel Gaudi's creativity and his love of nature.

13 위 글의 밑줄 친 ⓐ를 before[Before]를 사용하여 고치시오.

➡ _____
_____

14 위 글의 괄호 (A)~(C)에서 문맥이나 어법상 알맞은 낱말을 골라 쓰시오.

➡ (A) _____ (B) _____ (C) _____

[15~17] 다음 글을 읽고 물음에 답하시오.

The stadium was full of soccer fans. As we watched the match, we cheered by singing songs, waving our hands, and shouting with the other fans.

After we toured Madrid, we went to Seville. While we walked around the city, we saw many ___ⓐ___ buildings. We visited a flamenco museum and watched a flamenco dance. ⓑ A woman in a red dress was dancing the flamenco with wonderful movements.

<we = Jinwoo's family>

15 위 글의 빈칸 ⓐ에 history를 알맞은 형태로 쓰시오.

➡ _____

16 위 글의 밑줄 친 ⓑ를 다음과 같이 고칠 때 빈칸에 들어갈 알맞은 관계대명사를 쓰시오.

➡ A woman _____ was wearing a red dress

17 위 글을 읽고 진우의 가족이 마드리드와 세비야에서 한 일을 각각 우리말로 쓰시오.

➡ 마드리드: _____
세비야: _____

Enjoy Writing

How much do you know about Vietnam?

The capital of Vietnam is Hanoi. Vietnamese is spoken there. Pho and banh
→ 능동태: They speak Vietnamese there.

mi are popular dishes in Vietnam.
요리

Every year lots of tourists visit Halong Bay and Nha Trang.
= a lot of. many

Halong Bay has 1,969 islands and Nha Trang is well known for its beautiful
be well known for: ~으로 잘 알려져 있다

beaches. Vietnam is so beautiful that you should come someday.
so ~ that ...: 너무 ~해서 …하다

구문해설 · capital: 수도 · Vietnamese: 베트남어 · popular: 인기 있는 · island: 섬
· someday: 언젠가

당신은 베트남에 대해서 얼마나 많이 알고 있나요? 베트남의 수도는 하노이입니다. 그곳에서는 베트남어가 사용됩니다. 베트남에서는 pho(퍼, 베트남 쌀국수)와 banh mi(반미, 바게트 빵으로 만든 샌드위치)가 인기 있는 요리입니다. 매년 많은 관광객들이 하롱베이와 나트랑을 방문합니다. 하롱베이는 1,969개의 섬을 가지고 있고 나트랑은 아름다운 해변으로 잘 알려져 있습니다. 베트남은 너무 아름다워서 당신은 언젠가 꼭 오셔야 합니다.

Project Step 3

My group chose Hong Kong for a trip. Hong Kong is loved by many people
choose의 과거형   love의 수동태 be loved by: ~에 의해서 사랑받다

who want to do fun activities. We'll have great experiences at Mong Kok
주격 관계대명사   want는 to부정사를 목적어로 취한다.

Market, Victoria Peak, and Ocean Park.

구문해설 · choose 선택하다 · activity 활동 · experience 경험

우리 모둠은 여행 장소로 홍콩을 선택했다. 홍콩은 재밌는 활동을 하고 싶어 하는 많은 사람들에게 사랑받는다. 우리는 몽콕 시장, 빅토리아 피크 그리고 오션 파크에서 멋진 경험을 할 것이다.

Wrap Up

I was moved by a book. The title of the book is *The Old Man and the Sea*. It
수동태(= A book moved me.)

was written by Ernest Hemingway.
수동태(= Ernest Hemingway wrote it.)

The story was so great that I read it many times.
'so+형용사[부사]+that+주어+동사'의 형태로 원인과 결과를 나타낸다.(= Because the story was very great. I read
it many times.)

구문해설 · title 제목 · many times 여러 번

나는 어떤 책에 감동을 받았다. 그 책의 제목은 '노인과 바다'이다. 그것은 Ernest Hemingway에 의해 씌여졌다. 그 이야기는 너무도 대단해서 나는 그것을 여러 번 읽었다.

01 다음 중 밑줄 친 부분의 뜻풀이가 바르지 <u>않은</u> 것은?

① Let's <u>cheer for</u> our national team! (응원하다)

② How can I <u>get</u> there? (얻다, 획득하다)

③ I <u>designed</u> my house. (설계했다)

④ The <u>tea</u> has a wonderful flavor. (차)

⑤ What's the <u>title</u> of this song? (제목)

02 다음 제시된 단어를 사용하여 자연스러운 문장을 만들 수 없는 것은? (형태 변화 가능)

┌─ 보기 ─┐
| prefer   roll   slide   wave |
└──────┘

① The children are _____ over the frozen lake.

② The baby _____ to her mom.

③ They are _____ a big ball.

④ How about _____ a tour of the city then?

⑤ I _____ tea to coffee.

[03~04] 두 문장에 공통으로 들어갈 수 있는 단어를 쓰시오.

03

• Most people want to be famous _____ something.

• He is well known _____ his cool dancing and great music.

04

• Aren't there any ways I can get _____ the next flight to Sydney?

• It takes about ten minutes _____ foot.

05 다음 주어진 우리말에 맞게 빈칸을 채우시오.

(1) King Sejong is a _____ figure. (세종 대왕은 역사상 중요한 인물이다.)

(2) They went to the _____ last night. (그들은 어젯밤 극장에 갔다.)

(3) He looked up at the _____. (그는 천장을 올려다봤다.)

(4) They _____ _____ the players and shake hands with the _____. (그들은 선수들을 응원하고 팬들과 악수합니다.)

[06~07] 다음 대화를 읽고 물음에 답하시오.

B: Sally, I need to buy some candies for Halloween. (A)_____

G: You can buy them at Wendy's Candy Shop.

B: (B)_____

G: Go straight two blocks and turn right. It's across from the library.

06 빈칸 (A)와 (B)에 알맞은 것끼리 짝지어진 것을 고르시오.

(A) / (B)

① What can I buy? / Where is it?

② What can I buy? / Is there a candy shop near here?

③ How can I buy them? / What can I buy?

④ Where can I buy them? / What can I buy?

⑤ Where can I buy them? / Where is it?

07 위 대화의 내용과 일치하지 <u>않는</u> 것을 고르시오.

① Sally knows where Wendy's Candy Shop is.
② To get to Wendy's Candy Shop, the boy should go straight 2 blocks and turn right.
③ They are going to buy candies at Wendy's Candy Shop.
④ The boy wants to buy some candies for Halloween.
⑤ Wendy's Candy Shop is across from the library.

08 다음 그림과 일치하지 <u>않는</u> 대화를 고르시오.

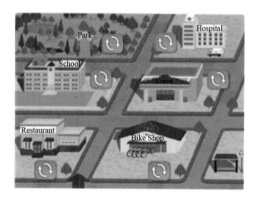

① A: Excuse me. Where is the bike shop?
   B: Go straight. It's on your right.
② A: Excuse me. Where is the school?
   B: Go straight one block and turn left. It's on your right. It's across from the restaurant.
③ A: Excuse me. Where is the hospital?
   B: Go straight two blocks and turn right. It's on your left. It's across from the school.
④ A: Excuse me. Where is the park?
   B: Go straight two blocks and turn left. It's on your right.
⑤ A: Excuse me. Where is the cinema?
   B: Go straight one block and turn right. It's on your left. It's across from the bike shop.

[09~11] 다음 대화를 읽고 물음에 답하시오.

Staff: How may I help you?
Hana's mom: We want to enjoy a good view of London. (①)
Hana: Where is the best place to go to?
Staff: We have two great places. (②) Which do you prefer? (③)
Hana's mom: Hmm... (④) I prefer the London Eye.
Hana: Me, too.
Staff: Good choice. You can get there by bus.
Hana's mom: 가장 가까운 버스 정거장은 어디 있나요?
Staff: (⑤) Go straight one block and turn right. It's on your left. Have a good trip!
Hana: Wow, I can see all of London. Look! There is a big clock.
Hana's mom: I think that's Big Ben. Why don't we go and visit it later?
Hana: That sounds great.

09 다음 영영풀이에 해당하는 단어를 대화에서 찾아 쓰시오.

> what you can see from a particular place or position, especially beautiful countryside

➡ _____

10 위 대화의 ①~⑤ 중 주어진 문장이 들어갈 알맞은 곳은?

> The London Eye is a Ferris wheel and the Sky Garden is a glass garden on top of a tall building.

①   ②   ③   ④   ⑤

11 밑줄 친 우리말을 주어진 단어를 이용하여 영작하시오. (5단어)

➡ _____ (stop, near)

12 주어진 문장 다음에 이어질 대화의 순서를 바르게 배열하시오.

> Let's go on a trip abroad.

> (A) I prefer Bangkok. The city is so colorful that we should go there.
> (B) Okay. Let's go there.
> (C) Which city do you prefer, Bangkok or Taiwan?

➡ _____

Grammar

13 다음 중 어법상 올바르지 <u>않은</u> 것은?

① The beautiful song was written by my friend.
② The plane stopped flying and turned into a restaurant.
③ Mary wasn't made to clean her room by her sister.
④ It rained so hard that we put off the picnic.
⑤ It was so noisy in the hall that I couldn't hear him speak.

14 다음 우리말을 주어진 어휘를 이용하여 영작했을 때 빈칸에 적절한 말을 쓰시오.

> • 그 문제들은 너무 어려워서 우리는 풀 수 없었다. (difficult, solve)
> = (1) The problems were _____
> _____ .
> = (2) The problems were _____
> _____ .

15 다음 빈칸에 알맞은 말이 바르게 짝지어진 것은?

> • The students were made _____ their homework by the teacher.
> • John started _____ early that he didn't need to hurry up.

① to do – so
② to do – very
③ did – too
④ doing – so
⑤ doing – very

16 Which is grammatically correct?

① The room was too cold that David turned on the heater.
② This story was so funny which I laughed a lot.
③ Arnold got up so late that he didn't miss the train.
④ The movie was so sad that Rachel cried a lot.
⑤ John is kind so that everyone likes him.

17 다음 두 문장의 의미가 같도록 빈칸에 들어갈 알맞은 말을 쓰시오.

> Because the city's night view is so beautiful, we should see it.
> = The city's night view is _____ we should see it.

18 다음 그림을 보고 괄호 안에 주어진 단어를 이용하여 빈칸을 채우시오.

(1) (*The Old Man and the Sea*, write)

→ *The Old Man and the Sea*
_____ Ernest Hemingway.

(2) (The pyramids, build)

→ The pyramids_____ the ancient Egyptians.

19 다음 중 밑줄 친 부분의 쓰임이 <u>어색한</u> 것은?

① The ball was caught by Jenny.
② Nha Trang is well known for its beautiful beaches.
③ I was written a long letter by my girl friend.
④ The animals in the cage were looked after by Aybek.
⑤ At first, I was surprised at the number of side dishes.

20 괄호 안에 주어진 단어를 이용하여 다음을 영작하시오.

(1) 전화는 누구에 의해 발명되었니? (the telephone, invent, 6 단어)

　➡ _____

(2) 그 집의 지붕은 눈으로 덮여 있었다. (the house, the roof, cover, 9 단어)

　➡ _____

(3) 너무 어두워서 아무 것도 보이지 않았다. (nothing, see, could, dark, that, 9 단어)

　➡ _____

(4) 그 달리기 선수는 너무 빨리 달려서 아무도 그를 따라잡을 수 없었다. (the runner, that, nobody, catch, 12 단어)

　➡ _____

Reading

[21~23] 다음 글을 읽고 물음에 답하시오.

My family traveled to Spain this summer. Spain is loved by lots of tourists. We visited many interesting places.

Our ⓐtrip started in Madrid. Madrid is the capital and is famous for soccer. We went to a stadium ⓑto watch a soccer match. My sister and I were excited because we could watch some of the world's most famous soccer players.　　　　<I = Park Jinwoo>

21 위 글의 밑줄 친 ⓐtrip과 바꿔 쓸 수 있는 단어를 본문에서 찾아 알맞은 형태로 쓰시오. (2개)

　➡ _____, _____

22 위 글의 밑줄 친 ⓑto watch와 to부정사의 용법이 다른 것을 <u>모두</u> 고르시오.

① There's no plan to build a new office.

② He cannot be a gentleman to do such a thing.

③ She lived long to see her son come back.

④ I have lots of homework to do today.

⑤ He promised me to do the dishes.

23 위 글의 내용과 일치하도록 다음 빈칸 (A)와 (B)에 알맞은 단어를 쓰시오.

During their trip to Spain, Jinwoo's family went to (A)_____ _____ in Madrid and watched (B)_____ _____ _____.

[24~25] 다음 글을 읽고 물음에 답하시오.

The stadium was full of soccer fans. ⓐAs we watched the match, we cheered by singing songs, waving our hands, and shouting with the other fans.

After we toured Madrid, we went to Seville. While we walked around the city, we saw many historic buildings. We visited a flamenco museum and watched a flamenco dance. A woman in a red dress was dancing the flamenco with wonderful movements.

<we = Jinwoo's family>

24 위 글의 밑줄 친 ⓐAs와 같은 의미로 쓰인 것을 고르시오.

① As he is honest, everyone liked him.

② Leave the papers as they are.

③ He came up to me as I was speaking.

④ I respect him as a teacher.

⑤ As she grew older, she became more beautiful.

25 위 글의 내용과 일치하지 <u>않는</u> 것은?

① Jinwoo's family watched a soccer match in Madrid.

② Jinwoo's family walked around the soccer stadium.

③ Jinwoo's family saw many historic buildings.

④ Jinwoo's family watched a flamenco dance.

⑤ A woman wearing a red dress was dancing the flamenco.

[26~27] 다음 글을 읽고 물음에 답하시오.

For dinner, we ate paella. It is a traditional Spanish dish with rice, vegetables, meat, and seafood. It tasted like (A)[frying / fried] rice in Korea. It was so delicious that we all enjoyed it.

In Barcelona, we took a tour of Park Guell and Sagrada Familia. ⓐBoth (B)[was / were] designed by Antoni Gaudi. In Park Guell, we saw some of Gaudi's (C)[common / creative] works like a colorful lizard.

26 위 글의 괄호 (A)~(C)에서 문맥이나 어법상 알맞은 낱말을 골라 쓰시오.

➡ (A)_____ (B)_____ (C)_____

27 위 글의 밑줄 친 ⓐBoth가 가리키는 것을 본문에서 찾아 쓰시오.

➡ _____

[01~02] 다음 빈칸에 공통으로 들어갈 수 있는 단어를 쓰시오.

출제율 95%

01

> • I'd like to _____ a walk with my dog.
> • You can _____ a class or join a club together after school.
> • They liked to _____ a tour of the castle.

출제율 90%

02

> • The 'Mona Lisa' was painted _____ Leonardo Da Vinci.
> • It took about 5 hours _____ bus.

출제율 95%

03 다음 우리말 해석에 맞게 빈칸을 완성하시오. (철자가 주어진 경우 그 철자로 시작할 것)

(1) All the people in the concert hall stood and _____ loudly. (콘서트홀에 있던 모든 사람이 일어나 크게 환호했다.)

(2) Would you like to _____ _____ this? (이걸 입어 보시겠습니까?)

(3) India is f_____ _____ curry. (인도는 카레로 유명하다.)

(4) Can I _____ there _____ _____? (거기까지 걸어서 갈 수 있나요?)

출제율 90%

04 다음 영영풀이에 해당하는 말을 주어진 철자로 시작하여 쓰고, 알맞은 것을 골라 문장을 완성하시오.

> • f_____ : a vigorous rhythmic dance style of the Andalusian Gypsies
> • p_____ : a mixture of blue and red color
> • V_____ : relating to the language, people or culture of Vietnam

(1) He enjoys dancing the _____.

(2) She learned _____ to get a job in Vietnam.

(3) She wore a dress of dark _____.

[05~06] 다음 대화를 읽고 물음에 답하시오.

> B: It's really hot here in Thailand. (①)
> G: Sounds good. (②) How do we get there? (③)
> B: We can go on foot or by bus. (④) Which do you prefer? (⑤)
> G: I prefer the bus.

출제율 100%

05 위 대화의 ①~⑤ 중 주어진 문장이 들어갈 알맞은 곳은?

> Let's go to the night market and have some fresh fruit juice.

①   ②   ③   ④   ⑤

출제율 85%

06 위 대화를 읽고 대답할 수 없는 질문을 고르시오.

① How will they go to the night market?

② Which does the boy prefer, bus or taxi?

③ Where are they?

④ Where are they going to go?

⑤ What are they going to drink?

[07~10] 그림을 참고하여 다음 대화를 읽고 물음에 답하시오.

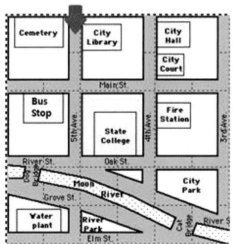

Staff: (A)_____ may I help you?

Hana's mom: We want to enjoy a good view of London. (①)

Hana: 가기에 가장 좋은 장소는 어디인가요?

Staff: We have two great places. The London Eye is a Ferris wheel and the Sky Garden is a glass garden on top of a tall building. (B)_____ do you prefer?

Hana's mom: Hmm... (②) I prefer the London Eye.

Hana: Me, too. (③)

Staff: Good choice. You can get there by bus. (④)

Hana's mom: (C)_____ is the nearest stop?

Staff: (D) _____ Have a good trip!

Hana: Wow, I can see all of London. Look! There is a big clock.

Hana's mom: I think that's Big Ben. (⑤)

Hana: That sounds great.

✏️ 출제율 100%

07 위 대화의 ①~⑤ 중 주어진 문장이 들어갈 알맞은 곳은?

> Why don't we go and visit it later?

①   ②   ③   ④   ⑤

✏️ 출제율 90%

08 빈칸 (A)~(C)에 알맞은 의문사를 쓰시오.

➡ (A)_____ (B)_____ (C)_____

✏️ 출제율 90%

09 밑줄 친 우리말과 의미가 같도록 영작하시오. (8단어)

➡ _____

✏️ 출제율 95%

10 그림을 보고 빈칸 (D)에 들어갈 말을 주어진 단어를 이용해 두 문장으로 쓰시오.

➡ _____

(block, go, your, turn, it)

✏️ 출제율 90%

11 주어진 문장 다음에 이어질 대화의 순서를 바르게 배열하시오.

> Excuse me. Can you tell me how to get to the Africa Museum?

(A) Go straight and turn right. And then?

(B) It's on your left. It's across from the shoe store.

(C) Sure. Go straight two blocks and turn right.

(D) I got it. Thank you very much.

➡ _____

출제율 95%

12 다음 중 태의 전환이 잘못된 것은?

① Those pictures were not painted by the artist.
→ The artist did not paint those pictures.
② Frank showed her the album.
→ The album was shown for her by Frank.
③ Edvard Munch painted *The Scream* in 1893.
→ *The Scream* was painted by Edvard Munch in 1893.
④ They saw Marianne dance on the stage.
→ Marianne was seen to dance on the stage by them.
⑤ Teresa took good care of the little babies.
→ Good care was taken of the little babies by Teresa.

출제율 90%

13 다음 두 문장을 'so ~ that' 구문을 사용하여 한 문장으로 연결하시오.

(1) • The shoes look really great.
• Sandra wants to buy them.
➡ _____

(2) • The stereo was very loud.
• It was impossible to sleep.
➡ _____

출제율 90%

14 다음 괄호 안의 어휘를 이용하여 빈칸에 알맞은 말을 쓰시오.

(1) The story was _____ I read it many times. (great)
(2) Many soldiers _____ in the war. (kill)

[15~17] 다음 글을 읽고 물음에 답하시오.

My family traveled to Spain this summer. Spain is loved by lots of tourists. We visited many interesting places.

Our trip started in Madrid. Madrid is the ⓐ capital and is famous for soccer. We went to a stadium to watch a soccer match. My sister and I were ___(A)___ because we could watch some of the world's most famous soccer players.

출제율 95%

15 위 글의 빈칸 (A)에 들어갈 알맞은 말을 고르시오.

① interesting
② disappointed
③ upset
④ excited
⑤ amusing

출제율 85%

16 위 글의 밑줄 친 ⓐcapital과 같은 의미로 쓰인 것을 고르시오.

① The cause of business failure is lack of capital.
② Paris is the fashion capital of the world.
③ He set up a business with a starting capital of £100,000.
④ I want to invest my capital in your business.
⑤ Please write in capital letters.

출제율 95%

17 What is Madrid well known for? Answer in English in a full sentence. (6 words)

➡ _____

[18~20] 다음 글을 읽고 물음에 답하시오.

The stadium was full of soccer fans. As we watched the match, we cheered by ⓐsinging songs, waving our hands, and shouting with the other fans.

ⓑAfter we toured of Madrid, we went to Seville. While we walked around the city, we saw many historic buildings. We visited a flamenco museum and watched a flamenco dance. A woman in a red dress was dancing the flamenco with wonderful movements.

<we = Jinwoo's family>

18 출제율 90%

위 글의 밑줄 친 ⓐsinging과 문법적 쓰임이 다른 것을 모두 고르시오.

① My son is singing songs on the musical stage.

② She is good at singing songs.

③ Do you know the boy singing songs there?

④ My dream is singing songs on the musical stage.

⑤ They always enjoy singing songs together.

19 출제율 90%

위 글의 밑줄 친 ⓑ에서 어법상 틀린 부분을 찾아 고치시오.

➡ _____

20 출제율 95%

위 글을 읽고 대답할 수 없는 질문은?

① Where did Jinwoo's family cheer?

② What did Jinwoo's family do when they cheered?

③ What did Jinwoo's family see while they walked around Seville?

④ How long did Jinwoo's family watch a flamenco dance?

⑤ What was the flamenco dancer wearing?

[21~24] 다음 글을 읽고 물음에 답하시오.

___ⓐ___ dinner, we ate paella. It is a traditional Spanish dish ___ⓑ___ rice, vegetables, meat, and seafood. It tasted like fried rice in Korea. It was so delicious that we all enjoyed it.

In Barcelona, we took a tour of Park Guell and Sagrada Familia. Both were designed by Antoni Gaudi. In Park Guell, we saw some of Gaudi's ___ⓒ___ works like a colorful lizard.

21 출제율 100%

위 글의 빈칸 ⓐ와 ⓑ에 들어갈 전치사가 바르게 짝지어진 것은?

① To – with　　② For – by

③ In – from　　④ To – by

⑤ For – with

22 출제율 90%

다음 중 paella의 재료가 아닌 것을 고르시오.

① 쌀　　　② 채소

③ 고기　　④ 국수

⑤ 해산물

23 출제율 95%

위 글의 빈칸 ⓒ에 create를 알맞은 형태로 쓰시오.

➡ _____

24 출제율 90%

By whom were Park Guell and Sagrada Familia designed? Answer in English.

➡ _____

서술형 실전문제

01 밑줄 친 부분에서 어법상 어색한 부분을 찾아 고치시오.

> M: Welcome to London City Tour. Today, we'll visit famous places in London. Can you see the London Eye? <u>It's on your right.</u> It's a Ferris wheel near the River Thames. <u>The view from the London Eye are amazing.</u> Many people visit it every year.

➡ _____

_____

02 그림을 보고 (A)와 (B)에 공통으로 들어갈 문장을 쓰시오. (목적지는 표시된 ③) (총 7 단어)

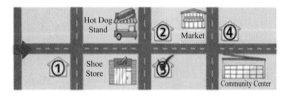

> B: Excuse me. Can you tell me how to get to the Africa Museum?
> G: Sure. (A)_____
> B: (B)_____ And then?
> G: It's on your left. It's across from the shoe store.
> B: I got it. Thank you very much.

➡ _____

03 주어진 문장 다음에 이어질 대화의 순서를 바르게 배열하시오.

> Jisu, why don't we watch the movie *Best Friends* on Saturday?

> (A) Sounds good. What time does it begin?
> (B) I prefer the seven showing.

> (C) On Saturday there are two showings, one at five and the other at seven. Which do you prefer?
> (D) Okay. Then let's meet at six.

➡ _____

04 그림을 참고하여 어떤 것을 더 선호하는지 묻는 질문을 완성하시오.

Roller Coaster **Scary House**

> A: _____
> _____
> B: I prefer the Scary House.

05 주어진 문장이 같은 뜻이 되도록 빈칸에 알맞은 말을 쓰시오.

(1) Because the city is so colorful, we should go there.
= The city is _____ we should go there.

(2) Emily was very tired. So, she couldn't do the dishes.
= Emily was _____ she couldn't do the dishes.
= Emily was _____ do the dishes.

06 다음 주어진 문장을 능동태는 수동태로, 수동태는 능동태로 바꾸시오.

(1) Hong Kong is loved by many people who want to do fun activities.

➡ _____

_____

(2) What did she promise to do last weekend?

➡ _____

(3) Ms. Grace taught us physics last year.

➡ _____

_____

[07~09] 다음 글을 읽고 물음에 답하시오.

ⓐThe stadium was full of soccer fans. As we watched the match, we cheered by singing songs, waving our hands, and shouting with the other fans.

After we toured Madrid, we went to Seville. While we walked around the city, we saw many historic buildings. We visited a flamenco museum and watched a flamenco dance. ⓑ빨간 드레스를 입은 여자가 멋진 동작으로 플라멩코를 추고 있었다.

<we = Jinwoo's family>

07 위 글의 밑줄 친 ⓐ를 다음과 같이 바꿔 쓸 때 빈칸에 들어갈 알맞은 말을 쓰시오.

➡ The stadium _____ _____ _____ soccer fans.

08 위 글의 밑줄 친 ⓑ의 우리말에 맞게 한 단어를 보충하여, 주어진 어휘를 알맞게 배열하시오.

movements / the flamenco / was / wonderful / dancing / a red dress / with / a woman

09 본문의 내용과 일치하도록 다음 빈칸 (A)와 (B)에 알맞은 단어를 쓰시오.

Jinwoo's family went to (A)_____ after they toured Madrid and they saw (B)_____ _____ _____ while they walked around the city.

[10~12] 다음 글을 읽고 물음에 답하시오.

For dinner, we ate paella. It is a traditional Spanish dish with rice, vegetables, meat, and seafood. It tasted ⓐ fried rice in Korea. It was so delicious that we all enjoyed it.

In Barcelona, we took a tour of Park Guell and Sagrada Familia. ⓑBoth were designed by Antoni Gaudi. In Park Guell, we saw some of Gaudi's creative works ⓒ a colorful lizard.

10 위 글의 빈칸 ⓐ와 ⓒ에 공통으로 들어갈 알맞은 말을 쓰시오.

➡ _____

11 다음 빈칸 (A)~(D)에 알맞은 단어를 넣어 paella에 대한 소개를 완성하시오.

Paella which is a traditional (A)_____ dish tastes like fried rice in (B)_____ and its ingredients are (C)_____, _____, _____ and (D)_____.

12 위 글의 밑줄 친 ⓑ를 능동태로 고치시오.

➡ _____

창의사고력 서술형 문제

01 주어진 정보와 그림을 이용해 빈칸에 알맞은 말을 쓰시오..

```
        BANK   POLICE   STORE
               STATION
              Main Street
LIBRARY  POST  DRUGSTORE  MOVIE        HOSPITAL
First Street  OFFICE            THEATER   Second Street
         SCHOOL    RESTAURANT
             Central Avenue
              TRAIN                    CHURCH
             STATION
```

<조건>

1. A는 은행을 가고 싶어 한다.

2. 'next'나 'across' 둘 중에서 하나의 단어가 반드시 들어가야 한다.

3. 'know'를 이용해 길을 물어보는 문장을 만든다.

A: Excuse me. _____

B: Of course. _____ It's on your left.

_____ / _____

---

02 주어진 정보를 이용해 호주를 소개하는 글을 쓰시오.

country: Australia

capital: Canberra

language: English

dish: meat pie, lamington

place • Sydney has the Sydney Opera House.

   • Melbourne has beautiful ocean roads.

How much do you know about Australia?

The (A)_____ of Australia is Canberra. (B)_____ is spoken there. (C)_____ are popular dishes in Australia. Every year lots of tourists visit Sydney and Melbourne. Sydney has (D)_____ and Melbourne is well known for its (E)_____. Australia is so wonderful that you should visit it someday.

---

03 <보기>에 주어진 어휘와 so와 that을 이용하여 3 문장 이상 쓰시오.

┌─ 보기 ───┐

practice dancing hard	thief	cartoon/interesting
become a B-boy dancer	run away/find	keep reading

└──┘

(1) _____

(2) _____

(3) _____

단원별 모의고사

01 다음 〈보기〉에 짝지어진 두 단어의 관계와 같도록 빈칸에 알맞은 단어를 쓰시오.

┌─ 보기 ─┐
nation – national

(1) use – _____
(2) hope – _____
(3) color – _____

02 〈보기〉의 주어진 단어를 이용해 빈칸을 채우시오.

┌─ 보기 ─┐
at   from   in   on   of   to

(1) The department store was full _____ customers.
(2) It's not very far _____ your home.
(3) The lamp is _____ top _____ the television.
(4) Turn _____ that fan.

03 다음 우리말 해석에 맞게 빈칸을 완성하시오. (철자가 주어진 경우 그 철자로 시작할 것)

(1) May I _____ _____ this shirt? (제가 이 셔츠를 입어 봐도 될까요?)
(2) The spring sale will g_____ _____ for a week. (봄 세일은 일주일 동안 계속될 것이다.)
(3) The museum is _____ _____ the park. (박물관은 공원 맞은편에 있습니다.)
(4) Melbourne _____ _____ _____ _____ its beautiful ocean roads. (멜버른은 아름다운 해안 도로로 잘 알려져 있다.)

04 다음 〈보기〉의 단어를 사용하여 자연스러운 문장을 만들 수 없는 것은?

┌─ 보기 ─┐
hamburger   match   movement   tour

① They are playing an important _____.
② The animal moved with quick _____s.
③ I can speak three _____s, English, Japanese and Korean.
④ On today's _____, we will see many rare animals.
⑤ They had _____s for lunch yesterday.

05 그림을 보고 대화의 빈칸을 완성하시오.

Water Slide Bumper Cars Tea Cups Ferris Wheel Roller Coaster Scary House

(1)
A: _____ is the Roller Coaster?
B: Go straight two blocks and turn _____. It's on _____ _____. _____ _____ _____ the 4D Movie Theater.

(2)
A: _____ _____ the Water Slide?
B: Go straight _____ _____ and _____. It's _____ _____. It's _____ from _____ _____.

[06~08] 다음 대화를 읽고 물음에 답하시오.

A: Let's go on a trip abroad.
B: (A)(do, Bangkok, city, prefer, which, or, Taiwan, you?)
A: I prefer Bangkok. The city is (B)[such / so] colorful (C)[what / that] we should go there.
B: Okay. Let's go there.

06 다음 영영풀이에 해당하는 단어를 대화에서 찾아 쓰시오.

> in or to a foreign country

➡ _____

07 괄호 (A) 안의 단어를 배열하여 알맞은 문장을 만드시오.

➡ _____

08 괄호 (B)와 (C)에서 알맞은 단어를 골라 쓰시오.

➡ (B)_____, (C)_____

[09~10] 다음 대화를 읽고 물음에 답하시오.

B: Jisu, why don't we (A)[watch / watching] the movie *Best Friends* on Saturday?
G: Sounds good. (B)[What time / Where] does it begin?
B: On Saturday there (C)[is / are] two showings, ⓐ_____ at five and ⓑ_____ at seven. Which do you prefer?
G: I prefer the seven showing.
B: Okay. Then let's meet at six.
G: Sounds good.

09 (A)~(C)에 알맞은 단어를 골라 쓰시오.

➡ (A)_____ (B)_____ (C)_____

10 빈칸 ⓐ와 ⓑ에 들어갈 말로 적절한 것끼리 짝지어진 것을 고르시오.

	ⓐ	ⓑ
①	one	another
②	one	the other
③	one	other
④	another	the other
⑤	another	some

[11~13] 다음 대화를 읽고 물음에 답하시오.

G: What is this long dress (A)_____(call)?
M: It is an Ao dai, a type of traditional clothing from Vietnam.
G: Can I try one (B)_____?
M: Sure. (C)<u>너는 보라색과 노란색 중 어느 것을 선호하니?</u>
G: The purple one, please.

11 빈칸 (A)에 주어진 단어를 어법에 맞게 쓰시오.

➡ _____

12 빈칸 (B)에 알맞은 전치사를 쓰시오.

➡ _____

13 밑줄 친 (C)의 우리말을 주어진 단어를 이용해 영작하시오.

➡ _____
_____ (one, prefer, which)

14 같은 의미가 되도록 빈칸에 알맞은 말을 쓰시오.

(1) I heard Jenny lock the door.
  = Jenny _____.

(2) Because Australia is very wonderful, you should visit it someday.
  = Australia is _____ you should visit it someday.

15 다음 중 어법상 <u>어색한</u> 것을 고르시오.

① The cake was so delicious that we all enjoyed it.
② This chair was made to Diana by my grandpa.
③ Vietnamese is spoken there.
④ The room was cleaned by Jenny.
⑤ Alex studied so hard that he could enter the university.

16 다음 두 문장을 한 문장으로 바르게 연결한 것은?

• Benjamin became very angry.
• His blood was boiling.

① Benjamin became very angry that his blood was boiling.
② Benjamin became angry enough to boil his blood.
③ Benjamin became too angry to boil his blood.
④ Benjamin became angry so that his blood was boiling.
⑤ Benjamin became so angry that his blood was boiling.

17 우리말과 일치하도록 괄호 안의 어구를 바르게 배열하시오.

(1) Sharon은 성공하기 위해 열심히 일했다. (Sharon, she, so, succeed, worked, might, hard, that)
  ➡ _____

(2) 상자가 너무 무거워서 아무도 움직일 수 없었다. (one, the box, it, that, no, heavy, could, was, move, so)
  ➡ _____

(3) 그 기계는 Kim 선생님에 의해 수리될 것이다. (Mr. Kim, the machine, repaired, will, be, by)
  ➡ _____

18 다음 밑줄 친 부분 중 생략할 수 있는 것은?

① Jessica is loved <u>by everybody</u>.
② I was moved <u>by a book</u>.
③ English is spoken there <u>by them</u>.
④ The apples were eaten <u>by Jenny</u>.
⑤ The room was cleaned <u>by the students</u>.

[19~20] 다음 글을 읽고 물음에 답하시오.

My family traveled to Spain (A)[this summer / in this summer]. Spain is loved by lots of tourists. We visited many (B)[interesting / interested] places.

Our trip started in Madrid. Madrid is the capital and is famous for soccer. We went to a stadium to watch a soccer match. My sister and I were (C)[exciting / excited] because we could watch some of the world's most famous soccer players.   <I = Park Jinwoo>

19 위 글의 괄호 (A)~(C)에서 어법상 알맞은 낱말을 골라 쓰시오.

➡ (A)_____ (B)_____ (C)_____

20 위 글을 읽고 대답할 수 없는 질문은?

① When did Jinwoo's family travel to Spain?

② Why did Jinwoo's family trip start in Madrid?

③ What is the capital of Spain?

④ Why did Jinwoo's family go to a stadium?

⑤ How did Jinwoo and his sister feel in the stadium?

[21~22] 다음 글을 읽고 물음에 답하시오.

The stadium was full of soccer fans. (①) As we watched the match, we cheered by singing songs, waving our hands, and shouting ⓐ the other fans. (②)

After we toured Madrid, we went to Seville. (③) We visited a flamenco museum and watched a flamenco dance. (④) A woman ⓑ a red dress was dancing the flamenco ⓐ wonderful movements. (⑤)

<we = Jinwoo's family>

21 위 글의 흐름으로 보아, 주어진 문장이 들어가기에 가장 적절한 곳은?

While we walked around the city, we saw many historic buildings.

①   ②   ③   ④   ⑤

22 위 글의 빈칸 ⓐ와 ⓑ에 들어갈 전치사가 바르게 짝지어진 것은?

① with – from   ② for – in

③ in – to   ④ for – to

⑤ with – in

[23~25] 다음 글을 읽고 물음에 답하시오.

For dinner, we ate paella. It is a ⓐtradition Spanish dish with rice, vegetables, meat, and seafood. ⓑIt tasted fried rice in Korea. It was so delicious that we all enjoyed it.

In Barcelona, we took a tour of Park Guell and Sagrada Familia. Both were designed by Antoni Gaudi. In Park Guell, we saw some of Gaudi's creative works like a colorful lizard.

<we = Jinwoo's family>

23 위 글의 밑줄 친 ⓐ를 알맞은 어형으로 고치시오.

➡ _____

24 위 글의 밑줄 친 ⓑ에서 어법상 틀린 부분을 고치시오.

➡ _____

25 위 글의 내용과 일치하지 않는 것은?

① 진우의 가족은 저녁 식사로 파에야를 먹었다.

② 파에야는 전통적인 스페인 요리이다.

③ 진우의 가족은 바르셀로나에서 구엘 공원과 사그라다 파밀리아를 둘러보았다.

④ Antoni Gaudi는 구엘 공원과 사그라다 파밀리아의 건설 자금을 지원했다.

⑤ 구엘 공원에서 Gaudi의 창의적인 작품들을 볼 수 있다.

Lesson 6

Wonders of Nature

 의사소통 기능

- 궁금증 표현하기
  I wonder what they are.
- 알고 있음 표현하기
  I heard it is the largest reed field in Korea.

 언어 형식

- 'It＋be동사＋형용사＋to＋동사원형' 구문
  It is important **to understand** the roles of mudflats.
- 'not only A but also B' 구문
  Not only very small living things like plankton **but also** crabs and fish live there.

Words & Expressions

Key Words

- **air cleaner** 공기 청정기
- **appear** [əpíər] 동 나타나다
- **bloom** [blu:m] 동 (꽃이) 피다
- **cave** [keiv] 명 동굴
- **cliff** [klif] 명 절벽
- **cover** [kʌ́vər] 동 (범위가) ~에 이르다, 차지하다
- **crab** [kræb] 명 게
- **creature** [krí:tʃər] 명 생물, 생명체
- **damage** [dǽmidʒ] 명 피해
- **during** [djúəriŋ] 전 ~ 동안(에)
- **else** [els] 부 그 밖의, 그것 이외의
- **environment** [inváiərənmənt] 명 환경
- **even** [í:vən] 부 ~조차(도)
- **fall** [fɔ:l] 명 (복수형으로) 폭포
- **feed** [fi:d] 동 먹이를 주다, 먹이다
- **filter** [fíltər] 동 ~을 여과하다, 거르다, 걸러 내다
- **flat** [flæt] 형 평평한
- **flood** [flʌd] 명 홍수
- **flow** [flou] 동 흐르다
- **fresh water** 민물, 담수
- **generous** [dʒénərəs] 형 관대한
- **greatly** [gréitli] 부 크게, 꽤
- **greet** [gri:t] 동 인사하다
- **guess** [ges] 동 추측하다, 알아맞히다
- **heavy** [hévi] 형 (양, 정도 등이 보통보다) 많은, 심한
- **heavy rain** 호우
- **high tide** 밀물
- **information** [ìnfərméiʃən] 명 정보
- **land** [lænd] 명 육지, 땅
- **large** [lɑ:rdʒ] 형 큰, 커다란
- **low tide** 썰물
- **lung** [lʌŋ] 명 폐
- **mess** [mes] 명 엉망진창
- **mud** [mʌd] 명 진흙
- **muddy** [mʌ́di] 형 진흙투성이인, 진흙의, 질퍽한
- **mudflat** [mʌ́dflæt] 명 갯벌
- **necessary** [nésəsèri] 형 필요한
- **occur** [əkə́:r] 동 일어나다, 발생하다
- **ocean** [óuʃən] 명 바다, 대양
- **oxygen** [áksidʒen] 명 산소
- **plain** [plein] 명 평원
- **plankton** [plǽŋktən] 명 플랑크톤
- **produce** [prədjú:s] 동 생산하다, 만들다
- **protect** [prətékt] 동 보호하다
- **provide** [prəváid] 동 제공하다, 주다
- **rain forest** 열대 우림
- **reach** [ri:tʃ] 동 ~에 이르다, 도달하다
- **reason** [rí:zn] 명 이유
- **reduce** [ridjú:s] 동 줄이다
- **reed** [ri:d] 명 갈대
- **regularly** [régjulərli] 부 규칙적으로
- **remove** [rimú:v] 동 제거하다
- **role** [roul] 명 역할, 임무
- **slide** [slaid] 동 미끄러지다
- **snake** [sneik] 명 뱀
- **southern** [sʌ́ðərn] 형 남쪽의, 남부의
- **stain** [stein] 명 얼룩
- **surf** [sə:rf] 동 서핑하다
- **surface** [sə́:rfis] 명 표면
- **surprising** [sərpráiziŋ] 형 놀라운
- **tide** [taid] 명 조수, 밀물과 썰물
- **trash** [træʃ] 명 쓰레기
- **truth** [tru:θ] 명 진실, 사실
- **unlike** [ənláik] 전 ~와는 달리
- **various** [vέəriəs] 형 각종의, 다양한
- **volume** [válju:m] 명 ~의 양, 용량, 용적
- **wonder** [wʌ́ndər] 명 놀라움, 경이 동 ~을 궁금해 하다

Key Expressions

- **a body of water** (바다나 호수 등의) 수역
- **a large number of** 다수의, 많은 수의
- **be famous for** ~로 유명하다
- **be good for** ~에 좋다, 유익하다
- **by the way** 그런데
- **get on** (버스 · 열차 등을) 타다
- **look like** +명사 ~처럼 보이다
- **make a living** 생계를 유지하다
- **not only A but also B** A뿐만 아니라 B도(= B as well as A)
- **such as** ~와 같은
- **take a trip** (**to** 장소) (~로) 여행하다[여행가다]
- **take off** (옷 등을) 벗다, 벗기다
- **thanks to** ~ 덕분에
- **turn** +형용사 ~한 상태로 변하다, ~하게 되다
- **work out** 운동하다

Word Power

※ make를 이용한 숙어들

□ **make a choice** (선택하다)

□ **make a living** (생계를 꾸리다)

□ **make a noise** (소음을 내다, 시끄럽게 하다)

□ **make a plan** (계획을 짜다)

□ **make an effort** (노력하다)

□ **make a decision** (결정하다)

□ **make a mistake** (실수하다)

□ **make a suggestion** (제안하다)

※ 접미사 '-y'가 붙어 형용사가 되는 명사

□ **cloud**(구름) – **cloudy**(흐린, 구름이 잔뜩 낀)

□ **health**(건강) – **healthy**(건강한)

□ **mess**(엉망진창) – **messy**(지저분한)

□ **wind**(바람) – **windy**(바람이 부는)

□ **dirt**(먼지, 때) – **dirty**(더러운)

□ **luck**(운, 행운) – **lucky**(운이 좋은)

□ **rain**(비) – **rainy**(비가 오는)

□ **scare**(두려움) – **scary**(무서운, 겁나는)

English Dictionary

□ **appear** 나타나다
  → begin to be seen suddenly
    갑자기 보이기 시작하다

□ **cliff** 절벽
  → a high steep rock, especially one facing the sea
    높고 가파른 암석, 특히 바다를 향하고 있는 것

□ **creature** 생물, 생명체
  → all living things except plants
    식물을 제외한 모든 살아있는 것

□ **else** 그 밖의, 그것 이외의
  → in addition to a person, place, or thing
    어떤 사람, 장소, 물건에 더하여

□ **filter** ~을 여과하다, 거르다
  → to pass something through a filter to remove particular things contained in it
    어떤 것 안에 있는 특정한 것을 제거하기 위해, 필터(여과장치)를 통과하게 하다

□ **flow** 흐르다
  → to move steadily without any interrupts, used to describe liquids, gas, electrical currents, etc.
    액체, 기체, 전류 등을 설명할 때 사용되는 것으로, 어떠한 방해 없이 꾸준히 움직이다

□ **generous** 관대한
  → willing to give something more than enough
    어떤 것을 충분한 것 이상으로 기꺼이 주는

□ **information** 정보
  → facts about something
    어떤 것에 대한 사실들

□ **land** 육지, 땅
  → the surface of the earth that is not water
    물이 아닌 땅의 표면

□ **large** 큰, 커다란
  → greater or bigger than usual in size, number, or amount
    크기, 숫자 또는 양에서 보통보다 더 많거나 큰

□ **lung** 폐
  → one of the two organs which you use to breathe
    숨을 쉴 때 사용하는 두 개의 장기 중 하나

□ **mud** 진흙
  → very soft wet earth 매우 부드럽고 젖은 흙

□ **muddy** 진흙투성이인, 진흙의
  → covered with mud, or full of mud
    진흙으로 덮인 또는 진흙으로 가득 찬

□ **mudflat** 갯벌
  → a level tract lying at little depth below the surface of water or alternately covered and left bare by the tide
    해수면 아래에 낮은 깊이로 펼쳐진 평평한 지역 또는 조수에 의해 번갈아 덮여지고 드러나게 되는 지역

□ **plain** 평원
  → a large flat area of land 넓은 평평한 땅

□ **provide** 제공하다, 주다
  → to give someone something that they need or want or make it available to them
    누군가에게 그들이 필요로 하거나 원하는 것을 주거나 그들에게 이용할 수 있도록 하다

□ **reed** 갈대
  → a tall thin plant like grass with a hollow stem that grows in or near water
    물속이나 근처에서 자라는 속이 빈 줄기를 가진 풀과 같은 길고 얇은 식물

□ **surface** 표면
  → the outer texture of anything 어떤 것의 바깥 면

□ **tide** 조수, 밀물과 썰물
  → the periodic rise and fall of the waters of the ocean
    바닷물이 주기적으로 올라가고 내려가는 것

01 짝지어진 단어의 관계가 나머지와 <u>다른</u> 하나를 고르시오.

① cloud – cloudy
② exact – exactly
③ dirt – dirty
④ luck – lucky
⑤ rain – rainy

[02~03] 다음 빈칸에 들어갈 말로 적절한 것은?

02
The earthquake causes _____ to the building.

① control   ② experience
③ cost   ④ effect
⑤ damage

03
Small _____ like shrimps eats these plants.

① sense   ② creature
③ snake   ④ place
⑤ trash

04 다음 영영풀이에 해당하는 단어를 고르시오.

a level tract lying at little depth below the surface of water or alternately covered and left bare by the tide

① wave   ② storm
③ shake   ④ field
⑤ mudflat

05 다음 〈보기〉의 단어를 사용하여 자연스러운 문장을 만들 수 없는 것은? (한 단어는 한 번 밖에 사용할 수 없음. 대·소문자 무시)

┤ 보기 ├
by for on out

① Exercise is good _____ both body and mind.
② I used to work _____ in the gym every day.
③ _____ the way, are you free for dinner tomorrow evening?
④ Thanks _____ your help, I was able to do it.
⑤ Isn't there any way I can get _____ the next flight to Sydney?

06 주어진 문장과 의미가 같은 것을 고르시오.

He can speak not only English but also Spanish.

① He can speak either English or Spanish.
② He can speak Spanish as well as English.
③ He can't speak both English and Spanish.
④ He can't speak English but Spanish.
⑤ He can speak Spanish but he can't speak English.

01 다음 밑줄 친 부분과 의미가 가까운 것을 주어진 철자로 시작하여 쓰시오.

> I <u>got rid of</u> the mud from my shoes.

➡ r_____

[02~03] 두 문장에 공통으로 들어갈 수 있는 단어를 쓰시오.

02
> • Tom and Lisa _____ a living as teachers.
> • I'll _____ a phone call to him to ask about his tomorrow's plans.

03
> • He was famous _____ playing classical music.
> • I believe that laughing is good _____ our health.

04 다음 주어진 우리말에 맞게 빈칸을 채우시오. (철자가 주어진 경우 그 철자로 시작할 것)

(1) 우리가 제시간에 공항에 도착할 수 있겠어.
➡ We could r_____ the airport on time.

(2) 산소는 인간의 삶에 있어 필수적이다.
➡ _____ is essential to human life.

(3) 나는 규칙적으로 운동을 하고 절대로 과식을 하지 않는다.
➡ I _____ _____ r_____ and never eat to excess.

(4) 셔츠의 얼룩이 제거하기 어렵다.
➡ The shirt s_____ is very difficult to _____.

(5) 그의 방은 엉망이었다.
➡ His room was a _____.

05 다음 빈칸에 알맞은 단어를 〈보기〉에서 골라 쓰시오. (한 단어는 한 번 밖에 사용할 수 없음)

> ┤ 보기 ├
> appear   bloom   cover   feed

(1) Hyenas _____ on small dead animals and birds.

(2) Forests _____ about 30 percent of the world's land area.

(3) Some colorful flowers _____ during the short summer.

(4) The moon _____ from behind the clouds.

06 다음 영영풀이에 해당하는 단어를 주어진 철자로 시작하여 쓰시오.

> facts about something

➡ i_____

Conversation

① 궁금증 표현하기

> **I wonder what they are.** 그것들이 뭔지 궁금해요.

■ 궁금증을 표현할 때 '~을 궁금해 하다'라는 의미의 동사 wonder를 사용하여 'I wonder ~.'라고 말한다.

■ 일반적으로 wonder 뒤에는 if절이나 의문사가 쓰인 절 등이 온다. 의문사가 쓰인 절을 사용할 때는 '의문사+주어+동사', 즉 간접의문문의 순서로 문장을 쓴다. 예를 들어, 'I wonder where was she from.'이 아니라 'I wonder where she was from.'이 옳은 문장이 된다.

■ 'I wonder ~.'와 비슷한 표현으로 'I want to know ~.', 'Can you tell me ~?' 또는 'I'd like to know ~.' 등이 있다.

궁금증 표현하기

- I wonder 의문사+주어+동사. (나는 ~가 궁금해요.)
- I want to know 의문사+주어+동사. (나는 ~을 알기를 원해요.)
- Can you tell me 의문사+주어+동사? (나에게 ~을 말해 줄 수 있나요?)
- I'd like to know 의문사+주어+동사. (나는 ~을 알기를 원해요.)

핵심 Check

1. 다음 우리말과 일치하도록 빈칸에 알맞은 말을 쓰시오.

   (1) **A:** I wonder_____ now. (우리가 지금 어디에 있는지 궁금해.)

   B: It seems that we are lost. (우리는 길을 잃은 것 같아.)

   (2) **A:** I _____ late. (나는 Tom이 왜 늦는지 궁금해.)

   B: I don't know. Maybe he got up late. (몰라. 아마도 늦게 일어났나봐.)

2. 괄호 안의 단어를 순서대로 배열하여 대화를 완성하시오.

   (1) **A:** _____ (this, are, how, in, wonder, many, events, I, festival) (이 축제에 얼마나 많은 행사가 있는지 궁금해.)

   B: There are 17. (17개가 있어.)

   (2) **A:** _____ (is, I, who, she, wonder) (나는 그녀가 누군지 궁금해.)

   B: I heard that she is our new science teacher. (나는 그녀가 우리의 새로운 과학 선생님이라고 들었어.)

2 알고 있음 표현하기

> **I heard it is the largest reed field in Korea.** 나는 그곳이 한국에서 가장 큰 갈대밭이라고 들었어.

■ 어떤 사실을 알고 있는지 말할 때 'I heard (that) ~.(나는 ~라고 들었어.)'라고 표현한다. 사실에 해당하는 내용으로 절이 나올 때는 'I heard that 주어+동사'를 사용하며, 여기서 that은 생략이 가능하다. 절이 아닌 구가 나올 경우에는 'be aware of'를 사용한다.

알고 있는 것 표현하기

- I heard (that) 주어 동사 ~. (나는 ~라는 것을 들었다.)
- I have heard (that) 주어 동사 ~. (나는 ~라는 것을 들었다.)
- I've been told (that) 주어 동사 ~. (나는 ~라는 것을 들었다.)
- I'm aware (that) 주어 동사 ~. (나는 ~라는 것을 알고 있다.)
- I'm aware of (동)명사 ~. (나는 ~을 알고 있다.)

■ 무언가에 대해 들어서 알고 있는지 물을 때는 'Did you hear about ~?(너는 ~에 대해 들었니?)'라고 말한다. 현재완료를 사용해 'Have you heard about ~?'으로 들어 본 적이 있는지 물을 수도 있다.

알고 있는지 묻기

- Did you hear (that) 주어 동사 ~? (~라는 것을 들었니?)
- Did you hear about (동)명사 ~? (~에 대해 들었니?)
- Have you heard (that) 주어 동사 ~? (~라는 것을 들었니?)
- Are you aware (that) 주어 동사 ~? (~라는 것을 알고 있니?)
- Are you aware of (동)명사 ~? (~을 알고 있니?)
- Do you know (that) 주어 동사 ~? (~라는 것을 알고 있니?)
- Do you know about (동)명사 ~? (~에 대해 알고 있니?)

핵심 Check

3. 다음 우리말과 일치하도록 빈칸에 알맞은 말을 쓰시오.

   A: I _____ the school tennis team won the match.

   (나는 학교 테니스 팀이 시합에서 이겼다는 것을 들었다.)

   B: Really? How wonderful! (정말? 멋지다!)

4. 괄호 안의 단어를 순서대로 배열하여 대화를 완성하시오.

   A: _____ today's lunch menu? (of, you, are, aware)

   (오늘의 점심 메뉴가 뭔지 알고 있니?)

   B: _____ today's lunch menu is kimchi fried rice. (heard, I, have,

   that) (나는 오늘 점심이 김치 볶음밥이라고 들었어.)

Listen & Speak 1 A-1

G: I ❶wonder what you did ❷during the summer vacation.

B: I ❸took a trip to Kenya and ❹saw many animals on the ❺plains.

G: Wonderful! ❻By the way, what are the plains?

B: ❼They are large areas of flat land.

G: I see.

G: 나는 네가 여름 방학 동안에 무엇을 했는지 궁금해.

B: 나는 케냐로 여행을 가서 평원에서 많은 동물들을 봤어.

G: 멋지구나! 그런데 평원이 무엇이니?

B: 그곳은 넓고 평평한 땅이야.

G: 그렇구나.

❶ wonder: ~을 궁금해 하다 wonder 다음에 궁금한 내용을 간접의문문(의문사(what)+주어(you)+동사(did))의 형식으로 사용하였다.

❷ during: ~ 동안(에) vacation: 방학

❸ take a trip (to 장소): (~로) 여행하다[여행가다]

❹ saw는 접속사 and로 동사 took a trip과 연결되어 있다.

❺ plain: 평원

❻ 'by the way'의 뜻은 '그런데'로 보통 대화의 화제를 바꿀 때 사용한다.

❼ 주어의 They는 앞 문장의 the plains를 가리키는 대명사이다. flat: 평평한

Check(√) True or False

(1) There are a lot of animals on the plains in Kenya.　　T ☐ F ☐

(2) The girl already knows what the boy did during the summer vacation.　　T ☐ F ☐

Listen & Speak 2 A-1

B: ❶Do you know how many oceans there are on the Earth?

G: The answer is four, isn't it?

B: No. ❷There are five oceans on the Earth. ❸They cover most of the Earth.

G: How much of the Earth do they ❹cover?

B: ❺I heard the oceans cover about 70% of the Earth's surface.

B: 너는 지구에 몇 개의 바다가 있는지 아니?

G: 정답은 네 개야. 그렇지 않니?

B: 아니야. 지구에는 다섯 개의 바다가 있어. 그곳은 지구의 대부분을 차지하고 있어.

G: 그곳이 지구의 얼마를 차지하고 있니?

B: 나는 바다가 지구 표면의 70%를 차지한다고 들었어.

❶ 'Do you know ~?'는 상대방이 어떠한 사실을 알고 있는지 묻는 표현이다. know의 목적어로 간접의문문(의문사+주어+동사)을 이용했다.

❷ There are ~: ~가 있다 ocean: 바다, 대양

❸ They = five oceans, most of ~: ~의 대부분

❹ cover: (범위가) ~에 이르다, 차지하다

❺ heard와 the oceans 사이에 접속사 that이 생략되어 있다. I heard (that) 주어 동사 ~: 나는 ~라는 것을 들었다 about 다음에 숫자가 나오면 '대략'의 의미이다. surface: 표면

Check(√) True or False

(3) There are four oceans on the Earth.　　T ☐ F ☐

(4) Oceans on the Earth cover most of the Earth.　　T ☐ F ☐

Listen & Speak 1 A-2

G: ❶Look at that lake! It's really beautiful.

B: It's not a lake. It's a ❷river.

G: ❸Is it? ❹I wonder how a river and a lake are different.

B: A river is ❺a long body of fresh water. ❻Unlike a lake, a river flows toward the ocean.

G: I got it.

❶ look at: ~을 보다 lake: 호수　❷ river: 강
❸ 'Is it' 다음에 'a lake'가 생략되어 있다.
❹ I wonder 의문사+주어+동사: 나는 ~가 궁금해요 'how a river and a lake are different'는 wonder의 목적어로 간접의문의 순서로 사용되었다.
❺ 'a body of water'는 강이나 호수, 바다 같이 물의 큰 지역을 의미한다.
❻ unlike: ~와는 달리 flow: 흐르다 toward: ~을 향해, ~쪽으로

Listen & Speak 2 A-2

G: ❶I heard the Amazon rain forest is called the lungs of the Earth.

B: Lungs? Why?

G: ❷Because it produces about 20% of the Earth's oxygen.

B: Wow! That's a lot.

❶ heard와 the Amazon rain forest 사이에 접속사 that이 생략되어 있다. 아마존 열대 우림이 지구의 폐라고 불리는 것이므로 that절의 동사는 수동태(be+called)로 써야 한다. rain forest: 열대 우림 lung: 폐
❷ 이유를 묻는 말에 접속사 because(~ 때문에)를 이용해 설명하고 있다. produce: 생산하다, 만들다 oxygen: 산소

Conversation A

M: ❶Guess what this is! It's not a tree. It is a plant ❷that looks like tall grass. ❸In fall, it turns yellow. It grows well in wet lands. I heard Suncheon Bay ❹is famous for this plant.

❶ guess의 목적어는 'what this is'이다. 의문문이 문장의 주어, 목적어, 보어 등으로 사용될 때 '의문사+주어+동사'의 어순으로 표현한다. guess: 추측하다, 알아맞히다

❷ 여기서 that은 주격 관계대명사이므로, 'that looks like tall grass'는 앞의 a plant(식물)를 수식한다. look like+명사: ~처럼 보이다
❸ 계절 앞에는 전치사 in을 사용한다. turn+형용사: ~한 상태로 변하다, ~하게 되다
❹ be famous for: ~로 유명하다

Conversation B

Dad: Do you ❶want to see an amazing place?

Karl & Sister: Sure!

Dad: Then let's ❷get on the train.

Sister: Look at the yellow plants! ❸I wonder what they are.

Dad: They are ❹reeds. Suncheon Bay has beautiful reed fields.

Karl: Wow, the reeds are ❺even taller than you, Dad.

Sister: They really are. ❻Let me take a picture of you.

Karl: This reed field is very large.

Dad: Yes. ❼I heard it is the largest one in Korea.

Karl: Look at the sky. It's ❽turning red.

Sister: Yes, it's beautiful.

❶ want는 뒤에 to부정사(to+동사원형)를 목적어로 취할 수 있지만 동명사는 목적어로 취할 수 없다.
❷ get on: (버스 · 지하철 등을) 타다
❸ I wonder 의문사+주어+동사: 나는 ~가 궁금해요
❹ reed: 갈대
❺ 형용사의 비교급은 바로 앞에 much, far, even, still, a lot 등을 사용해서 강조한다.
❻ let 목적어 목적격보어(동사원형): …가 ~하게 하다 take a picture: 사진을 찍다
❼ I heard (that) 주어 동사 ~: 나는 ~라는 것을 들었다 the largest는 large의 최상급 표현이다. 대명사 one은 reed field를 의미한다.
❽ turn+형용사: ~한 상태로 변하다, ~하게 되다

Communication Task Step 2

A: ❶I wonder what is special about Great Plains.

B: ❷I heard it ❸is good for raising animals.

❶ I wonder 의문사+주어+동사: 나는 ~가 궁금해요 special: 특별한
❷ I heard (that) 주어 동사 ~: 나는 ~라는 것을 들었다
❸ be good for: ~에 좋다, 유익하다 raise: 키우다, 기르다

● 다음 우리말과 일치하도록 빈칸에 알맞은 말을 쓰시오. (주어진 철자가 있으면 그 철자로 시작할 것)

Listen & Speak 1 A

1. G: I _____ _____ _____ _____ _____ the summer vacation.

   B: I _____ a _____ to Kenya and saw many animals on the plains.

   G: Wonderful! _____ the way, what are the _____?

   B: They are large areas of _____ land.

   G: I see.

2. G: Look _____ that lake! It's really beautiful.

   B: It's not a _____. It's a river.

   G: Is it? I _____ _____ a river and a lake _____ _____.

   B: A river is _____ _____ _____ _____ _____ water. Unlike a lake, a river flows _____ the ocean.

   G: I _____ _____.

Listen & Speak 1 B

1. A: I wonder _____ _____ _____ _____.

   B: It is a very _____ area of land.

2. A: _____ _____ _____ a _____ is.

   B: It is a large, _____ area of _____.

Listen & Talk 2 A

1. B: Do you know _____ _____ _____ _____ _____ on the Earth?

   G: The answer is four, isn't it?

   B: No. _____ _____ five oceans on the Earth. They _____ _____ of the Earth.

   G: How _____ of the Earth do they _____?

   B: I _____ the oceans _____ _____ 70% of the Earth's _____.

2. G: I heard the Amazon _____ _____ _____ _____ the _____ of the Earth.

   B: _____? Why?

   G: Because it _____ about 20% of the Earth's _____.

   B: Wow! That's a lot.

해석

1. G: 나는 네가 여름 방학 동안에 무엇을 했는지 궁금해.
   B: 나는 케냐로 여행을 가서 평원에서 많은 동물들을 봤어.
   G: 멋지구나! 그런데 평원이 무엇이니?
   B: 그곳은 넓고 평평한 땅이야.
   G: 그렇구나.

2. G: 저 호수를 봐. 정말 아름다워.
   B: 그것은 호수가 아니야. 그것은 강이야.
   G: 그래? 나는 강과 호수가 어떻게 다른지 궁금해.
   B: 강은 민물로 된 긴 물줄기야. 호수와 다르게 강은 바다로 흘러.
   G: 알겠어.

1. A: 나는 산이 무엇인지 궁금해.
   B: 그곳은 아주 높은 지대의 땅이야.

2. A: 나는 평원이 무엇인지 궁금해.
   B: 그곳은 넓고 평평한 지대의 땅이야.

1. B: 너는 지구에 몇 개의 바다가 있는지 아니?
   G: 정답은 네 개야, 그렇지 않니?
   B: 아니야. 지구에는 다섯 개의 바다가 있어. 그곳은 지구의 대부분을 차지하고 있어.
   G: 그곳이 지구의 얼마를 차지하고 있니?
   B: 나는 바다가 지구 표면의 70%를 차지한다고 들었어.

2. G: 나는 아마존 열대 우림이 지구의 허파라고 불린다고 들었어.
   B: 허파? 왜?
   G: 왜냐하면 그곳은 지구 산소의 약 20%를 생산하기 때문이야.
   B: 우와! 엄청나구나.

Listen & Talk 2 B

1. **A:** I _____ to go to Jecheon.
   B: Why?
   A: I _____ there are beautiful _____ in Jecheon.
2. **A:** I _____ _____ _____ _____ Danyang.
   B: Why?
   A: I heard there are _____ caves in Danyang.

Conversation A

M: Guess _____ this is! It's not a tree. It is a _____ that looks like tall _____. _____ fall, it _____ yellow. It grows well in _____ lands. I _____ Suncheon Bay is famous _____ this plant.

Conversation B

Dad: Do you want to see an _____ place?
Karl & Sister: Sure!
Dad: Then let's _____ _____ the train.
Sister: Look at the yellow plants! I _____ _____ _____ _____.
Dad: They are _____. Suncheon Bay has beautiful _____ fields.
Karl: Wow, the reeds are even _____ _____ you, Dad.
Sister: They really are. Let me _____ a picture of you.
Karl: This _____ _____ is very large.
Dad: Yes. I _____ it is _____ _____ _____ in Korea.
Karl: Look at the sky. It's _____ red.
Sister: Yes, it's beautiful.

Communication Task Step 1

A: What _____ do you have?
B: I have Moraine Lake. It's in Canada.
A: What is _____ about the place?
B: The color of the water _____ light blue.

해석

1. **A:** 나는 제천에 가고 싶어.
   B: 왜?
   A: 나는 제천에 아름다운 호수들이 있다고 들었어.

2. **A:** 나는 단양에 가고 싶어.
   B: 왜?
   A: 나는 단양에 유명한 동굴들이 있다고 들었어.

M: 이것이 무엇인지 추측해 봐! 그것은 나무가 아니야. 그것은 키가 큰 풀처럼 보이는 식물이야. 가을에는 노란색으로 변해. 그것은 습지에서 잘 자라. 나는 순천만이 이 식물로 유명하다고 들었어.

아빠: 너희들 멋진 곳을 보고 싶니?
Karl, 여동생: 물론이죠!
아빠: 그러면 기차를 타자.
여동생: 저 노란색 식물들을 봐요! 저게 무엇인지 궁금해요.
아빠: 그건 갈대야. 순천만에는 아름다운 갈대밭이 있어.
Karl: 와, 갈대가 아빠보다 키가 더 커요.
여동생: 진짜 그러네요. 제가 사진을 찍어 드릴게요.
Karl: 이 갈대밭은 정말 넓네요.
아빠: 그래. 나는 이곳이 한국에서 가장 큰 갈대밭이라고 들었어.
Karl: 하늘을 보세요. 빨갛게 변하고 있어요.
여동생: 그러네, 아름다워.

A: 너는 어떤 장소를 가지고 있니?
B: 나는 모레인호를 갖고 있어. 그곳은 캐나다에 있어.
A: 그곳은 어떤 것이 특별하니?
B: 물의 색이 연한 파랑색이야.

[01~02] 대화의 밑줄 친 부분의 의도로 알맞은 것은?

01

G: Look at that lake! It's really beautiful.
B: It's not a lake. It's a river.
G: <u>I wonder how a river and a lake are different.</u>
B: A river is a long body of fresh water. Unlike a lake, a river flows toward the ocean.
G: I got it.

① 방법 표현하기　② 당부하기　③ 이유 표현하기
④ 궁금증 표현하기　⑤ 모르는 것 말하기

02

A: I want to go to Jecheon.
B: Why?
A: <u>I heard there are beautiful lakes in Jecheon.</u>

① 궁금증 표현하기　② 불확실함 말하기　③ 놀람 표현하기
④ 충고하기　⑤ 알고 있음 표현하기

03 밑줄 친 부분과 바꿔 쓸 수 있는 것을 <u>모두</u> 고르시오.

Sister: Look at the yellow plants! <u>I wonder what they are.</u>
Dad: They are reeds. Suncheon Bay has beautiful reed fields.

① I have learned what they are.
② I'm very sure what they are.
③ I want to know what they are.
④ I'd like to know what they are.
⑤ I already know what they are.

04 다음 대화의 빈칸에 알맞은 말은?

A: I wonder what is special about Moraine Lake.
B: _____

① I heard the color of the water is light blue.
② I hope to visit the lake.
③ I don't think the color of the water is light blue.
④ I have been to Moraine lake.
⑤ I want to visit Moraine lake.

[01~03] 다음 대화를 읽고 물음에 답하시오.

B: I just finished making a plan for my trip. (①)
G: Sure. (②) (wonder, will, do, I, you, what) (③)
B: On the first day, I'm going to go fishing on a lake. (④) The next day, I'm going to climb a mountain.
G: Is that all?
B: No. On the last day, I'm going to go swimming. (⑤)
G: Wow. You will do a lot of activities.

01 위 대화의 ①~⑤ 중 다음 주어진 말이 들어갈 알맞은 곳은?

Do you want to hear it?

①   ②   ③   ④   ⑤

서답형
02 괄호 안에 주어진 단어를 배열하여 영작하시오.

➡ _____

서답형
03 위 대화를 읽고 대답할 수 있는 것을 모두 고르시오.

ⓐ For how many days will the boy take a trip?
ⓑ What will the boy do during his trip?
ⓒ Where will the boy go during his trip?
ⓓ When will the boy take a trip?
ⓔ What will the boy do on the first day of trip?

➡ _____

[04~07] 다음 대화를 읽고 물음에 답하시오.

G: I wonder what you did during the summer vacation. (①)
B: I (A)_____ a trip to Kenya and saw many animals on the plains. (②)
G: Wonderful! (③)
B: (④) They are large areas of flat land. (⑤)
G: I see.

중요
04 위 대화의 ①~⑤ 중 다음 주어진 말이 들어갈 알맞은 곳은?

By the way, what are the plains?

①   ②   ③   ④   ⑤

05 빈칸 (A)에 알맞은 말을 고르시오.

① made   ② took   ③ got
④ gave   ⑤ found

서답형
06 다음 영영풀이에 해당하는 단어를 대화에서 찾아 쓰시오.

the surface of the earth that is not water

➡ _____

중요
07 위 대화의 내용과 일치하지 않는 것을 고르시오.

① The girl didn't know what the plains are.
② There are plains in Kenya.
③ The plains are not flat.
④ The boy went to Kenya during the summer vacation.
⑤ There are many animals in Kenya.

[08~09] 다음 대화를 읽고 물음에 답하시오.

> B: Do you know how many oceans there are on the Earth?
> G: ⓐThe answer is four, isn't it?
> B: ⓑYes. There are five oceans on the Earth. ⓒThey cover most of the Earth.
> G: ⓓHow much of the Earth do they cover?
> B: ⓔI heard the oceans cover about 70% of the Earth's surface.

08 ⓐ~ⓔ 중 흐름상 어색한 것을 고르시오.

① ⓐ ② ⓑ ③ ⓒ ④ ⓓ ⑤ ⓔ

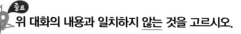 위 대화의 내용과 일치하지 <u>않는</u> 것을 고르시오.

① The most of the Earth is covered with oceans.
② The boy knows how much of the Earth oceans cover.
③ There are 5 oceans on the Earth.
④ The girl wants to know how much of the Earth oceans cover.
⑤ The girl correctly knew how many oceans there are on the Earth.

[10~12] 다음 대화를 읽고 물음에 답하시오.

> Dad: Do you want to see an amazing place?
> Karl & Sister: Sure! (①)
> Dad: Then let's (A)_____ on the train.
> Sister: Look at the yellow plants! (②)
> Dad: They are reeds. Suncheon Bay has beautiful reed fields.
> Karl: Wow, the reeds are even taller than you, Dad. (③)
> Sister: They really are. Let me take a picture of you. (④)
> Karl: This reed field is very large.
> Dad: Yes. I heard it is the largest one in Korea. (⑤)
> Karl: Look at the sky. It's turning red.
> Sister: Yes, it's beautiful.

 위 대화의 ①~⑤ 중 다음 주어진 말이 들어갈 알맞은 곳은?

> I wonder what they are.

① ② ③ ④ ⑤

11 빈칸 (A)에 알맞은 말을 고르시오.

① get ② give ③ take
④ pick ⑤ put

12 위 대화의 내용과 일치하지 <u>않는</u> 것을 고르시오.

① There are reed fields in Sunchen Bay.
② They travel by train.
③ Dad is shorter than the reeds.
④ Sunchen Bay has the second largest reed field in Korea.
⑤ They see the sunset.

 다음 중 짝지어진 대화가 어색한 것은?

① A: I wonder where my book is.
   B: Are you talking about the math book?
② A: I want to know why you called me last night.
   B: I had a question about our English homework.
③ A: I wonder who made this hamburger.
   B: Your mom made it for you.
④ A: Can you tell me where I can buy the snacks?
   B: You can buy them over there.
⑤ A: I would like to know what you did on Sunday.
   B: I am going to take a trip to Danyang.

Conversation 서술형 시험대비

[01~02] 다음 대화를 읽고 물음에 답하시오.

> A: (a) 나는 대평원의 특별한 점은 무엇인지 궁금해.
> (Great Plains, about, is, wonder, special, I, what)
> B: I heard it is good (A)_____ raising animals.

01 빈칸 (A)에 알맞은 전치사를 쓰시오.

➡ _____

02 (a)의 밑줄 친 우리말에 맞게 괄호 안에 주어진 단어를 배열하여 영작하시오.

➡ _____

03 ⓐ~ⓔ 중 어법상 어색한 것을 골라 고치시오.

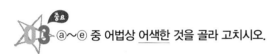

> G: ⓐI wonder what did you ⓑduring the summer vacation.
> B: ⓒI took a trip to Kenya ⓓand saw many animals on the plains.
> G: Wonderful! ⓔBy the way, what are the plains?
> B: They are large areas of flat land.
> G: I see.

➡ _____

[04~05] 다음 대화를 읽고 물음에 답하시오.

> G: Look at that lake! ⓐIt's really beautiful.
> B: ⓑIt's not a lake. It's a river.
> G: Is it? (A)I wonder how a river and a lake are different.
> B: ⓒA river is a long body of fresh water. ⓓLike a lake, ⓔa river flows toward the ocean.
> G: I got it.

04 ⓐ~ⓔ 중 흐름상 어색한 것을 바르게 고치시오.

➡ _____

05 밑줄 친 (A)와 같은 의미가 되도록 주어진 단어를 이용해서 문장을 만드시오.

➡ _____

(can, tell)

06 주어진 문장 이후에 이어질 대화의 순서를 바르게 배열하시오.

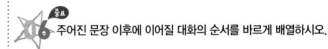

> Do you know how many oceans there are on the Earth?

> (A) I heard the oceans cover about 70% of the Earth's surface.
> (B) The answer is four, isn't it?
> (C) How much of the Earth do they cover?
> (D) No. There are five oceans on the Earth. They cover most of the Earth.

➡ _____

07 밑줄 친 우리말을 주어진 단어를 이용하여 영작하시오

> A: I want to go to Jejudo.
> B: Why?
> A: 나는 제주도에 여러 개의 오름이 있다고 들었어. (oreum, a lot of)

➡ _____

Grammar

① 'It+be동사+형용사+to+동사원형' 구문

> • **It** is important **to understand** the roles of mudflats. 갯벌의 역할을 이해하는 것이 중요하다.

■ 비교적 긴 to부정사 부분이 문장의 주어로 쓰일 때 그 to부정사 부분을 일반적인 주어의 자리인 문장의 맨 앞에 두지 않고 문장 뒤에 둔다. 대신 주어 자리에는 It을 넣어주는데 그것을 가주어 It이라고 부르고 문장 뒤로 간 to부정사 부분은 진주어라고 부른다. 이때 쓰인 It은 가주어이므로 구체적인 뜻이 없으며, '…하는 것은 ～하다'로 해석한다.

- **It** is not easy **to work out**. 운동하는 것은 쉽지 않다.
  = **To work out** is not easy.

- **It** is interesting **to play** soccer. 축구하는 것은 재미있다.
  = **To play** soccer is interesting.

■ to부정사의 의미상 주어

'to부정사'가 행하는 동작의 주체를 to부정사의 의미상 주어라고 한다. to부정사의 의미상 주어는 to부정사 바로 앞에 'for+목적격'의 형태로 쓴다. to부정사 구문에서 to부정사의 의미상 주어가 없는 경우는 특별한 사람이 아니라 일반적인 사람이기 때문이다. 문장에 쓰인 형용사가 kind, foolish, rude, careless, wise 등과 같이 사람의 성질을 나타내는 말일 때는 'of+목적격'을 쓴다. 또한 to부정사의 부정은 to부정사 앞에 not[never]을 써서 'not[never]+to V'로 나타내며 '…하지 않는 것은 ～하다'로 해석한다.

- **It** is necessary **for** you **to save** money. 너는 돈을 저축하는 것이 필요하다.

- **It** is nice **of** him **to say** so. 그렇게 말하다니 그는 참 착하구나.

- **It** is difficult **not to be** touched by the story. 그 이야기에 감동받지 않는 것은 어렵다.

핵심 Check

1. 다음 우리말과 일치하도록 빈칸에 알맞은 말을 쓰시오.

   (1) 축구를 하는 것은 재미있다.
   ➡ _____ is fun _____ _____ soccer.

   (2) 여기서 너를 보게 되어 좋다.
   ➡ It's great _____ _____ you here.

   (3) 당신은 돈을 저축하는 것이 필요하다.
   ➡ It is necessary _____ _____ _____ _____ money.

② 'not only A but also B' 구문

> **Not only** very small living things like plankton **but also** crabs and fish live there.
> 플랑크톤처럼 작은 생명체뿐만 아니라 게와 물고기도 그곳에 산다.

- ■ 'not only A but also B'의 형태로 'A뿐만 아니라 B도'라는 의미를 가지며 A와 B는 품사나 문장에서의 역할이 동일해야 한다. (이렇게 상호 호응 관계를 이루면서 한 쌍으로 이루어진 접속사를 상관접속사라고 한다.)
  - Amy is **not only** smart **but also** friendly. Amy는 똑똑할 뿐만 아니라 다정하다. (A와 B에 해당하는 smart와 friendly는 모두 형용사이며 보어의 역할을 한다.)

- ■ 초점이 but also 다음의 B에 놓이며 'B as well as A'로 바꿔 쓸 수 있다.
  - I like **not only** English **but also** math.
    = I like math **as well as** English. 나는 영어뿐 아니라 수학도 좋아한다.

- ■ 'not only A but also B'에서 A와 B 자리에는 명사(구)와 동사(구)를 비롯하여 다양한 표현이 사용될 수 있으며, but also에서 also가 생략되기도 한다.
  - Laura is **not only** pretty **but also** wise. Laura는 예쁠 뿐만 아니라 현명하다.
  - She **not only** wrote the text **but also** selected the pictures. 그녀는 그 본문을 썼을 뿐만 아니라 그림들을 선별하기도 했다.
  - He likes **not only** pizza **but also** spaghetti.
    = He likes **not only** pizza **but** spaghetti.
    = He likes **not simply[merely]** pizza **but (also)** spaghetti.
    = He likes spaghetti **as well as** pizza. 그는 피자뿐만 아니라 스파게티도 좋아한다.

- ■ 'not only A but also B'와 'B as well as A'가 주어로 쓰일 경우 B에 수를 일치시킨다.
  - **Not only** I **but also** my sister likes skating.
    = My sister **as well as** I likes skating. 나뿐만 아니라 내 여동생도 스케이트 타는 것을 좋아한다.

핵심 Check

2. 다음 우리말에 맞게 빈칸을 알맞게 채우시오.

(1) 그녀는 영어뿐만 아니라 불어도 한다.
  ➡ She speaks _____ _____ English but also French.

(2) 그들은 한국에서뿐만 아니라 일본에서도 인기가 있다.
  ➡ They are popular not only in Korea _____ _____ in Japan.

01 다음 빈칸에 알맞은 것을 고르시오.

> A: Is it interesting _____?
> B: Yes, of course.

① to draw cartoons
② to drawing cartoons
③ draws cartoons
④ you draw cartoons
⑤ of you to draw cartoons

02 다음 중 나머지와 의미가 <u>다른</u> 하나는?

① She is good at not only singing but also dancing.
② She is good at not only singing but dancing.
③ She is good at singing as well as dancing.
④ She is good at not simply singing but also dancing.
⑤ She is good at not merely singing but also dancing.

03 다음 문장에서 어법상 <u>어색한</u> 부분을 바르게 고쳐 쓰시오.

(1) Sam not only reads German but also write it.

_____ ➡ _____

(2) Mike is not only unkind but is stupid.

_____ ➡ _____

(3) Not only you but also Sophie like going shopping.

_____ ➡ _____

(4) It is impossible to crossing this river by swimming.

_____ ➡ _____

(5) That is great to cook for others.

_____ ➡ _____

(6) It is necessary of you to read the book.

_____ ➡ _____

01 다음 중 어법상 바르지 <u>않은</u> 것은?

① It was fun to find the information about these places.
② It's hard to take care of children.
③ That's necessary to know when to draw the line.
④ It became common to send texts instead of sending mails between students.
⑤ It's better to speak clearly.

02 다음 중 어법상 바른 것은?

① Ezra as well as his sisters was studying in the library.
② The book is not only an expensive one but uninteresting.
③ Not only I but also David like Julie.
④ Steve is not only smart but also generously.
⑤ Bill speaks rudely not only at home but also school.

03 다음 빈칸에 알맞은 말이 바르게 짝지어진 것은?

• My dog is not only _____ but also smart.
• It is great _____ a bike in the mountains.

① cutely – ride
② cute – to ride
③ cutely – riding
④ cute – to riding
⑤ cutely – riding

04 다음 문장의 빈칸에 들어갈 알맞은 것은?

_____ is important to wear long clothes in the jungle.

① What   ② This
③ That   ④ It
⑤ One

05 다음 대화의 빈칸에 들어갈 말로 알맞은 것은?

M: Who did you meet yesterday?
W: I met not _____ Molly but Heidi.

① also   ② simple   ③ as
④ very   ⑤ merely

06 다음 괄호 안에서 알맞은 말을 고르시오.

(1) (It / That) is not difficult to use this camera.
(2) It is important (understand / to understand) other cultures.
(3) It was clever (for / of) her to come early.
(4) It not only rained but (snowy / snowed) yesterday.
(5) I like not only English (and / but) math.
(6) Not only you but also Audrey (enjoy / enjoys) going shopping.

07 다음 중 어법상 옳은 것은?

① Amy is not only smartly but also friendly.

② It is fun to going into caves.

③ It is kind for him to say so.

④ She wants not only to dance but also to sing.

⑤ Not only you but also James play the piano.

08 다음 중 밑줄 친 부분의 쓰임이 다른 하나는?

① It is fun to go on a picnic.

② It was not such a nice party.

③ It's necessary to prepare for the worst.

④ It was not easy to win the race.

⑤ It is better to eat healthy food.

09 주어진 문장의 빈칸에 들어갈 알맞은 말을 고르시오.

• Mike was in need of not only food but _____ clothes.

① too ② also ③ so
④ as well ⑤ very

10 다음 우리말을 바르게 영작한 것을 고르시오.

힙합 댄스를 배우는 것은 신났었다.

① It was exciting learn hiphop dance.

② It was exciting learns hiphop dance.

③ It was exciting learned hiphop dance.

④ It was exciting to learn hiphop dance.

⑤ It was exciting to learning hiphop dance.

11 다음 두 문장을 한 문장으로 바르게 연결한 것은?

• She is good at singing.

• She is good at dancing, too.

① She is good at either singing or dancing.

② She is good at neither singing nor dancing.

③ She isn't good at both singing and dancing.

④ She is good at not singing but dancing.

⑤ She is good at not only singing but dancing.

12 다음 우리말과 일치하도록 빈칸에 알맞은 단어로 묶은 것은?

• 그녀가 프랑스어를 배운 것은 아주 현명했다.
= _____ was wise _____ her _____ French.

① It – for – learn

② It – of – to learn

③ This – for – learn

④ That – for – to learn

⑤ That – of – learning

서답형
13 주어진 어휘를 이용하여 빈칸에 알맞게 쓰시오.

I like not only reading stories but also _____ them. (write)

14 다음 문장에서 어법상 어색한 것을 바르게 고쳐 다시 쓰시오.

(1) It would be really stupid for you to help them.

➡ _____

(2) This is interesting to walk in the forest.

➡ _____

(3) It is important wear a hat to block the sun.

➡ _____

(4) Not only I but also Bella were enjoying taking a walk.

➡ _____

_____

(5) Harry is not only a great wizard but also very wise.

➡ _____

_____

15 다음 중 어법상 어색한 것을 고르시오. (2개)

① It was a lot of fun to swim in the pond with my friends.

② It was nice for you to help the elderly woman at the bus stop.

③ It looked necessary for him to go to the dentist.

④ My brother want not only to write Spanish but also speaks it.

⑤ They can build not only muscles but also mental strength.

16 다음 우리말을 영작했을 때 잘못된 것을 고르시오.

> 플랑크톤뿐만 아니라 게와 물고기도 그곳에 산다.

① Not only plankton but also crabs and fish live there.

② Not only plankton but crabs and fish live there.

③ Not merely plankton but also crabs and fish live there.

④ Not only plankton but simply crabs and fish live there.

⑤ Plankton as well as crabs and fish lives there.

17 다음 우리말을 바르게 영작한 것을 고르시오.

> 그가 그 산에 오르는 것은 위험하다.

① It is dangerous for him climb that mountain.

② It is dangerous he climbs that mountain.

③ It is dangerous for him to climb that mountain.

④ It is dangerous of him to climb that mountain.

⑤ To climb that mountain is dangerous of you.

18 다음 두 문장을 주어진 어휘를 이용하여 한 문장으로 바꿔 쓰시오.

> Gina is pretty. She is also kind. (well)

➡ _____

01 다음 우리말을 괄호 안에 주어진 어휘를 이용하여 (a) to부정사 주어를 써서, (b) 가주어를 써서 영작하시오.

(1) 좋은 친구를 사귀는 것은 어렵다. (difficult, make)

➡ (a) _____

(b) _____

(2) 남을 돕는 것은 중요하다. (important, others)

➡ (a) _____

(b) _____

(3) 맛을 설명하는 것은 불가능하다. (tastes, explain)

➡ (a) _____

(b) _____

02 다음 두 문장을 'not only A but also B' 구문을 사용하여 한 문장으로 연결하시오.

(1) Chris is friendly. He is good-looking, too.

➡ _____

(2) Marianne writes Korean well. She also speaks Korean well.

➡ _____

(3) Charlotte likes to play basketball. She enjoys watching soccer games on TV, too.

➡ _____

_____

03 그림을 보고 주어진 어휘를 이용하여 〈보기〉와 같이 쓰시오.

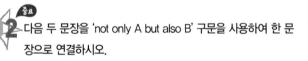

It is great to eat delicious food with friends.

(1) (exciting, watch fish swimming)

➡ _____

(2) (amazing, visit Giant's Causeway in Ireland)

➡ _____

04 두 문장의 의미가 같도록 빈칸에 알맞은 말을 쓰시오.

(1) This machine looks good. It also looks convenient.

= This machine looks not only good _____ _____ convenient.

(2) He can play the piano. He can play the violin, too.

= He can play not only the piano but the violin _____ _____.

05 다음 우리말에 맞게 주어진 단어를 바르게 배열하시오.

(1) 나의 가족과 함께 좋은 추억을 만드는 것은 중요하다. (it, memories, family, good, important, is, make, my, with, to)

➡ _____

(2) 성공하기 위해 영어를 잘하는 것은 필요하다. (it, English, is, speak, succeed, well, necessary, to, to)

➡ _____

(3) 나는 노래 부르는 것뿐 아니라 춤추는 것도 좋아한다. (I, only, but, like, dancing, singing, not)

➡ _____

(4) 너뿐만 아니라 네 동생도 설거지를 해야 한다. (you, your brother, dishes, wash, but, should, not, also, only, the)

➡ _____
_____

06 다음 문장을 It으로 시작하여 다시 쓰시오.

(1) To eat fruit and vegetables is easy.

➡ _____

(2) To know how to greet people in different countries will be necessary.

➡ _____
_____

(3) That knowledge is power is true.

➡ _____

07 다음 중 어법상 어색한 것을 바르게 고치시오.

(1) Build a new airport in the town is a bad idea.

_____
_____

(2) It is wise for Charles to select the book.

_____

(3) Betty should not only eat well but also working out regularly.

_____

(4) Emily as well as her sisters are good at tennis.

_____

08 다음 우리말을 괄호 안에 주어진 어휘를 이용하여 영작하시오.

(1) 적을 용서하는 것은 쉽지 않다. (forgive, an enemy, 8 단어)

➡ _____

(2) 에너지를 절약하는 것이 중요하다. (important, save, energy, 6 단어)

➡ _____

(3) 오늘은 크리스마스일 뿐만 아니라 내 생일이다. (only, Christmas, 9 단어)

➡ _____

(4) Jane뿐만 아니라 그녀의 남동생들도 친절하다. (kind, well, 8 단어)

➡ _____

Reading

Mudflats, Nature's Gift

Mudflats are large areas of <u>muddy</u> land at the seaside. They appear and
mud의 형용사형
<u>disappear</u> <u>with every tide</u>. During <u>low tides</u>, they show up, and <u>during</u>
→appear ~함에 따라, ~와 더불어, ~와 함께 썰물 ~ 동안
<u>high tides</u>, they <u>are covered by</u> the sea. Mudflats help sea creatures,
밀물 be동사+과거분사+by: 수동태 구문
people, and the Earth in many ways. <u>It is important to understand</u> the
It+be동사+형용사+to부정사
roles of mudflats. Let's see <u>what they do</u>.
간접의문문

Mudflats are home <u>to</u> a lot of <u>living things</u> at the seaside. <u>Not only</u>
~에게 생물
very small living things like plankton but also crabs and fish live there.
not only A but also B: A뿐만 아니라 B도, A와 B의 형태는 같아야 한다.
Mudflats <u>provide various types of food for</u> them. Also, many birds eat
주어+provide+직접목적어+for+간접목적어: 3형식 문장
food there.

Crab: Mudflats are my home sweet home.

mudflat: 갯벌
muddy: 진흙의, 질퍽한
appear: 나타나다, 출현하다
tide: 조수, 밀물과 썰물
creature: 생명체, 생물
role: 역할, 임무
plankton: 플랑크톤
crab: 게
provide: 제공하다, 주다
various: 각종의, 다양한

📎 **확인문제**

● 다음 문장이 본문의 내용과 일치하면 T, 일치하지 <u>않으면</u> F를 쓰시오.

1 Mudflats are large areas of muddy land at the seaside. ☐

2 Mudflats disappear during low tides. ☐

3 Mudflats are home to a lot of living things at the seaside. ☐

4 Not plankton but crabs and fish live on mudflats. ☐

Mudflats are good for people, too. People who live near mudflat areas make a living by catching fish and other sea animals nearby. Thanks to mudflats, people can get fresh seafood. People can enjoy fun activities, such as mud sliding and body painting on mudflats. They can also watch a large number of birds that feed on the sea animals there.

Boy: Mudflats are nature's gift to living things!

Mudflats help the environment greatly. Mudflats hold a lot of water, so they can reduce damage from floods. Also, mudflats filter water that flows from the land into the sea. They remove bad things in the water before it enters the sea. Thanks to mudflats, the water that reaches the sea is clean. Mudflats work as the Earth's lungs. They produce a huge volume of oxygen that is necessary for life on the Earth.

Earth: Mudflats keep me healthy and clean.

Mudflats are wonderful places, aren't they? They are a gift from nature to living things on the Earth. For all these reasons, it is necessary to protect mudflats.

mud: 진흙
slide: 미끄러지다
feed: 먹이를 먹다, 먹이다
make a living: 생계를 꾸리다
environment: 환경
reduce: 줄이다
damage: 피해, 손해
flood: 홍수
filter: 거르다, 걸러 내다
flow: 흐르다
remove: 제거하다
reach: ~에 이르다, 닿다, 도달하다
lung: 폐
volume: 용량, 용적
oxygen: 산소
necessary: 필요한
reason: 이유
protect: 보호하다

확인문제

● 다음 문장이 본문의 내용과 일치하면 T, 일치하지 <u>않으면</u> F를 쓰시오.

1 Mudflats enable people to get fresh seafood.

2 People can watch the sea animals that feed on birds on mudflats.

3 Mudflats filter water flowing from the land into the sea.

4 Thanks to mudflats, the water that arrives at the sea is clean.

5 Mudflats are a gift from living things on the Earth to nature.

● 우리말을 참고하여 빈칸에 알맞은 말을 쓰시오.

1 Mudflats, Nature's _____

2 Mudflats are large areas of _____ _____ at the seaside.

3 They appear and disappear _____ _____ _____.

4 During low tides, they _____ _____, and during _____ _____, they _____ _____ _____ the sea.

5 Mudflats help sea creatures, people, and the Earth _____ _____ _____.

6 It is important to understand _____ _____ _____ _____.

7 Let's see _____ _____ _____.

8 Mudflats _____ _____ _____ a lot of living things at the seaside.

9 _____ _____ very small living things like plankton _____ _____ crabs and fish live there.

10 Mudflats _____ various types of food _____ them.

11 _____, many birds eat food there.

12 Crab: Mudflats are my _____ _____ _____.

13 Mudflats _____ _____ _____ people, too.

1 갯벌, 자연의 선물

2 갯벌은 바닷가의 진흙이 있는 넓은 지역이다.

3 갯벌은 조수와 함께 나타나고 사라진다.

4 썰물일 때 갯벌이 드러나고, 밀물일 때 바다에 덮인다.

5 갯벌은 바다 생물과 사람, 지구를 많은 방면에서 돕는다.

6 갯벌의 역할을 이해하는 것이 중요하다.

7 갯벌이 무엇을 하는지 살펴보자.

8 갯벌은 바닷가에 있는 많은 생물들에게 집이다.

9 플랑크톤처럼 작은 생명체뿐만 아니라 게와 물고기도 그곳에 산다.

10 갯벌은 그들에게 다양한 종류의 먹이를 제공한다.

11 또한, 많은 새들도 그곳에서 먹이를 먹는다.

12 게: 갯벌은 나의 단란한 집이에요.

13 갯벌은 사람들에게도 유익하다.

14 People who live near mudflat areas _____ _____ _____ by catching fish and other sea animals _____ .

15 _____ _____ mudflats, people can get fresh seafood.

16 People can enjoy _____ _____ , _____ _____ mud sliding and body painting on mudflats.

17 They can also watch a large number of birds that _____ _____ the sea animals there.

18 Boy: Mudflats are _____ _____ to living things!

19 Mudflats _____ the environment _____ .

20 Mudflats _____ a lot of water, so they can _____ _____ from floods.

21 Also, mudflats _____ water that flows _____ the land _____ the sea.

22 They _____ _____ _____ in the water before it enters the sea.

23 Thanks to mudflats, the water _____ _____ _____ _____ is clean.

24 Mudflats work _____ _____ _____ _____ .

25 They produce _____ _____ _____ oxygen that is necessary for life on the Earth.

26 Earth: Mudflats keep me _____ and _____ .

27 Mudflats are wonderful places, _____ _____ ?

28 They are a gift _____ _____ _____ _____ on the Earth.

29 For all these reasons, it is necessary _____ _____ _____ .

14 갯벌 지역 인근에 사는 사람들은 근처에서 물고기와 다른 바다 동물들을 잡아 생계를 꾸린다.

15 갯벌 덕분에 사람들은 신선한 해산물을 얻을 수 있다.

16 사람들은 갯벌에서 진흙 미끄럼 타기나 보디 페인팅과 같은 즐거운 활동을 즐길 수 있다.

17 그들은 또한 그곳에서 바다 동물들을 먹는 수많은 새를 관찰할 수도 있다.

18 남자아이: 갯벌은 생명체에게 주는 자연의 선물이에요!

19 갯벌은 환경에 크게 도움이 된다.

20 갯벌은 많은 양의 물을 수용해서 홍수의 피해를 줄여 준다.

21 또한, 갯벌은 땅에서 바다로 흘러가는 물을 걸러내 준다.

22 물이 바다로 들어가기 전에 물 속에 있는 나쁜 물질을 갯벌이 제거한다.

23 갯벌 덕분에 바다에 도착한 물은 깨끗하다.

24 갯벌은 지구의 폐 역할을 한다.

25 그것들은 지구상의 생명에게 필요한 많은 양의 산소를 생산한다.

26 지구: 갯벌은 나를 건강하고 깨끗하게 지켜 줘요.

27 갯벌은 멋진 곳이다. 그렇지 않은가?

28 그곳은 자연이 지구상의 생물들에게 준 선물이다.

29 이러한 이유로, 갯벌을 보호하는 것은 필수이다.

• 우리말을 참고하여 본문을 영작하시오.

1 ▶ 갯벌, 자연의 선물

➡ _____

2 ▶ 갯벌은 바닷가의 진흙이 있는 넓은 지역이다.

➡ _____

3 ▶ 갯벌은 조수와 함께 나타나고 사라진다.

➡ _____

4 ▶ 썰물일 때 갯벌이 드러나고, 밀물일 때 바다에 덮인다.

➡ _____

5 ▶ 갯벌은 바다 생물과 사람, 지구를 많은 방면에서 돕는다.

➡ _____

6 ▶ 갯벌의 역할을 이해하는 것이 중요하다.

➡ _____

7 ▶ 갯벌이 무엇을 하는지 살펴보자.

➡ _____

8 ▶ 갯벌은 바닷가에 있는 많은 생물들에게 집이다.

➡ _____

9 ▶ 플랑크톤처럼 작은 생명체뿐만 아니라 게와 물고기도 그곳에 산다.

➡ _____

10 ▶ 갯벌은 그들에게 다양한 종류의 먹이를 제공한다.

➡ _____

11 ▶ 또한, 많은 새들도 그곳에서 먹이를 먹는다.

➡ _____

12 ▶ 게: 갯벌은 나의 단란한 집이에요.

➡ _____

13 ▶ 갯벌은 사람들에게도 유익하다.

➡ _____

14 갯벌 지역 인근에 사는 사람들은 근처에서 물고기와 다른 바다 동물들을 잡아 생계를 꾸린다.

➡ _____

15 갯벌 덕분에 사람들은 신선한 해산물을 얻을 수 있다.

➡ _____

16 사람들은 갯벌에서 진흙 미끄럼 타기나 보디 페인팅과 같은 즐거운 활동을 즐길 수 있다.

➡ _____

17 그들은 또한 그곳에서 바다 동물들을 먹는 수많은 새를 관찰할 수도 있다.

➡ _____

18 남자아이: 갯벌은 생명체에게 주는 자연의 선물이에요!

➡ _____

19 갯벌은 환경에 크게 도움이 된다.

➡ _____

20 갯벌은 많은 양의 물을 수용해서 홍수의 피해를 줄여 준다.

➡ _____

21 또한, 갯벌은 땅에서 바다로 흘러가는 물을 걸러내 준다.

➡ _____

22 물이 바다로 들어가기 전에 물속에 있는 나쁜 물질을 갯벌이 제거한다.

➡ _____

23 갯벌 덕분에 바다에 도착한 물은 깨끗하다.

➡ _____

24 갯벌은 지구의 폐 역할을 한다.

➡ _____

25 그것들은 지구상의 생명에게 필요한 많은 양의 산소를 생산한다.

➡ _____

26 지구: 갯벌은 나를 건강하고 깨끗하게 지켜 줘요.

➡ _____

27 갯벌은 멋진 곳이다, 그렇지 않은가?

➡ _____

28 그곳은 자연이 지구상의 생물들에게 준 선물이다.

➡ _____

29 이러한 이유로, 갯벌을 보호하는 것은 필수이다.

➡ _____

[01~04] 다음 글을 읽고 물음에 답하시오.

Mudflats are large areas of muddy land at the seaside. ⓐThey are appeared and disappeared with every tide. During low tides, they show up, and during high tides, they are covered by the sea. Mudflats help sea creatures, people, and the Earth in many ways. It is important to understand the roles of mudflats. Let's see what ⓑthey do.

서답형
01 위 글의 밑줄 친 ⓐ에서 어법상 틀린 부분을 찾아 고치시오.

➡ _____

_____

서답형
02 주어진 (1)과 (2)의 영영풀이에 해당하는 단어를 본문에서 찾아 각각 쓰시오.

(1) the inward flow of the tide or the time when the sea is at its highest level because the tide is in
(2) the outward flow of the tide or the time when the sea is at its lowest level because the tide is out

➡ (1) _____ (2) _____

중요
03 다음 중 갯벌에 대해 올바르게 이해하지 못한 사람을 고르시오.

① 수민: 갯벌은 바닷가의 진흙이 있는 넓은 지역이다.
② 희정: 갯벌은 조수간만이 없는 지역에서 드러난다.
③ 창수: 갯벌은 썰물일 때 드러난다.
④ 진호: 갯벌은 밀물일 때 사라진다.
⑤ 규진: 갯벌은 바다 생물과 사람, 지구를 많은 방면에서 돕는다.

04 위 글의 종류로 알맞은 것을 고르시오.

① an introduction to cultures
② geography experiment report
③ weather forecast
④ an introduction to the landform
⑤ field trip guide

[05~07] 다음 글을 읽고 물음에 답하시오.

Mudflats help the environment greatly. (①) Mudflats hold a lot of water, so they can reduce damage from floods. (②) Also, mudflats filter water ⓐthat flows from the land into the sea. (③) They remove bad things in the water before it enters the sea. (④) Thanks to mudflats, the water that reaches the sea is clean. (⑤) They produce a huge volume of oxygen that is necessary for life on the Earth.

중요
05 위 글의 흐름으로 보아, 주어진 문장이 들어가기에 가장 적절한 곳은?

Mudflats work as the Earth's lungs.

①   ②   ③   ④   ⑤

06 위 글의 밑줄 친 ⓐthat과 문법적 쓰임이 같은 것을 모두 고르시오.

① He said that the story was interesting.
② It's the best novel that I've ever read.
③ The people that I spoke to were very helpful.
④ Ann doesn't believe the fact that Tim is older than me.
⑤ The watch that you gave me keeps good time.

서답형

07 위 글을 읽고, 바다에 도착한 물이 깨끗해지는 이유를 우리말로 쓰시오. (40자 내외)

➡ _____

_____

[08~10] 다음 글을 읽고 물음에 답하시오.

Mudflats are good (A)[at / for] people, too. People who live near mudflat areas make a living by catching fish and (B)[another / other] sea animals nearby. Thanks to mudflats, people can get fresh seafood. People can enjoy fun activities, such as mud sliding and body painting on mudflats. They can also watch a __(a)__ number of birds that (C)[feed / food] on the sea animals there.

08 위 글의 빈칸 (a)에 들어갈 알맞은 말을 고르시오.

① many   ② much
③ high   ④ lot
⑤ large

서답형

09 위 글의 괄호 (A)~(C)에서 문맥이나 어법상 알맞은 낱말을 골라 쓰시오.

➡ (A)_____ (B)_____ (C)_____

중요
10 위 글의 앞에 올 내용으로 가장 알맞은 것을 고르시오.

① 갯벌이 유익한 다른 경우
② 갯벌의 정의
③ 갯벌의 생성 조건
④ 갯벌의 종류
⑤ 갯벌 보존의 필요성

[11~13] 다음 글을 읽고 물음에 답하시오.

All about Mudflats

Mudflats are muddy land at the seaside. ⓐNot only plants like *hamcho* but also animals such as crabs and fish live there. They show up during low tides and are covered by the sea during high tides. If you go to mudflats, it is important to wear long clothes ⓑto protect yourself from animals that can bite you.

서답형

11 위 글의 밑줄 친 ⓐ를 다음과 같이 바꿔 쓸 때 빈칸에 들어갈 알맞은 말을 쓰시오.

➡ Animals such as crabs and fish as well as plants like *hamcho* _____ there.

12 아래 보기에서 위 글의 밑줄 친 ⓑto protect와 to부정사의 용법이 다른 것의 개수를 고르시오.

┌─ 보기 ─┐
① He cannot be rich to ask you for some money.
② Give me something to eat.
③ I got up early to catch the train.
④ I am sorry to give you trouble.
⑤ I decided to help that poor woman.
└──────┘

① 1개   ② 2개   ③ 3개   ④ 4개   ⑤ 5개

서답형

13 What is important if you go to mudflats? Fill in the blanks with suitable words.

➡ It is important that you should _____ _____ to protect yourself from animals that can bite you.

[14~16] 다음 글을 읽고 물음에 답하시오.

Mudflats are home ⓐ a lot of living things at the seaside. ⓑNot only very small living things like plankton but also crabs and fish live there. Mudflats provide various types of food ⓒ them. Also, many birds eat food there.

 위 글의 빈칸 ⓐ와 ⓒ에 들어갈 전치사가 바르게 짝지어진 것은?

① to – with
② at – to
③ to – for
④ for – with
⑤ at – for

15 위 글의 밑줄 친 ⓑ와 의미가 <u>다른</u> 문장을 고르시오.

① Not merely very small living things like plankton but also crabs and fish live there.
② Not just very small living things like plankton but also crabs and fish live there.
③ Not simply very small living things like plankton but also crabs and fish live there.
④ Very small living things like plankton as well as crabs and fish live there.
⑤ Not only very small living things like plankton but crabs and fish live there.

16 위 글의 내용과 일치하지 <u>않는</u> 것은?

① 갯벌은 바닷가에 있는 많은 생물들에게 집이다.
② 플랑크톤처럼 작은 생명체는 갯벌에 살 수 없다.
③ 게와 물고기도 갯벌에 산다.
④ 갯벌은 게와 물고기 등에게 다양한 종류의 먹이를 제공한다.
⑤ 많은 새들도 갯벌에서 먹이를 먹는다.

[17~19] 다음 글을 읽고 물음에 답하시오.

Mudflats help the environment greatly. Mudflats hold a lot of water, so they can ① reduce damage from floods. (A) , mudflats filter water that flows from the land into the sea. They remove bad things in the water before it enters the sea. Thanks to mudflats, the water that ②reaches the sea is clean. Mudflats work as the Earth's lungs. They produce a ③huge volume of oxygen that is necessary for life on the Earth.

Earth: Mudflats keep me healthy and clean.

Mudflats are ④wonderful places, aren't they? They are a gift from nature to living things on the Earth. For all these reasons, it is necessary to ⑤protect mudflats.

17 위 글의 빈칸 (A)에 들어갈 알맞은 말을 고르시오.

① However
② Therefore
③ Also
④ For example
⑤ In other words

18 위 글의 밑줄 친 ①~⑤와 바꿔 쓸 수 <u>없는</u> 말을 고르시오.

① decrease
② gets to
③ large
④ awesome
⑤ prevent

19 본문의 내용과 일치하도록 다음 빈칸에 알맞은 단어를 쓰시오.

Mudflats can reduce damage from ____ by holding a lot of water.

➡ _____

[20~22] 다음 글을 읽고 물음에 답하시오.

Mudflats are large areas of muddy land at the seaside. They appear and disappear with every tide. During low tides, they show up, and during high tides, ⓐthey are covered by the sea. Mudflats help sea creatures, people, and the Earth in many ways. ⓑIt is important to understand the roles of mudflats. Let's see ___(A)___ they do.

20 위 글의 빈칸 (A)에 들어갈 알맞은 말을 고르시오.

① how   ② when
③ where   ④ what
⑤ why

서답형

21 위 글의 밑줄 친 ⓐ를 능동태로 고치시오.

➡ _____

22 위 글의 밑줄 친 ⓑ과 문법적 쓰임이 같은 것을 고르시오. (3개)

① It is time to go to bed.
② Is it difficult for you to do the work?
③ I made it a rule to exercise every day.
④ It was necessary to go there after school.
⑤ It was dangerous to swim in the river.

[23~25] 다음 글을 읽고 물음에 답하시오.

My group made a book about the longest river, the biggest cave, the tallest falls, and the highest mountain. ⓐThat was fun to find the information about these places. ⓑThey are not only beautiful but also surprising. We felt the wonder of nature.

서답형

23 위 글의 밑줄 친 ⓐ에서 어법상 틀린 부분을 찾아 고치시오.

➡ _____

서답형

24 위 글의 밑줄 친 ⓑThey의 예를 본문에서 찾아 쓰시오.

➡ _____
_____

서답형

25 주어진 영영풀이에 해당하는 단어를 본문에서 찾아 쓰시오.

something that is very surprising and unexpected

➡ _____

[26~27] 다음 글을 읽고 물음에 답하시오.

All about Deserts

Deserts are dry land with (A)[few / little] plants and (B)[few / little] water. Not only plants like elephant trees but also animals such as lizards and desert snakes live there. It is hot (C)[during / for] the day and cold at night. If you go to a desert, it is important to wear a hat to block the sun.

서답형

26 위 글의 괄호 (A)~(C)에서 어법상 알맞은 낱말을 골라 쓰시오.

➡ (A)_____ (B)_____ (C)_____

서답형

27 다음 문장에서 위 글의 내용과 다른 부분을 찾아서 고치시오.

• In the deserts, it is always hot day and night.

➡ _____
_____

[01~04] 다음 글을 읽고 물음에 답하시오.

Mudflats are large areas of muddy land at the seaside. They ⓐappear and disappear with every __(A)__ . During low tides, they show up, and during high tides, they are covered by the sea. Mudflats help sea creatures, people, and the Earth in many ways. It is important to understand the roles of mudflats. Let's see what ⓑthey do.

1 위 글의 빈칸 (A)에 들어갈 말을 본문에서 찾아 알맞은 형태로 쓰시오.

➡ _____

02 위 글의 밑줄 친 ⓐappear와 바꿔 쓸 수 있는 숙어를 본문에서 찾아 쓰시오.

➡ _____

03 다음 빈칸 (A)와 (B)에 알맞은 단어를 넣어 Mudflats에 대한 소개를 완성하시오.

> They are areas of flat empty land at the coast which appear during (A)_____ tides and (B)_____ during high tides.

04 위 글의 밑줄 친 ⓑthey가 가리키는 것을 본문에서 찾아 쓰시오.

➡ _____

[05~07] 다음 글을 읽고 물음에 답하시오.

Mudflats help the environment (A)[great / greatly]. ⓐMudflats hold a lot of water, as they can reduce damage from floods. Also, mudflats filter water that flows from the land into the sea. They (B)[generate / remove] bad

things in the water before it enters the sea. ⓑ 갯벌 덕분에 바다에 도착한 물은 깨끗하다. Mudflats work as the Earth's lungs. They produce a huge (C)[number / volume] of oxygen that is necessary for life on the Earth.

05 위 글의 괄호 (A)~(C)에서 문맥이나 어법상 알맞은 낱말을 골라 쓰시오.

➡ (A) _____ (B) _____ (C) _____

6 위 글의 밑줄 친 ⓐ에서 흐름상 어색한 부분을 찾아 고치시오.

➡ _____
  _____
  _____

07 위 글의 밑줄 친 ⓑ의 우리말에 맞게 주어진 어휘를 이용하여 11 단어로 영작하시오.

> Thanks to, that, reaches

➡ _____

[08~10] 다음 글을 읽고 물음에 답하시오.

Mudflats are home to a lot of living things at the seaside. ⓐNot only very small living things like plankton but also crabs and fish live there. ⓑMudflats provide various types of food for them. Also, many birds eat food ⓒthere.

08 위 글의 밑줄 친 ⓐ를 as well as를 사용하여 고치시오.

➡ _____

_____

09 위 글의 밑줄 친 ⓑ를 다음과 같이 바꿔 쓸 때 빈칸에 들어갈 알맞은 전치사를 쓰시오.

➡ Mudflats provide them _____ various types of food.

10 위 글의 밑줄 친 ⓒthere가 가리키는 장소를 본문에서 찾아 쓰시오.

➡ _____

[11~13] 다음 글을 읽고 물음에 답하시오.

Mudflats are good for people, too. People who live near mudflat areas make a living by (A)_____ fish and other sea animals nearby. Thanks to mudflats, people can get fresh seafood. People can enjoy ⓐfun activities, such as mud sliding and body painting (B)_____ mudflats. They can also watch a large number of birds that feed (C)_____ the sea animals there.

11 위 글의 빈칸 (A)에 catch를 알맞은 형태로 쓰시오.

➡ _____

12 위 글의 빈칸 (B)와 (C)에 공통으로 들어갈 전치사를 쓰시오.

➡ _____

13 위 글의 밑줄 친 ⓐfun activities의 예를 본문에서 찾아 쓰시오.

➡ _____

[14~17] 다음 글을 읽고 물음에 답하시오.

Mudflats help the environment greatly. Mudflats hold a lot of water, so they can reduce damage from floods. Also, mudflats filter water (A)_____ flows from the land into the sea. They remove bad things in the water before it enters the sea. Thanks to mudflats, the water (B)_____ reaches the sea is clean. Mudflats work as the Earth's lungs. They produce a huge volume of oxygen (C)_____ is necessary for life on the Earth.

Earth: ⓐMudflats keep me healthily and cleanly.

Mudflats are wonderful places, (D)_____? They are a gift from nature to living things on the Earth. For all these reasons, it is necessary to protect mudflats.

14 위 글의 빈칸 (A)~(C)에 공통으로 들어갈 알맞은 관계대명사를 쓰시오.

➡ _____

15 위 글의 빈칸 (D)에 들어갈 알맞은 부가의문문을 쓰시오.

➡ _____

16 위 글의 밑줄 친 ⓐ에서 어법상 틀린 부분을 찾아 고치시오.

➡ _____

17 다음 빈칸 (A)와 (B)에 알맞은 단어를 넣어 갯벌을 보호해야 하는 이유를 완성하시오.

As mudflats are a gift from (A)_____ to (B)_____ _____ on the Earth, it is necessary to protect mudflats.

Enjoy Writing B

Deserts are dry land with few plants and little water. Not only plants like
elephant trees but also animals such as lizards and desert snakes live there. It
is hot during the day and cold at night. If you go to a desert, it is important to
wear a hat to block the sun.

구문해설 • desert: 사막 • lizard: 도마뱀 • block: 막다, 차단하다

사막은 식물과 물이 거의 없는 건조한 땅이다. 코끼리 나무 같은 식물뿐만 아니라 도마뱀이나 사막뱀 같은 동물들도 그곳에 산다. 낮에는 덥고 밤에는 춥다. 만일 사막에 간다면 햇빛을 가리기 위해 모자를 쓰는 것이 중요하다.

Enjoy Writing B

All about Mudflats

Mudflats are muddy land at the seaside. Not only plants like *hamcho* but also
animals such as crabs and fish live there. They show up during low tides and
are covered by the sea during high tides. If you go to mudflats, it is important
to wear long clothes to protect yourself from animals that can bite you.

구문해설 • mudflat: 갯벌 • muddy: 진흙의, 질퍽한 • crab: 게 • show up: 나타나다 • low tides: 썰물
• high tides: 밀물 • bite: (이빨로) 물다

갯벌에 관한 모든 것

갯벌은 바닷가의 진흙이 있는 지역이다. 함초와 같은 식물들뿐만 아니라 게와 물고기와 같은 동물들도 그곳에 산다. 썰물일 때 갯벌이 드러나고, 밀물일 때 바다에 덮인다. 만약 당신이 갯벌에 간다면, 당신을 물 수 있는 동물들로부터 당신을 보호하기 위해 긴 옷을 입는 것이 중요하다.

Wrap Up 1

B: I just finished making a plan for my trip. Do you want to hear it?

G: Sure. I wonder what you will do.

B: On the first day, I'm going to go fishing on a lake. The next day, I'm going
to climb a mountain.

G: Is that all?

B: No. On the last day, I'm going to go swimming.

G: Wow. You will do a lot of activities.

B: 나는 방금 여행 계획 세우는 것을 끝냈어. 그것에 대해 듣고 싶니?
G: 물론이지. 나는 네가 무엇을 할지 궁금해.
B: 첫날에 나는 호수에서 낚시를 할 거야. 다음 날에 나는 산에 오를 거야.
G: 그게 전부니?
B: 아니. 마지막 날에 나는 수영을 할 거야.
G: 우와. 너는 많은 활동들을 할 거구나.

01 다음 중 밑줄 친 단어의 쓰임이 바르지 못한 것은?

① Please clean your <u>messy</u> desk.

② I have a <u>friendy</u> pet dog.

③ It is <u>windy</u> today.

④ I am very <u>lucky</u> to have such nice friends.

⑤ She exercises every day to become <u>healthy</u>.

02 다음 중 밑줄 친 부분의 뜻풀이가 바르지 <u>않은</u> 것은?

① The tree stands on the edge of a <u>cliff</u>. (절벽)

② It <u>filters</u> the seawater to keep it clean. (거르다)

③ The water will <u>flow</u> into the rivers. (흐르다)

④ The <u>falls</u> can supply 10 percent of all the electric power for the New York State. (떨어지다)

⑤ She <u>greeted</u> me with a smile. (인사했다)

03 다음 밑줄 친 부분과 의미가 가장 가까운 것을 주어진 철자로 시작하여 쓰시오.

> This can <u>take place</u> anywhere and at any time.

➡ o _____

04 다음 빈칸에 알맞은 말을 고르시오.

> The lake is probably the most polluted _____ of water in the world.

① wave　　② tide　　③ body

④ flood　　⑤ blood

[05~07] 다음 대화를 읽고 물음에 답하시오.

G: 나는 네가 여름 방학 동안에 무엇을 했는지 궁금해.

B: I took a trip to Kenya and (A)_____ (see) many animals on the plains.

G: Wonderful! (B)_____, what are the plains?

B: They are large areas of flat land.

G: I see.

05 빈칸 (A)에 알맞은 말을 주어진 단어를 이용해서 채우시오.

➡ _____

06 빈칸 (B)에 알맞은 말을 고르시오.

① Although

② In addition

③ On the contrary

④ Besides

⑤ By the way

07 밑줄 친 우리말을 주어진 단어를 이용하여 영작하시오. (9단어)

➡ _____

(wonder, do, during)

[08~10] 다음 대화를 읽고 물음에 답하시오.

B: Do you know how ⓐ<u>much</u> oceans ⓑ<u>are</u> there on the Earth?

G: The answer is four, ⓒ<u>isn't it?</u>

B: No. There ⓓ<u>are</u> five oceans on the Earth. They cover ⓔ<u>most</u> of the Earth.

G: (A)_____

B: I heard the oceans ⓕ<u>is covered</u> about 70% of the Earth's surface.

08 빈칸 (A)에 들어갈 말로 알맞은 것은?

① How do five oceans cover the Earth?
② How can oceans be found?
③ How big is the biggest ocean?
④ How much of the Earth do they cover?
⑤ Why is 70% of the Earth covered by oceans?

09 위 글의 ⓐ~ⓕ 중 어법상 틀린 것만 바르게 묶은 것은?

① ⓐ, ⓑ
② ⓒ, ⓓ
③ ⓔ, ⓕ
④ ⓐ, ⓑ, ⓕ
⑤ ⓒ, ⓓ, ⓔ

10 다음 영영풀이에 해당하는 단어를 대화에서 찾아 쓰시오.

> the flat top part of something or the outside of it

➡ _____

[11~12] 다음 대화를 읽고 물음에 답하시오.

Dad: Do you want to see an amazing place?

Karl & Sister: Sure!

Dad: Then let's get on the train.

Sister: Look at the yellow plants! I wonder what they are.

Dad: They are reeds. Suncheon Bay has beautiful reed fields.

Karl: Wow, the reeds are ___(A)___ taller than you, Dad.

Sister: They really are. Let me take a picture of you.

Karl: This reed field is very large.

Dad: Yes. (B)<u>나는 그곳이 한국에서 가장 큰 갈대밭이라고 들었어.</u>

Karl: Look at the sky. It's turning red.

Sister: Yes, it's beautiful.

11 빈칸 (A)에 들어가기에 어색한 것은?

① even
② far
③ still
④ very
⑤ a lot

12 밑줄 친 (B)의 우리말과 의미가 같도록 주어진 단어를 이용하여 영작하시오.

➡ _____

(9단어) (in, large, it, one, heard)

Grammar

13 다음 문장을 바르게 바꿔 쓴 것이 <u>아닌</u> 것은?

> Sam not only reads German but also writes it.

① Sam not only reads German but writes it.
② Sam not only reads German but writes it as well.
③ Sam reads German as well as writes it.
④ Sam not simply reads German but also writes it.
⑤ Sam not merely reads German but writes it.

14 다음 빈칸에 들어갈 표현이 순서대로 바르게 짝지어진 것을 고르시오.

> Hana is good at _____ math _____ art.

① not only — but
② not only — also
③ merely — also
④ simply — as well
⑤ not — too

15 밑줄 친 부분의 쓰임이 다른 하나는?

① It is exciting to play baseball.
② It's wonderful to make new friends.
③ It was not hard to work out every day.
④ He tried it several times only to fail.
⑤ Is it necessary to buy a ticket now?

16 다음 빈칸에 들어갈 말이 나머지와 다른 하나는?

① It is easy _____ me to learn how to ride a bike.
② It is rude _____ her to speak so loud in public.
③ It is impossible _____ Julie to work with them.
④ It is necessary _____ him to take care of others.
⑤ It is important _____ you to eat healthy food.

17 다음 ⓐ~ⓗ 중 옳은 것을 모두 고르면?

> ⓐ Not only you but also James play the piano.
> ⓑ Not only plants like *hamcho* but also animals such as crabs and fish live there.
> ⓒ Animals as well as plants lives in deserts.
> ⓓ They are not only beautiful but also surprising.
> ⓔ It was careless for you to break the window.
> ⓕ It will be dangerous swims in this lake.
> ⓖ That is easy for me to understand this book.
> ⓗ It is necessary for them to focus on the class.

① ⓐ, ⓒ
② ⓑ, ⓒ, ⓓ
③ ⓑ, ⓓ, ⓗ
④ ⓓ, ⓔ, ⓗ
⑤ ⓓ, ⓔ, ⓖ

18 다음 문장을 주어진 말로 시작하여 다시 쓰시오.

(1) You must be kind to other people.
➡ It is necessary _____.
(2) You should be careful when you drive a car.
➡ It is necessary _____
_____.

19 다음 중 어법상 어색한 문장은?

① It was foolish of him to think so.
② It was fun for us to go to an amusement park.
③ It is important to be nice to friends.
④ Not only plants like elephant trees but also animals such as lizards and desert snakes live there.
⑤ Dylan not only played computer games but also doing his homework.

[20~22] 다음 글을 읽고 물음에 답하시오.

Mudflats are large areas of muddy land at the seaside. They appear and disappear ⓐ_____ every tide. During low tides, they show up, and during high tides, they are covered by the sea. Mudflats help sea creatures, people, and the Earth ⓑ_____ many ways. ⓒIt is important to understand the roles of mudflats. Let's see what they do.

20 위 글의 빈칸 ⓐ와 ⓑ에 들어갈 알맞은 전치사를 고르시오.

① with – from
② in – by
③ in – from
④ with – in
⑤ on – through

21 위 글의 밑줄 친 ⓒ를 바르게 바꿔 쓴 문장을 <u>모두</u> 고르시오.

① Understanding the roles of mudflats are important.
② To understand the roles of mudflats is important.
③ That is important to understand the roles of mudflats.
④ To understand the roles of mudflats are important.
⑤ Understanding the roles of mudflats is important.

22 위 글을 읽고 대답할 수 <u>없는</u> 질문은?

① When do mudflats appear?
② When do mudflats disappear?
③ What are the roles of mudflats?
④ During high tides, what covers mudflats?
⑤ Are mudflats helpful to the Earth?

[23~24] 다음 글을 읽고 물음에 답하시오.

Mudflats help the environment greatly. Mudflats hold a lot of water, so they can (A)[increase / reduce] damage from floods. Also, mudflats filter water that flows from the land into the sea. They remove bad things in the water before it (B)[enters / enters into] the sea. Thanks to mudflats, the water that (C)[reaches / reaches to] the sea is clean. Mudflats work ⓐas the Earth's lungs. They produce a huge volume of oxygen that is necessary for life on the Earth.

23 위 글의 괄호 (A)~(C)에서 문맥이나 어법상 알맞은 낱말을 골라 쓰시오.

➡ (A)_____ (B)_____ (C)_____

24 위 글의 밑줄 친 ⓐas와 같은 의미로 쓰인 것을 고르시오.

① Do in Rome <u>as</u> the Romans do.
② He came up <u>as</u> I was speaking.
③ Susan is <u>as</u> pretty as Jane.
④ This box will serve <u>as</u> a table.
⑤ <u>As</u> we go up, the air grows colder.

[25~26] 다음 글을 읽고 물음에 답하시오.

Mudflats are good for people, too. People who live near mudflat areas make a living by ⓐ<u>catching</u> fish and other sea animals nearby. Thanks to mudflats, people can get fresh seafood. People can enjoy fun activities, ⓑ<u>such as</u> mud sliding and body painting on mudflats. They can also watch a large number of birds that feed on the sea animals there.

25 위 글의 밑줄 친 ⓐcatching과 문법적 쓰임이 <u>다른</u> 것을 모두 고르시오.

① The boy <u>sitting</u> under the tree is my brother.

② Thank you for <u>visiting</u> our website.

③ I saw her <u>walking</u> with her boyfriend.

④ I was <u>watching</u> TV in the living room.

⑤ <u>Mastering</u> foreign languages is not easy.

26 위 글의 밑줄 친 ⓑsuch as와 바꿔 쓸 수 있는 단어를 쓰시오.

➡ _____

[27~28] 다음 글을 읽고 물음에 답하시오.

Mudflats help the environment greatly. Mudflats hold a lot of water, so they can reduce damage from floods. Also, mudflats filter water that flows from the land into the sea. They remove bad things in the water before it enters the sea. Thanks to mudflats, the water that reaches the sea is clean. Mudflats work as the Earth's ___(A)___ . They produce a huge volume of oxygen that is necessary for life on the Earth.

27 위 글의 빈칸 (A)에 들어갈 알맞은 말을 고르시오.

① face   ② lungs

③ stomach   ④ head

⑤ hands and legs

28 위 글의 제목으로 알맞은 것을 고르시오.

① How to Reduce Damage from Floods

② Water Reaches the Sea through Mudflats

③ Oxygen, a Necessity for Life on the Earth

④ How Helpful Mudflats Are to the Environment!

⑤ Let's Protect the Environment

[29~31] 다음 글을 읽고 물음에 답하시오.

Mudflats are home to ①a lot of living things at the ②seaside. Not ③only very small living things ⓐlike plankton but also crabs and fish live there. Mudflats ④provide various types of food for them. ⑤Also, many birds eat food there.

29 위 글의 밑줄 친 ①~⑤와 바꿔 쓸 수 <u>없는</u> 말은?

① much   ② seashore

③ merely   ④ supply

⑤ In addition

30 위 글의 밑줄 친 ⓐlike와 같은 의미로 쓰인 것을 고르시오.

① I like hobbies <u>like</u> photography or painting.

② He is very <u>like</u> his father.

③ How did you <u>like</u> New York?

④ She responded in <u>like</u> manner.

⑤ Do it <u>like</u> this.

31 본문의 내용과 일치하도록 다음 빈칸에 알맞은 단어를 쓰시오.

Mudflats provide various types of _____ not only for living things at the seaside but also for many birds.

단원별 예상문제

01 다음 짝지어진 두 단어의 관계가 같도록 주어진 철자로 시작하여 빈칸에 알맞은 단어를 쓰시오.

> appear : disappear – high tide : _____

02 다음 빈칸에 알맞은 단어를 〈보기〉에서 골라 쓰시오. (필요하면 대문자를 사용하고, 단어는 한 번만 사용할 것)

> ┌─ 보기 ─┐
> as   during   else   unlike

(1) _____ its name, Greenland is covered with ice and snow.

(2) _____ the night, the pain sometimes wakes me up.

(3) He has many books, such _____ novels and cartoons.

(4) Nothing _____ is better than this.

[03~04] 두 문장에 공통으로 들어갈 수 있는 단어를 쓰시오.

03
> • I hope to _____ a trip to Europe.
> • Could you _____ a picture of us in front of the dinosaur?

04
> • I want to talk to you before I _____ a decision.
> • Don't be afraid to _____ a mistake.
> • It is rude to _____ a noise while eating.

05 다음 빈칸 어디에도 들어갈 수 <u>없는</u> 것은?

> G: Look at that lake! It's really ⓐ_____.
> B: It's not a lake. It's a river.
> G: Is it? I wonder ⓑ_____ a river and a lake are ⓒ_____.
> B: A river is a ⓓ_____ body of ⓔ_____ water. Unlike a lake, a river flows toward the ocean.
> G: I got it.

① fresh   ② beautiful
③ why   ④ different
⑤ long

[06~07] 다음 대화를 읽고 물음에 답하시오.

> A: 나는 숲이 무엇인지 궁금해.
> B: It is land who covered by plants and trees.

06 밑줄 친 우리말과 의미가 같도록 주어진 단어를 이용하여 영작하시오.

➡ _____ (wonder)

_____

(would, know)

07 밑줄 친 문장에서 어법상 <u>어색한</u> 부분을 고치시오.

➡ _____

[08~09] 다음 대화를 읽고 물음에 답하시오.

> G: 나는 아마존 열대 우림이 지구의 허파라고 불린다고 들었어. (heard, Earth, I, the, the, called, Amazon, is, of, lungs, rain, the, forest)

B: Lungs? Why?

G: (A)_____ it (B)_____ about 20% of the Earth's oxygen.

B: Wow! That's a lot.

출제율 90%

08 밑줄 친 우리말을 괄호 안의 단어를 배열하여 영작하시오.

➡ _____

_____

출제율 95%

09 빈칸 (A)와 (B)에 들어갈 말로 알맞은 것끼리 짝지어진 것을 고르시오.

	(A)	(B)
①	Because	protects
②	Because	removes
③	Because	produces
④	Because of	removes
⑤	Because of	produces

[10~11] 다음 대화를 읽고 물음에 답하시오.

A: I want (A)_____ to Danyang.

B: (B)_____?

A: (C)I heard there are famous caves in Danyang.

출제율 95%

10 빈칸 (A)와 (B)에 들어갈 말로 알맞은 것끼리 짝지어진 것을 고르시오.

	(A)	(B)
①	going	Why
②	going	Where
③	to go	Why
④	to go	Where
⑤	to go	How

출제율 100%

11 밑줄 친 (C)와 바꿔 쓸 수 없는 것을 모두 고르시오.

① I have heard

② I'm aware of

③ I'm aware that

④ I'm not sure

⑤ I've been told

출제율 85%

12 빈칸 (A)~(C)에 알맞은 말을 <보기>에서 골라 쓰시오.

M: Guess what this is! It's not a tree. It is a plant that looks (A)_____ tall grass. (B)_____ fall, it turns yellow. It grows well in wet lands. I heard Suncheon Bay is famous (C)_____ this plant.

┌ 보기 ┐

as   at   for   from   in   like

출제율 95%

13 다음 빈칸에 알맞은 말이 순서대로 짝지어진 것은?

• _____ is good to spend money wisely.

• It is very kind _____ you to help her.

① It – for   ② It – of

③ That – of   ④ That – for

⑤ This – for

출제율 100%

14 다음 중 어법상 적절한 문장은?

① It's important to protecting mudflats.

② It is exciting of me to play baseball.

③ Isn't it boring watch TV at home?

④ Ann felt disappointed as well as anger.

⑤ Cindy will not only go to the movies, but also meet her friends.

15 다음 우리말을 주어진 어휘를 이용하여 영작하시오. 출제율 90%

(1) 나는 이 책을 이해하는 것이 쉽다. (this book, me, it, understand)

➡ _____

(2) 그녀를 도와주다니 너는 참 친절하구나. (you, very kind, it, to)

➡ _____

(3) 네가 밤에 여기저기 걸어다니는 것은 위험하다. (walk around, it, to)

➡ _____

(4) 고양이는 깨끗할 뿐만 아니라 영리하다. (cats, clean, well, smart)

➡ _____

(5) Junsu는 춤뿐만 아니라 노래도 잘한다. (only, also, well)

➡ _____

(6) Eric뿐 아니라 그의 형들도 빨리 달린다. (his brothers, fast runners, only, also)

➡ _____

16 다음 두 문장이 같도록 할 때 빈칸에 알맞은 것은? 출제율 100%

> For all these reasons, to protect mudflats is necessary.
> → For all these reasons, it is necessary _____ mudflats.

① protect   ② protects
③ to protecting   ④ protected
⑤ to protect

[17~19] 다음 글을 읽고 물음에 답하시오.

Mudflats are large areas of muddy land at the seaside. They appear and disappear with every tide. During low tides, they show up, and during high tides, they are covered by the sea. Mudflats help sea creatures, people, and the Earth in many ways. It is important ⓐ to understand the roles of mudflats. Let's see what they do.

17 위 글의 밑줄 친 ⓐto understand와 to부정사의 용법이 다른 것을 모두 고르시오. 출제율 95%

① To understand the roles of mudflats is our chief concern.
② It is high time to understand the roles of mudflats.
③ It is not easy to understand the roles of mudflats.
④ This is the best way to understand the roles of mudflats.
⑤ He was wise enough to understand the roles of mudflats.

18 Why do mudflats disappear during high tides? Fill in the blank with suitable words. 출제율 90%

➡ It's because _____.

19 위 글의 뒤에 나올 내용으로 가장 알맞은 것을 고르시오. 출제율 100%

① the history of mudflats
② the importance of mudflats
③ the roles of mudflats
④ the meaning of mudflats
⑤ various kinds of mudflats

[20~22] 다음 글을 읽고 물음에 답하시오.

Mudflats are home to ⓐa lot of living things at the seaside. ⓑ플랑크톤처럼 작은 생명체뿐만 아니라 게와 물고기도 그곳에 산다. Mudflats provide various types of food for them. Also, many birds eat food there.

20 위 글의 밑줄 친 ⓐa lot of와 바꿔 쓸 수 없는 말을 고르시오.

① lots of
② a number of
③ plenty of
④ many
⑤ a great deal of

21 위 글의 밑줄 친 ⓑ의 우리말에 맞게 주어진 어휘를 이용하여 15 단어로 영작하시오.

> only, very small, like, also

➡ _____

_____

22 위 글의 제목으로 알맞은 것을 고르시오.

① Suitable Food for Many Living Things
② Mudflats, Sweet Home to Seaside Creatures
③ Various Types of Food Found at Mudflats
④ Mudflats, Paradise for Leisure
⑤ How about Going Camping at the Seaside?

[23~25] 다음 글을 읽고 물음에 답하시오.

Mudflats are good for people, too. People who live near mudflat areas make a living by catching fish and other sea animals nearby. ⓐThanks to mudflats, people can get fresh seafood. People can enjoy fun activities, such as mud sliding and body painting on mudflats. They can also watch a large number of birds that feed on the sea animals there.

23 위 글의 밑줄 친 ⓐ를 다음과 같이 바꿔 쓸 때 빈칸에 들어갈 알맞은 말을 쓰시오.

➡ Mudflats enable people _____
_____ fresh seafood.

24 How do people who live near mudflat areas make a living? Answer in English in a full sentence.

➡ _____

_____

25 위 글의 주제로 알맞은 것을 고르시오.

① Mudflats are large areas of muddy land at the seaside.
② Thanks to tides, mudflats appear and disappear.
③ Mudflats are nature's gift to living things.
④ Understanding the roles of mudflats is important.
⑤ We can enjoy many fun activities on mudflats.

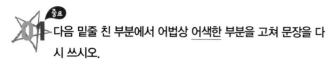

01 다음 밑줄 친 부분에서 어법상 <u>어색한</u> 부분을 고쳐 문장을 다시 쓰시오.

> G: <u>I wonder what did you do while the summer vacation.</u>
> B: I took a trip to Kenya and saw many animals on the plains.
> G: Wonderful! By the way, what are the plains?
> B: They are large areas of flat land.

➡ _____

_____

02 주어진 문장 다음에 이어질 대화의 순서를 바르게 배열하시오.

> Look at the yellow plants! I wonder what they are.

> (A) They really are. Let me take a picture of you.
> (B) Wow, the reeds are even taller than you, Dad.
> (C) They are reeds. Suncheon Bay has beautiful reed fields.

➡ _____

[03~04] 다음 대화를 읽고 물음에 답하시오.

> A: (A)_____ (about, wonder, is, special, what, I, the Yangze River)
> B: (B)<u>나는 그것이 세계에서 세 번째로 긴 강이라고 들었어.</u>(the world, long, in, heard)

03 위 대화의 빈칸 (A)에 주어진 단어를 배열하여 알맞은 문장을 만드시오.

➡ _____

04 위 대화의 밑줄 친 (B)의 우리말을 주어진 어구를 이용하여 영어로 쓰시오.

➡ _____

05 to부정사를 진주어로 하여 주어진 문장과 같은 의미가 되도록 쓰시오.

(1) The river is dangerous to swim in.
➡ _____

(2) She was wise to decide to be a nurse.
➡ _____

06 다음 문장을 'not only A but also B' 구문을 사용하여 한 문장으로 연결하시오.

(1) Midori can speak Japanese. She can speak English, too.
➡ _____

(2) Wendy studies hard at school. She also studies hard at home.
➡ _____

07 어법상 <u>틀린</u> 것을 바르게 고치시오.

> Jack as well as his friends are going to climb the mountain.

_____

ⓐMudflats are good for people, too. People ____(a)____ live (A)[near / nearly] mudflat areas make a living by catching fish and other sea animals (B)[nearby / nearly]. (C)[In spite of / Thanks to] mudflats, people can get fresh seafood. People can enjoy fun activities, such as mud sliding and body painting on mudflats. They can also watch a large number of birds ____(b)____ feed on the sea animals there.

08 위 글의 빈칸 (a)와 (b)에 공통으로 들어갈 알맞은 관계대명사를 쓰시오.

➡ _____

09 위 글의 밑줄 친 ⓐ에 해당하는 내용을 우리말로 쓰시오. (4가지)

➡ (1) _____
_____
(2) _____
(3) _____
_____
(4) _____
_____

10 위 글의 괄호 (A)~(C)에서 문맥이나 어법상 알맞은 낱말을 골라 쓰시오.

➡ (A)_____ (B)_____ (C)_____

Mudflats help the environment greatly. Mudflats hold a lot of water, so they can reduce damage from floods. Also, mudflats filter water that flows from the land into the sea. They ⓐremove bad things in the water before ⓑit enters the sea. Thanks to mudflats, the water that reaches the sea is clean. Mudflats work as the Earth's lungs. They produce a huge volume of oxygen that is necessary for life on the Earth.

Earth: Mudflats keep me healthy and clean.

Mudflats are wonderful places, aren't they? They are a gift from nature to living things on the Earth. For all these reasons, it is necessary to protect mudflats.

11 위 글의 밑줄 친 ⓐ와 바꿔 쓸 수 있는 한 단어를 본문에서 찾아 쓰시오.

➡ _____

12 위 글의 밑줄 친 ⓑit이 가리키는 것을 본문에서 찾아 쓰시오.

➡ _____

13 How do mudflats help the environment? Fill in the blanks with suitable words.

➡ (1) They can reduce damage from floods by _____.
(2) They remove bad things in the water before it enters the sea by _____.
(3) They work as the Earth's lungs by _____.

창의사고력 서술형 문제

01 주어진 조건에 맞춰서 빈칸을 완성하시오.

조건

1. 주어진 질문과 정보를 활용해야 함 2. 궁금증을 나타내는 표현이 반드시 포함되어야 함.

• What time does the mall open on the opening day?
• 개점일: 5월 18일 / 오전 8시

A: Do you know the mall in the downtown?
B: Yes, I'm aware that it opens _____.
A: _____
B: I'm aware that _____.
A: I see. Thank you.

02 주어진 어휘와 가주어를 이용하여 3 문장 이상을 쓰시오.

| watch the soccer game | exercise regularly | see such an old house |
| use water carefully | swim in the sea | wear a helmet |

(1) _____
(2) _____
(3) _____

03 다음 조사한 내용을 바탕으로 지형을 소개하는 글을 쓰시오.

• What are deserts?
  They are dry land with few plants and little water.
• What plants live there?
  Elephant trees live there.
• What animals live there?
  Lizards, desert snakes live there.
• What is special about them?
  It is hot during the day and cold at night.

All about Deserts

Deserts are dry land with (A)_____ plants and (B)_____ water. Not only plants like elephant trees but also animals such as (C)_____ live there. It is hot during the day and (D)_____ at night.

단원별 모의고사

[01~02] 다음 빈칸에 들어갈 말로 적절한 것을 고르시오.

01

His job is not _____ interesting but also very well-paid.

① only   ② well   ③ so

④ as   ⑤ very

02

A large _____ of people visit this museum every year.

① lots   ② much   ③ number

④ plenty   ⑤ deal

03 〈보기〉에 주어진 단어를 이용해 빈칸을 채우시오. (형태 변화 가능)

┌─ 보기 ─┐

flow occur protect provide reach

remove surf

(1) The road _____ down to the lake.

(2) The woman is _____ on the sea.

(3) A problem _____ during the setup.

(4) We have to _____ the environment from pollution.

(5) The river _____ into the sea.

(6) _____ your contact lenses and wear glasses.

(7) Cows _____ us with milk.

04 다음 중 영영풀이가 알맞지 <u>않은</u> 것은?

① appear: begin to be seen suddenly

② creature: all living things except plants

③ filter: to pass something through a filter to remove particular things contained in it

④ muddy: very soft wet earth

⑤ tide: the periodic rise and fall of the waters of the ocean

[05~06] 다음 대화를 읽고 물음에 답하시오.

B: I just finished making a plan for my trip. Do you want to hear it? (①)

G: Sure. <u>I wonder what did you do.</u> (②)

B: On the first day, I'm going to go fishing on a lake. (③)

G: Is that all?

B: No. On the last day, I'm going to go swimming. (④)

G: Wow. You will do a lot of activities. (⑤)

05 위 대화의 ①~⑤ 중 다음 주어진 말이 들어갈 알맞은 곳은?

The next day, I'm going to climb a mountain.

①   ②   ③   ④   ⑤

06 밑줄 친 부분에서 어법상 또는 문맥상 <u>어색한</u> 것을 찾아 바르게 고치시오.

➡ _____

_____

[07~09] 다음 대화를 읽고 물음에 답하시오.

G: Look at that lake! It's really beautiful.
B: It's not a lake. It's a river.
G: Is it? <u>나는 강과 호수가 어떻게 다른지 궁금해.</u>
B: A river is a long body of fresh water. Unlike a lake, a river flows toward the ocean.
G: I got it.

07 다음 영영풀이에 해당하는 단어를 대화에서 찾아 쓰시오.

> to move steadily without any interrupts, used to describe liquids, gas, electrical currents, etc.

➡ _____

08 밑줄 친 우리말을 'wonder'를 이용하여 영작하시오.

➡ _____

09 위 대화의 내용과 일치하지 <u>않는</u> 것을 고르시오.

① The boy knows the difference between a lake and a river.
② The lake doesn't flow toward the ocean.
③ They are looking at the lake.
④ The river is not sea water but fresh water.
⑤ The river and the lake are different.

10 다음 빈칸 어디에도 들어갈 수 <u>없는</u> 것은?

> M: Guess ⓐ_____! It's not a tree. It is a plant that ⓑ_____ tall grass. In fall, it ⓒ_____ yellow. It ⓓ_____ well in wet lands. I heard Suncheon Bay ⓔ_____ this plant.

① turns   ② is famous for
③ grows   ④ where they are
⑤ looks like

[11~12] 다음 대화를 읽고 물음에 답하시오.

Dad: Do you want to see an amazing place?
Karl & Sister: Sure!
Dad: Then let's (A)[get / have] on the train.
Sister: Look at the yellow plants! I wonder (B) [what are they / what they are].
Dad: They are reeds. Suncheon Bay has beautiful reed fields.
Karl: Wow, the reeds are even taller (C)[as / than] you, Dad.
Sister: They really are. Let me (D)[take / taken] a picture of you.
Karl: This reed field is very large.
Dad: Yes. I heard it is the largest one in Korea.
Karl: Look at the sky. It's turning red.
Sister: Yes, it's beautiful.

11 다음 영영풀이에 해당하는 단어를 대화에서 찾아 쓰시오.

> It is a tall thin plant that grows near water. Its stems can be used to make things.

➡ _____

12 (A)~(D)에 알맞은 것을 골라 쓰시오.

➡ (A)_____   (B)_____
   (C)_____   (D)_____

13 다음 중 어법상 <u>어색한</u> 것을 고르시오.

① It is fun to surf on sand in the desert.
② It was so foolish for Jane to do that.
③ I don't think it's a good idea to bring a smartphone to school.
④ We like not only playing soccer but also going hiking.
⑤ I as well as Sophie like to drink coffee.

14 그림을 보고 주어진 문장의 빈칸을 알맞게 채우시오. (빈칸 하나에 한 단어씩 쓸 것.)

Minhee likes to _____ _____ listen to music _____ _____ draw pictures.

15 다음 주어진 문장의 밑줄 친 부분과 쓰임이 같은 것은?

> <u>It</u> is a lot of fun to ride a bicycle.

① How far is <u>it</u> from your school to the station?
② <u>It</u> was three weeks later that he heard the news.
③ <u>It</u> was a pleasure to meet you at the party.
④ <u>It</u> took about 30 minutes to get to the park by bus.
⑤ I make <u>it</u> a rule to get up early.

16 다음 문장에서 어법상 어색한 것을 바르게 고치시오.

(1) Amy as well as her friends were looking forward to watching the movie.

_____

(2) It was foolish for him to believe such a story.

_____

17 다음 문장을 as well as를 사용하여 바꾸어 쓰시오.

(1) I saw not only *Avatar* but also *Alitar*.

➡ _____

(2) Not only his brothers but also Peter likes Minji.

➡ _____

[18~19] 다음 글을 읽고 물음에 답하시오.

Mudflats are large areas of muddy land at the seaside. They appear and disappear with every tide. During (A)[high / low] tides, they show up, and during (B)[high / low] tides, they are covered by the sea. Mudflats help sea creatures, people, and the Earth in many ways. It is important to understand the roles of mudflats. Let's see (C)[that / what] they do.

18 위 글의 괄호 (A)~(C)에서 문맥이나 어법상 알맞은 낱말을 골라 쓰시오.

➡ (A)_____ (B)_____ (C)_____

19 다음 중 위 글에 언급되어 있지 <u>않은</u> 것은?

① Mudflats appear when the tide goes out.
② Mudflats disappear when the tide comes in.
③ Mudflats help not only sea creatures but also people and the Earth.
④ It is important to protect mudflats from pollution.
⑤ Understanding the roles of mudflats is of importance.

[20~21] 다음 글을 읽고 물음에 답하시오.

Mudflats are home to a lot of living things at the seaside. ⓐ<u>Not only very small living things as plankton but also crabs and fish live there.</u> Mudflats provide ⓑ<u>various</u> types of food for them. Also, many birds eat food there.

20 위 글의 밑줄 친 ⓐ에서 어법상 틀린 부분을 찾아 고치시오.

➡ _____

21 위 글의 밑줄 친 ⓑvarious와 바꿔 쓸 수 <u>없는</u> 말을 고르시오.

① varied　　　　② diverse
③ similar　　　　④ different
⑤ a variety of

[22~23] 다음 글을 읽고 물음에 답하시오.

Mudflats are good for people, too. People who live near mudflat areas ⓐ생계를 꾸린다 by catching fish and other sea animals nearby. Thanks to mudflats, people can get fresh seafood. People can enjoy fun activities, such as mud sliding and body painting on mudflats. They can also watch a large number of birds that feed on the sea animals there.

22 위 글의 밑줄 친 ⓐ의 우리말을 세 단어로 쓰시오.

➡ _____

23 다음 중 갯벌에서 할 수 <u>없는</u> 것은?

① 물고기와 다른 바다 동물들을 잡기
② 수영을 즐기기
③ 진흙 미끄럼 타기
④ 보디 페인팅
⑤ 바다 동물들을 먹는 수많은 새를 관찰하기

[24~25] 다음 글을 읽고 물음에 답하시오.

Mudflats help the environment greatly. Mudflats hold a lot of water, so they can reduce damage from floods. Also, mudflats filter water that flows from the land into the sea. They remove bad things in the water before it enters the sea. Thanks to mudflats, the water that reaches the sea is clean. Mudflats work as the Earth's lungs. They produce a huge volume of oxygen that is necessary for life on the Earth.

Earth: Mudflats keep me healthy and clean.

Mudflats are wonderful places, aren't they? They are a gift from nature to living things on the Earth. For all these reasons, it is necessary to protect mudflats.

24 위 글의 주제로 가장 알맞은 것을 고르시오.

① Mudflats are very helpful to the environment.
② Mudflats can hold a lot of water.
③ Mudflats filter water.
④ Mudflats work as the Earth's lungs.
⑤ Oxygen is necessary for life on the Earth.

25 위 글에서 환경에 미치는 갯벌의 좋은 역할로 언급된 것을 <u>모두</u> 고르시오.

① 홍수로 인한 피해 축소
② 신선한 해산물 제공
③ 조류 관찰 장소 제공
④ 바다로 들어가는 물 정화
⑤ 산소 생성

Lesson 7

Work on Your Dreams

🎙 **의사소통 기능**

- 강조하기
  It's important that you never give up.
- 설명 요청하기
  What do you mean by that?

🎙 **언어 형식**

- 'ask/want+A+to부정사 구문
  Other teams **asked** African American players **to join** them.
- 목적격 관계대명사
  I will become a player **who** people like.

교과서
Words & Expressions

Key Words

□ **achieve**[ətʃíːv] 동 이루다, 달성하다

□ **although**[ɔːlðóu] 접 비록 ~일지라도

□ **American**[əmérikən] 명 미국인 형 미국의

□ **as**[əz] 전 ~로(자격)

□ **award**[əwɔ́ːrd] 명 상

□ **base**[beis] 명 야구의 루

□ **baseman**[béismən] 명 (1·2·3) 루수

□ **bat**[bæt] 동 (공을) 치다

□ **calm**[kɑːm] 형 침착한

□ **classical**[klǽsikəl] 형 (음악이) 클래식의

□ **color line** 인종 차별

□ **difficulty**[dífikʌlti] 명 어려움, 곤경, 장애

□ **earn**[əːrn] 동 얻다, 획득하다

□ **effort**[éfərt] 명 노력

□ **ever**[évər] 부 언젠가 한 번이라도

□ **excellence**[éksələns] 명 우수, 탁월, 뛰어남

□ **excellent**[éksələnt] 형 뛰어난

□ **face**[feis] 동 직면하다, 직시하다

□ **fail**[feil] 동 실패하다, ~하지 못하다

□ **finally**[fáinəli] 부 마침내

□ **gentle**[dʒéntl] 형 점잖은

□ **high five** 하이파이브(기쁨의 표시로 두 사람이 팔을 들어 서로 손바닥을 마주치는 것)

□ **honor**[ánər] 동 예우하다, ~을 공경하다

□ **lend**[lend] 동 빌려주다

□ **major**[méidʒər] 형 주요한

□ **Nobel Prize** 명 노벨상

□ **overcome**[óuvərkʌm] 동 극복하다

□ **pain**[pein] 명 아픔, 고통

□ **perfect**[pə́ːrfikt] 형 완벽한

□ **phrase**[freiz] 명 구, 구절

□ **plus**[plʌs] 전 게다가, 덧붙여

□ **positive**[pázətiv] 형 긍정적인

□ **present**[prizént] 동 주다, 수여하다, 증정하다

□ **recognize**[rékəgnàiz] 동 인정하다, 알아보다

□ **recycle**[riːsáikl] 동 재활용하다

□ **respect**[rispékt] 명 존경

□ **rudely**[rúːdli] 부 무례하게

□ **sentence**[séntəns] 명 문장

□ **skater**[skéitər] 명 스케이트 선수

□ **solve**[sɑlv] 동 풀다, 해결하다

□ **stadium**[stéidiəm] 명 경기장, 스타디움

□ **support**[səpɔ́ːrt] 명 지지

□ **talented**[tǽləntid] 형 재능이 있는

□ **team**[tiːm] 명 (경기 등의) 팀

□ **teammate**[tíːmeit] 명 팀 동료

□ **terrible**[térəbl] 형 무서운

□ **wish**[wiʃ] 동 바라다, 원하다

□ **with**[wið] 전 ~와 함께, ~함에 따라

Key Expressions

□ **achieve a goal** 목표를 달성하다

□ **at bat** 타석에서

□ **be good at** ~을 잘하다

□ **by 동사ing** ~함으로써

□ **cannot believe one's eyes** 눈을 의심하다(놀람)

□ **earn the respect** 존경을 얻다

□ **give up** 포기하다

□ **help+목적어+(to) 동사원형** (목적어)가 ~하는 것을 돕다

□ **keep calm** 평온을 유지하다

□ **keep 동명사** ~하는 것을 계속하다

□ **more than** ~보다 많이

□ **no longer** 더 이상 ~ 아닌

□ **one of 복수명사** ~중의 하나

□ **over and over** 반복해서

□ **present A with B** A에게 B를 수여하다, 증정하다

□ **shout at** ~을 향해 외치다

□ **take a class** 수업을 듣다

□ **thanks to** ~ 덕분에

□ **think to oneself** 마음속으로 생각하다

□ **turn down** ~을 거절하다, 거부하다, 소리를 줄이다

□ **win first place** 1등을 하다, 우승하다

Word Power

※ 형용사 - 명사
- [ ] **different**(다른) – **difference**(다름, 차이)
- [ ] **important**(중요한) – **importance**(중요성)
- [ ] **silent**(조용한) – **silence**(침묵)

- [ ] **excellent**(우수한) – **excellence**(우수, 장점)
- [ ] **significant**(중요한) – **significance**(중요성)

※ 비슷한 의미를 가진 어휘들
- [ ] **gentle**(점잖은) : **kind**(친절한)
- [ ] **respect**(존경) : **admiration**(존경)

- [ ] **finally**(마침내) : **in the end**(결국, 마침내)

English Dictionary

- [ ] **award** 상
  → a prize or other reward that is given to someone who has achieved something
  어떤 것을 달성한 사람에게 주어지는 상이나 다른 보상

- [ ] **baseman** (1·2·3) 루수
  → a player stationed at a base 베이스에 배치된 선수

- [ ] **bat** (공을) 치다
  → to hit the ball with a bat in a game such as baseball or cricket
  야구나 크리켓 경기에서 방망이로 공을 치다

- [ ] **calm** 침착한
  → not affected by strong emotions such as excitement, anger, shock, or fear
  흥분, 화, 충격 또는 공포 같은 강한 감정에 의해 영향을 받지 않은

- [ ] **classical** (음악이) 클래식의
  → relating to classical music 클래식 음악과 관련이 있는

- [ ] **earn** 얻다, 획득하다
  → to get something as a result of your efforts or your behavior 노력이나 행동의 결과로 어떤 것을 얻다

- [ ] **excellent** 뛰어난
  → unusually or extremely good 대단히 또는 극히 좋은

- [ ] **fail** 실패하다, ~하지 못하다
  → to be unable to do something 어떤 것을 할 수 없다

- [ ] **honor** 예우하다, ~을 공경하다
  → to show your respect or admiration for someone, especially by giving them a prize or title, or by praising them publicly
  특히 상이나 타이틀을 주거나, 공적으로 칭찬함으로써 어떤 사람에게 존경이나 칭찬을 보여주다

- [ ] **lend** 빌려주다
  → to give someone the use of something for a limited time 어떤 것을 제한된 시간 동안 사용하게 주다

- [ ] **major** 주요한
  → greater or more important than other people or things in a group
  한 그룹 안에서 다른 사람이나 사물보다 더 중요한

- [ ] **overcome** 극복하다
  → to succeed in dealing with or controlling a problem
  문제를 다루거나 통제하는 데 성공하다

- [ ] **pain** 아픔, 고통
  → a feeling that you have in a part of your body when you are hurt or ill 아프거나 다쳤을 때 몸의 일부에서 갖는 느낌

- [ ] **positive** 긍정적인
  → believing that good things will happen rather than bad ones 나쁜 일보다 좋은 일이 발생하리라 믿는

- [ ] **recognize** 인정하다, 알아보다
  → to see and know what someone or something is
  사람이나 사물이 무엇인지 알다

- [ ] **rudely** 무례하게
  → in a way that shows no respect for others
  다른 사람에 대한 존중을 보이지 않는 방식으로

- [ ] **sentence** 문장
  → a sequence of words forming a meaningful grammatical structure
  의미 있는 문법의 구조를 형성하는 일련의 단어들

- [ ] **support** 지지
  → help and kindness that you give to someone who is having a difficult time
  어려움을 겪고 있는 사람에게 주는 도움과 친절

- [ ] **team** (경기 등의) 팀
  → a group of people who work together or play a game or sport together
  같이 일하거나 게임이나 운동을 함께 하는 한 무리의 사람들

- [ ] **teammate** 팀 동료
  → a person who is in the same team 같은 팀에 있는 사람

[01~02] 다음 빈칸에 들어갈 말로 적절한 것은?

01

> He will _____ many difficulties in his life.

① celebrate ② achieve
③ increase ④ encourage
⑤ overcome

02 중요

> She doesn't _____ much money, but she enjoys the work.

① earn ② effort
③ experience ④ respect
⑤ turn

[03~04] 다음 빈칸에 공통으로 들어갈 말로 알맞은 것은?

03

> • She wanted to _____ his proposal, so she said 'no' to him.
> • Could you _____ the volume? I can't concentrate on my study.

① calm down ② break down
③ turn down ④ pick up
⑤ take up

04 중요

> • He took a deep breath and tried to _____ calm.
> • I don't know what I'll do if gas prices _____ going up.

① take ② keep ③ get
④ hold ⑤ have

05 중요 두 문장이 같은 의미가 되도록 빈칸에 알맞은 것을 고르시오.

> • _____ he has financial problems, he has bought a new car.
> = In spite of his financial problems, he has bought a new car.

① However ② Although
③ When ④ Therefore
⑤ Unless

[06~07] 다음 영영풀이에 해당하는 단어를 고르시오.

06

> not affected by strong emotions such as excitement, anger, shock, or fear

① calm ② nervous
③ serious ④ comfortable
⑤ quiet

07

> to show your respect or admiration for someone, especially by giving them a prize or title, or by praising them publicly

① award ② honor
③ solution ④ effort
⑤ contest

01 다음 밑줄 친 부분과 의미가 가장 가까운 것을 주어진 철자로 시작하여 쓰시오.

> The little boy was so <u>scared</u> that he made a lot of mistakes.

➡ a_____

02 두 문장에 공통으로 들어갈 수 있는 단어를 〈보기〉에서 골라 쓰시오.

┌─ 보기 ─┐

as at for from in to

- Who is the player _____ bat now?
- I'm really poor _____ math and I want to become good _____ it.

03 괄호 안에 주어진 단어를 알맞게 배열하시오.

(1) 그들은 연습을 통해 더 빨라졌다.
   (practice, they, faster, with, became)
   ➡ _____

(2) 난 여름방학 계획을 따르는 데 실패했다.
   (to, vacation, I, plan, the, failed, follow, summer)
   ➡ _____

(3) 내가 그걸 처음 봤을 때, 내 눈을 믿을 수 없었다.
   (couldn't, when, I, my, I, that, first, believe, eyes, saw)
   ➡ _____

04 다음 빈칸에 알맞은 단어를 〈보기〉에서 골라 쓰시오. (한 단어는 한 번 밖에 사용할 수 없음)

┌─ 보기 ─┐

excellent major positive talented

(1) He also spends a lot of time finding _____ artists.
(2) This is a _____ cause for concern.
(3) It's an _____ place to relax.
(4) Are you a _____ person or a negative person?

05 다음 우리말에 맞게 빈칸을 채우시오. (철자가 주어진 경우 그 철자로 시작할 것)

(1) 우리는 인종 차별을 하지 않는다.
   ➡ We do not draw the _____.
(2) Tony는 팀에서 1루수를 맡고 있다.
   ➡ Tony is the first _____ for the team.
(3) 비록 그들은 가난할지라도 행복하다.
   ➡ A_____ they are poor, they are happy.
(4) 그 프로젝트를 끝내는 데 많은 노력이 들었다.
   ➡ It took a lot of _____ to finish the project.
(5) 언젠가 우리 도움이 필요하면, 나한테 전화해.
   ➡ If you _____ need our help, just call me.

교과서

Conversation

1 강조하기

> **It's important that you never give up.** 절대 포기하지 않는 것이 중요해.

■ 'It's important ~.'는 '~가 중요해'의 의미이다. important 다음에는 to부정사나 that절이 올 수 있다. 여기서 it은 가주어이며, to부정사나 that절은 진주어이다.

■ important와 비슷한 뜻인 essential, critical, significant 등을 대신 사용할 수 있다.

강조하기

• It's important that 주어 동사 ~. (~하는 것이 중요해.)
• It's important to 동사원형 ~. (~하는 것이 중요해.)
• I want to stress ~. (~을 강조하고 싶어.)

■ 'It's important to 동사원형 ~.'에서 '~하지 않는 것이 중요하다.'의 의미이면 to부정사 앞에 not을 붙여 'It's important not to 동사원형 ~.'으로 문장을 만들 수 있다.

핵심 Check

1. 다음 우리말과 일치하도록 빈칸에 알맞은 말을 쓰시오.

   A: I'm sorry, Ms. Song. (송 선생님, 죄송해요.)

   B: You're late again. _____ on time. (또 늦었구나. 시간을 지키는 것이 중요하단다.)

2. 다음 대화의 순서를 바르게 배열하시오.

   (A) It's important to stay healthy.

   (B) But I have a big test tomorrow.

   (C) You need to rest.

   ➡ _____

3. 괄호 안의 단어를 순서대로 배열하여 대화를 완성하시오.

   A: What is important when I play soccer?

   B: _____ (is, a, to, it, lot, practice, important)

   (연습을 많이 하는 것이 중요해.)

114 Lesson 7. Work on Your Dreams

② 설명 요청하기

What do you mean by that? (그게 무슨 뜻이니?)

■ 'What do you mean by that?'은 '그게 무슨 뜻이니?'라는 뜻으로 상대방과의 대화에서 이해하지 못한 부분이 있거나, 의도를 파악하지 못했을 때 부연 설명을 요청하는 의미로 쓰는 표현이다. that은 상대방이 말한 내용을 언급하는 대명사이고 by that은 '그 말로써, 그것으로'라는 뜻으로, 직역하면 '그 말로써 너는 무엇을 의미하니?'라는 뜻이다.

설명 요청하기

- What do you mean (by that)? (그게 무슨 뜻이니?)
- What is that exactly? (그게 정확히 뭐니?)
- What exactly do you mean? (정확하게 무슨 뜻이니?)
- Could you explain about that in detail? (그것을 자세히 설명해 줄 수 있나요?)

■ 설명을 할 때는 '~을 의미하다'의 뜻을 가진 'mean'을 사용해 'It means ~. (그것은 ~ 뜻이야.)'로 대답할 수 있다.

설명하기

- It means ~. (~라는 뜻이야.) • I mean ~. (~라는 뜻이야.)

핵심 Check

4. 다음 대화의 순서를 바르게 배열하시오.

(A) She's a busy worker.

(B) She's a busy bee.

(C) What do you mean by that?

➡ _____

5. 괄호 안의 단어를 순서대로 배열하여 대화를 완성하시오.

A: When it rains, it pours.

B: _____ (that, could, about, you, explain)

(그것이 무슨 뜻인지 설명해 줄래?)

A: It means "When problems come, they come together."

 Listen & Speak 1 A-1

G: Hey, Minho. Did you find the answer to the math problem?

B: No. ❶It's too hard for me. ❷I'm not good at math.

G: ❸Let me see. ❹It's important that you use this math rule ❺to solve the problem.

B: Oh, I see. I'll use ❻it.

G: 이봐, 민호야. 이 수학 문제의 정답을 찾았니?

B: 아니. 그건 나에게 너무 어려워. 나는 수학을 잘하지 못 해.

G: 내가 한 번 볼게. 네가 그 문제를 풀기 위해선 이 수학 공식을 이용하는 것이 중요해.

B: 오, 알겠어. 그걸 사용해 볼게.

❶ It = The math problem, too: 너무, hard: 어려운
❷ be good at: ~을 잘하다
❸ 대화중에 질문을 받았을 때나 생각할 시간이 필요하면 'Let me think.'나 'Let me see.'라고 말할 수 있다
❹ that 이하의 내용을 강조할 때 'It's important that 주어 동사 ~.'를 사용하며, '~하는 것이 중요해.'의 의미이다.
❺ to부정사의 부사적 용법으로 '~하기 위해서'의 의미이다.
❻ it = this math rule

Check(√) True or False

(1) The math problem was too hard, so the boy didn't find the answer.　　T ☐ F ☐

(2) The girl is better at math than the boy.　　T ☐ F ☐

 Listen & Speak 2 A-1

G: Oh, this is hard to do.

B: ❶What's the matter?

G: Can you ❷teach me how to make cookies?

B: Sure. It's a walk in the park.

G: ❸What do you mean by that?

B: ❹I mean it's easy to do.

G: 오, 이것은 하기 어렵구나.

B: 무슨 일이야?

G: 쿠키를 만드는 방법을 나에게 가르쳐 줄 수 있니?

B: 물론이지. 그건 'a walk in the park'야.

G: 그게 무슨 뜻이니?

B: 하기 쉽다는 뜻이야.

❶ 상대방의 슬픔이나 불만족, 실망의 원인에 대해 물을 때 사용되는 표현으로 What's the matter?가 쓰이며 '무슨 일[문제] 있니?'라는 뜻이다 (= What's wrong? = What's the problem? = What happened?)
❷ teach(4형식동사)+me(간접목적어,~에게)+how to make cookies(직접목적어,~을, 를), how to 동사원형: ~하는 방법
❸ 상대방에게 설명을 요청할 때 'What do you mean by that?'이라고 말한다.
❹ 설명을 요청하는 질문에 대한 대답으로 'It means ~.'나 'I mean ~.'으로 대답할 수 있다.

Check(√) True or False

(3) The boy doesn't know how to make cookies.　　T ☐ F ☐

(4) "It's a walk in the park" means that it's easy to do.　　T ☐ F ☐

Listen & Speak 1 A-2

G: Your poster looks great.

B: Thanks, Kate. Did you finish ❶yours?

G: Not yet. ❷I can't draw well. How can I become good at drawing?

B: It ❸takes time. ❹It's important that you draw as often as you can.

G: ❺You mean I should keep practicing?

B: That's right.

❶ yours = your poster
❷ draw: (그림을) 그리다 well은 부사로 동사인 draw를 수식하고 있다.
❸ take: (얼마의 시간이) 걸리다
❹ 강조할 때는 'It's important that 주어 동사 ~.(~가 중요해.)'를 사용한다.
❺ You mean ~?: ~라는 뜻이니? keep 동명사: ~하는 것을 계속하다

Listen & Speak 2 A-2

B: I have a singing contest tomorrow. I really ❶want to win first place.

G: I'll keep my fingers crossed for you.

B: ❷What do you mean by "keep my fingers crossed"?

G: ❸It means I wish you good luck.

B: Thank you.

❶ want는 to부정사를 목적어로 취한다. win first place: 1등을 하다, 우승하다
❷ 'What do you mean by ~?(~가 무슨 뜻이니?)'는 상대방이 말한 것을 제대로 이해하지 못하여 설명을 요청할 때 사용하는 표현이다.
❸ means와 I 사이에 접속사 that이 생략되어 있다.

Conversation A

M: ❶To achieve my dream, I went to many auditions, but I often failed. ❷However, I never gave up. I ❸took acting and dancing classes. ❹Finally, I achieved my goal. ❺It's important that you never give up.

❶ to부정사의 부사적 용법(목적)을 사용하여 '~하기 위해서'로 해석한다. achieve: 이루다, 달성하다
❷ however: 하지만 give up: 포기하다
❸ take a class: 수업을 듣다
❹ finally: 마침내 achieve a goal: 목표를 달성하다
❺ It's important that 주어 동사 ~: ~하는 것이 중요하다

Conversation B

Hana: You ❶look sad, Jiho. What's wrong?

Jiho: ❷I don't think I can achieve my dream.

Amy: ❸What do you mean by that?

Jiho: I want to be an actor, but I ❹always fail auditions. Maybe I have to give up.

Amy: Do you know this actor?

Jiho: Sure. He's a famous movie star.

Amy: He failed ❺more than 100 auditions.

Jiho: Really? Maybe I ❻should keep trying. I will practice more for my next audition.

Hana: That's right! ❼It's important that you never give up.

❶ look+형용사: ~해 보이다
❷ think와 I 사이에 접속사 that이 생략되어 있다. think의 목적어는 'I can achieve my dream'이다.
❸ What do you mean by that?: 그게 무슨 뜻이니? (= What is that exactly? = What exactly do you mean? = Could you explain about that in detail?)
❹ always(항상)는 빈도부사로 be동사나 조동사 뒤에, 일반동사 앞에 위치한다. fail: 실패하다, ~하지 못하다
❺ more than: ~ 이상
❻ should+동사원형: ~해야 한다 keep 동명사: ~하는 것을 계속하다
❼ never: 결코 ~하지 않다 give up: 포기하다

Communication Task Step 2

A: Please ❶call me "Speedy Feet."

B: ❷What do you mean by "Speedy Feet"?

A: I mean I want to be a runner.

B: What is important to do to become a runner?

A: ❸It's important that I practice running every day.

B: I'm sure you'll ❹make it.

❶ call+목적어+목적격보어: ~을 …라고 부르다
❷ What do you mean by ~?: ~가 무슨 뜻이니?
❸ It's important that 주어 동사 ~: ~하는 것이 중요하다
❹ make it: 성공하다, 해내다

● 다음 우리말과 일치하도록 빈칸에 알맞은 말을 쓰시오.

Listen & Speak 1 A

1. **G:** Hey, Minho. Did you _____ the answer to the math _____?

   B: No. It's _____ _____ for me. _____ _____ _____

   _____ _____.

   G: Let me see. _____ _____ _____ you use this math rule

   to _____ the problem.

   B: Oh, I see. I'll use it.

2. **G:** Your poster _____ great.

   B: Thanks, Kate. Did you _____ yours?

   G: Not yet. I can't _____ well. _____ can I become _____

   at drawing?

   B: It _____ time. It's _____ that you draw _____ _____

   _____ you can.

   G: You mean I should _____ _____?

   B: That's right.

Listen & Speak 1 B

1. **A:** It's _____ _____ _____ a good dancer. _____ should

   I do?

   B: It's _____ that you _____ give up.

   A: Okay. I will _____ _____ that.

2. **A:** It's _____ _____ write a good story. What should I do?

   B: _____ _____ _____ you read many books.

   A: Okay. I _____ _____ forget that.

Listen & Talk 2 A

1. **G:** Oh, this is _____ _____ _____.

   B: What's the matter?

   G: Can you teach me _____ _____ make cookies?

   B: Sure. It's a walk in the park.

   G: _____ _____ _____ _____ _____ that?

   B: I _____ it's easy to do.

1. G: 이봐, 민호야. 이 수학 문제의 정답을 찾았니?
   B: 아니. 그건 나에게 너무 어려워. 나는 수학을 잘하지 못 해.
   G: 내가 한 번 볼게. 네가 그 문제를 풀기 위해선 이 수학 공식을 이용하는 것이 중요해.
   B: 오, 알겠어. 그걸 사용해 볼게.

2. G: 네 포스터가 멋져 보여.
   B: 고마워, Kate. 네 것은 끝냈니?
   G: 아직 못 끝냈어. 나는 그림을 잘 그리지 못 해. 어떻게 하면 내가 그림을 잘 그릴 수 있을까?
   B: 시간이 필요해. 네가 가능한 자주 그림을 그리는 것이 중요해.
   G: 내가 계속 연습해야 한다는 뜻이니?
   B: 맞아.

1. A: 훌륭한 댄서가 되는 것은 어려워. 내가 무엇을 해야 할까?
   B: 절대 포기하지 않는 것이 중요해.
   A: 알겠어. 그것을 잊지 않을게.

2. A: 좋은 이야기를 쓰는 것은 어려워. 내가 무엇을 해야 할까?
   B: 책을 많이 읽는 것이 중요해.
   A: 알겠어. 그것을 잊지 않을게.

1. G: 오, 이것은 하기 어렵구나.
   B: 무슨 일이야?
   G: 쿠키를 만드는 방법을 나에게 가르쳐 줄 수 있니?
   B: 물론이지. 그건 'a walk in the park'야.
   G: 그게 무슨 뜻이니?
   B: 하기 쉽다는 뜻이야.

2. **B:** I _____ a singing contest tomorrow. I really _____ _____ _____ first place.

　　G: I'll keep my fingers _____ for you.

　　B: _____ _____ _____ _____ _____ "keep my fingers crossed"?

　　G: It _____ I wish you good _____.

　　B: Thank you.

Listen & Talk 2 B

1. **A:** Two heads _____ better _____ one.

　　B: _____ do you _____ _____ "Two heads are better than one"?

　　A: I _____ working _____ is better _____ working _____.

2. **A:** _____ makes perfect.

　　B: What do you _____ by "Practice makes perfect"?

　　A: I _____ you learn something _____ _____ it _____ and over.

Conversation A

M: _____ _____ my dream, I went to many auditions, but I often _____. _____, I never gave _____. I _____ acting and dancing classes. _____, I _____ my goal. It's important that you _____ _____ up.

Conversation B

Hana: You _____ sad, Jiho. What's wrong?

Jiho: I don't think I can _____ my dream.

Amy: _____ _____ _____ _____ _____ _____ _____?

Jiho: I want to be an actor, but I always _____ _____. Maybe I have to _____ _____.

Amy: Do you know this actor?

Jiho: Sure. He's a _____ movie star.

Amy: He failed _____ _____ 100 auditions.

Jiho: Really? Maybe I should keep _____. I will _____ more for my next audition.

Hana: That's right! It's important that _____ _____ _____ _____.

해석

2. **B:** 나 내일 노래 경연 대회가 있어. 나는 정말 1등을 하고 싶어.
　　G: 너에게 'keep my fingers crossed'할게.
　　B: 'keep my fingers crossed'가 무슨 뜻이니?
　　G: 그건 내가 너에게 행운을 빈다는 뜻이야.
　　B: 고마워.

1. **A:** 두 개의 머리가 머리 하나보다 낫다.
　　B: "두 개의 머리가 머리 하나보다 낫다."가 무슨 뜻이니?
　　A: 함께 일하는 것이 혼자 일하는 것보다 낫다는 뜻이야.

2. **A:** 연습이 완벽함을 만든다.
　　B: "연습이 완벽함을 만든다."가 무슨 뜻이니?
　　A: 반복해서 무언가를 하면 배우게 된다는 뜻이야.

M: 내 꿈을 이루기 위해 나는 많은 오디션에 갔지만 자주 떨어졌다. 하지만 나는 절대 포기하지 않았다. 나는 연기와 춤 수업을 들었다. 마침내 나는 내 목표를 이뤘다. 절대 포기하지 않는 것이 중요하다.

하나: 너 슬퍼 보여, 지호야. 무슨 일이니?
지호: 내 생각에 나는 꿈을 이룰 수 없을 것 같아.
Amy: 그게 무슨 말이니?
지호: 나는 배우가 되고 싶지만 항상 오디션에서 떨어져. 어쩌면 나는 포기해야 할 거 같아.
Amy: 너 이 배우를 아니?
지호: 당연하지. 그는 유명한 영화배우잖아.
Amy: 그는 백 번 이상 오디션에서 떨어졌어.
지호: 정말? 그러면 나도 계속 노력해야겠구나. 나는 다음 오디션을 위해서 더 연습할 거야.
하나: 바로 그거야! 절대 포기하지 않는 것이 중요해.

Conversation 시험대비 기본평가

[01~02] 다음 대화의 빈칸에 알맞은 말은?

01

> G: Hey, Minho. Did you find the answer to the math problem?
> B: No. It's too hard for me. I'm not good at math.
> G: Let me see. _____
> B: Oh, I see. I'll use it.

① It's important to study math.

② It's important that you know many words.

③ It's important that you use this math rule to solve the problem.

④ It's important that you turn off the music when you study.

⑤ It's important that you decide what to do.

02

> G: Oh, this is hard to do.
> B: What's the matter?
> G: Can you teach me how to make cookies?
> B: Sure. It's a walk in the park.
> G: _____
> B: I mean it's easy to do.

① What do you mean by that?　② Where did you walk?

③ Why do you say so?　④ How is he doing?

⑤ What's the matter?

03 주어진 문장 다음에 이어질 대화의 순서로 알맞은 것을 고르시오.

> I have a singing contest tomorrow. I really want to win first place.

> (A) It means I wish you good luck.
> (B) What do you mean by "keep my fingers crossed"?
> (C) I'll keep my fingers crossed for you.
> (D) Thank you.

① (B) – (A) – (C) – (D)　② (B) – (C) – (A) – (D)

③ (C) – (A) – (B) – (D)　④ (C) – (B) – (A) – (D)

⑤ (C) – (D) – (B) – (A)

[01~03] 다음 대화를 읽고 물음에 답하시오.

G: Your poster looks great. (①)

B: Thanks, Kate. (②)

G: Not yet. I can't draw well. (③) How can I become good at drawing?

B: It takes (A)_____. (④) It's important that you draw as often as you can. (⑤)

G: You mean I should (B)_____ practicing?

B: That's right.

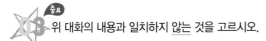 위 대화의 ①~⑤ 중 다음 주어진 말이 들어갈 알맞은 곳은?

> Did you finish yours?

①   ②   ③   ④   ⑤

02 빈칸 (A)와 (B)에 들어갈 말로 알맞은 것끼리 짝지어진 것을 고르시오.

	(A)	(B)
①	time	keep
②	time	enjoy
③	time	finish
④	money	keep
⑤	money	enjoy

 위 대화의 내용과 일치하지 <u>않는</u> 것을 고르시오.

① The boy finished drawing his poster.

② The girl thinks the poster which the boy drew is great.

③ The boy knows how to be good at drawing.

④ The girl can draw as well as the boy.

⑤ The boy gives her some advice for drawing well.

[04~06] 다음 대화를 읽고 물음에 답하시오.

Hana: You look sad, Jiho. What's wrong? (①)

Jiho: I don't think I can ⓐachieve my dream.

Amy: What do you mean by that?

Jiho: I want to be an actor, but I ⓑnever fail auditions. (②)

Amy: Do you know this actor?

Jiho: Sure. He's a famous movie star. (③)

Amy: He failed more than 100 auditions. (④)

Jiho: Really? Maybe I should keep ⓒtrying. (⑤) I will practice ⓓmore for my next audition.

Hana: That's right! It's important that you ⓔ never give up.

 위 대화의 ①~⑤ 중 다음 주어진 말이 들어갈 알맞은 곳은?

> Maybe I have to give up.

①   ②   ③   ④   ⑤

05 위 대화의 ⓐ~ⓔ 중 흐름상 어색한 것을 고르시오.

① ⓐ   ② ⓑ   ③ ⓒ   ④ ⓓ   ⑤ ⓔ

06 위 대화의 내용과 일치하지 <u>않는</u> 것을 고르시오.

① Hana thinks it's important not to give up.

② Jiho wants to become an actor.

③ Amy told Jiho the story about the famous movie star.

④ Jiho failed auditions more than 100 times.

⑤ Jiho will keep trying for the next audition.

07 빈칸에 공통으로 들어갈 알맞은 말을 고르시오.

> A: (A)_____.
> B: What do you mean by "(B)_____"?
> A: I mean working together is better than working alone.

① keep my fingers crossed
② It's a walk in the park
③ Will is power
④ Practice makes perfect
⑤ Two heads are better than one

[08~09] 다음 짝지어진 대화가 <u>어색한</u> 것은?

08 ① A: I bought this bag at the mall. It's a steal.
　　B: What do you mean by that?
　　A: It's very cheap.
② A: Mina is really nice. She is all ears.
　　B: What do you mean by that?
　　A: She listens very carefully.
③ A: What is important to do to be an scientist?
　　B: It's important to study math and science.
④ A: Practice makes perfect.
　　B: What do you mean by "Practice makes perfect"?
　　A: Yes, I do. I mean you learn something by doing it over and over.
⑤ A: I have an important exam tomorrow.
　　B: I'll keep my fingers crossed for you!
　　A: Thanks for saying that. I feel much better.

09 ① A: What is important to grow taller?
　　B: It is important to drink much milk.
② A: Is it important that I should prepare a lot for the contest?
　　B: Yes. I think practice makes perfect.
③ A: It's important to keep studying.
　　B: I'll turn off the music.
④ A: What does "No sweat, no sweet" mean?
　　B: It means "If you don't work hard, you can't achieve your goal."
⑤ A: What should we do to keep the air clean?
　　B: First of all, it's important to use public transportation.

[10~11] 다음 대화를 읽고 물음에 답하시오.

> A: It's hard to be a good dancer. (A)_____
> B: (B) <u>절대 포기하지 않는 것이 중요해.</u> (is, never, important, it, give, you, that, up)
> A: Okay. I will not forget that.

10 빈칸 (A)에 알맞은 말을 고르시오.

① What are you going to do?
② What should I do?
③ What do you mean by that?
④ What are you talking about?
⑤ What do you want to be?

서답형
11 밑줄 친 (B)의 우리말에 맞게 괄호 안에 주어진 단어를 배열하여 영작하시오.

➡ _____

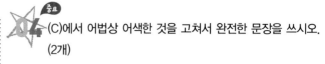
01 주어진 문장 이후에 이어질 대화의 순서를 바르게 배열하시오.

> Your poster looks great.

> (A) Not yet. I can't draw well. How can I become good at drawing?
> (B) That's right.
> (C) Thanks, Kate. Did you finish yours?
> (D) You mean I should keep practicing?
> (E) It takes time. It's important that you draw as often as you can.

➡ _____

[02~04] 다음 대화를 읽고 물음에 답하시오.

> A: Please call me "Speedy Feet."
> B: What do you mean (A)_____ "Speedy Feet"?
> A: I mean I want to be a runner.
> B: (B)달리기 선수가 되기 위해서 무엇을 하는 것이 중요하니? (to, become, runner, a, what, important, to, is, do)
> A: (C)It's important what I practice to run every day.
> B: I'm sure you'll make it.

02 빈칸 (A)에 알맞은 전치사를 쓰시오.

➡ _____

03 (B)의 밑줄 친 우리말에 맞게 괄호 안에 주어진 단어를 배열하여 영작하시오.

➡ _____

04 (C)에서 어법상 어색한 것을 고쳐서 완전한 문장을 쓰시오. (2개)

➡ _____

05 ⓐ~ⓔ 중 흐름상 어색한 것을 고치시오.

> G: Hey, Minho. ⓐDid you find the answer to the math problem?
> B: No. It's too hard for me. ⓑI'm good at math.
> G: ⓒLet me see. ⓓIt's important that you use this math rule to solve the problem.
> B: Oh, I see. ⓔI'll use it.

➡ _____
_____

06 다음 대화의 문맥상 또는 어법상 어색한 것을 고치시오. (2개)

> A: It's hard to make movies. What should I do?
> B: It's important that you think creative.
> A: Okay. I will forget that.

➡ (1) _____
_____
(2) _____

Grammar

① 'ask/want+A+to부정사' 구문

> **Other teams asked African American players to join them.**
> 다른 팀들은 아프리카계 미국인 선수들에게 자신들의 팀에 합류할 것을 요청했다.

- **'동사＋목적어＋to부정사' 구문**

  '주어＋동사＋목적어＋목적격보어'의 5형식 문장에서 want, ask, tell 등의 동사가 쓰이면 목적어와 목적격보어가 능동 관계일 때, 목적격보어로 to부정사가 온다.

  - Do you **want** me **to close** the shop? 내가 가게 문을 닫았으면 좋겠니?
  - He **asked** you **to wait** for him until 3:00. 그는 너에게 3시까지 기다려 달라고 부탁했어.

- **to부정사를 목적격보어로 취하는 동사**

  (1) 명령, 요청: tell, advise, warn, ask, request, allow 등
  - I **told** him **to do** it immediately. 나는 그에게 그것을 즉시 하라고 말했다.
  - Other players **advised** him **to stay** on the team. 다른 선수들은 그에게 팀에 남아 있으라고 충고했다.

  (2) 유도, 자극: lead, invite, encourage 등
  - He **encouraged** me **to write** poems. 그는 내게 시를 쓰도록 격려해 주었다.

  (3) 기대, 소망: like, expect, want, wish 등
  - Many people did not **expect** him **to do** well. 많은 사람들은 그가 잘하리라고 기대하지 않았다.

- **to부정사의 부정형은 'not[never]＋to 동사원형'이다.**

  - He **advised** me **not to go** there. 그는 나에게 거기에 가지 말라고 충고했다.
  - I **asked** him **not to tell** anybody. 나는 그에게 누구에게도 말하지 말라고 부탁했다.
  - The doctor **ordered** me **not to smoke**. 의사는 나에게 담배를 피우지 말라고 명령했다.

핵심 Check

1. 다음 우리말과 일치하도록 빈칸에 알맞은 말을 쓰시오.

   (1) 우리 부모님은 내가 그들과 함께 살기를 바라신다.
   ➡ My parents want me _____ _____ with them.

   (2) 나는 그에게 조심하라고 부탁했다.
   ➡ I asked him _____ _____ careful.

   (3) 어떻게 그런 생각을 하게 되었는가?
   ➡ What led you _____ _____ so?

② 목적격 관계대명사

> • I will become a player **who** people like. 나는 사람들이 좋아하는 선수가 될 거야.

■ **목적격 관계대명사의 뜻**

관계대명사는 절과 절을 연결하는 접속사와 대명사의 기능 두 가지를 겸하는데, 관계대명사 앞의 명사(선행사)가 뒤 문장의 목적어 역할을 할 때 이 관계대명사를 '목적격 관계대명사'라고 한다.

This is the book **which** I have chosen. 이것이 내가 고른 책이다.

■ **목적격 관계대명사의 종류**

선행사가 사람일 때 'who(m),' 사물일 때 'which,' 사람과 사물 모두에 'that'을 쓸 수 있다.

선행사	사람	사물, 동물	사람, 사물, 동물
목적격 관계대명사	who(m)/that	which/that	that

That man over there is the dentist **whom** I told you about. 저기 있는 사람이 내가 너에게 얘기했던 그 치과 의사야.

■ **목적격 관계대명사의 생략**

목적격 관계대명사는 생략이 가능하다.

• I know the novelist (**who/whom/that**) he mentioned. 나는 그가 언급한 소설가를 알고 있다.

■ 목적격 관계대명사절에서는 앞에 있는 관계대명사가 동사의 목적어 역할을 하기 때문에 동사 뒤에 목적어가 없다는 것에 특히 주의해야 한다.

• I cannot find the book. I put it(=the book) on the table.
= I cannot find the book (**which/that**) I put on the table. 나는 책상 위에 두었던 책을 찾을 수 없다.

■ 목적격 관계대명사가 전치사의 목적어인 경우 전치사는 관계대명사절의 끝에 오거나 관계대명사 앞에 올 수 있다. 전치사가 관계대명사절의 끝에 올 경우에는 관계대명사를 생략할 수 있지만 전치사가 관계대명사 앞에 올 경우에는 관계대명사를 생략하지 않으며 관계대명사 that을 쓸 수 없다.

• I had some animals (**which/that**) I took care **of**. (나는 내가 돌보던 동물들을 갖고 있었다.)
= I had some animals **of which** I took care.
= I had some animals of that I took care. (×)

핵심 Check

2. 다음 괄호 안에서 알맞은 말을 고르시오.

(1) He is the man (who / which) I met yesterday.

(2) The bag (whom / which) he is carrying is very old.

Grammar 시험대비 기본평가

01 다음 문장에서 어법상 <u>어색한</u> 부분을 바르게 고치시오.

(1) My mother told me bring my umbrella.

_____ ➡ _____

(2) I asked Sam borrow the book from the library

_____ ➡ _____

(3) She is an actress which I wanted to meet.

_____ ➡ _____

(4) Did you find the book who you wanted?

_____ ➡ _____

[02~03] 다음 문장의 빈칸에 들어갈 알맞은 말은?

02

Our English teacher advised us _____ harder.

① study   ② studies   ③ studied
④ studying   ⑤ to study

03

The bag _____ he is carrying is very old.

① that   ② what   ③ who
④ whom   ⑤ whose

04 다음 우리말에 맞게 빈칸에 알맞은 말을 쓰시오.

(1) 너는 내가 그 이야기를 믿으라고 기대하는 거야?

➡ Do you expect me _____ _____ the story?

(2) 그는 그들로 하여금 궁핍한 사람들을 도우라고 장려했다.

➡ He encouraged them _____ _____ the poor and needy.

(3) 소년은 한번 본 그 소녀와 사랑에 빠졌다.

➡ The boy fell in love with a girl _____ he saw once.

(4) 내가 어제 산 치마를 너에게 보여줄게.

➡ I'll show you the skirt _____ I bought yesterday.

01 다음 빈칸에 알맞은 것은?

> My father told me _____ TV for an
> hour a day.

① watch   ② watches
③ watched   ④ watching
⑤ to watch

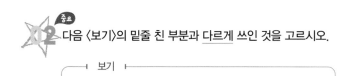**02** 다음 〈보기〉의 밑줄 친 부분과 다르게 쓰인 것을 고르시오.

> ┤ 보기 ├
> Everything that I said was true.

① The movie which I saw was interesting.
② The money was returned by the boy that
   had found it.
③ Ted wants to marry the lady whom he
   loves.
④ This is the movie that I really wanted to
   watch.
⑤ I am looking for a man who I met at the
   park yesterday.

03 다음 빈칸에 들어갈 수 있는 말이 다른 하나는?

① The bag _____ I bought yesterday is
   blue.
② She is the scientist _____ I want to
   meet.
③ An orphan is a child _____ parents
   are dead.
④ This is the pen _____ was on the
   desk.
⑤ Kate is the writer _____ I like most.

04 다음 우리말을 영어로 바르게 옮긴 것은?

> 그의 친구들은 그가 빚을 갚을 수 있도록 해줄 것
> 이다.

① His friends will enable him pay his
   debts.
② His friends will enable him pays his
   debts.
③ His friends will enable him paying his
   debts.
④ His friends will enable him to pay his
   debts.
⑤ His friends will enable him to paying his
   debts.

05 다음 중 어법상 바르지 않은 것은?

> Mark ①wanted ②me ③lend ④him ⑤
> some money.

①   ②   ③   ④   ⑤

서답형
06 다음 괄호 안에서 알맞은 말을 고르시오.

(1) The people (which / that) we met were
   very nice.
(2) The dress (who / which) she is wearing
   is pretty.
(3) This is the drama about (that / which) I
   spoke yesterday.
(4) His support helped Robinson (play /
   playing) harder.
(5) I (hoped / warned) the man to keep
   away from my dog.

07 다음 중 어법상 옳은 문장을 고르시오.

① But she had a dream who she couldn't give up.

② This is the house in that she lives.

③ We sometimes have to eat dishes whom we don't like.

④ Another important thing which we choose is time management.

⑤ There is something who you should remember.

08 다음 빈칸에 적절하지 <u>않은</u> 것은?

> Sena _____ me to start studying two weeks before the test.

① watched   ② encouraged   ③ told
④ expected   ⑤ persuaded

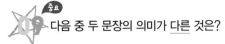다음 중 두 문장의 의미가 <u>다른</u> 것은?

① Mom expects that I will study hard.
   → Mom expects me to study hard.

② Sam advised her that she should not throw away the trash on the street.
   → Sam advised her not to throw away the trash on the street.

③ Ann told him that he must wear long clothes to protect himself from animals.
   → Ann told him to wear long clothes to protect himself from animals.

④ She allowed that I could eat ice cream for dessert.
   → I allowed her to eat ice cream for dessert.

⑤ Juliet told Romeo that he should come at once.
   → Juliet told Romeo to come at once.

10 다음 밑줄 친 that의 성격이 나머지 넷과 <u>다른</u> 것은?

① One idea is <u>that</u> a big rock from space hit the Earth.

② The phone <u>that</u> you picked up is mine.

③ An elephant is an animal <u>that</u> has a long nose.

④ Do you have some money <u>that</u> I can borrow?

⑤ The book <u>that</u> I read yesterday was very interesting.

11 서답형 괄호 안의 동사를 어법에 맞게 고쳐 쓰시오.

(1) They asked him (spend) the night in the house.

(2) Her doctors encouraged her (keep) learning Taekwondo.

(3) Why don't you help her (carry) the boxes?

(4) The teacher had the students (finish) their projects.

(5) We requested everyone in the office (assemble) in the lobby.

➡ (1) _____ (2) _____ (3) _____
   (4) _____ (5) _____

12 다음 중 어법상 <u>어색한</u> 부분을 찾아 바르게 고친 것은?

> He warned Cindy keep away from his dog.

① warned → has warned

② Cindy → Cindy's

③ keep → to keep

④ from → to

⑤ his → him

서답형

13 다음 문장에서 어법상 어색한 부분을 바르게 고쳐 다시 쓰시오.

(1) Sophie asked her dad help her to finish her homework.

➡ _____

(2) Mom wanted Lily coming home by 8.

➡ _____

(3) She invited me go to New York with her.

➡ _____

(4) The blue watch is the gift who I bought there for my brother.

➡ _____
_____

(5) The man which my mother is talking to is my art teacher.

➡ _____
_____

(6) The girl and her cat which I met this morning were playing in the park.

➡ _____
_____

14 괄호 안에 주어진 동사를 빈칸에 써 넣을 때 그 형태가 다른 하나는?

① The teacher wanted me _____ notes. (take)

② Jimin told me _____ a study group. (make)

③ Mom asked Rosa _____ some books to the library. (return)

④ Many people did not expect him _____ well. (do)

⑤ I feel something _____ up my back. (creep)

서답형

15 다음 문장에서 생략할 수 있는 것을 쓰시오.

(1) Mary is the girl who I met in Paris.

(2) My group thinks health is an important thing that we need for our dream.

(3) He is reading a book which is about the greenhouse gas.

➡ (1) _____ (2) _____ (3) _____

16 다음 중 어법상 어색한 것을 고르시오.

① The heavy rain caused the river overflow.

② Do not force them to agree to your opinion.

③ I warned him not to take any pictures here.

④ We want you to come and visit us.

⑤ After that season, other teams asked African American players to join them.

17 다음 두 문장을 한 문장으로 바르게 바꾸지 않은 것을 고르시오.

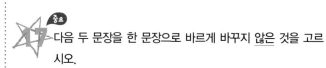

- Alice wishes to meet a boy.
- She went to the same school with him.

① Alice wishes to meet a boy she went to the same school with.

② Alice wishes to meet a boy who she went to the same school with.

③ Alice wishes to meet a boy that she went to the same school with.

④ Alice wishes to meet a boy with whom she went to the same school.

⑤ Alice wishes to meet a boy with that she went to the same school.

01 다음 문장에서 어법상 어색한 부분을 찾아 바르게 고쳐 다시 쓰시오.

(1) I want you are happy.

➡ _____

(2) Jack asked his mother woke him up at 8 o'clock.

➡ _____

(3) Tina told me finding a quiet place to study.

➡ _____

(4) Jessy got her dad drop her off at the bus stop.

➡ _____

(5) His teacher advised him not spend all his time on one subject.

➡ _____
_____

02 다음 두 문장을 관계대명사를 사용하여 한 문장으로 바꾸시오.

(1) • The man is my brother.
• You met the man on Sunday.

➡ _____
_____

(2) • That is the computer.
• I bought the computer last week.

➡ _____
_____

(3) • This is the cake.
• It was made by Ann.

➡ _____

(4) • I visited the church.
• I took some pictures of the church.

➡ _____
_____
_____

(5) • It is an experience.
• I look forward the experience.

➡ _____
_____
_____

(6) • Does Eddie have any friends?
• He can depend on them.

➡ _____
_____
_____

03 우리말에 맞게 괄호 안에 주어진 동사의 알맞은 형태를 빈칸에 쓰시오.

(1) 무엇을 가져오면 되나요?

➡ What would you like me _____? (bring)

(2) 그녀는 그들을 대회에 참가하도록 만들었다.

➡ She made them _____ part in the contest. (take)

(3) 무언가 탄내가 나는 것 같다.

➡ I think I smell something _____. (burn)

04 다음 문장에서 어법상 <u>어색한</u> 부분을 찾아 바르게 고쳐 다시 쓰시오.

(1) This is the bridge who my father built.

➡ _____

(2) They are the people which I met in the plane.

➡ _____

(3) I like the new computer that I bought it last week.

➡ _____

(4) Can you tell me about the church of that you took the picture last weekend?

➡ _____
_____
_____
_____

05 다음 두 문장이 비슷한 의미를 갖도록 빈칸을 알맞은 말로 채우시오.

(1) Mom told me that I must come back home by tonight.
➡ Mom told me _____ back home by tonight.

(2) His boss told him that he should be more careful for the future.
➡ His boss ordered him _____ more careful for the future.

(3) The teacher told Maria that she should not give up her dream.
➡ The teacher encouraged Maria _____ _____ her dream.

06 두 문장을 관계대명사를 사용하여 한 문장으로 썼을 때, 빈칸에 해당하는 문장을 쓰시오.

(1) • _____
• My favorite author wrote it.
→ I bought a book that my favorite author wrote.

(2) • That is the girl.
• _____
→ That is the girl whom I invited to the party.

(3) • There are three things.
• _____
_____
→ There are three things that I need to do to achieve my dream.

(4) • _____
• The famous author wrote it.
→ Is the novel which the famous author wrote fun?

07 괄호 안에 주어진 어휘를 이용하여 우리말에 맞게 영작하시오.

(1) 그녀는 너에게 자기 방 청소를 부탁했다. (ask, clean)

➡ _____

(2) 엄마는 내가 강아지를 돌볼 거라고 예상하신다. (expect, take care of)

➡ _____
_____

(3) 우리가 만났던 사람들은 매우 친절했다. (the people, nice)

➡ _____

(4) 내가 어제 산 가방은 파란색이다. (bag, buy)

➡ _____

Jackie Robinson Breaks the Color Line

It was New York City on April 15, 1947. Jackie Robinson, an African
날짜 앞에는 전치사 on을 쓴다.   'Jackie Robinson'을 부연 설명하는 동격.
American, went on the field as second baseman for the Brooklyn
동격 앞에는 콤마(,)를 쓴다.   as: ~로(자격)
Dodgers. People couldn't believe their eyes. He was the first African
                          '~의 눈을 의심하다'라는 뜻. 놀람을 나타낼 때 쓰인다.
American player to play on a Major League team. That day, the color
            to부정사의 형용사적 용법. on: 소속
line was broken.
수동태(be동사+과거분사). 과거시제이므로 be동사 was가 쓰였다.

Robinson faced many difficulties. Although Robinson was a talented
                                    =Though
player and a gentle person, his teammates did not want to play with
                                              want는 to부정사를 목적어로 취하는 동사
him. Every hotel turned the team down because Robinson was on
the team. When he was at bat, people in the stands rudely shouted at
him. Robinson thought to himself, 'I need to keep calm and focus on
                        재귀대명사   'need to': '~해야 한다'. 뒤에 동사원형이 온다.
baseball. I will try and become a player who people like. Then, next
                              목적격 관계대명사로 who 뒤의 절이 'a player'를 꾸며 준다.
season, there will be more African American players in the league.'
Robinson put all his time and energy into baseball. With practice, he
                                            with: ~함에 따라, ~와 더불어 with practice: 연습함에 따라서
became great at batting and base running.
          at의 목적어로 동명사 batting과 'base running'이 쓰임.

American: 미국인; 미국의
baseman: (1, 2, 3) 루수
major: 주요한, 중대한
color line: 인종 차별
although: (비록) ~이긴 하지만
talented: (타고난) 재능이 있는
teammate: 팀 동료
rudely: 무례하게, 예의 없이, 버릇없이
turn down: ~을 거절하다, 거부하다
at bat: 타석에 서서
shout at: ~에게 소리치다
think to oneself: 조용히 생각하다.
마음속으로 생각하다
keep calm: 평정을 유지하다

 확인문제

● 다음 문장이 본문의 내용과 일치하면 T, 일치하지 <u>않으면</u> F를 쓰시오.

1   Jackie Robinson was the first African American player to play on a Major League
    team. ☐

2   On April 15, 1947, the color line was made. ☐

3   Robinson experienced many difficulties. ☐

4   Robinson's teammates wanted to play with him. ☐

5   When Robinson was at bat, people in the stands rudely shouted at him. ☐

6   Robinson put all his time and energy into breaking the color line. ☐

Robinson's effort moved his teammates. When people shouted at Robinson, one of his teammates walked up to Robinson and tapped him on the shoulder. "Do not listen to them. You're doing fine," he said. His support helped Robinson to play harder. Finally, Robinson earned the respect of other players and fans.

'one of ~'는 '~ 중의 하나', 뒤에는 복수를 나타내는 명사가 와야 한다.
어깨를 두드렸다.
do fine: 잘하다
help+목적어+to부정사(동사원형): (목적어)가 ~하는 것을 돕다

Thanks to Robinson, the Dodgers won the National League Championship in 1947. The league recognized Robinson's excellence and presented him with the Rookie of the Year Award in the same year. After that season, other teams asked African American players to join them.

~ 덕분에
present A with B: A에게 B를 수여하다
주어+동사+목적어+목적격보어(5형식): ask는 목적격보어로 to부정사를 취함

Robinson's uniform number was 42. Baseball players in Major League teams no longer wear the number 42 to honor him. Every year, however, on April 15, every player wears the number that Robinson wore. The day is called "Jackie Robinson Day."

to부정사의 목적을 나타내는 부사적 용법. =Jackie Robinson
그러나(부사): 문장 중간에 쓸 때에는 앞과 뒤에 콤마(,)가 온다.
목적격 관계대명사
be동사+과거분사(수동태): ~라고 불리다

effort: 노력, 수고
support: 지지, 지원, 도움
recognize: 알아보다, 인정하다
excellence: 우수, 탁월, 뛰어남
earn the respect: 존경을 얻다
honor: 존경하다, 공경하다
no longer: 더 이상 ~ 아닌[하지 않는]

확인문제

• 다음 문장이 본문의 내용과 일치하면 T, 일치하지 <u>않으면</u> F를 쓰시오.

1 Robinson's effort moved his teammates. ☐

2 Some of Robinson's teammates walked up to Robinson and tapped him on the shoulder. ☐

3 Thanks to Robinson, the Dodgers won the National League Championship in 1947. ☐

4 The league didn't recognize Robinson's excellence. ☐

5 Baseball players in Major League teams no longer wear the number 42 to honor Robinson. ☐

6 "Jackie Robinson Day" is April 5 of each year. ☐

● 우리말을 참고하여 빈칸에 알맞은 말을 쓰시오.

1 Jackie Robinson _____ _____ _____

2 It was New York City _____ _____ _____, _____.

3 Jackie Robinson, an African American, went on the field _____ second baseman _____ the Brooklyn Dodgers.

4 People _____ _____ their eyes.

5 He was _____ _____ _____ _____ _____ to play on a Major League team.

6 That day, _____ _____ _____ _____ _____.

7 Robinson _____ _____ _____.

8 _____ Robinson was a talented player and a gentle person, his teammates did not want _____ _____ _____ _____.

9 Every hotel _____ _____ _____ _____ because Robinson was on the team.

10 When he _____ _____ _____, people in the stands rudely shouted at him.

11 Robinson _____ _____ _____, 'I need to keep calm and focus on baseball.

12 I will try and become a player _____ _____ _____.

13 Then, next season, _____ _____ _____ _____ African American players in the league.'

14 Robinson _____ all his time and energy _____ baseball.

---

1 Jackie Robinson 인종 차별을 깨다

2 1947년 4월 15일 뉴욕시에서 였다.

3 아프리카계 미국인 Jackie Robinson은 브루클린 다저스의 2루수로 경기장에 나갔다.

4 사람들은 자신들의 눈을 의심했다.

5 그는 메이저리그 팀에서 경기한 최초의 아프리카계 미국인 선수였다.

6 그날 인종 차별이 깨졌다.

7 Robinson은 많은 어려움에 직면했다.

8 Robinson은 재능 있는 선수이고 온화한 사람이었지만 그의 팀원들은 그와 함께 경기하기를 원하지 않았다.

9 Robinson이 팀에 있었기 때문에 모든 호텔에서 그 팀을 거절했다.

10 그가 타석에 있을 때, 관중석에 있는 사람들이 그에게 무례하게 소리치기도 했다.

11 Robinson은 마음속으로 생각했다. '나는 평정심을 유지하고 야구에 집중해야 해.

12 나는 노력해서 사람들이 좋아하는 선수가 될 거야.

13 그러면 다음 시즌에는 아프리카계 미국인 선수가 리그에 더 많이 생길 거야.'

14 Robinson은 자신의 모든 시간과 에너지를 야구에 집중했다.

15 _____ _____, he became great at _____ and _____

_____ .

16 Robinson's effort _____ his teammates.

17 When people shouted at Robinson, _____ _____ _____ walked up to Robinson and _____ _____ _____ _____ shoulder.

18 " _____ _____ _____ _____ them.

19 You're doing _____," he said.

20 His support helped Robinson _____ _____ harder.

21 Finally, Robinson _____ _____ _____ of other players and fans.

22 _____ _____ Robinson, the Dodgers won the National League Championship in 1947.

23 The league _____ Robinson's excellence and _____ him _____ the Rookie of the Year Award in the same year.

24 After that season, other teams _____ African American players _____ _____ them.

25 Robinson's _____ _____ was 42.

26 Baseball players in Major League teams _____ _____ wear the number 42 _____ _____ _____ .

27 Every year, _____, on April 15, every player wears the number that Robinson _____ .

28 The day _____ _____ "Jackie Robinson Day."

---

15 연습을 함으로써 그는 타격과 주루를 잘하게 되었다.

16 Robinson의 노력은 그의 팀원들을 감동시켰다.

17 사람들이 Robinson에게 소리쳤을 때, 그의 팀 동료 중 한 명이 Robinson에게 다가가 어깨를 두드렸다.

18 "그들 말을 듣지 마.

19 너는 잘하고 있어."라고 그가 말했다.

20 그의 지지는 Robinson이 더 열심히 경기하는 데 도움이 됐다.

21 마침내, Robinson은 다른 선수들과 팬들의 존경을 받았다.

22 Robinson 덕분에 다저스는 1947년에 내셔널리그 챔피언십에서 우승하게 되었다.

23 리그에서는 Robinson의 탁월함을 인정했고, 같은 해에 그에게 신인상을 수여했다.

24 그 시즌 이후, 다른 팀들은 아프리카계 미국인 선수들에게 자신들의 팀에 합류할 것을 요청했다.

25 Robinson의 등 번호는 42번이었다.

26 메이저리그 팀의 야구 선수들은 그에 대한 존경을 보여 주기 위해 더 이상 42번을 달지 않는다.

27 하지만 매년 4월 15일, 모든 선수들은 Robinson이 달았던 번호를 단다.

28 이 날을 '재키 로빈슨 데이'라고 부른다.

● 우리말을 참고하여 본문을 영작하시오.

1 Jackie Robinson 인종 차별을 깨다
➡ _____

2 1947년 4월 15일 뉴욕시에서였다.
➡ _____

3 아프리카계 미국인 Jackie Robinson은 브루클린 다저스의 2루수로 경기장에 나갔다.
➡ _____

4 사람들은 자신들의 눈을 의심했다.
➡ _____

5 그는 메이저리그 팀에서 경기한 최초의 아프리카계 미국인 선수였다.
➡ _____

6 그날 인종 차별이 깨졌다.
➡ _____

7 Robinson은 많은 어려움에 직면했다.
➡ _____

8 Robinson은 재능 있는 선수이고 온화한 사람이었지만 그의 팀원들은 그와 함께 경기하기를 원하지 않았다.
➡ _____

9 Robinson이 팀에 있었기 때문에 모든 호텔에서 그 팀을 거절했다.
➡ _____

10 그가 타석에 있을 때, 관중석에 있는 사람들이 그에게 무례하게 소리치기도 했다.
➡ _____

11 Robinson은 마음속으로 생각했다. '나는 평정심을 유지하고 야구에 집중해야 해.
➡ _____

12 나는 노력해서 사람들이 좋아하는 선수가 될 거야.
➡ _____

13 그러면 다음 시즌에는 아프리카계 미국인 선수가 리그에 더 많이 생길 거야.'
➡ _____

14 Robinson은 자신의 모든 시간과 에너지를 야구에 집중했다.
➡ _____

15 연습을 함으로써 그는 타격과 주루를 잘하게 되었다.
➡ _____

16 Robinson의 노력은 그의 팀원들을 감동시켰다.

➡ _____

17 사람들이 Robinson에게 소리쳤을 때, 그의 팀 동료 중 한 명이 Robinson에게 다가가 어깨를 두드렸다.

➡ _____

18 "그들 말을 듣지 마.

➡ _____

19 너는 잘하고 있어."라고 그가 말했다.

➡ _____

20 그의 지지는 Robinson이 더 열심히 경기하는 데 도움이 됐다.

➡ _____

21 마침내, Robinson은 다른 선수들과 팬들의 존경을 받았다.

➡ _____

22 Robinson 덕분에 다저스는 1947년에 내셔널리그 챔피언십에서 우승하게 되었다.

➡ _____

23 리그에서는 Robinson의 탁월함을 인정했고, 같은 해에 그에게 신인상을 수여했다.

➡ _____

24 그 시즌 이후, 다른 팀들은 아프리카계 미국인 선수들에게 자신들의 팀에 합류할 것을 요청했다.

➡ _____

25 Robinson의 등 번호는 42번이었다.

➡ _____

26 메이저리그 팀의 야구 선수들은 그에 대한 존경을 보여 주기 위해 더 이상 42번을 달지 않는다.

➡ _____

27 하지만 매년 4월 15일, 모든 선수들은 Robinson이 달았던 번호를 단다.

➡ _____

28 이 날을 '재키 로빈슨 데이'라고 부른다.

➡ _____

[01~03] 다음 글을 읽고 물음에 답하시오.

It was New York City __(A)__ April 15, 1947. Jackie Robinson, an African American, went on the field ⓐas second baseman for the Brooklyn Dodgers. People couldn't believe their eyes. He was the first African American player to play __(B)__ a Major League team. That day, the color line was broken.

서답형

01 위 글의 빈칸 (A)와 (B)에 공통으로 들어갈 알맞은 전치사를 쓰시오.

➡ _____

02 위 글의 밑줄 친 ⓐas와 같은 의미로 쓰인 것을 고르시오.

① Leave it as it is.
② Yesterday he attended the meeting as a reporter.
③ Her anger grew as she talked.
④ As I was tired, I soon fell asleep.
⑤ He trembled as he spoke.

 중요 위 글을 읽고 Jackie Robinson에 대해 알 수 없는 것을 고르시오.

① 혈통   ② 국적
③ 수비 위치   ④ 가족 관계
⑤ 소속팀

[04~06] 다음 글을 읽고 물음에 답하시오.

Robinson faced many difficulties. Although Robinson was a talented player and a gentle person, his teammates did not want to play with him. Every hotel turned the team down (A)[because / because of] Robinson was on the team. ⓐ그가 타석에 있을 때, people in the stands rudely shouted at him.

Robinson thought to (B)[him / himself], 'I need to keep calm and focus on baseball. I will try and become a player who people like. Then, next season, there will be more African American players in the league.' Robinson put all his time and energy into baseball. With practice, he became (C)[great / greatly] at batting and base running.

서답형

04 위 글의 괄호 (A)~(C)에서 어법상 알맞은 낱말을 골라 쓰시오.

➡ (A)_____ (B)_____ (C)_____

서답형

05 위 글의 밑줄 친 ⓐ의 우리말을 5단어로 쓰시오.

➡ _____

중요 위 글을 읽고 대답할 수 없는 질문은?

① Did Robinson have difficulties during his career as a major leaguer?
② Why did every hotel turn the team down?
③ When Robinson was at bat, did people in the stands welcome him?
④ Thanks to Robinson's effort, how many African American players could play on the Major League teams?
⑤ How did Robinson become a good batter and base runner?

[07~10] 다음 글을 읽고 물음에 답하시오.

Robinson's uniform number was 42. Baseball players in Major League teams no longer wear the number 42 ⓐto honor him. Every year, (A) , on April 15, every player wears the number that Robinson wore. ⓑThe day is called "Jackie Robinson Day."

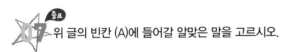 위 글의 빈칸 (A)에 들어갈 알맞은 말을 고르시오.

① therefore
② however
③ for example
④ in fact
⑤ in addition

08 아래 〈보기〉에서 위 글의 밑줄 친 ⓐto honor와 문법적 쓰임이 같은 것의 개수를 고르시오.

┌─── 보기 ├───
① He wept to see the sight.
② My hope is to work as a doctor in Africa.
③ I want something to write with.
④ I have nothing to do this afternoon.
⑤ I was very happy to hear the news.
└─────────────

① 1개   ② 2개   ③ 3개   ④ 4개   ⑤ 5개

서답형
09 Why do baseball players in Major League teams no longer wear the number 42? Fill in the blanks with a suitable word.

➡ They do so in order to _____ Robinson.

서답형
10 위 글의 밑줄 친 ⓑ를 능동태로 고치시오.

➡ _____

[11~13] 다음 글을 읽고 물음에 답하시오.

Robinson thought to himself, 'I need to keep calm and focus on baseball. I will try and become a player ___ⓐ___ people like. Then, next season, there will be more African American players in the league.' Robinson put all his time and energy into baseball. With practice, he became great at batting and base running.

11 위 글의 빈칸 ⓐ에 들어갈 알맞은 말을 모두 고르시오.

① what   ② who
③ whom   ④ which
⑤ that

12 위 글의 내용과 어울리는 속담을 고르시오.

① Better late than never.
② A stitch in time saves nine.
③ Do to others as you would be done by.
④ Practice makes perfect.
⑤ Look before you leap.

13 위 글의 내용과 일치하지 <u>않는</u> 것은?

① Robinson은 평정심을 유지하고 야구에 집중해야 한다고 마음속으로 생각했다.
② Robinson은 노력해서 사람들이 좋아하는 선수가 되려고 결심했다.
③ Robinson 덕분에 다음 시즌에 아프리카계 미국인 선수가 리그에 더 많이 생겼다.
④ Robinson은 자신의 모든 시간과 에너지를 야구에 집중했다.
⑤ 연습을 함으로써 Robinson은 타격과 주루를 잘하게 되었다.

[14~17] 다음 글을 읽고 물음에 답하시오.

How I Will Achieve My Dream

I want to be a designer. There are ⓐthree things (A)[that / what] I need to do ⓑto achieve my dream. I need to be healthy, be creative, and never give up. Being healthy will help me (B)[keep / keeping] going for my dream. Being creative will help me do something different. Plus, I will always tell myself never ___(A)___ because it will make me (C)[try / to try] harder.

서답형
14 위 글의 빈칸 (A)에 들어갈 알맞은 말을 쓰시오.

➡ _____

서답형
15 위 글의 괄호 (A)~(C)에서 어법상 알맞은 낱말을 골라 쓰시오.

➡ (A)_____ (B)_____ (C)_____

16 위 글의 밑줄 친 ⓐ에 해당하지 않는 것은? (2개)

① to be healthy
② to work well with others
③ to be creative
④ never to give up
⑤ to help others

중요
17 위 글의 밑줄 친 ⓑ를 바꿔 쓴 것으로 옳지 않은 것을 고르시오.

① so as to achieve my dream
② in order that I can achieve my dream
③ achieving my dream
④ so that I can achieve my dream
⑤ in order to achieve my dream

[18~20] 다음 글을 읽고 물음에 답하시오.

Robinson's effort ⓐmoved ①his teammates. When people shouted at Robinson, one of ②his teammates walked up to Robinson and tapped ③him on the shoulder. "Do not listen to them. ④You're doing fine," he said. ⑤His support helped Robinson to play harder. ⓑFinally, Robinson earned the respect of other players and fans.

18 위 글의 밑줄 친 ⓐmoved와 같은 의미로 쓰인 것을 고르시오.

① He moved towards the window.
② I moved the meeting to Wednesday.
③ Their deep friendship moved us a great deal.
④ They moved into a new house.
⑤ We moved our chairs a little nearer.

중요
19 밑줄 친 ①~⑤ 중에서 가리키는 대상이 나머지 넷과 다른 것은?

① ② ③ ④ ⑤

20 위 글의 밑줄 친 ⓑFinally와 바꿔 쓸 수 없는 말을 고르시오.

① Lastly ② In the long run
③ Eventually ④ In the end
⑤ At last

[21~22] 다음 글을 읽고 물음에 답하시오.

A: It's important that I manage my time well, practice hard, and have a strong ⓐwill to achieve my dream. How about you?
B: ⓑI think being healthy, working well with others, and being creative is important.

21 위 글의 밑줄 친 ⓐwill과 같은 의미로 쓰인 것을 고르시오.

① How long will you stay in Paris?

② Her decision shows great strength of will.

③ Will you send this letter for me, please?

④ It will be fine tomorrow.

⑤ I ought to draw up my will before I die.

서답형
22 위 글의 밑줄 친 ⓑ에서 어법상 틀린 부분을 찾아 고치시오.

➡ _____

[23~24] 다음 글을 읽고 물음에 답하시오.

Robinson's effort moved his teammates. (①) When people shouted at Robinson, one of his teammates walked up to Robinson and tapped him on the shoulder. (②) "Do not listen to them. (③) You're doing fine," he said. (④) Finally, Robinson earned the respect of other players and fans. (⑤)

Thanks to Robinson, the Dodgers won the National League Championship in 1947. The league recognized Robinson's __(A)__ and presented him with the Rookie of the Year Award in the same year. After that season, other teams asked African American players to join them.

서답형
23 위 글의 빈칸 (A)에 excellent를 알맞은 형태로 쓰시오.

➡ _____

중요
24 위 글의 흐름으로 보아, 주어진 문장이 들어가기에 가장 적절한 곳은?

> His support helped Robinson to play harder.

①   ②   ③   ④   ⑤

[25~27] 다음 글을 읽고 물음에 답하시오.

How I Will Achieve My Dream

I want to be a chef. There are ⓐthree things that I need to do to achieve my dream. I need to practice hard, work well with others, and manage my time well. (A)_____ hard will help me cook well and easily. (B)_____ well with others will make ⓑit easier to work at a restaurant. Plus, I will always tell myself (C)_____ my time well because it will help me make food in time to serve.

서답형
25 위 글의 빈칸 (A)~(C)에 들어갈 말을 각각 알맞은 형태로 쓰시오.

➡ (A) _____
   (B) _____
   (C) _____

서답형
26 위 글의 밑줄 친 ⓐthree things가 가리키는 것을 본문에서 찾아 쓰시오.

➡ _____
   _____

27 위 글의 밑줄 친 ⓑit과 문법적 쓰임이 같은 것을 모두 고르시오.

① It is very hard to give up smoking.

② It is easy to get a bad habit.

③ It is quite difficult to master a foreign language.

④ I found it useless to teach him English.

⑤ I make it a rule to take a walk early in the morning.

[01~03] 다음 글을 읽고 물음에 답하시오.

It was New York City on ⓐApril 15, 1947. Jackie Robinson, an African American, went on the field as second baseman for the Brooklyn Dodgers. People couldn't believe their eyes. He was the first African American player to play on a Major League team. That day, the (A)c_____ l_____ was broken.

01 주어진 영영풀이를 참고하여 빈칸 (A)에 주어진 철자로 시작하는 단어를 쓰시오.

barrier preventing blacks from participating in various activities with whites

➡ _____

02 위 글의 밑줄 친 ⓐ를 영어로 읽는 법을 쓰시오.

➡ _____

03 Why couldn't people believe their eyes when Jackie Robinson came out into the field? Fill in the blanks with suitable words.

➡ Because there was no _____ to play on a Major League team before him.

[04~07] 다음 글을 읽고 물음에 답하시오.

Thanks to Robinson, the Dodgers won the National League Championship in 1947. The league recognized Robinson's excellence and ⓐpresented him with the Rookie of the Year

Award in the same year. After that season, other teams asked African American players ___(A)___ ⓑthem.

04 위 글의 빈칸 (A)에 join을 알맞은 형태로 쓰시오.

➡ _____

05 위 글의 밑줄 친 ⓐ를 다음과 같이 바꿔 쓸 때 빈칸에 들어갈 알맞은 말을 쓰시오.

➡ presented the Rookie of the Year Award _____ him

06 위 글의 밑줄 친 ⓑ가 가리키는 것을 본문에서 찾아 쓰시오.

➡ _____

07 When did Robinson win the Rookie of the Year Award? Answer in English in a full sentence. (5 words)

➡ _____

[08~10] 다음 글을 읽고 물음에 답하시오.

Robinson faced many difficulties. Although Robinson was a talented player and a gentle person, his teammates did not want to play with him. ⓐ모든 호텔에서 그 팀을 거절했다 because Robinson was on the team. When he was at bat, people in the stands rudely shouted at him.

08 위 글에서 'gifted'와 바꿔 쓸 수 있는 단어를 찾아 쓰시오.

➡ _____

9 위 글의 밑줄 친 ⓐ의 우리말에 맞게 주어진 어휘를 이용하여 6단어로 영작하시오.

> Every, turned

➡ _____

_____

10 본문의 내용과 일치하도록 다음 빈칸 (A)와 (B)에 알맞은 단어를 쓰시오.

> In spite of his talent and (A)_____ personality, Robinson experienced many (B)_____. For example, his teammates did not want to play with him.

[11~14] 다음 글을 읽고 물음에 답하시오.

> ⓐRobinson's effort moved his teammates. When people shouted at Robinson, one of his teammates walked up to Robinson and tapped him on the shoulder. "Do not listen to ⓑthem. You're doing fine," he said. ⓒHis support helped Robinson to play harder. Finally, ⓓ Robinson은 다른 선수들과 팬들의 존경을 받았다.

11 위 글의 밑줄 친 ⓐ를 수동태로 고치시오.

➡ _____

_____

12 위 글의 밑줄 친 ⓑthem이 가리키는 것을 본문에서 찾아 쓰시오.

➡ _____

13 다음 빈칸 (A)와 (B)에 알맞은 단어를 넣어 ⓒHis support에 대한 설명을 완성하시오.

> One of Robinson's (A)_____ walked up to Robinson, tapped him on the shoulder, and told him not to listen to the people who (B)_____ _____ him, adding "You're doing fine."

14 위 글의 밑줄 친 ⓓ의 우리말에 맞게 주어진 어휘를 이용하여 9단어로 영작하시오.

> earn, respect, of

➡ _____

[15~17] 다음 글을 읽고 물음에 답하시오.

> Robinson ⓐ마음속으로 생각했다, 'I need to keep calm and focus on baseball. ⓑI will try and become a player who people like. Then, next season, there will be more African American players in the league.' Robinson put all his time and energy into baseball. With practice, he became great at (A)_____ and (B)_____.

15 위 글의 빈칸 (A)와 (B)에 bat와 base run을 각각 알맞은 형태로 쓰시오.

➡ (A) _____ (B) _____

16 위 글의 밑줄 친 ⓐ의 우리말을 세 단어로 쓰시오.

➡ _____

17 위 글의 밑줄 친 ⓑ에서 생략할 수 있는 단어를 생략하고 문장을 다시 쓰시오.

➡ _____

해석

Language in Use

I visited three countries last year. France was the first country which I visited.
the+서수 　　　목적격 관계대명사(= that)

Mary is the girl who I met in Paris. The blue watch is the gift which I bought
목적격 관계대명사(= whom/that)　　　　　　　　　　목적격 관계대명사(= that)

there for my brother.
= in Paris　buy A B(4형식) = buy B for A(3형식): A에게 B를 사주다

구문해설 • gift: 선물

작년에 나는 3개국을 방문했
다. 프랑스가 내가 방문한 첫
번째 국가였다. Mary는 내
가 파리에서 만났던 소녀이
다. 그 파란 시계는 그곳에서
내 동생을 위해 산 선물이다.

Enjoy Writing B

How I Will Achieve My Dream

I want to be a designer. There are three things that I need to do to achieve my
명사적 용법의 to부정사　　　　　　　　목적격 관계대명사　　　부사적 용법의 to부정사

dream. I need to be healthy, be creative, and never give up. Being healthy will
　　　　　　　　　　　　　　　　　　　　　　　　　동명사 주어

help me keep going for my dream. Being creative will help me do something
= to keep　　　　　　　　　　　　　help+목적어+to부정사(원형부정사)

different. Plus, I will always tell myself never to give up because it will make
주어와 목적어가 같으면 재귀대명사를 씀　　tell+목적어+to부정사

me try harder.
make+목적어+원형부정사

구문해설 • achieve: 성취하다 • creative: 창의적인 • give up: ~을 포기하다 • keep going: (힘들거나 고통스
러워도) 계속 살아가다[견디다]

**어떻게 나의 꿈을 성취할 것
인가**

나는 디자이너가 되기를 원한
다. 나의 꿈을 성취하기 위해
내가 할 필요가 있는 세 가
지가 있다. 나는 건강해야 하
고, 창의적이어야 하고, 그리
고 결코 포기하지 말아야 한
다. 건강한 것은 나의 꿈을 계
속 유지하도록 도와줄 것이
다. 창의적인 것은 내가 무언
가 다른 것을 하도록 도와줄
것이다. 더하여, 내 스스로에
게 결코 포기하지 말라고 항
상 말할 것인데, 이는 내가 더
열심히 노력하도록 해 줄 것
이기 때문이다.

Wrap Up 2

B: It's difficult to learn English.
가주어　　　　진주어

G: Rome was not built in a day.
be not p.p.(부정문 수동태)　하루 사이에, 하루 아침에

B: What do you mean by that?
그게 무슨 뜻이니? (= What is that exactly? = What exactly do you mean? = Could you explain about that in detail?)

G: I mean it takes time to achieve something.
take+시간: (얼마의 시간이) 걸리다　to부정사의 부사적 용법(목적): ~하기 위해서 (진주어로 쓰인 명사적 용법으로 볼 수도 있음)

B: I see.
= I understand.

B: 영어를 배우는 것은 어려
워.
G: 로마는 하루아침에 이루
어지지 않았어.
B: 그게 무슨 뜻이니?
G: 무언가를 이루는 데 시간
이 걸린다는 뜻이야.
B: 알겠어.

Words & Expressions

01 다음 빈칸에 들어갈 말이 순서대로 바르게 짝지어진 것은?

> • They gave _____ the game without scoring even one point.
> • I met a lot of nice people, thanks _____ you.

① in – to
② in – for
③ up – to
④ up – for
⑤ up – at

02 다음 중 밑줄 친 부분의 뜻풀이가 바르지 않은 것은?

① Sorry, we can no longer help you. (더 이상 ~ 아닌)
② I never expected your support. (지지)
③ No pain, no gain. (고통)
④ They will present him with an award for good citizenship. (선물)
⑤ She has a gentle heart. (점잖은)

03 다음 밑줄 친 부분과 의미가 가장 가까운 것을 주어진 철자로 시작하여 쓰시오.

> In the end, we all decided to organize a concert for Easter.

➡ F_____

04 다음 빈칸에 알맞은 말을 고르시오.

> One of the ways to _____ the respect is by showing responsibility for the community.

① believe ② present ③ keep
④ earn ⑤ win

Conversation

[05~06] 다음 대화를 읽고 물음에 답하시오.

> B: I have a singing contest tomorrow. I really want to win first place.
> G: I'll keep my fingers crossed for you.
> B: What do you mean by "keep my fingers crossed"?
> G: It means (A)_____.
> B: Thank you.

05 빈칸 (A)에 알맞은 말을 고르시오.

① it's easy to do
② working together is better than working alone
③ you learn something by doing it over and over
④ it takes time to achieve something
⑤ I wish you good luck

06 위 대화를 읽고 대답할 수 없는 질문은?

① Does the girl know the meaning of "keep my fingers crossed"?
② What does the boy want at a singing contest?
③ What kind of contest is the boy going to have?
④ Where is a singing contest held?
⑤ When is there a singing contest?

[07~08] 다음 대화를 읽고 물음에 답하시오.

> A: (A)_____.
> B: What do you mean ⓐ_____ "(B)_____"?
> A: I mean you learn something ⓑ_____ doing it over and over.

07 빈칸 (A)와 (B)에 공통으로 들어갈 말을 고르시오.

① Practice makes perfect
② Rome was not built in a day
③ Will is power
④ Two heads are better than one
⑤ It's a walk in the park

08 빈칸 ⓐ와 ⓑ에 공통으로 들어갈 전치사를 쓰시오.

➡ _____

[09~10] 다음 대화를 읽고 물음에 답하시오.

G: Your poster looks great. (①)
B: Thanks, Kate. (②) Did you finish yours?
G: Not yet. I can't draw well. (③)
B: It takes time. (④) It's important that
   (A)_____. (⑤)
G: You mean I should keep practicing?
B: That's right.

09 위 대화의 ①~⑤ 중 다음 주어진 말이 들어갈 알맞은 곳은?

How can I become good at drawing?

①   ②   ③   ④   ⑤

10 빈칸 (A)에 알맞은 말을 고르시오.

① you take an art class
② you draw as often as you can
③ you see a lot of pictures
④ you go to an art gallery
⑤ you buy expensive pictures

11 다음 상황에 어울리는 말이 <u>아닌</u> 것을 고르시오.

You and your friend are watching a soccer game in a stadium. Your friend shouts loudly, "Way to go!" but you do not know what he means. So, you want to ask him what it means.

① What is "Way to go" exactly?
② Will you "Way to go"?
③ What exactly do you mean by "Way to go"?
④ What do you mean by "Way to go"?
⑤ Could you explain about "Way to go" in detail?

12 다음 빈칸에 들어갈 말이 순서대로 바르게 짝지어진 것은?

B: It's difficult to learn English.
G: Rome was not built in a day.
B: What do you mean by that?
G: I mean it _____ time to _____ something.
B: I see.

① takes   mean
② takes   achieve
③ does   mean
④ does   achieve
⑤ does   expect

Grammar

13 다음 우리말을 주어진 어휘를 이용하여 영작하시오.

(1) 부모님이 내게 사 주신 컴퓨터가 고장 났다.
   (buy, for, break)
   ➡ _____
   _____

(2) 내가 사진을 찍어 준 남자와 그의 개가 1등을 차지했다. (the man, that, take a picture, win the first prize)

➡ _____

_____

(3) 네가 일요일에 만난 그 남자는 내 남동생이다. (meet, brother)

➡ _____

_____

(4) 그의 가족은 그가 수영 대회에 참가하기를 원했다. (take part in, the swimming competition)

➡ _____

_____

(5) 그녀는 나에게 파리에 함께 가자고 권유했다. (invite, go, her)

➡ _____

(6) 나는 그에게 시끄럽게 하지 말라고 말했다. (tell, make a noise)

➡ _____

14 다음 중 두 문장을 한 문장으로 만들었을 때 그 의미가 <u>다른</u> 하나는?

① It turned out to be a tiger shark. + It attacked her that morning.
   → It turned out to be a tiger shark which attacked her that morning.
② Those are the flowers. + Rebecca grows them in her garden.
   → Those are the flowers Rebecca grows in her garden.
③ Alice will send a letter to Alex. + Alice met him at the party.
   → Alice will send a letter to Alex whom she met at the party.
④ I will become a player. + People like the player.
   → I will become a player who people like.
⑤ The bag was sent to Wendy. + I bought the bag yesterday.
   → Wendy sent the bag that I bought yesterday.

15 다음 중 어법상 올바른 것은?

① I didn't expect him talk to you.
② They asked John did something for them.
③ Mom wanted Sam finishing his homework.
④ It will enable Jane to complete her project.
⑤ His doctor ordered Simon to takes some rest.

16 〈보기〉의 밑줄 친 that과 용법이 <u>다른</u> 하나는?

┌─ 보기 ─────────────────┐
France was the first country <u>that</u> I visited last year.
└───────────────────────┘

① The man <u>who</u> I admire the most is King Sejong.
② This is the dog <u>which</u> he often found in his garden.
③ Tom bought a backpack <u>which</u> has two side pockets.
④ You are the only person <u>that</u> I can trust.
⑤ This is the bike <u>that</u> Emily lost yesterday.

17 다음 ⓐ~ⓗ 중 옳은 것을 모두 고르면?

> ⓐ I told you to not make any noise.
> ⓑ My parents want me live with them.
> ⓒ I'll let you to go home early.
> ⓓ His wife asked him to wash the dishes.
> ⓔ His support helped Robinson to play harder.
> ⓕ He is the man which gave me a drink.
> ⓖ I didn't enjoy the movie which I saw it yesterday.
> ⓗ I will become a player that people like.

① ⓐ, ⓒ
② ⓑ, ⓒ, ⓓ
③ ⓑ, ⓓ, ⓗ
④ ⓓ, ⓔ, ⓖ
⑤ ⓓ, ⓔ, ⓗ

18 괄호 안에 주어진 어휘를 이용하여 우리말에 맞게 영작하시오.

(1) 그는 나에게 자기를 병원에 데려다 달라고 부탁했다. (ask, take, the hospital)

➡ _____

(2) 너는 그녀가 나가는 소리를 들었니? (hear, go out)

➡ _____

(3) 나는 로마에서 만난 그 여인을 잊을 수 없다. (forget, met, woman, Rome)

➡ _____

Reading

[19~20] 다음 글을 읽고 물음에 답하시오.

It was New York City on April 15, 1947. Jackie Robinson, an African American, went on the field as second baseman for the Brooklyn Dodgers. People couldn't believe their eyes. He was the first African American player ⓐto play on a Major League team. That day, the color line was broken.

19 위 글의 밑줄 친 ⓐto play와 to부정사의 용법이 다른 것을 모두 고르시오.

① He must be brave to do such a thing.
② At first, he had no friends to practice baseball together.
③ There are many African American players to play on a Major League team.
④ His dream was to be a major leaguer.
⑤ He put all his energy into baseball to become a player who people liked.

20 본문의 내용과 일치하도록 다음 빈칸 (A)와 (B)에 알맞은 단어를 쓰시오.

> On April 15, 1947, when (A)_____ _____ went on the field as second baseman for the Brooklyn Dodgers, the (B)_____ _____ was broken.

[21~23] 다음 글을 읽고 물음에 답하시오.

Robinson faced many difficulties. ⓐ Robinson was a talented player and a gentle person, his teammates did not want to play with him. Every hotel turned the team down because Robinson was on the team. When he was at bat, people in the stands rudely shouted at him.

(①) Robinson thought to himself, 'I need to keep calm and focus on baseball. (②) Then, next season, there will be more African American players in the league.' (③) Robinson put all his time and energy into baseball. (④) With practice, he became great at batting and base running. (⑤)

21 위 글의 빈칸 ⓐ에 들어갈 알맞은 말을 고르시오.

① As
② Although
③ If
④ Because
⑤ Since

22 위 글의 흐름으로 보아, 주어진 문장이 들어가기에 가장 적절한 곳은?

> I will try and become a player who people like.

①   ②   ③   ④   ⑤

23 위 글의 마지막 부분에서 알 수 있는 'Robinson'의 성격으로 가장 알맞은 것을 고르시오.

① curious   ② outgoing

③ sociable   ④ diligent

⑤ creative

[24~26] 다음 글을 읽고 물음에 답하시오.

Robinson's effort moved his teammates. When people shouted at Robinson, one of his teammates walked up to Robinson and tapped him ⓐ the shoulder. "Do not listen to them. You're doing fine," he said. His support helped Robinson to play harder. Finally, Robinson earned the respect of other players and fans.

Thanks to Robinson, the Dodgers won the National League Championship in 1947. The league recognized Robinson's excellence and presented him ⓑ the Rookie of the Year Award in the same year. After that season, ⓒ다른 팀들은 아프리카계 미국인 선수들에게 자신들의 팀에 합류할 것을 요청했다.

24 위 글의 빈칸 ⓐ와 ⓑ에 들어갈 전치사가 바르게 짝지어진 것은?

① on – with   ② by – to

③ in – for   ④ by – with

⑤ on – to

25 위 글의 밑줄 친 ⓒ의 우리말에 맞게 한 단어를 보충하여, 주어진 어휘를 알맞게 배열하시오.

> them / players / teams / asked / American / join / other / African

➡ _____

_____

26 위 글의 주제로 알맞은 것을 고르시오.

① Robinson's effort made him famous.

② Robinson earned people's recognition through his effort.

③ A teammate encouraged Robinson not to be disappointed.

④ The Dodgers won the National League Championship in 1947.

⑤ Robinson won the Rookie of the Year Award in 1947.

[27~28] 다음 글을 읽고 물음에 답하시오.

Robinson's uniform number was 42. Baseball players in Major League teams no longer wear the number 42 to honor him. Every year, however, on April 15, every player ⓐ_____ the number that Robinson ⓑ_____. The day is called "Jackie Robinson Day."

27 위 글의 빈칸 ⓐ와 ⓑ에 wear를 알맞은 형태로 쓰시오.

➡ ⓐ _____ ⓑ _____

28 다음 문장에서 위 글의 내용과 <u>다른</u> 부분을 찾아서 고치시오.

> Baseball players in Major League teams want to wear the number 42 to honor him.

➡ _____

✏️ 출제율 90%

01 다음 짝지어진 두 단어의 관계가 <u>다른</u> 하나를 고르시오.

① different – difference
② important – importance
③ silent – silence
④ allow – allowance
⑤ excellent – excellence

✏️ 출제율 95%

02 다음 중 밑줄 친 부분의 뜻풀이가 바르지 <u>않은</u> 것은?

① Writing a book requires a lot of time and <u>effort</u>. (노력)
② Everyone <u>recognized</u> his skill. (인정했다)
③ How many things do you <u>recycle</u> at your school? (재활용하다)
④ This is one of the <u>major</u> sources of energy. (주요한)
⑤ I know that they <u>face</u> lots of problems. (얼굴)

✏️ 출제율 85%

03 다음 빈칸에 알맞은 단어를 고르시오.

I thought _____, "I'm in trouble."

① to me
② for me
③ to myself
④ for myself
⑤ in me

✏️ 출제율 95%

04 두 문장에 공통으로 들어갈 수 있는 단어를 고르시오.

• She _____ first place in the swimming competition.
• She _____ the Best Actress award.

① won
② made
③ went
④ took
⑤ realized

✏️ 출제율 100%

05 다음 대화의 빈칸에 들어갈 말을 〈보기〉에서 골라 순서대로 바르게 배열한 것은?

G: Oh, this is hard to do.
B: _____
G: _____
B: _____
G: _____
B: I mean it's easy to do.

┌─── 보기 ───┐
(A) Can you teach me how to make cookies?
(B) Sure. It's a walk in the park.
(C) What's the matter?
(D) What do you mean by that?
└────────────┘

① (B) – (A) – (C) – (D)
② (B) – (C) – (A) – (D)
③ (C) – (A) – (B) – (D)
④ (C) – (B) – (A) – (D)
⑤ (C) – (D) – (B) – (A)

[06~07] 다음 글을 읽고 물음에 답하시오.

W: Do you want to ⓐ<u>achieve</u> your dream? Remember! Great people ⓑ<u>always stop</u> learning. The best way ⓒ<u>to learn</u> is by reading. Even ⓓ<u>when</u> you are busy, you have to find time to read. However, 네가 읽을 알맞은 책을 고르는 것도 중요하다. (choose, to, it's, that, books, read, important, you, the, right) Here is ⓔ<u>what</u> to choose the right books.

06 위 글에서 문맥상 또는 어법상 어색한 것을 <u>모두</u> 고르시오.

① ⓐ   ② ⓑ   ③ ⓒ   ④ ⓓ   ⑤ ⓔ

07 다음 밑줄 친 우리말에 맞게 주어진 단어를 바르게 배열하시오.

➡ _____

08 다음 대화의 빈칸에 들어갈 수 <u>없는</u> 것은?

> B: I have a singing contest tomorrow. I really want ⓐ_____ first place.
> G: I'll ⓑ_____ my fingers ⓒ_____ for you.
> B: What do you ⓓ_____ by "ⓑ_____ my fingers ⓒ_____"?
> G: ⓔ_____ I wish you good luck.
> B: Thank you.

① lucky   ② It means
③ to win   ④ mean
⑤ keep

[09~11] 다음 글을 읽고 물음에 답하시오.

> M: To achieve my dream, I went to many auditions, but I often failed. (A)_____, I never gave up. I took acting and dancing classes. (B)_____, I (C)_____ my goal. (D)<u>절대 포기하지 않는 것이 중요합니다.</u>

09 빈칸 (A)와 (B)에 들어갈 말로 알맞은 것끼리 짝지어진 것을 고르시오.

	(A)	(B)
①	However	Though
②	Therefore	Especially
③	However	Finally
④	Therefore	Especially
⑤	In addition	Finally

10 빈칸 (C)에 알맞은 말을 위의 대화에 나온 단어를 이용해서 채우시오.

➡ _____

11 밑줄 친 (D)의 우리말을 영작하시오.

➡ _____

12 다음 대화의 순서를 바르게 배열하시오.

> (A) It's important that you never give up.
> (B) Okay. I will not forget that.
> (C) It's hard to be a good dancer. What should I do?

➡ _____

13 다음 중 어법상 올바른 것은?

① Her parents were worried and asked her stop surfing.
② He also ordered us to tell the truth and never to lie.
③ Mr. Johnson told us shook hands after the game.
④ His parents encouraged him has an interest in art.
⑤ I didn't expect you understanding me at all.

출제율 95%

14 다음 중 어법상 <u>어색한</u> 문장은?

① I love the watch which my uncle bought for me.

② Paul is the boy who I often play soccer with.

③ Is this the book you were talking about it at that time?

④ I went to the office in which Anne was working.

⑤ Do you know the man your mother is talking to?

출제율 90%

15 다음 중 밑줄 친 that과 바꿔 쓸 수 있는 것은?

> The chair <u>that</u> I sat on was not comfortable.

① whom　　② whose　　③ who

④ which　　⑤ what

[16~18] 다음 글을 읽고 물음에 답하시오.

> It was New York City on April 15, 1947. Jackie Robinson, an African American, went on the field as second baseman for the Brooklyn Dodgers. People couldn't believe their eyes. He was the first ⓐ아프리카계 미국인 player to play on a Major League team. ⓑThat day, the color line __(A)__ .

출제율 100%

16 위 글의 빈칸 (A)에 들어갈 알맞은 말을 고르시오.

① was drawn　　② happened

③ was broken　　④ was made

⑤ appeared

출제율 90%

17 위 글의 밑줄 친 ⓐ의 우리말을 두 단어로 쓰시오.

➡ _____

출제율 90%

18 위 글의 밑줄 친 ⓑThat day가 가리키는 것을 본문에서 찾아 쓰시오.

➡ _____

[19~21] 다음 글을 읽고 물음에 답하시오.

> Robinson ⓐ<u>faced</u> many difficulties. Although Robinson was a talented player and a gentle person, his teammates did not want ⓑ<u>to play</u> with him. Every hotel ⓒ<u>turned the team down</u> because Robinson was on the team. When he was at bat, people in the stands rudely shouted at him.

출제율 90%

19 위 글의 밑줄 친 ⓐfaced와 바꿔 쓸 수 있는 말을 고르시오.

① expressed　　② encountered

③ accepted　　④ looked into

⑤ solved

출제율 95%

20 위 글의 밑줄 친 ⓑto play와 to부정사의 용법이 <u>다른</u> 것을 고르시오.

① I think it wrong to tell a lie.

② I decided to go to Madrid.

③ He wanted to buy a new smartphone.

④ This water is not good to drink.

⑤ It is necessary to finish the work now.

출제율 85%

21 위 글의 밑줄 친 ⓒturned the team down을 다음과 같이 바꿔 쓸 때 빈칸에 들어갈 알맞은 말을 쓰시오.

➡ _____ the team

[22~24] 다음 글을 읽고 물음에 답하시오.

> Robinson's effort ⓐ<u>moved</u> his teammates. When people shouted at Robinson, one of his teammates walked up to Robinson and tapped him on the shoulder. "Do not listen to them.

You're doing fine," he said. His support helped Robinson to play harder. Finally, Robinson earned the respect of other players and fans.

Thanks to Robinson, the Dodgers won the National League Championship in 1947. The league recognized Robinson's excellence and presented him with the Rookie of the Year Award in the same year. After that season, other teams asked African American players to join them.

출제율 100%

22 위 글의 제목으로 가장 알맞은 것을 고르시오.

① How to Earn the Respect of Others
② Robinson's Effort Bore Fruit
③ How Did the Dodgers Win the National League Championship?
④ Who Won the Rookie of the Year Award in 1947?
⑤ Many Teams Wanted African American Players.

출제율 90%

23 위 글의 밑줄 친 ⓐmoved와 바꿔 쓸 수 있는 단어를 쓰시오.

➡ _____

출제율 95%

24 위 글의 내용과 일치하지 않는 것은?

① When people shouted at Robinson, one of his teammates encouraged him.
② The teammate's support helped Robinson to play harder.
③ At last, other players and fans came to respect Robinson.
④ Thanks to the Dodgers, Robinson won the National League Championship in 1947.
⑤ After that season, other teams gave African American players a chance to join them.

[25~26] 다음 글을 읽고 물음에 답하시오.

Robinson's uniform number was 42. ⓐ Baseball players in Major League teams no longer wear the number 42 to honor him. Every year, however, on April 15, every player wears the number ⓑthat Robinson wore. The day is called "Jackie Robinson Day."

출제율 90%

25 위 글의 밑줄 친 ⓐ를 바르게 바꿔 쓴 문장을 모두 고르시오.

① Baseball players in Major League teams no more wear the number 42 to honor him.
② Baseball players in Major League teams don't wear the number 42 no longer to honor him.
③ Baseball players in Major League teams don't wear the number 42 any more to honor him.
④ Baseball players in Major League teams don't wear the number 42 no more to honor him.
⑤ Baseball players in Major League teams don't wear the number 42 any longer to honor him.

출제율 90%

26 위 글의 밑줄 친 ⓑthat과 문법적 쓰임이 같은 것을 모두 고르시오.

① Those are the books that you lent me.
② I am so tired that I cannot go on.
③ This is the house that we live in.
④ It is the movie that I want to see.
⑤ The trouble is that we have no money.

01 밑줄 친 우리말을 주어진 단어를 이용하여 영작하시오.

> A: Two heads are better than one.
> B: What do you mean by "Two heads are better than one"?
> A: 함께 일하는 것이 혼자 일하는 것보다 낫다는 뜻이야. (alone, together, working)

➡ _____

_____

[02~03] 다음 대화를 읽고 물음에 답하시오.

> G: Hey, Minho. ⓐDid you find the answer to the math problem?
> B: No. ⓑIt's too easy for me. ⓒI'm not good at math.
> G: ⓓLet me see. (A)네가 그 문제를 풀기 위해선 이 수학 공식을 이용하는 것이 중요해. (it's, that, rule, solve)
> B: Oh, I see. ⓔI'll use it.

02 ⓐ~ⓔ 중 흐름상 어색한 부분을 찾아 고치시오.

➡ _____

03 밑줄 친 우리말 (A)를 주어진 단어를 이용하여 영작하시오.

➡ _____

_____

04 밑줄 친 우리말을 주어진 단어를 이용하여 영작하시오.

> A: Practice makes perfect.
> B: What do you mean by "Practice makes perfect"?
> A: 반복해서 무언가를 하면 배우게 된다는 뜻이야. (over, by, I, something, learn) (11 words)

➡ _____

05 다음 두 문장을 관계대명사를 사용하여 한 문장으로 바꾸시오.

(1) • The Korean dishes tasted yummy.
  • We had them last night.

➡ _____

_____

(2) • I have a dog.
  • I take a walk with it every night.

➡ _____

_____

_____

06 다음 빈칸을 알맞은 말로 채워 비슷한 뜻을 갖는 문장으로 바꾸어 쓰시오.

(1) July told her daughter that she should not go out alone at night.
  ➡ July ordered her daughter _____

_____.

(2) We hope that Amy will win first prize at the singing contest.
  ➡ We expect Amy _____

_____.

Robinson faced @many difficulties. Although Robinson was a talented player and a gentle person, his teammates did not want to play with him. Every hotel turned the team (A)[down / up] because Robinson was on the team. When he was at bat, people in the stands (B)[rude / rudely] shouted at him.

Robinson thought to himself, 'I need to keep (C)[calm / calmly] and focus on baseball. I will try and become a player who people like. ⓑThen, next season, there will be more African American players in the league.' Robinson put all his time and energy into baseball. With practice, he became great at batting and base running.

07 위 글의 밑줄 친 @many difficulties의 예를 본문에서 찾아 우리말로 쓰시오.

➡ (1) _____

(2) _____

(3) _____

_____

⭐중요
08 위 글의 괄호 (A)~(C)에서 문맥이나 어법상 알맞은 낱말을 골라 쓰시오.

➡ (A)_____ (B)_____ (C)_____

09 위 글의 밑줄 친 ⓑThen이 가리키는 내용을 본문에서 찾아 다음 빈칸에 알맞게 쓰시오.

➡ If _____

Robinson's effort moved his teammates. When people shouted at Robinson, one of his teammates walked up to Robinson and tapped him on the shoulder. "Do not listen to them. You're doing fine," he said. @His support helped Robinson playing harder. Finally, Robinson earned the respect of other players and fans.

ⓑThanks to Robinson, the Dodgers won the National League Championship in 1947. The league recognized Robinson's excellence and presented him with the Rookie of the Year Award in the same year. After that season, other teams asked African American players to join them.

10 위 글의 밑줄 친 @에서 어법상 틀린 부분을 찾아 고치시오.

➡ _____

⭐중요
11 위 글을 읽고 1947년에 Robinson과 관련하여 일어난 일 두 가지를 우리말로 쓰시오.

➡ (1) _____

_____

(2) _____

_____

12 위 글의 밑줄 친 ⓑ를 다음과 같이 바꿔 쓸 때 빈칸에 들어갈 알맞은 말을 쓰시오

➡ Robinson's effort enabled the Dodgers _____ _____ the National League Championship in 1947.

01 다음 대화의 밑줄 친 우리말을 영작하시오. (주어진 어휘를 이용할 것)

> A: Are you studying now?
> B: Yes, I am.
> A: But you're listening to music now.
> B: Yes. 음악이 공부를 더 잘할 수 있게 도와준다고 생각해요. (study, help, better)_____
> A: I don't think so. 네가 공부할 때는 집중하는 것이 중요하다. (focus, when, it)
> _____
> B: Okay. 음악 소리를 줄일게요. (I'll, the music) _____

02 〈보기〉를 참고하여 다른 사람에게 기대하는 것을 expect를 이용하여 어법에 맞게 3 문장 이상 쓰시오.

> ┤ 보기 ├
> I expect my friend Sora to become a scientist.

(1) _____
(2) _____
(3) _____

03 다음 내용을 바탕으로 꿈을 이루기 위한 나의 다짐을 표현하는 글을 쓰시오.

> Q1 What is your dream? My dream is to become a chef.
> Q2 How can you achieve your dream?
> ☑ practicing hard, ☑ working well with others, ☑ managing my time well
> Q3 How can things from Q2 help you?
> ☑ practicing hard
> It will help me cook well and easily.
> ☑ working well with others
> It will make it easier to work at a restaurant.
> ☑ managing my time well
> It will help me make food in time to serve.

> **How I Will Achieve My Dream**
>   I want to be a chef. There are three things that I need to do to achieve my dream. I need (A)_____, work well with others, and manage my time well. Practicing hard will help me (B)_____. Working well with others will make it easier (C)_____. Plus, I will always tell myself to manage my time well because it will help me (D)_____.

단원별 모의고사

01 다음 빈칸에 들어갈 말로 적절한 것을 고르시오.

Why do you always shout _____ me?

① at ② by ③ of ④ from ⑤ to

02 빈칸 (A)와 (B)에 알맞은 것끼리 짝지어진 것을 고르시오.

- As a doctor, she (A)_____ the respect of her patients.
- If you have a dream, never (B)_____ up and pursue your passion.

	(A)	(B)
①	earned	give
②	accepted	give
③	earned	grow
④	accepted	grow
⑤	earned	count

03 우리말 해석을 보고 주어진 단어를 이용하여 빈칸을 채우시오.

(1) I'd like to have a strong will to overcome _____ like her. (나는 그녀처럼 어려움을 극복하는 강한 의지를 갖고 싶다.) (difficult)

(2) He got a prize for _____ in B-boy dancing. (그는 B-boy 댄스 부분에서 우수상을 탔다.) (excellent)

04 주어진 영영풀이의 어휘를 빈칸에 써 넣으시오.

help and kindness that you give to someone who is having a difficult time

I need his help and _____.

[05~06] 다음 대화를 읽고 물음에 답하시오.

A: (A)Will is power.
B: What do you mean by "Will is power"?
A: (B)강한 의지로 꿈을 이룰 수 있다는 뜻이야.
(mean, achieve, with)

05 위 대화의 밑줄 친 (A)'Will'과 같은 의미로 사용되지 않은 것을 고르시오.

① The decision was made of her free will.
② He will finish the report immediately.
③ The stronger will you have, the more you will learn.
④ Humans have the freedom of the will.
⑤ Where there is a will, there is a way.

06 밑줄 친 (B)의 우리말을 주어진 단어를 이용하여 영작하시오.

➡ _____

_____

07 주어진 대화 이후에 이어질 대화의 순서를 바르게 배열하시오.

A: Please call me "The Wizard of Goyang."
B: What do you mean by "The Wizard of Goyang"?

(A) What is important to do to become an inventor?
(B) I'm sure you'll make it.
(C) I mean I want to be an inventor.
(D) It's important that I think creatively.

➡ _____

08 ①~⑤ 중 다음 주어진 말이 들어갈 알맞은 곳은?

Do you want to achieve your dream? Remember! (①) Great people never stop learning. (②) The best way to learn is by reading. (③) Even when you are busy, you have to find time to read. (④) Here is how to choose the right books. (⑤)

However, it's important that you choose the right books to read.

①　　②　　③　　④　　⑤

[09~12] 다음 대화를 읽고 물음에 답하시오.

Hana: You look (A)_____, Jiho. What's wrong?

Jiho: I don't think I can achieve my dream.

Amy: (B)_____ that?

Jiho: I want to be an actor, but I always fail auditions. Maybe I have to give up.

Amy: Do you know this actor?

Jiho: Sure. He's a famous movie star.

Amy: (C)He failed much than 100 auditions.

Jiho: Really? Maybe I should keep trying. I will practice more for my next audition.

Hana: That's right! It's important that you never (D)_____.

09 빈칸 (A)에 알맞은 말을 고르시오.

① sleepy　　② happy　　③ sad
④ lonely　　⑤ lucky

10 빈칸 (B)에 알맞은 말을 고르시오.

① When are you going to tell me about
② Why are you telling him
③ What do you mean by
④ How do you know
⑤ Where did you hear about

11 밑줄 친 (C)에서 어법상 또는 문맥상 어색한 것을 찾아 바르게 고쳐서 완벽한 문장으로 쓰시오.

➡ _____

12 빈칸 (D)에 들어갈 말을 위의 대화에서 찾아 쓰시오.

➡ _____

13 다음 두 문장을 관계대명사를 사용하여 한 문장으로 바꾸시오.

(1) • She is the girl.
　　• I love her.
　　➡ _____

(2) • Have you ever fallen in love with a lady?
　　• You haven't even talked to her.
　　➡ _____
　　_____
　　_____

14 주어진 동사를 어법에 맞게 빈칸에 쓰시오.

(1) Mom asked David _____ the dishes. (do)

(2) Her dad allowed her _____ to the concert. (go)

(3) It caused them _____ on their freedom. (insist)

(4) I warned him _____ late. (be)

15 다음 중 어법상 어색한 문장은?

① Please allow me to stay here one more day.

② Becky asked you to clean your room.

③ He encouraged her to reveal her true feelings.

④ Everything that I said was true.

⑤ I love the jacket whom Hana is wearing.

16 다음 중 어법상 적절한 것을 고르시오.

① I will always tell myself manage my time well because it will help me to make food in time to serve.

② This is because people wanted her to become a role model for young people.

③ I like the cake who my mother made for my birthday.

④ Ryan sells oranges who he grew himself.

⑤ I will invite the friends who I met them at the party last weekend.

17 다음 문장에서 어법상 어색한 것을 바르게 고치시오.

(1) The doctor advised her drank more water.

　➡ _____

(2) The teacher encouraged her trying again.

　➡ _____

(3) He was not sure whether he wished her stay or go.

　➡ _____

(4) What is the name of the program who he is watching?

　➡ _____

[18~20] 다음 글을 읽고 물음에 답하시오.

Robinson faced many difficulties. ⓐAlthough Robinson was a talented player and a gentle person, his teammates did not want to play with him. Every hotel turned the team down because Robinson was on the team. When he was at bat, people in the stands rudely shouted ①at him.

Robinson thought to himself, 'I need to keep calm and focus ②on baseball. I will try and become a player who people like. Then, next season, there will be more African American players in the league.' Robinson put all his time and energy ③into baseball. ④With practice, he became great ⑤for ⓑbatting and base running.

18 위 글의 밑줄 친 ⓐ를 다음과 같이 바꿔 쓸 때 빈칸에 들어갈 알맞은 말을 쓰시오.

　➡ Robinson was a talented player and a gentle person, _____ his teammates did not want to play with him.

19 위 글의 밑줄 친 전치사 ①~⑤ 중에서 쓰임이 옳지 않은 것을 찾아 고치시오.

　➡ _____

20 아래 〈보기〉에서 위 글의 밑줄 친 ⓑbatting과 문법적 쓰임이 같은 것의 개수를 고르시오.

보기
① Kids are playing on the sand.
② I'm proud of being Korean.
③ Sally's hobby is talking about entertainers.
④ Being on time is very important in the business world.
⑤ Do you know the woman standing at the gate?

① 1개   ② 2개   ③ 3개   ④ 4개   ⑤ 5개

23 위 글을 읽고 대답할 수 없는 질문은?

① Who told Robinson not to listen to people who shouted at him?
② Could Robinson earn the respect of other players and fans?
③ When did the Dodgers win the National League Championship?
④ What award did Robinson win in 1947?
⑤ How many African American players joined other teams after that season?

[21~23] 다음 글을 읽고 물음에 답하시오.

Robinson's effort moved his teammates. When people shouted at Robinson, one of his teammates walked up to Robinson and tapped him on the shoulder. "Do not listen to them. You're doing fine," he said. His support helped Robinson to play harder. Finally, Robinson earned the respect of other players and fans.

Thanks to Robinson, the Dodgers won the National League Championship in 1947. The league recognized Robinson's excellence and presented him with the Rookie of the Year Award in the same year. After that season, other teams asked African American players to ⓐjoin them.

21 위 글의 밑줄 친 ⓐjoin과 바꿔 쓸 수 있는 어구들을 쓰시오.

➡ _____

22 위 글의 내용과 어울리는 속담을 고르시오.

① Sincerity moves heaven.
② Haste makes waste.
③ Don't cry over spilt milk.
④ Everybody's business is nobody's business.
⑤ Too many cooks spoil the broth.

[24~25] 다음 글을 읽고 물음에 답하시오.

Robinson's uniform number was 42. Baseball players in Major League teams no longer wear the number 42 to honor him. Every year, however, on April 15, every player wears ⓐ the number   (A)   Robinson wore. The day is called "Jackie Robinson Day."

24 위 글의 빈칸 (A)에 들어갈 알맞은 말을 모두 고르시오.

① who   ② what
③ that   ④ whom
⑤ which

25 위 글의 밑줄 친 ⓐthe number가 가리키는 것을 본문에서 찾아 쓰시오.

➡_____

Lesson 8

Science Is Making Big Changes

 의사소통 기능

- 놀람 표현하기
  I'm surprised that you can recommend books.

- 요청하기
  Can you recommend one, please?

 언어 형식

- 현재완료
  Have you ever **thought** about these changes?

- 조동사 may
  Let's see what our lives **may** be like in the near future.

교과서

Words & Expressions

Key Words

- **add** [æd] 동 더하다
- **advance** [ædvǽns] 명 발전
- **AI** 인공지능(= **artificial intelligence**)
- **app** [æp] 명 스마트폰 앱, 어플리케이션(**application**)
- **automatically** [ɔ̀ːtəmǽtikəli] 부 자동적으로
- **bottle** [bátl] 명 병
- **charge** [tʃɑːrdʒ] 동 (지불, 대금 등을) 청구하다
- **condition** [kəndíʃən] 명 상태, 조건
- **counter** [káuntər] 명 계산대
- **cover** [kávər] 동 덮다
- **decorate** [dékərèit] 동 장식하다, 꾸미다
- **deliver** [dilívər] 동 배달하다
- **difference** [dífərns] 명 차이, 차이점
- **drone** [droun] 명 (원격 조종의) 드론
- **drop** [drɑp] 동 떨어뜨리다
- **ever** [évər] 부 어느 때고, 언제든, 한번이라도
- **experience** [ikspíəriəns] 명 경험
- **fancy** [fǽnsi] 형 화려한, 공들인, 고급의
- **fit** [fit] 동 (치수 · 모양 등이) 꼭 맞다
- **gravity** [grǽvəti] 명 중력
- **guess** [ges] 동 추측하다
- **heavily** [hévili] 부 심하게, 아주 많이
- **huge** [hjuːdʒ] 형 거대한
- **later** [léitər] 부 나중에, 후에
- **law** [lɔː] 명 법칙, 법
- **librarian** [laibréəriən] 명 사서
- **list** [list] 명 목록, 리스트
- **lower** [lóuər] 동 낮추다

- **material** [mətíəriəl] 명 재료
- **medicine** [médisn] 명 약
- **method** [méθəd] 명 방법, 방식
- **offer** [ɔ́ːfər] 동 ~을 제공하다
- **patient** [péiʃənt] 명 환자
- **pay** [pei] 동 (돈을) 지불하다
- **price** [prais] 명 가격
- **print** [print] 동 ~을 인쇄하다
- **purchase** [pə́ːrtʃəs] 명 구입(품)
- **real** [ríːəl] 형 진짜의
- **recommend** [rèkəménd] 동 ~을 추천하다
- **rescue** [réskjuː] 동 구조하다
- **return** [ritə́ːrn] 동 돌아가다
- **save** [seiv] 동 구하다
- **since** [sins] 접 ~ 이후로
- **skill** [skil] 명 기술
- **society** [səsáiəti] 명 사회
- **station** [stéiʃən] 명 역, 정류장
- **suit** [suːt] 동 (입맛, 취향 등에) 맞다
- **taste** [teist] 동 맛보다
- **technology** [teknálədʒi] 명 과학 기술, 생산 기술
- **temperature** [témpərətʃər] 명 온도
- **tube** [tjuːb] 명 튜브
- **UFO** 미확인 비행 물체(= **Unidentified Flying Object**)
- **virtual** [və́ːrtʃuəl] 형 가상의
- **with** [wið] 전 ~을 써서, ~을 이용하여
- **work** [wəːrk] 동 작동하다

Key Expressions

- **add up** 합산하다
- **be good at** ~을 잘하다
- **be interested in** ~에 관심이 있다
- **be ready for** ~할 준비가 되다
- **be worried about** ~에 대해 걱정하다
- **by** 동명사 ~함으로써
- **don't have to** 동사원형 ~할 필요가 없다
- **forget to** 동사원형 ~할 것을 잊다
- **get lost** 길을 잃다
- **in space** 공중에
- **in the future** 미래에
- **in trouble** 곤경에 빠져서, 난처하여

- **look at** ~을 보다
- **look for** ~을 찾다
- **may+동사원형** ~일지도 모른다(추측)
- **move around** 돌아다니다
- **put on** 입다, 쓰다, 신다
- **take care of** ~을 돌보다
- **take place** 일어나다, 개최되다
- **talk to** ~ ~에게 말을 걸다
- **turn off** (전기 · 가스 · 수도 등을) 끄다
- **turn on** (전기 · 가스 · 수도 등을) 켜다
- **wait in line** 줄을 서서 기다리다
- **would like to** 동사원형 ~하고 싶다

Word Power

※ 명사에 접미사 –al을 붙여 형용사가 되는 어휘들

☐ **culture**(문화) – **cultural**(문화의, 문화적인)

☐ **music**(음악) – **musical**(음악의, 음악적인)

☐ **tradition**(전통) – **traditional**(전통의, 전통적인)

☐ **industry**(산업) – **industrial**(산업의)

☐ **person**(사람, 개인) – **personal**(개인의, 개인적인)

☐ **nation**(국가) – **national**(국가의)

※ 비슷한 의미를 가진 어휘들

☐ **deliver**(배달하다) – **carry**(나르다, 운반하다)

☐ **heavily**(심하게, 아주 많이) – **excessively**(지나치게, 심히)

☐ **huge**(거대한) – **large**(큰)

☐ **material**(재료) – **matter**(물질, 물체)

☐ **offer**(~을 제공하다) – **provide**(공급하다)

☐ **put on**(입다, 쓰다, 신다) – **wear**(입다)

☐ **guess**(추측하다) – **estimate**(추정하다)

☐ **law**(법칙, 법) – **principle**(원칙, 법칙)

☐ **method**(방법, 방식) – **manner**(방법, 방식)

☐ **take place**(일어나다) – **happen**(발생하다)

※ 반대 의미를 가진 어휘들

☐ **difference**(차이, 차이점) ↔ **similarity**(유사점)

☐ **ever**(어느 때고, 언제든, 한번이라도) ↔ **never**(지금까지[어느 때건] 한 번도 ~ 않다)

☐ **lower**(낮추다) ↔ **heighten**(강화하다, 높이다)

English Dictionary

☐ **advance** 발전
→ progress or an instance of progress in science, technology, human knowledge, etc.
과학, 기술, 인간의 지식의 진보나 그러한 순간

☐ **app** 애플리케이션
→ a piece of computer software that is designed to do a particular job
특별한 작업을 하기 위해 만들어진 컴퓨터 소프트웨어

☐ **automatically** 자동적으로
→ with operating by itself
저절로 작동되는

☐ **charge** (지불, 대금 등을) 청구하다
→ to ask someone to pay an amount of money for something that you are selling to them or doing for them
어떤 것을 팔거나, 어떤 일을 한 것에 대한 돈을 지불하라고 누군가에게 요청하다

☐ **decorate** 장식하다, 꾸미다
→ to add ornaments, etc. to something to make it more attractive 어떤 것을 더 매력적으로 만들기 위해서 장식을 더하다

☐ **deliver** 배달하다
→ to take something to somewhere to give it to someone 누군가에게 주기 위해 어딘가로 어떤 것을 가지고 가다

☐ **drone** (원격 조종의) 드론
→ an unmanned aircraft or ship guided by remote control or onboard computers
원격조종이나 내장 컴퓨터로 조종되는 무인의 항공기나 배

☐ **law** 법칙, 법
→ a statement of fact concerning what always happens in certain circumstances; a scientific principle
특정한 조건에서 항상 발생하는 것에 관련된 사실의 설명; 과학적 원리

☐ **material** 재료
→ a substance that is used for a particular purpose
특별한 목적을 위해 사용되는 물질

☐ **medicine** 약
→ a substance that you take to cure an illness
병을 치료하기 위해 먹는 물질

☐ **method** 방법, 방식
→ a way of doing something, especially a planned way
어떤 것을 하기 위한 방법, 특히 계획된 방법

☐ **patient** 환자
→ someone who is receiving medical treatment
의학적 치료를 받고 있는 사람

☐ **recommend** ~을 추천하다
→ to speak in favor of something
어떤 것을 지지하여 말하다

☐ **rescue** 구조하다
→ to save someone or something from danger or harm
위험이나 손상으로부터 누군가나 어떤 것을 구하다

☐ **station** 역, 정류장
→ a place where a bus or train stops to allow passengers to get on and off
버스나 기차가 승객을 태우거나 내리도록 멈추는 장소

☐ **virtual** 가상의
→ created by computers, or appearing on computers or the Internet
컴퓨터에 의해 만들어진 또는 컴퓨터나 인터넷에 나타나는

서답형

01 다음 〈보기〉와 같은 관계가 되도록 빈칸에 알맞은 말을 쓰시오.

┌─ 보기 ┐

huge – large

(1) wear – _____ (2 단어)

(2) happen – _____ (2 단어)

[02~03] 다음 빈칸에 들어갈 말로 적절한 것은?

02

He always tried to protect people _____ trouble.

① at ② for ③ on ④ in ⑤ to

03

It rained _____ last night, so it is a little cold today.

① nearly ② heavily

③ poorly ④ short

⑤ difficult

04 다음 중 밑줄 친 부분의 뜻풀이가 바르지 <u>않은</u> 것은?

① The <u>advances</u> in medicine are surprising. (발전)

② This is how the product <u>works</u>. (일하다)

③ I'm sorry, but can you tell me what the <u>difference</u> is? (차이점)

④ You can ask the woman at the <u>counter</u>. (계산대)

⑤ The door locks <u>automatically</u> when it is shut. (자동적으로)

[05~06] 다음 빈칸에 공통으로 들어갈 말로 알맞은 것은?

05

• I don't think I'll ever be ready _____ the exam tomorrow!

• I looked _____ my bag for three hours and finally found it.

① for ② at ③ to ④ on ⑤ like

06

• I need someone to _____ care of my daughter after school.

• A lot of cultural festivals _____ place during autumn.

① take ② give ③ get

④ find ⑤ have

07 〈보기〉의 밑줄 친 'may'와 같은 의미로 쓰인 것을 고르시오.

┌─ 보기 ┐

He's absent today. He <u>may</u> be sick.

① If you're finished, <u>may</u> I use the phone?

② <u>May</u> I come in two hours late tomorrow morning?

③ I <u>may</u> be late, so don't wait for me.

④ You <u>may</u> use this room.

⑤ <u>May</u> I use this computer for a while?

01 다음 밑줄 친 부분과 의미가 가장 가까운 것을 쓰시오. (3단어)

We need not change the meeting place.

➡ _____

02 다음 짝지어진 단어의 관계가 같도록 빈칸에 알맞은 말을 주어진 철자를 시작하여 쓰시오.

ever : never – difference : s_____

03 주어진 우리말에 맞게 빈칸을 채우시오. (철자가 주어진 경우 그 철자로 시작할 것)

(1) 그들은 박물관에 들어가는 데 너에게 20달러를 청구한다.

➡ They c_____ you $20 to get in the museum.

(2) 돌은 흔히 건축 재료로 사용된다.

➡ Stone is often used as a building m_____.

(3) 나의 친구가 이 레스토랑을 추천했다.

➡ My friend r_____ this restaurant.

(4) 이 가방이 내 취향에 가장 잘 맞는다.

➡ This bag s_____ my taste best.

(5) 이것을 할 수 있는 다른 방법이 있나요?

➡ Is there any other m_____ to do this?

04 빈칸에 들어갈 수 있는 단어를 〈보기〉에서 골라 쓰시오.

보기
as at by for of in on to

(1) In the summer, we turn _____ the fan to keep cool.

(2) Who takes care _____ the children while you're away?

(3) They can learn responsibility _____ doing their homework.

(4) I waited _____ line to buy a ticket.

05 우리말과 일치하도록 괄호 안에 주어진 단어를 알맞게 배열하시오.

(1) 지구는 태양 주위를 돈다.

(moves, the Sun, the Earth, around)

➡ _____

(2) 꽃집으로 가는 도중 길을 잃어버렸어.

(shop, lost, to, on, the, I, my, got, way, flower)

➡ _____

(3) 사람들은 대기 오염에 대해 걱정하지 않는다.

(are, pollution, people, about, worried, not, air)

➡ _____

(4) 안전 헬멧과 구명조끼를 입는 것을 명심해라.

(safety, life, sure, jackets, be, to, on, and, put, helmets)

➡ _____

Conversation

① 놀람 표현하기

I'm surprised that you can recommend books. 네가 책을 추천해 줄 수 있다니 놀라워.

- 예상하지 못한 일에 대한 놀라움을 나타낼 때 'I'm surprised that ~.'라고 말할 수 있다.
  접속사 that 다음에는 절(주어+동사)이 와야 하며, 명사구가 오는 경우에는 be surprised at을 쓴다.
  surprised 대신에 amazed나 shocked를 사용해도 된다.

- 비슷한 표현으로 'What a surprise!', 'How surprising!'이나 'I can't believe it.' 등이 있다.

놀람 표현하기

- I'm surprised that 주어 동사 ~. (~하는 것이 놀라워.)
- How surprising! (놀랍구나!)
- That's amazing! (놀랍구나!)
- What a surprise! (놀랍구나!)
- That's[It's] surprising! (놀랍구나!)
- I (just) can't believe this. (이걸 믿을 수 없어!)

핵심 Check

1. 다음 우리말과 일치하도록 빈칸에 알맞은 말을 쓰시오.

   A: _____ it has such a creative shape. (나는 그것이 그렇게 창의적인 형태를 가지고 있는 것에 놀랐어.)

   B: So am I. (나도 그래.)

2. 대화의 순서를 바르게 배열하시오.

   (A) Sure. I heard it from her.

   (B) No, I didn't. Is that true?

   (C) Wow! I'm surprised that Kate speaks four languages.

   (D) Did you know that Kate speaks four languages?

   ➡ _____

3. 괄호 안의 단어를 순서대로 배열하여 대화를 완성하시오.

   A: I think I need to study more. (나는 더 공부를 할 필요가 있는 것 같아.)

   B: _____ (so, I'm, that, surprised, think, you)
   (나는 네가 그렇게 생각하는 것이 놀라워.)

2 요청하기

Can you recommend one, please? (하나 추천해 줄 수 있니?)

■ 상대방에게 어떤 행동을 요청할 때는 'Can you 동사 ~?'로 말할 수 있다. 대답을 할 때는 긍정이면 'Sure.', 'Of course.' 등으로, 부정이면 'Sorry, I can't.' 등으로 말할 수 있다.

요청하기

- Can[Could/Will/Would] you 동사 ~? (~해 줄 수 있니?)
- Can[Could] I ask you to 동사 ~? (~을 부탁해도 될까?)
- Do[Would] you mind 동명사 ~? (~해 줄 수 있니?)
- (Please,) 동사 ~. (~해 줘.)

■ 'Do you mind 동명사 ~?'의 질문에 대답할 때 주의해야 할 점은 요청을 수락할 때 부정으로 대답해야 한다는 점이다. 즉, 'No, I don't (mind).', 'No problem.', 'Of course not.' 등으로 대답하는 것이 요청을 수락한 것이고, 요청을 거절할 때는 'Yes, I do.', 'I'm sorry I do.'라고 답한다.

요청에 답하기

수락
- Yes!
- Okay!
- Sure!
- All right!
- Of course.
- No problem.
- (That) Sounds good.

거절
- Of course not.
- Sorry, but ~.
- Thank you, but ~.
- (I'm) Sorry but I can't.
- I'm afraid I can't ~.

핵심 Check

4. 다음 우리말과 일치하도록 빈칸에 알맞은 말을 쓰시오.

   A: Can _____ with my English homework? (내 영어 숙제 좀 도와 줄 수 있니?)

   B: Of course. (물론이지.)

   A: Can you _____? (지금 내게 가르쳐 줄 수 있니?)

   B: _____ I have to go to the piano practice. (미안하지만, 못 할 것 같아. 피아노 연습에 가야 해.)

5. 괄호 안의 단어를 순서대로 배열하여 대화를 완성하시오.

   A: _____? (the, ask, could, door, to, I, you, open)

   (문 여는 것을 부탁해도 될까?)

   B: Sure! (물론이지!)

Listen & Speak 1 A-1

G: ❶Oh, I forgot to turn off the heater before I left home.

B: Really? Then do you ❷need to return home?

G: No. I can ❸turn it off ❹with my smartphone.

B: Wow, ❺I'm surprised that you can turn off the heater with your smartphone.

G: 아, 나는 집에서 나오기 전에 히터 끄는 것을 잊어버렸어.

B: 정말? 그러면 넌 집으로 돌아가야 하니?

G: 아니. 나는 내 스마트폰으로 히터를 끌 수 있어.

B: 우와, 나는 네가 스마트폰으로 히터를 끌 수 있다는 게 놀라워.

❶ forget+to동사원형: ~할 것을 잊다 turn off: (전기·가스·수도 등을) 끄다 / 여기서 before 뒤에 주어(I)+동사(left)가 나온 것으로 보아, before는 접속사로 사용되었다.

❷ need to 동사원형: ~할 필요가 있다 return: 돌아가다 need to 대신 should나 have to를 쓸 수도 있다.

❸ turn off는 이어동사로 '동사+부사(on, off, up, over 등)'로 이루어져 있다. '동사+부사+목적어'의 어순이나 '동사+목적어+부사'의 어순 둘 다 가능하다. 하지만 목적어 자리에 인칭대명사(it, them)가 올 때는 반드시 '동사+목적어+부사'의 어순으로 쓴다.

❹ with: ~을 써서[이용하여]

❺ I'm surprised that 주어 동사 ~: ~하는 것이 놀라워

Check(√) True or False

(1) The girl can turn the heater off with her smartphone.   T ☐ F ☐

(2) The boy is not surprised that the girl can turn off the heater with her smartphone.   T ☐ F ☐

 Listen & Speak 2 A-1

W: ❶May I help you?

B: Hi, I'm ❷looking for a smart watch. ❸Can you show me one?

W: Sure. ❹Look at this one. It can play music for you.

B: ❺Sounds cool.

W: ❻Also, you can search for anything just by talking to it.

B: That's great. I will ❼take it.

W: 도와드릴까요?

B: 안녕하세요, 저는 스마트 워치를 찾고 있어요. 하나 보여 주실래요?

W: 물론이죠. 이것을 보세요. 그것은 당신을 위해 음악을 연주할 수 있어요.

B: 멋지네요.

W: 또한 그것에게 말만 하면 어떤 것이든 검색할 수 있어요.

B: 멋지네요. 그것을 살게요.

❶ 어떤 일을 하기 전에 상대방에게 허락을 요청할 때는 'May I ~?', 'Can I ~?' 등을 사용할 수 있다.

❷ look for: ~을 찾다

❸ Can you 동사 ~?: ~해 줄 수 있니? show는 4형식 동사로 간접목적어(me)와 직접목적어(one)를 취한다.

❹ look at: ~을 보다

❺ sound+형용사: ~하게 들리다 cool: 멋진

❻ search for: ~을 찾다 just: 단지 by 동명사: ~함으로써

❼ take: 선택하다, 사다

Check(√) True or False

(3) The boy wants to buy a smart watch.   T ☐ F ☐

(4) The smart watch can't play music.   T ☐ F ☐

Listen & Speak 1 A-2

W: ❶Welcome to VR World. ❷Would you like to visit Niagara Falls?

B: Sure.

W: Okay, ❸put this on.

B: All right. Wow, it ❹looks so real.

W: It is ❺huge, isn't it?

B: Yes, and ❻I'm surprised that I feel water on my face.

❶ Welcome to: ~에 오신 것을 환영합니다
❷ would like to 동사원형: ~하고 싶다 visit: 방문하다
❸ put on: 입다, 쓰다, 신다
❹ look+형용사: ~하게 보이다 real: 진짜의
❺ huge: 거대한
❻ I'm surprised that 주어 동사 ~: ~하는 것이 놀라워

Listen & Speak 2 A-2

M: Welcome. This is our new smart light. You ❶don't have to use your hands ❷to turn it on and off.

W: Really? Then ❸can you tell me how to do it?

M: Just say, "Light on!" or "Light out!"

W: Light on or light out? That's very simple.

❶ don't have to 동사원형: ~할 필요가 없다
❷ to부정사의 부사적 용법(목적)으로 '~하기 위해서'로 해석한다. off 앞에 turn it이 생략되어 있다. turn on: (전기·가스·수도 등을) 켜다 turn off: (전기·가스·수도 등을) 끄다
❸ Can you 동사 ~?: ~해 줄 수 있니? tell+간접목적어(me)+직접목적어 (how to do it): 나에게 그것을 하는 방법을 말해주다

Conversation A

M: ❶These days, many things can work like humans. Some cars can travel without a human driver. We can ❷make smartphones do simple work only ❸by talking to them. ❹I'm surprised that we're already living in the future.

❶ these days: 요즘, 오늘날 like는 전치사로 '~처럼'의 의미이다.
❷ make(사역동사)+목적어+목적격보어(동사원형): …에게 ~하게 하다
❸ by 동명사: ~함으로써 talk to ~: ~에게 말을 걸다 them은 smartphones 를 받는 대명사이다
❹ I'm surprised that 주어 동사 ~: ~하는 것이 놀라워 in the future: 미래에

Conversation B

Amy: Wow, ❶there are so many books in this library.

Hana: You're right. Where can we find books about ❷gravity?

Terry: Hi, I'm Terry, the AI ❸librarian. Can I help you?

Amy: Hi. ❹We're looking for books about gravity. ❺Can you recommend one, please?

Terry: We have fifty seven books about gravity in this library. I think *The Law of Gravity* will be the best one for you.

Hana: I'm surprised that you can recommend books.

Amy: Right. That's ❻amazing. Where is the book, Terry?

Terry: It's ❼on the third floor. Come with me.

❶ there are 복수명사: ~가 있다
❷ gravity: 중력
❸ librarian: 사서
❹ look for: ~을 찾다
❺ Can you 동사 ~?: ~해 줄 수 있니? recommend: ~을 추천하다 one = a book
❻ amazing: 놀라운
❼ on the 서수 floor: ~층에

Communication Task Step 3

A: ❶Can you tell us about your item, please?

B: Sure. These are future shoes. People will run 100 meters in 5 seconds with these shoes.

C: Wow, ❷I'm surprised that humans will run that fast.

❶ 'Can you tell us about ~?'는 어떤 것에 대한 설명을 요청할 때 사용하는 표현이다. 요청이나 부탁의 표현을 할 때는 조동사 can 대신에 could, will, would를 사용하여 말할 수 있다.
❷ that: 그렇게

● 다음 우리말과 일치하도록 빈칸에 알맞은 말을 쓰시오.

Listen & Speak 1 A

1. G: Oh, I forgot _____ _____ _____ the heater before I left home.

   B: Really? Then do you need _____ _____ home?

   G: No. I can _____ it _____ with my smartphone.

   B: Wow, I'm _____ _____ you can turn _____ the heater with your smartphone.

2. W: Welcome to VR World. Would you like _____ visit Niagara Falls?

   B: Sure.

   W: Okay, _____ this on.

   B: All right. Wow, it looks so real.

   W: It is huge, isn't it?

   B: Yes, and _____ _____ that I feel water on my face.

해석

1. G: 아, 나는 집에서 나오기 전에 히터 끄는 것을 잊어버렸어.
   B: 정말? 그러면 넌 집으로 돌아가야 하니?
   G: 아니. 나는 내 스마트폰으로 히터를 끌 수 있어.
   B: 우와, 나는 네가 스마트폰으로 히터를 끌 수 있다는 게 놀라워.

2. W: VR 세계에 오신 것을 환영해요. 나이아가라 폭포를 방문하고 싶은가요?
   B: 물론이죠.
   W: 좋아요, 이걸 쓰세요.
   B: 알겠어요. 우와, 이것은 정말 진짜처럼 보여요.
   W: 거대하죠, 그렇지 않아요?
   B: 네, 그리고 얼굴에서 물이 느껴진다는 게 놀라워요.

Listen & Speak 1 B

1. A: Is _____ anything in these pictures that _____ you?

   B: Yes. I'm _____ that this drone can _____ a dog.

2. A: Is _____ _____ in these pictures _____ _____ you?

   B: Yes. _____ _____ _____ this car can drive _____ automatically.

1. A: 이 사진들에서 너를 놀라게 한 것이 있니?
   B: 응, 나는 이 드론이 개를 산책시킬 수 있는 게 놀라워.

2. A: 이 사진들에서 너를 놀라게 한 것이 있니?
   B: 응, 나는 이 차가 자동으로 운전할 수 있는 게 놀라워.

Listen & Talk 2 A

1. W: May I _____ you?

   B: Hi, I'm _____ _____ a smart watch. Can you show me one?

   W: Sure. Look at this one. It can play music _____ you.

   B: Sounds cool.

   W: Also, you can _____ _____ anything just _____ talking to it.

   B: That's great. I will take it.

1. W: 도와드릴까요?
   B: 안녕하세요, 저는 스마트 워치를 찾고 있어요. 하나 보여 주실래요?
   W: 물론이죠. 이것을 보세요. 그것은 당신을 위해 음악을 연주할 수 있어요.
   B: 멋지네요.
   W: 또한 그것에게 말만 하면 어떤 것이든 검색할 수 있어요.
   B: 멋지네요. 저 그거 살게요.

2. M: Welcome. This is our new smart light. You _____ _____ to use your hands to turn it on and off.

   W: Really? Then can you _____ me _____ to do it?

   M: Just say, "Light on!" or "Light out!"

   W: Light _____ or light out? That's very simple.

Listen & Talk 2 B

1. A: I want to _____ go. Can you _____ go with me, please?
   B: Sure.

2. A: My room is _____. Can you _____ it, please?
   B: Sure.

3. A: The dog wants to go _____. Can you _____ the dog, please?
   B: Sure.

Conversation A

M: These days, many things can _____ _____ humans. Some cars can _____ without a human driver. We can make smartphones do _____ work only_____ _____ _____ them. _____ _____ _____ we're already _____ in the future.

Conversation B

Amy: Wow, there _____ so many _____ in this library.

Hana: You're right. _____ _____ we find books about _____?

Terry: Hi, I'm Terry, the AI _____. Can I help you?

Amy: Hi. We're _____ _____ books about _____. Can you _____ one, please?

Terry: We have fifty seven books about gravity in this library. I think *The Law of Gravity* will be the best one for you.

Hana: I'm surprised _____ _____ _____ _____ _____.

Amy: Right. That's _____. Where is the book, Terry?

Terry: It's _____ the third floor. Come with me.

해석

2. M: 환영해요. 이것은 우리의 새로운 스마트 전등이에요. 그것을 켜고 끄기 위해 손을 사용할 필요가 없어요.

   W: 정말로요? 그러면 그것을 켜고 끄는 방법을 나에게 말해 줄 수 있나요?

   M: "불 켜!" 또는 "불 꺼"라고 말해요.

   W: 불 켜 또는 불 꺼? 정말 간단하네요.

1. A: 나는 바둑을 두고 싶어. 나와 함께 바둑을 둘 수 있니?
   B: 물론이지.

2. A: 나의 방은 지저분해. 청소해 줄 수 있니?
   B: 물론이지.

3. A: 개가 나가고 싶어 해. 개를 산책 시켜 줄 수 있니?
   B: 물론이지.

M: 오늘날, 많은 것들이 인간처럼 작동한다. 어떤 차들은 인간 운전자 없이 이동할 수 있다. 우리는 스마트폰에 말하는 것만으로 스마트폰이 간단한 일을 하게 할 수 있다. 나는 우리가 이미 미래에 살고 있다는 게 놀랍다.

Amy: 와, 이 도서관에는 책이 아주 많구나.

하나: 네 말이 맞아. 우리가 중력에 관한 책들을 어디에서 찾을 수 있을까?

Terry: 안녕, 나는 AI 사서인 Terry라고 해. 내가 도와줄까?

Amy: 안녕, 우리는 중력에 관한 책들을 찾고 있어. 추천해 줄 수 있니?

Terry: 이 도서관에는 중력에 관한 책이 57권 있단다. 나는 'The Law of Gravity'라는 책이 너희들에게 가장 좋은 책일 거라고 생각해.

하나: 나는 네가 책을 추천해 줄 수 있다니 놀라워.

Amy: 맞아. 놀랍다. Terry야, 그 책은 어디에 있니?

Terry: 그건 3층에 있어. 나를 따라와.

Conversation 시험대비 기본평가

[01~02] 다음 대화의 빈칸에 알맞은 말은?

01

G: Oh, I forgot to turn off the heater before I left home.

B: Really? Then do you need to return home?

G: No. I can turn it off with my smartphone.

B: Wow, I'm _____ that you can turn off the heater with your smartphone.

① interesting   ② boring   ③ exciting

④ surprised   ⑤ satisfied

02

W: May I help you?

B: Hi, I'm looking for a smart watch. _____

W: Sure. Look at this one. It can play music for you.

B: Sounds cool.

W: Also, you can search for anything just by talking to it.

B: That's great. I will take it.

① Can you tell me how to do it?   ② Can you show me one?

③ Can you show me how it works?   ④ Can I recommend one?

⑤ Can I clean it?

03 주어진 문장 다음에 이어질 대화의 순서로 알맞은 것을 고르시오.

Are you ready for your trip to London?

(A) Can you show me one?

(B) Yes, but I'm worried about getting lost. I'm not good at finding places.

(C) Don't worry. There are many good smartphone apps you can use.

(D) Sure. Use this one. It shows you a map of the city and pictures of streets.

① (B) – (A) – (C) – (D)   ② (B) – (C) – (A) – (D)

③ (C) – (A) – (B) – (D)   ④ (C) – (B) – (A) – (D)

⑤ (C) – (D) – (B) – (A)

[01~03] 다음 대화를 읽고 물음에 답하시오.

> W: Welcome to VR World. Would you like to visit Niagara Falls?
> B: Sure.
> W: Okay, (A)_____.
> B: All right. Wow, it looks so real.
> W: It is huge, isn't it?
> B: Yes, and (B)_____

01 빈칸 (A)에 들어갈 말로 알맞은 것을 고르시오.

① work this out
② put this away
③ put this on
④ give this up
⑤ turn it down

02 빈칸 (B)에 들어갈 말로 알맞은 것을 고르시오.

① I'm surprised that you did that.
② I'm surprised to learn that I can visit Niagara Falls.
③ I'm surprised that you can help me.
④ I'm surprised that I won the game.
⑤ I'm surprised that I feel water on my face.

03 위 대화의 내용과 일치하지 <u>않는</u> 것을 고르시오. (2개)

① 남자아이는 VR을 이용해 나이아가라 폭포를 보고 있다.
② VR을 통해 본 나이아가라 폭포는 진짜처럼 보인다.
③ 남자아이는 나이아가라 폭포에 직접 갔다.
④ VR을 통해 본 나이아가라 폭포는 그리 크지 않다.
⑤ VR을 통해 나이아가라 폭포를 볼 때 남자아이는 물을 느꼈다.

04 다음 중 짝지어진 대화가 <u>어색한</u> 것은?

① A: Can you help me to do this?
　 B: I'm sorry. I can't.
② A: Did you know that Nick speaks four languages?
　 B: No, I didn't. I'm surprised that he speaks four languages.
③ A: Can you come to my house this weekend?
　 B: Of course.
④ A: Can you go to the store for me?
　 B: Sure. I'm busy now.
⑤ A: Did you see Tom at the school festival?
　 B: Yeah, I was surprised that he was like a real singer.

05 빈칸 (A)와 (B)에 공통으로 들어갈 말로 알맞은 것을 고르시오.

> A: Is there anything in these pictures (A)_____ surprises you?
> B: Yes. I'm surprised (B)_____ this car can drive itself automatically.

① which
② what
③ that
④ how
⑤ why

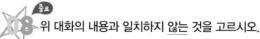

06 대화의 빈칸에 들어갈 말을 〈보기〉에서 골라 순서대로 바르게 배열한 것은?

> W: May I help you?
> B: _____
> W: _____
> B: _____
> W: _____
> B: That's great. I will take it.

┤ 보기 ├
(A) Also, you can search for anything just by talking to it.
(B) Sounds cool.
(C) Hi, I'm looking for a smart watch. Can you show me one?
(D) Sure. Look at this one. It can play music for you.

① (B) – (A) – (C) – (D)
② (B) – (C) – (A) – (D)
③ (C) – (A) – (B) – (D)
④ (C) – (B) – (A) – (D)
⑤ (C) – (D) – (B) – (A)

[07~08] 다음 대화를 읽고 물음에 답하시오.

> M: Welcome. (①) This is our new smart light. (②) You don't have to use your hands to turn it on and off. (③)
> W: Really? (④)
> M: Just say, "Light on!" or "Light out!" (⑤)
> W: Light on or light out? That's very simple.

07 위 대화의 ①~⑤ 중 다음 주어진 말이 들어갈 알맞은 곳은?

> Then can you tell me how to do it?

①   ②   ③   ④   ⑤

08 위 대화의 내용과 일치하지 <u>않는</u> 것을 고르시오.

① The man knows how to turn on and off the new smart light.
② The woman should use her hands to turn on and off the new smart light.
③ The woman at first didn't know the way to turn on and off the new smart light.
④ The woman thinks that the way to turn on and off the new smart light is simple.
⑤ By saying "Light on", the woman can turn the new smart light on.

[09~10] 다음 대화를 읽고 물음에 답하시오.

> G: Oh, I forgot to turn off the heater before I left home. (①)
> B: Really? (②) Then do you need to return home? (③)
> G: No. (④)
> B: Wow, I'm surprised that you can turn off the heater with your smartphone. (⑤)

09 위 대화의 ①~⑤ 중 다음 주어진 말이 들어갈 알맞은 곳은?

> I can turn it off with my smartphone.

①   ②   ③   ④   ⑤

10 위 대화의 내용과 일치하는 것을 고르시오.

① The girl is in her house now.
② The girl is going to return home to turn off the heater.
③ The boy already knows that the heater can be turned off by the smartphone.
④ The boy forgot to turn the heater off.
⑤ The boy is surprised to learn that the girl can turn off the heater with her smartphone.

Conversation 서술형 시험대비

01 다음 대화의 (A)~(C)에서 적절한 것을 고르시오.

> G: Oh, I forgot to turn (A)[on / off] the heater before I left home.
>
> B: Really? Then do you need to return home?
>
> G: (B)[Yes / No]. I can turn it off with my smartphone.
>
> B: Wow, I'm (C)[surprised / frustrated] that you can turn off the heater with your smartphone.

➡ (A) _____ (B) _____ (C) _____

02 다음 우리말에 맞게 주어진 단어를 바르게 배열하시오.

> A: Is there anything in these pictures that surprises you?
>
> B: Yes. 나는 이 드론이 물건을 배달할 수 있다는 게 놀라워. (this, things, I'm, can, that, deliver, surprised, drone)

➡ _____

03 ⓐ~ⓔ 중 흐름상 어색한 것을 고치시오.

> M: Welcome. ⓐThis is our new smart light. ⓑYou have to use your hands to turn it on and off.
>
> W: Really? ⓒThen can you tell me how to do it?
>
> M: ⓓJust say, "Light on!" or "Light out!"
>
> W: ⓔLight on or light out? That's very simple.

➡ _____

[04~05] 다음 대화를 읽고 물음에 답하시오.

> Amy: Wow, there are so many books in this library.
>
> Hana: You're right. Where can we find books about gravity?
>
> Terry: Hi, I'm Terry, the AI librarian. Can I help you?
>
> Amy: Hi. We're looking for books about gravity. (A)Can you recommend one, please?
>
> Terry: We have fifty seven books about gravity in this library. I think *The Law of Gravity* will be the best one for you.
>
> Hana: (B)나는 네가 책을 추천해 줄 수 있다니 놀라워. (you, I'm, recommend, that, books, surprised, can)
>
> Amy: Right. That's amazing. Where is the book, Terry?
>
> Terry: It's on the third floor. Come with me.

04 밑줄 친 (A)와 같은 의미를 가진 문장으로 쓰고자 한다. 주어진 단어를 이용해 문장을 만드시오.

➡ (1) _____ (can, ask)
  (2) _____ (mind)
  (3) _____ (will)

05 (B)의 밑줄 친 우리말에 맞게 괄호 안에 주어진 단어를 배열하여 영작하시오.

➡ _____

Grammar

1 현재완료

Have you ever **thought** about these changes?
여러분은 이러한 변화들에 대해 생각해 본 적이 있는가?

- 현재완료는 'have[has]+과거분사'의 형태로 과거의 어느 한 시점에 일어난 일이 현재까지 영향을 미칠 때 사용한다.

- 의문문은 'Have[Has]+주어+과거분사 ~?'이며, 부정문은 'have[has]+not[never]+과거분사'로 나타낸다.

  • I **haven't forgotten** his warning yet. 나는 그의 경고를 아직 잊지 않았다.

  • How many times **have** you **done** this kind of work? 이런 일을 몇 번이나 해보셨어요?

- 현재완료는 의미에 따라 완료(막[벌써] ~했다), 경험(~한 적이 있다), 계속(~해 왔다), 결과(~해 버렸다) 등으로 구분할 수 있다.

  완료 용법은 과거에 시작한 일이 이미 끝난 것을 나타내며, 보통 'just(막, 방금), already(이미, 벌써), yet(아직, 벌써)' 등과 같은 부사와 쓰이고, 경험 용법은 과거에서부터 지금까지의 경험을 나타내며, 'ever(이제껏), never(한 번도 ~ 아닌), before(전에), once(한 번), twice(두 번), three times(세 번)' 등과 같은 부사(구)와 함께 쓰이며, 계속 용법은 과거에 일어난 일이 현재까지 계속되고 있는 것을 나타내며, 보통 'for(~ 동안)+기간 명사'나 'since(~부터, ~ 이래로)+시간 명사'와 함께 쓰인다. 결과 용법은 과거의 일이 원인이 되어, 그 결과가 현재에 영향을 미칠 때 쓴다.

  • I **have never been** here before. <경험> 저는 전에 이곳에 와 본 적이 없습니다.

  • He **has studied** Japanese for three years. <계속> 그는 3년 동안 일본어를 공부하고 있다.

  • The man **has lost** his cowboy hat. <결과> 그 남자는 그의 카우보이 모자를 잃어버렸다. (그 결과 (그의 카우보이 모자가) 지금 없다.)

- 현재완료는 과거에 시작된 동작과 그 동작의 현재 상태를 동시에 표현하므로 명백한 과거를 나타내는 yesterday, ~ ago, last week 등의 부사(구)나 의문사 when과는 함께 쓰이지 않는다.

  • I **was** ill yesterday. (○) 나는 어제 아팠다.
    I have been ill yesterday. (×)

  *have[has] been to vs. have[has] gone to
  have[has] been to는 '~에 가 본 적이 있다'는 경험을 나타내고, have[has] gone to는 '~에 가고 없다'는 결과를 나타낸다. 그러므로 have[has] gone to는 3인칭만 주어로 쓸 수 있다.

핵심 Check

1. 주어진 동사를 빈칸에 어법에 맞게 쓰시오.
   (1) She _____ already _____ all her money. (spend)
   (2) I _____ not _____ from my brother for about two months. (hear)
   (3) _____ you ever _____ about becoming a teacher? (think)

② 조동사 may

> Let's see what our lives **may** be like in the near future.
> 가까운 미래에 우리의 삶이 어떻게 될지 살펴보자.

■ 'may'는 조동사로 뒤에 'be'동사나 일반동사와 함께 쓰이며, 이때 'be'동사와 일반동사는 동사원형으로 쓴다.

• You **may** do as you like. 너 하고 싶은 대로 해도 괜찮다.

■ 조동사 '**may**'의 의미

(1) '추측'을 나타내어 '~일지도 모른다, 아마 ~일 것이다'의 뜻을 나타낸다.
• A friend today **may** turn against you tomorrow. 오늘의 친구가 내일의 적이 될지도 모른다.

(2) '허가'를 나타내어 '~해도 좋다'의 뜻을 나타낸다.
• If you're finished, **may** I use the phone? 전화 끝나셨으면 제가 좀 써도 될까요?

■ 부정문은 'may' 다음에 'not'을 쓰고 의문문은 may를 문두에 둔다.

• You **may not** believe it, but that's true. 믿지 않을지 모르지만 그것은 사실이다.

• **May** I ask where you bought it? 그걸 어디서 샀는지 물어봐도 될까요?

핵심 Check

2. 다음 괄호 안에서 알맞은 말을 고르시오.

(1) He worked a lot today. He (may / can) be tired now.

(2) May I (use / using) your phone?

(3) The math problem may (be / is) easy for him.

01 다음 대화의 빈칸에 알맞은 말을 쓰시오.

> M: _____ I speak to Mr. Kim, please?
>
> W: Wait a moment, please.

02 다음 두 문장을 한 문장으로 바르게 연결한 것은?

> • Robert went to America.
> • And he is there now.

① Robert went to America.

② Robert went to America already.

③ Robert hasn't been to America yet.

④ Robert hasn't come back to America.

⑤ Robert has gone to America.

03 다음 빈칸에 알맞은 것을 고르시오.

> It is possible that they are in the garden.
> = They _____ in the garden.

① may be   ② must be   ③ have been

④ are   ⑤ were

04 다음 대화의 빈칸에 들어갈 말로 알맞은 것은?

> M: Did you finish doing the dishes?
>
> W: I'm sorry, but I have not finished doing the dishes _____.

① for   ② since   ③ just

④ yet   ⑤ already

05 다음 빈칸에 가장 알맞은 것은?

> He didn't take a rest for long. He _____ tired.

① has   ② has been   ③ may be

④ may is   ⑤ should be

01 다음 중 어법상 바르지 <u>않은</u> 것은?

① Melanie has gone to her home country already.

② Most people have never heard of these laws.

③ She has studied Spanish for three years.

④ When have you parked your car at the garage?

⑤ Ann has caught a big fish at the lake.

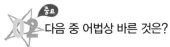 다음 중 어법상 바른 것은?

① He mays know my e-mail address.

② It may not raining in Seoul.

③ Paul may do not be in the classroom.

④ Jane may not is at home now.

⑤ I may not be able to work again.

03 다음 빈칸에 알맞은 말이 바르게 짝지어진 것은?

• _____ you finished your homework already?

• What do you think may _____ in the future?

① Is – happen

② Is – happens

③ Have – happen

④ Have – happens

⑤ Has – happening

 다음 괄호 안에서 알맞은 말을 고르시오.

(1) Jack (have / has) just drawn her portrait.

(2) I (don't have / haven't) improved much in speaking English.

(3) Matthew is not here. He has (been / gone) to a far country over the sea.

(4) A lot of things (have happened / happened) in 2010.

(5) Something good may (happens / happen) to you.

(6) Tony (not may / may not) be interested in music.

05 다음 질문에 대한 응답으로 알맞은 것은?

• Has Charlotte lived a difficult life since childhood?

① Yes, she is.

② Yes, she has.

③ Yes, she does.

④ No, she doesn't.

⑤ No, she may be.

 다음 우리말을 영어로 옮길 때, 빈칸에 알맞은 말을 고르시오.

Smith 씨와 통화할 수 있을까요?
_____ I speak to Mr. Smith?

① May   ② Am   ③ Must

④ Will   ⑤ Do

서답형

07 다음 문장에서 어법상 어색한 부분을 바르게 고치시오.

(1) People have already start to pay with virtual cards.

⟶ _____

(2) What have you done last week, Allen?

⟶ _____

(3) How long do you have been employed here?

⟶ _____

(4) I haven't heard from him for last year.

⟶ _____

(5) I have been out of work since five months.

⟶ _____

중요

08 다음 중 밑줄 친 부분의 의미가 다른 하나는?

① How <u>may</u> I help you?

② You <u>may</u> not use my pen.

③ You <u>may</u> play computer games after you finish your homework.

④ <u>May</u> I call you later tonight?

⑤ Jason worked all day. He <u>may</u> be tired now.

09 다음 빈칸에 알맞은 말이 순서대로 짝지어진 것은?

• She has lived in a 3D printed house _____ 5 years.
• She has lived in a 3D printed house _____ 2025.

① after – for   ② for – after

③ since – for   ④ for – since

⑤ as – for

[10~11] 다음 우리말에 맞게 영작한 것을 고르시오.

10

내 여동생은 중국에 가 본 적이 있다.

① My sister went to China.

② My sister was in China.

③ My sister has been to China.

④ My sister has gone to China.

⑤ My sister has went to China.

11

드론들이 학교에서 학생들과 선생님들을 도와줄지도 모른다.

① Drones must help students and teachers at schools.

② Drones may help students and teachers at schools.

③ Drones can help students and teachers at schools.

④ Drones will help students and teachers at schools.

⑤ Drones should help students and teachers at schools.

중요

12 다음 중 어법상 어색한 문장은?

① Julie has known Mr. Brown since ten years.

② Don't you mean that Peter has met a famous person before?

③ He has never played tennis.

④ Something bad may happen to you when you are alone.

⑤ When it rains heavily, people may cover the whole city with the huge umbrella.

13 다음 〈보기〉의 밑줄 친 부분과 용법이 같은 것은?

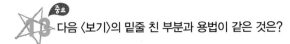

> He has managed the small but nice hotel for about 10 years.

① She has lost her smartphone on the bus.
② Mike has been in the hospital since last month.
③ Julie has been to Amsterdam ten times.
④ Andy has just finished decorating his bedroom.
⑤ Linda has gone back to her home country.

서답형
14 다음 문장에서 어법상 어색한 부분을 바르게 고치시오.

(1) She mays be angry with me.
　　_____ ➡ _____
(2) Look at the sky. It may rains soon.
　　_____ ➡ _____
(3) She does not may use my computer.
　　_____ ➡ _____
(4) She may is upset with you.
　　_____ ➡ _____

15 다음 글의 밑줄 친 ⓐ, ⓑ를 알맞은 형태로 바꿔 쓰시오.

> • Christine and Thomas ⓐhas visited the Technology Fair yesterday. But we have never ⓑgone there.

➡ ⓐ _____　　ⓑ _____

서답형
16 주어진 어휘를 이용하여 다음 두 문장을 비슷한 뜻을 가진 한 문장으로 바꿔 쓰시오.

(1) Bill first knew Alice in 2017. He still knows her. (since)
　　➡ _____
(2) Olivia started to live in Seoul three years ago. And she still lives there. (for)
　　➡ _____

17 다음 밑줄 친 부분과 바꾸어 쓸 수 있는 것을 고르시오.

> May I help you?

① Do　　② Must　　③ Will
④ Can　　⑤ Should

서답형
18 다음 문장을 지시한 대로 바꾸어 쓰시오.

(1) Cleaning drones may help students at school. (부정문으로)
　　➡ _____
(2) I may see your passport. (의문문으로)
　　➡ _____

19 다음 밑줄 친 부분의 쓰임이 나머지 넷과 다른 것은?

① We have known each other since 2004.
② He has taught math for 20 years.
③ Sasha has been in Seoul for long.
④ I have been to Japan before.
⑤ Jack has grown tomatoes since then.

Grammar **181**

01 다음 우리말에 맞게 주어진 어휘를 이용하여 영작하시오.

(1) 그는 15살 이래로 부산에 살고 있다.
(live, Busan, old)

➡ _____

(2) 너는 기린을 본 적이 있니? (see, giraffes)

➡ _____

(3) 나는 아직 숙제를 끝내지 못했다. (finish, my)

➡ _____

(4) 나는 내 일기장을 잃어버렸다. (그래서 지금 일기장이 없다.) (lose)

➡ _____

(5) Paul은 교실에 없을지도 모른다. (be, classroom)

➡ _____

(6) 제가 에어컨을 켜도 될까요? (turn, the air conditioner)

➡ _____

03 그림을 보고, 주어진 어휘를 이용하여 자신의 경험에 대해 쓰시오. (현재완료 시제로 주어와 동사를 갖춘 완전한 문장으로 쓸 것.)

(1) (use, naver, drone)

➡ _____

(2) (to, the tomato festival)

➡ _____

_____

02 주어진 두 문장을 한 문장으로 바꿔 쓰시오.

(1) • It began to rain last Thursday.
• It still rains.

➡ _____

(2) • Did William go to buy sandwiches?
• So, he isn't here now.

➡ _____

04 다음 밑줄 친 단어의 의미를 쓰시오.

(1) Students <u>may</u> learn many different subjects that are not taught now such as 3D printing, drone design, etc.

➡ _____

(2) You <u>may</u> go for a swim this afternoon.

➡ _____

05 다음 두 문장이 비슷한 뜻을 갖도록 빈칸에 알맞은 말을 쓰시오.

(1) It is probable that she will come to the party.

➡ She _____ to the party.

(2) You can't park your car here.

➡ You _____ your car here.

(3) Maybe they will sell delicious food.

➡ They _____ delicious food.

06 다음 문장을 어법에 맞게 고쳐 쓰시오.

(1) When have you started working at the company?

➡ _____

(2) She has worked as a drone designer for 2035.

➡ _____

(3) Have you ever gone to Vietnam before?

➡ _____

(4) So there maybe traffic lights for drones in the sky.

➡ _____

(5) Schools may are open only three days a week, so students don't may go to school every day.

➡ _____
_____

07 다음 문장을 부정문과 의문문으로 각각 바꿔 쓰시오.

> You have ever thought of how schools may change over the next 20 years.

부정문: _____
_____

의문문: _____
_____

08 다음 우리말을 괄호 안에 주어진 어휘를 이용하여 영작하시오.

(1) 나는 6년 동안 영어를 공부해 왔다. (study, years, 7 단어)

➡ _____

(2) 나는 그 편지를 아직 보내지 않았다. (send, the letter, 7 단어)

➡ _____

(3) 너는 바다에서 수영해 본 적이 있니? (ever, the sea, 7 단어)

➡ _____

(4) 어떤 변화들은 이미 일어나기 시작했고 반면 다른 것들은 가까운 미래에 일어날지도 모른다. (some, take place, while, 16 단어)

➡ _____
_____

09 두 문장의 의미가 같도록 빈칸에 알맞은 말을 쓰시오.

(1) I visited the restaurant again. It was my fourth visit.

= I _____ the restaurant _____.

(2) It is likely to rain today.

= We _____ rain today.

Changing Society

Advances in science and technology <u>have caused</u> many changes in
have+과거분사: 현재완료 계속 용법
our lives <u>so far</u>. In the future, science and technology will make more
지금까지
changes. Let's see <u>what our lives may be like</u> in the near future.
간접의문문: 의문사+주어(our lives)와 조동사(may). may: ~일지도 모른다(추측)

Sangho in the Shopping Center

Shopping is <u>much</u> easier. There are no lines and no counters.
비교급 강조('훨씬')
Sangho enters a shop with his smartphone <u>which</u> has a special
주격 관계대명사
shopping app. In the shop, he takes <u>the items he wants</u>. The items are
'the items'와 'he' 사이에 목적격 관계대명사 'which[that]'가 생략.
automatically <u>added</u> to a virtual card on his smartphone. If Sangho puts
수동태(be동사+과거분사)
an item back, <u>it is automatically removed</u> from his list of purchases.
if가 쓰인 문장의 주절에는 일반적으로 조동사가 쓰이지만, 어떤 조건이 주어졌을 때 예외 없이 발생하는 상황을 묘사할 때는 조동사 생략 가능. it = an item
When he finishes <u>shopping</u>, Sangho does not need to wait in line <u>to</u>
finish는 목적어로 동명사를 취한다.
<u>pay</u>. His virtual card adds up all the prices and will charge him <u>later</u>.
부사적 용법(목적)   latter(X)
Isn't that fancy?

society: (공동체를 이루는 일반적인) 사회
advance: 발전, 진보, 발달
technology: 과학 기술, 생산 기술
counter: 계산대, 판매대
app: 스마트폰 앱, 어플리케이션
(=application)
automatically: 자동(적)으로
virtual: (컴퓨터를 이용한) 가상의
list: 목록, 리스트
purchase: 구입; 구입하다
charge: 청구하다
fancy: 멋진
wait in line: 줄을 서서 기다리다
add up: 더하다

 확인문제

● 다음 문장이 본문의 내용과 일치하면 T, 일치하지 <u>않으면</u> F를 쓰시오.

1 Advances in science and technology have caused many changes in our lives until

now. ☐

2 Shopping has become more complex. ☐

3 Sangho enters a shop with his smartphone which has a special shopping app. ☐

4 When he finishes shopping, Sangho needs to wait in line to pay. ☐

Sumin's 3D Printed House and Clothes

Sumin lives in a 3D printed house. Building a 3D printed house is
faster and cheaper than building a house with traditional methods.
Sumin's house looks fantastic because of its unique design. A 3D
printer can produce house shapes that people cannot make with
traditional building methods and materials. Sumin also likes to make
her clothes at home by using a 3D printer. She can choose colors and
materials and can design clothes that fit her body and suit her tastes.
Sumin is now a fashion designer!

Dongmin in the Hospital

Dongmin is visiting his grandfather in the hospital. An AI nurse
enters the room. It moves around the room and checks the patients'
conditions. When the AI nurse finds that Dongmin's grandfather
has a high temperature, it gives him some medicine to lower his
temperature.

Have you ever thought about these changes? Some changes have
already started to take place while others may start in the near future.
Can you imagine other changes? Take some time to think about them.

method: 방법
material: 재료
fit: (모양·크기가 어떤 사람·사물에) 맞다
suit: (~에게) 맞다, 어울리다
AI: 인공 지능(= artificial intelligence)
patient: 환자; 인내심이 있는
medicine: 약
ever: 어느 때고, 언제든, 한번이라도
move around: 돌아다니다
take place: 일어나다(= happen), 개최되다

 확인문제

● 다음 문장이 본문의 내용과 일치하면 T, 일치하지 <u>않으면</u> F를 쓰시오.

1 Sumin's house looks strange because of its unique design. ☐

2 Sumin designs clothes for others by using a 3D printer. ☐

3 An AI nurse moves around the room and checks the patients' conditions. ☐

4 When the AI nurse finds that Dongmin's grandfather has a low temperature, it gives some medicine to raise his temperature. ☐

5 Some changes have already started to happen while others may start in the near future. ☐

● 우리말을 참고하여 빈칸에 알맞은 말을 쓰시오.

1 _____ Society

2 _____ in science and technology _____ _____ many changes in our lives _____ _____.

3 In the future, science and technology will _____ _____ _____.

4 Let's see what our lives _____ _____ _____ in the near future.

5 Sangho in the _____ _____

6 Shopping is _____ _____.

7 There are _____ _____ and _____ _____.

8 Sangho enters a shop with his smartphone which has a _____ _____ _____.

9 In the shop, he _____ _____ _____ he wants.

10 The items _____ _____ _____ _____ _____ a virtual card on his smartphone.

11 If Sangho _____ an item _____, it _____ _____ _____ _____ his list of purchases.

12 When he finishes _____, Sangho does not need to wait _____ _____ to pay.

13 His virtual card _____ _____ all the prices and will _____ him later.

14 Isn't that _____?

1	변화하는 사회
2	과학과 기술의 발전은 지금까지 우리의 삶에 많은 변화를 초래해 왔다.
3	미래에 과학 기술은 더 많은 변화를 만들 것이다.
4	가까운 미래에 우리의 삶이 어떻게 될지 살펴보자.
5	쇼핑 센터에 있는 상호
6	쇼핑이 훨씬 쉽다.
7	줄도 없고 계산대도 없다.
8	상호는 특별한 쇼핑 앱이 있는 스마트폰을 가지고 가게로 들어간다.
9	가게에서 그는 그가 원하는 물건들을 집는다.
10	그 물건들은 자동으로 그의 스마트폰에 있는 가상 카드에 더해진다.
11	만약 상호가 물건을 되돌려 놓으면 그것은 자동으로 그의 구매 목록에서 제거된다.
12	쇼핑을 끝냈을 때 상호는 돈을 지불하기 위해 줄을 설 필요가 없다.
13	그의 가상 카드가 모든 가격을 더해서 나중에 그에게 청구할 것이다.
14	정말 멋지지 않은가?

15 Sumin's _____ _____ House and Clothes

16 Sumin lives in a _____ _____ house.

17 _____ a 3D printed house is _____ _____ _____ than building a house _____ _____ _____ .

18 Sumin's house _____ _____ because of its unique design.

19 A 3D printer can produce _____ _____ that people cannot make with _____ _____ _____ _____ _____ .

20 Sumin also likes to make her clothes at home _____ _____ a 3D printer.

21 She can choose colors and materials and can design clothes _____ _____ her body and _____ her tastes.

22 Sumin is now a _____ _____ !

23 Dongmin _____ _____ _____

24 Dongmin _____ _____ his grandfather in the hospital.

25 _____ _____ nurse enters the room.

26 It moves around the room and _____ the patients' _____ .

27 When the AI nurse finds that Dongmin's grandfather has a _____ _____ , it gives him some medicine _____ _____ his temperature.

28 _____ _____ _____ _____ about these changes?

29 Some changes have already started to _____ _____ while others may start _____ _____ _____ _____ .

30 Can you _____ other changes?

31 _____ _____ _____ to think about them.

---

15 수민이의 3D 프린터로 만든 집과 옷

16 수민이는 3D 프린터로 만든 집에 산다.

17 3D 프린터로 집을 짓는 것은 전통적인 방법으로 집을 짓는 것보다 더 빠르고 저렴하다.

18 수민이의 집은 독특한 디자인 때문에 멋져 보인다.

19 3D 프린터는 사람들이 전통 건축 방법과 재료들로 만들 수 없는 집 모양을 만들어 낼 수 있다.

20 수민이는 또한 집에서 3D 프린터를 사용해 옷을 만드는 것을 좋아한다.

21 그녀는 색깔과 재료를 고를 수 있고 자신의 몸과 취향에 맞는 옷을 디자인할 수 있다.

22 수민이는 이제 패션 디자이너이다!

23 병원에 있는 동민

24 동민이는 병원에 계시는 그의 할아버지를 방문하고 있다.

25 AI 간호사가 병실로 들어온다.

26 그것은 병실을 돌아다니고, 환자들의 상태를 확인한다.

27 AI 간호사가 동민이 할아버지가 열이 높다는 것을 알았을 때 그것은 그의 체온을 낮추기 위해 그에게 약을 준다.

28 여러분은 이러한 변화에 대해 생각해 본 적 있는가?

29 어떤 변화는 이미 일어나기 시작했고 반면 다른 것들은 가까운 미래에 일어날지도 모른다.

30 여러분은 다른 변화들을 상상할 수 있는가?

31 그것들에 대해 잠깐 생각해 보자.

● 우리말을 참고하여 본문을 영작하시오.

1 변화하는 사회
➡ _____

2 과학과 기술의 발전은 지금까지 우리의 삶에 많은 변화를 초래해 왔다.
➡ _____

3 미래에 과학 기술은 더 많은 변화를 만들 것이다.
➡ _____

4 가까운 미래에 우리의 삶이 어떻게 될지 살펴보자.
➡ _____

5 쇼핑 센터에 있는 상호
➡ _____

6 쇼핑이 훨씬 쉽다.
➡ _____

7 줄도 없고 계산대도 없다.
➡ _____

8 상호는 특별한 쇼핑 앱이 있는 스마트폰을 가지고 가게로 들어간다.
➡ _____

9 가게에서 그는 그가 원하는 물건들을 집는다.
➡ _____

10 그 물건들은 자동으로 그의 스마트폰에 있는 가상 카드에 더해진다.
➡ _____

11 만약 상호가 물건을 되돌려 놓으면 그것은 자동으로 그의 구매 목록에서 제거된다.
➡ _____

12 쇼핑을 끝냈을 때 상호는 돈을 지불하기 위해 줄을 설 필요가 없다.
➡ _____

13 그의 가상 카드가 모든 가격을 더해서 나중에 그에게 청구할 것이다.
➡ _____

14 정말 멋지지 않은가?
➡ _____

15 수민이의 3D 프린터로 만든 집과 옷
➡ _____

16 수민이는 3D 프린터로 만든 집에 산다.
➡ _____

17 3D 프린터로 집을 짓는 것은 전통적인 방법으로 집을 짓는 것보다 더 빠르고 저렴하다.
➡ _____

18 수민이의 집은 독특한 디자인 때문에 멋져 보인다.

➡ _____

19 3D 프린터는 사람들이 전통 건축 방법과 재료들로 만들 수 없는 집 모양을 만들어 낼 수 있다.

➡ _____

20 수민이는 또한 집에서 3D 프린터를 사용해 옷을 만드는 것을 좋아한다.

➡ _____

21 그녀는 색깔과 재료를 고를 수 있고 자신의 몸과 취향에 맞는 옷을 디자인할 수 있다.

➡ _____

22 수민이는 이제 패션 디자이너이다!

➡ _____

23 병원에 있는 동민

➡ _____

24 동민이는 병원에 계시는 그의 할아버지를 방문하고 있다.

➡ _____

25 AI 간호사가 병실로 들어온다.

➡ _____

26 그것은 병실을 돌아다니고, 환자들의 상태를 확인한다.

➡ _____

27 AI 간호사가 동민이 할아버지가 열이 높다는 것을 알았을 때 그것은 그의 체온을 낮추기 위해 그에게 약을 준다.

➡ _____

28 여러분은 이러한 변화에 대해 생각해 본 적 있는가?

➡ _____

29 어떤 변화는 이미 일어나기 시작했고 반면 다른 것들은 가까운 미래에 일어날지도 모른다.

➡ _____

30 여러분은 다른 변화들을 상상할 수 있는가?

➡ _____

31 그것들에 대해 잠깐 생각해 보자.

➡ _____

[01~03] 다음 글을 읽고 물음에 답하시오.

Advances in science and technology ⓐhave caused many changes in our lives so far. In the future, science and technology will make more changes. Let's see what our lives may be like in the near future.

01 위 글의 밑줄 친 ⓐhave caused와 현재완료의 용법이 다른 것을 모두 고르시오.

① She has been in Seoul since 2000.
② We have visited Paris before.
③ Have you solved it yet?
④ We have known her for a long time.
⑤ He has lost his pen.

02 위 글의 제목으로 알맞은 것을 고르시오.

① Too Much Information in Changing Society
② Changes Due to Advances in Science and Technology
③ Various Kinds of Advances
④ What Changes Do You Like Most?
⑤ Rapid Advances in Science and Technology

03 위 글의 뒤에 올 내용으로 가장 알맞은 것을 고르시오.

① 과학과 기술의 발전이 지금까지 우리의 삶에 가져온 변화
② 현재의 과학과 기술이 발전하는 모습
③ 전 세계의 과학과 기술의 발전 가능성
④ 가까운 미래의 우리 삶의 모습
⑤ 과학 기술 발전의 장단점

[04~06] 다음 글을 읽고 물음에 답하시오.

Sumin's 3D Printed House and Clothes

Sumin lives in a 3D printed house. ⓐ Building a 3D printed house is faster and cheaper than building a house with traditional methods. ⓑ수민이의 집은 독특한 디자인 때문에 멋져 보인다. A 3D printer can produce house shapes   (A)   people cannot make with traditional building methods and materials. Sumin also likes to make her clothes at home by using a 3D printer. She can choose colors and materials and can design clothes   (B)   fit her body and suit her tastes. Sumin is now a fashion designer!

04 위 글의 빈칸 (A)와 (B)에 공통으로 들어갈 알맞은 말을 모두 고르시오.

① that   ② who
③ what   ④ which
⑤ whom

05 위 글의 밑줄 친 ⓐBuilding과 문법적 쓰임이 다른 것을 모두 고르시오.

① The sleeping girl is so pretty.
② I heard him singing on the stage.
③ He enjoyed studying with his friends.
④ Look at the boy sitting under the tree.
⑤ Thank you for showing me the way to the subway station.

서답형
06 위 글의 밑줄 친 ⓑ의 우리말에 맞게 주어진 어휘를 이용하여 9단어로 영작하시오.

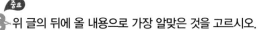
fantastic, because, unique

➡ _____

[07~09] 다음 글을 읽고 물음에 답하시오.

Dongmin in the Hospital

Dongmin is visiting his grandfather in the hospital. An AI nurse enters the room. It moves around the room and checks the patients' conditions. When the AI nurse finds that Dongmin's grandfather has a high temperature, ⓐit gives him some medicine ⓑ to lower his temperature.

Have you ever thought about these changes? __(A)__ changes have already started to take place while __(B)__ may start in the near future. Can you imagine other changes? Take some time to think about them.

07 위 글의 빈칸 (A)와 (B)에 들어갈 말로 바르게 짝지어진 것은?

① Some – other
② Another – other
③ Some – others
④ Another – others
⑤ One – the other

서답형

08 위 글의 밑줄 친 ⓐit이 가리키는 것을 본문에서 찾아 쓰시오.

➡ _____

서답형

09 위 글의 밑줄 친 ⓑ를 다음과 같이 바꿔 쓸 때 빈칸에 들어갈 알맞은 말을 쓰시오.

➡ _____ it _____ his
temperature

[10~12] 다음 글을 읽고 물음에 답하시오.

Sangho in the Shopping Center

Shopping is ⓐmuch easier. There are no lines and no counters. Sangho enters a shop with his smartphone which has a special shopping app. In the shop, he takes the items he wants. The items are automatically added __(A)__ a virtual card on his smartphone. If Sangho puts an item back, it is automatically removed __(B)__ his list of purchases. When he finishes shopping, Sangho does not need to wait in line to pay. His virtual card adds up all the prices and will charge him later. Isn't that fancy?

10 위 글의 빈칸 (A)와 (B)에 들어갈 전치사가 바르게 짝지어진 것은?

① to – from
② at – for
③ at – from
④ on – by
⑤ to – for

11 위 글의 밑줄 친 ⓐmuch와 바꿔 쓸 수 없는 말을 고르시오.

① even
② far
③ still
④ very
⑤ a lot

12 미래에 쇼핑하는 방법으로 위 글의 내용과 일치하지 <u>않는</u> 것은?

① 특별한 쇼핑 앱이 있는 스마트폰을 가지고 가게로 들어간다.
② 원하는 물건들을 집으면, 그 물건들은 자동으로 스마트폰에 있는 가상 카드에 더해진다.
③ 물건을 되돌려 놓으면, 나중에 그 금액을 반환받으면 된다.
④ 돈을 지불하기 위해 줄을 설 필요가 없다.
⑤ 가상 카드가 모든 가격을 더해서 나중에 청구할 것이다.

[13~15] 다음 글을 읽고 물음에 답하시오.

Sumin's 3D Printed House and Clothes

Sumin lives in a 3D printed house. Building a 3D printed house is faster and cheaper than building a house with traditional methods. Sumin's house looks fantastic because of its unique design. A 3D printer can produce house shapes ⓐthat people cannot make with traditional building methods and materials. Sumin also likes to make her clothes at home by using a 3D printer. She can choose colors and materials and can design clothes ⓑthat fit her body and suit her tastes. Sumin is now a fashion designer!

서답형
13 다음 보기에서 위 글의 밑줄 친 ⓐthat, ⓑthat과 문법적 쓰임이 같은 것을 각각 고르시오.

① This is the pen that you gave me yesterday.
② The dog that is running there is mine.
③ I want to read the book that he was reading.
④ He is the man that wants to see you.
⑤ Where's the letter that came yesterday.

➡ ⓐthat과 같은 것: _____
ⓑthat과 같은 것: _____

서답형
14 Which is faster and cheaper, building a 3D printed house or building a house with traditional methods? Answer in English in a full sentence. (9 words)

➡ _____

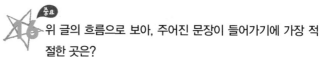
중요
위 글을 읽고 대답할 수 없는 질문은?

① What kind of house does Sumin live in?
② How long does it take to build a 3D printed house?
③ Why does Sumin's house look fantastic?
④ How does Sumin make her clothes at home?
⑤ Who chooses colors and materials of Sumin's clothes?

[16~19] 다음 글을 읽고 물음에 답하시오.

Sangho in the Shopping Center

Shopping is much easier. There are no lines and no counters. (①) Sangho enters a shop with his smartphone which has a special shopping (A)[app / list]. (②) In the shop, he takes the items he wants. (③) If Sangho puts an item back, it is automatically removed from his list of purchases. (④) When he finishes shopping, Sangho (B)[needs / does not need] to wait in line to pay. (⑤) His virtual card adds up all the prices and will ⓐcharge him (C)[later / latter]. Isn't that fancy?

중요
16 위 글의 흐름으로 보아, 주어진 문장이 들어가기에 가장 적절한 곳은?

The items are automatically added to a virtual card on his smartphone.

①   ②   ③   ④   ⑤

서답형
17 위 글의 괄호 (A)~(C)에서 문맥상 알맞은 낱말을 골라 쓰시오.

➡ (A)_____ (B)_____ (C)_____

18 위 글의 밑줄 친 ⓐcharge와 같은 의미로 쓰인 것을 고르시오.

① We will charge at the enemy.
② We won't charge you for delivery.
③ He took charge of the farm after his father's death.
④ You can use it free of charge.
⑤ I need to charge a storage battery.

위 글의 주제로 알맞은 것을 고르시오.

① The use of the smartphone will increase.
② Many fancy shopping apps are now available.
③ Using a virtual card will increase.
④ It's difficult to live without a smartphone.
⑤ Shopping will be a lot easier in the future.

[20~21] 다음 글을 읽고 물음에 답하시오.

Schools in 20 Years

ⓐHave you ever thought of how schools may change over the next 20 years? Students may learn drone design. Cleaning drones may help students at school. ⓑ모든 학교에 AI 선생님들 교무실이 있을지도 모릅니다. Students may go to school only two or three times a week.

20 아래 〈보기〉에서 위 글의 밑줄 친 ⓐ와 현재완료의 용법이 같은 것의 개수를 고르시오.

┌─── 보기 ───┐
① He has just broken the window.
② She has never eaten spaghetti.
③ He has studied English for three hours.
④ I have lost my key.
⑤ How many times have you seen it?
└──────────┘

① 1개 ② 2개 ③ 3개 ④ 4개 ⑤ 5개

서답형
21 위 글의 밑줄 친 ⓑ의 우리말에 맞게 주어진 어휘를 이용하여 10단어로 영작하시오.

┌──────────────────┐
│ there, AI teachers' room │
└──────────────────┘

➡ _____

[22~24] 다음 글을 읽고 물음에 답하시오.

Dongmin in the Hospital

Dongmin is visiting his grandfather in the hospital. An AI nurse enters the room. It moves around the room and checks the patients' conditions. When the AI nurse finds that Dongmin's grandfather has a high temperature, ⓐit gives him some medicine to lower his temperature.

Have you ever thought about these changes? Some changes have already started to take place ⓑwhile others may start in the near future. Can you imagine other changes? Take some time to think about them.

서답형
22 위 글의 밑줄 친 ⓐ를 3형식 문장으로 고치시오.

➡ _____

23 위 글의 밑줄 친 ⓑwhile과 같은 의미로 쓰인 것을 고르시오.

① Strike while the iron is hot.
② Did anyone call while I was away?
③ While you are eating, you shouldn't speak.
④ Her parents died while she was still at school.
⑤ I've read fifty pages, while he's read only twenty.

서답형
24 본문의 내용과 일치하도록 다음 빈칸 (A)와 (B)에 알맞은 단어를 쓰시오.

┌──────────────────────┐
│ The AI nurse gives Dongmin's grandfather some medicine to (A)_____ his temperature when it finds that he has a (B)_____ temperature. │
└──────────────────────┘

[01~03] 다음 글을 읽고 물음에 답하시오.

Advances in science and technology ⓐ_____ many changes in our lives so far. In the future, science and technology will make more changes. ⓑLet's see what our lives may be like in the near future.

01 위 글의 빈칸 ⓐ에 cause를 알맞은 형태로 쓰시오.

➡ _____

02 본문의 내용과 일치하도록 다음 빈칸 (A)와 (B)에 알맞은 단어를 쓰시오.

> Because of (A)_____ in science and technology, there have been many (B)_____ in our lives so far.

03 위 글의 밑줄 친 ⓑ를 다음과 같이 바꿔 쓸 때 빈칸에 들어갈 알맞은 말을 쓰시오.

(1) How about _____ what our lives may be like in the near future?

(2) _____ _____ _____ see what our lives may be like in the near future?

[04~06] 다음 글을 읽고 물음에 답하시오.

Sangho in the Shopping Center

Shopping is much easier. There are no lines and no counters. Sangho enters a shop with his smartphone which has a special shopping app. ⓐIn the shop, he takes the items he wants. The items are automatically added to a virtual card on his smartphone. If Sangho puts an item back, it is automatically removed from his list of purchases. When he finishes shopping, ⓑ돈을 지불하기 위해 줄을 설 필요가 없다. His virtual card adds up all the prices and will charge him later. Isn't that fancy?

04 위 글을 읽고 상호가 쇼핑 센터에서 장을 보는 방법을 우리말로 쓰시오.

➡ (1) _____
(2) _____
(3) _____
_____
_____
(4) _____
_____

05 위 글의 밑줄 친 문장 ⓐ에 생략된 단어를 넣어 문장을 다시 쓰시오.

➡ _____

06 위 글의 밑줄 친 ⓑ의 우리말에 맞게 주어진 어휘를 이용하여 10단어로 영작하시오.

> need, line, to

➡ _____

[07~09] 다음 글을 읽고 물음에 답하시오.

Sumin's 3D Printed House and Clothes

Sumin lives in a 3D printed house. Building a 3D printed house is faster and cheaper than building a house with traditional methods. Sumin's house looks fantastic because of its unique design. A 3D printer can produce house shapes that people cannot make with traditional building methods and materials. Sumin also likes to make her clothes at home by using a 3D printer. ⓐShe can choose colors and materials and can design clothes that fits her body and suits her tastes. Sumin is now a fashion designer!

07 본문의 내용과 일치하도록 다음 빈칸에 알맞은 단어를 쓰시오.

> The _____ _____ of Sumin's house makes it look fantastic.

08 위 글의 밑줄 친 ⓐ에서 어법상 틀린 부분을 찾아 고치시오. (두 군데)

> ➡ _____, _____

09 위 글을 읽고 수민이가 집에서 자신의 옷을 만드는 방법을 우리말로 쓰시오.

> ➡ (1) _____
>   (2) _____
>   (3) _____

[10~12] 다음 글을 읽고 물음에 답하시오.

Sangho in the Shopping Center

Shopping is much easier. There are no lines and no counters. Sangho enters a shop with his smartphone which has a special shopping ⓐapp. In the shop, he takes the items he wants. The items are automatically added to a virtual card on his smartphone. If Sangho puts an item back, ⓑit is automatically removed from his list of purchases. ⓒWhen he finishes to shop, Sangho does not need to wait in line to pay. His virtual card adds up all the prices and will charge him later. Isn't that fancy?

10 위 글의 밑줄 친 ⓐapp을 줄이지 않은 본래 형태로 쓰시오.

> ➡ _____

11 다음 빈칸에 알맞은 단어를 넣어 위 글의 밑줄 친 ⓑit이 가리키는 것을 완성하시오.

> the _____ that Sangho puts back

12 위 글의 밑줄 친 ⓒ에서 어법상 틀린 부분을 찾아 고치시오.

> ➡ _____

[13~15] 다음 글을 읽고 물음에 답하시오.

Schools in 20 Years

Have you ever thought of ⓐ다음 20년에 걸쳐 학교의 모습이 어떻게 변할지? Students (A) learn 3D printing. AI teachers (B) help students at school. There (C) be a drone station in every school. ⓑStudents may not carry paper textbooks anymore.

13 위 글의 빈칸 (A)~(C)에 공통으로 들어갈 알맞은 조동사를 쓰시오.

> ➡ _____

14 위 글의 밑줄 친 ⓐ의 우리말에 맞게 한 단어를 보충하여, 주어진 어휘를 알맞게 배열하시오.

> may / 20 years / schools / over / the / how / change

> ➡ _____

15 위 글의 밑줄 친 ⓑ를 다음과 같이 바꿔 쓸 때 빈칸에 들어갈 알맞은 말을 쓰시오.

> ➡ Students may _____ _____ carry paper textbooks.

Enjoy Writing B

Schools in 20 Years

Have you ever thought of <u>how schools may change over the next 20 years?</u>
간접의문문: 의문사+주어+동사

Students <u>may</u> learn drone design. Cleaning drones may help students at
추측을 나타내는 조동사

school. <u>There may be</u> an AI teachers' room in every school. Students may go
〜이 있을지도 모른다

to school only <u>two or three times</u> <u>a week</u>.
배수: 〜번   일주일에(=per week)

구문해설 • over: [기간] … 동안, …에 걸쳐 • teachers' room: 교무실 • two or three times: 두세 번

20년 후 학교의 모습

다음 20년에 걸쳐 학교의 모습이 어떻게 변할지 생각해 본 적이 있나요? 학생들은 드론 디자인을 배울지도 모릅니다. 청소 드론이 학교에서 학생들을 도울지도 모릅니다. 모든 학교에 AI 선생님들 교무실이 있을지도 모릅니다. 학생들은 일주일에 오직 두세 번만 학교에 갈지도 모릅니다.

Project

Have you ever <u>imagined</u> life in the future? People <u>may</u> use personal drones in
현재완료(경험)   추측

their daily <u>lives</u>. So there <u>may be</u> traffic lights for drones in the sky. <u>A lot of</u> AI
life의 복수형   추측   = Many

helpers <u>may</u> <u>be created</u> soon and they <u>may</u> help humans in <u>lots of</u> ways.
추측   수동태   추측   = many

구문해설 • personal: 개인의 • daily life: 일상 생활

미래의 삶을 상상해 본 적이 있나요? 사람들은 매일의 삶에서 개인 드론을 사용할지도 모릅니다. 그래서 하늘에는 드론들을 위한 교통 신호등이 있을지도 모릅니다. 많은 AI 도우미들이 곧 만들어져서 많은 방식으로 인간을 도울지 모릅니다.

Wrap Up 1

G: <u>Are you ready for</u> your trip to London?
be ready for: 〜의 준비가 되다

B: Yes, but I'm worried about getting lost. I'm not good at finding places.
be worried about: 〜에 대해 걱정하다 get lost: 길을 잃다 be good at: 〜을 잘하다

G: Don't worry. There are many good smartphone apps you can use.
There are+복수명사: 〜가 있다   apps와 you can use 사이에 목적격
관계대명사(which, that)가 생략되어 있다.

B: <u>Can you show me one?</u>
Can you 동사 〜?: 〜해 줄 수 있니?[요청하기] one = a smartphone app

G: Sure. Use this one. It shows you a map of the city and pictures of streets.
shows(4형식 동사)+간접목적어(you, 〜에게)+직접목적어(a map of the city and picture of streets, 〜을.를)

B: Oh, thanks.

G: 너의 런던 여행은 준비됐니?
B: 응, 하지만 나는 길을 잃는 것에 대해 걱정하고 있어. 나는 장소 찾는 것을 잘 못해.
G: 걱정 마. 네가 사용할 수 있는 좋은 스마트폰 앱이 많이 있어.
B: 나에게 하나 보여줄 수 있니?
G: 물론이지. 이것을 사용해 봐. 그것은 도시의 지도와 길의 사진을 보여줘.
B: 오, 고마워.

영역별 핵심문제

Words & Expressions

01 다음 짝지어진 단어의 관계가 나머지와 <u>다른</u> 하나는?

① difference – similarity
② ever – never
③ law – principle
④ lower – heighten
⑤ true – false

02 다음 중 〈보기〉에 있는 단어를 사용하여 자연스러운 문장을 만들 수 <u>없는</u> 것은? (형태 변화 가능하며 필요하다면 대문자를 쓸 것)

┌─── 보기 ───┐
　　add　get　move　wait
└────────────┘

① You don't _____ to bring your lunch.
② They are _____ in line to order food.
③ _____ up the following numbers.
④ If you _____ lost, call my mobile phone at 010-744-2996.
⑤ We _____ around classrooms for every subject.

[03~04] 다음 빈칸에 알맞은 말을 고르시오.

03

> Seawater _____ about 70 percent of the Earth's surface.

① spreads　　② covers　　③ grows
④ charges　　⑤ fits

04

> He enjoyed the work which _____ his personality perfectly.

① saved　　② worked　　③ paid
④ lowered　　⑤ suited

Conversation

05 다음 대화에서 흐름상 어색한 것을 고르시오.

> G: ⓐAre you ready for your trip to London?
> B: Yes, but I'm worried about getting lost. ⓑI'm good at finding places.
> G: ⓒDon't worry. There are many good smartphone apps you can use.
> B: ⓓCan you show me one?
> G: Sure. Use this one. ⓔIt shows you a map of the city and pictures of streets.
> B: Oh, thanks.

① ⓐ　　② ⓑ　　③ ⓒ　　④ ⓓ　　⑤ ⓔ

[06~07] 대화의 순서를 바르게 배열하시오.

06

> (A) Sure. These are future shoes. People will run 100 meters in 5 seconds with these shoes.
> (B) Wow, I'm surprised that humans will run that fast.
> (C) Can you tell us about your item, please?

➡ _____

07

(A) Oh, I forgot to turn off the heater before I left home.

(B) No. I can turn it off with my smartphone.

(C) Wow, I'm surprised that you can turn off the heater with your smartphone.

(D) Really? Then do you need to return home?

➡ _____

08 다음 대화에서 어법상 알맞은 것을 고르시오.

W: Welcome to VR World. Would you like ⓐvisiting Niagara Falls?

B: Sure.

W: Okay, ⓑput on this.

B: All right. Wow, it looks so ⓒreally.

W: It is huge, ⓓdoesn't it?

B: Yes, and ⓔI'm surprised that I feel water on my face.

① ⓐ ② ⓑ ③ ⓒ ④ ⓓ ⑤ ⓔ

[09~12] 다음 대화를 읽고 물음에 답하시오.

G: Uncle Jack! Your new drone looks cool.

M: Thanks. I designed it to (A)_____ people's lives.

G: (B)_____ people's lives?

M: Yes. It watches the ocean. 만약 곤경에 빠진 사람이 있다면 그것은 날아가서 튜브를 떨어뜨린단다. (drops, is, it, if, and, a person, a tube, over, in, there, flies, trouble)

G: I'm surprised that drones can rescue people. (C)Can you show me how it works?

M: Sure. Watch this.

09 빈칸 (A)와 (B)에 공통으로 들어갈 말로 적절한 것을 고르시오. (대·소문자 무시)

① spend ② charge ③ take
④ save ⑤ deliver

10 다음 영영풀이에 해당하는 단어를 대화에서 찾아 쓰시오.

to save someone or something from danger or harm

➡ _____

11 밑줄 친 우리말과 같은 뜻이 되도록 괄호 안의 어구를 바르게 배열하시오.

➡ _____
_____

12 밑줄 친 (C)와 같은 의미가 되도록 주어진 단어를 이용해 문장을 완성하시오.

➡ _____

(ask, can)

[13~14] 다음 대화를 읽고 물음에 답하시오.

G: Are you ready (A)____ your trip to London?

B: Yes, but I'm worried (B)____ getting lost. I'm not good (C)____ finding places.

G: Don't worry. There are many good smartphone apps you can use.

B: Can you show me one?

G: Sure. Use this one. It shows you a map of the city and pictures of streets.

B: Oh, thanks.

13 빈칸 (A)~(C)에 알맞은 말을 〈보기〉에서 골라 쓰시오.

> ┌ 보기 ┐
> about at for from in along

➡ (A)_____ (B)_____ (C)_____

14 위 대화를 읽고 답할 수 <u>없는</u> 질문을 고르시오.

① What is the boy worried about?

② Where is the boy going to travel?

③ What isn't the boy good at?

④ What does the app that the girl recommends to the boy show?

⑤ How many apps can the boy use?

Grammar

15 다음 빈칸에 들어갈 표현이 순서대로 바르게 짝지어진 것을 고르시오.

> He _____ the bridge since he _____ 42 years old.

① has built   –   was

② has built   –   has been

③ is building   –   was being

④ built   –   was

⑤ built   –   has been

16 다음 ⓐ~ⓗ 중 옳은 것을 <u>모두</u> 고르면?

> ⓐ He mays be late for school.
> ⓑ There may are other people that I don't know.
> ⓒ I've never gone to Paris before.
> ⓓ They may invite me to the party.
> ⓔ I have eaten traditional Korean food before.
> ⓕ Jim has worked at the company for 2015.
> ⓖ She may not use my computer.
> ⓗ He has met his old roommate for dinner last week.

① ⓐ, ⓒ   ② ⓑ, ⓒ, ⓓ

③ ⓑ, ⓓ, ⓗ   ④ ⓓ, ⓔ, ⓗ

⑤ ⓓ, ⓔ, ⓖ

17 밑줄 친 부분의 쓰임이 나머지 넷과 <u>다른</u> 것은?

① They <u>may</u> know my name.

② The news <u>may</u> be true.

③ I think schools <u>may</u> change a lot over the next 20 years.

④ Buses and trains <u>may</u> run at 500km per hour.

⑤ <u>May</u> we have a short break now?

18 다음 문장에서 어법상 어색한 것을 바르게 고쳐 쓰시오.

(1) I have bought it only a couple of hours ago.

➡ _____

(2) She has studied science and technology since 10 years.

➡ _____

(3) Have you ever gone to Paris?

➡ _____

(4) There may is an AI teachers' room in every school.

➡ _____

19 다음 우리말을 주어진 어휘를 이용하여 영작하시오.

(1) 그는 복권을 사 본 적이 없다. (never, a lottery ticket)

➡ _____

(2) 나는 공항에서 여권을 잃어버렸다. (지금 여권이 없다.) (lose, my passport, at)

➡ _____

(3) 우리는 1999년부터 서로 알고 지냈다. (know, each, 7 단어)

➡ _____

(4) 그는 과학 프로젝트를 막 마쳤다. (finish, his science project, just)

➡ _____

(5) 그들은 내일 돌아올지도 모른다. (come back)

➡ _____

(6) 제가 당신의 스마트폰을 써도 될까요? (use)

➡ _____

Reading

[20~21] 다음 글을 읽고 물음에 답하시오.

ⓐ과학과 기술의 발전은 지금까지 우리의 삶에 많은 변화를 초래해 왔다. In the future, science and technology will make more changes. Let's see what our lives ⓑmay be like in the near future.

20 위 글의 밑줄 친 ⓐ의 우리말에 맞게 한 단어를 보충하여, 주어진 어휘를 알맞게 배열하시오.

advances / in our lives / so far / many changes / in science and technology / caused

➡ _____

_____

21 위 글의 밑줄 친 ⓑmay와 같은 의미로 쓰인 것을 모두 고르시오.

① May I come in?
② He works so that he may succeed.
③ It may rain at any moment.
④ May she rest in peace.
⑤ It may be true.

[22~24] 다음 글을 읽고 물음에 답하시오.

Sangho in the Shopping Center

Shopping is much easier. There are no lines and no counters. Sangho enters a shop with his smartphone which has a special shopping app. In the shop, he takes the items he wants. The items are automatically (A)[adding / added] to a virtual card on his smartphone. ⓐIf Sangho puts an item back, it automatically removes from his list of purchases. When he finishes shopping, Sangho does not need to wait in line to pay. His (B)[actual / virtual] card adds up all the prices and will (C)[change / charge] him later. Isn't that fancy?

22 위 글의 괄호 (A)~(C)에서 문맥이나 어법상 알맞은 낱말을 골라 쓰시오.

➡ (A)_____ (B)_____ (C)_____

23 위 글의 밑줄 친 ⓐ에서 어법상 틀린 부분을 찾아 고치시오.

➡ _____

24 다음 문장에서 위 글의 내용과 다른 부분을 찾아서 고치시오.

> • When Sangho finishes shopping, he needs to pay at the counter.

➡ _____

_____

[25~27] 다음 글을 읽고 물음에 답하시오.

Sumin's 3D Printed House and Clothes

Sumin lives in a 3D printed house. ⓐBuilding a 3D printed house is faster and cheaper than building a house with traditional methods. Sumin's house looks fantastic because of its unique design. ⓑA 3D printer can produce house shapes that people cannot make them with traditional building methods and materials. Sumin also likes to make her clothes at home by using a 3D printer. She can choose colors and materials and can design clothes that fit her body and suit her tastes. Sumin is now a fashion designer!

25 위 글의 밑줄 친 문장 ⓐ를 바르게 바꿔 쓴 문장을 모두 고르시오.

① To build a 3D printed house is faster and cheaper than to build a house with traditional methods.

② Building a house with traditional methods is faster and cheaper than building a 3D printed house.

③ Building a 3D printed house is not as fast and cheap as building a house with traditional methods.

④ Building a house with traditional methods is not as fast and cheap as building a 3D printed house.

⑤ Building a 3D printed house is as fast and cheap as building a house with traditional methods.

26 위 글의 밑줄 친 ⓑ에서 어법상 틀린 부분을 찾아 고치시오.

➡ _____

27 위 글의 내용과 일치하지 않는 것은?

① 수민이는 3D 프린터로 만든 집에 산다.

② 수민이의 집은 독특한 디자인 때문에 멋져 보인다.

③ 3D 프린터는 사람들이 전통적인 건축 방법과 재료들로 만들 수 있는 집 모양을 만들어 낼 수 없다.

④ 수민이는 또한 집에서 3D 프린터를 사용해 옷을 만드는 것을 좋아한다.

⑤ 수민이는 자신의 몸과 취향에 맞는 옷을 디자인할 수 있다.

[28~29] 다음 글을 읽고 물음에 답하시오.

Dongmin in the Hospital

Dongmin is visiting his grandfather in the hospital. An AI nurse enters the room. It moves around the room and checks the patients' conditions. When the AI nurse finds that Dongmin's grandfather has a high temperature, it gives ⓐhim some medicine to __(A)__ his temperature.

Have you ever thought about these changes? Some changes have already started to take place while others may start in the near future. Can you imagine other changes? Take some time to think about ⓑthem.

28 위 글의 빈칸 (A)에 low를 알맞은 형태로 쓰시오.

➡ _____

29 위 글의 밑줄 친 ⓐhim과 ⓑthem이 가리키는 것을 본문에서 찾아 쓰시오.

➡ ⓐ _____ ⓑ _____

01 출제율 90%

다음 짝지어진 단어의 관계가 같도록 빈칸에 알맞은 말을 주어진 철자로 시작하여 쓰시오.

(1) | farm : farmer – library : l_____ |

(2) | material : matter – provide : o_____ |

02 출제율 95%

다음 빈칸에 들어갈 말로 적절한 것은?

I haven't played rugby _____ I left university.

① when ② before ③ as
④ since ⑤ although

03 출제율 100%

다음 우리말에 맞게 빈칸에 알맞은 말을 쓰시오.

(1) 나는 드론에 관심이 있다.
➡ I'm _____ _____ _____.

(2) 십대들은 새로운 과학 기술을 이용하는 데 어려움이 없다.
➡ Teens have no difficulty using new _____.

(3) 나의 선생님은 많은 다른 교육 자료를 사용한다.
➡ My teacher uses a lot of different teaching _____.

(4) 그녀는 화려한 스포츠카를 갖고 있다.
➡ She has a f_____ sports car.

04 출제율 90%

우리말과 일치하도록 주어진 단어를 바르게 배열하시오.

(1) 기술의 발전은 우리에게 많은 좋은 것들을 가져다주었다.
(have, things, in, us, good, technology, many, advances, brought)
➡ _____

(2) 이 시계는 스마트폰처럼 많은 애플리케이션을 작동할 수 있다.
(can, like, applications, this, many, watch, run, smartphones)
➡ _____

[05~06] 다음 대화를 읽고 물음에 답하시오.

G: Oh, I forgot to turn off the heater (A)[before / after] I left home.
B: Really? Then do you need to return home?
G: No. I can (B)[turn it off / turn off it] with my smartphone.
B: Wow, (C)나는 네가 스마트폰으로 히터를 끌 수 있다는 게 놀라워.

05 출제율 95%

위 글의 괄호 (A)~(C)에서 문맥이나 어법상 알맞은 낱말을 골라 쓰시오.

➡ (A) _____ (B) _____

06 출제율 90%

밑줄 친 (C)의 우리말에 맞게 주어진 단어를 이용해서 영작하시오.

➡ _____

_____

(can, with, surprised, that)

[07~10] 다음 대화를 읽고 물음에 답하시오.

Amy: Wow, there are so many books in this library. (①)

Hana: You're right. (②) Where can we find books about gravity?

Terry: Hi, I'm Terry, the AI librarian. Can I help you?

Amy: Hi. We're looking for books about gravity. (③)

Terry: We have fifty seven books about gravity in this library. (④) I think *The Law of Gravity* will be the best one for you.

Hana: I'm (A)_____(surprise) that you can recommend books. (⑤)

Amy: Right. That's (B)_____(amaze). Where is the book, Terry?

Terry: It's on the third floor. Come with me.

출제율 100%
07 위 대화의 ①~⑤ 중 주어진 문장이 들어갈 알맞은 곳은?

> Can you recommend one, please?

①   ②   ③   ④   ⑤

출제율 85%
08 다음 영영풀이에 해당하는 단어를 위 대화에서 찾아 쓰시오.

> to speak in favor of something

➡ _____

출제율 90%
09 빈칸 (A)와 (B)를 괄호 안에 주어진 단어를 이용하여 채우시오.

➡ (A) _____ (B) _____

출제율 90%
10 위 대화의 내용과 일치하지 <u>않는</u> 것을 고르시오.

① There are a lot of books about gravity in the library.

② Hana and Amy are looking for books about gravity.

③ Terry is the AI librarian.

④ Hana and Amy are in the library.

⑤ Terry is amazed that AI recommends a book.

출제율 90%
11 다음 빈칸에 알맞은 말이 순서대로 짝지어진 것은?

> • I have known Cindy _____ a long time.
> • I have known Cindy _____ 1999.

① for – during   ② during – for

③ for – since   ④ since – for

⑤ since – during

출제율 95%
12 다음 중 어법상 적절한 문장은?

① Koreans have played *jegichagi*, a traditional Korean game, since a long time.

② The children have yet had dinner.

③ He has left for New York last night.

④ Does he have done his homework?

⑤ My sister has been to China.

출제율 100%
13 다음 중 어법상 바르지 <u>않은</u> 것은?

① Tony may leave early.

② The math problem is difficult. Chris must not know the answer.

③ Students may go to school only two or three times a week.

④ She may know the truth.

⑤ A lot of AI helpers may be created soon and they may help humans in lots of ways.

[14~16] 다음 글을 읽고 물음에 답하시오.

___ⓐ___ in science and technology have caused many changes in our lives ⓑ<u>so far</u>. In the future, science and technology will make more changes. Let's see what our lives may be ⓒ<u>like</u> in the near future.

14 주어진 영영풀이를 참고하여 빈칸 ⓐ에 철자 A로 시작하는 단어를 쓰시오.

> changes for the better; progress in development

➡ _____

15 위 글의 밑줄 친 ⓑ<u>so far</u>와 바꿔 쓸 수 있는 말을 고르시오.

① lately
② until then
③ until now
④ for now
⑤ recently

16 위 글의 밑줄 친 ⓒ<u>like</u>와 같은 의미로 쓰인 것을 모두 고르시오.

① She's very <u>like</u> her mother.
② I don't <u>like</u> the way he's looking at me.
③ Do you <u>like</u> this dress?
④ She bought a bag <u>like</u> yours.
⑤ I <u>like</u> playing tennis.

[17~19] 다음 글을 읽고 물음에 답하시오.

Sangho in the Shopping Center

ⓐ<u>Shopping is much easier.</u> There are no lines and no counters. Sangho enters a shop with his smartphone which has a special shopping app. In the shop, he takes the items he wants. ⓑ그 물건들은 자동으로 그의 스마트폰에 있는 가상 카드에 더해진다. If Sangho puts an item back, it is automatically

removed from his list of purchases. When he finishes shopping, Sangho does not need to wait in line to pay. His virtual card adds up all the prices and will charge him later. Isn't that ___(A)___ ?

17 위 글의 빈칸 (A)에 들어갈 알맞은 말을 고르시오.

① boring
② fancy
③ plain
④ terrible
⑤ complex

18 다음 중 위 글의 밑줄 친 문장 ⓐ의 이유로 옳지 <u>않은</u> 것을 고르시오.

① There are no lines.
② There are many counters.
③ A shopper can purchase the items by using the smartphone which has a special shopping app.
④ If a shopper puts an item back, it is automatically removed from his or her list of purchase.
⑤ When a shopper finishes shopping, his or her virtual card adds up all the prices and will charge him or her later.

19 위 글의 밑줄 친 ⓑ의 우리말에 맞게 한 단어를 보충하여, 주어진 어휘를 알맞게 배열하시오.

> a virtual card / added / on / the items / his smartphone / are / to

➡ _____
_____

[20~22] 다음 글을 읽고 물음에 답하시오.

Sumin's 3D Printed House and Clothes

Sumin lives in a 3D printed house. (①) Building a 3D printed house is faster and cheaper than building a house with traditional methods. (②) Sumin's house looks fantastic because of its unique design. (③) A 3D printer can produce house shapes ⓐthat people cannot make with traditional building methods and materials. (④) She can choose colors and materials and can design clothes that fit her body and suit her tastes. (⑤) Sumin is now a fashion designer!

출제율 95%

20 위 글의 흐름으로 보아, 주어진 문장이 들어가기에 가장 적절한 곳은?

> Sumin also likes to make her clothes at home by using a 3D printer.

①   ②   ③   ④   ⑤

출제율 90%

21 위 글의 밑줄 친 ⓐthat과 문법적 쓰임이 같은 것을 모두 고르시오.

① The point is that you are still responsible.
② I believe that you'll succeed in the future.
③ He is the only man that I love.
④ It was beyond doubt that he was in error.
⑤ Look at the boy and the dog that are running over there.

출제율 100%

22 위 글의 요지로 알맞은 것을 고르시오.

① Building a 3D printed house is the best way to protect the environment.
② Using a 3D printer, Sumin builds her house and makes her clothes.
③ Building a 3D printed house is good because it is faster and cheaper.
④ Using a 3D printer is good for recycling resources.
⑤ 3D printed things reduce waste of resources.

[23~24] 다음 글을 읽고 물음에 답하시오.

Dongmin in the Hospital

Dongmin is visiting his grandfather in the hospital. An AI nurse enters the room. It moves around the room and checks the patients' conditions. When the AI nurse finds that Dongmin's grandfather has a high temperature, it gives him some medicine to lower his temperature.

Have you ever thought about these changes? Some changes ⓐhave already started to take place while others may start in the near future. Can you imagine other changes? Take some time to think about them.

출제율 95%

23 위 글을 읽고 AI 간호사가 하는 일을 우리말로 쓰시오.

➡ _____

_____

_____

출제율 90%

24 아래 〈보기〉에서 위 글의 밑줄 친 ⓐ와 현재완료의 용법이 같은 것의 개수를 고르시오.

> ┤ 보기 ├
> ① She hasn't cleaned her room yet.
> ② My sister has gone to New York.
> ③ Tom has just finished his homework.
> ④ He has driven a car before.
> ⑤ He has played basketball for two hours.

① 1개   ② 2개   ③ 3개   ④ 4개   ⑤ 5개

서술형 실전문제

01 그림을 보고 주어진 단어를 이용하여 영작하시오.

> A: Is there anything in these pictures that surprises you?
> B: Yes. _____
> _____
>
> (automatic, surprise, this, itself)

[02~03] 다음 대화를 읽고 물음에 답하시오.

> M: Welcome. ⓐThis is our new smart light. ⓑYou don't have to use your hands to turn it on and off.
> W: Really? (A)Then can you tell me how to do it?
> M: ⓒJust say, "Light on!" or "Light out!"
> W: ⓓLight on or light out? ⓔThat's very difficult.

02 ⓐ~ⓔ 중 흐름상 어색한 부분을 찾아 고치시오.

➡ _____

03 밑줄 친 (A)와 같은 의미가 되도록 주어진 단어를 이용하여 영작하시오.

➡ _____ (mind)
_____ (can, ask)

04 다음 빈칸에 알맞은 단어를 〈보기〉에서 골라 쓰시오.

┌─ 보기 ─────────────────┐
│   before   ago   since   for   │
└───────────────────────┘

(1) I started to live in Canada five years ago. I have lived in Canada _____ five years.

(2) We became friends in 2011. We have been friends _____ 2011.

(3) I have never eaten African food _____.

05 다음 우리말을 주어진 어휘를 이용하여 영작하시오.

(1) 당신은 지금 이 방을 나가서는 안 된다. (may, leave)

➡ _____

(2) 내 친구는 그 소식 때문에 슬플지도 모른다. (sad, of)

➡ _____

(3) 부모님은 내가 태어난 이후로 그 개를 길러 오셨다. (born, raise)

➡ _____

(4) 그녀는 영화를 보러 갔다. (그래서 현재 여기에 없다.) (to see the movie)

➡ _____

(5) 그녀는 강에서 수영해 본 적이 한 번 있다. (the river, once, swim)

➡ _____

(6) 그 아이들은 아직 저녁을 먹지 않았다. (have, dinner)

➡ _____

06 다음 대화의 빈칸에 철자 m으로 시작하여 알맞은 말을 쓰시오.

(1) A: Do you know where Anne is?
    B: I'm not sure. She _____ be taking a walk in the park.

(2) A: What are you looking for, Son?
    B: I cannot find my smartphone. _____ I lost it on my way home.

[07~09] 다음 글을 읽고 물음에 답하시오.

Sangho in the Shopping Center

ⓐShopping is much more difficult. There are no lines and no counters. Sangho enters a shop with his smartphone which has a special shopping app. In the shop, he takes the items he wants. The items are automatically added to a virtual card on his smartphone. If Sangho puts an item back, it is automatically removed from his list of purchases. ⓑWhen he finishes shopping, Sangho does not need to wait in line to pay. His virtual card adds up all the prices and will charge him later. Isn't that fancy?

07 위 글의 밑줄 친 ⓐ에서 흐름상 어색한 부분을 찾아 고치시오.

➡ _____

08 주어진 영영풀이에 해당하는 단어를 본문에서 찾아 쓰시오.

> done or seen using computers or the Internet instead of going to a place, meeting people in person, etc.

➡ _____

09 위 글의 밑줄 친 문장 ⓑ의 이유를 우리말로 쓰시오.

➡ _____
_____

[10~12] 다음 글을 읽고 물음에 답하시오.

Sumin's 3D Printed House and Clothes

Sumin lives in a 3D printed house. Building a 3D printed house is faster and cheaper than building a house with traditional methods. ⓐSumin's house looks like fantastic because of its unique design. A 3D printer can produce house shapes that people cannot make with traditional building methods and materials. Sumin also likes to make her clothes at home by __(A)__ a 3D printer. She can choose colors and materials and can design clothes that fit her body and suit her tastes. Sumin is now a fashion designer!

10 위 글의 빈칸 (A)에 use를 알맞은 형태로 쓰시오.

➡ _____

11 위 글의 밑줄 친 ⓐ에서 어법상 틀린 부분을 찾아 고치시오.

➡ _____

12 위 글을 읽고 3D 프린터로 집을 짓는 것의 장점 세 가지를 우리말로 쓰시오.

➡ (1) _____
_____
  (2) _____
  (3) _____
_____

01 다음 대화의 밑줄 친 우리말을 영작하시오. (주어진 어휘와 조건을 이용할 것)

> A: Look! This is closing its leave.
> B: I heard about this plant. It's a fly eater.
> A: <u>그것이 나뭇잎 같이 생겼는데 움직여서 놀라워</u>. (surprise, like, 놀람 표현하기, 현재진행형)
> _____

02 주어진 어휘와 현재완료 시제를 이용하여 3 문장 이상을 쓰시오.

Advances in science and technology	life in the future	to Austria
finish my homework	visit Jejudo	

(1) _____
(2) _____
(3) _____

03 다음 내용을 바탕으로 20년 후 학교의 모습을 설명하는 글을 쓰시오.

> Q1: What do students learn?
> A: They learn 3D printing.
> Q2: Who helps students at school?
> A: AI teachers help students at school.
> Q3: What new place is in every school?
> A: There is a drone station in every school.
> Q4: What other ideas do you have about future schools?
> A: Students may not carry paper textbooks anymore.

Schools in 20 Years

  Have you ever thought of how schools may change over the next 20 years? Students may learn (A)_____ . (B)_____ may help students at school. There may be (C)_____ in every school. Students may not carry (D)_____ anymore.

단원별 모의고사

01 빈칸 (A)와 (B)에 들어갈 말로 알맞은 것끼리 짝지어진 것을 고르시오.

> • The jacket (A)_____ me pretty well.
> • How much are we (B)_____ for delivery for items ordered from our Web site?

	(A)	(B)
①	fits	paying
②	fits	charging
③	fits	saving
④	follow	paying
⑤	follow	charging

02 다음 주어진 우리말에 맞게 빈칸을 채우시오. (철자가 주어진 것이 있으면 그 철자로 시작할 것)

(1) 나의 과학 선생님이 중력의 법칙에 대해 가르쳐 주셨다.

➡ My science teacher taught us about the l_____ of _____.

(2) 그 환자는 위독한 상태였다.

➡ The _____ was in a critical condition.

(3) 그의 가르치는 방식은 항상 창의적이다.

➡ His teaching m_____ is always creative.

(4) 그 축제는 다음 주 목요일에 개최될 것이다.

➡ The festival will _____ place next Thursday.

03 주어진 영영풀이의 어휘를 빈칸에 써 넣으시오.

> created by computers, or appearing on computers or the Internet

> _____ reality technology needs very powerful computers.

04 다음 우리말에 맞게 주어진 단어를 바르게 배열하시오.

(1) 그들은 커피를 뽑으려고 줄을 서서 기다리고 있다.
(in, waiting, line, get, are, coffee, to, they)

➡ _____

(2) 내가 곤경에 빠졌을 때, 그녀는 나를 많이 지원해주려고 노력했다. (when으로 시작할 것)
(when, me, lot, to, in, was, a, trouble, support, she, I, tried)

➡ _____

(3) 그 여자는 자기의 구입품을 교환하려고 노력 중이다.
(exchange, purchase, woman, the, her, is, to, trying)

➡ _____

(4) 이 약을 식후에 복용해라.
(meals, medicine, this, after, take)

➡ _____

05 밑줄 친 우리말에 맞게 주어진 단어를 이용하여 영작하시오.

> M: These days, many things can work like humans. Some cars can travel without a human driver. We can make smartphones do simple work only by talking to them. 나는 우리가 이미 미래에 살고 있다는 게 놀랍다.

➡ _____

(that, future, living)

[06~08] 다음 대화를 읽고 물음에 답하시오.

Amy: Wow, there are so many books in this library. (①)

Hana: You're right. Where can we find books about gravity? (②)

Terry: Hi, I'm Terry, the AI librarian. Can I help you?

Amy: Hi. We're looking for books about gravity. (③) Can you recommend one, please?

Terry: We have fifty seven books about gravity in this library. I think The Law of Gravity will be the best one for you.

Hana: I'm surprised that you can recommend books. (④)

Amy: Right. That's amazing. (⑤)

Terry: It's on the third floor. Come with me.

06 위 대화의 ①~⑤ 중 주어진 말이 들어갈 알맞은 곳은?

> Where is the book, Terry?

①   ②   ③   ④   ⑤

07 다음 영영풀이에 해당하는 단어를 위 대화에서 찾아 쓰시오.

> a statement of fact concerning what always happens in certain circumstances; a scientific principle

➡ _____

08 위 대화를 읽고 답할 수 <u>없는</u> 질문을 고르시오.

① How many books are there in the library?
② Where are Amy and Hana?
③ What book was recommended by Terry?
④ After the dialogue, where are they going to go?
⑤ What floor is *The Law of Gravity* on?

[09~10] 다음 대화를 읽고 물음에 답하시오.

G: Uncle Jack! Your new drone looks cool.

M: Thanks. I designed it ⓐ<u>to saving people's lives</u>.

G: Save people's lives?

M: Yes. It watches the ocean. If there is ⓑ<u>a person in trouble</u>, it flies over and ⓒ<u>drop a tube</u>.

G: ⓓ<u>I'm surprised what</u> drones can rescue people. Can you ⓔ<u>show me how it works</u>?

M: Sure. Watch this.

09 다음 영영풀이에 해당하는 단어를 위 대화에서 찾아 쓰시오.

> an unmanned aircraft or ship guided by a remote control or onboard computers

➡ _____

10 ⓐ~ⓔ 중 어법상 <u>어색한</u> 것의 개수를 고르시오.

① 1개   ② 2개   ③ 3개   ④ 4개   ⑤ 5개

11 다음 우리말에 맞게 주어진 단어를 바르게 배열하시오.

> A: I think shoes will change our lives in the future.
> B: 미래에 어떻게 신발이 우리의 생활을 바꿀 수 있는지 말해 줄 수 있니?
> A: I think we will run 100 meters in 5 seconds.

➡ _____

_____

12 다음 대화의 순서를 바르게 배열하시오.

> (A) Light on or light out? That's very simple.
> (B) Just say, "Light on!" or "Light out!"
> (C) Welcome. This is our new smart light. You don't have to use your hands to turn it on and off.
> (D) Really? Then can you tell me how to do it?

➡ _____

13 다음 중 어법상 어색한 것을 고르시오.

① I have never used a chatting robot before.
② I have met a famous person then.
③ Technological developments have changed our lives.
④ We have been good friends for ten years.
⑤ Advances in science and technology have caused many changes in our lives so far.

14 다음 주어진 문장의 밑줄 친 부분과 쓰임이 같은 것은?

> • You <u>may</u> leave early.

① She <u>may</u> know the truth.
② They <u>may</u> invite me to the party.
③ You <u>may</u> not read my diary.
④ All types of diseases like cancer <u>may</u> be cured.
⑤ Students <u>may</u> get help from not only human teachers but also AI teachers.

15 그림을 보고, 'may'와 주어진 단어를 이용하여 추측하는 문장을 완성하시오.

(Cindy, live, a 3D printed house, future)

➡ _____

16 다음 두 문장을 해석하고 그 차이를 설명하시오.

(1) I lost my smartphone.
(2) I have lost my smartphone.

➡ 해석: (1) _____
해석: (2) _____
차이: _____
_____
_____

[17~19] 다음 글을 읽고 물음에 답하시오.

Sangho in the Shopping Center

Shopping is much easier. There are no lines and no counters. Sangho enters a shop with his smartphone which has a special shopping app. In the shop, he takes the items he wants. The items are automatically added to a virtual card on his smartphone. If Sangho puts an item back, it is automatically removed from his list of purchases. When he finishes shopping, Sangho does not need to wait in line ⓐ<u>to pay</u>. His virtual card adds up all the prices and will charge him later. Isn't that fancy?

17 아래 보기에서 위 글의 밑줄 친 ⓐto pay와 to부정사의 용법이 <u>다른</u> 것의 개수를 고르시오.

보기
① <u>To hear</u> him talk, you would think him a foreigner.
② She has many children to <u>look</u> after.
③ He began <u>to read</u> the book.
④ She must be honest <u>to say</u> so.
⑤ I didn't know where <u>to go</u>.

① 1개   ② 2개   ③ 3개   ④ 4개   ⑤ 5개

18 본문의 내용과 일치하도록 다음 빈칸 (A)와 (B)에 알맞은 단어를 쓰시오.

In the shop, the items Sangho (A)_____ are automatically added to a virtual card on his smartphone, and the items Sangho (B)_____ _____ are automatically removed from his list of purchases.

19 위 글을 읽고 대답할 수 <u>없는</u> 질문은?

① Are there lines or counters in the shopping center?
② Does Sangho need a special app to shop at the shopping center?
③ What operation method does the app use to automatically add the items to a virtual card on Sangho's smartphone?
④ Is the item Sangho puts back automatically removed from his list of purchases?
⑤ How does Sangho pay when he buys things at a shopping center?

[20~22] 다음 글을 읽고 물음에 답하시오.

Sumin's 3D Printed House and Clothes
Sumin lives in a 3D printed house. Building a 3D printed house is faster and cheaper than building a house with traditional methods. Sumin's house looks fantastic ⓐbecause of its unique design. A 3D printer can produce house shapes that people cannot make with traditional building methods and materials. Sumin also likes to make her clothes at home by using a 3D printer. She can choose colors and materials and can design clothes that fit her body and suit her ⓑtastes. Sumin is now   (A) !

20 위 글의 빈칸 (A)에 들어갈 알맞은 말을 고르시오.

① an architect   ② a fashion model
③ an engineer   ④ a fashion designer
⑤ a painter

21 위 글의 밑줄 친 ⓐbecause of와 바꿔 쓸 수 <u>없는</u> 말을 고르시오.

① on account of   ② thanks to
③ in spite of   ④ owing to
⑤ due to

22 위 글의 밑줄 친 ⓑtastes와 같은 의미로 쓰인 것을 고르시오.

① She has very unique <u>taste</u> in clothes.
② The soup <u>tastes</u> of onion.
③ It <u>tastes</u> sweet.
④ I don't like the <u>tastes</u> of vegetables.
⑤ She <u>tastes</u> with her tongue.

Special

The 100th Customer

🪶 언어 형식

- 지각동사

  Mr. Kang **watched** them **eat**.

- 'too＋형용사/부사＋to＋동사원형' 구문

  She was **too** poor **to** pay for two bowls.

Words & Expressions

Key Words

- □ **bedroom**[bédrùːm] 몡 침실
- □ **bowl**[boul] 몡 (우묵한) 그릇, 통
- □ **break**[breik] 몡 휴식, (학교의) 쉬는 시간
- □ **chair**[tʃɛər] 몡 의지
- □ **chew**[tʃuː] 통 (음식을) 씹다
- □ **count**[kaunt] 통 수를 세다, 계산하다
- □ **counter**[káuntər] 몡 계산대
- □ **customer**[kʌ́stəmər] 몡 손님, 고객
- □ **elderly**[éldərli] 혱 연세가 드신
- □ **even**[íːvən] 뷔 (예상 밖의 놀라운 일을 나타내어) ~도, ~조차
- □ **grandson**[grǽndsʌn] 몡 손자
- □ **if**[if] 젭 만일 ~라면

- □ **meal**[miːl] 몡 식사
- □ **novel**[nάvəl] 몡 소설
- □ **order**[ɔ́ːrdər] 통 (음식, 음료 등을) 주문하다
- □ **owner**[óunər] 몡 주인, 소유주
- □ **player**[pléiər] 몡 참가자, 선수, 배우
- □ **producer**[prədjúːsər] 몡 생산자, 제작자
- □ **raise**[reiz] 통 (자금 등을) 모으다
- □ **single**[síŋgl] 혱 단 하나의, 단일의
- □ **tap**[tæp] 통 (가볍게) 톡톡 두드리다, 치다
- □ **treat**[triːt] 통 대접하다, 다루다
- □ **turn**[təːrn] 몡 (무엇을 할) 차례, 순번
- □ **yet**[jet] 뷔 (부정문, 의문문에서) 아직

Key Expressions

- □ **be about to** 막 ~하려는 참이다
- □ **can't wait to** 동사원형 빨리 ~하고 싶다, ~하는 것이 기다려지다
- □ **have to** 동사원형 ~해야 한다
- □ **help**+목적어+동사원형 (목적어)가 ~하는 것을 돕다
- □ **pick up** 들어올리다, 집다, ~을 (차에) 태우러 가다

- □ **say to oneself** 혼잣말을 하다
- □ **think up** ~을 생각해 내다
- □ **too**+형용사/부사+**to** 동사원형 너무 …해서 ~할 수 없다
- □ **treat A(사람) to B(사물)** A에게 B를 대접하다

Word Power

※ 접미사 -er을 붙여 '~하는 사람'이라는 뜻의 명사가 되는 동사들

□ **own** (소유하다) – **owner** (주인, 소유주)

□ **play** (경기하다, (연극 등을) 상연[공연]하다) – **player** (선수, 배우)

□ **produce** (생산하다, 만들다) – **producer** (생산자, 제작자)

□ **write** (쓰다, (작품·문서 등을) 저술하다) – **writer** (작가)

□ **teach** (가르치다) – **teacher** (교사)

□ **paint** (그림을 그리다) – **painter** (화가)

(*cf.*) 접미사 -er을 붙여 '~하는 것'이라는 뜻의 명사가 되는 동사

□ **clean** (청소하다) – **cleaner** (청소기)

□ **dry** (건조시키다) – **dryer** (건조기, 드라이어)

※ 비슷한 뜻을 가진 어휘들

□ **elderly** (연세가 드신) – **old** (나이든)

□ **producer** (생산자, 제작자) – **maker** (제조업자, 만드는 사람)

□ **raise** ((자금 등을) 모으다) – **collect** ((돈·기부·인원을) 모으다)

□ **single** (단 하나의, 단일의) – **only** (유일한)

□ **treat** (대접하다, 다루다) – **deal with** ((문제 등을) 다루다)

English Dictionary

□ **bedroom** 침실
→ a room that you sleep in
당신이 자는 방

□ **chair** 의자
→ a piece of furniture for one person to sit on, with a back, legs, and sometimes two arms
한 사람이 앉기 위한, 등받이와 다리, 때때로 팔걸이가 있는 가구

□ **chew** (음식을) 씹다
→ to break food etc. with the teeth before swallowing
음식을 삼키기 전에 이로 음식을 부수다

□ **counter** 계산대
→ the place where customers are served or pay in a restaurant or shop
식당이나 가게에서 손님들이 시중을 받고 돈을 지불하는 장소

□ **customer** 손님, 고객
→ a person who buys goods from a shop, etc.
가게에서 물건을 사는 사람

□ **grandson** 손자
→ a son of one's son or daughter
어떤 사람의 아들이나 딸의 아들

□ **meal** 식사
→ an occasion when you eat food such as breakfast, lunch, and dinner
아침, 점심, 저녁 같은 음식을 먹는 것

□ **novel** 소설
→ a book telling a long story in prose
산문의 형식으로 긴 이야기를 하는 책

□ **single** 단 하나의
→ comprising only one part
오직 하나의 부분으로만 이루어진

□ **think up** ~을 생각해 내다
→ to invent or to imagine something, especially an excuse
특히 변명으로 어떤 것을 지어내거나 상상해 내다

□ **treat** 대접하다
→ to buy or give someone something special
어떤 사람에게 특별한 것을 사 주거나 주다

교과서
Reading

The 100th Customer

One day, an elderly woman walked into a restaurant. She was with
<u>old보다 정중한 표현, 나이가 드신</u>

her grandson. Quietly, the woman asked <u>Mr. Kang</u>, <u>the owner of the</u>
'Mr. Kang'과 'the owner of the restaurant'는 동격. 콤마(,)가 쓰였다.

<u>restaurant</u>.

"How much is a bowl of Gukbap'?"
How much ~?: 양이나 가격을 물을 때 쓰임. 여기에서는 국밥 한 그릇의 가격을 묻고 있다.

"It's 4,000 won, ma'am," Mr. Kang answered <u>with a smile</u>. She
미소 지으며

was <u>too poor to pay</u> for two bowls. She ordered a single bowl for her
too+형용사/부사+to+동사원형: 너무 ~해서 …할 수 없다

grandson.

"Are you <u>sure you</u> are not hungry, Grandma?" the boy asked, as he
sure와 you 사이에 접속사 that이 생략

ate the hot soup.

"No, I'm not hungry. Don't worry about me." She picked up some

Gimchi and <u>chewed on</u> it happily.
~을 씹었다. 입에 물었다

Mr. Kang <u>watched them eat</u>, and a warm feeling <u>came over</u> him.
지각동사+목적어+동사원형: 목적격보어로 동사원형이나 현재분사가 온다.   come over: (격한 감정 등이) ~에게 밀려오다

He thought up <u>a plan to give</u> the boy a free meal. When the woman
to부정사(형용사적 용법)

was about to pay, Mr. Kang waved his hands and said, "No need,

ma'am. In my restaurant, you don't pay <u>if</u> you're the 100th customer
만일 ~라면(조건을 나타내는 접속사)

of the day." The woman and her grandson thanked Mr. Kang and left.

---

owner: 주인
order: 주문하다
single: 단 하나의, 단일의
chew: ~을 씹다
meal: 식사
pick up: 집다
think up: ~을 생각해 내다
be about to: 막 ~하려는 참이다

확인문제

● 다음 문장이 본문의 내용과 일치하면 T, 일치하지 <u>않으면</u> F를 쓰시오.

1 One day, an elderly woman walked into a restaurant with her grandson. ☐

2 She had enough money to pay for two bowls. ☐

3 Mr. Kang thought up a plan to give the boy a free meal. ☐

4 It was true that the woman was the 100th customer of the day. ☐

A month later, Mr. Kang saw the boy in the street outside the restaurant. The boy was gathering stones.

"What are you doing?" asked Mr. Kang.

"I'm counting the number of customers who enter your restaurant. Today is my grandma's birthday."

'He wants to be the 100th customer and treat his grandmother to a bowl of Gukbap!' Mr. Kang said to himself.

Mr. Kang looked down. He could see that the number of stones was not yet even fifty. He had to do something to help the boy gather 100 stones. Mr. Kang went back into the restaurant and called his friends.

"Come to my restaurant now and bring everyone who works with you. There is a boy who needs your help."

People began to arrive at the restaurant. When the 99th customer arrived, Mr. Kang heard the boy say, "It's our turn, Grandma." Mr. Kang welcomed them and served the woman a free bowl of Gukbap.

"Are you sure you're not hungry?" the woman asked the boy.

The boy chewed loudly on some Gimchi and said with a smile,

"No, I'm not hungry, Grandma. Don't worry about me. Happy birthday!"

outside: ~ 밖에
stone: 돌
treat: 대접하다
yet: 아직
even: ~도, ~조차

확인문제

● 다음 문장이 본문의 내용과 일치하면 T, 일치하지 <u>않으면</u> F를 쓰시오.

1 The boy was counting the number of customers who entered Mr. Kang's restaurant.

2 The number of stones was already over fifty. ☐

3 Mr. Kang went back into the restaurant and called his friends. ☐

4 Mr. Kang welcomed the boy and his grandmother and served them two free bowls of Gukbap. ☐

● 우리말을 참고하여 빈칸에 알맞은 말을 쓰시오.

1 The _____ Customer

2 One day, an _____ woman walked into a restaurant.

3 She was _____ _____ _____.

4 _____, the woman asked Mr. Kang, _____ _____ of the restaurant.

5 "_____ _____ is a bowl of Gukbap?"

6 "It's 4,000 won, ma'am," Mr. Kang answered _____ _____ _____.

7 She was _____ _____ _____ _____ for two bowls.

8 She ordered a single bowl _____ _____ _____.

9 "_____ _____ _____ you are not hungry, Grandma?" the boy asked, as he ate the hot soup.

10 "_____, I'm not hungry.

11 _____ _____ about me."

12 She picked up some Gimchi and _____ _____ it happily.

13 Mr. Kang watched them _____, and a warm feeling _____ _____ him.

14 He thought up a plan _____ _____ _____ _____ _____ _____ _____.

15 When the woman _____ _____ _____ _____, Mr. Kang waved his hands and said, "No need, ma'am.

16 In my restaurant, you don't pay if you're _____ _____ of the day."

17 The woman and her grandson _____ _____ _____ and left.

1 백 번째 손님

2 어느 날 한 할머니가 식당으로 걸어 들어왔다.

3 그녀는 손자와 함께 있었다.

4 그녀는 조용히 식당 주인인 강 씨에게 물었다.

5 "국밥 한 그릇이 얼마인가요?"

6 "4,000원입니다. 할머니." 강 씨는 미소 지으며 답했다.

7 그녀는 너무 가난해서 두 그릇 값을 지불할 수 없었다.

8 그녀는 손자를 위해 한 그릇을 주문했다.

9 "정말 배고프지 않으세요, 할머니?" 남자아이는 따뜻한 국물을 먹으며 물었다.

10 "응, 난 배고프지 않단다.

11 내 걱정하지 마라."

12 그녀는 행복하게 김치를 집어서 먹었다.

13 강 씨는 그들이 먹는 것을 지켜보았고, 따뜻한 감정이 밀려왔다.

14 그는 남자아이에게 무료로 식사를 주기 위해 계획을 생각해 냈다.

15 할머니가 돈을 내려고 할 때, 강 씨는 손을 흔들며 말했다. "필요 없습니다. 할머니.

16 저희 식당에서는 그 날의 백 번째 손님이 되면 돈을 내지 않아도 됩니다."

17 할머니와 손자는 강 씨에게 감사 하며 떠났다.

18 _____ _____ _____, Mr. Kang saw the boy in the street _____ the restaurant.

19 The boy _____ _____ stones.

20 "_____ are you doing?" asked Mr. Kang.

21 "I'm _____ the number of customers _____ enter your restaurant.

22 _____ _____ my grandma's birthday."

23 'He wants to be the 100th customer and _____ his grandmother to a bowl of Gukbap!' Mr. Kang _____ _____ _____.

24 Mr. Kang _____ _____.

25 He could see that _____ _____ of stones _____ not yet even fifty.

26 He had to do something _____ _____ the boy gather 100 stones.

27 Mr. Kang _____ _____ _____ the restaurant and called his friends.

28 "Come to my restaurant now and _____ _____ _____ works with you.

29 There is a boy _____ _____ your help."

30 People began _____ _____ _____ the restaurant.

31 When the 99th customer arrived, Mr. Kang heard the boy say, "_____ _____ _____, Grandma."

32 Mr. Kang _____ _____ and served the woman _____ _____ _____ _____ _____.

33 "_____ _____ _____ you're not hungry?" the woman asked the boy.

34 The boy chewed loudly on some Gimchi and said _____ _____ _____, "No, I'm not hungry, Grandma.

35 _____ _____ about me. Happy birthday!"

18 한 달 후, 강 씨는 식당 밖 거리에서 그 남자아이를 보았다.
19 그 남자아이는 돌멩이를 모으고 있었다.
20 너 뭐 하고 있니?" 강 씨가 물었다.
21 "저는 아저씨 식당에 들어가는 손님들의 수를 세고 있어요.
22 오늘이 우리 할머니 생신이거든요."
23 '저 아이는 백 번째 손님이 되어서 할머니께 공짜 국밥 한 그릇을 대접하고 싶어 하는구나.' 강 씨는 혼잣말을 했다.
24 강 씨는 아래를 내려다보았다.
25 그는 돌멩이의 개수가 아직 오십 개도 안 되는 것을 볼 수 있었다.
26 그는 남자아이가 돌멩이 백 개를 모으는 것을 돕기 위해 무언가를 해야 했다.
27 강 씨는 식당으로 되돌아가 그의 친구들에게 전화했다.
28 "지금 내 식당으로 오고, 자네와 함께 일하는 모든 사람들을 데려와 주게.
29 자네 도움이 필요한 남자아이가 있어."
30 사람들이 식당에 도착하기 시작했다.
31 아흔아홉 번째 손님이 도착했을 때 강 씨는 남자아이가 "우리 차례예요, 할머니."라고 말하는 것을 들었다.
32 강 씨는 그들을 반기며 할머니께 공짜 국밥 한 그릇을 제공했다.
33 "너 정말 배고프지 않니?" 할머니가 남자아이에게 물었다.
34 남자아이는 큰 소리로 김치를 씹고 미소 지으며 말했다. "네, 전 배고프지 않아요, 할머니.
35 제 걱정 마세요. 생신 축하드려요!"

● 우리말을 참고하여 본문을 영작하시오.

1 백 번째 손님
➡ _____

2 어느 날 한 할머니가 식당으로 걸어 들어왔다.
➡ _____

3 그녀는 손자와 함께 있었다.
➡ _____

4 그녀는 조용히 식당 주인인 강 씨에게 물었다.
➡ _____

5 "국밥 한 그릇이 얼마인가요?"
➡ _____

6 "4,000원입니다, 할머니." 강 씨는 미소 지으며 답했다.
➡ _____

7 그녀는 너무 가난해서 두 그릇 값을 지불할 수 없었다.
➡ _____

8 그녀는 손자를 위해 한 그릇을 주문했다.
➡ _____

9 "정말 배고프지 않으세요, 할머니?" 남자아이는 따뜻한 국물을 먹으며 물었다.
➡ _____

10 "응, 난 배고프지 않단다.
➡ _____

11 내 걱정하지 마라."
➡ _____

12 그녀는 행복하게 김치를 집어서 먹었다.
➡ _____

13 강 씨는 그들이 먹는 것을 지켜보았고, 따뜻한 감정이 밀려왔다.
➡ _____

14 그는 남자아이에게 무료로 식사를 주기 위해 계획을 생각해 냈다.
➡ _____

15 할머니가 돈을 내려고 할 때, 강 씨는 손을 흔들며 말했다. "필요 없습니다, 할머니.
➡ _____

16 저희 식당에서는 그 날의 백 번째 손님이 되면 돈을 내지 않아도 됩니다."
➡ _____

17 할머니와 손자는 강 씨에게 감사해 하며 떠났다.
➡ _____

18 한 달 후, 강 씨는 식당 밖 거리에서 그 남자아이를 보았다.

➡ _____

19 그 남자아이는 돌멩이를 모으고 있었다.

➡ _____

20 "너 뭐 하고 있니?" 강 씨가 물었다.

➡ _____

21 "저는 아저씨 식당에 들어가는 손님들의 수를 세고 있어요.

➡ _____

22 오늘이 우리 할머니 생신이거든요."

➡ _____

23 '저 아이는 백 번째 손님이 되어서 할머니께 공짜 국밥 한 그릇을 대접하고 싶어 하는구나.' 강 씨는 혼잣말을 했다.

➡ _____

_____

24 강 씨는 아래를 내려다보았다.

➡ _____

25 그는 돌멩이의 개수가 아직 오십 개도 안 되는 것을 볼 수 있었다.

➡ _____

26 그는 남자아이가 돌멩이 백 개를 모으는 것을 돕기 위해 무언가를 해야 했다.

➡ _____

27 강 씨는 식당으로 되돌아가 그의 친구들에게 전화했다.

➡ _____

28 "지금 내 식당으로 오고, 자네와 함께 일하는 모든 사람들을 데려와 주게.

➡ _____

29 자네 도움이 필요한 남자아이가 있어."

➡ _____

30 사람들이 식당에 도착하기 시작했다.

➡ _____

31 아흔아홉 번째 손님이 도착했을 때 강 씨는 남자아이가 "우리 차례예요, 할머니."라고 말하는 것을 들었다.

➡ _____

32 강 씨는 그들을 반기며 할머니께 공짜 국밥 한 그릇을 제공했다.

➡ _____

33 "너 정말 배고프지 않니?" 할머니가 남자아이에게 물었다.

➡ _____

34 남자아이는 큰 소리로 김치를 씹고 미소 지으며 말했다. "네, 전 배고프지 않아요, 할머니.

➡ _____

35 제 걱정 마세요. 생신 축하드려요!"

➡ _____

01 밑줄 친 부분과 의미가 가장 가까운 단어를 주어진 철자로 시작하여 쓰시오.

(1) This is the <u>only</u> bank in the area.

➡ s_____

(2) There are new ways of <u>dealing with</u> the problem of street crime.

➡ t_____

(3) Sarah takes care of her <u>old</u> parents.

➡ e_____

02 빈칸에 공통으로 들어갈 단어를 쓰시오.

(1)
• Who thought _____ names for new products?
• Passengers are picking _____ their bags.

(2)
• I'll treat them _____ dinner tonight.
• Johnson always says _____ himself.

03 다음 빈칸에 알맞은 단어를 〈보기〉에서 골라 쓰시오.

┌─ 보기 ─┐
chew   count   order   raise

(1) They hoped to _____ one million dollars to buy land.

(2) I can't _____ my food well because of the toothache.

(3) _____ whatever you want regardless of expense.

(4) John had to _____ the number of animals.

04 주어진 문장과 비슷한 의미가 되도록 빈칸을 알맞게 채우시오.

I'm looking forward to taking the trip.

➡ I _____ wait _____ _____ the trip.

05 다음 주어진 우리말에 맞게 빈칸을 채우시오.

(1) 거기는 여름에도 춥다.

➡ It is cold there _____ in summer.

(2) 식사 사이에 먹지 않도록 노력해라.

➡ Try not to eat between _____.

(3) 너의 차례가 오면, 한 칸을 움직여라.

➡ When it's your _____, move one space.

(4) 버스 운전사가 아직 안 왔다.

➡ The bus driver isn't here _____.

06 다음 영영풀이에 해당하는 말을 주어진 철자로 시작하여 쓰시오.

a piece of furniture for one person to sit on, with a back, legs, and sometimes two arms

➡ c_____

to break food etc. with the teeth before swallowing

➡ c_____

★**7** 다음 문장에서 어법상 어색한 부분을 바르게 고쳐 쓰시오.

(1) I saw you to enter the museum.

➡ _____

(2) I heard my friend laughed loudly in English class.

➡ _____

_____

(3) The kid is very short to reach that book.

➡ _____

(4) I am too tired that I can't get up early.

➡ _____

08 주어진 동사를 빈칸에 알맞게 쓰시오.

(A) The cook smelled soup _____.
(burn)
(B) The chair is too heavy _____.
(carry)

09 다음 우리말을 주어진 어휘를 이용하여 영작하시오.

(1) 그 셔츠는 너무 커서 입을 수 없다. (wear, large, to)

➡ _____

(2) 나는 Tom이 나에 대해 얘기하는 것을 들었다. (talk)

➡ _____

(3) 그는 사실을 말할 만큼 정직하다. (enough, tell)

➡ _____

[10~12] 다음 글을 읽고 물음에 답하시오.

One day, an elderly woman walked into a restaurant. She was ⓐ her grandson. Quietly, the woman asked Mr. Kang, the owner of the restaurant.

"ⓑHow much is a bowl of Gukbap?"

"It's 4,000 won, ma'am," Mr. Kang answered ⓒ a smile. ⓓShe was too poor to pay for two bowls. She ordered a single bowl for her grandson.

10 위 글의 빈칸 ⓐ와 ⓒ에 공통으로 들어갈 알맞은 전치사를 쓰시오.

➡ _____

11 위 글의 밑줄 친 ⓑ를 다음과 같이 바꿔 쓸 때 빈칸에 들어갈 알맞은 말을 쓰시오.

➡ What's the _____ of a bowl of Gukbap?

★**12** 위 글의 밑줄 친 ⓓ를 다음과 같이 바꿔 쓸 때 빈칸에 들어갈 알맞은 말을 쓰시오.

➡ She was _____ poor _____ she _____ pay for two bowls.

[13~15] 다음 글을 읽고 물음에 답하시오.

"Are you sure you are not hungry, Grandma?" the boy asked, as he ate the hot soup.

"(A)[Yes / No], I'm not hungry. Don't worry about me." She picked up some Gimchi and chewed on it happily.

ⓐMr. Kang watched them to eat, and a warm feeling came over him. He thought up ⓑa plan to give the boy a free meal. When the woman was about (B)[to pay / paying], Mr. Kang waved his hands and said, "No need, ma'am. In my restaurant, you don't pay if you're the 100th (C)[customer / guest] of the day." The woman and her grandson thanked Mr. Kang and left.

13 위 글의 괄호 (A)~(C)에서 문맥이나 어법상 알맞은 낱말을 골라 쓰시오.

➡ (A) _____ (B) _____ (C) _____

14 위 글의 밑줄 친 ⓐ에서 어법상 **틀린** 부분을 찾아 고치시오.

➡ _____

15 위 글의 밑줄 친 ⓑa plan의 구체적인 내용을 우리말로 쓰시오.

➡ _____

_____

[16~18] 다음 글을 읽고 물음에 답하시오.

A month later, Mr. Kang saw the boy in the street outside the restaurant. The boy was gathering stones.

"What are you doing?" asked Mr. Kang.

"I'm counting the number of customers ⓐ _____ enter your restaurant. Today is my grandma's birthday."

'He wants to be the 100th customer and treat his grandmother to a bowl of Gukbap!' Mr. Kang said to himself.

Mr. Kang looked down. He could see ⓑ_____ the number of stones was not yet even fifty. He had to do ⓒsomething to help the boy gather 100 stones. Mr. Kang went back into the restaurant and called his friends.

"Come to my restaurant now and bring everyone who works with you. There is a boy ⓓ_____ needs your help."

16 빈칸 ⓐ, ⓑ, ⓓ에 공통으로 들어갈 알맞은 말을 쓰시오.

➡ _____

17 밑줄 친 ⓒ가 구체적으로 가리키는 내용을 우리말로 쓰시오.

➡ _____

_____

18 Why did Mr. Kang call his friends and ask them to come to his restaurant? Fill in the blanks with suitable words.

➡ Because he wanted to make the boy _____ _____ _____ of the day.

[19~21] 다음 글을 읽고 물음에 답하시오.

People began to ⓐarrive at the restaurant. When the 99th customer arrived, Mr. Kang heard the boy __(A)__, "It's our turn, Grandma." Mr. Kang welcomed them and ⓑserved the woman a free bowl of Gukbap.

19 빈칸 (A)에 say를 알맞은 형태로 쓰시오.

➡ _____

20 밑줄 친 ⓐarrive at과 바꿔 쓸 수 있는 단어를 쓰시오.

➡ _____

21 밑줄 친 ⓑ를 3형식으로 고치시오.

➡ _____

출제율 95%

01 다음 중 단어의 관계가 나머지 넷과 다른 하나는?

① own – owner
② dry – dryer
③ write – writer
④ teach – teacher
⑤ produce – producer

출제율 95%

02 다음 빈칸에 공통으로 들어갈 말로 알맞은 것을 주어진 철자로 시작하여 쓰시오.

(1)
- I will p_____ my sister at the airport.
- We have to p_____ the trash on the street.

(2)
- R_____ your hand if you know the right answer.
- They r_____d funds to help the flood victim.

출제율 90%

03 다음 우리말에 맞게 주어진 단어를 바르게 배열하시오.

(1) 그녀는 그에게 점심을 대접했다. (to, she, him, lunch, treated)

➡ _____

(2) 그가 나한테 전화했을 때, 나는 막 나가려는 참이었다. (I, about, he, was, me, leave, when, to, called) (when으로 시작할 것)

➡ _____

(3) 소녀는 여동생이 케이크 만드는 것을 도왔다. (a cake, helped, make, her, the girl, sister)

➡ _____

(4) 나는 그것을 정말 보고 싶어. (can't, to, I, it, wait, watch)

➡ _____

출제율 90%

04 다음 중 밑줄 친 부분의 뜻풀이가 바르지 않은 것은?

① Put the vegetables in the salad bowl. (그릇)
② We had a very warm welcome from the owner of the house. (주인)
③ I had to think up a better excuse. (추측하다)
④ I ordered a cup of coffee and a sandwich. (주문했다)
⑤ He sent her a single red rose. (하나의)

출제율 95%

05 다음 두 문장에 공통으로 알맞은 것은?

- The plane was _____ to take off.
- What _____ going on a picnic?

① of
② with
③ from
④ along
⑤ about

출제율 100%

06 밑줄 친 부분과 의미가 가장 가까운 것을 고르시오.

He held a concert to collect money for charity.

① protect
② carry
③ raise
④ drop
⑤ create

07 다음 중 어법상 바른 것은? (출제율 100%)

① It is so hot to go out today.
② He was too poor that he couldn't buy a car.
③ The problem is so easy that he can solve.
④ Mike felt someone tapped him on the shoulder.
⑤ Harry heard his friend speak on the phone.

08 다음 중 어법상 <u>어색한</u> 것은? (출제율 85%)

① It was too late to save the man.
② Sarah is so sick that she can't go to school today.
③ I felt the ground shook once.
④ He listened to the teacher talk.
⑤ When I arrived there, I saw him leaving the room.

09 주어진 두 문장을 한 문장으로 바꿔 쓰시오. (접속사나 관계대명사 사용 금지) (출제율 90%)

(1) • I felt something.
  • It was biting my leg.
  ➡ _____

(2) • We enjoyed listening to the bird.
  • The bird sang.
  ➡ _____

(3) • Did you see the children?
  • The children were playing soccer on the ground.
  ➡ _____

10 다음 우리말에 맞게 주어진 어휘를 이용하여 영작하시오. (출제율 90%)

(1) Kate는 누군가가 그녀의 가방을 만지는 것을 느꼈다. (feel, touch, someone)
  ➡ _____

(2) 나는 네가 나를 부르는 것을 듣지 못했다. (hear, call)
  ➡ _____

(3) 나는 해변에서 그 소년이 모래성을 쌓고 있는 것을 보았다. (watch, a sandcastle, build)
  ➡ _____

(4) 나는 너무 어려서 그 영화를 볼 수 없었다. (so, young, watch the movie)
  ➡ _____

(5) 그녀는 첫 기차를 탈 만큼 충분히 일찍 일어났다. (get, early, enough, catch)
  ➡ _____

(6) 차가 너무 뜨거워서 마실 수가 없다. (the tea, hot, too)
  ➡ _____

11 다음 문장을 같은 뜻을 갖는 문장으로 바꿔 쓰시오. (출제율 95%)

(1) She is too shy to ask for help.
  ➡ _____

(2) The stars in the sky are too many to count.
  ➡ _____

(3) The problem is easy enough for him to solve.
  ➡ _____

[12~15] 다음 글을 읽고 물음에 답하시오.

"Are you sure you are not hungry, Grandma?" the boy asked, ⓐas he ate the hot soup.

"No, I'm not hungry. Don't worry about me." She picked up some Gimchi and chewed on it happily.

Mr. Kang watched them __(A)__ , and a warm feeling came over him. He thought up a plan ⓑto give the boy a free meal. When the woman was about to pay, Mr. Kang waved his hands and said, "No need, ma'am. In my restaurant, you don't pay if you're the 100th customer of the day." The woman and her grandson thanked Mr. Kang and left.

출제율 90%

12 위 글의 빈칸 (A)에 들어갈 말을 모두 고르시오.

① eaten   ② eat

③ ate   ④ to eat

⑤ eating

출제율 95%

13 위 글의 밑줄 친 ⓐas와 같은 의미로 쓰인 것을 고르시오.

① Do as you are told.

② It can be used as a chair.

③ She came up as I was speaking.

④ I regard him as a fool.

⑤ I love you as much as she does.

출제율 85%

14 위 글의 밑줄 친 ⓑ를 3형식으로 고치시오.

➡ _____

출제율 90%

15 위 글에서 할머니와 Mr. Kang이 보여준 배려의 행동을 각각 우리말로 쓰시오.

➡ 할머니: _____

  Mr. Kang : _____

  _____

[16~18] 다음 글을 읽고 물음에 답하시오.

A month later, Mr. Kang saw the boy in the street outside the restaurant. The boy was gathering stones.

"What are you doing?" asked Mr. Kang.

"I'm counting the number of customers who enter your restaurant. (①) Today is my grandma's birthday."

(②) 'He wants to be the 100th customer and treat his grandmother __ⓐ__ a bowl of Gukbap!' Mr. Kang said __ⓑ__ himself.

(③) Mr. Kang looked down. (④) He could see that the number of stones was not yet even fifty. (⑤) Mr. Kang went back into the restaurant and called his friends.

"Come to my restaurant now and bring everyone who works with you. There is a boy who needs your help."

출제율 90%

16 위 글의 빈칸 ⓐ와 ⓑ에 공통으로 들어갈 전치사를 쓰시오.

➡ _____

출제율 100%

17 위 글의 흐름으로 보아, 주어진 문장이 들어가기에 가장 적절한 곳은?

He had to do something to help the boy gather 100 stones.

①   ②   ③   ④   ⑤

18 위 글에서 알 수 있는 'Mr. Kang'의 성격으로 가장 알맞은 것을 고르시오. *출제율 95%*

① patient   ② considerate

③ funny   ④ curious

⑤ outgoing

[19~21] 다음 글을 읽고 물음에 답하시오.

People began to arrive at the restaurant. When the 99th customer arrived, Mr. Kang heard the boy say, "It's our ⓐturn, Grandma." Mr. Kang welcomed them and ⓑ할머니께 공짜 국밥 한 그릇을 제공했다.

19 위 글의 밑줄 친 ⓐturn과 같은 의미로 쓰인 것을 고르시오. *출제율 90%*

① The wheels of the car began to turn.

② Ann and Jane turn 21 in June.

③ Please wait your turn.

④ Why did she turn the wheel to the left?

⑤ The car made a turn to the right.

20 위 글의 밑줄 친 ⓑ의 우리말에 맞게 한 단어를 보충하여, 주어진 어휘를 알맞게 배열하시오. *출제율 95%*

> Gukbap / a / served / bowl / woman / of / the

➡ _____

21 위 글의 분위기로 가장 알맞은 것을 고르시오. *출제율 100%*

① moving   ② depressing

③ comic   ④ miserable

⑤ boring

[22~24] 다음 글을 읽고 물음에 답하시오.

ⓐMr. Kang watched them eat, and a warm feeling came over him. He thought up a plan to give the boy a ⓑfree meal. When the woman was about to pay, Mr. Kang waved his hands and said, "No need, ma'am. In my restaurant, you don't pay ⓒ그 날의 백 번째 손님이 되면." The woman and her grandson thanked Mr. Kang and left.

22 위 글의 밑줄 친 문장 ⓐ에서 알 수 있는 'Mr. Kang'의 심경으로 가장 알맞은 것을 고르시오. *출제율 100%*

① ashamed   ② excited

③ disappointed   ④ bored

⑤ touched

23 위 글의 밑줄 친 ⓑfree와 같은 의미로 쓰인 것을 고르시오. *출제율 90%*

① You are free to come and go.

② Keep Friday night free for my party.

③ She struggled to free herself.

④ Admission is free.

⑤ The researchers set the birds free.

24 위 글의 밑줄 친 ⓒ의 우리말에 맞게 주어진 어휘를 이용하여 8단어로 영작하시오. *출제율 95%*

> you're, 100th, the day

➡ _____

[25~27] 다음 글을 읽고 물음에 답하시오.

A month later, Mr. Kang saw the boy in the street outside the restaurant. The boy was gathering stones.

"What are ①you doing?" asked Mr. Kang.

"I'm counting the number of customers who enter your restaurant. Today is ②my grandma's birthday."

'③He wants to be the 100th customer and treat ④his grandmother to a bowl of Gukbap!' Mr. Kang said to (A)[him / himself].

Mr. Kang looked down. He could see that the number of stones (B)[was / were] not yet even fifty. He had to do something to help the boy (C)[gather / gathering] 100 stones. Mr. Kang went back into the restaurant and called ⑤his friends.

"Come to my restaurant now and bring everyone who works with you. There is a boy who needs your help."

25 밑줄 친 ①~⑤ 중에서 가리키는 대상이 나머지 넷과 <u>다른</u> 것은?

①   ②   ③   ④   ⑤

26 위 글의 괄호 (A)~(C)에서 어법상 알맞은 낱말을 골라 쓰시오.

➡ (A) _____ (B) _____ (C) _____

27 위 글의 내용과 일치하지 <u>않는</u> 것은?

① 한 달 후, 강 씨는 식당 밖 거리에서 그 남자아이를 보았다.

② 그 남자아이는 돌멩이를 모으고 있었다.

③ 그 남자아이는 식당에 들어가는 손님들의 수를 세고 있었다.

④ 식당의 손님은 이미 오십 명을 넘었다.

⑤ 강 씨는 남자아이가 돌멩이 백 개를 모으는 것을 돕기 위해 식당으로 되돌아가 그의 친구들에게 전화했다.

[28~30] 다음 글을 읽고 물음에 답하시오.

People began ⓐto arrive at the restaurant. When the 99th customer arrived, Mr. Kang heard the boy say, "It's our turn, Grandma." Mr. Kang welcomed ⓑthem and served the woman a __(A)__ bowl of Gukbap.

"Are you sure you're not hungry?" the woman asked the boy. The boy chewed loudly on some Gimchi and said with a smile, "No, I'm not hungry, Grandma. Don't worry about me. Happy birthday!"

28 아래 〈보기〉에서 위 글의 밑줄 친 ⓐto arrive와 문법적 쓰임이 같은 것의 개수를 고르시오.

┌─── 보기 ───┐
① There is no water to drink.

② To see is to believe.

③ To tell a lie again, you will be punished.

④ He must be foolish to say such a thing.

⑤ He promised to buy me new shoes.
└─────────┘

① 1개   ② 2개   ③ 3개   ④ 4개   ⑤ 5개

29 위 글의 밑줄 친 ⓑthem이 가리키는 것을 영어로 쓰시오.

➡ _____

31 위 글의 종류로 알맞은 것을 고르시오.

① e-mail　　　② article
③ essay　　　④ diary
⑤ review

30 주어진 영영풀이를 참고하여 빈칸 (A)에 철자 f로 시작하는 단어를 쓰시오.

> costing nothing

➡ _____

32 위 글의 내용과 일치하지 <u>않는</u> 것은?

① 한 달 전에 한 부인이 그녀의 손자에게 줄 국밥 한 그릇을 주문했다.
② Mr. Kang은 그 부인이 그 날의 백 번째 손님이기 때문에 돈을 내지 않아도 된다고 말했다.
③ 오늘 소년은 국밥을 먹고 싶다고 Mr. Kang에게 말했다.
④ Mr. Kang은 소년을 그 날의 백 번째 손님으로 만들기 위해 친구들에게 전화했다.
⑤ 아흔아홉 번째 손님이 도착했을 때 소년과 할머니가 들어왔다.

[31~32] 다음 글을 읽고 물음에 답하시오.

> 20XX. 10. 15.
> A month ago, a woman ordered a bowl of Gukbap for her grandson. She was too poor to pay for two bowls. A warm feeling came over me. I told her not to pay because she was the 100th customer of the day.
> Today I saw the boy count the number of customers who entered my restaurant. He wanted to treat his grandmother to a free bowl of Gukbap. I called my friends to make the boy the 100th customer of the day. When the 99th customer arrived, the boy and his grandmother came in. I welcomed them and served them a free bowl of Gukbap.
>
> I= Mr. Kang

[33~34] 다음 글을 읽고 물음에 답하시오.

> Mr. Kang was ⓐmoved and wanted to give the boy ⓑ공짜 국밥 한 그릇. He said to the boy, "You don't pay if today is someone's birthday," and served the boy ⓑ공짜 국밥 한 그릇.

33 위 글의 밑줄 친 ⓐmoved와 바꿔 쓸 수 있는 단어를 쓰시오.

➡ _____

34 위 글의 밑줄 친 ⓑ의 우리말을 다섯 단어로 쓰시오.

➡ _____

MEMO

중간 + 기말
plus
영어 기출문제집

영어 중 2

시사 | 박준언

Best Collection

내용문의 중등영어발전소 적중100 편집부 TEL 070-7707-0457

INSIGHT
on the textbook

교과서 파헤치기

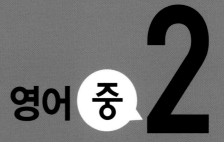

영어 중 2

시사 | 박준언

INSIGHT
on the textbook

교과서 파헤치기

※ 다음 영어를 우리말로 쓰시오.

01 tourist	22 prefer
02 care	23 helpful
03 abroad	24 stadium
04 wave	25 movement
05 excuse	26 ceiling
06 tour	27 slide
07 traditional	28 purple
08 experience	29 Vietnamese
09 historic	30 design
10 column	31 near
11 island	32 theater
12 roll	33 dish
13 capital	34 lizard
14 view	35 be full of
15 cheer	36 across from
16 work	37 be famous for
17 language	38 try on
18 unique	39 be known for
19 match	40 put off
20 shine	41 on foot
21 careful	42 cheer for
	43 far from

※ 다음 우리말을 영어로 쓰시오.

01 빛나다

02 역사적인

03 경험; 경험하다

04 섬

05 전통적인

06 구르다, 굴리다

07 돌봄, 보살핌

08 미끄러지다, 활주하다

09 근처에

10 도움이 되는

11 ~을 용서하다

12 보라색

13 여행객

14 조심하는, 주의 깊은

15 흔들다; 파도

16 여행, 관광하다

17 전망, 경치

18 환호하다; 환호

19 음식, 접시

20 경기, 시합

21 수도

22 설계하다

23 동작

24 천장

25 도마뱀

26 기둥

27 선호하다

28 일하다; 작품

29 언어

30 외국으로(에서)

31 독특한

32 극장

33 정거장; 멈추다

34 베트남어; 베트남의

35 ~의 맞은편에

36 ~으로 가득 차다

37 ~의 위에, ~의 꼭대기에

38 ~을 응원하다

39 (시간, 날짜를) 미루다

40 ~로부터 멀리

41 ~로 알려져 있다

42 입어 보다

43 ~로 유명하다

※ 다음 영영풀이에 알맞은 단어를 <보기>에서 골라 쓴 후, 우리말 뜻을 쓰시오.

1 _____ : to produce bright light: _____

2 _____ : in or to a foreign country: _____

3 _____ : to move along smoothly: _____

4 _____ : the upper inside surface of a room: _____

5 _____ : a mixture of blue and red color: _____

6 _____ : the main city of a country where its government is: _____

7 _____ : a reptile that has a rough skin and a long tail: _____

8 _____ : relating to the language, people or culture of Spain: _____

9 _____ : to give a shout out of pleasure, praise, or support: _____

10 _____ : relating to the language, people or culture of Vietnam: _____

11 _____ : a building with a big screen or stage where many people watch movies
        or plays: _____

12 _____ : an outlook onto, or picture of a scene: _____

13 _____ : a spicy Indian food with meat and vegetables in sauce: _____

14 _____ : to like something or someone better than another: _____

15 _____ : a journey for pleasure during which various places of interest are visited:
        _____

16 _____ : to forgive someone for something bad that they have done, especially
        something that is not very serious: _____

보기

theater	abroad	shine	prefer
view	cheer	tour	purple
curry	lizard	capital	Vietnamese
Spanish	ceiling	slide	excuse

※ 다음 우리말과 일치하도록 빈칸에 알맞은 말을 쓰시오.

Listen & Speak 1 A

1. **B:** _____ me. _____ the Picasso Museum _____ here?

   G: Yes. It's not _____ _____ here.

   B: _____ I _____ _____ ?

   G: _____ one block and _____ _____ . It's _____

   _____ _____ .

2. **B:** Sally, I _____ _____ _____ some candies for Halloween.

   _____ I _____ them?

   G: You can _____ _____ _____ Wendy's Candy Shop.

   B: _____ _____ _____ ?

   G: _____ _____ two _____ and turn right. It's _____

   _____ _____ _____ .

Listen & Speak 1 B

1. **A:** _____ . _____ _____ _____ the park?

   B: _____ _____ _____ _____ and turn left. It's _____

   _____ _____ .

2. **A:** Excuse me. _____ _____ the school?

   B: Go _____ _____ _____ and turn left. _____ _____

   your right. _____ _____ _____ the restaurant.

Listen & Talk 2 A

1. **B:** _____ really hot here in Thailand. _____ _____ to the

   night market and _____ some _____ _____ _____ .

   G: Sounds _____ . _____ do we _____ _____ ?

   B: We can go _____ _____ _____ .

   _____ _____ _____ _____ ?

   G: I _____ the bus.

2. **G:** _____ _____ this long dress _____ ?

   M: It is an Ao dai, a _____ of _____ _____ from Vietnam.

   G: Can I _____ _____ _____ ?

   M: Sure. _____ _____ _____ _____ , the purple one or the

   _____ ?

   G: The _____ _____ , please.

1. **B:** 실례할게. 이 근처에 피카소 박물관이 있니?
   G: 응, 여기서 멀지 않아.
   B: 그곳에 어떻게 가니?
   G: 한 블록 직진한 후 좌회전해. 오른편에 있어.

2. **B:** Sally야, 나는 할로윈에 필요한 사탕을 사야 해. 그것들을 어디서 살 수 있니?
   G: 넌 그것들을 Wendy's 사탕 가게에서 살 수 있어.
   B: 그곳은 어디에 있니?
   G: 두 블록 직진한 후 우회전해. 도서관 맞은편에 있어.

1. **A:** 실례합니다. 공원이 어디에 있나요?
   B: 두 블록 직진한 후 좌회전하세요. 오른편에 있어요.

2. **A:** 실례합니다. 학교가 어디에 있나요?
   B: 한 블록 직진한 후 좌회전하세요. 오른편에 있어요. 식당 맞은편이에요.

1. **B:** 태국은 정말 더워. 야시장에 가서 신선한 과일 주스를 마시자.
   G: 좋아. 우리는 그곳에 어떻게 가지?
   B: 우리는 걸어가거나 버스를 탈 수 있어. 어떤 것을 선호하니?
   G: 나는 버스를 선호해.

2. **G:** 이 긴 드레스를 뭐라고 부르나요?
   M: 그것은 베트남 전통 의상의 한 종류인 아오자이야.
   G: 제가 한 번 입어볼 수 있나요?
   M: 물론이지. 너는 보라색과 노란색 중 어떤 것을 선호하니?
   G: 보라색이요.

Listen & Talk 2 B

1. A: _____ _____ _____ _____, hamburgers or spaghetti?

   B: I _____ _____.

2. A: _____ _____ _____ _____ , curry _____ paella?

   B: I _____ _____.

1. A: 햄버거와 스파게티 중 어느 것을
   선호하니?
   B: 나는 햄버거를 선호해.

2. A: 카레와 파에야 중 어느 것을 선호
   하니?
   B: 나는 파에야를 선호해.

Conversation A

M: _____ _____ London City Tour. Today, _____ _____
famous places in London. Can you _____ the London Eye? It's
_____ _____ _____. It's a Ferris wheel _____ the River
Thames. The _____ _____ the London Eye is _____. Many
people visit it _____ _____.

M: 런던 시티 투어에 오신 걸 환영합니
다. 오늘 우리는 런던에서 유명한 장
소들을 방문할 거예요. 런던 아이
가 보이죠? 오른편에 있어요. 그것
은 템스강 근처에 있는 대관람차예
요. 런던 아이에서의 전망은 놀라워
요. 매년 많은 사람들이 그곳을 방문
해요.

Conversation B

Staff: _____ _____ I _____ you?

Hana's mom: We _____ _____ _____ _____ a good _____ _____
   London.

Hana: Where is the _____ _____ _____ _____ _____ _____?

Staff: We have two _____ _____. The London Eye is a Ferris
   wheel and the Sky Garden is a glass garden _____ _____
   _____ a tall building. _____ _____ you _____?

Hana's mom: Hmm... I _____ the London Eye.

Hana: _____, _____.

Staff: Good choice. You can _____ there _____ _____.

Hana's mom: _____ is the _____ _____?

Staff: Go _____ _____ and _____ _____. It's
   _____ _____ _____. Have a good trip!

Hana: Wow, I _____ all of London. Look! _____
   _____ a big clock.

Hana's mom: _____ _____ that's Big Ben. _____ _____
   _____ _____ and _____ it _____?

Hana: That _____ great.

직원: 무엇을 도와드릴까요?
엄마: 우리는 런던의 멋진 경치를 즐기
고 싶어요.
하나: 가기에 가장 좋은 장소는 어디인
가요?
직원: 두 곳이 있습니다. 런던 아이는 대
관람차이고 스카이 가든은 높은
건물 꼭대기에 있는 유리 정원이
에요. 어느 것을 선호하시나요?
엄마: 흠... 저는 런던 아이가 좋아요.
하나: 저도요.
직원: 좋은 선택이에요. 그곳에 버스로
갈 수 있답니다.
엄마: 가장 가까운 버스 정거장은 어디
있나요?
직원: 여기서 한 블록 직진한 후 오른쪽
으로 도세요. 왼편에 있어요. 좋은
여행하세요!
하나: 와, 런던 전체를 다 볼 수 있어요.
보세요! 커다란 시계가 있어요.
엄마: 내 생각에 저것은 빅벤 같아. 우리
나중에 가서 그곳을 방문해 볼래?
하나: 좋아요.

※ 다음 우리말에 맞도록 대화를 영어로 쓰시오.

 해석

Listen & Speak 1 A

1. B: _____

   G: _____

   B: _____

   G: _____

2. B: _____

   G: _____

   B: _____

   G: _____

1. B: 실례할게. 이 근처에 피카소 박물관이 있니?
   G: 응, 여기서 멀지 않아.
   B: 그곳에 어떻게 가니?
   G: 한 블록 직진한 후 좌회전해. 오른편에 있어.

2. B: Sally야, 나는 할로윈에 필요한 사탕을 사야 해. 그것들을 어디서 살 수 있니?
   G: 넌 그것들을 Wendy's 사탕 가게에서 살 수 있어.
   B: 그곳은 어디에 있니?
   G: 두 블록 직진한 후 우회전해. 도서관 맞은편에 있어.

Listen & Speak 1 B

1. A: _____

   B: _____

2. A: _____

   B: _____

      _____

1. A: 실례합니다. 공원이 어디에 있나요?
   B: 두 블록 직진한 후 좌회전하세요. 오른편에 있어요.

2. A: 실례합니다. 학교가 어디에 있나요?
   B: 한 블록 직진한 후 좌회전하세요. 오른편에 있어요. 식당 맞은편이에요.

Listen & Talk 2 A

1. B: _____

      _____

   G: _____

   B: _____

   G: _____

2. G: _____

   M: _____

   G: _____

   M: _____

   G: _____

1. B: 태국은 정말 더워. 야시장에 가서 신선한 과일 주스를 마시자.
   G: 좋아. 우리는 그곳에 어떻게 가지?
   B: 우리는 걸어가거나 버스를 탈 수 있어. 어떤 것을 선호하니?
   G: 나는 버스를 선호해.

2. G: 이 긴 드레스를 뭐라고 부르나요?
   M: 그것은 베트남 전통 의상의 한 종류인 아오자이야.
   G: 제가 한 번 입어볼 수 있나요?
   M: 물론이지. 너는 보라색과 노란색 중 어떤 것을 선호하니?
   G: 보라색이요.

Listen & Talk 2 B

1. A: _____

   B: _____

2. A: _____

   B: _____

1. A: 햄버거와 스파게티 중 어느 것을 선호하니?
   B: 나는 햄버거를 선호해.

2. A: 카레와 파에야 중 어느 것을 선호하니?
   B: 나는 파에야를 선호해.

Conversation A

M: _____

_____

_____

_____

M: 런던 시티 투어에 오신 걸 환영합니다. 오늘 우리는 런던에서 유명한 장소들을 방문할 거예요. 런던 아이가 보이죠? 오른편에 있어요. 그것은 템스강 근처에 있는 대관람차예요. 런던 아이에서의 전망은 놀라워요. 매년 많은 사람들이 그곳을 방문해요.

Conversation B

Staff: _____

Hana's mom: _____

Hana: _____

Staff: _____

_____

Hana's mom: _____

Hana: _____

Staff: _____

Hana's mom: _____

Staff: _____

Hana: _____

Hana's mom: _____

Hana: _____

직원: 무엇을 도와드릴까요?
엄마: 우리는 런던의 멋진 경치를 즐기고 싶어요.
하나: 가기에 가장 좋은 장소는 어디인가요?
직원: 두 곳이 있습니다. 런던 아이는 대관람차이고 스카이 가든은 높은 건물 꼭대기에 있는 유리 정원이에요. 어느 것을 선호하시나요?
엄마: 흠... 저는 런던 아이가 좋아요.
하나: 저도요.
직원: 좋은 선택이에요. 그곳에 버스로 갈 수 있답니다.
엄마: 가장 가까운 버스 정거장은 어디 있나요?
직원: 여기서 한 블록 직진한 후 오른쪽으로 도세요. 왼편에 있어요. 좋은 여행하세요!
하나: 와, 런던 전체를 다 볼 수 있어요. 보세요! 커다란 시계가 있어요.
엄마: 내 생각에 저것은 빅벤 같아. 우리 나중에 가서 그곳을 방문해 볼래?
하나: 좋아요.

Step1

※ 다음 우리말과 일치하도록 빈칸에 알맞은 것을 골라 쓰시오.

1 My _____ _____ in Spain – _____ Park Jinwoo

    A. Days   B. by   C. happy

2 My family _____ _____ Spain _____ summer.

    A. to   B. traveled   C. this

3 Spain is _____ _____ lots _____ tourists.

    A. of   B. by   C. loved

4 We _____ many _____ _____.

    A. places   B. visited   C. interesting

5 _____ _____ started _____ Madrid.

    A. in   B. trip   C. our

6 Madrid is the _____ and is _____ _____ soccer.

    A. for   B. capital   C. famous

7 We _____ to a stadium to _____ a soccer _____.

    A. match   B. watch   C. went

8 My sister and I were _____ because we could watch some of the _____ _____ _____ soccer player.

    A. most   B. excited   C. famous   D. world's

9 The stadium was _____ _____ soccer _____.

    A. of   B. full   C. fans

10 As we watched the match, we cheered _____ _____ songs, _____ our hands, and _____ with the other fans.

    A. waving   B. singing   C. shouting   D. by

11 _____ we _____ Madrid, we _____ to Seville.

    A. went   B. after   C. toured

12 _____ we _____ _____ the city, we saw many historic buildings.

    A. walked   B. while   C. around

13 We _____ a flamenco _____ and _____ a flamenco dance.

    A. museum   B. watched   C. visited

14 A woman _____ a red dress was _____ the flamenco _____ wonderful _____.

    A. with   B. in   C. movements   D. dancing

---

1 스페인에서의 행복한 날들 – 박진우

2 나의 가족은 이번 여름에 스페인을 여행했다.

3 스페인은 수많은 관광객들에게 사랑받는다.

4 우리는 여러 흥미로운 장소를 방문했다.

5 우리의 여행은 마드리드에서 시작했다.

6 마드리드는 수도이며 축구로 유명하다.

7 우리는 축구 경기를 보기 위해서 경기장으로 갔다.

8 나의 여동생과 나는 세계에서 가장 유명한 축구 선수 몇몇을 볼 수 있었기 때문에 신이 났다.

9 경기장은 축구 팬들로 가득 차 있었다.

10 우리는 경기를 보는 동안 노래를 부르고, 손을 흔들고, 다른 팬들과 함께 소리를 치며 응원을 했다.

11 마드리드를 여행하고 난 후, 우리는 세비야로 갔다.

12 우리는 도시를 걸어다니는 동안, 역사상 중요한 많은 건물들을 보았다.

13 우리는 플라멩코 박물관을 방문해서 플라멩코 춤을 보았다.

14 빨간 드레스를 입은 여자가 멋진 동작으로 플라멩코를 추고 있었다.

15 _____ dinner, we _____ paella.

    A. ate   B. for

16 It is a _____ Spanish _____ _____ rice, vegetables, meat, and seafood.

    A. with   B. dish   C. traditional

17 It _____ _____ fried rice _____ Korea.

    A. in   B. like   C. tasted

18 It was _____ delicious _____ we _____ enjoyed it.

    A. that   B. so   C. all

19 In Barcelona, we _____ a _____ _____ Park Guell and Sagrada Familia.

    A. of   B. tour   C. took

20 _____ were _____ _____ Antoni Gaudi.

    A. designed   B. both   C. by

21 In Park Guell, we saw some of Gaudi's _____ works _____ a _____ lizard.

    A. like   B. colorful   C. creative

22 _____ Park Guell, we _____ Sagrada Familia.

    A. visited   B. after

23 _____ on the building started in 1883 and is still _____ _____ today.

    A. going   B. work   C. on

24 I was _____ by _____ size and _____ design.

    A. unique   B. impressed   C. its

25 The _____ inside Sagrada Familia _____ _____ the night sky _____ bright stars.

    A. with   B. shone   C. ceiling   D. like

26 Its stone _____ _____ _____ big trees.

    A. like   B. stood   C. colomns

27 At Park Guell and Sagrada Familia I could _____ Gaudi's _____ and his _____ of _____.

    A. feel   B. nature   C. love   D. creativity

28 _____ in Spain was a _____ _____.

    A. experience   B. wonderful   C. traveling

29 _____ I was there, I learned _____ _____ about Spain.

    A. lot   B. while   C. a

30 I want to _____ the _____ _____.

    A. country   B. visit   C. again

---

15 저녁 식사로 우리는 파에야를 먹었다.

16 그것은 쌀과 채소, 고기, 해산물이 들어간 전통적인 스페인 요리이다.

17 그것은 한국의 볶음밥과 같은 맛이 났다.

18 너무 맛있어서 우리 모두는 그것을 즐겼다.

19 바르셀로나에서 우리는 구엘 공원과 사그라다 파밀리아를 둘러보았다.

20 두 곳 모두 Antoni Gaudi에 의해 설계되었다.

21 구엘 공원에서 우리는 형형색색의 도마뱀과 같은 몇몇 Gaudi의 창의적인 작품들을 보았다.

22 구엘 공원을 본 다음, 우리는 사그라다 파밀리아를 방문했다.

23 건물 공사는 1883년에 시작되었고 오늘날까지도 여전히 진행 중이다.

24 나는 건물의 크기와 독특한 디자인에 감명 받았다.

25 사그라다 파밀라아 안의 천장은 밝은 별이 있는 밤하늘처럼 빛났다.

26 돌기둥은 큰 나무처럼 서 있었다.

27 구엘 공원과 사그라다 파밀리아에서 나는 Gaudi의 창의성과 자연에 대한 사랑을 느낄 수 있었다.

28 스페인 여행은 훌륭한 경험이었다.

29 나는 그곳에서 스페인에 대해 많은 것을 배웠다.

30 나는 그 나라를 다시 방문하고 싶다.

※ 다음 우리말과 일치하도록 빈칸에 알맞은 말을 쓰시오.

1 My _____ _____ in Spain – _____ Park Jinwoo

2 My family _____ _____ _____ this summer.

3 Spain _____ _____ _____ _____ _____ _____ tourists.

4 We _____ many _____ _____.

5 _____ _____ _____ _____ Madrid.

6 Madrid is the _____ and _____ _____ _____ soccer.

7 We went to a stadium _____ _____ a _____ _____.

8 My sister and I _____ _____ we could watch some of _____ _____ _____ _____ _____ _____ _____.

9 The stadium _____ _____ _____ soccer fans.

10 As we watched the match, we _____ _____ _____ songs, _____ our hands, and _____ with the _____ _____.

11 _____ we _____ Madrid, we _____ _____ Seville.

12 _____ we _____ _____ the city, we saw _____ _____ _____.

13 We _____ a flamenco museum and _____ a flamenco dance.

14 A woman _____ _____ _____ _____ _____ the flamenco _____ _____ _____.

1 스페인에서의 행복한 날들 – 박진우

2 나의 가족은 이번 여름에 스페인을 여행했다.

3 스페인은 수많은 관광객들에게 사랑받는다.

4 우리는 여러 흥미로운 장소를 방문했다.

5 우리의 여행은 마드리드에서 시작했다.

6 마드리드는 수도이며 축구로 유명하다.

7 우리는 축구 경기를 보기 위해서 경기장으로 갔다.

8 나의 여동생과 나는 세계에서 가장 유명한 축구 선수 몇몇을 볼 수 있었기 때문에 신이 났다.

9 경기장은 축구 팬들로 가득 차 있었다.

10 우리는 경기를 보는 동안 노래를 부르고, 손을 흔들고, 다른 팬들과 함께 소리를 치며 응원을 했다.

11 마드리드를 여행하고 난 후, 우리는 세비야로 갔다.

12 우리는 도시를 걸어다니는 동안, 역사상 중요한 많은 건물들을 보았다.

13 우리는 플라멩코 박물관을 방문해서 플라멩코 춤을 보았다.

14 빨간 드레스를 입은 여자가 멋진 동작으로 플라멩코를 추고 있었다.

15 _____, we _____ paella.

16 It is a _____ _____ _____ _____ rice, vegetables, _____, and _____.

17 It _____ _____ _____ _____ in Korea.

18 It was _____ delicious _____ we _____ _____ it.

19 In Barcelona, we _____ _____ _____ _____ Park Guell and Sagrada Familia.

20 Both _____ _____ _____ Antoni Gaudi.

21 In Park Guell, we saw some of Gaudi's _____ _____ _____ a _____ _____.

22 _____ Park Guell, we _____ Sagrada Familia.

23 _____ _____ the building started in 1883 and _____ _____ _____ _____ today.

24 I _____ _____ _____ _____ _____ _____ and unique design.

25 The ceiling inside Sagrada Familia _____ _____ the night sky _____ _____ _____.

26 Its _____ _____ _____ _____ big trees.

27 At Park Guell and Sagrada Familia I _____ _____ Gaudi's _____ and _____ _____ _____ _____.

28 _____ in Spain was _____ _____ _____.

29 _____ I was there, I learned _____ _____ about Spain.

30 I want _____ _____ the country again.

---

15 저녁 식사로 우리는 파에야를 먹었다.

16 그것은 쌀과 채소, 고기, 해산물이 들어간 전통적인 스페인 요리이다.

17 그것은 한국의 볶음밥과 같은 맛이 났다.

18 너무 맛있어서 우리 모두는 그것을 즐겼다.

19 바르셀로나에서 우리는 구엘 공원과 사그라다 파밀리아를 둘러보았다.

20 두 곳 모두 Antoni Gaudi에 의해 설계되었다.

21 구엘 공원에서 우리는 형형색색의 도마뱀과 같은 몇몇 Gaudi의 창의적인 작품들을 보았다.

22 구엘 공원을 본 다음, 우리는 사그라다 파밀리아를 방문했다.

23 건물 공사는 1883년에 시작되었고 오늘날까지도 여전히 진행 중이다.

24 나는 건물의 크기와 독특한 디자인에 감명 받았다.

25 사그라다 파밀라아 안의 천장은 밝은 별이 있는 밤하늘처럼 빛났다.

26 돌기둥은 큰 나무처럼 서 있었다.

27 구엘 공원과 사그라다 파밀리아에서 나는 Gaudi의 창의성과 자연에 대한 사랑을 느낄 수 있었다.

28 스페인 여행은 훌륭한 경험이었다.

29 나는 그곳에서 스페인에 대해 많은 것을 배웠다.

30 나는 그 나라를 다시 방문하고 싶다.

※ 다음 문장을 우리말로 쓰시오.

1   My Happy Days in Spain – by Park Jinwoo

➡ _____

2   My family traveled to Spain this summer.

➡ _____

3   Spain is loved by lots of tourists.

➡ _____

4   We visited many interesting places.

➡ _____

5   Our trip started in Madrid.

➡ _____

6   Madrid is the capital and is famous for soccer.

➡ _____

7   We went to a stadium to watch a soccer match.

➡ _____

8   My sister and I were excited because we could watch some of the world's most famous soccer players.

➡ _____

9   The stadium was full of soccer fans.

➡ _____

10   As we watched the match, we cheered by singing songs, waving our hands, and shouting with the other fans.

➡ _____

11   After we toured Madrid, we went to Seville.

➡ _____

12   While we walked around the city, we saw many historic buildings.

➡ _____

13   We visited a flamenco museum and watched a flamenco dance.

➡ _____

14   A woman in a red dress was dancing the flamenco with wonderful movements.

➡ _____

15   For dinner, we ate paella.

➡ _____

16   It is a traditional Spanish dish with rice, vegetables, meat, and seafood.

➡ _____

17 It tasted like fried rice in Korea.

➡ _____

18 It was so delicious that we all enjoyed it.

➡ _____

19 In Barcelona, we took a tour of Park Guell and Sagrada Familia.

➡ _____

20 Both were designed by Antoni Gaudi.

➡ _____

21 In Park Guell, we saw some of Gaudi's creative works like a colorful lizard.

➡ _____

22 After Park Guell, we visited Sagrada Familia.

➡ _____

23 Work on the building started in 1883 and is still going on today.

➡ _____

24 I was impressed by its size and unique design.

➡ _____

25 The ceiling inside Sagrada Familia shone like the night sky with bright stars.

➡ _____

26 Its stone columns stood like big trees.

➡ _____

27 At Park Guell and Sagrada Familia I could feel Gaudi's creativity and his love of nature.

➡ _____

28 Traveling in Spain was a wonderful experience.

➡ _____

29 While I was there, I learned a lot about Spain.

➡ _____

30 I want to visit the country again.

➡ _____

※ 다음 괄호 안의 단어들을 우리말에 맞도록 바르게 배열하시오.

1 (happy / my / in / Days / by / – / Spain / Jinwoo / Park)
➡ _____

2 (family / my / to / traveled / Spain / summer. / this)
➡ _____

3 (is / Spain / by / loved / lots / tourists. / of)
➡ _____

4 (visited / we / interesting / many / places.)
➡ _____

5 (trip / our / Madrid. / in / started)
➡ _____

6 (is / Madrid / capital / the / is / and / soccer. / for / famous)
➡ _____

7 (went / we / a / to / stadium / watch / to / match. / soccer / a)
➡ _____

8 (sister / my / and / were / I / excited / we / because / could / some / watch / of / world's / the / famous / most / / players. / soccer)
➡ _____

9 (stadium / the / full / was / fans. / soccer / of)
➡ _____

10 (we / as / the / watched / match, / cheered / we / singing / by / songs, / waving / hands, / our / and / with / shouting / the / fans. / other)
➡ _____

11 (we / after / Madrid, / toured / went / we / Seville. / to)
➡ _____

12 (we / while / walked / the / around / city, / saw / we / many / buildings. / historic)
➡ _____

13 (visited / we / flamenco / a / museum / and / a / watched / dance. / flamenco)
➡ _____

14 (woman / a / in / red / a / dress / dancing / was / flamenco / the / movements. / wonderful / with)
➡ _____

1 스페인에서의 행복한 날들 – 박진우
2 나의 가족은 이번 여름에 스페인을 여행했다.
3 스페인은 수많은 관광객들에게 사랑받는다.
4 우리는 여러 흥미로운 장소를 방문했다.
5 우리의 여행은 마드리드에서 시작했다.
6 마드리드는 수도이며 축구로 유명하다.
7 우리는 축구 경기를 보기 위해서 경기장으로 갔다.
8 나의 여동생과 나는 세계에서 가장 유명한 축구 선수 몇몇을 볼 수 있었기 때문에 신이 났다.
9 경기장은 축구 팬들로 가득 차 있었다.
10 우리는 경기를 보는 동안 노래를 부르고, 손을 흔들고, 다른 팬들과 함께 소리를 치며 응원을 했다.
11 마드리드를 여행하고 난 후, 우리는 세비야로 갔다.
12 우리는 도시를 걸어다니는 동안, 역사상 중요한 많은 건물들을 보았다.
13 우리는 플라멩코 박물관을 방문해서 플라멩코 춤을 보았다.
14 빨간 드레스를 입은 여자가 멋진 동작으로 플라멩코를 추고 있었다.

15 (dinner, / for / paella. / ate / we)
➡ _____

16 (is / it / Spanish / traditional / a / with / dish / rice, / meat, / vegetables, / seafood. / and)
➡ _____

17 (tasted / it / fried / like / Korea. / in / rice)
➡ _____

18 (was / it / delicious / so / that / all / we / it. / enjoyed)
➡ _____

19 (Barcelona, / in / took / we / tour / a / Park / of / and / Guell / Familia. / Sagrada)
➡ _____

20 (were / both / by / designed / Gaudi. / Antoni)
➡ _____

21 (Guell, / Park / in / saw / we / of / some / creative / Gaudi's / works / a / like / lizard. / colorful)
➡ _____

22 (Park / after / Guell, / visited / we / Familia. / Sagrada)
➡ _____

23 (on / work / building / the / in / started / 1883 / is / and / going / still / today. / on)
➡ _____

24 (was / I / by / impressed / size / its / and / design. / unique)
➡ _____

25 (ceiling / the / Sagrada / inside / Familia / like / shone / night / the / sky / stars. / bright / with)
➡ _____

26 (stone / its / stood / columns / trees. / big / like)
➡ _____

27 (Park / at / and / Guell / Familia / Sagrada / could / I / Gaudi's / feel / creativity / his / and / of / nature. / love)
➡ _____

28 (in / traveling / Spain / was / experiece. / wonderful / a)
➡ _____

29 (I / while / there, / was / learned / I / about / a / Spain. / lot)
➡ _____

30 (I / to / want / the / visit / again. / country)
➡ _____

15 저녁 식사로 우리는 파에야를 먹었다.

16 그것은 쌀과 채소, 고기, 해산물이 들어간 전통적인 스페인 요리이다.

17 그것은 한국의 볶음밥과 같은 맛이 났다.

18 너무 맛있어서 우리 모두는 그것을 즐겼다.

19 바르셀로나에서 우리는 구엘 공원과 사그라다 파밀리아를 둘러보았다.

20 두 곳 모두 Antoni Gaudi에 의해 설계되었다.

21 구엘 공원에서 우리는 형형색색의 도마뱀과 같은 몇몇 Gaudi의 창의적인 작품들을 보았다.

22 구엘 공원을 본 다음, 우리는 사그라다 파밀리아를 방문했다.

23 건물 공사는 1883년에 시작되었고 오늘날까지도 여전히 진행 중이다.

24 나는 건물의 크기와 독특한 디자인에 감명 받았다.

25 사그라다 파밀리아 안의 천장은 밝은 별이 있는 밤하늘처럼 빛났다.

26 돌기둥은 큰 나무처럼 서 있었다.

27 구엘 공원과 사그라다 파밀리아에서 나는 Gaudi의 창의성과 자연에 대한 사랑을 느낄 수 있었다.

28 스페인 여행은 훌륭한 경험이었다.

29 나는 그곳에서 스페인에 대해 많은 것을 배웠다.

30 나는 그 나라를 다시 방문하고 싶다.

※ 다음 우리말을 영어로 쓰시오.

1 스페인에서의 행복한 날들 – 박진우

➡ _____

2 나의 가족은 이번 여름에 스페인을 여행했다.

➡ _____

3 스페인은 수많은 관광객들에게 사랑받는다.

➡ _____

4 우리는 여러 흥미로운 장소를 방문했다.

➡ _____

5 우리의 여행은 마드리드에서 시작했다.

➡ _____

6 마드리드는 수도이며 축구로 유명하다.

➡ _____

7 우리는 축구 경기를 보기 위해서 경기장으로 갔다.

➡ _____

8 나의 여동생과 나는 세계에서 가장 유명한 축구 선수 몇몇을 볼 수 있었기 때문에 신이 났다.

➡ _____

9 경기장은 축구 팬들로 가득 차 있었다.

➡ _____

10 우리는 경기를 보는 동안 노래를 부르고, 손을 흔들고, 다른 팬들과 함께 소리를 치며 응원을 했다.

➡ _____

11 마드리드를 여행하고 난 후, 우리는 세비야로 갔다.

➡ _____

12 우리는 도시를 걸어다니는 동안, 역사상 중요한 많은 건물들을 보았다.

➡ _____

13 우리는 플라멩코 박물관을 방문해서 플라멩코 춤을 보았다.

➡ _____

14 빨간 드레스를 입은 여자가 멋진 동작으로 플라멩코를 추고 있었다.

➡ _____

15 저녁 식사로 우리는 파에야를 먹었다.

➡ _____

16 그것은 쌀과 채소, 고기, 해산물이 들어간 전통적인 스페인 요리이다.

➡ _____

17 그것은 한국의 볶음밥과 같은 맛이 났다.

➡ _____

18 너무 맛있어서 우리 모두는 그것을 즐겼다.

➡ _____

19 바르셀로나에서 우리는 구엘 공원과 사그라다 파밀리아를 둘러보았다.

➡ _____

20 두 곳 모두 Antoni Gaudi에 의해 설계되었다.

➡ _____

21 구엘 공원에서 우리는 형형색색의 도마뱀과 같은 몇몇 Gaudi의 창의적인 작품들을 보았다.

➡ _____

22 구엘 공원을 본 다음, 우리는 사그라다 파밀리아를 방문했다.

➡ _____

23 건물 공사는 1883년에 시작되었고 오늘날까지도 여전히 진행 중이다.

➡ _____

24 나는 건물의 크기와 독특한 디자인에 감명 받았다.

➡ _____

25 사그라다 파밀라아 안의 천장은 밝은 별이 있는 밤하늘처럼 빛났다.

➡ _____

26 돌기둥은 큰 나무처럼 서 있었다.

➡ _____

27 구엘 공원과 사그라다 파밀리아에서 나는 Gaudi의 창의성과 자연에 대한 사랑을 느낄 수 있었다.

➡ _____

28 스페인 여행은 훌륭한 경험이었다.

➡ _____

29 나는 그곳에서 스페인에 대해 많은 것을 배웠다.

➡ _____

30 나는 그 나라를 다시 방문하고 싶다.

➡ _____

※ 다음 우리말과 일치하도록 빈칸에 알맞은 말을 쓰시오.

Enjoy Writing

1. _____ _____ do you _____ _____ Vietnam?

2. The _____ _____ _____ is Hanoi. Vietnamese _____ _____ there.

3. Pho and banh mi _____ _____ _____ in Vietnam.

4. _____ _____ _____ _____ tourists visit Halong Bay and Nha Trang.

5. Halong Bay has 1,969 islands and Nha Trang _____ _____ _____ _____ its beautiful beaches.

6. Vietnam is _____ _____ _____ you _____ come someday.

1. 당신은 베트남에 대해서 얼마나 많이 알고 있나요?
2. 베트남의 수도는 하노이입니다. 그곳에서는 베트남어가 사용됩니다.
3. 베트남에서는 pho(퍼, 베트남 쌀국수)와 banh mi(반미, 바게트 빵으로 만든 샌드위치)가 인기 있는 요리입니다.
4. 매년 많은 관광객들이 하롱베이와 나트랑을 방문합니다.
5. 하롱베이는 1,969개의 섬을 가지고 있고 나트랑은 아름다운 해변으로 잘 알려져 있습니다.
6. 베트남은 너무 아름다워서 당신은 언젠가 꼭 오셔야 합니다.

Project Step 3

1. My group _____ Hong Kong _____ _____ _____.

2. Hong Kong _____ _____ _____ many people _____ want _____ _____ fun activities.

3. We'll _____ _____ _____ _____ Mong Kok Market, Victoria Peak, and Ocean Park.

1. 우리 모둠은 여행 장소로 홍콩을 선택했다.
2. 홍콩은 재밌는 활동을 하고 싶어 하는 많은 사람들에게 사랑받는다.
3. 우리는 몽콕 시장, 빅토리아 피크 그리고 오션 파크에서 멋진 경험을 할 것이다.

Wrap Up

1. I _____ _____ _____ a book.

2. The _____ _____ _____ _____ is *The Old Man and the Sea*.

3. It _____ _____ _____ Ernest Hemingway.

4. The story was _____ great _____ I read it _____ _____.

1. 나는 어떤 책에 감동을 받았다.
2. 그 책의 제목은 '노인과 바다'이다.
3. 그것은 Ernest Hemingway에 의해 씌여졌다.
4. 그 이야기는 너무도 대단해서 나는 그것을 여러 번 읽었다.

※ 다음 우리말을 영어로 쓰시오.

Enjoy Writing

1. 당신은 베트남에 대해서 얼마나 많이 알고 있나요?
   ➡ _____

2. 베트남의 수도는 하노이입니다. 그곳에서는 베트남어가 사용됩니다.
   ➡ _____

3. 베트남에서는 pho(퍼, 베트남 쌀국수)와 banh mi(반미, 바게트 빵으로 만든 샌드위치)가 인기 있는 요리입니다.
   ➡ _____

4. 매년 많은 관광객들이 하롱베이와 나트랑을 방문합니다.
   ➡ _____

5. 하롱베이는 1,969개의 섬을 가지고 있고 나트랑은 아름다운 해변으로 잘 알려져 있습니다.
   ➡ _____

6. 베트남은 너무 아름다워서 당신은 언젠가 꼭 오셔야 합니다.
   ➡ _____

Project Step 3

1. 우리 모둠은 여행 장소로 홍콩을 선택했다.
   ➡ _____

2. 홍콩은 재밌는 활동을 하고 싶어 하는 많은 사람들에게 사랑받는다.
   ➡ _____

3. 우리는 몽콕 시장, 빅토리아 피크 그리고 오션 파크에서 멋진 경험을 할 것이다.
   ➡ _____

Wrap Up

1. 나는 어떤 책에 감동을 받았다.
   ➡ _____

2. 그 책의 제목은 '노인과 바다'이다.
   ➡ _____

3. 그것은 Ernest Hemingway에 의해 씌여졌다.
   ➡ _____

4. 그 이야기는 너무도 대단해서 나는 그것을 여러 번 읽었다.
   ➡ _____

※ 다음 영어를 우리말로 쓰시오.

01	bloom	22	regularly
02	reed	23	protect
03	damage	24	mess
04	greet	25	lung
05	cliff	26	stain
06	oxygen	27	information
07	plain	28	feed
08	crab	29	muddy
09	trash	30	necessary
10	creature	31	occur
11	truth	32	provide
12	remove	33	tide
13	surface	34	wonder
14	environment	35	work out
15	various	36	such as
16	appear	37	be good for
17	reason	38	not only A but also B
19	flood	39	by the way
18	reduce	40	a large number of
20	produce	41	take off
21	generous	42	be famous for
		43	make a living

※ 다음 우리말을 영어로 쓰시오.

01 동굴	22 먹이를 주다, 먹이다
02 나타나다	23 진실, 사실
03 피해	24 얼룩
04 절벽	25 줄이다
05 환경	26 인사하다
06 제거하다	27 폐
07 (꽃이) 피다	28 엉망진창
08 ~을 여과하다	29 갈대
09 각종의, 다양한	30 진흙투성이인, 진흙의
10 표면	31 필요한
11 생물, 생명체	32 일어나다, 발생하다
12 흐르다	33 제공하다, 주다
13 규칙적으로	34 크게, 꽤
14 관대한	35 그런데
15 이유	36 생계를 유지하다
16 홍수	37 ~로 유명하다
17 쓰레기	38 ~와 같은
18 생산하다, 만들다	39 ~에 좋다, 유익하다
19 보호하다	40 다수의, 많은 수의
20 놀라움, 경이	41 운동하다
21 산소	42 (옷 등을) 벗다, 벗기다
	43 A뿐만 아니라 B도

※ 다음 영영풀이에 알맞은 단어를 <보기>에서 골라 쓴 후, 우리말 뜻을 쓰시오.

1 _____ : very soft wet earth: _____

2 _____ : a large flat area of land: _____

3 _____ : begin to be seen suddenly: _____

4 _____ : facts about something: _____

5 _____ : the outer texture of anything: _____

6 _____ : a high steep rock, especially one facing the sea: _____

7 _____ : the surface of the earth that is not water: _____

8 _____ : all living things except plants: _____

9 _____ : willing to give something more than enough: _____

10 _____ : one of the two organs which you use to breathe: _____

11 _____ : covered with mud, or full of mud: _____

12 _____ : a tall thin plant like grass with a hollow stem that grows in or near water
    : _____

13 _____ : the periodic rise and fall of the waters of the ocean: _____

14 _____ : to pass something through a filter to remove particular things contained
    in it: _____

15 _____ : to move steadily without any interrupts, used to describe liquids, gas,
    electrical currents, etc.: _____

16 _____ : to give someone something that they need or want or make it available
    to them: _____

보기			
provide	muddy	surface	creature
cliff	flow	reed	lung
appear	information	filter	generous
plain	tide	mud	land

※ 다음 우리말과 일치하도록 빈칸에 알맞은 말을 쓰시오.

Listen & Speak 1 A

1. G: I _____ _____ _____ _____ _____ the summer vacation.

   B: I _____ a _____ to Kenya and saw many animals on the plains.

   G: Wonderful! _____ the way, what are the _____?

   B: They are large areas of _____ _____.

   G: I see.

2. G: _____ _____ that lake! It's really _____.

   B: It's not a _____. It's a river.

   G: Is it? I _____ _____ a river and a lake _____ _____.

   B: A river is _____ _____ _____ _____ _____ water. _____ a lake, a river _____ _____ the ocean.

   G: I _____ _____.

Listen & Speak 1 B

1. A: I wonder _____ _____ _____ _____.

   B: It is a very _____ area of land.

2. A: _____ _____ _____ a _____ is.

   B: It is a _____, _____ area of _____.

Listen & Talk 2 A

1. B: Do you know _____ _____ _____ _____ _____ on the Earth?

   G: The answer is four, _____ _____?

   B: No. _____ _____ five oceans on the Earth. They _____ _____ of the Earth.

   G: _____ _____ of the Earth do they _____?

   B: I _____ the oceans _____ _____ 70% of the Earth's _____.

2. G: I _____ the Amazon _____ _____ _____ _____ the _____ of the Earth.

   B: _____? Why?

   G: _____ it _____ about 20% of the Earth's _____.

   B: Wow! That's _____ _____.

1. G: 나는 네가 여름 방학 동안에 무엇을 했는지 궁금해.
   B: 나는 케냐로 여행을 가서 평원에서 많은 동물들을 봤어.
   G: 멋지구나! 그런데 평원이 무엇이니?
   B: 그곳은 넓고 평평한 땅이야.
   G: 그렇구나.

2. G: 저 호수를 봐. 정말 아름다워.
   B: 그것은 호수가 아니야. 그것은 강이야.
   G: 그래? 나는 강과 호수가 어떻게 다른지 궁금해.
   B: 강은 민물로 된 긴 물줄기야. 호수와 다르게 강은 바다로 흘러.
   G: 알겠어.

1. A: 나는 산이 무엇인지 궁금해.
   B: 그곳은 아주 높은 지대의 땅이야.

2. A: 나는 평원이 무엇인지 궁금해.
   B: 그곳은 넓고 평평한 지대의 땅이야.

1. B: 너는 지구에 몇 개의 바다가 있는지 아니?
   G: 정답은 네 개야, 그렇지 않니?
   B: 아니야. 지구에는 다섯 개의 바다가 있어. 그곳은 지구의 대부분을 차지하고 있어.
   G: 그곳이 지구의 얼마를 차지하고 있니?
   B: 나는 바다가 지구 표면의 70%를 차지한다고 들었어.

2. G: 나는 아마존 열대 우림이 지구의 허파라고 불린다고 들었어.
   B: 허파? 왜?
   G: 왜냐하면 그곳은 지구 산소의 약 20%를 생산하기 때문이야.
   B: 우와! 엄청나구나.

Listen & Talk 2 B

1. **A:** I _____ to go to Jecheon.

   B: Why?

   A: I _____ there are beautiful _____ in Jecheon.

2. **A:** I _____ _____ _____ _____ Danyang.

   B: Why?

   A: I heard there _____ _____ _____ in Danyang.

1. A: 나는 제천에 가고 싶어.
   B: 왜?
   A: 나는 제천에 아름다운 호수들이 있다고 들었어.

2. A: 나는 단양에 가고 싶어.
   B: 왜?
   A: 나는 단양에 유명한 동굴들이 있다고 들었어.

Conversation A

M: Guess _____ this is! It's not a tree. It is a _____ that _____ _____ tall _____. _____ fall, it _____ yellow. It grows well in _____ lands. I _____ Suncheon Bay _____ _____ _____ this plant.

M: 이것이 무엇인지 추측해 봐! 그것은 나무가 아니야. 그것은 키가 큰 풀처럼 보이는 식물이야. 가을에는 노란색으로 변해. 그것은 습지에서 잘 자라. 나는 순천만이 이 식물로 유명하다고 들었어.

Conversation B

Dad: Do you want to see an _____ _____?

Karl & Sister: Sure!

Dad: Then _____ _____ _____ the train.

Sister: _____ _____ the yellow plants! I _____ _____ _____ _____.

Dad: They are _____. Suncheon Bay has beautiful _____ fields.

Karl: Wow, the reeds are even _____ _____ you, Dad.

Sister: They really are. _____ me _____ a picture _____ you.

Karl: This _____ _____ is very large.

Dad: Yes. I _____ it is _____ _____ _____ in Korea.

Karl: _____ _____ the sky. It's _____ red.

Sister: Yes, it's _____.

아빠: 너희들 멋진 곳을 보고 싶니?
Karl, 여동생: 물론이죠!
아빠: 그러면 기차를 타자.
여동생: 저 노란색 식물들을 봐요! 저게 무엇인지 궁금해요.
아빠: 그건 갈대야. 순천만에는 아름다운 갈대밭이 있어.
Karl: 와, 갈대가 아빠보다 키가 더 커요.
여동생: 진짜 그러네요. 제가 사진을 찍어 드릴게요.
Karl: 이 갈대밭은 정말 넓네요.
아빠: 그래. 나는 이곳이 한국에서 가장 큰 갈대밭이라고 들었어.
Karl: 하늘을 보세요. 빨갛게 변하고 있어요.
여동생: 그러네, 아름다워.

Communication Task Step 1

A: What _____ do you have?

B: I have Moraine Lake. It's in Canada.

A: What is _____ _____ the place?

B: The color of the water _____ _____ _____.

A: 너는 어떤 장소를 가지고 있니?
B: 나는 모레인호를 갖고 있어. 그곳은 캐나다에 있어.
A: 그곳은 어떤 것이 특별하니?
B: 물의 색이 연한 파랑색이야.

※ 다음 우리말에 맞도록 대화를 영어로 쓰시오.

해석

Listen & Speak 1 A

1. G: _____

   B: _____

   G: _____

   B: _____

   G: _____

2. G: _____

   B: _____

   G: _____

   B: _____

   _____

   G: _____

1. G: 나는 네가 여름 방학 동안에 무엇을 했는지 궁금해.
   B: 나는 케냐로 여행을 가서 평원에서 많은 동물들을 봤어.
   G: 멋지구나! 그런데 평원이 무엇이니?
   B: 그곳은 넓고 평평한 땅이야.
   G: 그렇구나.

2. G: 저 호수를 봐. 정말 아름다워.
   B: 그것은 호수가 아니야. 그것은 강이야.
   G: 그래? 나는 강과 호수가 어떻게 다른지 궁금해.
   B: 강은 민물로 된 긴 물줄기야. 호수와 다르게 강은 바다로 흘러.
   G: 알겠어.

Listen & Speak 1 B

1. A: _____

   B: _____

2. A: _____

   B: _____

1. A: 나는 산이 무엇인지 궁금해.
   B: 그곳은 아주 높은 지대의 땅이야.

2. A: 나는 평원이 무엇인지 궁금해.
   B: 그곳은 넓고 평평한 지대의 땅이야.

Listen & Talk 2 A

1. B: _____

   G: _____

   B: _____

   G: _____

   B: _____

2. G: _____

   B: _____

   G: _____

   B: _____

1. B: 너는 지구에 몇 개의 바다가 있는지 아니?
   G: 정답은 네 개야. 그렇지 않니?
   B: 아니야. 지구에는 다섯 개의 바다가 있어. 그곳은 지구의 대부분을 차지하고 있어.
   G: 그곳이 지구의 얼마를 차지하고 있니?
   B: 나는 바다가 지구 표면의 70%를 차지한다고 들었어.

2. G: 나는 아마존 열대 우림이 지구의 허파라고 불린다고 들었어.
   B: 허파? 왜?
   G: 왜냐하면 그곳은 지구 산소의 약 20%를 생산하기 때문이야.
   B: 우와! 엄청나구나.

Listen & Talk 2 B

1. A: _____

   B: _____

   A: _____

2. A: _____

   B: _____

   A: _____

Conversation A

M: _____

_____

_____

Conversation B

Dad: _____

Karl & Sister: _____

Dad: _____

Sister: _____

Dad: _____

Karl: _____

Sister: _____

Karl: _____

Dad: _____

Karl: _____

Sister: _____

Communication Task Step 1

A: _____

B: _____

A: _____

B: _____

※ 다음 우리말과 일치하도록 빈칸에 알맞은 것을 골라 쓰시오.

1 Mudflats, _____ _____
A. Gift   B. Nature's

2 Mudflats are large _____ of _____ land at the _____.
A. muddy   B. areas   C. seaside

3 They _____ and disappear _____ every _____.
A. tide   B. appear   C. with

4 During low tides, they _____ _____, and during high _____, they are _____ by the sea.
A. covered   B. up   C. tides   D. show

5 Mudflats help sea _____, people, and the Earth _____ many _____.
A. ways   B. creatures   C. in

6 It is _____ to understand the _____ of _____.
A. roles   B. important   C. mudflats

7 _____ see _____ they _____.
A. what   B. let's   C. do

8 Mudflats are _____ to a lot of _____ things at the _____.
A. living   B. home   C. seaside

9 _____ _____ very small living things like plankton _____ _____ crabs and fish live there.
A. but   B. not   C. also   D. only

10 Mudflats _____ various _____ of food _____ them.
A. types   B. for   C. provide

11 _____, many birds _____ food _____.
A. there   B. also   C. eat

12 Crab: Mudflats are _____ home _____ _____.
A. home   B. sweet   C. my

13 Mudflats are _____ _____ people, _____.
A. too   B. for   C. good

14 People who live near _____ areas _____ a _____ by catching fish and other sea animals _____.
A. make   B. nearby   C. mudflat   D. living

15 _____ _____ mudflats, people can get _____ seafood.
A. fresh   B. thanks   C. to

1 갯벌, 자연의 선물

2 갯벌은 바닷가의 진흙이 있는 넓은 지역이다.

3 갯벌은 조수와 함께 나타나고 사라진다.

4 썰물일 때 갯벌이 드러나고, 밀물일 때 바다에 덮인다.

5 갯벌은 바다 생물과 사람, 지구를 많은 방면에서 돕는다.

6 갯벌의 역할을 이해하는 것이 중요하다.

7 갯벌이 무엇을 하는지 살펴보자.

8 갯벌은 바닷가에 있는 많은 생물들에게 집이다.

9 플랑크톤처럼 작은 생명체뿐만 아니라 게와 물고기도 그곳에 산다.

10 갯벌은 그들에게 다양한 종류의 먹이를 제공한다.

11 또한, 많은 새들도 그곳에서 먹이를 먹는다.

12 게: 갯벌은 나의 단란한 집이에요.

13 갯벌은 사람들에게도 유익하다.

14 갯벌 지역 인근에 사는 사람들은 근처에서 물고기와 다른 바다 동물들을 잡아 생계를 꾸린다.

15 갯벌 덕분에 사람들은 신선한 해산물을 얻을 수 있다.

16 People can enjoy _____ _____, _____ _____ mud sliding and body painting on mudflats.

A. as　　　　　B. fun　　　　　C. such　　　　　D. activities

17 They can also watch a _____ _____ of birds that _____ _____ the sea animals there.

A. feed　　　　　B. number　　　　　C. on　　　　　D. large

18 Boy: Mudflats are _____ _____ to _____ things!

A. living　　　　　B. gift　　　　　C. nature's

19 Mudflats _____ the environment _____.

A. greatly　　　　　B. help

20 Mudflats _____ a lot of water, so they can _____ _____ from _____.

A. damage　　　　　B. hold　　　　　C. floods　　　　　D. reduce

21 Also, mudflats _____ water that flows _____ the land _____ the sea.

A. from　　　　　B. filter　　　　　C. into

22 They _____ bad _____ in the water _____ it enters the sea.

A. before　　　　　B. things　　　　　C. remove

23 _____ to mudflats, the water that _____ the sea is _____.

A. reaches　　　　　B. thanks　　　　　C. clean

24 Mudflats _____ _____ the Earth's _____.

A. as　　　　　B. lungs　　　　　C. work

25 They produce a _____ volume of _____ that is _____ for life on the Earth.

A. oxygen　　　　　B. huge　　　　　C. necessary

26 Earth: Mudflats _____ me _____ and _____.

A. healthy　　　　　B. keep　　　　　C. clean

27 _____ are wonderful places, _____ _____?

A. they　　　　　B. mudflats　　　　　C. aren't

28 They are a _____ from _____ to _____ things on the Earth.

A. living　　　　　B. gift　　　　　C. nature

29 For all these _____, it is _____ to _____ mudflats.

A. reasons　　　　　B. protect　　　　　C. necessary

16 사람들은 갯벌에서 진흙 미끄럼 타기나 보디 페인팅과 같은 즐거운 활동을 즐길 수 있다.

17 그들은 또한 그곳에서 바다 동물들을 먹는 수많은 새를 관찰할 수도 있다.

18 남자아이: 갯벌은 생명체에게 주는 자연의 선물이에요!

19 갯벌은 환경에 크게 도움이 된다.

20 갯벌은 많은 양의 물을 수용해서 홍수의 피해를 줄여 준다.

21 또한, 갯벌은 땅에서 바다로 흘러가는 물을 걸러내 준다.

22 물이 바다로 들어가기 전에 물 속에 있는 나쁜 물질을 갯벌이 제거한다.

23 갯벌 덕분에 바다에 도착한 물은 깨끗하다.

24 갯벌은 지구의 폐 역할을 한다.

25 그것들은 지구상의 생명에게 필요한 많은 양의 산소를 생산한다.

26 지구: 갯벌은 나를 건강하고 깨끗하게 지켜 줘요.

27 갯벌은 멋진 곳이다. 그렇지 않은가?

28 그곳은 자연이 지구상의 생물들에게 준 선물이다.

29 이러한 이유로, 갯벌을 보호하는 것은 필수이다.

※ 다음 우리말과 일치하도록 빈칸에 알맞은 말을 쓰시오.

1 Mudflats, _____ _____

2 Mudflats are large areas of _____ _____ at the seaside.

3 They appear and _____ _____ _____ _____ .

4 _____ low tides, they _____ _____, and during _____ _____, they _____ _____ _____ the sea.

5 Mudflats help _____ _____, people, and the Earth _____ _____ _____ .

6 It is important _____ _____ _____ _____ _____ _____ .

7 _____ see _____ _____ _____ .

8 Mudflats _____ _____ _____ a lot of _____ _____ at the seaside.

9 _____ _____ very small living things like plankton _____ _____ crabs and fish live there.

10 Mudflats _____ various _____ _____ food _____ them.

11 _____, many birds eat food there.

12 Crab: Mudflats are my _____ _____ _____ .

13 Mudflats _____ _____ _____ people, _____ .

14 People who live near mudflat areas _____ _____ _____ _____ fish and other sea animals _____ .

15 _____ _____ mudflats, people can get _____ _____ .

1 갯벌, 자연의 선물

2 갯벌은 바닷가의 진흙이 있는 넓은 지역이다.

3 갯벌은 조수와 함께 나타나고 사라진다.

4 썰물일 때 갯벌이 드러나고, 밀물일 때 바다에 덮인다.

5 갯벌은 바다 생물과 사람, 지구를 많은 방면에서 돕는다.

6 갯벌의 역할을 이해하는 것이 중요하다.

7 갯벌이 무엇을 하는지 살펴보자.

8 갯벌은 바닷가에 있는 많은 생물들에게 집이다.

9 플랑크톤처럼 작은 생명체뿐만 아니라 게와 물고기도 그곳에 산다.

10 갯벌은 그들에게 다양한 종류의 먹이를 제공한다.

11 또한, 많은 새들도 그곳에서 먹이를 먹는다.

12 게: 갯벌은 나의 단란한 집이에요.

13 갯벌은 사람들에게도 유익하다.

14 갯벌 지역 인근에 사는 사람들은 근처에서 물고기와 다른 바다 동물들을 잡아 생계를 꾸린다.

15 갯벌 덕분에 사람들은 신선한 해산물을 얻을 수 있다.

16 People can enjoy _____ _____, _____ _____ mud sliding and body painting _____ _____.

17 They can also watch _____ _____ _____ _____ birds that _____ _____ the sea animals there.

18 Boy: Mudflats are _____ _____ to living things!

19 Mudflats _____ the _____ _____.

20 Mudflats _____ a lot of water, so they can _____ _____ _____ _____.

21 Also, mudflats _____ water that _____ _____ the land _____ the sea.

22 They _____ _____ _____ in the water before it _____ the sea.

23 _____ _____ mudflats, the water _____ _____ _____ _____ is clean.

24 Mudflats work _____ _____ _____ _____.

25 They produce _____ _____ _____ _____ oxygen that is _____ for life on the Earth.

26 Earth: Mudflats _____ _____ _____ and _____.

27 Mudflats are wonderful places, _____ _____?

28 They are a gift _____ _____ _____ _____ on the Earth.

29 For all these reasons, it is necessary _____ _____ _____.

16 사람들은 갯벌에서 진흙 미끄럼 타기나 보디 페인팅과 같은 즐거운 활동을 즐길 수 있다.

17 그들은 또한 그곳에서 바다 동물들을 먹는 수많은 새를 관찰할 수도 있다.

18 남자아이: 갯벌은 생명체에게 주는 자연의 선물이에요!

19 갯벌은 환경에 크게 도움이 된다.

20 갯벌은 많은 양의 물을 수용해서 홍수의 피해를 줄여 준다.

21 또한, 갯벌은 땅에서 바다로 흘러가는 물을 걸러내 준다.

22 물이 바다로 들어가기 전에 물 속에 있는 나쁜 물질을 갯벌이 제거한다.

23 갯벌 덕분에 바다에 도착한 물은 깨끗하다.

24 갯벌은 지구의 폐 역할을 한다.

25 그것들은 지구상의 생명에게 필요한 많은 양의 산소를 생산한다.

26 지구: 갯벌은 나를 건강하고 깨끗하게 지켜 줘요.

27 갯벌은 멋진 곳이다. 그렇지 않은가?

28 그곳은 자연이 지구상의 생물들에게 준 선물이다.

29 이러한 이유로, 갯벌을 보호하는 것은 필수이다.

※ 다음 문장을 우리말로 쓰시오.

1 Mudflats, Nature's Gift

➡ _____

2 Mudflats are large areas of muddy land at the seaside.

➡ _____

3 They appear and disappear with every tide.

➡ _____

4 During low tides, they show up, and during high tides, they are covered by the sea.

➡ _____

5 Mudflats help sea creatures, people, and the Earth in many ways.

➡ _____

6 It is important to understand the roles of mudflats.

➡ _____

7 Let's see what they do.

➡ _____

8 Mudflats are home to a lot of living things at the seaside.

➡ _____

9 Not only very small living things like plankton but also crabs and fish live there.

➡ _____

10 Mudflats provide various types of food for them.

➡ _____

11 Also, many birds eat food there.

➡ _____

12 Crab: Mudflats are my home sweet home.

➡ _____

13 Mudflats are good for people, too.

➡ _____

14 People who live near mudflat areas make a living by catching fish and other sea animals nearby.

➡ _____

15 Thanks to mudflats, people can get fresh seafood.

➡ _____

16 People can enjoy fun activities, such as mud sliding and body painting on mudflats.

➡ _____

17 They can also watch a large number of birds that feed on the sea animals there.

➡ _____

18 Boy: Mudflats are nature's gift to living things!

➡ _____

19 Mudflats help the environment greatly.

➡ _____

20 Mudflats hold a lot of water, so they can reduce damage from floods.

➡ _____

21 Also, mudflats filter water that flows from the land into the sea.

➡ _____

22 They remove bad things in the water before it enters the sea.

➡ _____

23 Thanks to mudflats, the water that reaches the sea is clean.

➡ _____

24 Mudflats work as the Earth's lungs.

➡ _____

25 They produce a huge volume of oxygen that is necessary for life on the Earth.

➡ _____

26 Earth: Mudflats keep me healthy and clean.

➡ _____

27 Mudflats are wonderful places, aren't they?

➡ _____

28 They are a gift from nature to living things on the Earth.

➡ _____

29 For all these reasons, it is necessary to protect mudflats.

➡ _____

※ 다음 괄호 안의 단어들을 우리말에 맞도록 바르게 배열하시오.

1 (Nature's / Gift / Mudflats,)
➡ _____

2 (are / mudflats / areas / large / muddy / of / at / land / seaside. / the)
➡ _____

3 (appear / they / and / with / disappear / tide. / every)
➡ _____

4 (low / during / tides, / show / they / up, / and / high / during / tides, / are / they / by / sea. / the / covered)
➡ _____
_____

5 (help / mudflats / creatures, / sea / people, / the / and / Earth / in / ways. / many)
➡ _____
_____

6 (is / it / important / understand / to / roles / the / mudfalts. / of)
➡ _____

7 (see / let's / they / what / do.)
➡ _____

8 (are / mudflats / home / a / to / lot / living / of / things / the / seaside. / at)
➡ _____
_____

9 (only / not / small / very / things / living / like / but / plankton / also / crabs / and / live / there. / fish)
➡ _____
_____

10 (provide / mudflats / types / various / food / of / them. / for)
➡ _____

11 (also, / birds / many / food / there. / eat)
➡ _____

12 (Crab: / are / mudflats / home / my / home. / sweet)
➡ _____

13 (are / mudflats / for / good / too. / people,)
➡ _____

14 (who / people / near / live / areas / mudflat / a / make / living / catching / by / fish / and / sea / other / nearby. / animals)
➡ _____
_____

15 (to / thanks / mudflats, / can / people / fresh / seafood. / get)
➡ _____

1 갯벌, 자연의 선물

2 갯벌은 바닷가의 진흙이 있는 넓은 지역이다.

3 갯벌은 조수와 함께 나타나고 사라진다.

4 썰물일 때 갯벌이 드러나고, 밀물일 때 바다에 덮인다.

5 갯벌은 바다 생물과 사람, 지구를 많은 방면에서 돕는다.

6 갯벌의 역할을 이해하는 것이 중요하다.

7 갯벌이 무엇을 하는지 살펴보자.

8 갯벌은 바닷가에 있는 많은 생물들에게 집이다.

9 플랑크톤처럼 작은 생명체뿐만 아니라 게와 물고기도 그곳에 산다.

10 갯벌은 그들에게 다양한 종류의 먹이를 제공한다.

11 또한, 많은 새들도 그곳에서 먹이를 먹는다.

12 게: 갯벌은 나의 단란한 집이에요.

13 갯벌은 사람들에게도 유익하다.

14 갯벌 지역 인근에 사는 사람들은 근처에서 물고기와 다른 바다 동물들을 잡아 생계를 꾸린다.

15 갯벌 덕분에 사람들은 신선한 해산물을 얻을 수 있다.

16 (can / people / fun / enjoy / activities, / as / such / sliding / mud / and / body / on / painting / mudflats.)

➡ _____

_____

17 (they / also / watch / can / a / number / large / birds / of / that / on / feed / sea / the / there. / animals)

➡ _____

_____

18 (Boy: / are / mudflats / gift / nature's / to / things! / living)

➡ _____

19 (help / mudflats / environment / the / greatly.)

➡ _____

20 (hold / mudflats / lot / a / of / water, / they / so / reduce / can / from / damage / floods.)

➡ _____

21 (mudflats / also, / water / filter / that / from / flows / the / into / land / sea. / the)

➡ _____

22 (remove / they / things / bad / the / in / water / before / enters / it / sea. / the)

➡ _____

23 (to / thanks / mudflats, / water / the / reaches / that / sea / the / clean. / is)

➡ _____

24 (work / mudflats / the / as / lungs. / Earth's)

➡ _____

25 (produce / they / huge / a / of / volume / oxygen / is / that / for / necessary / life / the / Earth. / on)

➡ _____

_____

26 (Earth: / keep / mudflats / me / clean. / and / healthy)

➡ _____

27 (are / mudflats / places, / wonderful / they? / aren't)

➡ _____

28 (are / they / gift / a / from / nature / living / to / things / the / Earth. / on)

➡ _____

29 (all / for / reasons, / these / is / it / necessary / protect / to / mudflats.)

➡ _____

16 사람들은 갯벌에서 진흙 미끄럼 타기나 보디 페인팅과 같은 즐거운 활동을 즐길 수 있다.

17 그들은 또한 그곳에서 바다 동물들을 먹는 수많은 새를 관찰할 수도 있다.

18 남자아이: 갯벌은 생명체에게 주는 자연의 선물이에요!

19 갯벌은 환경에 크게 도움이 된다.

20 갯벌은 많은 양의 물을 수용해서 홍수의 피해를 줄여 준다.

21 또한, 갯벌은 땅에서 바다로 흘러가는 물을 걸러내 준다.

22 물이 바다로 들어가기 전에 물 속에 있는 나쁜 물질을 갯벌이 제거한다.

23 갯벌 덕분에 바다에 도착한 물은 깨끗하다.

24 갯벌은 지구의 폐 역할을 한다.

25 그것들은 지구상의 생명에게 필요한 많은 양의 산소를 생산한다.

26 지구: 갯벌은 나를 건강하고 깨끗하게 지켜 줘요.

27 갯벌은 멋진 곳이다, 그렇지 않은가?

28 그곳은 자연이 지구상의 생물들에게 준 선물이다.

29 이러한 이유로, 갯벌을 보호하는 것은 필수이다.

※ 다음 우리말을 영어로 쓰시오.

1 갯벌, 자연의 선물

➡ _____

2 갯벌은 바닷가의 진흙이 있는 넓은 지역이다.

➡ _____

3 갯벌은 조수와 함께 나타나고 사라진다.

➡ _____

4 썰물일 때 갯벌이 드러나고, 밀물일 때 바다에 덮인다.

➡ _____

5 갯벌은 바다 생물과 사람, 지구를 많은 방면에서 돕는다.

➡ _____

6 갯벌의 역할을 이해하는 것이 중요하다.

➡ _____

7 갯벌이 무엇을 하는지 살펴보자.

➡ _____

8 갯벌은 바닷가에 있는 많은 생물들에게 집이다.

➡ _____

9 플랑크톤처럼 작은 생명체뿐만 아니라 게와 물고기도 그곳에 산다.

➡ _____

10 갯벌은 그들에게 다양한 종류의 먹이를 제공한다.

➡ _____

11 또한, 많은 새들도 그곳에서 먹이를 먹는다.

➡ _____

12 게: 갯벌은 나의 단란한 집이에요.

➡ _____

13 갯벌은 사람들에게도 유익하다.

➡ _____

14 갯벌 지역 인근에 사는 사람들은 근처에서 물고기와 다른 바다 동물들을 잡아 생계를 꾸린다.

➡ _____

15 갯벌 덕분에 사람들은 신선한 해산물을 얻을 수 있다.

➡ _____

16 사람들은 갯벌에서 진흙 미끄럼 타기나 보디 페인팅과 같은 즐거운 활동을 즐길 수 있다.

➡ _____

17 그들은 또한 그곳에서 바다 동물들을 먹는 수많은 새를 관찰할 수도 있다.

➡ _____

18 남자아이: 갯벌은 생명체에게 주는 자연의 선물이에요!

➡ _____

19 갯벌은 환경에 크게 도움이 된다.

➡ _____

20 갯벌은 많은 양의 물을 수용해서 홍수의 피해를 줄여 준다.

➡ _____

21 또한, 갯벌은 땅에서 바다로 흘러가는 물을 걸러내 준다.

➡ _____

22 물이 바다로 들어가기 전에 물속에 있는 나쁜 물질을 갯벌이 제거한다.

➡ _____

23 갯벌 덕분에 바다에 도착한 물은 깨끗하다.

➡ _____

24 갯벌은 지구의 폐 역할을 한다.

➡ _____

25 그것들은 지구상의 생명에게 필요한 많은 양의 산소를 생산한다.

➡ _____

26 지구: 갯벌은 나를 건강하고 깨끗하게 지켜 줘요.

➡ _____

27 갯벌은 멋진 곳이다, 그렇지 않은가?

➡ _____

28 그곳은 자연이 지구상의 생물들에게 준 선물이다.

➡ _____

29 이러한 이유로, 갯벌을 보호하는 것은 필수이다.

➡ _____

※ 다음 우리말과 일치하도록 빈칸에 알맞은 말을 쓰시오.

Enjoy Writing B

1. Deserts are dry land _____ _____ plants and _____ water.

2. _____ _____ plants like elephant trees _____ _____ animals _____ _____ lizards and desert snakes live there.

3. It is hot _____ _____ _____ and cold at night.

4. If you go to a desert, _____ is important _____ _____ a hat _____ _____ the sun.

1. 사막은 식물과 물이 거의 없는 건조한 땅이다.
2. 코끼리 나무 같은 식물뿐만 아니라 도마뱀이나 사막뱀 같은 동물들도 그곳에 산다.
3. 낮에는 덥고 밤에는 춥다.
4. 만일 사막에 간다면 햇빛을 가리기 위해 모자를 쓰는 것이 중요하다.

Enjoy Writing B

1. All _____ _____

2. Mudflats are _____ _____ at the _____.

3. _____ _____ plants like *hamcho* _____ _____ animals _____ _____ crabs and fish live there.

4. They _____ _____ during low tides and _____ _____ _____ the sea during high tides.

5. If you go to mudflats, it is important _____ _____ long clothes _____ _____ _____ from animals that _____ _____ you.

1. 갯벌에 관한 모든 것
2. 갯벌은 바닷가의 진흙이 있는 지역이다.
3. 함초와 같은 식물들뿐만 아니라 게와 물고기와 같은 동물들도 그곳에 산다.
4. 썰물일 때 갯벌이 드러나고, 밀물일 때 바다에 덮인다.
5. 만약 당신이 갯벌에 간다면, 당신을 물 수 있는 동물들로부터 당신을 보호하기 위해 긴 옷을 입는 것이 중요하다.

Wrap Up 1

1. B: I just _____ _____ a plan for my trip. Do you _____ _____ _____ it?

2. G: Sure. I _____ _____ _____ _____ _____ _____.

3. B: On the first day, I'm _____ to _____ _____ on a lake. The next day, I'm going to _____ _____ _____.

4. G: _____ that _____?

5. B: No. _____ the last day, I'm _____ _____ _____ _____.

6. G: Wow. You will do _____ _____ _____ activities.

1. B: 나는 방금 여행 계획 세우는 것을 끝냈어. 그것에 대해 듣고 싶니?
2. G: 물론이지. 나는 네가 무엇을 할지 궁금해.
3. B: 첫날에 나는 호수에서 낚시를 할 거야. 다음 날에 나는 산에 오를 거야.
4. G: 그게 전부니?
5. B: 아니. 마지막 날에 나는 수영을 할 거야.
6. G: 우와. 너는 많은 활동들을 할 거구나.

※ 다음 우리말을 영어로 쓰시오.

Enjoy Writing B

1. 사막은 식물과 물이 거의 없는 건조한 땅이다.
➡ _____

2. 코끼리 나무 같은 식물뿐만 아니라 도마뱀이나 사막뱀 같은 동물들도 그곳에 산다.
➡ _____

3. 낮에는 덥고 밤에는 춥다.
➡ _____

4. 만일 사막에 간다면 햇빛을 가리기 위해 모자를 쓰는 것이 중요하다.
➡ _____

Enjoy Writing B

1. 갯벌에 관한 모든 것
➡ _____

2. 갯벌은 바닷가의 진흙이 있는 지역이다.
➡ _____

3. 함초와 같은 식물들뿐만 아니라 게와 물고기와 같은 동물들도 그곳에 산다.
➡ _____

4. 썰물일 때 갯벌이 드러나고, 밀물일 때 바다에 덮인다.
➡ _____

5. 만약 당신이 갯벌에 간다면, 당신을 물 수 있는 동물들로부터 당신을 보호하기 위해 긴 옷을 입는 것이 중요하다.
➡ _____
_____

Wrap Up 1

1. B: 나는 방금 여행 계획 세우는 것을 끝냈어. 그것에 대해 듣고 싶니?
➡ _____

2. G: 물론이지. 나는 네가 무엇을 할지 궁금해.
➡ _____

3. B: 첫날에 나는 호수에서 낚시를 할 거야. 다음 날에 나는 산에 오를 거야.
➡ _____

4. G: 그게 전부니?
➡ _____

5. B: 아니. 마지막 날에 나는 수영을 할 거야.
➡ _____

6. G: 우와. 너는 많은 활동들을 할 거구나.
➡ _____

※ 다음 영어를 우리말로 쓰시오.

01	teammate	22	present
02	perfect	23	effort
03	calm	24	honor
04	achieve	25	lend
05	difficulty	26	major
06	face	27	excellent
07	award	28	respect
08	terrible	29	solve
09	fail	30	rudely
10	finally	31	support
11	positive	32	talented
12	gentle	33	phrase
13	base	34	color line
14	recognize	35	think to oneself
15	sentence	36	no longer
16	although	37	win first place
17	recycle	38	turn down
18	overcome	39	give up
19	earn	40	over and over
20	excellence	41	present A with B
21	pain	42	at bat
		43	cannot believe one's eyes

※ 다음 우리말을 영어로 쓰시오.

01 이루다, 달성하다

02 침착한

03 인정하다, 알아보다

04 어려움, 곤경, 장애

05 완벽한

06 얻다, 획득하다

07 비록 ~일지라도

08 우수, 탁월, 뛰어남

09 아픔, 고통

10 상

11 뛰어난

12 긍정적인

13 직면하다, 직시하다

14 재활용하다

15 존경

16 예우하다, ~을 공경하다

17 실패하다

18 풀다, 해결하다

19 재능이 있는

20 지지

21 마침내

22 점잖은

23 수여하다, 증정하다

24 무례하게

25 팀 동료

26 문장

27 (공을) 치다

28 노력

29 빌려주다

30 주요한

31 극복하다

32 무서운

33 경기장, 스타디움

34 야구의 루

35 포기하다

36 마음속으로 생각하다

37 더 이상 ~ 아닌

38 ~ 덕분에

39 반복해서

40 1등을 하다, 우승하다

41 ~을 거절하다, 소리를 줄이다

42 A에게 B를 수여하다

43 수업을 듣다

※ 다음 영영풀이에 알맞은 단어를 <보기>에서 골라 쓴 후, 우리말 뜻을 쓰시오.

1 _____ : unusually or extremely good: _____

2 _____ : a person who is in the same team: _____

3 _____ : a player stationed at a base: _____

4 _____ : to be unable to do something: _____

5 _____ : in a way that shows no respect for others: _____

6 _____ : relating to classical music: _____

7 _____ : a feeling that you have in a part of your body when you are hurt or ill : _____

8 _____ : to give someone the use of something for a limited time: _____

9 _____ : greater or more important than other people or things in a group: _____

10 _____ : to succeed in dealing with or controlling a problem: _____

11 _____ : to hit the ball with a bat in a game such as baseball or cricket: _____

12 _____ : believing that good things will happen rather than bad ones: _____

13 _____ : to see and know what someone or something is: _____

14 _____ : a prize or other reward that is given to someone who has achieved something: _____

15 _____ : not affected by strong emotions such as excitement, anger, shock, or fear: _____

16 _____ : help and kindness that you give to someone who is having a difficult time: _____

보기			
bat	lend	baseman	teammate
support	excellent	positive	calm
fail	award	pain	overcome
recognize	classical	rudely	major

※ 다음 우리말과 일치하도록 빈칸에 알맞은 말을 쓰시오.

Listen & Speak 1 A

1. G: Hey, Minho. Did you _____ the answer to the _____ _____?

   B: No. It's _____ _____ for me. _____ _____ _____

   _____ _____.

   G: _____ me _____. _____ _____ _____ you use this

   math rule _____ _____ the problem.

   B: Oh, I see. I'll _____ it.

2. G: Your poster _____ _____.

   B: Thanks, Kate. Did you _____ _____?

   G: Not yet. I can't _____ well. _____ can I become _____

   _____ _____?

   B: It _____ time. It's _____ that you draw _____ _____

   _____ _____ _____.

   G: You _____ I should _____ _____?

   B: That's _____.

Listen & Speak 1 B

1. A: It's _____ _____ _____ a good dancer. _____ should

   I do?

   B: It's _____ that you _____ _____ _____.

   A: Okay. I will _____ _____ that.

2. A: It's _____ _____ write a good story. What _____ I do?

   B: _____ _____ _____ you read many books.

   A: Okay. I _____ _____ _____ that.

Listen & Talk 2 A

1. G: Oh, this is _____ _____ _____.

   B: What's the _____?

   G: Can you teach me _____ _____ _____ cookies?

   B: Sure. It's a walk in the park.

   G: _____ _____ _____ _____ _____ _____ that?

   B: I _____ it's _____ _____ _____.

1. G: 이봐, 민호야. 이 수학 문제의 정답을 찾았니?
   B: 아니. 그건 나에게 너무 어려워. 나는 수학을 잘하지 못 해.
   G: 내가 한 번 볼게. 네가 그 문제를 풀기 위해선 이 수학 공식을 이용하는 것이 중요해.
   B: 오, 알겠어. 그걸 사용해 볼게.

2. G: 네 포스터가 멋져 보여.
   B: 고마워, Kate. 네 것은 끝냈니?
   G: 아직 못 끝냈어. 나는 그림을 잘 그리지 못 해. 어떻게 하면 내가 그림을 잘 그릴 수 있을까?
   B: 시간이 필요해. 네가 가능한 자주 그림을 그리는 것이 중요해.
   G: 내가 계속 연습해야 한다는 뜻이니?
   B: 맞아.

1. A: 훌륭한 댄서가 되는 것은 어려워. 내가 무엇을 해야 할까?
   B: 절대 포기하지 않는 것이 중요해.
   A: 알겠어. 그것을 잊지 않을게.

2. A: 좋은 이야기를 쓰는 것은 어려워. 내가 무엇을 해야 할까?
   B: 책을 많이 읽는 것이 중요해.
   A: 알겠어. 그것을 잊지 않을게.

1. G: 오, 이것은 하기 어렵구나.
   B: 무슨 일이야?
   G: 쿠키를 만드는 방법을 나에게 가르쳐 줄 수 있니?
   B: 물론이지. 그건 'a walk in the park'야.
   G: 그게 무슨 뜻이니?
   B: 하기 쉽다는 뜻이야.

2. **B:** I _____ a singing contest tomorrow. I really _____ _____

   _____ _____ _____.

   G: I'll keep my fingers _____ for you.

   B: _____ _____ _____ _____ _____ _____ "keep my fingers

   crossed"?

   G: It _____ I _____ you _____ _____.

   B: Thank you.

Listen & Talk 2 B

1. **A:** Two heads _____ _____ _____ one.

   B: _____ do you _____ _____ "Two heads are better than

   one"?

   A: I _____ working _____ is better _____ _____ _____ _____.

2. **A:** _____ makes _____.

   B: What do you _____ _____ "Practice makes perfect"?

   A: I _____ you learn something _____ _____ it _____

   _____ _____.

Conversation A

M: _____ _____ my dream, I went to many auditions, but I often

_____. _____, I never _____ _____. I _____ acting

and dancing _____. _____, I _____ my goal. It's important

_____ you _____ _____ _____.

Conversation B

Hana: You _____ sad, Jiho. What's _____?

Jiho: I _____ _____ I can _____ my dream.

Amy: _____ _____ _____ _____ _____ _____ _____ _____?

Jiho: I want to be an actor, but I always _____ _____. Maybe I

_____ _____ _____ _____.

Amy: Do you know this _____?

Jiho: Sure. He's a _____ movie star.

Amy: He _____ _____ _____ 100 auditions.

Jiho: Really? Maybe I _____ _____ _____. I will _____

more for my next audition.

Hana: That's right! _____ _____ _____ _____ _____

_____ _____.

44 Lesson 7. Work on Your Dreams

2. B: 나 내일 노래 경연 대회가 있어. 나는 정말 1등을 하고 싶어.
   G: 너에게 'keep my fingers crossed'할게.
   B: 'keep my fingers crossed'가 무슨 뜻이니?
   G: 그건 내가 너에게 행운을 빈다는 뜻이야.
   B: 고마워.

1. A: 두 개의 머리가 머리 하나보다 낫다.
   B: "두 개의 머리가 머리 하나보다 낫다."가 무슨 뜻이니?
   A: 함께 일하는 것이 혼자 일하는 것보다 낫다는 뜻이야.

2. A: 연습이 완벽함을 만든다.
   B: "연습이 완벽함을 만든다."가 무슨 뜻이니?
   A: 반복해서 무언가를 하면 배우게 된다는 뜻이야.

M: 내 꿈을 이루기 위해 나는 많은 오디션에 갔지만 자주 떨어졌다. 하지만 나는 절대 포기하지 않았다. 나는 연기와 춤 수업을 들었다. 마침내 나는 내 목표를 이뤘다. 절대 포기하지 않는 것이 중요하다.

하나: 너 슬퍼 보여, 지호야. 무슨 일이니?
지호: 내 생각에 나는 꿈을 이룰 수 없을 것 같아.
Amy: 그게 무슨 말이니?
지호: 나는 배우가 되고 싶지만 항상 오디션에서 떨어져. 어쩌면 나는 포기해야 할 거 같아.
Amy: 너 이 배우를 아니?
지호: 당연하지. 그는 유명한 영화배우잖아.
Amy: 그는 백 번 이상 오디션에서 떨어졌대.
지호: 정말? 그러면 나도 계속 노력해야겠구나. 나는 다음 오디션을 위해서 더 연습할 거야.
하나: 바로 그거야! 절대 포기하지 않는 것이 중요해.

※ 다음 우리말에 맞도록 대화를 영어로 쓰시오.

Listen & Speak 1 A

1. G: _____
   B: _____
   G: _____
   B: _____

2. G: _____
   B: _____
   G: _____
   B: _____
   G: _____
   B: _____

Listen & Speak 1 B

1. A: _____
   B: _____
   A: _____

2. A: _____
   B: _____
   A: _____

Listen & Talk 2 A

1. G: _____
   B: _____
   G: _____
   B: _____
   G: _____
   B: _____

해석

1. G: 이봐, 민호야. 이 수학 문제의 정답을 찾았니?
   B: 아니. 그건 나에게 너무 어려워. 나는 수학을 잘하지 못 해.
   G: 내가 한 번 볼게. 네가 그 문제를 풀기 위해선 이 수학 공식을 이용하는 것이 중요해.
   B: 오, 알겠어. 그걸 사용해 볼게.

2. G: 네 포스터가 멋져 보여.
   B: 고마워, Kate. 네 것은 끝냈니?
   G: 아직 못 끝냈어. 나는 그림을 잘 그리지 못 해. 어떻게 하면 내가 그림을 잘 그릴 수 있을까?
   B: 시간이 필요해. 네가 가능한 자주 그림을 그리는 것이 중요해.
   G: 내가 계속 연습해야 한다는 뜻이니?
   B: 맞아.

1. A: 훌륭한 댄서가 되는 것은 어려워. 내가 무엇을 해야 할까?
   B: 절대 포기하지 않는 것이 중요해.
   A: 알겠어. 그것을 잊지 않을게.

2. A: 좋은 이야기를 쓰는 것은 어려워. 내가 무엇을 해야 할까?
   B: 책을 많이 읽는 것이 중요해.
   A: 알겠어. 그것을 잊지 않을게.

1. G: 오, 이것은 하기 어렵구나.
   B: 무슨 일이야?
   G: 쿠키를 만드는 방법을 나에게 가르쳐 줄 수 있니?
   B: 물론이지. 그건 'a walk in the park'야.
   G: 그게 무슨 뜻이니?
   B: 하기 쉽다는 뜻이야.

2. B: _____

   G: _____

   B: _____

   G: _____

   B: _____

2. B: 나 내일 노래 경연 대회가 있어. 나는 정말 1등을 하고 싶어.
   G: 너에게 'keep my fingers crossed'할게.
   B: 'keep my fingers crossed'가 무슨 뜻이니?
   G: 그건 내가 너에게 행운을 빈다는 뜻이야.
   B: 고마워.

Listen & Talk 2 B

1. A: _____

   B: _____

   A: _____

2. A: _____

   B: _____

   A: _____

1. A: 두 개의 머리가 머리 하나보다 낫다.
   B: "두 개의 머리가 머리 하나보다 낫다."가 무슨 뜻이니?
   A: 함께 일하는 것이 혼자 일하는 것보다 낫다는 뜻이야.

2. A: 연습이 완벽함을 만든다.
   B: "연습이 완벽함을 만든다."가 무슨 뜻이니?
   A: 반복해서 무언가를 하면 배우게 된다는 뜻이야.

Conversation A

M: _____

_____

_____

M: 내 꿈을 이루기 위해 나는 많은 오디션에 갔지만 자주 떨어졌다. 하지만 나는 절대 포기하지 않았다. 나는 연기와 춤 수업을 들었다. 마침내 나는 내 목표를 이뤘다. 절대 포기하지 않는 것이 중요하다.

Conversation B

Hana: _____

Jiho: _____

Amy: _____

Jiho: _____

Amy: _____

Jiho: _____

Amy: _____

Jiho: _____

Hana: _____

하나: 너 슬퍼 보여, 지호야. 무슨 일이니?
지호: 내 생각에 나는 꿈을 이룰 수 없을 것 같아.
Amy: 그게 무슨 말이니?
지호: 나는 배우가 되고 싶지만 항상 오디션에서 떨어져. 어쩌면 나는 포기해야 할 거 같아.
Amy: 너 이 배우를 아니?
지호: 당연하지. 그는 유명한 영화배우잖아.
Amy: 그는 백 번 이상 오디션에서 떨어졌대.
지호: 정말? 그러면 나도 계속 노력해야겠구나. 나는 다음 오디션을 위해서 더 연습할 거야.
하나: 바로 그거야! 절대 포기하지 않는 것이 중요해.

※ 다음 우리말과 일치하도록 빈칸에 알맞은 것을 골라 쓰시오.

1 Jackie Robinson _____ the _____ _____
A. Color   B. Breaks   C. Line

2 _____ was New York City _____ _____ 15, 1947.
A. April   B. it   C. on

3 Jackie Robinson, an African American, _____ _____ the field _____ second baseman _____ the Brooklyn Dodgers.
A. on   B. for   C. went   D. as

4 People _____ _____ their _____.
A. believe   B. couldn't   C. eyes

5 He was the _____ African _____ player to _____ _____ a Major League team.
A. American   B. play   C. first   D. on

6 That day, the _____ _____ was _____.
A. line   B. broken   C. color

7 Robinson _____ _____ _____.
A. difficulties   B. faced   C. many

8 _____ Robinson was a _____ player and a _____ person, his teammates did not want to play _____ him.
A. gentle   B. although   C. talented   D. with

9 _____ hotel _____ the team _____ _____ Robinson was on the team.
A. because   B. turned   C. down   D. every

10 When he was at _____, people in the stands _____ shouted _____ him.
A. rudely   B. at   C. bat

11 Robinson _____ to _____, 'I need to _____ calm and _____ on baseball.
A. keep   B. thought   C. focus   D. himself

12 I will _____ and _____ a player who people _____.
A. like   B. try   C. become

13 Then, next season, _____ will _____ African American players in the _____.'
A. there   B. more   C. league   D. be

14 Robinson _____ all his time and _____ _____ baseball.
A. into   B. put   C. energy

1 Jackie Robinson 인종 차별을 깨다

2 1947년 4월 15일 뉴욕시에 서였다.

3 아프리카계 미국인 Jackie Robinson은 브루클린 다저스의 2루수로 경기장에 나갔다.

4 사람들은 자신들의 눈을 의심했다.

5 그는 메이저리그 팀에서 경기한 최초의 아프리카계 미국인 선수였다.

6 그날 인종 차별이 깨졌다.

7 Robinson은 많은 어려움에 직면했다.

8 Robinson은 재능 있는 선수이고 온화한 사람이었지만 그의 팀원들은 그와 함께 경기하기를 원하지 않았다.

9 Robinson이 팀에 있었기 때문에 모든 호텔에서 그 팀을 거절했다.

10 그가 타석에 있을 때, 관중석에 있는 사람들이 그에게 무례하게 소리치기도 했다.

11 Robinson은 마음속으로 생각했다. '나는 평정심을 유지하고 야구에 집중해야 해.

12 나는 노력해서 사람들이 좋아하는 선수가 될 거야.

13 그러면 다음 시즌에는 아프리카계 미국인 선수가 리그에 더 많이 생길 거야.'

14 Robinson은 자신의 모든 시간과 에너지를 야구에 집중했다.

15 _____ _____, he became great at _____ and base _____.

    A. batting   B. with   C. running   D. practice

16 Robinson's _____ _____ his _____.

    A. moved   B. effort   C. teammates

17 When people shouted at Robinson, _____ of his teammates walked _____ to Robinson and _____ him _____ the shoulder.

    A. on   B. up   C. one   D. tapped

18 "_____ not _____ _____ them.

    A. to   B. do   C. listen

19 You're _____ _____," he said.

    A. fine   B. doing

20 His _____ _____ Robinson _____ play _____.

    A. harder   B. helped   C. support   D. to

21 _____, Robinson _____ the _____ of _____ players and fans.

    A. other   B. earned   C. finally   D. respect

22 _____ _____ Robinson, the Dodgers _____ the National League Championship _____ 1947.

    A. won   B. to   C. thanks   D. in

23 The league _____ Robinson's excellence and _____ him _____ the Rookie of the Year Award in the _____ year.

    A. presented   B. recognized   C. same   D. with

24 After that season, _____ teams _____ African American players _____ _____ them.

    A. join   B. asked   C. other   D. to

25 Robinson's _____ _____ was 42.

    A. number   B. uniform

26 Baseball players in Major League teams _____ _____ wear the number 42 _____ _____ him.

    A. honor   B. longer   C. to   D. no

27 Every year, _____, on April 15, _____ player _____ the number that Robinson _____.

    A. wears   B. however   C. wore   D. every

28 The day _____ _____ "Jackie Robinson Day."

    A. called   B. is

---

15 연습을 함으로써 그는 타격과 주루를 잘하게 되었다.

16 Robinson의 노력은 그의 팀원들을 감동시켰다.

17 사람들이 Robinson에게 소리쳤을 때, 그의 팀 동료 중 한 명이 Robinson에게 다가가 어깨를 두드렸다.

18 "그들 말을 듣지 마.

19 너는 잘하고 있어."라고 그가 말했다.

20 그의 지지는 Robinson이 더 열심히 경기하는 데 도움이 됐다.

21 마침내, Robinson은 다른 선수들과 팬들의 존경을 받았다.

22 Robinson 덕분에 다저스는 1947년에 내셔널리그 챔피언십에서 우승하게 되었다.

23 리그에서는 Robinson의 탁월함을 인정했고, 같은 해에 그에게 신인상을 수여했다.

24 그 시즌 이후, 다른 팀들은 아프리카계 미국인 선수들에게 자신들의 팀에 합류할 것을 요청했다.

25 Robinson의 등 번호는 42번이었다.

26 메이저리그 팀의 야구 선수들은 그에 대한 존경을 보여 주기 위해 더 이상 42번을 달지 않는다.

27 하지만 매년 4월 15일, 모든 선수들은 Robinson이 달았던 번호를 단다.

28 이 날을 '재키 로빈슨 데이'라고 부른다.

※ 다음 우리말과 일치하도록 빈칸에 알맞은 말을 쓰시오.

1 Jackie Robinson _____ _____ _____ _____

2 It was New York City _____ _____ _____, _____.

3 Jackie Robinson, an _____ _____, went on the field _____ second baseman _____ the Brooklyn Dodgers.

4 People _____ _____ _____ _____.

5 He was _____ _____ _____ _____ to play on a Major League team.

6 That day, _____ _____ _____ _____ _____ _____.

7 Robinson _____ _____ _____.

8 _____ Robinson was a _____ _____ and a gentle person, his teammates did not want _____ _____ _____ _____.

9 Every hotel _____ _____ _____ _____ because Robinson was on the team.

10 When he _____ _____ _____, people in the stands _____ _____ _____ him.

11 Robinson _____ _____ _____, 'I need to _____ _____ and _____ _____ baseball.

12 I will try and _____ a player _____ _____ _____.

13 Then, next season, _____ _____ _____ _____ African American players in the league.'

14 Robinson _____ all his time and energy _____ baseball.

1 Jackie Robinson 인종 차별을 깨다

2 1947년 4월 15일 뉴욕시에서였다.

3 아프리카계 미국인 Jackie Robinson은 브루클린 다저스의 2루수로 경기장에 나갔다.

4 사람들은 자신들의 눈을 의심했다.

5 그는 메이저리그 팀에서 경기한 최초의 아프리카계 미국인 선수였다.

6 그날 인종 차별이 깨졌다.

7 Robinson은 많은 어려움에 직면했다.

8 Robinson은 재능 있는 선수이고 온화한 사람이었지만 그의 팀원들은 그와 함께 경기하기를 원하지 않았다.

9 Robinson이 팀에 있었기 때문에 모든 호텔에서 그 팀을 거절했다.

10 그가 타석에 있을 때, 관중석에 있는 사람들이 그에게 무례하게 소리치기도 했다.

11 Robinson은 마음속으로 생각했다. '나는 평정심을 유지하고 야구에 집중해야 해.

12 나는 노력해서 사람들이 좋아하는 선수가 될 거야.

13 그러면 다음 시즌에는 아프리카계 미국인 선수가 리그에 더 많이 생길 거야.'

14 Robinson은 자신의 모든 시간과 에너지를 야구에 집중했다.

15 _____ _____, he became great _____ _____ and _____ _____.

16 Robinson's _____ _____ his _____.

17 When people _____ _____ Robinson, _____ _____ _____ _____ walked _____ _____ Robinson and _____ _____ _____ _____ _____.

18 "_____ _____ _____ _____ them.

19 You're _____ _____," he said.

20 His support _____ Robinson _____ _____ _____.

21 Finally, Robinson _____ _____ _____ of other players and fans.

22 _____ _____ Robinson, the Dodgers _____ the National League Championship in 1947.

23 The league _____ Robinson's excellence and _____ him _____ the Rookie of the Year Award in the _____ _____.

24 After that season, _____ teams _____ African American players _____ _____ them.

25 Robinson's _____ _____ was 42.

26 Baseball players in Major League teams _____ _____ _____ the number 42 _____ _____ _____.

27 _____ year, _____, on April 15, every player _____ the number that Robinson _____.

28 The day _____ _____ "Jackie Robinson Day."

---

15 연습을 함으로써 그는 타격과 주루를 잘하게 되었다.

16 Robinson의 노력은 그의 팀원들을 감동시켰다.

17 사람들이 Robinson에게 소리쳤을 때, 그의 팀 동료 중 한 명이 Robinson에게 다가가 어깨를 두드렸다.

18 "그들 말을 듣지 마.

19 너는 잘하고 있어."라고 그가 말했다.

20 그의 지지는 Robinson이 더 열심히 경기하는 데 도움이 됐다.

21 마침내, Robinson은 다른 선수들과 팬들의 존경을 받았다.

22 Robinson 덕분에 다저스는 1947년에 내셔널리그 챔피언십에서 우승하게 되었다.

23 리그에서는 Robinson의 탁월함을 인정했고, 같은 해에 그에게 신인상을 수여했다.

24 그 시즌 이후, 다른 팀들은 아프리카계 미국인 선수들에게 자신들의 팀에 합류할 것을 요청했다.

25 Robinson의 등 번호는 42번이었다.

26 메이저리그 팀의 야구 선수들은 그에 대한 존경을 보여 주기 위해 더 이상 42번을 달지 않는다.

27 하지만 매년 4월 15일, 모든 선수들은 Robinson이 달았던 번호를 단다.

28 이 날을 '재키 로빈슨 데이'라고 부른다.

※ 다음 문장을 우리말로 쓰시오.

1 Jackie Robinson Breaks the Color Line

➡ _____

2 It was New York City on April 15, 1947.

➡ _____

3 Jackie Robinson, an African American, went on the field as second baseman for the Brooklyn Dodgers.

➡ _____

4 People couldn't believe their eyes.

➡ _____

5 He was the first African American player to play on a Major League team.

➡ _____

6 That day, the color line was broken.

➡ _____

7 Robinson faced many difficulties.

➡ _____

8 Although Robinson was a talented player and a gentle person, his teammates did not want to play with him.

➡ _____

9 Every hotel turned the team down because Robinson was on the team.

➡ _____

10 When he was at bat, people in the stands rudely shouted at him.

➡ _____

11 Robinson thought to himself, 'I need to keep calm and focus on baseball.

➡ _____

12 I will try and become a player who people like.

➡ _____

13 Then, next season, there will be more African American players in the league.'

➡ _____

14 Robinson put all his time and energy into baseball.

➡ _____

15 With practice, he became great at batting and base running.

➡ _____

16 Robinson's effort moved his teammates.

➡ _____

17 When people shouted at Robinson, one of his teammates walked up to Robinson and tapped him on the shoulder.

➡ _____

18 "Do not listen to them.

➡ _____

19 You're doing fine," he said.

➡ _____

20 His support helped Robinson to play harder.

➡ _____

21 Finally, Robinson earned the respect of other players and fans.

➡ _____

22 Thanks to Robinson, the Dodgers won the National League Championship in 1947.

➡ _____

23 The league recognized Robinson's excellence and presented him with the Rookie of the Year Award in the same year.

➡ _____

24 After that season, other teams asked African American players to join them.

➡ _____

25 Robinson's uniform number was 42.

➡ _____

26 Baseball players in Major League teams no longer wear the number 42 to honor him.

➡ _____

27 Every year, however, on April 15, every player wears the number that Robinson wore.

➡ _____

28 The day is called "Jackie Robinson Day."

➡ _____

※ 다음 괄호 안의 단어들을 우리말에 맞도록 바르게 배열하시오.

1 (Robinson / Jackie / Breaks / Color / the / Line)
➡ _____

2 (was / it / York / New / City / April / on / 1947. / 15,)
➡ _____

3 (Robinson, / Jackie / African / an / American, / on / went / field / the / second / as / baseman / the / for / Dodgers. / Brooklyn)
➡ _____
_____

4 (couldn't / people / their / believe / eyes.)
➡ _____

5 (was / he / first / the / American / African / to / player / on / play / a / League / Major / team.)
➡ _____

6 (day, / that / color / the / was / broken. / line)
➡ _____

7 (faced / Robinson / difficulties. / many)
➡ _____

8 (Robinson / although / a / was / player / talented / and / gentle / a / person, / teammates / his / not / did / to / want / him. / with / play)
➡ _____
_____

9 (hotel / every / the / turned / team / down / because / was / Robinson / on / team. / the)
➡ _____

10 (he / when / at / was / bat, / in / people / the / stands / shouted / rudely / him. / at)
➡ _____

11 (thought / Robinson / himself, / to / 'I / to / need / calm / keep / and / on / focus / baseball.)
➡ _____

12 (I / try / will / and / a / become / player / people / who / like.)
➡ _____

13 (next / then, / season, / will / there / more / be / American / African / players / in / league.' / the)
➡ _____

14 (put / Robinson / all / time / his / and / into / baseball. / energy)
➡ _____

1　Jackie Robinson 인종 차별을 깨다

2　1947년 4월 15일 뉴욕시에 서였다.

3　아프리카계 미국인 Jackie Robinson은 브루클린 다저스의 2루수로 경기장에 나갔다.

4　사람들은 자신들의 눈을 의심했다.

5　그는 메이저리그 팀에서 경기한 최초의 아프리카계 미국인 선수 였다.

6　그날 인종 차별이 깨졌다.

7　Robinson은 많은 어려움에 직면했다.

8　Robinson은 재능 있는 선수이고 온화한 사람이었지만 그의 팀원들은 그와 함께 경기하기를 원하지 않았다.

9　Robinson이 팀에 있었기 때문에 모든 호텔에서 그 팀을 거절했다.

10　그가 타석에 있을 때, 관중석에 있는 사람들이 그에게 무례하게 소리치기도 했다.

11　Robinson은 마음속으로 생각했다. '나는 평정심을 유지하고 야구에 집중해야 해.

12　나는 노력해서 사람들이 좋아하는 선수가 될 거야.

13　그러면 다음 시즌에는 아프리카계 미국인 선수가 리그에 더 많이 생길 거야.'

14　Robinson은 자신의 모든 시간과 에너지를 야구에 집중했다.

15 (practice, / with / became / he / at / great / batting / and / running. / base)
➡ _____

16 (effort / Robinson's / moved / teammates. / his)
➡ _____

17 (people / when / at / shouted / Robinson, / of / one / teammates / his / up / walked / to / Robinson / and / him / tapped / the / on / shoulder.)
➡ _____

18 (not / "do / to / listen / them.)
➡ _____

19 (doing / you're / fine," / said. / he)
➡ _____

20 (support / his / Robinson / helped / play / harder. / to)
➡ _____

21 (Robinson / finally, / the / earned / respect / other / of / fans. / and / players)
➡ _____

22 (to / thanks / Robinson, Dodgers / the / the / won / National / Championship / League / 1947. / in)
➡ _____

23 (league / the / Robinson's / recognized / presented / and / excellence / with / him Rookie / the / of / the / Award / Year / the / in / year. / same)
➡ _____
_____

24 (that / after / season, / teams / other / African / asked / players / American / to / them. / join)
➡ _____

25 (uniform / Robinson's / was / number / 42.)
➡ _____

26 (players / baseball / Major / in / League / no / teams / wear / longer / number / the / to / 42 / him. / honor)
➡ _____
_____

27 (year, / every / on / however, / 15, / April / player / every / the / wears / that / number / wore. / Robinson)
➡ _____
_____

28 (day / the / called / is / "Jackie / Robinson / Day." / Robinson)
➡ _____

15 연습을 함으로써 그는 타격과 주루를 잘하게 되었다.

16 Robinson의 노력은 그의 팀원들을 감동시켰다.

17 사람들이 Robinson에게 소리쳤을 때. 그의 팀 동료 중 한 명이 Robinson에게 다가가 어깨를 두드렸다.

18 "그들 말을 듣지 마.

19 너는 잘하고 있어."라고 그가 말했다.

20 그의 지지는 Robinson이 더 열심히 경기하는 데 도움이 됐다.

21 마침내, Robinson은 다른 선수들과 팬들의 존경을 받았다.

22 Robinson 덕분에 다저스는 **1947**년에 내셔널리그 챔피언십에서 우승하게 되었다.

23 리그에서는 Robinson의 탁월함을 인정했고, 같은 해에 그에게 신인상을 수여했다.

24 그 시즌 이후. 다른 팀들은 아프리카계 미국인 선수들에게 자신들의 팀에 합류할 것을 요청했다.

25 Robinson의 등 번호는 **42**번이었다.

26 메이저리그 팀의 야구 선수들은 그에 대한 존경을 보여 주기 위해 더 이상 **42**번을 달지 않는다.

27 하지만 매년 **4**월 **15**일. 모든 선수들은 Robinson이 달았던 번호를 단다.

28 이 날을 '재키 로빈슨 데이'라고 부른다.

※ **다음 우리말을 영어로 쓰시오.**

1 Jackie Robinson 인종 차별을 깨다

➡ _____

2 1947년 4월 15일 뉴욕시에서였다.

➡ _____

3 아프리카계 미국인 Jackie Robinson은 브루클린 다저스의 2루수로 경기장에 나갔다.

➡ _____

4 사람들은 자신들의 눈을 의심했다.

➡ _____

5 그는 메이저리그 팀에서 경기한 최초의 아프리카계 미국인 선수였다.

➡ _____

6 그날 인종 차별이 깨졌다.

➡ _____

7 Robinson은 많은 어려움에 직면했다.

➡ _____

8 Robinson은 재능 있는 선수이고 온화한 사람이었지만 그의 팀원들은 그와 함께 경기하기를 원하지 않았다.

➡ _____

9 Robinson이 팀에 있었기 때문에 모든 호텔에서 그 팀을 거절했다.

➡ _____

10 그가 타석에 있을 때, 관중석에 있는 사람들이 그에게 무례하게 소리치기도 했다.

➡ _____

11 Robinson은 마음속으로 생각했다. '나는 평정심을 유지하고 야구에 집중해야 해.

➡ _____

12 나는 노력해서 사람들이 좋아하는 선수가 될 거야.

➡ _____

13 그러면 다음 시즌에는 아프리카계 미국인 선수가 리그에 더 많이 생길 거야.'

➡ _____

14 Robinson은 자신의 모든 시간과 에너지를 야구에 집중했다.

➡ _____

15 연습을 함으로써 그는 타격과 주루를 잘하게 되었다.

➡ _____

16 Robinson의 노력은 그의 팀원들을 감동시켰다.

➡ _____

17 사람들이 Robinson에게 소리쳤을 때, 그의 팀 동료 중 한 명이 Robinson에게 다가가 어깨를 두드렸다.

➡ _____

18 "그들 말을 듣지 마.

➡ _____

19 너는 잘하고 있어."라고 그가 말했다.

➡ _____

20 그의 지지는 Robinson이 더 열심히 경기하는 데 도움이 됐다.

➡ _____

21 마침내, Robinson은 다른 선수들과 팬들의 존경을 받았다.

➡ _____

22 Robinson 덕분에 다저스는 1947년에 내셔널리그 챔피언십에서 우승하게 되었다.

➡ _____

23 리그에서는 Robinson의 탁월함을 인정했고, 같은 해에 그에게 신인상을 수여했다.

➡ _____

24 그 시즌 이후, 다른 팀들은 아프리카계 미국인 선수들에게 자신들의 팀에 합류할 것을 요청했다.

➡ _____

25 Robinson의 등 번호는 42번이었다.

➡ _____

26 메이저리그 팀의 야구 선수들은 그에 대한 존경을 보여 주기 위해 더 이상 42번을 달지 않는다.

➡ _____

27 하지만 매년 4월 15일, 모든 선수들은 Robinson이 달았던 번호를 단다.

➡ _____

28 이 날을 '재키 로빈슨 데이'라고 부른다.

➡ _____

※ 다음 우리말과 일치하도록 빈칸에 알맞은 말을 쓰시오.

Language in Use

1. I visited three countries _____ _____.

2. France was _____ _____ _____ _____ I _____.

3. Mary is the girl _____ I _____ in Paris.

4. The blue watch is the _____ _____ _____ _____ there _____ my brother.

1. 작년에 나는 3개국을 방문했다.
2. 프랑스가 내가 방문한 첫 번째 국가였다.
3. Mary는 내가 파리에서 만났던 소녀이다.
4. 그 파란 시계는 그곳에서 내 동생을 위해 산 선물이다.

Enjoy Writing B

1. _____ I Will _____ My Dream

2. I _____ _____ _____ a designer.

3. There are three things _____ I _____ _____ do _____ _____ my dream.

4. I need to be _____, be _____, and never _____ _____.

5. _____ healthy will _____ me _____ _____ for my dream.

6. Being creative will _____ _____ _____ something different.

7. Plus, I will always tell _____ never _____ _____ _____ because it will _____ _____ _____ harder.

1. 어떻게 나의 꿈을 성취할 것인가
2. 나는 디자이너가 되기를 원한다.
3. 나의 꿈을 성취하기 위해 내가 할 필요가 있는 세 가지가 있다.
4. 나는 건강해야 하고, 창의적이어야 하고, 그리고 결코 포기하지 말아야 한다.
5. 건강한 것은 나의 꿈을 계속 유지하도록 도와줄 것이다.
6. 창의적인 것은 내가 무언가 다른 것을 하도록 도와줄 것이다.
7. 더하여, 내 스스로에게 결코 포기하지 말라고 항상 말할 것인데, 이는 내가 더 열심히 노력하도록 해 줄 것이기 때문이다.

Wrap Up 2

1. B: _____ difficult _____ _____ English.

2. G: Rome _____ _____ _____ in a day.

3. B: _____ do you _____ _____ that?

4. G: I mean it _____ time _____ _____ _____.

5. B: I _____.

1. B: 영어를 배우는 것은 어려워.
2. G: 로마는 하루아침에 이루어지지 않았어.
3. B: 그게 무슨 뜻이니?
4. G: 무언가를 이루는 데 시간이 걸린다는 뜻이야.
5. B: 알겠어.

※ 다음 우리말을 영어로 쓰시오.

Language in Use

1. 작년에 나는 3개국을 방문했다.
➡ _____

2. 프랑스가 내가 방문한 첫 번째 국가였다.
➡ _____

3. Mary는 내가 파리에서 만났던 소녀이다.
➡ _____

4. 그 파란 시계는 그곳에서 내 동생을 위해 산 선물이다.
➡ _____

Enjoy Writing B

1. 어떻게 나의 꿈을 성취할 것인가
➡ _____

2. 나는 디자이너가 되기를 원한다.
➡ _____

3. 나의 꿈을 성취하기 위해 내가 할 필요가 있는 세 가지가 있다.
➡ _____

4. 나는 건강해야 하고, 창의적이어야 하고, 그리고 결코 포기하지 말아야 한다.
➡ _____

5. 건강한 것은 나의 꿈을 계속 유지하도록 도와줄 것이다.
➡ _____

6. 창의적인 것은 내가 무언가 다른 것을 하도록 도와줄 것이다.
➡ _____

7. 더하여, 내 스스로에게 결코 포기하지 말라고 항상 말할 것인데, 이는 내가 더 열심히 노력하도록 해 줄 것이기 때문이다.
➡ _____

Wrap Up 2

1. B: 영어를 배우는 것은 어려워.
➡ _____

2. G: 로마는 하루아침에 이루어지지 않았어.
➡ _____

3. B: 그게 무슨 뜻이니?
➡ _____

4. G: 무언가를 이루는 데 시간이 걸린다는 뜻이야.
➡ _____

5. B: 알겠어.
➡ _____

※ 다음 영어를 우리말로 쓰시오.

01	counter	
02	automatically	
03	condition	
04	price	
05	recommend	
06	decorate	
07	medicine	
08	material	
09	society	
10	rescue	
11	technology	
12	fit	
13	advance	
14	temperature	
15	experience	
16	charge	
17	fancy	
18	lower	
19	skill	
20	purchase	
21	huge	

22	later	
23	virtual	
24	difference	
25	heavily	
26	law	
27	since	
28	gravity	
29	deliver	
30	pay	
31	method	
32	work	
33	patient	
34	real	
35	forget to 동사원형	
36	in space	
37	take care of	
38	be ready for	
39	put on	
40	move around	
41	take place	
42	in the future	
43	would like to 동사원형	

※ 다음 우리말을 영어로 쓰시오.

01 심하게, 아주 많이 _____

02 자동적으로 _____

03 (지불, 대금 등을) 청구하다 _____

04 사서 _____

05 상태, 조건 _____

06 작동하다 _____

07 경험 _____

08 구하다 _____

09 발전 _____

10 (차수·모양 등이) 꼭 맞다 _____

11 중력 _____

12 거대한 _____

13 ~ 이후로 _____

14 가격 _____

15 배달하다 _____

16 장식하다, 꾸미다 _____

17 낮추다 _____

18 구조하다 _____

19 기술 _____

20 온도 _____

21 ~을 추천하다 _____

22 약 _____

23 환자 _____

24 차이, 차이점 _____

25 가상의 _____

26 구입(품) _____

27 방법, 방식 _____

28 사회 _____

29 맛보다 _____

30 재료 _____

31 ~을 제공하다 _____

32 추측하다 _____

33 (돈을) 지불하다 _____

34 과학 기술, 생산 기술 _____

35 일어나다, 개최되다 _____

36 ~할 준비가 되다 _____

37 입다, 쓰다, 신다 _____

38 합산하다 _____

39 ~을 돌보다 _____

40 ~할 필요가 없다 _____

41 돌아다니다 _____

42 ~에 대해 걱정하다 _____

43 곤경에 빠져서, 난처하여 _____

※ 다음 영영풀이에 알맞은 단어를 <보기>에서 골라 쓴 후, 우리말 뜻을 쓰시오.

1 _____ : a substance that you take to cure an illness: _____

2 _____ : to save someone or something from danger or harm: _____

3 _____ : with operating by itself: _____

4 _____ : someone who is receiving medical treatment: _____

5 _____ : a substance that is used for a particular purpose: _____

6 _____ : to speak in favor of something: _____

7 _____ : a way of doing something, especially a planned way: _____

8 _____ : to take something to somewhere to give it to someone: _____

9 _____ : to add ornaments, etc. to something to make it more attractive:

_____

10 _____ : a piece of computer software that is designed to do a particular job:

_____

11 _____ : created by computers, or appearing on computers or the Internet:

_____

12 _____ : a place where a bus or train stops to allow passengers to get on and off:

_____

13 _____ : progress or an instance of progress in science, technology, human

knowledge, etc.: _____

14 _____ : an unmanned aircraft or ship guided by remote control or onboard

computers: _____

15 _____ : a statement of fact concerning what always happens in certain

circumstances; a scientific principle: _____

16 _____ : to ask someone to pay an amount of money for something that you are

selling to them or doing for them: _____

보기			
law	station	advance	recommend
automatically	charge	patient	medicine
deliver	rescue	method	app
material	drone	decorate	virtual

※ 다음 우리말과 일치하도록 빈칸에 알맞은 말을 쓰시오.

Listen & Speak 1 A

1. G: Oh, I _____ _____ _____ _____ the heater before I
      left home.
   B: Really? Then do you _____ _____ _____ home?
   G: No. I can _____ it _____ with my smartphone.
   B: Wow, I'm _____ _____ you can turn _____ the heater
      _____ your smartphone.

2. W: _____ _____ VR World. Would you _____ _____
      _____ Niagara Falls?
   B: Sure.
   W: Okay, _____ this _____.
   B: All _____. Wow, it _____ so real.
   W: It is huge, _____ _____?
   B: Yes, and _____ _____ that I feel water on my face.

Listen & Speak 1 B

1. A: Is _____ anything in these pictures that _____ you?
   B: Yes. I'm _____ that this drone can _____ a dog.

2. A: Is _____ _____ in these pictures _____ _____ you?
   B: Yes. _____ _____ _____ this car can drive _____
      _____.

Listen & Speak 2 A

1. W: May I _____ you?
   B: Hi, I'm _____ _____ a smart watch. Can you _____
      _____ _____?
   W: Sure. _____ _____ this one. It can play music _____ you.
   B: _____ cool.
   W: Also, you can _____ _____ anything just _____ _____
      to it.
   B: That's great. I _____ _____ it.

1. G: 아, 나는 집에서 나오기 전에 히터 끄는 것을 잊어버렸어.
   B: 정말? 그러면 넌 집으로 돌아가야 하니?
   G: 아니. 나는 내 스마트폰으로 히터를 끌 수 있어.
   B: 우와, 나는 네가 스마트폰으로 히터를 끌 수 있다는 게 놀라워.

2. W: VR 세계에 오신 것을 환영해요. 나이아가라 폭포를 방문하고 싶은가요?
   B: 물론이죠.
   W: 좋아요, 이걸 쓰세요.
   B: 알겠어요. 우와, 이것은 정말 진짜처럼 보여요.
   W: 거대하죠, 그렇지 않아요?
   B: 네, 그리고 얼굴에서 물이 느껴진다는 게 놀라워요.

1. A: 이 사진들에서 너를 놀라게 한 것이 있니?
   B: 응, 나는 이 드론이 개를 산책시킬 수 있는 게 놀라워.

2. A: 이 사진들에서 너를 놀라게 한 것이 있니?
   B: 응, 나는 이 차가 자동으로 운전할 수 있는 게 놀라워.

1. W: 도와드릴까요?
   B: 안녕하세요, 저는 스마트 워치를 찾고 있어요. 하나 보여 주실래요?
   W: 물론이죠. 이것을 보세요. 그것은 당신을 위해 음악을 연주할 수 있어요.
   B: 멋지네요.
   W: 또한 그것에게 말만 하면 어떤 것이든 검색할 수 있어요.
   B: 멋지네요. 저 그거 살게요.

2. M: Welcome. This is our new smart light. You _____ _____ _____ your hands to _____ it _____ and _____.

W: Really? Then can you _____ me _____ _____ do it?

M: Just say, "Light _____!" or "Light _____!"

W: Light _____ or light out? That's very _____.

Listen & Speak 2 B

1. A: I want to _____ go. Can you _____ go with me, please?
   B: _____.

2. A: My room is _____. Can you _____ it, please?
   B: Sure.

3. A: The dog wants _____ _____ _____. Can you _____ the dog, please?
   B: Sure.

Conversation A

M: These days, many things can _____ _____ humans. Some cars can _____ _____ a human driver. We can make smartphones do _____ work only_____ _____ _____ them. _____ _____ _____ we're _____ _____ in the future.

Conversation B

Amy: Wow, there _____ so many _____ in this library.

Hana: You're right. _____ _____ we find books about _____?

Terry: Hi, I'm Terry, the AI _____. Can I help you?

Amy: Hi. We're _____ _____ books about _____. Can you _____ one, please?

Terry: We have _____ _____ _____ about gravity in this library. I think *The Law of Gravity* will be the best one for you.

Hana: I'm surprised _____ _____ _____ _____ _____ _____.

Amy: Right. That's _____. Where is the book, Terry?

Terry: It's _____ the _____ _____. Come with me.

2. M: 환영해요. 이것은 우리의 새로운 스마트 전등이에요. 그것을 켜고 끄기 위해 손을 사용할 필요가 없어요.
   W: 정말로요? 그러면 그것을 켜고 끄는 방법을 나에게 말해 줄 수 있나요?
   M: "불 켜!" 또는 "불 꺼!"라고 말해요.
   W: 불 켜 또는 불 꺼? 정말 간단하네요.

1. A: 나는 바둑을 두고 싶어. 나와 함께 바둑을 둘 수 있니?
   B: 물론이지.

2. A: 나의 방은 지저분해. 청소해 줄 수 있니?
   B: 물론이지.

3. A: 개가 나가고 싶어 해. 개를 산책시켜 줄 수 있니?
   B: 물론이지.

M: 오늘날, 많은 것들이 인간처럼 작동한다. 어떤 차들은 인간 운전자 없이 이동할 수 있다. 우리는 스마트폰에 말하는 것만으로 스마트폰이 간단한 일을 하게 할 수 있다. 나는 우리가 이미 미래에 살고 있다는 게 놀랍다.

Amy: 와, 이 도서관에는 책이 아주 많구나.
하나: 네 말이 맞아. 우리가 중력에 관한 책들을 어디에서 찾을 수 있을까?
Terry: 안녕, 나는 AI 사서인 Terry라고 해. 내가 도와줄까?
Amy: 안녕, 우리는 중력에 관한 책들을 찾고 있어. 추천해 줄 수 있니?
Terry: 이 도서관에는 중력에 관한 책이 57권 있단다. 나는 'The Law of Gravity'라는 책이 너희들에게 가장 좋은 책일 거라고 생각해.
하나: 나는 네가 책을 추천해 줄 수 있다니 놀라워.
Amy: 맞아. 놀랍다. Terry야, 그 책은 어디에 있니?
Terry: 그건 3층에 있어. 나를 따라와.

※ 다음 우리말에 맞도록 대화를 영어로 쓰시오.

Listen & Speak 1 A

1. G: _____
   B: _____
   G: _____
   B: _____

2. W: _____
   B: _____
   W: _____
   B: _____
   W: _____
   B: _____

1. G: 아, 나는 집에서 나오기 전에 히터 끄는 것을 잊어버렸어.
   B: 정말? 그러면 넌 집으로 돌아가야 하니?
   G: 아니. 나는 내 스마트폰으로 히터를 끌 수 있어.
   B: 우와, 나는 네가 스마트폰으로 히터를 끌 수 있다는 게 놀라워.

2. W: VR 세계에 오신 것을 환영해요. 나이아가라 폭포를 방문하고 싶은가요?
   B: 물론이죠.
   W: 좋아요, 이걸 쓰세요.
   B: 알겠어요. 우와, 이것은 정말 진짜처럼 보여요.
   W: 거대하죠, 그렇지 않아요?
   B: 네, 그리고 얼굴에서 물이 느껴진다는 게 놀라워요.

Listen & Speak 1 B

1. A: _____
   B: _____

2. A: _____
   B: _____

1. A: 이 사진들에서 너를 놀라게 한 것이 있니?
   B: 응, 나는 이 드론이 개를 산책시킬 수 있는 게 놀라워.

2. A: 이 사진들에서 너를 놀라게 한 것이 있니?
   B: 응, 나는 이 차가 자동으로 운전할 수 있는 게 놀라워.

Listen & Speak 2 A

1. W: _____
   B: _____
   W: _____
   B: _____
   W: _____
   B: _____

1. W: 도와드릴까요?
   B: 안녕하세요, 저는 스마트 워치를 찾고 있어요. 하나 보여 주실래요?
   W: 물론이죠. 이것을 보세요. 그것은 당신을 위해 음악을 연주할 수 있어요.
   B: 멋지네요.
   W: 또한 그것에게 말만 하면 어떤 것이든 검색할 수 있어요.
   B: 멋지네요. 저 그거 살게요.

2. M: _____
   _____
   W: _____
   M: _____
   W: _____

Listen & Speak 2 B

1. A: _____
   B: _____
2. A: _____
   B: _____
3. A: _____
   B: _____

Conversation A

M: _____
_____
_____

Conversation B

Amy: _____
Hana: _____
Terry: _____
Amy: _____
Terry: _____

Hana: _____
Amy: _____
Terry: _____

2. M: 환영해요. 이것은 우리의 새로운 스마트 전등이에요. 그것을 켜고 끄기 위해 손을 사용할 필요가 없어요.
   W: 정말로요? 그러면 그것을 켜고 끄는 방법을 나에게 말해 줄 수 있나요?
   M: "불 켜!" 또는 "불 꺼!"라고 말해요.
   W: 불 켜 또는 불 꺼? 정말 간단하네요.

1. A: 나는 바둑을 두고 싶어. 나와 함께 바둑을 둘 수 있니?
   B: 물론이지.

2. A: 나의 방은 지저분해. 청소해 줄 수 있니?
   B: 물론이지.

3. A: 개가 나가고 싶어 해. 개를 산책시켜 줄 수 있니?
   B: 물론이지.

M: 오늘날, 많은 것들이 인간처럼 작동한다. 어떤 차들은 인간 운전자 없이 이동할 수 있다. 우리는 스마트폰에 말하는 것만으로 스마트폰이 간단한 일을 하게 할 수 있다. 나는 우리가 이미 미래에 살고 있다는 게 놀랍다.

Amy: 와, 이 도서관에는 책이 아주 많구나.
하나: 네 말이 맞아. 우리가 중력에 관한 책들을 어디에서 찾을 수 있을까?
Terry: 안녕, 나는 AI 사서인 Terry라고 해. 내가 도와줄까?
Amy: 안녕, 우리는 중력에 관한 책들을 찾고 있어. 추천해 줄 수 있니?
Terry: 이 도서관에는 중력에 관한 책이 57권 있단다. 나는 'The Law of Gravity'라는 책이 너희들에게 가장 좋은 책일 거라고 생각해.
하나: 나는 네가 책을 추천해 줄 수 있다니 놀라워.
Amy: 맞아. 놀랍다. Terry야, 그 책은 어디에 있니?
Terry: 그건 3층에 있어. 나를 따라와.

※ 다음 우리말과 일치하도록 빈칸에 알맞은 것을 골라 쓰시오.

1 _____ _____

A. Society   B. Changing

2 _____ in science and technology have _____ many changes in our lives _____ _____.

A. far   B. advances   C. so   D. caused

3 In the _____, science and technology will _____ more _____.

A. make   B. future   C. changes

4 Let's see _____ our lives may be _____ in the _____ future.

A. like   B. what   C. near

5 Sangho in the _____ _____

A. Center   B. Shopping

6 Shopping is _____ _____.

A. easier   B. much

7 _____ are no _____ and no _____.

A. lines   B. there   C. counters

8 Sangho _____ a shop _____ his smartphone which has a _____ shopping _____.

A. with   B. special   C. app   D. enters

9 In the _____, he _____ the _____ he wants.

A. items   B. shop   C. takes

10 The _____ are _____ _____ to a _____ card on his smartphone.

A. virtual   B. automatically   C. items   D. added

11 If Sangho _____ an item _____, it is _____ _____ from his list of purchases.

A. removed   B. back   C. puts   D. automatically

12 When he finishes _____, Sangho does not _____ to wait in _____ to _____.

A. line   B. shopping   C. pay   D. need

13 His virtual card _____ _____ all the prices and will _____ him _____.

A. up   B. later   C. charge   D. adds

14 _____ that _____?

A. fancy   B. isn't

---

1 변화하는 사회

2 과학과 기술의 발전은 지금까지 우리의 삶에 많은 변화를 초래해 왔다.

3 미래에 과학 기술은 더 많은 변화를 만들 것이다.

4 가까운 미래에 우리의 삶이 어떻게 될지 살펴보자.

5 쇼핑 센터에 있는 상호

6 쇼핑이 훨씬 쉽다.

7 줄도 없고 계산대도 없다.

8 상호는 특별한 쇼핑 앱이 있는 스마트폰을 가지고 가게로 들어간다.

9 가게에서 그는 그가 원하는 물건들을 집는다.

10 그 물건들은 자동으로 그의 스마트폰에 있는 가상 카드에 더해진다.

11 만약 상호가 물건을 되돌려 놓으면 그것은 자동으로 그의 구매 목록에서 제거된다.

12 쇼핑을 끝냈을 때 상호는 돈을 지불하기 위해 줄을 설 필요가 없다.

13 그의 가상 카드가 모든 가격을 더해서 나중에 그에게 청구할 것이다.

14 정말 멋지지 않은가?

15 Sumin's 3D _____ _____ and _____

A. Clothes　　　　B. House　　　　C. Printed

16 Sumin _____ in a _____ _____ house.

A. lives　　　　B. printed　　　　C. 3D

17 _____ a 3D printed house is faster and _____ than building a house _____ traditional _____.

A. cheaper　　　B. building　　　C. methods　　　D. with

18 Sumin's house _____ _____ because of its _____ design.

A. unique　　　　B. fantastic　　　C. looks

19 A 3D printer can _____ house _____ that people cannot make with _____ building methods and _____.

A. traditional　　B. shapes　　　C. materials　　　D. produce

20 Sumin _____ likes to make her _____ at home _____ _____ a 3D printer.

A. clothes　　　B. using　　　C. by　　　D. also

21 She can _____ colors and materials and can design clothes that _____ her body and _____ her _____.

A. fit　　　　B. suit　　　C. choose　　　D. tastes

22 Sumin is now a _____ _____!

A. designer　　　B. fashion

23 Dongmin _____ the _____

A. Hospital　　　B. in

24 Dongmin is _____ his _____ in the _____.

A. grandfather　　B. hospital　　　C. visiting

25 An _____ _____ _____ the room.

A. enters　　　B. nurse　　　C. AI

26 It _____ _____ the room and _____ the patients' _____.

A. checks　　　B. around　　　C. conditions　　　D. moves

27 When the AI nurse finds that Dongmin's grandfather has a _____ _____, it gives him some _____ to _____ his temperature.

A. temperature　　B. lower　　　C. medicine　　　D. high

28 _____ you ever _____ about these _____?

A. changes　　　B. have　　　C. thought

29 Some changes have already started to _____ _____ while _____ may start in the _____ future.

A. place　　　B. near　　　C. others　　　D. take

30 Can you _____ _____ _____?

A. other　　　B. changes　　　C. imagine

31 _____ some time to _____ _____ them.

A. think　　　B. take　　　C. about

15 수민이의 3D 프린터로 만든 집과 옷

16 수민이는 3D 프린터로 만든 집에 산다.

17 3D 프린터로 집을 짓는 것은 전통적인 방법으로 집을 짓는 것보다 더 빠르고 저렴하다.

18 수민이의 집은 독특한 디자인 때문에 멋져 보인다.

19 3D 프린터는 사람들이 전통 건축 방법과 재료들로 만들 수 없는 집 모양을 만들어 낼 수 있다.

20 수민이는 또한 집에서 3D 프린터를 사용해 옷을 만드는 것을 좋아한다.

21 그녀는 색깔과 재료를 고를 수 있고 자신의 몸과 취향에 맞는 옷을 디자인할 수 있다.

22 수민이는 이제 패션 디자이너이다!

23 병원에 있는 동민

24 동민이는 병원에 계시는 그의 할아버지를 방문하고 있다.

25 AI 간호사가 병실로 들어온다.

26 그것은 병실을 돌아다니고, 환자들의 상태를 확인한다.

27 AI 간호사가 동민이 할아버지가 열이 높다는 것을 알았을 때 그것은 그의 체온을 낮추기 위해 그에게 약을 준다.

28 여러분은 이러한 변화에 대해 생각해 본 적 있는가?

29 어떤 변화는 이미 일어나기 시작했고 반면 다른 것들은 가까운 미래에 일어날지도 모른다.

30 여러분은 다른 변화들을 상상할 수 있는가?

31 그것들에 대해 잠깐 생각해 보자.

※ 다음 우리말과 일치하도록 빈칸에 알맞은 말을 쓰시오.

1 _____ Society

2 _____ in science and _____ _____ _____ many _____ in our lives _____ _____.

3 _____ _____ _____, science and technology will _____ _____ _____.

4 _____ see what our lives _____ _____ _____ in the _____ future.

5 Sangho in the _____ _____

6 Shopping is _____ _____.

7 There are _____ _____ and _____ _____.

8 Sangho enters a shop _____ his smartphone which has a _____ _____ _____.

9 In the shop, he _____ _____ _____ he wants.

10 The items _____ _____ _____ _____ a _____ card on his smartphone.

11 If Sangho _____ an item _____, it _____ _____ _____ his _____ _____ _____.

12 When he finishes _____, Sangho _____ _____ _____ _____ wait _____ _____ to pay.

13 His virtual card _____ _____ all the _____ and will _____ him _____.

14 _____ that _____?

1 변화하는 사회

2 과학과 기술의 발전은 지금까지 우리의 삶에 많은 변화를 초래해 왔다.

3 미래에 과학 기술은 더 많은 변화를 만들 것이다.

4 가까운 미래에 우리의 삶이 어떻게 될지 살펴보자.

5 쇼핑 센터에 있는 상호

6 쇼핑이 훨씬 쉽다.

7 줄도 없고 계산대도 없다.

8 상호는 특별한 쇼핑 앱이 있는 스마트폰을 가지고 가게로 들어간다.

9 가게에서 그는 그가 원하는 물건들을 집는다.

10 그 물건들은 자동으로 그의 스마트폰에 있는 가상 카드에 더해진다.

11 만약 상호가 물건을 되돌려 놓으면 그것은 자동으로 그의 구매 목록에서 제거된다.

12 쇼핑을 끝냈을 때 상호는 돈을 지불하기 위해 줄을 설 필요가 없다.

13 그의 가상 카드가 모든 가격을 더해서 나중에 그에게 청구할 것이다.

14 정말 멋지지 않은가?

15 Sumin's _____ _____ House and _____

16 Sumin _____ in a _____ _____ house.

17 _____ a 3D printed house is _____ _____ _____ than building a house _____ _____ _____ .

18 Sumin's house _____ _____ because of its unique design.

19 A 3D printer can produce _____ _____ that people cannot make with _____ _____ _____ _____ _____ .

20 Sumin also likes to make _____ _____ at home _____ _____ a 3D printer.

21 She can choose colors and materials and can design clothes _____ _____ her body and _____ her _____ .

22 Sumin is now a _____ _____ !

23 Dongmin _____ _____ _____

24 Dongmin _____ _____ his grandfather in the hospital.

25 _____ _____ nurse _____ the room.

26 It _____ _____ the room and _____ the patients' _____ .

27 When the AI nurse finds that Dongmin's grandfather has a _____ _____ , it gives him some medicine _____ _____ _____ _____ .

28 _____ _____ _____ _____ about these changes?

29 Some changes have already started to _____ _____ while _____ may start _____ _____ _____ _____ .

30 Can you _____ _____ _____ ?

31 _____ _____ _____ _____ _____ about them.

---

15 수민이의 3D 프린터로 만든 집과 옷

16 수민이는 3D 프린터로 만든 집에 산다.

17 3D 프린터로 집을 짓는 것은 전통적인 방법으로 집을 짓는 것보다 더 빠르고 저렴하다.

18 수민이의 집은 독특한 디자인 때문에 멋져 보인다.

19 3D 프린터는 사람들이 전통 건축 방법과 재료들로 만들 수 없는 집 모양을 만들어 낼 수 있다.

20 수민이는 또한 집에서 3D 프린터를 사용해 옷을 만드는 것을 좋아한다.

21 그녀는 색깔과 재료를 고를 수 있고 자신의 몸과 취향에 맞는 옷을 디자인할 수 있다.

22 수민이는 이제 패션 디자이너이다!

23 병원에 있는 동민

24 동민이는 병원에 계시는 그의 할아버지를 방문하고 있다.

25 AI 간호사가 병실로 들어온다.

26 그것은 병실을 돌아다니고, 환자들의 상태를 확인한다.

27 AI 간호사가 동민이 할아버지가 열이 높다는 것을 알았을 때 그것은 그의 체온을 낮추기 위해 그에게 약을 준다.

28 여러분은 이러한 변화에 대해 생각해 본 적 있는가?

29 어떤 변화는 이미 일어나기 시작했고 반면 다른 것들은 가까운 미래에 일어날지도 모른다.

30 여러분은 다른 변화들을 상상할 수 있는가?

31 그것들에 대해 잠깐 생각해 보자.

※ 다음 문장을 우리말로 쓰시오.

1 ▶ Changing Society

➡ _____

2 ▶ Advances in science and technology have caused many changes in our lives so far.

➡ _____

3 ▶ In the future, science and technology will make more changes.

➡ _____

4 ▶ Let's see what our lives may be like in the near future.

➡ _____

5 ▶ Sangho in the Shopping Center

➡ _____

6 ▶ Shopping is much easier.

➡ _____

7 ▶ There are no lines and no counters.

➡ _____

8 ▶ Sangho enters a shop with his smartphone which has a special shopping app.

➡ _____

9 ▶ In the shop, he takes the items he wants.

➡ _____

10 ▶ The items are automatically added to a virtual card on his smartphone.

➡ _____

11 ▶ If Sangho puts an item back, it is automatically removed from his list of purchases.

➡ _____

12 ▶ When he finishes shopping, Sangho does not need to wait in line to pay.

➡ _____

13 ▶ His virtual card adds up all the prices and will charge him later.

➡ _____

14 ▶ Isn't that fancy?

➡ _____

15 ▶ Sumin's 3D Printed House and Clothes

➡ _____

16 ▶ Sumin lives in a 3D printed house.

➡ _____

17 ▶ Building a 3D printed house is faster and cheaper than building a house with traditional methods.

➡ _____

18 Sumin's house looks fantastic because of its unique design.

➡ _____

19 A 3D printer can produce house shapes that people cannot make with traditional building methods and materials.

➡ _____

20 Sumin also likes to make her clothes at home by using a 3D printer.

➡ _____

21 She can choose colors and materials and can design clothes that fit her body and suit her tastes.

➡ _____

22 Sumin is now a fashion designer!

➡ _____

23 Dongmin in the Hospital

➡ _____

24 Dongmin is visiting his grandfather in the hospital.

➡ _____

25 An AI nurse enters the room.

➡ _____

26 It moves around the room and checks the patients' conditions.

➡ _____

27 When the AI nurse finds that Dongmin's grandfather has a high temperature, it gives him some medicine to lower his temperature.

➡ _____

28 Have you ever thought about these changes?

➡ _____

29 Some changes have already started to take place while others may start in the near future.

➡ _____

30 Can you imagine other changes?

➡ _____

31 Take some time to think about them.

➡ _____

※ 다음 괄호 안의 단어들을 우리말에 맞도록 바르게 배열하시오.

1 (Society / Changing)
➡ _____

2 (in / advances / science / and / have / technology / caused / changes / many / our / in / lives / far. / so)
➡ _____
_____

3 (the / in / future, / technology / and / science / make / will / changes. / more)
➡ _____
_____

4 (see / let's / our / what / lives / be / may / like / the / in / future. / near)
➡ _____

5 (in / Sangho / the / Center / Shopping)
➡ _____

6 (is / shopping / easier. / much)
➡ _____

7 (are / there / lines / no / and / countries. / no)
➡ _____

8 (enters / Sangho / shop / a / with / smartphone / his / has / which / special / a / app. / shopping)
➡ _____
_____

9 (the / in / shop, / takes / he / items / the / wants. / he)
➡ _____

10 (items / the / automatically / are / to / added / a / card / virtual / on / smartphone. / his)
➡ _____

11 (Sangho / if / an / puts / back, / item / is / it / removed / automatically / from / list / his / purchases. / of)
➡ _____

12 (he / when / shopping, / finishes / does / Sangho / need / not / wait / to / line / in / pay. / to)
➡ _____

13 (virtual / his / adds / card / all / up / the / and / prices / charge / will / later. / him)
➡ _____

14 (that / isn't / fancy?)
➡ _____

15 (3D / Sumin's / House / Printed / Clothes / and)
➡ _____

16 (lives / Sumin / a / in / 3D / house. / printed)
➡ _____

17 (a / building / printed / 3D / house / faster / is / and / than / cheaper / building / house / a / traditional / with / methods.)
➡ _____
_____

1 변화하는 사회

2 과학과 기술의 발전은 지금까지 우리의 삶에 많은 변화를 초래해 왔다.

3 미래에 과학 기술은 더 많은 변화를 만들 것이다.

4 가까운 미래에 우리의 삶이 어떻게 될지 살펴보자.

5 쇼핑 센터에 있는 상호

6 쇼핑이 훨씬 쉽다.

7 줄도 없고 계산대도 없다.

8 상호는 특별한 쇼핑 앱이 있는 스마트폰을 가지고 가게로 들어간다.

9 가게에서 그는 그가 원하는 물건들을 집는다.

10 그 물건들은 자동으로 그의 스마트폰에 있는 가상 카드에 더해진다.

11 만약 상호가 물건을 되돌려 놓으면 그것은 자동으로 그의 구매 목록에서 제거된다.

12 쇼핑을 끝냈을 때 상호는 돈을 지불하기 위해 줄을 설 필요가 없다.

13 그의 가상 카드가 모든 가격을 더해서 나중에 그에게 청구할 것이다.

14 정말 멋지지 않은가?

15 수민이의 3D 프린터로 만든 집과 옷

16 수민이는 3D 프린터로 만든 집에 산다.

17 3D 프린터로 집을 짓는 것은 전통적인 방법으로 집을 짓는 것보다 더 빠르고 저렴하다.

18 (house / Sumin's / fantastic / looks / of / because / its / design. / unique)

➡ _____

19 (3D / a / can / printer / produce / shapes / house / that / cannot / people / with / make / building / traditional / materials. / and / methods)

➡ _____

20 (also / Sumin / to / likes / her / make / at / clothes / home / using / by / 3D / printer. / a)

➡ _____

21 (she / choose / can / materials / and / colors / and / design / can / that / clothes / her / fit / body / and / her / suit / tastes.)

➡ _____

22 (is / Sumin / a / now / designer! / fashion)

➡ _____

23 (in / Dongmin / Hospital / the)

➡ _____

24 (is / Dongmin / his / visiting / grandfather / the / hospital. / in)

➡ _____

25 (AI / an / and / enters / nurse / room. / the)

➡ _____

26 (moves / it / the / around / room / checks / and / patients' / the / conditions.)

➡ _____

27 (the / when / nurse / AI / that / finds / grandfather / Dongmin's / has / a / temperature, / high / gives / it / some / him / to / medicine / lower / temperature. / his)

➡ _____

28 (you / have / thought / ever / these / about / changes?)

➡ _____

29 (changes / some / already / have / to / started / place / take / while / may / others / start / the / in / future. / near)

➡ _____

30 (you / can / other / imagine / changes?)

➡ _____

31 (some / take / to / time / them. / about / think)

➡ _____

18 수민이의 집은 독특한 디자인 때문에 멋져 보인다.

19 3D 프린터는 사람들이 전통 건축 방법과 재료들로 만들 수 없는 집 모양을 만들어 낼 수 있다.

20 수민이는 또한 집에서 3D 프린터를 사용해 옷을 만드는 것을 좋아한다.

21 그녀는 색깔과 재료를 고를 수 있고 자신의 몸과 취향에 맞는 옷을 디자인할 수 있다.

22 수민이는 이제 패션 디자이너이다!

23 병원에 있는 동민

24 동민이는 병원에 계시는 그의 할아버지를 방문하고 있다.

25 AI 간호사가 병실로 들어온다.

26 그것은 병실을 돌아다니고, 환자들의 상태를 확인한다.

27 AI 간호사가 동민이 할아버지가 열이 높다는 것을 알았을 때 그것은 그의 체온을 낮추기 위해 그에게 약을 준다.

28 여러분은 이러한 변화에 대해 생각해 본 적 있는가?

29 어떤 변화는 이미 일어나기 시작했고 반면 다른 것들은 가까운 미래에 일어날지도 모른다.

30 여러분은 다른 변화들을 상상할 수 있는가?

31 그것들에 대해 잠깐 생각해 보자.

※ 다음 우리말을 영어로 쓰시오.

1 변화하는 사회

➡ _____

2 과학과 기술의 발전은 지금까지 우리의 삶에 많은 변화를 초래해 왔다.

➡ _____

3 미래에 과학 기술은 더 많은 변화를 만들 것이다.

➡ _____

4 가까운 미래에 우리의 삶이 어떻게 될지 살펴보자.

➡ _____

5 쇼핑 센터에 있는 상호

➡ _____

6 쇼핑이 훨씬 쉽다.

➡ _____

7 줄도 없고 계산대도 없다.

➡ _____

8 상호는 특별한 쇼핑 앱이 있는 스마트폰을 가지고 가게로 들어간다.

➡ _____

9 가게에서 그는 그가 원하는 물건들을 집는다.

➡ _____

10 그 물건들은 자동으로 그의 스마트폰에 있는 가상 카드에 더해진다.

➡ _____

11 만약 상호가 물건을 되돌려 놓으면 그것은 자동으로 그의 구매 목록에서 제거된다.

➡ _____

12 쇼핑을 끝냈을 때 상호는 돈을 지불하기 위해 줄을 설 필요가 없다.

➡ _____

13 그의 가상 카드가 모든 가격을 더해서 나중에 그에게 청구할 것이다.

➡ _____

14 정말 멋지지 않은가?

➡ _____

15 수민이의 3D 프린터로 만든 집과 옷

➡ _____

16 수민이는 3D 프린터로 만든 집에 산다.

➡ _____

17 3D 프린터로 집을 짓는 것은 전통적인 방법으로 집을 짓는 것보다 더 빠르고 저렴하다.

➡ _____

18 수민이의 집은 독특한 디자인 때문에 멋져 보인다.

➡ _____

19 3D 프린터는 사람들이 전통 건축 방법과 재료들로 만들 수 없는 집 모양을 만들어 낼 수 있다.

➡ _____

20 수민이는 또한 집에서 3D 프린터를 사용해 옷을 만드는 것을 좋아한다.

➡ _____

21 그녀는 색깔과 재료를 고를 수 있고 자신의 몸과 취향에 맞는 옷을 디자인할 수 있다.

➡ _____

22 수민이는 이제 패션 디자이너이다!

➡ _____

23 병원에 있는 동민

➡ _____

24 동민이는 병원에 계시는 그의 할아버지를 방문하고 있다.

➡ _____

25 AI 간호사가 병실로 들어온다.

➡ _____

26 그것은 병실을 돌아다니고, 환자들의 상태를 확인한다.

➡ _____

27 AI 간호사가 동민이 할아버지가 열이 높다는 것을 알았을 때 그것은 그의 체온을 낮추기 위해 그에게 약을 준다.

➡ _____

28 여러분은 이러한 변화에 대해 생각해 본 적 있는가?

➡ _____

29 어떤 변화는 이미 일어나기 시작했고 반면 다른 것들은 가까운 미래에 일어날지도 모른다.

➡ _____

30 여러분은 다른 변화들을 상상할 수 있는가?

➡ _____

31 그것들에 대해 잠깐 생각해 보자.

➡ _____

※ 다음 우리말과 일치하도록 빈칸에 알맞은 말을 쓰시오.

Enjoy Writing B

1. Schools _____ 20 _____

2. _____ you ever _____ of _____ _____ _____ _____
   over the next 20 years?

3. Students _____ _____ drone design.

4. _____ drones _____ _____ students at school.

5. _____ _____ _____ an AI teachers' room _____ _____
   _____ .

6. Students _____ _____ to school only _____ _____
   _____ _____ a week.

1. 20년 후 학교의 모습
2. 다음 20년에 걸쳐 학교의 모습이 어떻게 변할지 생각해 본 적이 있나요?
3. 학생들은 드론 디자인을 배울지도 모릅니다.
4. 청소 드론이 학교에서 학생들을 도울지도 모릅니다.
5. 모든 학교에 AI 선생님들 교무실이 있을지도 모릅니다.
6. 학생들은 일주일에 오직 두세 번만 학교에 갈지도 모릅니다.

Project

1. _____ you ever _____ life _____ _____ _____ ?

2. People _____ use personal drones _____ _____ _____
   _____ .

3. So there _____ _____ _____ _____ for drones in the sky.

4. _____ _____ _____ AI helpers _____ _____ _____
   soon and they may help humans _____ _____ _____
   _____ .

1. 미래의 삶을 상상해 본 적이 있나요?
2. 사람들은 매일의 삶에서 개인 드론을 사용할지도 모릅니다.
3. 그래서 하늘에는 드론들을 위한 교통 신호등이 있을지도 모릅니다.
4. 많은 AI 도우미들이 곧 만들어져서 많은 방식으로 인간을 도울지 모릅니다.

Wrap Up 1

1. G: _____ you _____ _____ your trip to London?

2. B: Yes, but I'm _____ _____ _____ _____ . I'm not
   _____ _____ _____ places.

3. G: _____ worry. _____ _____ many good smartphone
   _____ _____ _____ _____ .

4. B: Can you _____ _____ _____ ?

5. G: Sure. Use this one. It _____ _____ _____ _____ of
   the city and _____ _____ _____ .

6. B: Oh, _____ .

1. G: 너의 런던 여행은 준비됐니?
2. B: 응, 하지만 나는 길을 잃는 것에 대해 걱정하고 있어. 나는 장소 찾는 것을 잘 못해.
3. G: 걱정 마. 네가 사용할 수 있는 좋은 스마트폰 앱이 많이 있어.
4. B: 나에게 하나 보여줄 수 있니?
5. G: 물론이지. 이것을 사용해 봐. 그것은 도시의 지도와 길의 사진을 보여줘.
6. B: 오, 고마워.

※ 다음 우리말을 영어로 쓰시오.

Enjoy Writing B

1. 20년 후 학교의 모습
   ➡ _____

2. 다음 20년에 걸쳐 학교의 모습이 어떻게 변할지 생각해 본 적이 있나요?
   ➡ _____

3. 학생들은 드론 디자인을 배울지도 모릅니다.
   ➡ _____

4. 청소 드론이 학교에서 학생들을 도울지도 모릅니다.
   ➡ _____

5. 모든 학교에 AI 선생님들 교무실이 있을지도 모릅니다.
   ➡ _____

6. 학생들은 일주일에 오직 두세 번만 학교에 갈지도 모릅니다.
   ➡ _____

Project

1. 미래의 삶을 상상해 본 적이 있나요?
   ➡ _____

2. 사람들은 매일의 삶에서 개인 드론을 사용할지도 모릅니다.
   ➡ _____

3. 그래서 하늘에는 드론들을 위한 교통 신호등이 있을지도 모릅니다.
   ➡ _____

4. 많은 AI 도우미들이 곧 만들어져서 많은 방식으로 인간을 도울지 모릅니다.
   ➡ _____

Wrap Up 1

1. G: 너의 런던 여행은 준비됐니?
   ➡ _____

2. B: 응, 하지만 나는 길을 잃는 것에 대해 걱정하고 있어. 나는 장소 찾는 것을 잘 못해.
   ➡ _____

3. G: 걱정 마. 네가 사용할 수 있는 좋은 스마트폰 앱이 많이 있어.
   ➡ _____

4. B: 나에게 하나 보여줄 수 있니?
   ➡ _____

5. G: 물론이지. 이것을 사용해 봐. 그것은 도시의 지도와 길의 사진을 보여줘.
   ➡ _____

6. B: 오, 고마워.
   ➡ _____

※ 다음 영어를 우리말로 쓰시오.

01 single

02 break

03 tap

04 chair

05 producer

06 owner

07 turn

08 yet

09 count

10 order

11 elderly

12 grandson

13 chew

14 if

15 even

16 raise

17 meal

18 customer

19 novel

20 bedroom

21 player

22 counter

23 treat

24 bowl

25 have to 동사원형

26 be about to

27 treat A(사람) to B(사물)

28 can't wait to 동사원형

29 pick up

30 say to oneself

31 help+목적어+동사원형

32 think up

※ 다음 우리말을 영어로 쓰시오.

01 침실

02 계산대

03 생산자, 제작자

04 (음식을) 씹다

05 (가볍게) 톡톡 두드리다

06 (무엇을 할) 차례, 순번

07 아직

08 (음식을) 주문하다

09 참가자, 선수

10 의자

11 대접하다, 다루다

12 연세가 드신

13 수를 세다, 계산하다

14 (우묵한) 그릇, 통

15 (자금 등을) 모으다

16 주인, 소유주

17 휴식, (학교의) 쉬는 시간

18 손자

19 만일 ~라면

20 식사

21 손님, 고객

22 소설

23 ~도, ~조차

24 단 하나의, 단일의

25 ~을 생각해 내다

26 ~해야 한다

27 들어올리다, 집다

28 A에게 B를 대접하다

29 (목적어)가 ~하는 것을 돕다

30 빨리 ~하고 싶다

31 막 ~하려는 참이다

32 혼잣말을 하다

※ 다음 영영풀이에 알맞은 단어를 <보기>에서 골라 쓴 후, 우리말 뜻을 쓰시오.

1 _____ : someone who owns something: _____

2 _____ : comprising only one part: _____

3 _____ : a son of one's son or daughter: _____

4 _____ : a room that you sleep in: _____

5 _____ : a book telling a long story in prose: _____

6 _____ : a person who buys goods from a shop, etc.: _____

7 _____ : to buy or give someone something special: _____

8 _____ : to break food etc. with the teeth before swallowing: _____

9 _____ : an occasion when you eat food such as breakfast, lunch, and dinner: _____

10 _____ : the place where customers are served or pay in a restaurant or shop: _____

11 _____ : to invent or to imagine something, especially an excuse: _____

12 _____ : a piece of furniture for one person to sit on, with a back, legs, and sometimes two arms: _____

보기			
chair	counter	think up	grandson
novel	treat	bedroom	chew
single	owner	meal	customer

※ 다음 우리말과 일치하도록 빈칸에 알맞은 것을 골라 쓰시오.

1　The _____ _____
　　A. Customer　　　B. 100th

2　One day, an _____ woman _____ _____ a restaurant.
　　A. into　　　B. elderly　　　C. walked

3　She was _____ _____ _____ .
　　A. her　　　B. with　　　C. grandson

4　_____ , the woman _____ Mr. Kang, the _____ of the restaurant.
　　A. asked　　　B. owner　　　C. quietly

5　"_____ _____ is a _____ of Gukbap?"
　　A. bowl　　　B. much　　　C. how

6　"It's 4,000 won, ma'am," Mr. Kang _____ _____ a _____ .
　　A. with　　　B. smile　　　C. answered

7　She was too _____ to _____ for two _____ .
　　A. bowls　　　B. pay　　　C. poor

8　She _____ a _____ bowl for her _____ .
　　A. single　　　B. ordered　　　C. grandson

9　"Are you _____ you are not _____ , Grandma?" the boy asked, _____ he _____ the hot soup.
　　A. as　　　B. sure　　　C. hungry　　　D. ate

10　"_____ , I'm not _____ .
　　A. hungry　　　B. no

11　_____ _____ about me."
　　A. worry　　　B. don't

12　She _____ _____ some Gimchi and _____ _____ it happily.
　　A. up　　　B. on　　　C. chewed　　　D. picked

13　Mr. Kang watched them _____ , and a warm _____ came _____ him.
　　A. over　　　B. eat　　　C. feeling

14　He _____ _____ a plan to give the boy a _____ _____ .
　　A. free　　　B. up　　　C. meal　　　D. thought

15　When the woman was _____ to _____ , Mr. Kang _____ his hands and said, "No _____ , ma'am.
　　A. about　　　B. need　　　C. pay　　　D. waved

16　In my restaurant, you don't _____ _____ you're the _____ _____ of the day."
　　A. if　　　B. pay　　　C. customer　　　D. 100th

17　The _____ and her grandson _____ Mr. Kang and _____ .
　　A. left　　　B. thanked　　　C. woman

1　백 번째 손님

2　어느 날 한 할머니가 식당으로 걸어 들어왔다.

3　그녀는 손자와 함께 있었다.

4　그녀는 조용히 식당 주인인 강 씨에게 물었다.

5　"국밥 한 그릇이 얼마인가요?"

6　"4,000원입니다. 할머니." 강 씨는 미소 지으며 답했다.

7　그녀는 너무 가난해서 두 그릇 값을 지불할 수 없었다.

8　그녀는 손자를 위해 한 그릇을 주문했다.

9　"정말 배고프지 않으세요, 할머니?" 남자아이는 따뜻한 국물을 먹으며 물었다.

10　"응, 난 배고프지 않단다.

11　내 걱정하지 마라."

12　그녀는 행복하게 김치를 집어서 먹었다.

13　강 씨는 그들이 먹는 것을 지켜보았고, 따뜻한 감정이 밀려왔다.

14　그는 남자아이에게 무료로 식사를 주기 위해 계획을 생각해 냈다.

15　할머니가 돈을 내려고 할 때, 강 씨는 손을 흔들며 말했다. "필요 없습니다, 할머니.

16　저희 식당에서는 그 날의 백 번째 손님이 되면 돈을 내지 않아도 됩니다."

17　할머니와 손자는 강 씨에게 감사해 하며 떠났다.

18 A _____ _____ , Mr. Kang _____ the boy in the street _____ the restaurant.

A. outside   B. later   C. saw   D. month

19 The boy _____ _____ _____ .

A. gathering   B. stones   C. was

20 " _____ are you _____ ?" _____ Mr. Kang.

A. doing   B. what   C. asked

21 "I'm _____ the _____ of customers _____ _____ your restaurant.

A. number   B. enter   C. counting   D. who

22 _____ my _____ birthday."

A. grandma's   B. is   C. today

23 'He wants to be the 100th customer and _____ his grandmother _____ a _____ of Gukbap!' Mr. Kang said to _____ .

A. himself   B. treat   C. bowl   D. to

24 Mr. Kang _____ _____ .

A. down   B. looked

25 He could see that the _____ of stones _____ not yet _____ fifty.

A. even   B. number   C. was

26 He _____ to do something _____ _____ the boy _____ 100 stones.

A. gather   B. had   C. help   D. to

27 Mr. Kang _____ _____ _____ the restaurant and _____ his friends.

A. back   B. went   C. called   D. into

28 "Come to my restaurant now and _____ _____ who _____ you.

A. bring   B. with   C. everyone   D. works

29 _____ is a boy who _____ your _____ ."

A. help   B. there   C. needs

30 People began _____ _____ _____ the restaurant.

A. arrive   B. to   C. at

31 When the 99th customer _____ , Mr. Kang _____ the boy say, "It's our _____ , Grandma."

A. heard   B. turn   C. arrived

32 Mr. Kang _____ them and _____ the woman a _____ _____ of Gukbap.

A. served   B. free   C. welcomed   D. bowl

33 "Are you _____ you're not _____ ?" the woman _____ the boy.

A. asked   B. sure   C. hungry

34 The boy _____ _____ _____ on some Gimchi and said _____ a _____ , "No, I'm not hungry, Grandma.

A. loudly   B. with   C. chewed   D. smile

35 _____ _____ about _____ . Happy birthday!"

A. me   B. worry   C. don't

18 한 달 후, 강 씨는 식당 밖 거리에서 그 남자아이를 보았다.

19 그 남자아이는 돌멩이를 모으고 있었다.

20 너 뭐 하고 있니?" 강 씨가 물었다.

21 "저는 아저씨 식당에 들어가는 손님들의 수를 세고 있어요.

22 오늘이 우리 할머니 생신이거든요."

23 '저 아이는 백 번째 손님이 되어서 할머니께 공짜 국밥 한 그릇을 대접하고 싶어 하는구나.' 강 씨는 혼잣말을 했다.

24 강 씨는 아래를 내려다보았다.

25 그는 돌멩이의 개수가 아직 오십 개도 안 되는 것을 볼 수 있었다.

26 그는 남자아이가 돌멩이 백 개를 모으는 것을 돕기 위해 무언가를 해야 했다.

27 강 씨는 식당으로 되돌아가 그의 친구들에게 전화했다.

28 "지금 내 식당으로 오고, 자네와 함께 일하는 모든 사람들을 데려와 주게.

29 자네 도움이 필요한 남자아이가 있어."

30 사람들이 식당에 도착하기 시작했다.

31 아흔아홉 번째 손님이 도착했을 때 강 씨는 남자아이가 "우리 차례예요, 할머니."라고 말하는 것을 들었다.

32 강 씨는 그들을 반기며 할머니께 공짜 국밥 한 그릇을 제공했다.

33 "너 정말 배고프지 않니?" 할머니가 남자아이에게 물었다.

34 남자아이는 큰 소리로 김치를 씹고 미소 지으며 말했다. "네, 전 배고프지 않아요, 할머니.

35 제 걱정 마세요. 생신 축하드려요!"

※ 다음 우리말과 일치하도록 빈칸에 알맞은 말을 쓰시오.

1 The _____ _____

2 One day, an _____ woman _____ _____ a restaurant.

3 She was _____ _____ _____ .

4 _____, the woman _____ Mr. Kang, _____ _____ of the restaurant.

5 "_____ _____ is _____ _____ _____ Gukbap?"

6 "It's 4,000 won, ma'am," Mr. Kang answered _____ _____ _____ .

7 She was _____ _____ _____ _____ for two bowls.

8 She ordered a _____ bowl _____ _____ _____ .

9 "_____ _____ _____ you are not hungry, Grandma?" the boy asked, as he _____ the hot soup.

10 "_____, I'm _____ _____ .

11 _____ _____ _____ me."

12 She picked up some Gimchi and _____ _____ it _____ .

13 Mr. Kang _____ them _____, and a warm feeling _____ _____ him.

14 He _____ _____ a plan _____ _____ _____ _____ _____ _____ .

15 When the woman _____ _____ _____ _____, Mr. Kang _____ his hands and said, "No need, ma'am.

16 In my restaurant, you don't _____ if you're _____ _____ _____ of the day."

17 The woman and her grandson _____ _____ _____ and left.

---

1 백 번째 손님

2 어느 날 한 할머니가 식당으로 걸어 들어왔다.

3 그녀는 손자와 함께 있었다.

4 그녀는 조용히 식당 주인인 강 씨에게 물었다.

5 "국밥 한 그릇이 얼마인가요?"

6 "4,000원입니다. 할머니." 강 씨는 미소 지으며 답했다.

7 그녀는 너무 가난해서 두 그릇 값을 지불할 수 없었다.

8 그녀는 손자를 위해 한 그릇을 주문했다.

9 "정말 배고프지 않으세요, 할머니?" 남자아이는 따뜻한 국물을 먹으며 물었다.

10 "응. 난 배고프지 않단다.

11 내 걱정하지 마라."

12 그녀는 행복하게 김치를 집어서 먹었다.

13 강 씨는 그들이 먹는 것을 지켜 보았고, 따뜻한 감정이 밀려왔다.

14 그는 남자아이에게 무료로 식사를 주기 위해 계획을 생각해 냈다.

15 할머니가 돈을 내려고 할 때, 강 씨는 손을 흔들며 말했다. "필요 없습니다. 할머니.

16 저희 식당에서는 그 날의 백 번 째 손님이 되면 돈을 내지 않아 도 됩니다."

17 할머니와 손자는 강 씨에게 감 사해 하며 떠났다.

18 _____ _____ _____, Mr. Kang _____ the boy in the street _____ the restaurant.

19 The boy _____ _____ _____.

20 "_____ are you _____?" asked Mr. Kang.

21 "I'm _____ the number of customers _____ enter your restaurant.

22 _____ _____ my grandma's birthday."

23 'He wants to be the 100th customer and _____ his grandmother to a bowl of Gukbap!' Mr. Kang _____ _____ _____.

24 Mr. Kang _____ _____.

25 He could see that _____ _____ of stones _____ not yet _____ _____.

26 He had to do something _____ _____ the boy gather 100 stones.

27 Mr. Kang _____ _____ _____ the restaurant and _____ his friends.

28 "Come to my restaurant now and _____ _____ _____ _____ _____ you.

29 There is a boy _____ _____ _____ _____."

30 People _____ _____ _____ _____ the restaurant.

31 When the 99th customer arrived, Mr. Kang heard the boy say, "_____ _____ _____, Grandma."

32 Mr. Kang _____ _____ and _____ the woman _____ _____ _____ _____.

33 "_____ _____ _____ you're not hungry?" the woman asked the boy.

34 The boy _____ _____ on some Gimchi and said _____ _____ _____, "No, I'm not hungry, Grandma.

35 _____ _____ about me. Happy birthday!"

18 한 달 후, 강 씨는 식당 밖 거리에서 그 남자아이를 보았다.

19 그 남자아이는 돌멩이를 모으고 있었다.

20 너 뭐 하고 있니?" 강 씨가 물었다.

21 "저는 아저씨 식당에 들어가는 손님들의 수를 세고 있어요.

22 오늘이 우리 할머니 생신이거든요."

23 '저 아이는 백 번째 손님이 되어서 할머니께 공짜 국밥 한 그릇을 대접하고 싶어 하는구나.' 강 씨는 혼잣말을 했다.

24 강 씨는 아래를 내려다보았다.

25 그는 돌멩이의 개수가 아직 오십 개도 안 되는 것을 볼 수 있었다.

26 그는 남자아이가 돌멩이 백 개를 모으는 것을 돕기 위해 무언가를 해야 했다.

27 강 씨는 식당으로 되돌아가 그의 친구들에게 전화했다.

28 "지금 내 식당으로 오고, 자네와 함께 일하는 모든 사람들을 데려와 주게.

29 자네 도움이 필요한 남자아이가 있어."

30 사람들이 식당에 도착하기 시작했다.

31 아흔아홉 번째 손님이 도착했을 때 강 씨는 남자아이가 "우리 차례예요, 할머니."라고 말하는 것을 들었다.

32 강 씨는 그들을 반기며 할머니께 공짜 국밥 한 그릇을 제공했다.

33 "너 정말 배고프지 않니?" 할머니가 남자아이에게 물었다.

34 남자아이는 큰 소리로 김치를 씹고 미소 지으며 말했다. "네, 전 배고프지 않아요, 할머니.

35 제 걱정 마세요, 생신 축하드려요!"

※ 다음 문장을 우리말로 쓰시오.

1 The 100th Customer
➡ _____

2 One day, an elderly woman walked into a restaurant.
➡ _____

3 She was with her grandson.
➡ _____

4 Quietly, the woman asked Mr. Kang, the owner of the restaurant.
➡ _____

5 "How much is a bowl of Gukbap?"
➡ _____

6 "It's 4,000 won, ma'am," Mr. Kang answered with a smile.
➡ _____

7 She was too poor to pay for two bowls.
➡ _____

8 She ordered a single bowl for her grandson.
➡ _____

9 "Are you sure you are not hungry, Grandma?" the boy asked, as he ate the hot soup.
➡ _____

10 "No, I'm not hungry.
➡ _____

11 Don't worry about me."
➡ _____

12 She picked up some Gimchi and chewed on it happily.
➡ _____

13 Mr. Kang watched them eat, and a warm feeling came over him.
➡ _____

14 He thought up a plan to give the boy a free meal.
➡ _____

15 When the woman was about to pay, Mr. Kang waved his hands and said, "No need, ma'am.
➡ _____

16 In my restaurant, you don't pay if you're the 100th customer of the day."
➡ _____

17 The woman and her grandson thanked Mr. Kang and left.
➡ _____

18 A month later, Mr. Kang saw the boy in the street outside the restaurant

➡ _____

19 The boy was gathering stones.

➡ _____

20 "What are you doing?" asked Mr. Kang.

➡ _____

21 "I'm counting the number of customers who enter your restaurant.

➡ _____

22 Today is my grandma's birthday."

➡ _____

23 'He wants to be the 100th customer and treat his grandmother to a bowl of Gukbap!' Mr. Kang said to himself.

➡ _____

24 Mr. Kang looked down.

➡ _____

25 He could see that the number of stones was not yet even fifty.

➡ _____

26 He had to do something to help the boy gather 100 stones.

➡ _____

27 Mr. Kang went back into the restaurant and called his friends.

➡ _____

28 "Come to my restaurant now and bring everyone who works with you.

➡ _____

29 There is a boy who needs your help."

➡ _____

30 People began to arrive at the restaurant.

➡ _____

31 When the 99th customer arrived, Mr. Kang heard the boy say, "It's our turn, Grandma."

➡ _____

32 Mr. Kang welcomed them and served the woman a free bowl of Gukbap.

➡ _____

33 "Are you sure you're not hungry?" the woman asked the boy.

➡ _____

34 The boy chewed loudly on some Gimchi and said with a smile, "No, I'm not hungry, Grandma.

➡ _____

35 Don't worry about me. Happy birthday!"

➡ _____

※ 다음 괄호 안의 단어들을 우리말에 맞도록 바르게 배열하시오.

1 (100th / The / Customer)
➡ _____

2 (day, / one / elderly / an / walked / woman / into / restaurant. / a)
➡ _____

3 (was / she / her / with / grandson.)
➡ _____

4 (the / quietly, / asked / woman / Kang, / Mr. / owner / the / of / restaurant. / the)
➡ _____

5 (much / "how / a / is / bowl / Gukbap?" / of)
➡ _____

6 (4,000 / "it's / ma'am," / won, / Kang / Mr. / with / answered / smile. / a)
➡ _____

7 (was / she / poor / too / pay / to / two / bowls. / for)
➡ _____

8 (ordered / she / single / a / for / bowl / grandson. / her)
➡ _____

9 ("are / sure / you / are / you / not / Grandma?" / hungry, / boy / the / asked, / he / as / ate / hot / the / soup.)
➡ _____

10 ("no, / not / I'm / hungry.)
➡ _____

11 (worry / don't / me." / about)
➡ _____

12 (picked / she / up / Gimchi / some / and / on / chewed / happily. / it)
➡ _____

13 (Kang / Mr. / them / watched / eat, / a / and / warm / came / feeling / him. / over)
➡ _____

14 (thought / he / a / up / plan / give / to / boy / the / free / a / meal.)
➡ _____

15 (the / when / woman / was / to / about / pay, / Kang / Mr. / his / waved / hands / said, / and / "no / ma'am. / need,)
➡ _____

16 (my / in / restaurant, / don't / you / pay / you're / if / 100th / the / of / customer / day." / the)
➡ _____

17 (woman / the / and / grandson / her / Mr. / thanked / Kang / left. / and)
➡ _____

1 백 번째 손님

2 어느 날 한 할머니가 식당으로 걸어 들어왔다.

3 그녀는 손자와 함께 있었다.

4 그녀는 조용히 식당 주인인 강 씨에게 물었다.

5 "국밥 한 그릇이 얼마인가요?"

6 "4,000원입니다. 할머니." 강 씨는 미소 지으며 답했다.

7 그녀는 너무 가난해서 두 그릇 값을 지불할 수 없었다.

8 그녀는 손자를 위해 한 그릇을 주문했다.

9 "정말 배고프지 않으세요, 할머니?" 남자아이는 따뜻한 국물을 먹으며 물었다.

10 "응, 난 배고프지 않단다.

11 내 걱정하지 마라."

12 그녀는 행복하게 김치를 집어서 먹었다.

13 강 씨는 그들이 먹는 것을 지켜보았고, 따뜻한 감정이 밀려왔다.

14 그는 남자아이에게 무료로 식사를 주기 위해 계획을 생각해 냈다.

15 할머니가 돈을 내려고 할 때, 강 씨는 손을 흔들며 말했다. "필요 없습니다. 할머니.

16 저희 식당에서는 그 날의 백 번째 손님이 되면 돈을 내지 않아도 됩니다."

17 할머니와 손자는 강 씨에게 감사해 하며 떠났다.

18 (month / a / later, / Kang / Mr. / the / saw / boy / the / in / street / the / outside / restaurant.)
➡ _____

19 (boy / the / was / stones. / gathering)
➡ _____

20 (are / "what / doing?" / you / Mr. / asked / Kang.)
➡ _____

21 ("I'm / the / counting / number / customers / of / enter / who / restaurant. / your)
➡ _____

22 (is / today / grandma's / my / birthday.")
➡ _____

23 (wants / 'he / be / to / 100th / the / customer / and / his / treat / grandmother / a / to / bowl / Gukbap!' / of / Kang / Mr. / to / said / himself.)
➡ _____

24 (Kang / Mr. / down. / looked)
➡ _____

25 (could / he / see / the / that / of / number / stones / not / was / yet / fifty. / even)
➡ _____

26 (had / he / do / to / to /something / help / boy / the / gather / stones. / 100)
➡ _____

27 (Kang / Mr. / back / went / the / into / restaurant / called / and / friends. / his)
➡ _____

28 (to / "come / restaurant / my / now / and / everyone / bring / who / with / works / you.)
➡ _____

29 (is / there / boy / a / who / your / needs / help.")
➡ _____

30 (began / people / arrive / to / the / at / restaurant.)
➡ _____

31 (when / 99th / the / arrived, / customer / Kang / Mr. / the / heard / boy / say, / "it's / our / Grandma." / turn,)
➡ _____

32 (Kang / Mr. / them / welcomed / and / the / served / woman / a / bowl / free / Gukbap. / of)
➡ _____

33 (you / "are / sure / not / you're / hungry?" / woman / the / the / asked / boy.)
➡ _____

34 (boy / the / loudly / chewed / some / on / Gimchi / said / and / a / with / smile, / "no, / not / I'm / Grandma. / hungry)
➡ _____

35 (worry / don't / me. / about // birthday!" / happy)
➡ _____

18 한 달 후, 강 씨는 식당 밖 거리에서 그 남자아이를 보았다.

19 그 남자아이는 돌멩이를 모으고 있었다.

20 너 뭐 하고 있니?" 강 씨가 물었다.

21 "저는 아저씨 식당에 들어가는 손님들의 수를 세고 있어요.

22 오늘이 우리 할머니 생신이거든요"

23 '저 아이는 백 번째 손님이 되어서 할머니께 공짜 국밥 한 그릇을 대접하고 싶어 하는구나.' 강 씨는 혼잣말을 했다.

24 강 씨는 아래를 내려다보았다.

25 그는 돌멩이의 개수가 아직 오십 개도 안 되는 것을 볼 수 있었다.

26 그는 남자아이가 돌멩이 백 개를 모으는 것을 돕기 위해 무언가를 해야 했다.

27 강 씨는 식당으로 되돌아가 그의 친구들에게 전화했다.

28 "지금 내 식당으로 오고, 자네와 함께 일하는 모든 사람들을 데려와 주게.

29 자네 도움이 필요한 남자아이가 있어."

30 사람들이 식당에 도착하기 시작했다.

31 아흔아홉 번째 손님이 도착했을 때 강 씨는 남자아이가 "우리 차례예요, 할머니."라고 말하는 것을 들었다.

32 강 씨는 그들을 반기며 할머니께 공짜 국밥 한 그릇을 제공했다.

33 "너 정말 배고프지 않니?" 할머니가 남자아이에게 물었다.

34 남자아이는 큰 소리로 김치를 씹고 미소 지으며 말했다. "네, 전 배고프지 않아요, 할머니.

35 제 걱정 마세요, 생신 축하드려요!"

※ 다음 우리말을 영어로 쓰시오.

1 백 번째 손님

➡ _____

2 어느 날 한 할머니가 식당으로 걸어 들어왔다.

➡ _____

3 그녀는 손자와 함께 있었다.

➡ _____

4 그녀는 조용히 식당 주인인 강 씨에게 물었다.

➡ _____

5 "국밥 한 그릇이 얼마인가요?"

➡ _____

6 "4,000원입니다, 할머니." 강 씨는 미소 지으며 답했다.

➡ _____

7 그녀는 너무 가난해서 두 그릇 값을 지불할 수 없었다.

➡ _____

8 그녀는 손자를 위해 한 그릇을 주문했다.

➡ _____

9 "정말 배고프지 않으세요, 할머니?" 남자아이는 따뜻한 국물을 먹으며 물었다.

➡ _____

10 "응, 난 배고프지 않단다.

➡ _____

11 내 걱정하지 마라."

➡ _____

12 그녀는 행복하게 김치를 집어서 먹었다.

➡ _____

13 강 씨는 그들이 먹는 것을 지켜보았고, 따뜻한 감정이 밀려왔다.

➡ _____

14 그는 남자아이에게 무료로 식사를 주기 위해 계획을 생각해 냈다.

➡ _____

15 할머니가 돈을 내려고 할 때, 강 씨는 손을 흔들며 말했다. "필요 없습니다, 할머니.

➡ _____

16 저희 식당에서는 그 날의 백 번째 손님이 되면 돈을 내지 않아도 됩니다."

➡ _____

17 할머니와 손자는 강 씨에게 감사해 하며 떠났다.

➡ _____

18 한 달 후, 강 씨는 식당 밖 거리에서 그 남자아이를 보았다.

➡ _____

19 그 남자아이는 돌멩이를 모으고 있었다.

➡ _____

20 "너 뭐 하고 있니?" 강 씨가 물었다.

➡ _____

21 "저는 아저씨 식당에 들어가는 손님들의 수를 세고 있어요.

➡ _____

22 오늘이 우리 할머니 생신이거든요."

➡ _____

23 '저 아이는 백 번째 손님이 되어서 할머니께 공짜 국밥 한 그릇을 대접하고 싶어 하는구나.'
강 씨는 혼잣말을 했다.

➡ _____

_____

24 강 씨는 아래를 내려다보았다.

➡ _____

25 그는 돌멩이의 개수가 아직 오십 개도 안 되는 것을 볼 수 있었다.

➡ _____

26 그는 남자아이가 돌멩이 백 개를 모으는 것을 돕기 위해 무언가를 해야 했다.

➡ _____

27 강 씨는 식당으로 되돌아가 그의 친구들에게 전화했다.

➡ _____

28 "지금 내 식당으로 오고, 자네와 함께 일하는 모든 사람들을 데려와 주게.

➡ _____

29 자네 도움이 필요한 남자아이가 있어."

➡ _____

30 사람들이 식당에 도착하기 시작했다.

➡ _____

31 아흔아홉 번째 손님이 도착했을 때 강 씨는 남자아이가 "우리 차례예요, 할머니."라고 말하는 것을 들었다.

➡ _____

32 강 씨는 그들을 반기며 할머니께 공짜 국밥 한 그릇을 제공했다.

➡ _____

33 "너 정말 배고프지 않니?" 할머니가 남자아이에게 물었다.

➡ _____

34 남자아이는 큰 소리로 김치를 씹고 미소 지으며 말했다. "네, 전 배고프지 않아요, 할머니.

➡ _____

35 제 걱정 마세요. 생신 축하드려요!"

➡ _____

MEMO

영어 기출 문제집

적중100 plus
2학기 전과정

2학기

정답 및 해설

시사 | 박준언

중 2

적중100

영어 기출 문제집

적중 100

2학기

정답 및 해설

시사 | 박준언

중 2

Lesson
5

Different Countries, Different Cultures

시험대비 실력평가　　　　　　　　　　p.08

01 ③	02 ⑤	03 ⑤	04 ①
05 (1) capital	(2) Spanish	06 ④	
07 (1) (d)ish	(2) (u)nique	08 ④	

01 unique: 독특한 unusual: 특이한, 흔치 않은 / 각 등장인물은 독특한 성격을 갖고 있다.

02 Excuse me: (모르는 사람의 관심을 끌려고 할 때) 실례합니다 / 실례지만, 가장 가까운 지하철역이 어느 쪽인가요?

03 ceiling: 천장 / 방의 위쪽 내부 표면

04 shine: 빛나다 / 밝은 빛을 만들어 내다

05 (1) capital: 수도 (2) Spanish: 스페인의

06 ① coaster: (롤러) 코스터 / 그 남자는 롤러 코스터를 타고 있다. ② lizard: 도마뱀 / 도마뱀은 네 개의 다리와 긴 꼬리를 가지고 있다. ③ curry: 카레 / 그 카레는 나한테 너무 맵다. ④ view: 전망, 경치 / 나는 전망이 좋은 방을 원한다. ⑤ column: 기둥 / 그 기둥은 흰 대리석으로 만들어졌다.

07 (1) dish: 음식, 요리 / 가장 대표적인 한국 음식이 무엇이라고 생각하니? (2) unique: 독특한 / Rachel은 독특한 장미의 향을 사랑한다.

08 ④ friend는 뒤에 ly를 붙여 형용사로 만들 수 있다. friend: 친구 friendly: 친절한 ① help: 도움 helpful: 도움이 되는 ② care: 조심 careful: 조심하는 ③ wonder: 놀라움 wonderful: 놀랄 만한, 멋진 ⑤ peace: 평화 peaceful: 평화로운

서술형 시험대비　　　　　　　　　　p.09

01 (1) traditional　(2) historic[historical]

02 (1) cheers　(2) match　(3) works　(4) waves
　(5) experience

03 (1) Do you know how many tourists visit Boston every day?
　(2) The sun shines and the tree grows.
　(3) The crowd cheered up at the good news.
　(4) I want to study abroad.

04 (1) take　(2) turn　(3) put　(4) try

01 둘은 명사와 형용사의 관계이다. use: 사용 useful: 유용한

(1) tradition: 전통 traditional: 전통적인 (2) history: 역사 historic: 역사적인, 역사상 중요한 historical: 역사상, 역사와 관련된

02 (1) cheer: 격려하다, 환호하다, 갈채하다; 환호 (2) match: 경기, 시합; 어울리다 (3) work: 일하다, 작품 (4) wave: 흔들다; 파도 (5) experience: 경험; 경험하다

03 (1) tourist: 여행객 (2) shine: 빛나다 (3) cheer up: 기운을 내다 (4) abroad: 외국으로[에서]

04 (1) take a tour: 관광하다, 여행을 가다 / 너는 여행을 가고 싶니? (2) turn off: (전기, 가스, 수도 등을) 끄다 / TV를 꺼라. 잠잘 시간이 지났어. (3) put off: (시간, 날짜를) 미루다, 연기하다 / 다음 25일까지 여행을 미룰 수 있을까요? (4) try on: 입어 보다 / 이 재킷을 입어 봐도 돼요?

교과서
Conversation

핵심 Check　　　　　　　　　　p.10~11

1 Where, bank / Go straight / next to
2 (1) Which, (p)refer / prefer, to
　(2) like better / prefer

교과서 대화문 익히기

Check(√) True or False　　　　　　p.12

1 F　2 T　3 F　4 F　5 T　6 T

교과서 확인학습　　　　　　　　　　p.14~15

Listen & Speak 1 A
1. Is, near / far from / How / Go straight, left, on
2. to buy, Where can / them at / Where is it / Go straight, blocks, across from

Listen & Speak 1 B
1. Where is / Go straight two blocks, on
2. Where is / straight, It's on, It's across from

Listen & Talk 2 A
1. It's, Let's go / good, How, get there / on foot or by bus , Which do you prefer / prefer
2. What is, called / type, traditional clothing / try one on / Which do you prefer

1. Which do you prefer
2. Which do you prefer, or

Conversation A

we'll visit, see, on your right, view from

Conversation B

How, help / want to enjoy / to go to / on top of, Which / prefer / get, by bus / Where, nearest stop / straight, turn right / There is / Why don't we

---

시험대비 기본평가   p.16

01 ②   02 ⑤   03 ①, ③, ⑤
04 (C) → (D) → (A) → (B)

01 'Where is ~?'는 '~가 어디에 있나요?'라는 의미로 길이나 위치를 물어볼 때 사용하는 표현이다.

02 I think hamburgers are less preferable to spaghetti. → I think hamburgers are preferable to spaghetti. less preferable은 덜 선호한다는 의미이므로, less를 빼야 햄버거를 스파게티보다 더 좋아한다는 의미가 된다.

03 ② Do you know when to go to the school? → Do you know where the school is? ④ Could I tell you where the school is? → Could you tell me where the school is?로 바꾸면 길을 물어보는 표현이 될 수 있다.

04 (C) 근처에 피카소 박물관이 있는지 묻는 질문에 (D) 그렇다고 대답한 후 여기서 멀지 않다고 언급한다. (A) 이어서 피카소 박물관을 어떻게 가는지 묻자 (B) 가는 방법을 알려준다.

시험대비 실력평가   p.17~18

01 ②   02 ②   03 ③   04 ④
05 ⑤   06 ④   07 ②
08 (A) why, (B) let's   09 ②   10 Where
11 ③   12 across from

01 far from: ~에서 먼

02 How can I get there?: 그곳에 어떻게 가니? 'Where is ~?'와 같이 'How can I get ~?'도 길이나 위치를 물어볼 때 사용하는 표현이다.

03 주어진 문장은 야시장에 어떻게 갈 수 있는지 물어보는 질문이다. 이에 대한 대답으로 가는 방법에 대한 언급이 나와야 한다. 그러므로 걸어가거나 버스를 타서 갈 수 있다는 대답 앞에 오는 것이 적절하다.

04 What do you prefer? → Which do you prefer? 걸어가거나 버스를 타는 것 중 하나를 선택하는 것이므로 의문사 Which

05 여자아이가 아니라 남자아이가 야시장에 가는 방법을 알고 있다.

06 길을 물어보는 질문에, 'I'm a stranger here, too. (저도 여기 처음이에요.)'라고 말한 후에 길을 알려 주는 것은 어울리지 않는다.

07 주어진 문장은 그것(*Best Friends*)이 언제 시작하는지 시간에 대한 정보를 묻고 있다. 그러므로 5시와 7시에 시작한다는 답이 이어지는 ②번이 적절하다.

08 (A)와 (B)에 사용된 'Why don't we ~?'와 'Let's ~'는 둘 다 '~ 하자'라고 제안을 할 때 사용할 수 있는 말이다. How about 다음에는 동명사가 나와야 하므로 (B)에는 let's가 적절하다.

09 ① 영화 Best Friends가 토요일 몇 시에 시작하는가? ② 어디서 그들이 토요일에 만날 것인가? ③ 여자아이는 5시나 7시 중 어떤 시간을 선호하는가? ④ 그들은 토요일 몇 시에 만날 것인가? ⑤ 그들은 토요일에 어떤 영화를 볼 것인가?

10 where: 어디서

11 Go straight two blocks: 두 블록 직진하세요. turn right: 우회전하세요.

12 across from: ~의 맞은편에

서술형 시험대비   p.19

01 'Yes, I do.'를 생략
02 Can you tell me how to get to the African Museum?
03 (A) right, (B) left, (C) across from
04 (A) on, (B) by
05 How can I get there? / Do you know how to get there? / Can you tell me how to get there?
06 or   07 to curry

01 'Which do you prefer, A or B?'는 어느 것을 선호하는지 묻는 표현으로 'Yes.'나 'No.'로 대답할 수 없다.

02 Can you tell me how to get to ~?: ~에 어떻게 가는지 말해 줄 수 있나요? / how to 동사원형: ~하는 방법 / get to 장소명사: ~에 도착하다

03 그림을 참고해 보면 ③은 두 블록 직진한 후, 우회전하면, 왼편에 있다. across from: ~의 맞은편에

04 on foot: 걸어서, by bus: 버스로

05 How can/do I get to ~?: ~에 어떻게 가나요? Do you know how to get to ~?: ~에 어떻게 가는지 아나요? Can you tell me how to get to ~?: ~에 어떻게 가는지 말해 줄 수 있나요?

06 Which do you prefer, A or B?: A와 B 중 어떤 것을 선호하니?

07 두 가지 중에서 어떤 것을 더 선호하는지 말할 때 'I prefer A to B.'를 사용한다. to B는 생략할 수 있다.

Grammar
교과서

핵심 Check
p.20~21

1 (1) built (2) will be

2 (1) The water was so clear that you could see the bottom.

　(2) He worked so hard that he became a lawyer.

　(3) I 'll drive fast so that you can get there in time.

시험대비 기본평가
p.22

01 (1) cleans → is cleaned

　(2) is → was

　(3) very → so

　(4) so that → so that she

02 ④　　　　03 ②

04 (1) The water was so clean that we could drink it.

　(2) He was injured during the soccer match.

01 (1) 방이 청소하는 것이 아니라 청소되는 것이므로 수동태가 적절하다. (2) in 1908이라는 과거를 나타내는 부사구가 있으므로 시제를 과거로 써야 한다. (3) 'so+형용사[부사]+that+주어+동사'의 형태로 원인과 결과를 나타내는 것이 적절하다. (4) so that 다음에는 '주어+동사'가 나와야 한다.

02 tomorrow가 있으므로 'will be sent'가 되어야 한다.

03 '…해서 ~하다'의 의미인 'so … that ~' 구문이다.

04 (1) 물이 깨끗해서 그 결과 마실 수 있었던 것이므로 'so … that ~' 구문으로 쓰는 것이 적절하다. (2) 부상을 입은 것이므로 수동태가 적절하다.

시험대비 실력평가
p.23~25

01 ④　　02 ③　　03 ⑤

04 weak so → so weak

05 (1) excited (2) consider (3) to (4) for (5) of

　(6) so (7) that　06 ①　　07 ①

08 ④　　09 ②　　10 ⑤

11 (1) Antoni Gaudi designed both.

　(2) James took this photo.

　(3) A beautiful dress was made for her by her mom.

　(4) They will hold the book fair in Seoul.

　(5) Who considers it to be dangerous?

12 (1) so (2) such (3) couldn't　13 ⑤

14 ③, ⑤

15 (1) invented → was invented

　(2) was happened → happened

　(3) too careless → careless enough

16 ⑤　　　17 ⑤　　　18 ③

01 영어가 말하는 것이 아니라 말해지는 것이므로 수동태가 적절하다.

02 세차되는 것이므로 수동태가 적절하고 원인과 결과를 나타내는 'so+형용사[부사]+that+주어+동사' 구문이 적절하다.

03 The pictures drawn in France were sent to me by Jenny. sent가 능동태의 동사이므로 수동태로 바꾸면 'were sent'가 되어야 한다.

04 'so+형용사[부사]+that+주어+동사'는 원인과 결과를 나타내지만 'so that+주어+동사'는 목적을 나타낸다.

05 (1) 내가 신나게 되는 것이므로 수동태가 적절하다. (2) We가 주어이므로 능동태가 적절하다. (3) 직접목적어를 주어로 한 수동태에서 간접목적어 앞에 teach는 전치사 to를, (4) choose는 전치사 for를, (5) ask는 of를 쓴다. (6), (7) 'so+형용사[부사]+that+주어+동사' 구문이다.

06 원인과 결과를 나타내는 'so ~ that …' 구문이 적절하다.

07 by 이외의 전치사를 사용하는 수동태에 유의한다. be pleased with: ~에 기뻐하다 be satisfied with: ~에 만족하다

08 'so+형용사[부사]+that+주어+동사' 구문은 '너무 ~해서 …하다'라는 뜻으로 원인과 결과를 나타낸다.

09 'so that+주어+동사'는 목적을 나타내어 '~하기 위해서' 혹은 '~하도록'이라는 의미로 쓰인다. 부사적 용법의 '목적'과 바꿔 쓸 수 있다. 원인과 결과를 나타내는 'so ~ that …'과 혼동하지 않도록 유의한다.

10 turn off는 구동사로 하나의 단어처럼 취급하여 be turned off로 나타낸다. off를 빠뜨리지 않도록 주의한다.

11 (3) make는 직접목적어를 주어로 하는 수동태만 가능하며 간접목적어 앞에 전치사 for를 쓴다. (4) 미래 시제의 수동태는 'will be+과거분사'이며 수동태에서 일반인이 행위자일 경우 보통 'by+일반인 주어'를 생략한다. (5) 수동태의 by whom이 who로 바뀌는 것에 주의한다.

12 (1) 원인과 결과를 나타내는 'so ~ that …' 구문이다. (2) 'so ~ that …' 구문에서 that 앞에 형용사나 부사 대신 명사가 오면 so 대신 such를 쓴다. (3) so+형용사[부사]+that+주어+can't+동사원형: 너무 ~하여 …할 수 없다.

13 목적격보어가 원형부정사인 경우, 수동태 문장에서는 to부정사로 바뀐다. We were made to do our homework by our teacher.

14 ① He was seen to put the bag on the table by Ann. ② The storybook was read to him every night by his mom. ④ It was such a nice day that we went for a walk.

15 (1) WWW가 발명되는 것이므로 수동태가 적절하다. (2) happen은 자동사이므로 수동태로 쓰이지 않는다. (3) so+형용

사[부사]+that+주어+can ~ = '형용사[부사]+enough+to 동사원형', so+형용사[부사]+that+주어+can't ~ = too+형용사[부사]+to 동사원형

16 choose는 직접목적어를 주어로 한 수동태에서는 간접목적어 앞에 for를 쓴다.

17 시제가 과거이므로 was heard로 쓰고, 원형부정사인 목적격보어는 to부정사로 쓴다.

18 이유를 나타내는 Because절이므로 'so+형용사[부사]+that+주어+동사' 구문으로 원인과 결과를 나타낼 수 있다

서술형 시험대비 p.26~27

01 (1) Someone stole the painting last week.
   (2) I was impressed by its size and unique design.
   (3) Peter was heard to open the window by Eva.
   (4) A present will be given to me by Angie on my birthday.
   (5) The baby was taken care of by Cathy.

02 (1) so stupid that
   (2) tall enough to
   (3) too shocked to

03 (1) hard so that (2) so hard that

04 (1) Cake is made from flour, milk, eggs and sugar.
   (2) The shirts will be ironed by John tomorrow morning.
   (3) Mike was seen to be hit by a car by Ms. Brown.
   (4) Our dog was run over by a truck.
   (5) The matter will be discussed by us tommorow.

05 (1) easy enough to (2) so fast that

06 (1) The novel was written by Ernest Hemingway.
   (2) The first World Cup took place in Uruguay in 1930.
   (3) A fairy tale book was read to her daughter by Laura.
   (4) Kimberly was disappointed at the news.
   (5) Was Allie heard to sing by you?
   (6) It was so cold that he caught a cold.

07 (1) Claire got up too late to get on the train.
   (2) Chuck spoke so low that I could not hear him.
   (3) Bill was smart enough to solve the difficult math problems.
   (4) Juliet is so rich that she can buy the house.

08 (1) The sweater was made for me by my grandmother.
   (2) Are these rooms cleaned by her every day?
   (3) Dan was made to prepare dinner by Mariel.
   (4) Joakim was pleased with your recent success a lot.

01 (3) 목적격보어가 원형부정사인 경우 수동태에서는 to부정사로 쓴다. (4) 미래 시제의 수동태는 'will be+과거분사'이다. (5) 구동사(take care of)는 하나의 동사처럼 취급한다는 것에 주의한다.

02 (1) 'so+형용사[부사]+that+주어+동사'의 형태로 원인과 결과를 나타낸다. (2) so+형용사[부사]+that+주어+can ~ = '형용사[부사]+enough+to 동사원형' (3) so+형용사[부사]+that+주어+can't ~ = too+형용사[부사]+to 동사원형

03 (1) 목적을 나타내는 'so that'을 사용한다. (2) 원인과 결과를 나타내는 'so ~ that …'을 사용한다.

04 (1) be made of: ~로 만들어지다(물리적 변화), be made from: ~로 만들어지다(화학적 변화) (2) shirts가 다림질을 하는 것이 아니라 다림질 되는 것이므로 수동태가 적절하며 미래의 일이므로 'will be+pp' 형태가 적절하다. (3) 목적격보어가 원형부정사인 경우, 수동태 문장에서는 to부정사로 바뀐다. (4) ran over는 이어동사이다. (5) 'will be +pp' 형태가 되어야 한다.

05 (1) so+형용사[부사]+that+주어+can ~ = 형용사[부사]+enough+to 동사원형 (2) so+형용사[부사]+that+주어+can't ~ = too+형용사[부사]+to 동사원형

06 (1) 소설이 씌여지는 것이므로 수동태가 적절하다. (2) take place는 자동사로 쓰이므로 수동태로 쓰면 안 된다. (3) read는 직접목적어를 주어로 하는 수동태만 가능하다. fairy tale book: 동화책 (4) be disappointed at: ~에 실망하다, 낙담하다 (5) 목적격보어가 원형부정사인 경우, 수동태 문장에서는 to부정사로 바뀐다 (6) so ~ that: 너무 ~해서 …하다

07 so ~ that 주어 can't … = too ~ to …, ~ enough to부정사 = so ~ that 주어 can … 이때 to부정사 앞에 for 목적격으로 쓰인 것은 to부정사의 의미상의 주어로 that 이하의 절로 바꿀 때는 주격으로 바꿔야 하며, to부정사로 썼을 때 생략된 동사의 목적어는 써 주어야 한다.

08 (1) 직접목적어를 주어로 한 수동태에서 make는 간접목적어 앞에 전치사 for를 쓴다. (2) 의문문을 수동태로 바꿀 때는 평서문으로 바꿔서 고친 후에 다시 의문문으로 바꾸면 쉽다. (3) 목적격보어가 원형부정사인 경우, 수동태 문장에서는 to부정사로 바뀐다. (4) please는 수동태에서 by가 아니라 보통 with를 쓴다. be pleased with: ~로 기뻐하다

교과서
Reading

확인문제 p.28

1 F 2 T 3 T 4 F 5 T 6 F

1 T 2 F 3 T 4 F 5 T 6 F

교과서 확인학습 A   p.30~31

01 Happy Days, by   02 traveled to
03 is loved by
04 visited, interesting   05 Our trip
06 is famous for   07 to watch
08 were excited, the world's most famous soccer players
09 was full of
10 by singing, shouting   11 After
12 While, walked around
13 visited, watched
14 in a red dress, with wonderful movements
15 For
16 traditional Spanish dish with
17 tasted like   18 so, that   19 took a tour of
20 were designed by
21 creative works like   22 After
23 is still going on
24 was impressed by
25 shone like   26 stood like
27 creativity, his love of nature
28 Traveling, a wonderful experience
29 While, a lot   30 to visit

교과서 확인학습 B   p.32~33

1 My Happy Days in Spain by Park Jinwoo
2 My family traveled to Spain this summer.
3 Spain is loved by lots of tourists.
4 We visited many interesting places.
5 Our trip started in Madrid.
6 Madrid is the capital and is famous for soccer.
7 We went to a stadium to watch a soccer match.
8 My sister and I were excited because we could watch some of the world's most famous soccer players.
9 The stadium was full of soccer fans.
10 As we watched the match, we cheered by singing songs, waving our hands, and shouting with the other fans.
11 After we toured Madrid, we went to Seville.
12 While we walked around the city, we saw many

historic buildings.
13 We visited a flamenco museum and watched a flamenco dance.
14 A woman in a red dress was dancing the flamenco with wonderful movements.
15 For dinner, we ate paella.
16 It is a traditional Spanish dish with rice, vegetables, meat, and seafood.
17 It tasted like fried rice in Korea.
18 It was so delicious that we all enjoyed it.
19 In Barcelona, we took a tour of Park Guell and Sagrada Familia.
20 Both were designed by Antoni Gaudi.
21 In Park Guell, we saw some of Gaudi's creative works like a colorful lizard.
22 After Park Guell, we visited Sagrada Familia.
23 Work on the building started in 1883 and is still going on today.
24 I was impressed by its size and unique design.
25 The ceiling inside Sagrada Familia shone like the night sky with bright stars.
26 Its stone columns stood like big trees.
27 At Park Guell and Sagrada Familia I could feel Gaudi's creativity and his love of nature.
28 Traveling in Spain was a wonderful experience.
29 While I was there, I learned a lot about Spain.
30 I want to visit the country again.

시험대비 실력평가   p.34~37

01 ③   02 ①, ⑤   03 ③
04 saw them in Seville.   05 ②   06 ③
07 It was so delicious that we all[all of us] enjoyed it.
08 ②   09 ③
10 (A) Barcelona   (B) a colorful lizard
11 They speak Vietnamese there.   12 ②
13 ②   14 (A) ceiling   (B)there   (C) about
15 ①, ④   16 ⓐ size, ⓑ unique design
17 ③   18 ④   19 ②   20 ④
21 creativity   22 ①   23 ④
24 is spoken
25 Australia is so wonderful that you should visit it someday.
26 (A) the Sydney Opera House, (B) ocean roads

01 위 글은 '기행문'이다. ① (책·연극·영화 등에 대한) 논평[비평], 감상문, ② 수필, ④ 전기, ⑤ (신문·잡지의) 글, 기사

02 ① 약간의, ④ a number of: (수가) 많은, ⑤ (양이) 많은, lots of = a lot of = plenty of: (수와 양이) 많은

03 ③ 진우의 가족 여행은 마드리드에서 '시작했다.'

04 '세비야'에서 많은 역사상 중요한 건물들을 보았다.

05 ⓐ와 ②번: …하는 동안, ① …인 데 반하여(둘 사이의 대조를 나타냄), ③과 ⑤ [주절 뒤에서 반대·비교·대조를 나타내어] 그런데, 한편(으로는), ④ 잠깐, 잠시

06 ⓑ와 ②, ③, ⑤번: 현재분사, ①, ④: 동명사

07 so ~ that …: 너무 ~해서 …하다

08 ⓓ와 ②번: 작품들(명사), ① 근무하다, 취직해 있다(동사), ③ (건설) 공사[작업](명사), ④ (약 따위가) 작용하다, 듣다[on] (동사), ⑤ (기계 따위가) 움직이다, 작동하다(동사)

09 ③ 위 글은 '진우의 가족이 즐긴 요리와 장소를 소개'하는 글이다.

10 그것은 '바르셀로나'에 있고 Antoni Gaudi에 의해 설계되었다. 그곳에서 진우의 가족은 '형형색색의 도마뱀'과 같은 몇몇 Gaudi의 창의적인 작품들을 보았다.

11 일반인을 나타내는 They를 주어로 해서 바꾸는 것이 적절하다.

12 be well known for: ~으로 잘 알려져 있다

13 ② 베트남에서는 '베트남어'가 사용된다.

14 (A) 사그라다 파밀리아 안의 '천장'이라고 해야 하므로 ceiling 이 적절하다. ceiling: 천장, sealing: (봉투 등을) 밀봉[밀폐] 하기, (B) there는 부사이므로 전치사 없이 쓰는 것이 적절하다. (C) 스페인에 '대해' 많은 것을 배웠다고 해야 하므로 about 이 적절하다. a lot of: 많은

15 ① 가주어 It을 사용하여 바꾸거나, ④ to부정사를 주어로 하여 바꾸는 것이 적절하다.

16 진우에게, 사그라다 파밀리아의 '크기'와 '독특한 디자인'은 인상적이었다. impressive: 인상적인, 인상[감명] 깊은

17 ① They visited Park Guell. ② It started in 1883. ③ 사그라다 파밀리아의 건물 공사가 오늘날까지도 여전히 진행 중인 이유는 알 수 없다. ④ Stone. ⑤ At Park Guell and Sagrada Familia.

18 주어진 문장의 Both에 주목한다. ④번 앞 문장의 Park Guell 과 Sagrada Familia를 받고 있으므로 ④번이 적절하다.

19 ② paella의 조리법이 무엇인지는 대답할 수 없다. ① Rice, vegetables, meat, and seafood. ingredient: 재료, ③ They took a tour of Park Guell and Sagrada Familia. ④ Both were designed by Antoni Gaudi. ⑤ They saw some of Gaudi's creative works like a colorful lizard.

20 ④ go on = continue: 계속하다, ② remain: (처리·이행 등을 해야 할 일이) 남아 있다

21 소유격 다음에 명사를 써야 하는데, creation은 '창조, 창작'의 뜻 이므로 creativity(창의성, 독창력)를 쓰는 것이 적절하다.

22 스페인 여행은 훌륭한 경험이었다며, 그 나라를 다시 방문하고 싶

다고 했으므로 '만족한' 심정이라고 하는 것이 적절하다. ① 만족한, ② 겁먹은, 무서워하는, ③ 지루한, ④ 부끄러운, ⑤ 실망한

23 ④ '사그라다 파밀리아'에서 Gaudi의 창의성과 자연에 대한 사랑을 느낄 수 있었다.

24 영어가 '사용된다'고 해야 하므로 수동태로 쓰는 것이 적절하다.

25 'so'를 보충하면 된다.

26 시드니의 관광명소는 '시드니 오페라하우스'이고 멜버른은 아름다운 '해안 도로들'로 유명하다.

서술형 시험대비   p.38~39

01 Lots of tourists love Spain.

02 (A)visited (B)to watch (C)were

03 well known

04 ⓐ singing ⓑ waving ⓒ shouting

05 After

06 Seville

07 Spanish

08 felt → tasted

09 toured

10 It tasted like fried rice in Korea.

11 paella

12 such as

13 We visited Park Guell before Sagrada Familia. 또는 Before Sagrada Familia, we visited Park Guell.

14 (A) impressed (B) shone (C) stood

15 historic

16 who[that]

17 축구 경기장에서 경기를 보며 응원했다 / 도시를 걸어다니는 동안 많은 역사상 중요한 건물 들을 보았고, 플라멩코 박물관을 방문해서 플라멩코 춤을 보았다.

01 by 다음의 'lots of tourists'를 주어로 해서 고치는 것이 적절하다.

02 (A) visit는 타동사이므로 전치사 없이 바로 목적어를 쓰는 것이 적절하다. (B) 축구 경기를 '보기 위해서'라고 해야 하므로 to watch가 적절하다. (C) 'My sister and I'가 주어이므로 were가 적절하다.

03 be famous for = be well known for: ~로 유명하다, ~로 잘 알려져 있다

04 전치사 by 뒤에 동명사로 쓰는 것이 적절하다.

05 우리는 세비야로 가기 '전에' 마드리드를 관광했다. = 마드리드를 관광하고 난 '후', 우리는 세비야로 갔다..

06 '세비야'를 가리킨다.

07 형용사 Spanish로 쓰는 것이 적절하다. Spanish: 스페인의

08 한국의 볶음밥과 같은 '맛이 났다'고 하는 것이 적절하다. feel like: (촉감이) …하다

09 tour = take a tour of

10 'like'를 보충하면 된다.

11 '파에야'를 가리킨다.

12 like = such as: ~와 같은

13 '사그라다 파밀리아를 보기 전에 우리는 구엘 공원을 방문했다'라고 고치는 것이 적절하다.

14 (A) '감명 받았다'고 해야 하므로 impressed가 적절하다. impressing: 감동시키는, (B) 밤하늘처럼 '빛났다'고 해야 하므로 shone이 적절하다. shine - shone: 빛나다, 반짝이다, shine - shined: 윤[광]을 내다, 닦다, (C) stand는 자동사라서 수동태를 만들 수 없으므로 stood가 적절하다.

15 'history'의 형용사형 historic을 쓰는 것이 적절하다. historic: 역사적으로 중요한, 역사적인, historical은 '역사에 바탕을 둔'이라는 뜻으로, 보통 과거와 관련된 것, 역사 연구와 관련된 것 또는 과거에 실제 있었던 일을 묘사할 때 사용하므로 적절하지 않다.

16 주격 관계대명사 'who'나 'that'을 쓰는 것이 적절하다.

17 마드리드의 축구 경기장에서 경기를 보며 응원했고, 세비야를 걸어 다니는 동안 많은 역사상 중요한 건물들을 보았고 플라멩코 박물관을 방문해서 플라멩코 춤을 보았다.

영역별 핵심문제   p.41~45

01 ② 02 ④ 03 for 04 on
05 (1) historic (2) theater (3) ceiling (4) cheer for, fans
06 ⑤ 07 ③ 08 ③ 09 view
10 ② 11 Where is the nearest bus stop?
12 (C) → (A) → (B) 13 ②
14 (1) so difficult that we couldn't solve them
    (2) too difficult for us to solve. 15 ①
16 ④ 17 so beautiful that
18 (1) was written by (2) were built by 19 ③
20 (1) By whom was the telephone invented?
    (2) The roof of the house was covered with snow.
    (3) It was so dark that nothing could be seen.
    (4) The runner ran so fast that nobody could
      catch up with him.
21 travel, tour 22 ①, ④, ⑤
23 (A) a stadium, (B) a soccer match
24 ③ 25 ②
26 (A) fried (B) were (C) creative
27 Park Guell and Sagrada Familia

01 ① cheer for: ~을 응원하다 / 우리의 국가 대표팀을 응원해요! ② get 장소 부사: ~에 도착하다 / 그곳에 어떻게 가니? ③ design: 설계하다, 디자인하다 / 나는 나의 집을 설계했다. ④ tea: 차 / 그 차는 훌륭한 맛을 지니고 있다. ⑤ title: 제목 / 이 노래의 제목이 무엇이니?

02 ① sliding, slide: 미끄러지다, 활주하다 / 아이들은 얼어붙은 호수에서 미끄럼을 타고 있다. ② waved, wave: 흔들다 / 아기는 그녀의 엄마에게 손을 흔들었다. ③ rolling, roll: 구르다, 굴리다 / 그들은 큰 공을 굴리고 있다. ④ taking, take a tour: 관광하다, 여행을 가다 / 시내 구경을 하시는 게 어때요? ⑤ prefer: 선호하다 / 나는 커피보다 차를 선호한다.

03 be famous for: ~로 유명하다 be well known for: ~로 잘 알려져 있다

04 get on: ~에 타다 on foot: 걸어서

06 (A) 할로윈에 필요한 사탕을 사야 하는데 그것을 어디서 살 수 있는지 물어보고, 이에 대한 대답으로 Wendy's 사탕 가게에서 살 수 있다는 대답을 들었다. (B) Wendy's 사탕 가게가 어디 있는지 질문하고 이에 대한 대답을 듣는 것이 적절하다.

07 할로윈에 필요한 사탕을 사기 위해 Wendy's 사탕 가게에 가야 할 사람은 남자아이이다.

08 ③ It's across from the school. → It's across from the cinema. 병원은 영화관 맞은편에 있다.

09 view: 전망, 경치 / 어떤 특정한 장소나 위치에서 볼 수 있는 것, 특히 아름다운 전원

10 주어진 문장은 런던 아이와 스카이 가든에 대해서 간략히 설명하고 있다. 직원이 런던의 멋진 경치를 즐기기에 좋은 장소가 두 곳이 있다고 먼저 말한 후, 이에 대해 설명하는 것이 자연스러우므로 ②가 적절하다.

11 Where is ~?: ~가 어디에 있나요? the 최상급(형용사+est): 가장 ~한 stop: 정거장

12 해외 여행을 가자는 말에. (C) 어떤 도시(방콕이나 대만)를 선호하는지 묻는다. (A) 방콕을 더 좋아한다고 대답하고, 너무 화려해서 가야 한다고 말한다. (B) 그곳(방콕)에 가자고 대답한다.

13 비행기가 식당으로 바뀐 것이므로 수동태가 적절하다. The plane stopped flying and was turned into a restaurant.

14 'so+형용사[부사]+that+주어+can't ~'는 'too+형용사[부사]+to 동사원형'으로 바꿔 쓸 수 있다. 이때 to부정사의 목적어가 주어와 같을 경우 따로 써주지 않는 것에 유의한다.

15 첫 번째 문장에서는 목적격보어가 원형부정사인 경우, 수동태 문장에서는 to부정사로 바뀐다. 두 번째 문장에서는 'so+형용사[부사]+that+주어+동사'의 형태로 원인과 결과를 나타내는 것이 적절하다.

16 ① The room was so cold that David turned on the heater. ② This story was so funny that I laughed a lot. ③ Arnold got up so late that he missed the train. ⑤ John is so kind that everyone likes him.

17 'so+형용사[부사]+that+주어+동사'의 형태로 원인과 결과를 나타낸다.

18 (1) 책이 씌여진 것이고 (2) 피라미드가 건설된 것이므로

'be+pp' 형태의 수동태로 쓴다.

19 ③ write는 직접목적어를 주어로 하는 수동태만 가능하다. A long letter was written to me by my girl friend.

20 (1) 수동태의 의문문은 능동태의 평서문을 수동태로 고친 후에 다시 의문문으로 바꾸면 쉽다. (2) be covered with: ~로 덮여 있다 (3), (4) 'so+형용사[부사]+that+주어+동사' 구문은 '너무 ~해서 …하다'라는 뜻으로 원인과 결과를 나타낸다.

21 trip = travel = tour: 여행

22 ⓑ와 ②, ③번은 부사적 용법, ①, ④ 형용사적 용법 ⑤ 명사적 용법

23 진우의 가족은 스페인 여행 도중에 마드리드에 있는 '경기장'에 가서 '축구 경기'를 보았다.

24 ④와 ③번: …할 때(접속사), ① …이므로, …이기 때문에(접속사), ② …하는 대로(접속사), ④ (자격·기능 등이)

25 ② 진우의 가족은 '세비야'를 걸어다녔다.

26 (A) 한국의 '볶음밥'과 같은 맛이 났다고 해야 하므로 fried가 적절하다. fried rice: 볶음밥, frying: (기름에) 굽는, 튀기는, (B) Both는 복수로 취급하므로 were가 적절하다. (C) Gaudi 의 '창의적인' 작품들을 보았다고 해야 하므로 creative가 적절하다. common: 흔한, 공통의, creative: 창의적인

27 '구엘 공원'과 '사그라다 파밀리아'를 가리킨다.

단원별 예상문제
p.46~49

01 take　　　**02** by

03 (1) cheered　(2) try on　(3) (f)amous for
　　(4) get, on foot

04 (f)lamenco, (p)urple, (V)ietnamese
　　(1) flamenco　(2) Vietnamese　(3) purple

05 ①　　　　**06** ②　　　　**07** ⑤

08 (A) How　(B) Which　(C) Where

09 Where is the best place to go to?

10 Go straight one block and turn right. It's on your left.　**11** (C) → (A) → (B) → (D)　**12** ②

13 (1) The shoes look so great that Sandra wants to buy them.
　　(2) The stereo was so loud that it was impossible to sleep.

14 (1) so great that　(2) were killed　　**15** ④

16 ②　　　　　**17** It is well known for soccer.

18 ①, ③

19 toured of → toured 또는 took a tour of

20 ④　　　**21** ⑤　　　**22** ④

23 creative

24 They were designed by Antoni Gaudi.

01 take a walk: 산책하다 / 나는 나의 개와 산책하고 싶다. take a class: 수업을 받다 / 방과 후에 너는 수업을 듣거나 함께 클럽

에 가입할 수 있어. take a tour: 관광하다, 여행을 가다 / 그들은 그 성을 관광했던 것을 좋아했다.

02 수동태(be+p.p+by 행위자): …에 의해서 ~되다, by+교통수단: 교통수단으로 → by bus: 버스로

03 (1) cheer: 환호하다, 갈채하다 (2) try on: 입어 보다 (3) be famous for: ~로 유명하다 (4) on foot: 걸어서 get 장소 부사: ~에 도착하다

04 (1) flamenco: 플라멩코 (스페인 남부 Andalusia 지방 집시의 춤) / 안달루시아 집시의 격렬한 리듬을 가진 춤 / 그는 플라멩코 춤을 즐겨 춘다. (2) Vietnamese: 베트남어; 베트남의 / 베트남 언어, 사람 또는 문화와 관련된 / 그녀는 베트남에서 일자리를 구하기 위해 베트남어를 배웠다. (3) purple: 보라색 / 파란색과 빨간색을 섞은 색 / 그녀는 짙은 보라색 옷을 입었다.

05 주어진 문장은 야시장에 가서 신선한 과일 주스를 마시자고 제안하는 말이다. 날씨가 정말 덥다고 얘기하면서 이러한 제안을 하고, 이 제안에 대해서 'Sounds good.(좋아)'이라고 대답을 하고 있으므로 ①이 적절하다.

06 ② 위의 대화에서는 버스와 걷는 것 중의 선호를 물었기 때문에 버스와 택시 중에 무엇을 더 좋아하는지에 대해 대답할 수 없다. ① 그들은 야시장에 어떻게 갈 것인가? ② 남자아이는 버스와 택시 중 어떤 것을 선호하니? ③ 그들은 어디에 있는가? ④ 그들은 어디에 갈 것인가? ⑤ 그들은 무엇을 마실 것인가?

07 주어진 문장은 나중에 그곳을 방문하자고 제안하는 말이다. 여기서 그곳으로 지칭할 수 있는 장소는 런던 아이와 빅벤이며, 제안에 수락이나 거절하는 표현이 나와야 한다. 그러므로 'That sounds great.(좋아요)'라고 제안을 수락한 문장 앞에 들어가는 것이 적절하다.

08 (A) How may I help you?: 무엇을 도와드릴까요? (B) Which do you prefer(, A or B)?: (A와 B 중) 어떤 것을 선호하니? (C) Where is ~?: ~가 어디에 있나요?

09 'to go to'는 앞의 the best place를 꾸며주는 형용사적 용법으로 쓰인 to부정사이다. Where is ~?: ~가 어디에 있나요? best: 최고의, 가장 좋은

10 Go straight: 직진하세요. Turn right: 우회전하세요. It is on your left: 왼편에 있어요.

11 아프리카 박물관에 가는 방법을 물어보는 질문에 (C) 물론 가르쳐 준다고 대답하며 두 블록 직진한 후 우회전하라고 얘기한다. (A) 두 블록 직진한 후 우회전하고 그 다음에는 어떻게 하는지 질문하자. (B) 아프리카 박물관이 왼편에 있고, 신발 가게 맞은편에 있다는 추가적인 정보를 준다. (D) 길을 알려 준 것에 대해 감사를 표한다.

12 ③ 간접목적어 앞에 for 대신 to를 써야 한다.

13 (1), (2) 'so+형용사[부사]+that+주어+동사' 구문을 이용하여 원인과 결과를 나타낸다.

14 (1) 'so+형용사[부사]+that+주어+동사'로 원인과 결과를 나타낸다. (2) 누가 그 동작을 했는지 중요하지 않거나 잘 모를 때,

수동태 문장으로 표현한다.

15 ④ 세계에서 가장 유명한 축구 선수 몇몇을 볼 수 있었기 때문에 '신이 났다'고 하는 것이 적절하다. ① 재미있는, 흥미로운, ② 실망한, ③ 속상한, 마음이 상한, ⑤ 재미있는, 즐거운, amused(재미있어 하는, 즐거워하는)

16 ⓐ와 ②번: 수도, ①, ③, ④ 자본금, 자본 ⑤ 대문자

17 마드리드는 '축구'로 유명하다. be famous for = be well known for: ~로 유명하다, ~로 잘 알려져 있다

18 ⓐ와 ②, ④, ⑤번: 동명사, ①, ③번: 현재분사

19 tour = take a tour of

20 ④ 진우의 가족이 얼마나 오래 플라멩코 춤을 보았는지는 대답할 수 없다. ① At the soccer stadium. ② They sang songs, waved their hands, and shouted with the other fans. ③ They saw many historic buildings. ⑤ She was wearing a red dress.

21 ⓐ For dinner: 저녁 식사로, ⓑ with: '~로, ~이 있는'이라는 뜻의 전치사

22 파에야는 '쌀'과 '채소', '고기', '해산물'이 들어간 전통적인 스페인 요리이다.

23 뒤의 명사를 수식하는 형용사로 쓰는 것이 적절하다.

서술형 실전문제   p.50~51

01 The view from the London Eye are amazing. →
The view from the London Eye is amazing.

02 Go straight two blocks and turn right.

03 (A) → (C) → (B) → (D)

04 Which do you prefer, the Roller Coaster or the Scary House?

05 (1) so colorful that   (2) so tired that, too tired to

06 (1) Many people who want to do fun activities love Hong Kong.

(2) What was promised to do by her last weekend?

(3) We were taught physics by Ms. Grace last year. 또는 Physics wes taught (to) us by Ms. Grace last year.

07 was filled with

08 A woman in a red dress was dancing the flamenco with wonderful movements.

09 (A) Seville   (B) many historic buildings

10 like

11 (A) Spanish   (B) Korea   (C) rice, vegetables, meat (D) seafood

12 Antoni Gaudi designed both.

01 The view가 문장의 주어로 단수형이기 때문에 are가 아니라 is가 적절하다.

02 Go straight.: 직진하세요. Turn right.: 우회전하세요.

03 지수에게 토요일에 영화를 보자고 제안한다. (A) 좋다고 대답하며 영화가 몇 시에 시작하는지 질문하자 (C) 토요일에 5시와 7시가 있다고 말하며 어떤 시간을 더 선호하는지 물어본다. (B) 7시를 더 선호한다고 대답하고 (D) 그러면 6시에 만나자고 약속 시간을 정한다.

04 Which do you prefer, A or B?: A와 B중 어떤 것을 선호하니?

05 'so+형용사[부사]+that+주어+동사' 구문을 이용하여 원인과 결과를 나타낸다.

06 (2) 의문문의 수동태는 능동태의 의문문을 평서문으로 바꾼 후 이것을 수동태로 고치고, 다시 의문문으로 바꾸면 쉽다. (3) 4형식 문장의 수동태는 간접목적어와 직접목적어 각각을 주어로 하는 수동태가 가능하며 직접목적어를 주어로 한 수동태에서 teach 동사는 간접목적어 앞에 전치사 to를 쓴다. 이때의 to는 생각할 수도 있다.

07 be full of = be filled with: ~로 가득 차 있다

08 'in'을 보충하면 된다.

09 진우의 가족은 마드리드를 여행하고 난 후, '세비야'로 가서 도시를 걸어다니는 동안, '많은 역사상 중요한 건물들'을 보았다.

10 ⓐ tasted like: ~와 같은 맛이 났다, ⓒ like: ~와 같은

11 전통적인 '스페인' 요리인 파에야는 '한국'의 볶음밥과 같은 맛이 나고, 그것의 재료는 '쌀'과 '채소', '고기', '해산물'이다. ingredient: (특히 요리 등의) 재료[성분]

12 Antoni Gaudi를 주어로 해서 고치는 것이 적절하다.

창의사고력 서술형 문제   p.52

|모범답안|

01 (A) Do you know how to get to the bank?

(B) Go straight two blocks and turn right. / It's next to the police station. / It's across from the post office.

02 (A) capital

(B) English

(C) Meat pie and lamington

(D) the Sydney Opera House

(E) beautiful ocean roads.

03 (1) He practiced dancing so hard that he became a B-boy dancer.

(2) The thief ran away so that no one could find him.

(3) The cartoon was so interesting that I kept reading it.

01 Do you know how to get to ~?: ~에 어떻게 가는지 아나요? Go straight: 직진하세요. Turn right: 우회전 하세요. next to: ~옆에 across from: ~의 맞은편에

p.53~56

01 (1) useful (2) hopeful (3) colorful
02 (1) of (2) from (3) on, of (4) on
03 (1) try on (2) (g)o on (3) across from
　　(4) is well known for
04 ③
05 (1) Where / right, your left. It's next to
　　(2) Where is / one block, turn left, on your right,
　　　　across, the Flower Garden　　06 abroad
07 Which city do you prefer, Bangkok or Taiwan?
08 (B) so, (C) that
09 (A) watch (B) What time (C) are
10 ②　　　　　　11 called　　12 on
13 Which do you prefer, the purple one or the
　　yellow one?
14 (1) was heard to lock the door by me
　　(2) so wonderful that
15 ②　　　　　16 ⑤
17 (1) Sharon worked hard so that she might succeed.
　　(2) The box was so heavy that no one could move it.
　　(3) The machine will be repaired by Mr. Kim.
18 ③
19 (A) this summer (B) interesting (C) excited
20 ②　　　　21 ③　　　　22 ⑤
23 traditional　　　　　24 tasted → tasted like
25 ④

07 Which do you prefer, A or B?: A와 B 중 어떤 것을 선호하니?
08 so 형용사/부사 that 주어 동사: 너무 ~해서 그 결과 ~하다
09 (A) Why don't we 동사원형 ~?: ~할래?(제안하기) (B) What time: 몇 시에, 질문에 대한 대답이 '토요일에는 5시와 7시 두 번 상영해.'라는 것으로 보아 시간에 대해 질문하고 있다. (C) 'There be ~'는 be동사 다음에 주어가 나온다. two showings가 주어이므로 복수동사 are가 적절하다.
10 토요일에 영화가 5시와 7시로 2개를 선택할 수 있다. 이렇게 2개가 있을 때 먼저 언급한 것은 one, 나머지는 the other로 받는다.
11 긴 드레스가 이름이 뭐라고 불리는지 묻고 있는 것이므로 수동태가 어울린다.
12 try ~ on: ~을 입어 보다
13 Which do you prefer, A or B?: A와 B 중 어느 것을 선호하니? 대명사 one은 앞서 나온 Ao dai를 의미한다.
14 (1) hear는 지각동사이므로 목적격보어로 원형부정사를 쓰지만 수동태에서는 원형부정사를 to부정사로 바꿔 주어야 한다. (2) 원인과 결과를 나타내는 'so ~ that …' 구문이 적절하다.
15 ② 직접목적어를 주어로 한 수동태에서 make는 간접목적어 앞에 전치사 for를 쓴다.
16 'so … that ~'은 '너무[매우] …해서 ~하다'의 의미로 원인과 결과를 나타낸다.
17 (1) 'so that+주어+동사' 구문은 목적을 나타내어 '~하기 위해서' 혹은 '~하도록'이라는 의미로 쓰인다. (2) 'so+형용사[부사]+that+주어+동사' 구문은 '너무 ~해서 …하다'라는 뜻으로 원인과 결과를 나타낸다. (3) 조동사가 있는 문장의 수동태는 '조동사+be+p.p.' 형식을 갖는다.
18 일반 사람이 주어인 능동태를 수동태로 바꿀 때 'by+일반 사람'은 생략 가능하다.
19 (A) 때를 나타내는 this, last, next 등의 앞에는 전치사를 붙이지 않으므로 this summer가 적절하다. (B) 감정을 나타내는 동사가 무생물을 수식할 때는 보통 현재분사를 쓰므로 interesting이 적절하다. (C) 감정을 나타내는 동사가 사람을 수식할 때는 보통 과거분사를 쓰므로 excited가 적절하다.
20 진우의 가족 여행이 왜 마드리드에서 시작했는지는 대답할 수 없다. ① This summer. ③ Madrid. ④ To watch a soccer match. ⑤ They felt excited.
21 주어진 문장의 the city에 주목한다. ③번 앞 문장의 Seville를 받고 있으므로 ③번이 적절하다.
22 ⓐ with the other fans: 다른 팬들과 함께, with wonderful movements: 멋진 동작으로, ⓑ in: '착용'을 나타내는 전치사
23 명사를 수식하므로 형용사가 되어야 한다. traditional: 전통적인
24 한국의 볶음밥과 같은 맛이 났다고 해야 하므로 tasted like로 고치는 것이 적절하다. taste like+명사: ~와 같은 맛이 나다
25 ④ Antoni Gaudi는 구엘 공원과 사그라다 파밀리아를 '설계했다.'

01 주어진 두 단어의 관계는 명사와 형용사의 관계이다. use, hope, color는 모두 명사이고 뒤에 ful을 붙여서 형용사가 된다. (1) use: 사용 useful: 유용한 (2) hope: 희망, 기대 hopeful: 희망에 찬, 기대하는 (3) color: 색깔 colorful: 다채로운
02 (1) be full of: ~으로 가득 차다 (2) far from: ~로부터 먼 (3) on top of: ~의 위에, ~의 꼭대기에 (4) turn on: ~을 켜다
03 (1) try on: 입어 보다 (2) go on: (어떤 일이) 계속되다 (3) across from: ~의 맞은편에 (4) be well known for: ~로 잘 알려져 있다
04 ① match: 경기, 시합 / 그들은 중요한 시합을 하는 중이다. ② movement: 동작 / 그 동물은 빠른 동작으로 움직였다. ③ language: 언어 / 나는 영어, 일본어, 한국어 세 가지 언어를 할 수 있다. ④ tour: 여행 / 오늘 여행에서 우리는 많은 희귀 동물을 볼 것이다. ⑤ hamburger: 햄버거 / 그들은 어제 점심으로 햄버거를 먹었다.
05 Where is ~?: ~가 어디에 있나요? Go straight: 직진하세요. Turn left/right: 좌회전/우회전 하세요. next to: ~옆에 across from: ~의 맞은편에
06 abroad: 외국으로[에서] / 외국에서 또는 외국으로

11

Wonders of Nature

01 ②번 이외의 보기들은 명사에 접미사 '-y'가 붙어 형용사가 된 단어이지만 ②번은 형용사에 '-ly'를 붙여 부사가 되었다. exact: 정확한 exactly: 정확히 ① cloud: 구름 cloudy: 흐린, 구름이 잔뜩 낀 ③ dirt: 먼지, 때 dirty: 더러운 ④ luck: 운, 행운 lucky: 운이 좋은 ⑤ rain: 비 rainy: 비가 오는

02 damage: 피해 / 지진은 건물에 해를 가한다.

03 creature: 생물, 생명체 / 새우 같은 작은 생명체는 이 식물을 먹는다.

04 mudflat: 갯벌 / 해수면 아래에 낮은 깊이로 펼쳐진 평평한 지역 또는 조수에 의해 번갈아 덮여지고 드러나게 되는 지역

05 ① be good for: ~에 좋다, 유익하다 / 운동은 몸과 마음 둘 다에 유익하다. ② work out: 운동하다 / 나는 매일 체육관에서 운동하곤 했다. ③ by the way: 그런데 /그런데, 너 내일 저녁에 저녁식사 같이 할 시간 있니? ④ thanks to 명사: ~ 덕분에 / 네 도움 덕분에 나는 그것을 할 수 있었다. ⑤ get on: (버스·지하철 등을) 타다 / 다음 번 시드니행 비행기를 탈 수 있는 방법이 없나요?

06 not only A but also B: A뿐만 아니라 B도(= B as well as A) / 그는 영어뿐만 아니라 스페인어도 말할 수 있다.

01 remove: 제거하다 get rid of: 제거하다 / 나는 내 신발의 진흙을 제거했다.

02 make a living: 생계를 꾸리다 / Tom과 Lisa는 교사로 생계를 꾸려나간다. make a phone call: 전화를 걸다 / 나는 그에게 내일 계획을 물어보기 위해서 전화를 걸 것이다.

03 be famous for: ~로 유명하다 / 그는 클래식 음악 연주자로 유명했다. be good for: ~에 좋다, 유익하다 / 나는 웃음이 우리의 건강에 좋다고 믿는다.

04 (1) reach: ~에 이르다, 도달하다 (2) oxygen: 산소 (3) work out: 운동하다 regularly: 규칙적으로 (4) stain: 얼룩 remove: 제거하다 (5) mess: 엉망진창

05 (1) feed on: ~을 먹고 살다 / 하이에나는 죽어 있는 작은 동물과 새를 먹고 산다. (2) cover: (범위가) ~에 이르다, 차지하다 / 숲은 전세계 육지 면적의 30퍼센트를 차지하고 있다. (3) bloom: (꽃이) 피다 / 몇몇 화려한 꽃들은 짧은 여름 동안 꽃이 핀다. (4) appear: 나타나다 / 구름 뒤에서 달이 나타났다.

06 information: 정보 / 어떤 것에 대한 사실들

교과서 Conversation

교과서 대화문 익히기

교과서 확인학습   p.66~67

Listen & Speak 1 A

1. wonder what you did during / took, trip / By, plains / flat

2. at / lake / wonder how, are different / a long body of fresh, toward / got it

Listen & Speak 1 B

1. what a mountain is / high

2. I wonder what, plain / flat, land

Listen & Talk 2 A

1. how many oceans there are / There are, cover most / much, cover / heard, cover about, surface

2. rain forest is called, lungs / Lungs / produces, oxygen

Listen & Talk 2 B

1. want / heard, lakes
2. want to go to / famous

Conversation A

what, plant, grass / In, turns, wet / heard, for

Conversation B

amazing / get on / wonder what they are / reeds, reed / taller than / take / reed field / heard, the largest one / turning

Communication Task Step 1

place / special / is

시험대비 기본평가

01 ④	02 ⑤	03 ③, ④	04 ①

01 궁금증을 표현할 때 '~를 궁금해 하다'라는 의미의 동사 wonder를 사용하여 'I wonder 의문사+주어+동사 ~.'라고 말한다.

02 어떤 사실을 알고 있는지 말할 때 'I heard (that) ~.(나는 ~라고 들었어.)'라고 표현한다.

03 I want to know 의문사+주어+동사, I'd like to know 의문사+주어+동사: 나는 ~를 알기를 원해요

04 모레인호의 특별한 점을 궁금해 하는 말에, 물의 색깔이 연한 파랑색이라고 들었다고 대답해 준다. hope: 희망하다 have been to ~: ~에 가 본 경험이 있다

시험대비 실력평가
p.69~70

01 ①	02 I wonder what you will do.		
03 ⓐ, ⓑ, ⓔ	04 ③	05 ②	06 land
07 ③	08 ②	09 ⑤	10 ②
11 ①	12 ④	13 ⑤	

01 주어진 문장은 'Do you want to hear it?(그것에 대해 듣고 싶니?)'인데 내용상 it은 a plan을 의미한다. 듣고 싶은지 묻는 질문에 여자아이가 'Sure.(물론이지.)'로 대답하는 것이 어울린다.

02 I wonder 의문사+주어+동사: 나는 ~가 궁금해

03 ⓐ 남자아이는 며칠 동안 여행을 할 것인가?(3일) ⓑ 여행 기간 동안 남자아이는 무엇을 할 것인가?(첫째 날은 낚시, 둘째 날은 등산, 셋째 날은 수영) ⓒ 여행 중에 그는 어디로 갈 것인가? ⓓ 남자아이는 언제 여행을 갈 것인가? ⓔ 여행 첫 번째 날 남자아이는 무엇을 할 것인가?(호수에서 낚시)

04 주어진 문장은 평원이 무엇인지 물어보는 질문이다. 이에 대해 남자아이가 'They are large areas of flat land.(그곳은 넓고 평평한 땅이야.)'라고 대답한다.

05 take a trip (to 장소): (~로) 여행하다[여행가다]

06 land: 육지, 땅 / 물이 아닌 땅의 표면

07 평원은 넓고 평평한 땅이다. flat: 평평한

08 ⓑ Yes. → No.

09 여자아이는 4개의 바다가 있다고 생각했는데 실제로는 5개였으므로 정확하게 알고 있지 않았다.

10 주어진 문장은 그것들(노란색 식물들)이 무엇인지 궁금증을 표현하는 문장이다. 이 궁금증을 아빠가 갈대라고 알려주는 것이 적절하므로 ②가 어울린다.

11 get on: (버스·기차 등을) 타다

12 ④ 순천만은 한국에서 2번째로 큰 갈대밭이 아니라 가장 큰 갈대밭을 가지고 있다.

13 일요일에 무엇을 했는지 묻는 질문에, 단양에 갈 계획이라고 대답하는 것은 어색하다 I am going to take a trip to Danyang. → I took a trip to Danyang.

서술형 시험대비

01 for
02 I wonder what is special about Great Plains.
03 ⓐ I wonder what did you → I wonder what you did
04 ⓓ Like a lake → Unlike a lake
05 Can you tell me how a river and a lake are different?
06 (B) → (D) → (C) → (A)
07 I heard there are a lot of *oreums* in Jejudo.

01 be good for: ~에 좋다, 유익하다

02 I wonder 의문사+주어+동사: 나는 ~가 궁금해요 special: 특별한 about: ~에 대해서

03 I wonder 의문사+주어+동사: 나는 ~가 궁금해요

04 강과 호수가 어떻게 다른지 궁금한 여자아이에게 차이점을 설명해 주고 있다. 그러므로 like(~와 같이)가 아니라 unlike(~와는 달리)의 의미인 전치사를 사용하여 차이점을 얘기하는 것을 어울린다.

05 'I wonder 의문사+주어+동사.(나는 ~가 궁금해요.)'와 'Can you tell me 의문사+주어+동사?(나에게 ~를 말해줄 수 있나요?)'의 둘 다 궁금증을 표현하는 데 사용하는 표현들이다.

06 지구에 몇 개의 바다가 있는지 아는지 물어보는 질문에 (B) 4개라고 대답하자 (D) 아니라며 지구에 5개의 바다가 있고, 지구의 대부분을 차지하고 있다고 말한다. (C) 이어서 바다가 지구의 얼마를 차지하고 있는지 질문하자 (A) 지구 표면의 70%를 바다가 차지한다고 대답한다.

07 I heard (that) 주어 동사 ~: 나는 ~라는 것을 들었다 there are 복수 명사: ~가 있다 a lot of: 많은

핵심 Check
p.72~73

1 (1) It, to play (2) to see (3) for you to save
2 (1) not only (2) but also

시험대비 기본평가
p.74

01 ① **02** ③

03 (1) write → writes (2) is stupid → stupid

(3) like → likes (4) to crossing → to cross

(5) That → it (6) of → for

01 It을 가주어로 하고 to부정사를 진주어로 이용할 수 있는 ①번이 적절하다.

02 'not only A but also B'는 'B as well as A'로 바꿔 쓸 수 있다. ③번은 She is good at dancing as well as singing.으로 써야 초점이 같은 dancing에 놓인다.

03 (1) Sam을 주어로 하는 동사가 연결된 것이므로 writes가 되어야 한다. (2) 'not only A but also B' 구문에서 A와 B는 품사나 문장에서의 역할이 동일해야 한다. is의 보어로 stupid만 나와야 한다. (3) 'not only A but also B'가 주어로 쓰일 경우 B에 수를 일치시킨다. (4) 진주어로 to부정사가 적절하다. (5) 가주어로는 That이 아니라 It을 쓴다. (6) 문장에 쓰인 형용사가 사람의 성질을 나타내는 말이 아니므로 to부정사의 의미상 주어로 'for+목적격'을 써야 한다.

시험대비 실력평가
p.75~77

01 ③ **02** ① **03** ②

04 ④ **05** ⑤ **06** (1) It (2) to understand

(3) of (4) snowed (5) but (6) enjoys **07** ④

08 ② **09** ② **10** ④ **11** ⑤

12 ② **13** writing

14 (1) It would be really stupid of you to help them.

(2) It is interesting to walk in the forest.

(3) It is important to wear a hat to block the sun.

(4) Not only I but also Bella was enjoying taking a walk.

(5) Harry is not only a great wizard but also a very wise man.

15 ②, ④ **16** ⑤ **17** ③

18 Gina is kind as well as pretty

01 가주어로는 That이 아니라 It이 적절하다.

02 ② The book is not only expensive but interesting. ③ Not only I but also David likes Julie. ④ Steve is not only smart but also generous. ⑤ Bill speaks rudely not only at home but also at school.

03 'not only A but also B' 구문에서 A와 B는 품사나 문장에서의 역할이 동일해야 한다. is의 보어로 형용사가 나와야 한다. It이 나와 있으므로 It을 가주어로 하고 빈칸에는 진주어로 이용할 수 있는 to부정사가 적절하다.

04 가주어로 It이 적절하다.

05 'not only A but also B'는 'not only A but B', 'not simply[merely] A but (also) B', 'B as well as A' 등으로 바꿔 쓸 수 있다.

06 (1) 가주어로 It이 적절하다. (2) 진주어로 to부정사가 적절하다. (3) 문장에 쓰인 형용사가 사람의 성질을 나타내는 말일 때 to부정사의 의미상 주어를 'of+목적격'을 쓴다. (4) 'not only A but also B' 구문에서 A와 B는 품사나 문장에서의 역할이 동일해야 한다. (5) 'not only A but also B'에서 also가 생략되기도 한다. (6) 'not only A but also B'가 주어로 쓰일 경우 B에 수를 일치시킨다.

07 ① Amy is not only smart but also friendly. ② It is fun to go into caves. ③ It is kind of him to say so. ⑤ Not only you but also James plays the piano.

08 ②번은 인칭대명사로 '그것'이라고 해석 가능하지만 나머지는 모두 가주어로 쓰인 it이다.

09 not only A but also B: A뿐만 아니라 B도

10 '힙합 댄스를 배우는 것(to learn hiphop dance)'을 진주어로 하고 가주어 It을 이용하여 'It ~ to ...' 형식으로 쓴다.

11 not only A but (also) B'의 형태로 'A뿐만 아니라 B도'라는 의미를 갖는다.

12 가주어로 it을 쓰고 진주어로 to부정사를 쓰고 문장에 쓰인 형용사가 wise로 사람의 성질을 나타내는 말이므로 to부정사의 의미상 주어로 'of+목적격'을 쓰는 것이 적절하다.

13 'not only A but also B' 구문에서 A와 B는 품사나 문장에서의 역할이 동일해야 하므로 reading에 맞추어 writing이 적절하다.

14 (1) stupid가 사람의 성질을 나타내는 형용사이므로 의미상의 주어로 'of+목적격'을 쓴다. (2) 가주어로는 this가 아니라 it을 쓴다. (3) 진주어로 to부정사를 쓴다. (4) 'not only A but also B'가 주어로 쓰일 경우 B에 수를 일치시킨다. (5) 'not only A but also B'에서 A와 B는 문법적으로 동등한 구조를 연결해야 한다.

15 문장에 쓰인 형용사가 사람의 성질을 나타내는 말일 때는 to부정사의 의미상의 주어로 'of+목적격'을 쓴다. 'not only A but also B' 구문에서 A와 B는 품사나 문장에서의 역할이 동일해야 한다.

16 'not only A but also B'는 'not only A but B', 'not simply[merely] A but (also) B', 'B as well as A' 등으로 바꿔 쓸 수 있다.

17 산에 오르는 것(to climb that mountain)'을 진주어로 하고 가주어 It을 이용하여 'It ~ to …' 형식으로 쓴다.

18 'not only A but also B'는 'B as well as A'로 바꿔 쓸 수 있다.

서술형 시험대비
p.78~79

01 (1) (a) To make good friends is difficult.
　　 (b) It is difficult to make good friends.
　 (2) (a) To help others is important.
　　 (b) It is important to help others.
　 (3) (a) To explain tastes is impossible.
　　 (b) It is impossible to explain tastes.

02 (1) Chris is not only friendly but also good-looking.
　 (2) Marianne not only writes but also speaks Korean well.
　 (3) Charlotte not only likes to play basketball but also enjoys watching soccer games on TV.

03 (1) It is exciting to watch fish swimming.
　 (2) It is amazing to visit Giant's Causeway in Ireland.

04 (1) but also
　 (2) as well

05 (1) It is important to make good memories with my family.
　 (2) It is necessary to speak English well to succeed.
　 (3) I like not only singing but dancing.
　 (4) Not only you but also your brother should wash the dishes.

06 (1) It is easy to eat fruit and vegetables.
　 (2) It will be necessary to know how to greet people in different countries.
　 (3) It is true that knowledge is power.

07 (1) Build → To build, 또는 전체 문장 → It is a bad idea to build a new airport in the town.
　 (2) for → of
　 (3) working → work
　 (4) are → is

08 (1) It is not easy to forgive an enemy.
　 (2) It is important to save energy.
　 (3) Today is not only Christmas but also my birthday.
　 (4) Her brothers as well as Jane are kind.

01 to부정사가 문장의 주어로 쓰일 때 주어 자리에 가주어 it을 두고 to부정사 부분(진주어)을 문장 뒤로 보내어 쓸 수 있다.

02 'not only A but also B' 구문에서 A와 B는 품사나 문장에서의 역할이 동일해야 한다.

03 it을 가주어로 하고 to부정사를 진주어로 하여 쓴다.

04 'not only A but also B'는 'not only A but B as well'로 바꿔 쓸 수 있다.

05 (1)~(2) '가주어(it) ~ 진주어(to부정사) …' 구문을 이용한다. (3)~(4) 'not only A but also B'를 이용하여 배열한다.

06 (1)~(2) 문장의 주어로 쓰인 to부정사를 뒤로 보내고 대신 주어 자리에 가주어 It을 쓴다. (3) 주어로 쓰인 that절의 경우에도 긴 that절을 뒤로 보내고 주어 자리에 가주어 It을 쓴다.

07 (1) to부정사를 주어로 하거나 전체 문장을 '가주어(It) ~ 진주어(to부정사) …' 구문으로 고쳐 쓴다. (2) 사람의 성질을 나타내는 wise가 쓰였으므로 to부정사의 의미상 주어로 'of+목적격'을 써야 한다. (3) 'not only A but also B' 구문에서 A와 B는 품사나 문장에서의 역할이 동일해야 한다. should에 이어지는 work로 고쳐야 한다. (4) 'B as well as A'가 주어로 쓰일 경우 B에 수를 일치시킨다.

08 (1), (2) '가주어(It) ~ 진주어(to부정사) …' 구문을 이용한다. (3) 'not only A but also B' 구문을 이용한다. (4) 'B as well as A'가 주어로 쓰일 경우 B에 수를 일치시킨다.

교과서 Reading

확인문제
p.80

1 T　2 F　3 T　4 F

확인문제
p.81

1 T　2 F　3 T　4 T　5 F

교과서 확인학습 A
p.82~83

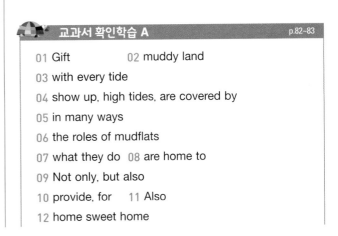

01 Gift　　　　　02 muddy land
03 with every tide
04 show up, high tides, are covered by
05 in many ways
06 the roles of mudflats
07 what they do　08 are home to
09 Not only, but also
10 provide, for　　11 Also
12 home sweet home

15

13 are good for
14 make a living, nearby
15 Thanks to
16 fun activities, such as   17 feed on
18 nature's gift   19 help, greatly
20 hold, reduce damage
21 filter, from, into
22 remove bad things
23 that reaches the sea
24 as the Earth's lungs
25 a huge volume of   26 healthy, clean
27 aren't they
28 from nature to living things
29 to protect mudflats

into the sea.

22 They remove bad things in the water before it enters the sea.

23 Thanks to mudflats, the water that reaches the sea is clean.

24 Mudflats work as the Earth's lungs.

25 They produce a huge volume of oxygen that is necessary for life on the Earth.

26 Earth: Mudflats keep me healthy and clean.

27 Mudflats are wonderful places, aren't they?

28 They are a gift from nature to living things on the Earth.

29 For all these reasons, it is necessary to protect mudflats.

교과서 확인학습 B

1 Mudflats, Nature's Gift

2 Mudflats are large areas of muddy land at the seaside.

3 They appear and disappear with every tide.

4 During low tides, they show up, and during high tides, they are covered by the sea.

5 Mudflats help sea creatures, people, and the Earth in many ways.

6 It is important to understand the roles of mudflats.

7 Let's see what they do.

8 Mudflats are home to a lot of living things at the seaside.

9 Not only very small living things like plankton but also crabs and fish live there.

10 Mudflats provide various types of food for them.

11 Also, many birds eat food there.

12 Crab: Mudflats are my home sweet home.

13 Mudflats are good for people, too.

14 People who live near mudflat areas make a living by catching fish and other sea animals nearby.

15 Thanks to mudflats, people can get fresh seafood.

16 People can enjoy fun activities, such as mud sliding and body painting on mudflats.

17 They can also watch a large number of birds that feed on the sea animals there.

18 Boy: Mudflats are nature's gift to living things!

19 Mudflats help the environment greatly.

20 Mudflats hold a lot of water, so they can reduce damage from floods.

21 Also, mudflats filter water that flows from the land

시험대비 실력평가

01 are appeared and disappeared → appear and disappear

02 (1) high tide (2) low tide   03 ②   04 ④

05 ⑤   06 ②, ③, ⑤

07 땅에서 바다로 물이 흘러들어가기 전에 물속에 있는 나쁜 물질을 갯벌이 제거해 주기 때문이다.

08 ⑤   09 (A) for (B) other (C) feed

10 ①   11 live   12 ②

13 wear long clothes   14 ③   15 ④

16 ②   17 ③   18 ⑤

19 floods   20 ④   21 the sea covers them

22 ②, ④, ⑤   23 That → It

24 the longest river, the biggest cave, the tallest falls, and the highest mountain

25 wonder   26 (A) few (B) little (C) during

27 it is always hot day and night → it is hot during the day and cold at night

01 appear와 disappear는 수동태로 만들 수 없는 동사들이다.

02 (1) 밀물, 조수가 안으로 들어오는 흐름 또는 조수가 들어와서 바다가 가장 높은 수위에 도달한 때, (2) 썰물, 조수가 밖으로 빠져나가는 흐름 또는 조수가 빠져나가서 바다가 가장 낮은 수위에 도달한 때

03 갯벌은 '조수와 함께' 나타나고 사라진다고 했으므로, 갯벌의 의미를 올바르게 이해하지 못한 사람은 '희정'이다.

04 위 글은 '지형을 소개하는 글'이다. ① 문화에 대한 소개서, ② 지리 실험 보고서, ③ 일기 예보, 기상 통보, ⑤ 현장학습 안내서

05 주어진 문장이 ⑤번 다음 문장의 이유에 해당하므로 ⑤번이 적절하다.

16 정답 및 해설

06 ⓐ와 ②, ③, ⑤번: 관계대명사, ①, ④: 접속사

07 갯벌 덕분에 바다에 도착한 물은 깨끗하다.

08 number는 'large'와 'small'을 사용하여 수량을 표현하는 명사이다.

09 (A) '유익하다'고 해야 하므로 for가 적절하다. be good at: ~을 잘하다, be good for: ~에 좋다, (B) '다른 바다 동물들'이라고 해야 하므로 other가 적절하다. another+단수명사, (C) 동사를 써야 하므로 feed가 적절하다. food: feed의 명사

10 ① 'Mudflats are good for people, too.'로 글이 시작하고 있으므로, 위 글의 앞에도 '갯벌이 유익한 다른 경우'에 대한 내용이 나왔을 것이라고 하는 것이 적절하다.

11 not only A but (also) B = B as well as A: A뿐만 아니라 B도, 'not only A but also B'나 'B as well as A'가 주어로 쓰일 경우 B에 수를 일치시킨다.

12 ⓑ와 ①, ③, ④: 부사적 용법, ② 형용사적 용법, ⑤ 명사적 용법

13 만약 당신이 갯벌에 간다면, 당신을 물 수 있는 동물들로부터 당신을 보호하기 위해 '긴 옷을 입는 것'이 중요하다.

14 ⓐ 'to'는 '~에게'라는 의미이다. ⓒ provide+사람(대상)+with 사물 = provide+사물+for[to] 사람[대상]: ~에게 …을 제공[공급]하다

15 not only[merely/just/simply] A but (also) B = B as well as A: A뿐만 아니라 B도, ④ 'Crabs and fish as well as very small living things like plankton live there.'라고 하는 것이 적절하다.

16 플랑크톤처럼 작은 생명체뿐만 아니라 게와 물고기도 갯벌에 산다.

17 앞에 나오는 내용에 추가하는 내용이 뒤에 이어지므로 Also가 가장 적절하다. ② 그러므로, ⑤ 즉, 다시 말해

18 ④ awesome: 경탄할 만한, 기막히게 좋은, 굉장한, ⑤ protect: 보호하다, prevent: 막다[예방/방지하다]

19 갯벌은 많은 양의 물을 수용해서 '홍수'의 피해를 줄여 준다.

20 앞 문장에서 갯벌의 '역할'을 이해하는 것이 중요하다고 했기 때문에, 갯벌이 '무엇을' 하는지 살펴보자고 하는 것이 적절하다. ① how는 부사이므로 do의 목적어로 쓰일 수 없고, how they do them처럼 따로 목적어를 써야 한다.

21 'the sea'를 주어로 해서 고치는 것이 적절하다.

22 ⓑ와 ②, ④, ⑤번: 가주어 , ① 비인칭 주어, ③ 가목적어

23 'That'을 가주어 'It'으로 고치는 것이 적절하다.

24 '가장 긴 강, 가장 큰 동굴, 가장 높은 폭포, 그리고 가장 높은 산'을 가리킨다.

25 wonder: 경이(로운 것), 경탄, 매우 놀라운 그리고 예상 밖의 어떤 것

26 (A) 'plants'는 셀 수 있는 명사이므로 few가 적절하다. (B) 'water'는 셀 수 없는 명사이므로 little이 적절하다. (C) during the day: 낮 동안, during+기간을 나타내는 명사, for+숫자

27 사막에서 낮에는 덥고 밤에는 춥다. day and night: 밤낮으로

01 tide
02 show up
03 (A) low　(B) disappear
04 mudflats
05 (A) greatly　(B) remove　(C) volume
06 as → so 또는 Mudflats hold a lot of water, as they can reduce damage from floods. → As[Because] mudflats hold a lot of water, they can reduce damage from floods.
07 Thanks to mudflats, the water that reaches the sea is clean.
08 Crabs and fish as well as very small living things like plankton live there.
09 with
10 Mudflats[mudflats]
11 catching
12 on
13 mud sliding and body painting
14 that 또는 which
15 aren't they
16 healthily and cleanly → healthy and clean
17 (A) nature　(B) living things

01 every 뒤에 단수형을 쓰는 것이 적절하다. 갯벌은 '조수'와 함께 나타나고 사라진다.

02 appear = show up: 나타나다

03 갯벌은 '썰물'일 때 나타나고 밀물일 때 '사라지는' 해안의 평평하고 빈 땅의 지역이다.

04 '갯벌'을 가리킨다.

05 (A) 동사 help를 수식하므로 부사 greatly가 적절하다. (B) 나쁜 물질을 '제거한다'고 해야 하므로 remove가 적절하다. generate: 발생시키다, 만들어 내다, (C) 'oxygen'은 셀 수 없는 명사이므로 volume이 적절하다.

06 '갯벌은 많은 양의 물을 수용해서 홍수의 피해를 줄여 준다'고 해야 하므로 as를 so로 고치거나 문장을 As나 Because 등으로 시작하여 쓰는 것이 적절하다.

07 Thanks to: ~ 덕분에

08 not only A but also B = B as well as A: A뿐만 아니라 B도

09 provide+사람(대상)+with 사물 = provide+사물+for[to] 사람(대상): ~에게 …을 제공[공급]하다

10 '갯벌'을 가리킨다.

11 전치사 by 뒤에 동명사를 쓰는 것이 적절하다.

12 (B) on mudflats: 갯벌에서, (C) feed on: ~을 먹다[먹고 살다]

13 '진흙 미끄럼 타기'와 '보디 페인팅'

17

14 관계대명사 that이나 which를 쓰는 것이 적절하다.

15 문장의 동사가 be동사이므로, be동사를 사용하여 부가의문문을 만드는 것이 적절하다.

16 keep의 목적격보어이므로 형용사로 고치는 것이 적절하다.

17 갯벌은 '자연'이 지구상의 '생물들'에게 준 선물이므로, 갯벌을 보호하는 것은 필수이다.

영역별 핵심문제
p.93~97

01 ② **02** ④ **03** (o)ccur **04** ③

05 saw **06** ⑤

07 I wonder what you did during the summer vacation.

08 ④ **09** ④ **10** surface **11** ④

12 I heard it is the largest one in Korea.

13 ③ **14** ① **15** ④ **16** ②

17 ③

18 (1) for you to be kind to other people
(2) for you to be careful when you drive a car.

19 ⑤ **20** ④ **21** ②, ⑤ **22** ③

23 (A)reduce (B)enters (C)reaches

24 ④ **25** ①, ③, ④ **26** like **27** ②

28 ④ **29** ① **30** ① **31** food

01 ② 이외의 보기들은 접미사 '-y'가 붙어 형용사가 되는 명사들이다. friend는 '-ly'가 붙어 형용사가 된다. ① mess: 엉망진창 messy: 지저분한 ② friend: 친구 friendly: 친근한 ③ wind: 바람 windy: 바람이 부는 ④ luck: 운, 행운 lucky: 운이 좋은 ⑤ health: 건강 healthy: 건강한

02 fall: (복수형으로) 폭포 / 폭포는 뉴욕 주의 총 전력의 10 퍼센트를 공급할 수 있습니다.

03 take place: 일어나다, 개최되다 occur: 일어나다 / 이것은 언제 어디서든 일어날 수 있다.

04 a body of water: (바다나 호수 등의) 수역

05 took a trip과 접속사 and로 연결되어 있으므로 과거형 동사가 어울린다.

06 ① Although: ~에도 불구하고 ② In addition: 게다가 ③ On the contrary: 이와 반대로 ④ Besides: 게다가 ⑤ By the way: 그런데 (대화에서 화제를 바꿀 때 씀)

07 I wonder 의문사+주어+동사: 나는 ~가 궁금해요 during+명사: ~ 중에, ~ 동안에

08 cover: (범위가)~에 이르다, 차지하다 How much of the Earth do they cover?: 그것들이 지구의 얼마를 차지하고 있니?

09 ⓐ many, oceans는 셀 수 있는 명사이므로 much가 아니라 many의 수식을 받는다. ⓑ there are, 간접의문문의 순서는 '의문사+주어+동사'이다. ⓕ cover, 'is covered'는 수동태로 '덮여지다'의 의미이다. 바다가 지구의 표면의 70%를 차지한다는

10 surface: 표면 / 어떤 것의 평평한 윗부분 또는 그것의 바깥쪽

11 형용사의 비교급은 바로 앞에 much, far, even, still, a lot 등을 사용해서 강조한다. very는 원급을 강조할 때 사용한다.

12 I heard (that) 주어 동사 ~: 나는 ~라는 것을 들었다 the 최상급 형용사: 가장 ~한

13 'not only A but also B'는 'B as well as A'로 바꿔 쓸 수 있다. Sam writes German as well as reads it.

14 'not only A but also B'는 'not only A but B', 'not simply[merely] A but (also) B', 'B as well as A' 등으로 바꿔 쓸 수 있다.

15 ④번은 to부정사의 부사적 용법(결과)이지만 나머지는 모두 진주어로 쓰인 명사적 용법으로 쓰였다.

16 ②에는 사람의 성격이나 성질을 나타내는 형용사(rude)가 왔으므로 의미상의 주어로 'of+목적격'을 써야 한다. 나머지는 모두 for가 들어간다.

17 ⓐ play → plays ⓒ lives → live ⓔ for → of ⓕ swims → to swim ⓖ That → It

18 '~해야 한다'는 의미를 가주어 It을 이용하여 '~할 필요가 있다'라고 쓰려면 진주어로 to부정사를 이용한다. 이때 의미상의 주어를 빠뜨리지 않도록 주의한다.

19 'not only A but also B' 구문에서 A와 B는 품사나 문장에서의 역할이 동일해야 한다. Dylan not only played computer games but also did his homework.

20 ⓐ with every tide: 조수와 '함께', ⓑ in many ways: 많은 방면에서

21 to부정사와 동명사가 주어일 때 단수 취급하는 것이 적절하다.

22 갯벌의 역할이 무엇인지는 대답할 수 없다. ① During low tides. ② During high tides. ④ The sea. ⑤ Yes.

23 (A) 홍수의 피해를 '줄여 준다'고 해야 하므로 reduce가 적절하다. (B) 물이 바다로 '들어가기 전에'라고 해야 하므로 enters가 적절하다. enter = go into, enter into: (논의·처리 등을) 시작하다, (C) reach는 타동사이므로 전치사 없이 바로 목적어를 가지는 것이 적절하다. reach = get to: ~에 도착하다

24 ⓐ와 ④번: 전치사 'as'는 자격·기능 등을 나타내어 '~로(서)'라는 뜻이다. ① (접속사) [양태] …처럼, …하는 대로, …와 같이, ② (접속사) …할 때, ③ 앞의 as가 지시부사, 뒤의 as는 접속사, ⑤ (접속사) [비례] …함에 따라, …할수록

25 ⓐ와 ②, ⑤: 동명사, ①, ③, ④: 현재분사

26 such as = like: ~와 같은

27 갯벌은 지구상의 생명에게 필요한 많은 양의 산소를 생산한다고 했기 때문에, 그것들은 지구의 '폐' 역할을 한다고 하는 것이 적절하다. ③ 위(胃), 복부, 배

28 이 글은 '갯벌이 환경에 크게 도움이 된다.'는 내용의 글이다.

29 ① things가 복수명사이므로 much 대신 many를 써야 한다. ② seashore: 해변, 해안, 바닷가, ③ not only A but also B = not merely[simply] A but also B ④ supply: 공급[제공]

18 정답 및 해설

하다, ⑤ In addition: 게다가

30 ⓐ와 ①: (전치사) …와 같은(such as), ② (전치사) …와 비슷한, ③ (동사) (…을) 좋아하다, ④ (형용사) 비슷한, ⑤ (전치사) …와 (똑)같이[마찬가지로], …처럼

31 갯벌은 바닷가에 있는 많은 생물들뿐만 아니라 많은 새들에게도 다양한 종류의 '먹이'를 제공한다.

단원별 예상문제

p.98~101

01 low tide   **02** (1) Unlike (2) During (3) as (4) else

03 take   **04** make   **05** ③

06 I wonder what a forest is. /
I would like to know what a forest is.

07 who covered → that[which] is covered

08 I heard the Amazon rain forest is called the lungs of the Earth.

09 ③   **10** ③   **11** ②, ④

12 (A) like (B) In (C) for   **13** ②   **14** ⑤

15 (1) It is easy for me to understand this book.
(2) It is very kind of you to help her.
(3) It is dangerous for you to walk around at night.
(4) Cats are smart as well as clean.
(5) Junsu not only dances but also sings well.
(6) Not only Eric but also his brothers are fast runners.

16 ⑤   **17** ②, ④, ⑤

18 they are covered by the sea.   **19** ③

20 ⑤

21 Not only very small living things like plankton but also crabs and fish live there.

22 ②   **23** to get

24 They make a living by catching fish and other sea animals nearby.

25 ③

01 두 단어는 반의어 관계이다. appear: 나타나다 disappear: 사라지다 high tide: 밀물 low tide: 썰물

02 (1) unlike: ~와는 달리 / 그것의 이름과 달리, 그린랜드는 얼음과 눈으로 덮여 있습니다. (2) during: ~ 동안(에), ~ 중에 / 밤중에 통증으로 간혹 깨곤 합니다. (3) such as: ~와 같은 / 그는 소설, 만화 같은 많은 책을 갖고 있다. (4) else: 그 밖의, 그것 이외의 / 이보다 더 좋을 순 없다

03 take a trip (to 장소): (~로) 여행하다[여행가다] / 나는 유럽으로 여행 갈 희망하고 있다. take a picture: 사진을 찍다 / 저 공룡 앞에서 저희들 사진 좀 찍어 주실래요?

04 make a decision: 결정하다 / 나는 결정을 내리기 전에 너와 이야기하고 싶다. make a mistake: 실수하다 / 실수하는 것을

두려워하지 마. make a noise: 소음을 내다, 시끄럽게 하다 / 음식을 먹으면서 시끄러운 소리를 내는 것은 실례이다.

05 ③ why → how ⓐ beautiful ⓑ how ⓒ different ⓓ long ⓔ fresh. a body of water: (바다나 호수 등의) 수역 fresh water: 민물

06 I wonder 의문사+주어+동사: 나는 ~가 궁금해요 I'd like to know 의문사+주어+동사: 나는 ~을 알기를 원해요. forest: 숲

07 land는 사물이므로 주격 관계대명사 which나 that이 어울린다. '식물과 나무로 덮여진 땅'이므로 수동태(be+p.p)의 형태로 사용해야 한다.

08 I heard (that) 주어 동사 ~: 나는 ~라는 것을 들었다 rain forest: 열대 우림 lung: 폐

09 Why로 질문하였으므로 이유를 설명하는 단어가 어울리며, (A) 뒤에 주어와 동사가 나오므로 접속사 Because가 어울린다. produce: 생산하다, 만들다 protect: 보호하다 remove: 제거하다

10 want는 to부정사를 목적어로 취하는 동사이다. 단양에 가고 싶다는 말에 단양에 유명한 동굴이 있다고 들었다고 대답하므로, 단양에 왜 가고 싶은지 이유를 묻는 것이 어울린다.

11 'I heard (that) 주어 동사 ~. / 'I'm aware (that) 주어 동사 ~. / 'I'm aware of (동)명사 ~. / 'I have heard (that) 주어 동사 ~. / 'I've been told (that) 주어 동사 ~. 모두 알고 있는 것을 표현하는 말들이다. ②번은 of 다음에 (동)명사가 와야 하므로 나올 수 없다. ④ I'm not sure ~: 나는 ~을 확신하지 않는다.

12 look like+명사: ~처럼 보이다 in+계절: ~ 계절에 be famous for: ~로 유명하다

13 가주어로는 That이 아니라 It을 쓰며 문장에 쓰인 형용사가 사람의 성질을 나타내는 말일 때는 to부정사의 의미상 주어로 'of+목적격'을 쓴다.

14 ① It's important to protect mudflats. ② It is exciting for me to play baseball. ③ Isn't it boring to watch TV at home? ④ Ann felt disappointed as well as angry.

15 (1) it을 가주어로 하고 to부정사를 진주어로 이용한다. (2) 형용사 kind가 있으므로 to부정사의 의미상 주어로 'of+목적격'을 쓴다. (3) 가주어 it이 있으므로 to부정사의 의미상 주어로 'for you'를 빠뜨리면 안 된다. (4) B as well as A: A뿐만 아니라 B도 (5) not only A but also B: A뿐만 아니라 B도 (6) 'not only A but also B'나 'B as well as A'가 주어로 쓰일 경우 B에 수를 일치시킨다.

16 가주어 it을 이용하여 바꿔 쓰는 것으로 원래 문장의 to부정사를 진주어로 쓴다.

17 ⓐ와 ①, ③: 명사적 용법, ②, ④: 형용사적 용법, ⑤: 부사적 용법

18 밀물일 때 '바다에 덮이기' 때문이다.

19 갯벌의 역할을 이해하는 것이 중요하다며 갯벌이 무엇을 하는지

살펴보자고 했기 때문에, 이 글의 뒤에는 '갯벌의 역할'에 대한 내용이 이어질 것이라고 하는 것이 적절하다.

20 뒤에 복수 명사가 나오므로, (양이) 많은 것을 나타내는 ⑤는 적절하지 않다. ⓐ와 ①, ③: (수나 양이) 많은, ②, ④: (수가) 많은, ⑤ a great deal of: (양이) 많은

21 not only A but also B: A뿐만 아니라 B도

22 이 글은 '갯벌은 바닷가에 있는 많은 생물들에게 집'이라는 내용의 글이므로, 제목으로는 '갯벌, 바닷가에 있는 생물들의 집'이 적절하다.

23 enable+목적어+to부정사: ~에게 …할 수 있게 하다

24 그들은 근처에서 물고기와 다른 바다 동물들을 잡아 생계를 꾸린다.

25 이 글은 갯벌의 많은 유익한 점에 관한 글이므로, 주제로는 '갯벌은 생명체에게 주는 자연의 선물'이라고 하는 것이 적절하다.

🦉 서술형 실전문제
p.102~103

01 I wonder what you did during the summer vacation.

02 (C) → (B) → (A)

03 I wonder what is special about the Yangze River.

04 I heard it is the third longest river in the world.

05 (1) It is dangerous to swim in the river.
(2) It was wise of her to be a nurse.

06 (1) Midori can speak not only Japanese but also English.
(2) Wendy studies hard not only at school but also at home.

07 are → is

08 that

09 (1) 갯벌 지역 인근에 사는 사람들은 근처에서 물고기와 다른 바다 동물들을 잡아 생계를 꾸린다.
(2) 갯벌 덕분에 사람들은 신선한 해산물을 얻을 수 있다.
(3) 사람들은 갯벌에서 진흙 미끄럼 타기나 보디 페인팅과 같은 즐거운 활동을 즐길 수 있다.
(4) 사람들은 갯벌에서 바다 동물을 먹는 수많은 새를 관찰할 수도 있다.

10 (A) near (B) nearby (C) Thanks to

11 filter

12 the water

13 (1) holding a lot of water
(2) filtering water
(3) producing a huge volume of oxygen

---

01 I wonder 의문사+주어+동사 ~.: 나는 ~가 궁금해요. while과 during은 '~ 동안에'로 뜻은 같지만, 'the summer vacation'은 명사이므로 전치사인 during이 어울린다.

---

02 노란색 식물들이 무엇인지 궁금하다고 말하니까, (C) 그건 갈대라고 대답해 주며, 순천만에는 아름다운 갈대밭이 있다고 말한다. (B) 갈대가 아빠의 키보다 더 크다고 말하니까 (A) 정말 그렇다고 동의하며 사진을 찍어 준다고 말한다.

03 I wonder 의문사+주어+동사 ~.: 나는 ~가 궁금해요. special: 특별한

04 I heard (that)+주어+동사 ~.: 나는 ~라는 것을 들었다. the 서수+최상급 형용사: ~ 번째로 가장 ~한

05 (1) It을 가주어로 하고 in의 목적어로 the river를 쓴다. (2) to decide의 주어가 she이므로 of her로 의미상의 주어를 나타내야 한다.

06 'not only A but also B' 구문에서 A와 B는 품사나 문장에서의 역할이 동일해야 한다. (1) Japanese와 English를 A와 B 자리에 쓴다. (2) at school과 at home을 A와 B 자리에 쓴다.

07 'B as well as A'가 주어로 쓰일 경우 B에 수를 일치시킨다.

08 관계대명사 that은 선행사가 사람, 동물, 사물일 때 다 사용할 수 있다.

09 ⓐ 다음에 이어지는 내용을 쓰면 된다.

10 (A) 갯벌 지역 '가까이에서'라고 해야 하므로 전치사 near가 적절하다. near: (전치사) ~에서 가까이, (부사) 가까이, nearly: (부사) 거의, (B) '근처에서'라고 해야 하므로 nearby가 적절하다. (형용사) 인근의, 가까운 곳의, (부사) 인근에, 가까운 곳에, nearly: (부사) 거의, (C) 갯벌 '덕분에'라고 해야 하므로 Thanks to가 적절하다. In spite of: ~에도 불구하고

11 물속에 있는 나쁜 물질을 제거한다 = 물을 걸러내 준다 filter: 거르다, 걸러내다

12 '물'을 가리킨다.

13 (1) '많은 양의 물을 수용해서' 홍수의 피해를 줄여 준다. (2) '물을 걸러냄으로써' 물이 바다로 들어가기 전에 물속에 있는 나쁜 물질을 갯벌이 제거한다. (3) '많은 양의 산소를 생산함으로써' 지구의 폐 역할을 한다.

🐇 창의사고력 서술형 문제
p.104

|모범답안|

01 on May 18th / I wonder what time the mall opens on the opening day? / it opens at 8 a.m

02 (1) |모범답안| It is exciting to watch the soccer game. / It's necessary for you to do exercise regularly.
(2) |모범답안| It was amazing to see such an old house. / It is important to use water carefully.
(3) |모범답안| It's dangerous to swim in the sea. / It's safe to wear a helmet while riding a bike.

03 (A) |모범답안| few (B) |모범답안| little
(C) |모범답안| lizards and desert snakes live
(D) |모범답안| cold

01 I heard (that) 주어 동사 ~: 나는 ~라는 것을 들었다 I wonder 의문사+주어+동사: 나는 ~가 궁금해요 날짜 앞에는 전치사 on을, 시간 앞에는 전치사 at을 사용한다.

단원별 모의고사   p.105~108

01 ①　　　　　02 ③

03 (1) reaches　(2) surfing　(3) occurred　(4) protect
　　(5) flows　(6) Remove　(7) provide

04 ④　　　　　05 ③

06 I wonder what you will do. 또는 I wonder what you are going to do.

07 flow

08 I wonder how a river and a lake are different.

09 ③　　　　10 ④　　　　　11 reed

12 (A) get　(B) what they are　(C) than　(D)take

13 ②

14 not only[simply, merely, just] , but also

15 ③

16 (1) were → was　(2) for → of

17 (1) I saw Alitar as well as Avatar.
　　(2) Peter as well as his brothers likes Minji.

18 (A) low　(B) high　(C) what

19 ④　　　　　20 as → like 또는 such as

21 ③　　　　　22 make a living

23 ②　　　　　24 ①　　　　　25 ①, ④, ⑤

01 not only A but also B: A뿐만 아니라 B도(= B as well as A) / 그의 직업은 재미있을 뿐 아니라 보수도 매우 좋다.

02 a large number of: 다수의, 많은 수의 / 매년 많은 사람들이 이 박물관을 찾는다.

03 (1) reach: ~에 이르다, 도달하다 (2) surf: 서핑하다 (3) occur: 일어나다 (4) protect: 보호하다 (5) flow: 흐르다 (6) remove: 제거하다 (7) provide: 제공하다, 주다

04 ④의 영영풀이는 mud에 대한 설명이다. mud: 진흙, muddy: 진흙투성이인, 진흙의, 질퍽한, covered with mud, or full of mud(진흙으로 덮인 또는 진흙으로 가득 찬)

05 남자아이는 여행 계획을 말하고 있다. 주어진 문장에서 다음 날에 산에 오를 것이라고 말하고 있다. 내용상 첫날의 일정을 말하고 그 다음 날에 대해 얘기하고, 상대방이 'Is that all?(그게 전부니?)'이라고 묻고 마지막 날의 계획을 말하는 것이 자연스럽다.

06 I wonder 의문사+주어+동사: 나는 ~가 궁금해요. 여행을 가서 미래에 할 내용을 궁금해 하고 있으므로 미래 시제를 표현하는 'will+동사원형'이나 'be going to 동사원형'을 사용한다.

07 flow: 흐르다 / 액체, 기체, 전류 등을 설명할 때 사용되는 것으로, 어떠한 방해 없이 꾸준히 움직이다

08 I wonder 의문사+주어+동사: 나는 ~가 궁금해요 how: 어떻게 different: 다른

09 그들은 호수가 아니라 강을 보고 있다.

10 ⓐ what this is ⓑ looks like ⓒ turns ⓓ grows ⓔ is famous for

11 reed: 갈대 / 그것은 물 근처에서 사는 길고 얇은 식물이다. 그것의 줄기는 물건을 만들기 위해 사용될 수 있다.

12 (A) get on: (버스·지하철 등을) 타다 (B) I wonder 의문사+주어+동사: 나는 ~가 궁금해요 (C) 비교급 than: ~보다 더 ~한 (D) let+목적어+목적격보어(동사원형): ~가 …하게 하다

13 문장에 쓰인 형용사가 사람의 성질을 나타내는 말일 때 to부정사의 의미상 주어로 'of+목적격'을 쓴다. It was so foolish of Jane to do that.

14 'not only A but also B(A뿐만 아니라 B도)' 구문을 이용한다.

15 주어진 문장과 ③번은 가주어로 쓰이고 있다. ①, ④ 비인칭주어 ② It ~ that 강조 구문 ⑤ 가목적어

16 (1) 'B as well as A'가 주어로 쓰일 경우 B에 수를 일치시킨다. (2) 문장에 쓰인 형용사가 사람의 성질을 나타내는 말일 때는 to부정사의 의미상 주어로 'of+목적격'을 쓴다.

17 (1) not only A but (also) B = B as well as A 여기서 A와 B는 문법적으로 같은 성격의 것이어야 한다. (2) 'not only A but also B'나 B as well as A가 주어로 쓰일 경우 B에 수를 일치시킨다.

18 (A) '썰물'일 때 갯벌이 드러난다고 해야 하므로 'low'가 적절하다. (B) '밀물'일 때 사라진다고 해야 하므로 'high'가 적절하다. (C) 갯벌이 '무엇을' 하는지 살펴보자고 해야 하므로 what이 적절하다.

19 '갯벌을 오염으로부터 보호하는 것이 중요하다'는 내용은 언급되어 있지 않다.

20 like: (전치사) …와 같은(=such as)

21 ③ '비슷한', '유사한', ⓑ와 나머지: '다양한'

22 make a living: 생계를 꾸리다

23 갯벌에서 수영은 할 수 없다.

24 이 글은 '갯벌은 환경에 크게 도움이 된다.'는 내용의 글이다.

25 갯벌은 홍수로 인한 피해를 축소해 주고, 바다로 들어가는 물을 정화하고, 산소를 생성한다.

Work on Your Dreams

01 overcome: 극복하다 / 그는 인생에서 많은 어려움을 극복할 것입니다.

02 earn: 얻다, 획득하다 / 그녀는 많은 돈을 벌지는 못하지만 일을 즐긴다.

03 turn down: ~을 거절하다, 거부하다, 소리를 줄이다 / • 그녀는 그의 제안을 거절하기를 원해서, 그에게 'no'라고 말했다. • 소리 좀 줄여주시겠어요? 내가 공부에 집중할 수 없어요.

04 keep calm: 평온을 유지하다 / • 그는 심호흡을 하며 평온을 유지하려고 노력했다. keep 동명사: ~하는 것을 계속하다 / • 휘발유 값이 계속 올라간다면, 어떻게 해야 할지 모르겠어요.

05 although: 비록 ~일지라도 in spite of: ~에도 불구하고 / 재정상의 문제들에도 불구하고, 그는 새 차를 구입했다.

06 calm: 침착한 / 흥분, 화, 충격 또는 공포 같은 강한 감정에 의해 영향을 받지 않은

07 honor: 예우하다, ~을 공경하다 / 특히 상이나 타이틀을 주거나, 공적으로 칭찬함으로써 어떤 사람에게 존경이나 칭찬을 보여주다

서술형 시험대비 p.113

01 (a)fraid

02 at

03 (1) They became faster with practice.
　(2) I failed to follow the summer vacation plan.
　(3) I couldn't believe my eyes when I first saw that.

04 (1) talented (2) major (3) excellent (4) positive

05 (1) color line (2) baseman (3) (A)lthough
　(4) effort (5) ever

01 그 꼬마 사내아이는 너무 무서워서 많은 실수를 했다. / scared: 무서운

02 at bat: 타석에서 / 지금 타석에 있는 선수는 누구인가? be poor at: ~을 못하다 become good at: ~을 잘하게 되다 / 나는 수학을 정말 못해서 수학을 잘하고 싶어.

03 (1) with: ~함에 따라 (2) fail: 실패하다, ~하지 못하다 (3) cannot believe one's eyes: ~ 눈을 의심하다

04 (1) talented: 재능이 있는 / 그는 또한 재능 있는 예술가를 찾는 데 많은 시간을 보내고 있습니다. (2) major: 주요한 / 이것은 주요한 우려의 원인이다. (3) excellent: 뛰어난 / 그곳은 휴식을 취하기에 최적의 장소입니다. (4) positive: 긍정적인 / 당신은 긍정적인 사람인가요 아니면 부정적인 사람인가요?

05 (1) color line: 인종 차별 (2) baseman: (1·2·3) 루수 (3) although: 비록 ~일지라도 (4) effort: 노력 (5) ever: 언젠가, 한 번이라도

교과서
Conversation

핵심 Check p.114~115

1 It's important to be

2 (C) → (B) → (A)

3 It is important to practice a lot.

4 (B) → (C) → (A)

5 Could you explain about that?

교과서 대화문 익히기

Check(√) True or False p.116

1 T　2 T　3 F　4 T

교과서 확인학습 p.118~119

Listen & Speak 1 A

1. find, problem / too hard, I'm not good at math / It's important that, solve

2. looks / finish / draw, How, good / takes, important, as often as / keep practicing

Listen & Speak 1 B

1. hard to be, What / important, never / not forget

2. hard to / It's important that / will not

Listen & Talk 2 A

1. hard to do / how to / What do you mean by / mean

2. have, want to win / crossed / What do you mean by / means, luck

Listen & Talk 2 B

1. are, than / What, mean by / mean, together, than, alone

2. Practice / mean / mean, by doing, over

시험대비 기본평가　　　　　　　　　p.120

01 ③　　　　02 ①　　　　03 ④

01 It's important that 주어 동사 ~: ~하는 것이 중요해 use: 사용하다 rule: 규칙 solve: 풀다, 해결하다

02 'I mean ~.(그것은 ~ 뜻이야.)'은 설명을 요청할 때의 대답이므로 설명을 요청하는 질문이 어울린다. What do you mean by that?: 그게 무슨 뜻이니?

03 노래 경연 대회에서 1등을 하고 싶다는 말에 (C) "keep my fingers crossed"한다고 말하니 (B) "keep my fingers crossed"가 무슨 뜻인지 물어보고 (A) 행운을 빈다는 뜻이라고 대답한다. (D) 행운을 빌어줘 고맙다고 대답한다.

시험대비 실력평가　　　　　　　　p.121~122

01 ②　　02 ①　　03 ④　　04 ②
05 ②　　06 ④　　07 ⑤　　08 ④
09 ③　　10 ②

11 It is important that you never give up.

01 yours는 your poster를 의미한다. 너의 포스터를 다 끝냈는지 물어보는 질문에 'Not yet.(아직 못 끝냈어.)'이 어울리므로 ②가 적절하다.

02 (A) 그림을 잘 그리기 위해서 자주 그림을 그리는 것이 중요하다고 했으므로 시간이 걸린다는 말이 적절하다. (B) keep 동명사: ~하는 것을 계속하다

03 여자아이는 그림을 잘 그리지 못하고, 그림을 잘 그리기를 원한다. 남자아이의 포스터는 멋져 보였고, 그림을 잘 그리기 위한 조언을 해 주는 것을 보아 남자아이는 잘 그리는 것으로 유추할 수 있다.

04 지호는 배우가 되고 싶지만, 항상 오디션에 떨어져서 포기를 하고 싶다는 말을 하고 있다.

05 ⓑ always fail

06 지호가 아닌 유명한 영화배우가 백 번 이상 오디션에서 떨어졌다.

07 Two heads are better than one: 두 개의 머리가 머리 하나보다 낫다(= 백지장도 맞들면 낫다)

08 'What do you mean by ~?(~이 무슨 뜻이니?)'는 Yes나 No로 대답할 수 없다.

09 계속 공부하는 것이 중요하다는 말에 음악을 끌 것이라고 대답하는 것은 어색하다.

10 What should I do?: 내가 무엇을 해야 할까? 훌륭한 댄서가 되기 위해 무엇을 해야 할지 묻자, 절대 포기하지 않는 것이 중요하다고 대답한다.

11 It's important that 주어 동사 ~: ~하는 것이 중요해. give up: 포기하다

서술형 시험대비　　　　　　　　　　p.123

01 (C) → (A) → (E) → (D) → (B)

02 by

03 What is important to do to become a runner?

04 It's important that I practice running every day.

05 ⓑI'm good at math. → I'm not good at math. / I'm poor at math.

06 (1) It's important that you think creative. → It's important that you think creatively.

　(2) I will forget that. → I will not[won't] forget that.

01 포스터가 멋져 보인다는 말에 (C) 고맙다고 대답하며, 상대방도 포스터를 끝냈는지 물어본다. (A) 아직 안 끝냈다고 대답하고, 그림을 잘 그리지 못 한다며 어떻게 해야 그림을 잘 그릴 수 있는지 질문한다. (E) 가능한 한 자주 그리는 것이 중요하다는 말을 하자, (D) 계속 그리는 연습을 해야 한다는 의미인지 질문하고 (B) 맞다고 대답한다.

02 What do you mean by ~?: ~이 무슨 뜻이니?

03 important: 중요한 become: ~이 되다 'to become a runner'는 to부정사의 부사적 용법(목적, ~하기 위해)으로 사용하였다.

04 'It은 가주어 that절이 진주어로 사용되었다. practice는 동명사를 목적어로 받는다.

05 남자아이는 수학 문제의 정답을 찾지 못했고, 너무 어렵다고 말하고 있으므로, 수학을 잘하지 못한다는 말과 어울린다. be good at: ~을 잘하다

06 (1) 동사를 수식할 수 있는 것은 부사이므로 creative가 아니라 creatively를 사용해야 한다. (2) 영화를 만드는 것이 어렵다는 상대방에게 창의적으로 생각하는 것이 중요하다는 말을 했는데, 이에 'I will forget that.(그것을 잊을게.)'은 어색하다.

23

핵심 Check   p.124~125

1 (1) to live (2) to be (3) to think
2 (1) who (2) which

시험대비 기본평가   p.126

01 (1) bring → to bring (2) borrow → to borrow
  (3) which → who, whom 또는 that
  (4) who → which 또는 that
02 ⑤   **03** ①
04 (1) to believe (2) to help (3) who(m)[that]
  (4) which[that]

01 (1), (2) 목적어와 목적격보어가 능동 관계일 때 tell과 ask의 목적격보어로 to부정사가 적절하다. (3) 선행사가 사람일 때 목적격 관계대명사로 which가 아니라 who, whom이나 that을 쓴다. (4) 선행사가 사물일 때 목적격 관계대명사로 who가 아니라 which나 that을 쓴다.

02 목적어와 목적격보어가 능동 관계일 때 advise의 목적격보어는 to부정사이다.

03 선행사가 사물일 때 목적격 관계대명사로 which나 that을 쓴다.

04 (1) 목적어와 목적격보어가 능동 관계일 때 expect의 목적격보어로 to부정사가 적절하다. (2) 목적어와 목적격보어가 능동 관계일 때 encourage의 목적격보어로 to부정사가 적절하다. (3) 선행사가 사람일 때 목적격 관계대명사로 who, whom이나 that을 쓴다. (4) 선행사가 사물일 때 목적격 관계대명사로 which나 that을 쓴다.

시험대비 실력평가   p.127~129

01 ⑤   **02** ②   **03** ③   **04** ④
05 ③
06 (1) that (2) which (3) which (4) play (5) warned
07 ④   **08** ①   **09** ④   **10** ①
11 (1) to spend (2) to keep (3) (to) carry (4) finish
  (5) to assemble   **12** ③
13 (1) Sophie asked her dad to help her to finish her homework.
  (2) Mom wanted Lily to come home by 8.
  (3) She invited me to go to New York with her.
  (4) The blue watch is the gift which[that] I bought there for my brother.

---

  (5) The man who[whom/that] my mother is talking to is my art teacher.
  (6) The girl and her cat that I met this morning were playing in the park.
14 ⑤   **15** (1) who (2) that (3) which is
16 ①   **17** ⑤

01 목적어와 목적격보어가 능동 관계일 때 tell은 목적격보어로 to부정사가 나온다.

02 <보기>와 나머지는 목적격 관계대명사이지만, ②번은 주격 관계대명사이다.

03 모두 주격이나 목적격으로 사용된 관계대명사 that이 들어갈 수 있지만 ③번은 소유격 관계대명사 whose가 들어가야 한다.

04 enable은 목적격보어로 to부정사가 나온다.

05 want는 목적격보어로 동사원형이 아니라 to부정사가 나온다. to lend가 되어야 한다.

06 (1) 선행사가 사람이므로 that, (2) 선행사가 사물이므로 which, (3) 전치사 about이 있으므로 that은 쓸 수 없다. (4) 'help'는 목적격보어로 원형부정사와 to부정사 둘 다 취할 수 있다. (5) to부정사를 목적격보어로 쓸 수 있는 것은 warn이다. hope는 5형식으로 쓰이지 않는다.

07 관계대명사의 선행사가 사람이면 who, whom이나 that을 쓰고 사물이면 which나 that을 쓴다. ② This is the house in which she lives. 또는 This is the house which[that] she lives in.

08 빈칸에는 to부정사를 목적격보어로 취할 수 있는 동사가 들어가야 한다. watch는 목적격보어로 동사원형이나 현재분사가 나와야 한다.

09 She allowed me to eat ice cream for dessert.

10 ①번은 접속사이지만 나머지는 모두 관계대명사이다.

11 (1), (2), (5) ask, encourage, request는 to부정사를 목적격보어로 취하는 동사이다. (3) help는 to부정사나 동사원형을 쓸 수 있다. (4) have는 사역동사로 목적격보어로 원형부정사를 쓴다.

12 warn은 목적격보어로 to부정사를 쓴다.

13 (1), (2), (3) ask, want, invite는 모두 목적격보어로 to부정사가 나와야 한다. (4) 선행사가 사물일 때 목적격 관계대명사로 who가 아니라 which나 that을 쓴다. (5) 선행사가 사람일 때 목적격 관계대명사로 which가 아니라 who, whom이나 that을 쓴다. (6) 선행사가 '사람+동물'일 경우 목적격 관계대명사로 that을 쓴다.

14 feel은 지각동사로 동사원형이나 현재분사를 목적격보어로 취한다. 나머지는 모두 to부정사를 목적격보어로 취하는 동사들로 부정사의 형태가 들어가야 한다.

15 목적격 관계대명사와 '주격 관계대명사+be동사'는 생략할 수 있다.

16 cause, force, warn, want, ask는 모두 목적격보어로 to부정사를 취하는 동사이다. The heavy rain caused the river to overflow.

17 관계대명사 that은 전치사 다음에는 쓰지 않는다. 또한 목적격 관계대명사는 생략될 수 있다.

p.130~131

서술형 시험대비

01 (1) I want you to be happy.
(2) Jack asked his mother to wake him up at 8 o'clock.
(3) Tina told me to find a quiet place to study.
(4) Jessy got her dad to drop her off at the bus stop.
(5) His teacher advised him not to spend all his time on one subject.

02 (1) The man who[whom/that] you met on Sunday is my brother.
(2) That is the computer which[that] I bought last week.
(3) This is the cake which[that] was made by Ann.
(4) I visited the church which[that] I took some pictures of. 또는 I visited the church of which I took some pictures.
(5) It is an experience which[that] I look forward to. 또는 It is an experience to which I look forward.
(6) Does Eddie have any friends who[whom/that] he can depend on? 또는 Does Eddie have any friends on whom he can depend?

03 (1) to bring (2) take (3) burning

04 (1) This is the bridge which[that] my father built.
(2) They are the people who[whom/that] I met in the plane.
(3) I like the new computer that I bought last week.
(4) Can you tell me about the church of which you took the picture last weekend? 또는 Can you tell me about the church (which/that) you took the picture of last weekend?

05 (1) to come (2) to be (3) not to give up

06 (1) I bought a book.
(2) I invited her to the party.
(3) I need to do them[three things] to achieve my dream.
(4) Is the novel fun?

07 (1) She asked you to clean her room.
(2) Mom[My mom] expects me to take care of the puppy.
(3) The people who(m)[that] we met were very

nice.
(4) The bag (which/that) I bought yesterday is blue.

01 (1) want는 that절을 목적어로 하는 3형식으로 쓰이지 않으며 목적어와 목적격보어가 능동 관계일 때 목적격보어로 to부정사가 나와야 한다. (2) ask, (3) tell, (4) get (5) advise 등의 동사도 목적어와 목적격보어가 능동 관계일 때 목적격보어로 to부정사가 나와야 한다. 또한 to부정사의 부정형은 'not to 동사원형'으로 쓴다.

02 목적격 관계대명사는 수식하는 선행사가 사람이면 who나 whom, that을, 사람이나 동물이면 which나 that을 쓴다. 일반적으로 목적격 관계대명사는 생략될 수 있다. 목적격 관계대명사가 전치사의 목적어인 경우 전치사는 관계대명사절의 끝에 오거나 관계대명사 앞에 올 수 있다. 전치사가 관계대명사절의 끝에 올 경우에는 관계대명사를 생략할 수 있다. 전치사가 관계대명사 앞에 올 경우에는 관계대명사 that을 쓸 수 없으며, 관계대명사를 생략하지 않는다.

03 목적어와 목적격보어가 능동 관계일 때 (1) would like는 목적격보어로 to부정사를 쓴다. (2) make는 사역동사로 목적격보어로 원형부정사를 쓴다. (3) smell은 목적격보어로 현재분사를 쓴다.

04 (1) 선행사가 사물이므로 which나 that, (2) 선행사가 사람이므로 who, whom이나 that, (3) 관계대명사가 접속사와 대명사의 역할을 하므로 목적어로 쓰인 it을 삭제해야 한다. (4) 전치사가 관계대명사 앞에 올 경우에는 관계대명사 that을 쓸 수 없으며, 관계대명사를 생략하지 않는다.

05 (1) tell (2) order (3) encourage 모두 목적격보어로 to부정사를 쓴다.

06 목적격 관계대명사는 선행사가 사람이면 who나 whom, that, 사물이나 동물이면 which나 that을 쓰고 관계대명사절에서 목적어 역할을 한다.

07 (1), (2) ask와 expect의 목적격보어로 to부정사를 쓴다. (3), (4) 선행사가 사람이면 who, whom이나 that, 사물이나 동물이면 which나 that을 쓴다.

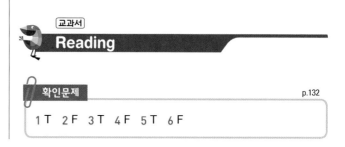

교과서
Reading

확인문제
p.132

1 T 2 F 3 T 4 F 5 T 6 F

1 T　2 F　3 T　4 F　5 T　6 F

교과서 확인학습 A　　　　　p.134~135

01 Breaks the Color Line

02 on April 15, 1947

03 as, for　　　　04 couldn't believe

05 the first African American player

06 the color line was broken

07 faced many difficulties

08 Although, to play with him

09 turned the team down

10 was at bat　　11 thought to himself

12 who people like

13 there will be more

14 put, into

15 With practice, batting, base running

16 moved

17 one of his teammates, tapped him on the

18 Do not listen to　　　　19 fine

20 to play　　　21 earned the respect

22 Thanks to　　23 recognized, presented, with

24 asked, to join

25 uniform number

26 no longer, to honor him

27 however, wore　　　　　28 is called

교과서 확인학습 B　　　　　p.136~137

1 Jackie Robinson Breaks the Color Line

2 It was New York City on April 15, 1947.

3 Jackie Robinson, an African American, went on the field as second baseman for the Brooklyn Dodgers.

4 People couldn't believe their eyes.

5 He was the first African American player to play on a Major League team.

6 That day, the color line was broken.

7 Robinson faced many difficulties.

8 Although Robinson was a talented player and a gentle person, his teammates did not want to play with him.

9 Every hotel turned the team down because Robinson was on the team.

10 When he was at bat, people in the stands rudely shouted at him.

11 Robinson thought to himself, 'I need to keep calm and focus on baseball.

12 I will try and become a player who people like.

13 Then, next season, there will be more African American players in the league.'

14 Robinson put all his time and energy into baseball.

15 With practice, he became great at batting and base running.

16 Robinson's effort moved his teammates.

17 When people shouted at Robinson, one of his teammates walked up to Robinson and tapped him on the shoulder.

18 "Do not listen to them.

19 You're doing fine," he said.

20 His support helped Robinson to play harder.

21 Finally, Robinson earned the respect of other players and fans.

22 Thanks to Robinson, the Dodgers won the National League Championship in 1947.

23 The league recognized Robinson's excellence and presented him with the Rookie of the Year Award in the same year.

24 After that season, other teams asked African American players to join them.

25 Robinson's uniform number was 42.

26 Baseball players in Major League teams no longer wear the number 42 to honor him.

27 Every year, however, on April 15, every player wears the number that Robinson wore.

28 The day is called "Jackie Robinson Day."

시험대비 실력평가　　　　　p.138~139

01 on　　　　02 ②　　　　03 ④

04 (A) because (B) himself (C) great

05 When he was at bat　　06 ④

07 ②　　　　08 ②　　　　09 honor

10 People[They] call the day "Jackie Robinson Day."

11 ②, ③, ⑤　　12 ④　　　13 ③

14 to give up　15 (A) that (B) keep (C) try　16 ②, ⑤

17 ③　　　　18 ③　　　19 ⑤　　　20 ①

21 ②　　　22 is → are　23 excellence 24 ④

25 (A) Practicing[To Practice] (B) Working[To Work] (C) to manage

26 to practice hard, work well with others, and manage my time well　　27 ④, ⑤

01 (A) 날짜 앞에 on을 쓰는 것이 적절하다. (B) '소속'을 나타내는 on을 쓰는 것이 적절하다.

02 ⓐ와 ②번: (전치사) '~로(서)'라는 뜻으로 자격을 나타낸다. ① (접속사) [상태] …인 대로, …인 채로, ③ (접속사) [비례] …함에 따라, …할수록, ④ (접속사) [이유] …이므로, …이기 때문에, ⑤ (접속사) 때

03 ④ 가족 관계는 알 수 없다. ① 아프리카계, ② 미국, ③ 2루수, ⑤ 브루클린 다저스

04 (A) 뒤에 절(주어+동사)이 나오므로 because가 적절하다. because of+구, (B) Robinson은 '마음속으로 생각했다'고 해야 하므로 himself가 적절하다. think to oneself: 조용히 생각하다, 마음속으로 생각하다, (C) become의 보어로 형용사를 써야 하므로 great가 적절하다.

05 at bat: 타석에 서서

06 ④ Robinson의 노력 덕분에 몇 명의 아프리카계 미국인들이 메이저리그 팀에서 경기할 수 있었는지는 대답할 수 없다. ① Yes, he did. ② Because Robinson was on the team. ③ No, they didn't. ⑤ With practice, he became great at batting and base running.

07 ② 앞에 나오는 내용과 상반되는 내용이 뒤에 이어지므로 however가 가장 적절하다. ① 그러므로, ④ 사실은, ⑤ 게다가

08 ⓐ와 ①, ⑤: 부사적 용법 ② 명사적 용법 ③, ④ 형용사적 용법

09 메이저리그 팀의 야구 선수들은 Robinson에 대한 '존경을 보여주기 위해' 더 이상 42번을 달지 않는다.

10 People[They]을 주어로 해서 고치는 것이 적절하다.

11 선행사가 사람이고 목적어 자리이므로, 목적격 관계대명사 who, whom, that을 쓰는 것이 적절하다.

12 ④ 연습이 완벽하게 만들어 준다. ① 늦어도 안 하는 것보다 낫다. ② 제때의 바늘 한 뜸이 아홉 번의 수고를 던다. (때를 놓치지 않고 신속하게 행동해야 생길 수 있는 문제를 예방할 수 있다.) ③ 남에게 받고 싶은 대로 남에게 해 주어라. ⑤ 뛰기 전에 살펴봐라. (신중하게 행동하라.)

13 Robinson은 '자신이 노력해서 사람들이 좋아하는 선수가 되면, 다음 시즌에는 아프리카계 미국인 선수가 리그에 더 많이 생길 것'이라고 마음속으로 생각했다.

14 꿈을 성취하기 위해 필요한 세 가지인 to be healthy, to be creative, and never to give up 중에서 세 번째인 never to give up을 쓰는 것이 적절하다. tell + 목적어 + to부정사

15 (A) 선행사가 있기 때문에 that이 적절하다. (B) 'help+목적어+to부정사 또는 원형부정사'이므로 keep이 적절하다. (C) 'make+목적어+원형부정사'이므로 try가 적절하다.

16 ② '남들과 잘 일하기'와 ⑤ '남들은 돕기'는 디자이너의 꿈을 성취하기 위해 필요한 요소에 속하지 않는다.

17 so as to 동사원형 = in order to 동사원형 = in order that 주어 can = so that 주어 can: ~하기 위하여

18 ⓐ와 ③번: 감동시켰다, ① (몸을) 움직였다, ② 바꿨다, ④ 이사했다, ⑤ 옮겼다

19 ⑤는 Robinson의 팀 동료 중 한 명을 가리키고, 나머지는 다 Robinson을 가리킨다.

20 ① 마지막으로, 끝으로(무엇을 열거하면서 마지막 요소 앞에 붙이는 말), ⓐ와 나머지: 마침내

21 ⓐ와 ②번: 의지(명사), ①, ④: …일[할] 것이다(조동사), ③ 무엇을 해 달라는 부탁을 할 때 씀. ⑤ 유언장(명사)

22 주어가 being, working, and being이므로 are로 고치는 것이 적절하다.

23 소유격 다음이므로 명사를 쓰는 것이 적절하다. excellence: 우수, 탁월, 뛰어남

24 주어진 문장의 His support에 주목한다. ④번 앞 문장의 내용을 받고 있으므로 ④번이 적절하다.

25 꿈을 성취하기 위해 필요한 세 가지인 to practice hard, to work well with others, and to manage my time well을 알맞은 형태로 쓰는 것이 적절하다. (A)와 (B)는 주어, (C)는 tell+목적어+to부정사

26 꿈을 성취하기 위해 필요한 세 가지인 to practice hard, to work well with others, and to manage my time well을 가리킨다.

27 ⓑ와 ④, ⑤번: 가목적어, ①, ②, ③: 가주어

서술형 시험대비
p.142~143

01 color line
02 April fifteen(th), nineteen forty-seven
03 African American player
04 to join
05 to
06 other teams
07 He won it in 1947.
08 talented
09 Every hotel turned the team down 또는 Every hotel turned down the team
10 (A) gentle   (B) difficulties
11 Robinson's teammates were moved by his effort. 또는 His teammates were moved by Robinson's effort.
12 people
13 (A) teammates (B) shouted at
14 Robinson earned the respect of other players and fans.
15 (A) batting (B) base running
16 thought to himself
17 I will try and become a player people like.

01 a color line: 인종 차별, (정치적·사회적) 흑인과 백인의 차별, 흑인들이 백인과 함께 다양한 활동에 참여하는 것을 막는 장벽

02 날짜는 서수로 읽는 것이 원칙이지만 기수로도 읽는다. 그리고

27

April the fifteenth도 가능하다(보통 April 15th, 1947로 표기된 경우).

03 come out into the field: 출전하다, 그 이전에 메이저리그 팀에서 경기한 '아프리카계 미국인 선수'가 없었기 때문이다. (그는 메이저리그 팀에서 경기한 최초의 아프리카계 미국인 선수였다.)

04 ask+목적어+to부정사

05 present A with B = present B to A: A에게 B를 수여하다

06 '다른 팀들'을 가리킨다.

07 그는 1947년에 신인상을 수여했다.

08 talented = gifted: 재능이 있는

09 이어동사 turned down의 목적어인 'the team'을 turned down 사이에 써도 되고 뒤에 써도 된다.

10 그의 재능과 '온화한' 성격에도 불구하고, Robinson은 많은 '어려움'을 경험했다. 예를 들면, 그의 팀원들은 그와 함께 경기하기를 원하지 않았다. in spite of: ~에도 불구하고, personality: 성격

11 Robinson's teammates[his teammates]를 주어로 해서 고치는 것이 적절하다.

12 '사람들'을 가리킨다.

13 Robinson의 '팀 동료' 중 한 명이 Robinson에게 다가가 어깨를 두드리고, "너는 잘하고 있어."라고 덧붙이면서 그에게 소리치고 있는 사람들 말을 듣지 말라고 말했다.

14 earn the respect: 존경을 얻다

15 전치사 'at'의 목적어로 동명사 'batting'과 'base running'을 쓰는 것이 적절하다.

16 think to oneself: 조용히 생각하다, 마음속으로 생각하다

17 목적격 관계대명사 'whom' 대신에 쓰인 'who'를 생략할 수 있다.

영역별 핵심문제 p.145~149

01 ③	02 ④	03 (F)inally	04 ④
05 ⑤	06 ④	07 ①	08 by
09 ③	10 ②	11 ②	12 ②

13 (1) The computer (which/that) my parents bought for me is broken.
　(2) The man and his dog that I took a picture of won the first prize.
　(3) The man (who/whom/that) you met on Sunday is my brother.
　(4) His family wanted him to take part in the swimming competition.
　(5) She invited me to go to Paris with her.
　(6) I told him not to make a noise.

| 14 ⑤ | 15 ④ | 16 ③ | 17 ⑤ |

18 (1) He asked me to take him to the hospital.
　(2) Did you hear her go[going] out?
　(3) I can't forget the woman who[whom/that] I met in Rome.

19 ①, ④, ⑤

20 (A) Jackie Robinson　(B) color line

| 21 ② | 22 ② | 23 ④ |

24 ①

25 other teams asked African American players to join them

| 26 ② | 27 ⓐ wears ⓑ wore |

28 want to wear → no longer wear

01 give up: 포기하다 / 그들은 1점도 득점하지 못하고 경기를 포기했어요. thanks to: ~ 덕분에 / 당신 덕분에, 나는 많은 좋은 사람들을 만났다.

02 present A with B: A에게 B를 수여하다 / 그들은 그에게 훌륭한 시민상을 수여할 것이다.

03 finally: 마침내 / 결국, 우리 모두는 부활절 콘서트를 조직하기로 결정했다.

04 earn the respect: 존경을 얻다 / 존경을 얻기 위한 방법들 중 하나는 사회를 위한 책임감을 보여주는 것이다.

05 'keep my fingers crossed'는 행운을 빈다는 뜻이다.

06 ① 여자아이는 "keep my fingers crossed"의 뜻을 알고 있는가? ② 남자아이는 경연 대회에서 무엇을 원하는가? ③ 남자 아이는 어떤 종류의 대회에 나갈 것인가? ④ 어디서 노래 경연 대회가 열리는가? ⑤ 언제 노래 경연 대회가 있는가?

07 반복해서 무언가를 하면 배우게 된다는 뜻을 가진 말은 'Practice makes perfect.(연습이 완벽함을 만든다.)'이다.

08 What do you mean by ~?: ~가 무슨 뜻이니? by 동사-ing: ~함으로써

09 주어진 문장은 어떻게 하면 그림을 잘 그릴 수 있는지 묻는 질문이다. 이 질문에 대한 대답으로 그림을 잘 그릴 수 있도록 하는 조언이 어울린다. 여기서는 시간이 많이 걸리고 자주 그림을 그리라고 조언했다.

10 뒤에 나오는 You mean I should keep practicing?과 어울리는 것은 가능한 한 자주 그림을 그리라는 것이다.

11 ② 이외의 보기들은 설명을 요청할 때 사용하는 표현들이다.

12 take: (얼마의 시간이) 걸리다 achieve: 이루다, 달성하다 Rome was not built in a day.: 로마는 하루아침에 이루어지지 않았다.(= 무언가를 이루는 데는 시간이 걸린다.)

13 (1) 선행사가 사물일 때 목적격 관계대명사로 which나 that을 쓰며, 생략할 수 있다. (2) 선행사가 '사람+동물'일 때 목적격 관계대명사로 that을 쓰며, 생략할 수 있다. (3) 선행사가 사람일 때 목적격 관계대명사로 who, whom이나 that을 쓴다. (4), (5), (6) want, tell, invite는 목적격보어로 to부정사가 나온다. to부정사의 부정형은 'not to 동사원형'으로 쓴다.

14 ⑤ The bag (which/that) I bought yesterday was sent

to Wendy.

15 ① I didn't expect him to talk to you. ② They asked John to do something for them. ③ Mom wanted Sam to finish his homework. ⑤ His doctor ordered Simon to take some rest.

16 ③번은 주격 관계대명사이고 나머지는 모두 목적격 관계대명사이다.

17 ⓐ to not → not to ⓑ live → to live ⓒ to go → go ⓕ which → who ⓖ it → 삭제

18 (1) ask의 목적격 보어로 to부정사가 나와야 한다. (2) 지각동사 hear의 목적격 보어로 동사원형이나 현재분사가 나와야 한다. (3) 선행사가 사람이므로 목적격 관계대명사로 who나 whom 또는 that을 쓴다.

19 ⓐ와 ②, ③: 형용사적 용법, ①, ⑤: 부사적 용법, ④ 명사적 용법, a major leaguer: 메이저 리그 선수

20 1947년 4월 15일, 'Jackie Robinson'이 브루클린 다저스의 2루수로 경기장에 나갔을 때, '인종 차별'이 깨졌다.

21 'Robinson은 재능 있는 선수이고 온화한 사람이었지만 그의 팀원들은 그와 함께 경기하길 원하지 않았다.'고 해야 하므로 'Although'를 쓰는 것이 적절하다.

22 ②번 다음 문장의 Then에 주목한다. 주어진 문장의 내용을 받고 있으므로 ②번이 적절하다.

23 ④ diligent: 근면한, 성실한, Robinson은 자신의 모든 시간과 에너지를 야구에 집중했고, 연습을 함으로써 타격과 주루를 잘하게 되었다고 했으므로 성격이 '성실하다'고 하는 것이 적절하다. ① 호기심 많은, ② 외향적인, ③ 사교적인, ⑤ 창의적인

24 ⓐ 정관사가 다른 사람의 신체의 일부를 나타내는 명사 앞에서 소유격 대명사를 대신한 구문이고, tap이나 pat과 같이 '두드리다'는 뜻일 때는 전치사 'on'을 사용하는 것이 적절하다. ⓑ present A with B = present B to A: A에게 B를 수여[제공]하다

25 'to'를 보충하면 된다. ask+목적어+to부정사

26 이 글은 Robinson이 자신의 노력을 통해 사람들의 인정을 얻었다는 내용의 글이다.

27 ⓐ every는 단수로 취급하므로 wears, ⓑ Robinson이 예전에 42번을 달았던 것이므로 wore

28 메이저리그 팀의 야구 선수들은 그에 대한 존경을 보여 주기 위해 '더 이상' 42번을 '달지 않는다.'

단원별 예상문제
p.150~153

01 ④   02 ⑤   03 ③   04 ①
05 ③   06 ②, ⑤
07 it's important that you choose the right books to read.
08 ①   09 ③   10 achieved
11 It's important that you never give up.
12 (C) → (A) → (B)   13 ②   14 ③

15 ④   16 ③   17 African American
18 April 15, 1947   19 ②   20 ④
21 refused(rejected)   22 ②
23 touched
24 ④   25 ①, ③, ⑤   26 ①, ③, ④

01 ④번은 동사와 명사의 관계이고 나머지 보기는 형용사와 명사의 관계이다. ① different: 다른 difference: 다름, 차이 ② important: 중요한 importance: 중요성 ③ silent: 조용한 silence: 침묵 ④ allow: 허락하다 allowance: 허용 ⑤ excellent: 우수한 excellence: 우수, 장점

02 face: 직면하다, 직시하다 / 나는 그들이 많은 문제들에 직면해 있다는 것을 안다.

03 think to oneself: 마음속으로 생각하다

04 win first place: 1등을 하다, 우승하다 / 그녀는 수영대회에서 1등을 했다. award: 상 win an award: 상을 타다 / 그녀는 최고의 여배우 상을 받았다.

05 이것을 하기 어렵다는 말에 (C) 무슨 일인지 물어보자 (A) 쿠키를 만드는 방법을 가르쳐 줄 수 있는지 물었다. (B) 물론이라고 대답하며, 그것이 'a walk in the park'라고 말한다. (D) 'a walk in the park'가 무슨 뜻인지 물어보자 그것은 하기 쉽다는 뜻이라고 대답한다.

06 ⓑ never stop ⓔ how

07 It's important that 주어 동사 ~: ~하는 것이 중요하다 choose: 고르다

08 ⓐ to win ⓑ keep ⓒ crossed ⓓ mean ⓔ It means

09 빈칸 (A)의 앞, 뒤의 말이 역접의 관계이므로('많은 오디션에 갔지만 자주 떨어졌다'와 '나는 절대 포기하지 않았다.') 그러므로 However(하지만)가 어울린다.

10 achieve: 이루다, 달성하다 achieve a goal: 목표를 달성하다

11 It's important that 주어 동사 ~: ~하는 것이 중요하다 give up: 포기하다

12 (C) 훌륭한 댄서가 되는 것이 어렵다고 말하면서 무엇을 해야 하는지 상대방에게 질문했다. (A) 절대로 포기하지 않는 것이 중요하다고 말하자 (B) 알았다고 잊지 않겠다고 대답한다.

13 ① Her parents were worried and asked her to stop surfing. ③ Mr. Johnson told us to shake hands after the game. ④ His parents encouraged him to have an interest in art. ⑤ I didn't expect you to understand me at all.

14 ③번은 목적격 관계대명사가 생략된 것이므로 it이 없어야 한다.

15 선행사가 사물일 때 목적격 관계대명사로 which나 that을 쓴다.

16 ③ 인종 차별이 '깨졌다'고 해야 하므로, break를 과거 수동태로 쓰는 것이 적절하다.

17 African American: 아프리카계 미국인

18 '1947년 4월 15일'을 가리킨다.

19 ⓐ face: 직면하다, ② encounter: 만나다, 마주치다, ① express: 표현하다, ③ accept: 수락하다, 받아들이다, ④ look into: ~을 조사하다, ⑤ solve: 해결하다

20 ④ 부사적 용법, ⓑ와 나머지: 명사적 용법

21 turn down = refuse = reject: 거절하다

22 이 글은 'Robinson이 자신의 노력을 통해 사람들의 인정을 얻었다'는 내용의 글이므로, 제목으로는 'Robinson의 노력이 결실을 맺었다'가 적절하다. bear fruit: 결실을 맺다

23 move = touch: 감동시키다

24 ④ Thanks to Robinson, the Dodgers won the National League Championship in 1947.

25 no longer = no more = not ~ any longer = not ~ any more: 더 이상 ~ 않다

26 ⓑ와 ①, ③, ④번: 관계대명사, ②, ⑤: 접속사

01 I mean[It means] working together is better than working alone.

02 ⓑIt's too easy for me. → It's too hard[difficult] for me.

03 It's important that you use this math rule to solve the problem.

04 I mean you learn something by doing it over and over.

05 (1) The Korean dishes which[that] we had last night tasted yummy.
   (2) I have a dog with which I take a walk every night. 또는 I have a dog which[that] I take a walk with every night.

06 (1) not to go out alone at night
   (2) to win first prize at the singing contest

07 (1) 그의 팀원들은 그와 함께 경기하기를 원하지 않았다.
   (2) Robinson이 팀에 있었기 때문에 모든 호텔에서 그 팀을 거절했다.
   (3) 그가 타석에 있을 때, 관중석에 있는 사람들이 그에게 무례 하게 소리치기도 했다.

08 (A) down (B) rudely (C) calm

09 I try and become a player who people like

10 playing → (to) play

11 (1) Robinson 덕분에 다저스는 1947년에 내셔널리그 챔피언십에서 우승하게 되었다.
   (2) 리그에서는 Robinson의 탁월함을 인정했고, 같은 해에 그에게 신인상을 수여했다.

12 to win

01 설명을 할 때는 '~을 의미하다'의 뜻을 가진 'mean'을 사용해 'It means ~.'나 'I mean ~.'으로 대답할 수 있다. better than: ~보다 나은

02 ⓑ의 수학 문제가 너무 쉽다는 말과 ⓒ의 수학을 못한다는 말은 반대의 말이므로 어색하다. 여자아이가 수학 문제에 대한 조언을 해 주고 있으므로, 수학이 어렵다는 말이 어울린다.

03 It's important that 주어 동사 ~: ~하는 것이 중요하다 use: 사용하다 solve: 풀다, 해결하다

04 by 동사ing: ~함으로써 over and over: 반복해서

05 목적격 관계대명사는 수식하는 선행사가 사람이면 who나 whom, that을, 사람이 아니면 which나 that을 쓴다. 일반적으로 목적격 관계대명사는 생략될 수 있다. 목적격 관계대명사가 전치사의 목적어인 경우 전치사는 관계대명사절의 끝에 오거나 관계대명사 앞에 올 수 있다. 전치사가 관계대명사절의 끝에 올 경우에는 관계대명사를 생략할 수 있다. 전치사가 관계대명사 앞에 올 경우에는 관계대명사 that을 쓸 수 없으며, 관계대명사를 생략하지 않는다.

06 order와 expect는 목적어와 목적격보어가 능동 관계일 때 목적격보어로 to부정사를 쓴다.

07 뒤에 이어지는 내용을 쓰는 것이 적절하다.

08 (A) 'Robinson이 팀에 있었기 때문에 모든 호텔에서 그 팀을 거절했다.'고 해야 하므로 down이 적절하다. turn down: ~을 거절하다, 거부하다, turn up: 나타나다, (B) 동사 shouted를 수식하므로 부사 rudely가 적절하다. (C) keep의 보어이므로 형용사 calm이 적절하다.

09 때나 조건을 나타내는 부사절에서는 현재시제가 미래를 대신한다.

10 help+목적어+to부정사 또는 원형부정사

11 두 번째 단락의 내용을 쓰면 된다.

12 Robinson의 노력이 다저스가 1947년에 내셔널리그 챔피언십에서 우승하도록 해주었다.

|모범답안|

01 I think music helps me to study better. /
   It's important to focus when you study. /
   I'll turn down the music.

02 (1) I expect Mina to get good grades.
   (2) I expect Luke to do exercise regularly.
   (3) I expect my mom to be healthy. / I expect my dad to stop smoking.

03 (A) to practice hard (B) cook well and easily
   (C) to work at a restaurant
   (D) make food in time to serve

01 help+목적어+(to)동사원형: (목적어)가 ~하는 것을 돕다 It's important that 주어 동사 ~: ~하는 것이 중요해 focus: 집중하다 turn down: 소리를 줄이다

01 ①　　　　　　　　02 ①

03 (1) difficulties　(2) excellence

04 support　　　05 ②

06 I mean[It means] you can achieve your dream with a strong will.

07 (C) → (A) → (D) → (B)　　08 ④　　　　09 ③

10 ③　　　　　11 He failed more than 100 auditions.

12 give up

13 (1) She is the girl who[whom/that] I love.

　　(2) Have you ever fallen in love with a lady to whom you haven't even talked? 또는 Have you ever fallen in love with a lady who[whom/that] you haven't even talked to?

14 (1) to do　(2) to go　(3) to insist　(4) not to be

15 ⑤　　　　　　16 ②

17 (1) drank → to drink　(2) trying → to try

　　(3) stay → to stay　(4) who → which[that]

18 but　　　　19 ⑤번 → at　20 ③

21 take part in 또는 participate in　　　　22 ①

23 ⑤　　　　　24 ③, ⑤　　　25 42

---

01 shout at: ~을 향해 외치다 / 너는 왜 항상 나에게 소리를 지르니?

02 earn the respect: 존경을 얻다 / 그녀는 의사로서 환자들의 존경을 얻었다. give up: 포기하다 pursue: 추구하다 / 당신이 꿈을 갖고 있다면, 절대 포기하지 말고 당신의 열정을 추구하세요.

03 (1) difficult: 어려운 difficulty: 어려움, 곤경, 장애 (2) excellent: 뛰어난 excellence: 우수, 탁월, 뛰어남

04 support: 지지 / 어려움을 겪고 있는 사람에게 주는 도움과 친절 / 나는 그의 도움과 지지가 필요하다.

05 대화의 will은 '의지'의 뜻이다. ② ~할 것이다 / 그는 보고서를 즉시 끝낼 것이다. ① 그 결정은 그녀의 자유 의지로 되었다. ③ 의지가 강할수록 더 많이 배울 것이다. ④ 사람은 의지의 자유가 있다. ⑤ 의지가 있는 곳에 길이 있습니다.

06 achieve: 이루다, 달성하다 will: 의지

07 A가 자신을 "The Wizard of Goyang"으로 불러달라고 하자 B가 그것이 무슨 뜻인지 물어본다. (C) "The Wizard of Goyang"의 뜻이 자신이 발명가가 되고 싶다는 의미라고 설명한다. (A) 상대방에게 발명가가 되기 위해서는 무엇이 중요한지 질문하자 (D) 창의적으로 생각하는 것이 중요하다고 말하고 (B) 상대방이 성공할 것을 확신한다고 대답한다.

08 주어진 문장은 '하지만, 읽을 알맞은 책을 고르는 것이 중요하다.'란 의미이다. ④번 다음 문장에서 책을 고르는 법을 언급하고 있으므로 ④번이 적절하다. It's important that 주어 동사 ~: ~하는 것이 중요하다 right: 올바른, 알맞은

09 하나가 지호에게 무슨 일인지 묻는 질문에 꿈을 이룰 수 없을 것

같다고 대답한 것을 보았을 때 슬퍼 보인다는 것을 유추할 수 있다. ① 졸린 ② 행복한 ③ 슬픈 ④ 외로운 ⑤ 운이 좋은

10 What do you mean by ~?: ~가 무슨 뜻이니?

11 fail: 실패하다, ~하지 못하다 more than: ~보다 많이

12 give up: 포기하다

13 목적격 관계대명사는 수식하는 선행사가 사람이면 who나 whom, that을, 사람이 아니면 which나 that을 쓴다. 일반적으로 목적격 관계대명사는 생략될 수 있다. 목적격 관계대명사가 전치사의 목적어인 경우 전치사는 관계대명사절의 끝에 오거나 관계대명사 앞에 올 수 있다. 전치사가 관계대명사절의 끝에 올 경우에는 관계대명사를 생략할 수 있다. 전치사가 관계대명사 앞에 올 경우에는 관계대명사 that을 쓸 수 없으며, 관계대명사를 생략하지 않는다.

14 ask, allow, cause, warn의 목적격보어로 to부정사가 적절하다. to부정사의 부정형은 'not to 동사원형'으로 쓴다.

15 I love the jacket which[that] Hana is wearing.

16 ① tell의 목적격보어로 to부정사가 적절하다. ③, ④ 선행사가 사물일 때 목적격 관계대명사로 which나 that을 쓴다. ⑤ 목적어로 쓰인 them을 삭제해야 한다.

18 Although 대신 문장 중간에 but을 쓰는 것이 적절하다.

19 연습을 함으로써 그는 타격과 주루를 '잘하게 되었다'라고 해야 하므로, at으로 고치는 것이 적절하다. become great for: ~에 좋게 되다, become great at: ~에 잘하게 되다

20 전치사의 목적어로 동명사 'batting'과 'base running'이 쓰였다. ⓑ와 ②, ③, ④: 동명사, ①, ⑤: 현재분사

21 join = take part in = participate in: ~에 참가하다

22 ① 지성이면 감천이다. ② 서두르면 일을 그르친다. ③ 엎질러진 우유를 놓고 울어봐야 소용없다.(되돌릴 수 없는 잘못을 하고 후회해 봐야 아무 소용이 없다.) ④ 모두의 일은 어느 누구의 일도 아니다.(누군가에게 직접 책임이 지워지지 않은 일은 서로 미루다가 결국은 아무도 하지 않게 된다.) ⑤ 요리사가 너무 많으면 국을 망친다.(사공이 많으면 배가 산으로 올라간다.)

23 ⑤ 그 시즌 이후, 몇 명의 아프리카계 미국인 선수들이 다른 팀에 합류했는지는 대답할 수 없다. ① One of his teammates. ② Yes. ③ In 1947. ④ The Rookie of the Year Award.

24 목적격 관계대명사 that이나 which가 적절하다.

25 Robinson의 등 번호 '42번'을 가리킨다.

Lesson
8

Science Is Making Big Changes

시험대비 실력평가　p.164

01 (1) put on　(2) take place　02 ④　　03 ②
04 ②　　　　05 ①　　　　06 ①　　　　07 ③

01 <보기>의 단어들은 유의어 관계이다. huge: 거대한 large: 큰 (1) wear: 입다 put on: 입다, 쓰다, 신다 (2) happen: 발생하다 take place: 일어나다

02 in trouble: 곤경에 빠져서, 난처하여 / 그는 항상 어려움에 처한 사람들을 보호하려고 노력했습니다.

03 heavily: 심하게, 아주 많이 / 간밤에 비가 심하게 왔다, 그래서 오늘은 좀 춥다.

04 work: 작동하다 / 이것이 그 제품이 작동하는 방법입니다.

05 be ready for: ~할 준비가 되다 / • 아무래도 내일 시험은 잘 못 볼 것 같아! look for: ~을 찾다 / • 나는 3시간 동안 나의 가방을 찾았고, 마침내 그것을 발견했다.

06 take care of: ~을 돌보다 / • 방과 후에 나의 딸을 보살펴 줄 사람이 필요하다. take place: 일어나다, 개최되다 / • 많은 문화 축제들이 가을 동안 개최된다.

07 <보기>의 문장의 may의 뜻은 '~일지도 모른다'로 사용되었다. 그는 오늘 결석이다. 아플지도 모른다. ③ 이외의 may는 '~해도 좋다'로 허락의 의미를 지닌다. ① 전화 끝나셨으면 제가 좀 써도 될까요? ② 제가 내일 두 시간 늦게 출근해도 될까요? ③ 늦을 지도 몰라, 그러니 기다리지 마. ④ 이 방을 사용해도 좋다. ⑤ 이 컴퓨터 잠시 좀 써도 될까요?

서술형 시험대비　p.165

01 don't have to
02 (s)imilarity
03 (1) (c)harge　(2) (m)aterial　(3) (r)ecommended
　　(4) (s)uits　(5) (m)ethod
04 (1) on　(2) of　(3) by (4) in
05 (1) The Earth moves around the Sun.
　　(2) I got lost on my way to the flower shop.
　　(3) People are not worried about air pollution.
　　(4) Be sure to put on safety helmets and life jackets.

01 don't have to 동사원형: ~할 필요가 없다(= need not) / 우리는 만나는 장소를 바꿀 필요가 없다.

02 반의어 관계이다. ever: 어느 때고, 언제든, 한번이라도 never: 지금까지[어느 때건] 한 번도 ~ 않다 difference: 차이점 similarity: 유사점

03 (1) charge: (지불, 대금 등을) 청구하다 (2) material: 물질, 물체 (3) recommend: ~을 추천하다 (4) suit: (입맛, 취향 등에) 맞다 (5) method: 방법, 방식

04 (1) turn on: (전기·가스·수도 등을) 켜다 / 여름에 우리는 선풍기를 틀어 시원하게 한다. (2) take care of: ~을 돌보다 / 당신이 없는 동안 아이들은 누가 돌보나요? (3) by 동명사: ~함으로써 / 그들은 그들의 숙제를 함으로써 책임감을 배울 수 있다. (4) wait in line: 줄을 서서 기다리다 / 나는 표를 사기 위해 줄을 서서 기다렸다.

05 (1) move around: ~의 주위를 돌다 (2) get lost: 길을 잃다 (3) be worried about: ~에 대해 걱정하다 (4) put on: 입다, 쓰다; 신다

교과서
Conversation

핵심 Check　p.166~167

1 I'm surprised th at
2 (D) → (B) → (A) → (C)
3 I'm surprised that you think so.
4 you help me / teach me now / I'm afraid I can't.
5 Could I ask you to open the door

교과서 대화문 익히기

Check(√) True or False　p.168

1 T　2 F　3 T　4 F

교과서 확인학습
p.170~171

Listen & Speak 1 A

1. to turn off / to return / turn, off / surprised that, off
2. to / put / I'm surprised

Listen & Speak 1 B

1. there, surprises / surprised, walk
2. there anything, that surprises / I'm surprised that, itself

시험대비 기본평가 p.172

01 ④   02 ②   03 ②

01 I'm surprised that 주어 동사 ~: ~하는 것이 놀라워 / 놀람을 표현할 때는 'I'm surprised that ~.' 또는 'I'm amazed that ~.'이라고 표현한다.

02 스마트 워치를 찾고 있는 남자아이가 스마트 워치 하나를 보여 줄 수 있는지 여직원에게 묻는 말이 적절하다. Can you 동사 ~?: ~해 줄 수 있니? show: 보여주다

03 런던 여행 준비가 다 되었는지 묻는 질문에 (B) 준비는 다 되었지만, 길을 잃는 것을 걱정하고 있다고 말한다. (C) 상대방은 걱정 말라고 말하며, 좋은 스마트폰 앱을 추천한다. (A) 스마트폰 앱 하나를 보여 달라는 요청에 (D) 물론이라고 대답하면서, 도시의 지도와 길의 사진을 보여주는 앱을 사용해 보라고 권한다.

시험대비 실력평가 p.173~174

01 ③   02 ⑤   03 ③, ④   04 ④
05 ③   06 ⑤   07 ④   08 ②
09 ④   10 ⑤

01 put on: 입다, 쓰다, 신다 남자아이는 VR(Virtual Reality: 가상현실)로 나이아가라 폭포를 보기 위해서 어떤 것을 쓰고 체험하고 있다.

02 I'm surprised that 주어 동사 ~: ~하는 것이 놀라워 feel: ~을 느끼다

03 ③ VR(가상현실)을 이용해 나이아가라 폭포를 보고 있다. ④ VR(가상현실)을 통해 본 나이가라 폭포는 거대했다.

04 가게에 가 달라고 요청하는 말에 'Sure.(물론이지.)'라고 긍정의

대답을 하고 'I'm busy now.(난 지금 바빠.)'라고 말하는 것은 어울리지 않는다.

05 (A)는 anything을 수식하는 주격 관계대명사 that이 어울린다. I'm surprised that 주어 동사 ~: ~하는 것이 놀라워

06 (C) 스마트 워치를 찾고 있고, 하나를 보여 달라고 요청했다. (D) 하나를 보여주면서, 음악의 연주 기능에 대해 언급한다. (B) 멋지다고 대답하고 (A) 점원이 스마트 워치가 말로 검색하는 또 다른 기능을 가지고 있다고 말한다. 남자아이는 그것을 산다고 말하며 대화가 끝난다.

07 스마트 전등을 켜고 끄기 위해 손을 사용할 필요가 없다는 말에 대한 응답으로 그것을 켜고 끄는 방법을 묻는 것이 어울린다.

08 새로운 스마트 전등을 켜기 위해서 "불 켜!"라고 말해도 되므로 손을 꼭 사용할 필요는 없다. should: ~해야 한다

09 히터 끄는 것을 잊어버렸다는 여자아이의 말에 남자아이가 집으로 돌아가야 하는지 물었고 'No'라고 대답했으므로, 이어서 집에 안 가고 끌 수 있는 방법인 스마트폰으로 히터를 끌 수 있다는 말을 하는 것이 어울린다.

10 ① 여자아이는 지금 그녀의 집에 있다. ② 여자아이는 히터를 끄기 위해 집에 갈 것이다. ③ 남자아이는 이미 스마트폰으로 히터를 끌 수 있다는 것을 알고 있었다. ④ 남자아이는 히터 끄는 것을 잊어버렸다. ⑤ 남자아이는 여자아이가 스마트폰으로 히터를 끌 수 있다는 것에 놀랐다.

서술형 시험대비 p.175

01 (A) off   (B) No   (C) surprised
02 I'm surprised that this drone can deliver things.
03 ⓑ have to → don't have to
04 (1) Can I ask you to recommend one
   (2) Do[Would] you mind recommending one
   (3) Will you recommend one
05 I'm surprised that you can recommend books.

01 (A) turn off: (전기·가스·수도 등을) 끄다 (B) 남자아이가 히터를 끄기 위해 집에 가야 하는지 묻자, 여자 아이가 스마트폰을 이용해 끌 수 있다고 말하므로 'No'가 어울린다. (C) I'm surprised that 주어 동사 ~: ~하는 것이 놀라워

02 I'm surprised that 주어 동사 ~: ~하는 것이 놀라워 drone: (원격 조종의) 드론 deliver: 배달하다

03 don't have to 동사원형: ~할 필요가 없다

04 요청하는 표현에는 'Can[Will] you 동사 ~?(~해 줄 수 있니?)', 'Could[Can] I ask you to 동사 ~?(~을 부탁해도 될까?)', 'Do[Would] you mind 동명사 ~?(~해 줄 수 있니?)' 등이 있다.

05 I'm surprised that 주어 동사 ~: ~하는 것이 놀라워 can+동사원형: ~할 수 있다 recommend: ~을 추천하다

핵심 Check   p.176~177

1 (1) has, spent   (2) have, heard   (3) Have, thought
2 (1) may   (2) use   (3) be

시험대비 기본평가   p.178

01 May   02 ⑤   03 ①   04 ④
05 ③

01 may의 '허가' 용법을 이용한다. Can을 May 대신 쓸 수도 있다.

02 현재완료의 결과적 용법(…해서 (그 결과) 지금 ~하다)을 이용하여 과거에 미국으로 간 것이 아직도 거기에 있다는 현재의 결과를 나타내도록 한다.

03 '그들이 정원에 있을 가능성이 있다.'는 말은 '그들이 어쩌면 정원에 있을지도 모른다.'고 말할 수 있다. may의 '추측' 용법을 이용한다.

04 부정문이므로 yet이 적절하다.

05 may의 '추측' 용법을 이용한다. 조동사 다음에는 동사원형이 나온다.

시험대비 실력평가   p.179~181

01 ④   02 ⑤   03 ③
04 (1) has   (2) haven't   (3) gone   (4) happened
    (5) happen   (6) may not
05 ②   06 ①
07 (1) start → started
    (2) have you done → did you do
    (3) do you have been → have you been
    (4) for → since   (5) since → for
08 ⑤   09 ④   10 ③   11 ②
12 ①   13 ②
14 (1) mays → may   (2) rains → rain
    (3) does not may → may not   (4) is → be
15 ⓐ visited   ⓑ been
16 (1) Bill has known Alice since 2017.
    (2) Olivia has lived in Seoul for three years.
17 ④
18 (1) Cleaning drones may not help students at school.
    (2) May I see your passport?
19 ④

01 언제 주차했는지 묻는 문장으로 특정한 과거의 한 시점을 묻는 것이므로 현재완료가 아니라 과거시제가 되어야 한다. 보통 when은 현재완료와 쓰이지 않는다. When did you park your car at the garage?

02 조동사는 인칭에 따른 변화가 없고 조동사 다음에는 항상 동사원형이 나와야 하며 'may' 다음에 'not'을 써서 부정문을 만든다.

03 현재완료의 의문문은 'Have[Has]+주어+과거분사~?'이다. 조동사 'may'가 나와 있으므로 그 다음에는 동사원형이 나와야 한다. 그러므로 ③번이 적절하다.

04 (1) 주어가 3인칭 단수이므로 has가 적절하다. (2) 현재완료의 부정문은 'have[has]+not[never]+과거분사'로 나타낸다. (3) have[has] gone to는 '~에 가고 없다'는 결과를 나타낸다. (4) 현재완료는 과거를 나타내는 어구(in 2010)와 함께 쓸 수 없다. (5) 조동사 다음에는 동사원형이 나와야 한다. (6) 'may' 다음에 'not'을 써서 부정문을 만든다.

05 현재완료 시제의 의문문에 대한 답은 have를 이용하여 답한다.

06 '허가(~해도 좋다)'를 나타내는 may를 이용한다.

07 (1) 현재완료는 'have[has]+과거분사'의 형태이다. (2) 현재완료는 과거를 나타내는 어구와 함께 쓸 수 없다. (3) 현재완료의 의문문은 have 동사를 주어 앞으로 보낸다. (4), (5) 현재완료에서 'since+시간 명사', 'for+기간 명사'를 쓴다.

08 ⑤번은 '추측'의 의미로 쓰였다. 나머지는 '허가'의 의미이다.

09 현재완료에서 'since+시간 명사', 'for+기간 명사'로 쓰는 것이 적절하다.

10 'have[has] been to'는 '~에 가 본 적이 있다'는 경험을 나타내고, 'have[has] gone to'는 '~에 가고 없다'는 결과를 나타내며 현재완료는 'have[has]+과거분사'의 형태이다.

11 '~일지도 모른다, 아마 ~일 것이다'라는 '추측'의 의미로 쓰일 수 있는 것은 may이다.

12 현재완료에서 'since+시간 명사', 'for+기간 명사'로 쓰는 것이 적절하다.

13 <보기>와 ②는 계속 용법이다. ①, ⑤ 결과 용법 ③ 경험 용법 ④ 완료 용법

14 (1) 조동사는 인칭이나 시제에 따른 어형 변화가 없다. (2), (4) 조동사 뒤에 나오는 be동사나 일반동사는 동사원형으로 쓴다. (3) 'may' 다음에 'not'을 써서 부정문을 만든다.

15 ⓐ yesterday라는 과거를 나타내는 말이 있으므로 과거형으로 써야 한다. ⓑ 'have gone to'는 결과를 나타내는 말로 1인칭을 주어로 쓸 수 없다. 여기서 there는 to the Technology Fair를 의미한다.

16 (1) 2017년에 Alice를 처음 알았고 지금도 알고 있으므로 현재완료의 '계속' 용법으로 나타낸다. (2) 3년 전에 살기 시작해서 아직도 살고 있으므로 현재완료의 '계속' 용법으로 나타낸다. 현재완료에서 'since+시간 명사', 'for+기간 명사'를 쓴다는 것에 유의한다.

17 '허가'를 나타내어 '~해도 좋다'의 뜻을 나타내는 may 대신에 can을 사용할 수도 있다.

18 (1) 'may' 다음에 'not'을 써서 부정문을 만든다. (2) 'may'의 의문문은 'may'를 문두로 옮겨 'May+주어+동사 ~?'의 어순으로 쓴다.

19 ④번은 현재완료의 '경험' 용법이고, 나머지는 모두 '계속' 용법이다.

01 (1) He has lived in Busan since he was 15 years old.

(2) Have you ever seen giraffes?

(3) I haven't finished my homework yet.

(4) I have lost my diary.

(5) Paul may not be in the classroom.

(6) May[Can] I turn on the air conditioner?

02 (1) It has rained since last Thursday.

(2) Has William gone to buy sandwiches?

03 (1) I have never used a drone before.

(2) I have been to the tomato festival once. 등 어법에 맞게 쓰면 정답

04 (1) '~할지도 모른다' (추측)

(2) '~해도 좋다' (허가)

05 (1) may come　(2) may not park　(3) may sell

06 (1) When did you start working at the company?

(2) She has worked as a drone designer since 2035.

(3) Have you ever been to Vietnam before?

(4) So there may be traffic lights for drones in the sky.

(5) Schools may be open only three days a week, so students may not go to school every day.

07 부정문: You have never[haven't] thought of how schools may change over the next 20 years.

의문문: Have you ever thought of how schools may change over the next 20 years?

08 (1) I have studied English for 6 years.

(2) I have not sent the letter yet.

(3) Have you ever swum in the sea?

(4) Some changes have already started to take place while others may start in the near future.

09 (1) have visited, four times

(2) may have

01 (1)~(4) 현재완료를 이용하여 영작한다. 각각 '계속', '경험', '완

료', '결과' 용법이다. (5)~(6) may를 이용한다. (5)번은 '추측'을, (6)번은 '허가'를 의미한다. '허가'의 경우에는 may 대신 can을 쓸 수 있다.

02 (1) 지난 목요일에 비가오기 시작해서 지금도 오고 있는 것이므로 현재완료의 '계속'을 이용한다. (2) 샌드위치를 사러 가서 지금 여기 없는 것이므로 현재완료의 '결과'를 이용한다.

03 현재완료의 '경험' 용법을 이용하여 쓴다.

04 조동사 'may'는 '추측'과 '허가'의 의미로 쓰인다.

05 (1) '올 것 같다'는 것을 '올지도 모른다'라고 may를 써서 나타낸다. (2) '허가'를 나타내는 can과 may를 이용한다. (3) maybe는 '아마도'라는 뜻으로 may를 이용하여 나타낼 수 있다.

06 (1) 현재완료는 과거의 특정 시점을 나타내는 의문사 when과 함께 쓸 수 없다. (2) 현재완료에서 'since+시간 명사', 'for+기간 명사' (3) have[has] been to는 '~에 가 본적이 있다'는 경험을 나타내고, have[has] gone to는 '~에 가고 없다'는 결과를 나타내므로 3인칭만 주어가 될 수 있다. 주어가 you이므로 have been to로 고쳐야 한다. (4) maybe는 부사로 '어쩌면, 아마'라는 뜻이다. 동사가 없으므로 'maybe'를 'may be'로 고쳐 쓴다. (5) 조동사 다음에는 동사원형이 나와야 하고 'may' 다음에 'not'을 써서 부정문을 만든다.

07 현재완료의 부정문은 'have[has]+not[never]+과거분사'로, 의문문은 'Have[Has]+주어+과거분사 ~?'로 나타낸다.

08 (1) 현재완료의 '계속' 용법, (2) 현재완료의 '완료' 용법, (3) 현재완료의 '경험' 용법을 이용한다. (4) 현재완료의 '완료' 용법과 '추측'의 may를 이용한다.

09 (1) 현재완료의 '경험' 용법을 이용한다. (2) '추측'의 may를 이용한다. be likely to: ~할 것 같다

📎 **확인문제**　　　　　　　　　　　　　　　p.184

1 T　2 F　3 T　4 F

📎 **확인문제**　　　　　　　　　　　　　　　p.185

1 F　2 F　3 T　4 F　5 T

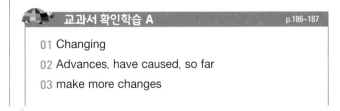

01 Changing

02 Advances, have caused, so far

03 make more changes

04 may be like   05 Shopping Center

06 much easier   07 no lines, no counters

08 special shopping app

09 takes the items

10 are automatically added to

11 puts, back, is automatically removed from

12 shopping, in line

13 adds up, charge

14 fancy   15 3D Printed

16 3D printed

17 Building, faster and cheaper, with traditional methods

18 looks fantastic

19 house shapes, traditional building methods and materials

20 by using   21 that fit, suit

22 fashion designer   23 in the Hospital

24 is visiting   25 An AI

26 checks, conditions

27 high temperature, to lower

28 Have you ever thought

29 take place, in the near future

30 imagine

31 Take some time

교과서 확인학습 B p.188~189

1 Changing Society

2 Advances in science and technology have caused many changes in our lives so far.

3 In the future, science and technology will make more changes.

4 Let's see what our lives may be like in the near future.

5 Sangho in the Shopping Center

6 Shopping is much easier.

7 There are no lines and no counters.

8 Sangho enters a shop with his smartphone which has a special shopping app.

9 In the shop, he takes the items he wants.

10 The items are automatically added to a virtual card on his smartphone.

11 If Sangho puts an item back, it is automatically removed from his list of purchases.

12 When he finishes shopping, Sangho does not need to wait in line to pay.

13 His virtual card adds up all the prices and will

charge him later.

14 Isn't that fancy?

15 Sumin's 3D Printed House and Clothes

16 Sumin lives in a 3D printed house.

17 Building a 3D printed house is faster and cheaper than building a house with traditional methods.

18 Sumin's house looks fantastic because of its unique design.

19 A 3D printer can produce house shapes that people cannot make with traditional building methods and materials.

20 Sumin also likes to make her clothes at home by using a 3D printer.

21 She can choose colors and materials and can design clothes that fit her body and suit her tastes.

22 Sumin is now a fashion designer!

23 Dongmin in the Hospital

24 Dongmin is visiting his grandfather in the hospital.

25 An AI nurse enters the room.

26 It moves around the room and checks the patients' conditions.

27 When the AI nurse finds that Dongmin's grandfather has a high temperature, it gives him some medicine to lower his temperature.

28 Have you ever thought about these changes?

29 Some changes have already started to take place while others may start in the near future.

30 Can you imagine other changes?

31 Take some time to think about them.

시험대비 실력평가 p.190~193

01 ②, ③, ⑤   02 ②   03 ④   04 ①, ④

05 ①, ②, ④

06 Sumin's house looks fantastic because of its unique design.

07 ③   08 the AI nurse

09 in order that[so that], may[can] lower

10 ①   11 ④   12 ③

13 ①, ③ / ②, ④, ⑤

14 Building a 3D printed house is faster and cheaper.

15 ②   16 ③

17 (A) app   (B) does not need   (C) later   18 ②

19 ⑤   20 ②

21 There may be an AI teachers' room in every

school.

22 it gives some medicine to him   23 ⑤

24 (A) lower   (B) high

---

01 ⓐ와 ①, ④번: 계속 용법, ② 경험 용법, ③ 완료 용법, ⑤ 결과 용법

02 이 글은 '과학과 기술의 발전으로 인한 변화'에 관한 글이다.

03 본문 끝에서 '가까운 미래에 우리의 삶이 어떻게 될지 살펴보자'라고 했으므로, ④번이 적절하다.

04 (A)에는 목적격 관계대명사를, (B)에는 주격 관계대명사를 써야 하고, 선행사가 사물이므로 that이나 which가 적절하다.

05 ⓐ와 ③, ⑤번: 동명사, ①, ②, ④: 현재분사

06 look+형용사: ~하게 보이다, because of+명사구

07 '어떤' 변화는 이미 일어나기 시작했고 반면 '다른 것들'은 가까운 미래에 일어날지도 모른다고 해야 하므로, some과 others가 적절하다.

08 'AI 간호사'를 가리킨다.

09 목적을 나타내는 to부정사는 'in order that 주어 may[can]'나 'so that 주어 may[can]'로 고치는 것이 적절하다.

10 (A) add A to B: A를 B에 더하다, (B) remove A from B: B로부터 A를 제거하다

11 very는 원급을 강조하고, ⓐ와 나머지는 비교급을 강조한다.

12 물건을 되돌려 놓으면 그것은 자동으로 구매 목록에서 제거된다.

13 ⓐ와 ①, ③: 목적격 관계대명사, ⓑ와 ②, ④, ⑤: 주격 관계대명사

14 '3D 프린터로 집을 짓는 것'이 전통적인 방법으로 집을 짓는 것보다 더 빠르고 저렴하다.

15 ② 3D 프린터로 집을 짓는 것이 얼마나 걸리는지는 대답할 수 없다. ① In a 3D printed house. ③ Because of its unique design. ④ By using a 3D printer. ⑤ Sumin does.

16 주어진 문장의 The items에 주목한다. ③번 앞 문장의 the items를 받고 있으므로 ③번이 적절하다.

17 (A) 특별한 쇼핑 '앱'이 있는 스마트폰을 가지고 가게로 들어간다고 해야 하므로 app이 적절하다. list: 목록, (B) 가상 카드가 모든 가격을 더해서 나중에 그에게 청구한다고 했으므로, 돈을 지불하기 위해 줄을 설 '필요가 없다'고 하는 것이 적절하다. (C) 가상 카드가 모든 가격을 더해서 '나중에' 그에게 청구할 것이라고 해야 하므로 later가 적절하다. later: 나중에, latter: 후자의

18 ⓐ와 ②번: (요금, 값을) 청구하다, ① 돌격[공격]하다, ③ 책임(명사), ④ 청구 금액, 대가(명사), free of charge: 무료로, ⑤ <축전지에> 충전하다

19 이 글은 '훨씬 쉬워진 미래의 쇼핑'에 관한 글이다.

20 ⓐ와 ②, ⑤번: 경험 용법, ① 완료 용법, ③ 계속 용법, ④ 결과 용법

21 There may be: ~이 있을지도 모른다

22 give는 'to'를 사용하여 3형식으로 고친다.

23 ⓐ와 ⑤번: [주절 뒤에서 반대·비교·대조를 나타내어] 그런데, 한편(으로는), ①, ②, ③, ④: …하는 동안, …하는 사이, …와 동시에

24 AI 간호사는 동민이 할아버지가 열이 '높다'는 것을 알았을 때 그것은 그의 체온을 '낮추기' 위해 그에게 약을 준다.

🦉 서술형 시험대비   p.194~195

01 have caused

02 (A) advances   (B) changes

03 (1) seeing   (2) Why don't we

04 (1) 특별한 쇼핑 앱이 있는 스마트폰을 가지고 가게로 들어간다.
   (2) 가게에서 그가 원하는 물건들을 집는다.
   (3) 그 물건들은 자동으로 그의 스마트폰에 있는 가상 카드에 더 해지고, 만약 그가 물건을 되돌려 놓으면 그것은 자동으로 그의 구매 목록에서 제거된다.
   (4) 쇼핑을 끝내면 돈을 지불하기 위해 줄을 설 필요가 없고, 그의 가상 카드가 모든 가격을 더해서 나중에 그에게 청구할 것이다.

05 In the shop, he takes the items that[which] he wants.

06 he does not need to wait in line to pay

07 unique design

08 fits → fit, suits → suit

09 (1) 색깔과 재료를 고른다.
   (2) 자신의 몸과 취향에 맞는 옷을 디자인한다.
   (3) 3D 프린터를 사용해 집에서 옷을 만든다.

10 application

11 item

12 to shop → shopping

13 may

14 how schools may change over the next 20 years

15 no more[longer]

---

01 뒤에 'so far'가 있으므로 현재완료 시제로 쓰는 것이 적절하다.

02 과학과 기술의 '발전' 때문에 지금까지 우리의 삶에 많은 '변화들'이 있어 왔다.

03 Let's see ~. = How[What] about seeing ~? = Why don't we see ~?: ~을 보는 게 어때?

04 본문에서 소개하고 있는 쇼핑 방법을 쓰는 것이 적절하다.

05 생략된 목적격 관계대명사 that[which]을 넣어 문장을 다시 쓰는 것이 적절하다.

06 wait in line: 줄을 서서 기다리다

07 수민이의 집의 '독특한 디자인'이 집을 멋져 보이게 만든다.

08 선행사가 clothes이므로 fit과 suit으로 고치는 것이 적절하다.

09 수민이는 색깔과 재료를 고를 수 있고 자신의 몸과 취향에 맞는 옷을 디자인하여 집에서 **3D 프린터**를 사용해 옷을 만들 수 있다고 했다.

10 app: 스마트폰 앱, 어플리케이션(application)

11 상호가 되돌려 놓는 '물건'을 가리킨다.

12 finish는 목적어로 동명사를 취한다.

13 추측을 표현하는 'may'를 쓰는 것이 적절하다.

14 'next'를 보충하면 된다.

15 not ~ anymore = no more[longer]: 더 이상 ~ 아닌

영역별 핵심문제   p.197~201

01 ③   02 ①   03 ②   04 ⑤
05 ②   06 (C) → (A) → (B)
07 (A) → (D) → (B) → (C)   08 ⑤
09 ④   10 rescue
11 If there is a person in trouble, it flies over and drops a tube.
12 Can I ask you to show me how it works?
13 (A) for   (B) about   (C) at
14 ⑤   15 ①   16 ⑤   17 ⑤
18 (1) I bought it only a couple of hours ago.
   (2) She has studied science and technology for 10 years.
   (3) Have you ever been to Paris?
   (4) There may be an AI teachers' room in every school.
19 (1) He has never bought a lottery ticket.
   (2) I have lost my passport at the airport.
   (3) We have known each other since 1999.
   (4) He has just finished his science project.
   (5) They may come back tomorrow.
   (6) May[Can] I use your smartphone?
20 Advances in science and technology have caused many changes in our lives so far.
21 ③, ⑤   22 (A) added (B) virtual (C) charge
23 automatically removes → is automatically removed
24 he needs to pay at the counter → he does not need to wait in line to pay
25 ①, ④   26 make them → make
27 ③   28 lower
29 ⓐ Dongmin's grandfather   ⓑ other changes

---

01 ③은 유의어 관계이며, 나머지 보기들은 반의어 관계이다. ① difference: 차이, 차이점 similarity: 유사점 ② ever: 어느 때고, 언제든, 한번이라도 never: 지금까지[어느 때건] 한 번도 ~ 않다 ③ law: 법칙, 법 principle: 원칙, 법칙 ④ lower: 낮

추다 heighten: 강화하다, 높이다 ⑤ true: 참된 false: 거짓의

02 ① have, don't have to 동사원형: ~할 필요가 없다 / 너는 도시락을 가져올 필요는 없다. ② waiting, wait in line: 줄을 서서 기다리다 / 그들은 음식을 주문하기 위해 줄서서 기다리고 있다. ③ Add, add up: 합산하다 / 다음의 숫자를 합산하세요. ④ get, get lost: 길을 잃다 / 만약 길을 잃으시면 제 휴대폰 010-744-2996으로 전화주세요. ⑤ move, move around: 돌아다니다 / 우리는 모든 과목마다 교실을 옮겨다닌다.

03 cover: 덮다 / 바다는 지구 표면의 70% 정도를 덮고 있습니다.

04 suit: (입맛, 취향 등에) 맞다 / 그는 자기 적성에 맞는 그 일을 좋아했다.

05 ⓑ I'm good at finding places. → I'm not good at finding places. 길을 잃을 것에 대해 걱정하는 말을 했으므로, 장소를 잘 찾는다는 말이 나오는 것은 어색하다.

06 (C) 상대의 물건에 대해 설명을 요청하는 말에 (A) 미래의 신발이라고 말하며, 이 신발을 신은 사람은 100미터를 5초 안에 달릴 것이라고 설명한다. (B) 그 정도로 빨리 달릴 수 있는 것에 대해 놀람을 표현한다.

07 (A) 집에 나오기 전에 히터 끄는 것을 잊어버렸고 말한다. (D) 그러면 히터를 끄기 위해 집으로 돌아가야 하는지 질문하자, (B) 스마트폰으로 히터를 끌 수 있다고 말한다. (C) 상대방이 스마트폰으로 히터를 끌 수 있다는 사실에 대해 놀라워한다.

08 ⓐ to visit, would like to 동사원형: ~하고 싶다 ⓑ put this on, 이어동사는 '동사+부사(on, off, up, over 등)'로 이루어져 있다. '동사+부사+목적어'의 어순이나 '동사+목적어+부사'의 어순 둘 다 가능하지만 목적어 자리에 대명사(it, them, this 등)가 올 때는 '동사+목적어+부사'의 어순으로 쓴다. ⓒ real, look+형용사: ~하게 보이다 ⓓ isn't it ⓔ I'm surprised that 주어 동사 ~: ~하는 것이 놀라워

09 save: 구하다

10 rescue: 구조하다 / 위험이나 손상으로부터 누군가나 어떤 것을 구하다

11 if: ~라면 there is+단수 명사: ~가 있다 in trouble: 곤경에 빠져서, 난처하여 drop: 떨어뜨리다 tube: 튜브

12 Can[Could/Will/Would] you 동사 ~?(~해 줄 수 있니?)', 'Could[Can] I ask you to 동사 ~?(~을 부탁해도 될까?)'는 상대방에게 어떤 행동을 요청할 때 사용하는 표현들이다.

13 be ready for: ~의 준비가 되다 be worried about: ~에 대해 걱정하다 be good at: ~을 잘하다

14 ① 남자아이는 무엇을 걱정하는가?(길을 잃는 것) ② 남자 아이는 어디를 여행할 것인가?(런던) ③ 남자아이는 무엇을 잘 못하는가?(장소 찾는 것) ④ 여자아이가 남자아이에게 추천해 준 앱은 무엇을 보여주는가?(도시의 지도와 길의 사진) ⑤ 남자아이는 얼마나 많은 스마트폰 앱을 사용할 수 있는가?

15 since(~ 이래로)는 보통 현재완료와 함께 많이 쓰인다. 이때 since절에는 과거 시제가 쓰인다.

16 ⓐ mays → may ⓑ are → be ⓒ gone → been ⓕ for →

since ⓗ has met → met

17 ⑤번은 '허가'의 의미로 쓰였지만 나머지는 모두 '추측'의 의미로 쓰였다.

18 (1) 현재완료는 과거를 나타내는 ~ ago와는 함께 쓰이지 않는다. (2) 현재완료의 '계속' 용법이다. 'since+시간 명사', 'for+ 기간 명사'임에 유의한다. (3) have[has] been to는 '~에 가 본 적이 있다'는 경험을 나타내고, have[has] gone to는 '~에 가고 없다'는 결과를 나타내므로 have been to로 고쳐야 한다. (4) 조동사 may 다음에는 동사원형이 나와야 한다.

19 (1) 현재완료의 '경험' 용법을 이용한다. (2) 현재완료의 '결과' 용법을 이용한다. (3) 현재완료의 '계속' 용법을 이용한다. (4) 현재완료의 '완료' 용법을 이용한다. (5) '추측'의 may를 이용한다. (6) '허가'의 may를 이용한다. '허가'의 경우에는 may 대신 can을 쓸 수 있다.

20 'have'를 보충하면 된다.

21 ⓑ와 ③, ⑤번: (추측) ~일지도 모른다, ① (허락) …해도 되다[좋다], ② [목적을 나타내는 부사절에서] …하기 위하여, …할 수 있도록, ④ (바람, 소망) …이기를 (빌다)

22 (A) 그의 스마트폰에 있는 가상 카드에 '더해진다'라고 수동태로 써야 하므로 added가 적절하다. (B) 그의 '가상' 카드라고 해야 하므로 virtual이 적절하다. actual: 실제의, virtual: (컴퓨터를 이용한) 가상의, (C) 나중에 그에게 '청구할 것'이라고 해야 하므로 charge가 적절하다.

23 자동으로 그의 구매 목록에서 '제거된다'고 해야 하므로, 수동태로 고치는 것이 적절하다.

24 쇼핑을 끝냈을 때 상호는 '돈을 지불하기 위해 줄을 설 필요가 없다.'

25 ① 주어 자리에 동명사와 to부정사를 쓸 수 있다. ④ 전통적인 방법으로 집을 짓는 것은 3D 프린터로 집을 짓는 것만큼 빠르고 저렴하지 않다.

26 목적격 관계대명사 that이 있으므로, them을 삭제하는 것이 적절하다.

27 3D 프린터는 사람들이 전통적인 건축 방법과 재료들로 만들 수 '없는' 집 모양을 만들어 낼 수 '있다'.

28 체온을 '낮추기' 위해 그에게 약을 준다고 하는 것이 적절하다. lower: …을 내리다[낮추다]

29 ⓐ는 '동민이 할아버지'를, ⓑ는 '다른 변화들'을 가리킨다.

🪨 단원별 예상문제　　　　　　　　p.202~205

01 (1) (l)ibrarian　(2) (o)ffer　　02 ④

03 (1) interested in drones　(2) technology
　　(3) materials　(4) (f)ancy

04 (1) Advances in technology have brought us many good things.
　　(2) This watch can run many applications like smartphones.

05 (A) before　(B) turn it off

---

06 I'm surprised that you can turn off the heater with your smartphone.

07 ③　　　　08 recommend

09 (A) surprised　(B) amazing　　　　10 ⑤

11 ③　　　12 ⑤　　　13 ②

14 Advances　15 ③　　16 ①, ④　　17 ②

18 ②

19 The items are automatically added to a virtual card on his smartphone. 또는 The items are added to a virtual card on his smartphone automatically.

20 ④　　　　21 ③, ⑤　　　22 ②

23 AI 간호사는 병실을 돌아다니면서 환자들의 상태를 확인하고, 환자의 열이 높다는 것을 알면 체온을 낮추기 위해 환자에게 약을 준다.

24 ②

---

01 (1) 장소와 직업의 관계이다. farm: 농장 farmer: 농부 library: 도서관 librarian: 사서 (2) 동의어 관계이다 material: 재료 matter: 물질, 물체 provide: 공급하다 offer: 제공하다

02 since: ~ 이후로 / 대학교를 떠난 이후로 럭비를 하지 않았다.

03 (1) be interested in: ~에 관심이 있다 drone: (원격 조종의) 드론 (2) technology: 과학 기술, 생산 기술 (3) different: 다른 material: 재료 (4) fancy: 화려한, 공들인, 고급의

04 (1) advance: 발전 technology: 과학 기술, 생산 기술 (2) app: 스마트폰 앱, 어플리케이션(application)

05 (A) 집에서 나오기 전에 히터를 끄는 것을 잊어버린 것을 말하고, 이어 상대방이 히터를 끄기 위해 집에 다시 가야 하는지 물어 보는 것이 어울리므로 before가 적절하다. (B) turn off는 이어동사로 '동사+부사'로 이루어져 있다. 목적어 자리에 대명사가 올 때는 '동사+목적어+부사'의 어순으로 쓴다.

06 I'm surprised that 주어 동사 ~: ~하는 것이 놀라워 with: ~을 써서, 이용하여

07 주어진 문장은 '추천해 줄 수 있니?'라는 의미의 문장이다. 여기서 one은 a book about gravity이며, 이 질문에 대한 대답으로 책을 추천해야 하므로, 'The Law of Gravity'를 추천하는 말 앞에 나와야 어울린다.

08 recommend: ~을 추천하다 / 어떤 것을 지지하여 말하다

09 I'm surprised that 주어 동사 ~: ~하는 것이 놀라워 amazing: 놀라운 감정을 나타내는 동사의 경우 현재분사는 '~하게 하는'의 뜻으로 감정을 유발하는 대상에 쓰이고, 과거분사는 '~하게 된'의 뜻으로 감정을 느끼는 대상에 쓰인다.

10 AI가 책을 추천해서 놀라움을 표현한 것은 하나와 Amy이다.

11 현재완료에서 'since+시간 명사', 'for+기간 명사'

12 ① Koreans have played *jegichagi*, a traditional Korean

39

game, for a long time. ② The children have already had dinner. ③ He left for New York last night. ④ Has he done his homework?

13 ② The math problem is difficult. Chris may not know the answer.

14 더 나은 쪽으로의 변화; 발달에 있어서의 진전 / advance: 발달, 진보

15 ③ so far = until now: 지금까지, ①과 ⑤: 최근에, ② 그 때까지, ④ 우선은, 현재로는, 당분간은

16 ©와 ①, ④번: (외관·내용 등이) …을 닮아, …와 유사하여(전치사), ②, ③, ⑤: ~을 좋아하다(동사)

17 쇼핑이 훨씬 쉬워진 것이므로, '정말 멋지지 않은가?'라고 하는 것이 적절하다. ① 지루한, ③ 소박한, ④ 끔찍한, ⑤ 복잡한

18 ② 계산대는 없다.

19 'automatically'를 보충하면 된다.

20 ④번 다음 문장부터 3D 프린터를 사용해 옷을 만드는 내용이 나오므로 ④번이 적절하다.

21 ⓐ와 ③, ⑤번: 관계대명사, ①, ②, ④: 접속사

22 이 글은 '수민이가 3D 프린터를 사용하여 집을 짓고 옷을 만든다'는 내용의 글이다.

23 첫 단락의 내용을 쓰는 것이 적절하다.

24 ⓐ와 ①, ③번: 완료 용법, ② 결과 용법, ④ 경험 용법, ⑤ 계속 용법

서술형 실전문제 p.206~207

01 I'm surprised that this car can drive itself automatically.

02 ⓔ That's very difficult. → That's very simple[easy].

03 Then do you mind telling me how to do it? /
Then can I ask you to tell me how to do it?

04 (1) for (2) since (3) before

05 (1) You may not leave this room now.
   (2) My friend may be sad because of the news.
   (3) My parents have raised the dog since I was born.
   (4) She has gone to see the movie.
   (5) She has swum in the river once.
   (6) The children have not had dinner yet.

06 (1) may (2) Maybe

07 more difficult → easier

08 virtual

09 그의 가상 카드가 모든 가격을 더해서 나중에 그에게 청구할 것이기 때문이다.

10 using

11 looks like → looks

12 (1) 3D 프린터로 집을 짓는 것은 전통적인 방법으로 집을 짓는 것보다 더 빠르고 저렴하다.
   (2) 독특한 디자인 때문에 멋져 보인다.
   (3) 3D 프린터는 사람들이 전통적인 건축 방법과 재료들로 만들 수 없는 집 모양을 만들어 낼 수 있다.

01 I'm surprised that 주어 동사 ~: ~하는 것이 놀라워
automatically: 자동적으로 itself: 그 자신, 스스로

02 전등을 켜고 끄기 위해서 단지 "불 켜!" 또는 "불 꺼!"라고 말하는 것은 간단한[쉬운] 일이다.

03 요청하는 표현에는 'Could[Can] I ask you to 동사 ~?(~을 부탁해도 될까?)', 'Do[Would] you mind 동명사 ~?(~해 줄 수 있니?)' 등이 있다.

04 (1), (2) 현재완료에서 'since+시간 명사', 'for+ 기간 명사' (3) ago는 현재완료와 함께 사용할 수 없으나 before는 사용할 수 있다.

05 (1) '허가'의 may를 이용한다. (2) '추측'의 may를 이용한다. (3) 현재완료의 '계속' 용법을 이용한다. (4) 현재완료의 '결과' 용법을 이용한다. have[has] been to는 '~에 가 본 적이 있다'는 경험을 나타내고, have[has] gone to는 '~에 가고 없다'는 결과를 나타낸다. (5) 현재완료의 '경험' 용법을 이용한다. (6) 현재완료의 '완료' 용법을 이용한다. 부정문이므로 yet을 쓰는 것에 주의한다.

06 (1) '추측'의 may를 쓰는 것이 적절하다. (2) maybe를 이용한다. maybe는 부사로 '어쩌면, 아마'라는 뜻이다.

07 줄도 없고 계산대도 없다고 했기 때문에 쇼핑이 '훨씬 쉽다'고 하는 것이 적절하다.

08 어떤 장소에 가거나 직접 사람들을 만나지 않고 컴퓨터나 인터넷을 사용하여 행해지거나 보여지는, virtual: (컴퓨터를 이용한) 가상의

09 뒷문장의 내용을 쓰는 것이 적절하다.

10 전치사 다음에 동명사를 쓰는 것이 적절하다.

11 look+형용사: ~하게 보이다

12 본문의 앞부분의 내용을 쓰는 것이 적절하다.

창의사고력 서술형 문제 p.208

|모범답안|

01 I'm surprised that it looks like a leaf but it's moving.

02 (1) Advances in science and technology have caused many changes.
   (2) Have you ever imagined life in the future? / I have never been to Austria.
   (3) I have finished my homework. / I have visited Jejudo twice.

03 (A) 3D printing (B) AI teachers
   (C) a drone station (D) paper textbooks

01 ②

02 (1) (l)aw, gravity (2) patient (3) (m)ethod (4) take

03 Virtual

04 (1) They are waiting in line to get coffee.

(2) When I was in trouble, she tried to support me a lot.

(3) The woman is trying to exchange her purchase.

(4) Take this medicine after meals.

05 I'm surprised that we're already living in the future.

06 ⑤   07 law   08 ①   09 drone

10 ③

11 Can you tell me how shoes will change our lives in the future?

12 (C) → (D) → (B) → (A)

13 ②   14 ③

15 Cindy may live in a 3D printed house in the future.

16 해석: (1) 나는 스마트폰을 잃어버렸다.

해석: (2) 나는 스마트폰을 잃어버렸다.

차이: (1)번은 '스마트폰을 잃어버렸다'는 사실만을 나타내지만, (2)번은 '스마트폰을 잃어버려서 현재 스마트폰이 없다'는 현재의 상황까지 나타낸다.

17 ③   18 (A) takes   (B) puts back

19 ③   20 ④   21 ③   22 ①

01 fit: (치수·모양 등이) 꼭 맞다 / 이 재킷은 나에게 꽤 잘 맞는다. charge: (지불·대금 등을) 청구하다 / 우리 웹사이트에 들어온 주문품을 배달하는 비용을 얼마나 청구하지요?

02 (1) law: 법칙, 법 gravity: 중력 (2) patient: 환자 condition: 상태, 조건 (3) method: 방법, 방식 (4) take place: 일어나다, 개최되다

03 virtual: 가상의 / 컴퓨터에 의해 만들어진 또는 컴퓨터나 인터넷에 나타나는 / 가상 현실 기술은 아주 우수한 컴퓨터를 필요로 한다.

04 (1) wait in line: 줄을 서서 기다리다 (2) in trouble: 곤경에 빠져서, 난처하여 (3) purchase: 구입(품) (4) medicine: 약

05 I'm surprised that 주어 동사 ~: ~하는 것이 놀라워 in the future: 미래에

06 주어진 문장은 책이 어디에 있는지 위치를 묻는 질문이므로, 'It's on the third floor.(그건 3층에 있어.)'의 대답과 잘 어울린다.

07 law: 법칙, 법 / 특정한 조건에서 항상 발생하는 것에 관련된 사실의 진술; 과학적 원리

08 중력에 관한 책이 57권이 있다고 말했지만, 도서관에 책이 몇 권 있는지는 언급되지 않았다. ① 도서관에 책이 몇 권 있니? ② Amy와 하나는 어디에 있는가? ③ 어떤 책이 Terry에 의해

추천되었는가? ④ 대화 후에 그들은 어디에 갈 것인가? ⑤ The Law of Gravity는 몇 층에 있는가?

09 drone: (원격 조종의) 드론 / 원격조종이나 내장 컴퓨터로 조종되는 무인의 항공기나 배

10 ⓐ to save people's lives, to부정사의 부사적 용법 (~하기 위해서) ⓒ drops a tube, flies와 병렬 관계 ⓓ I'm surprised that, I'm surprised that 주어 동사 ~: ~하는 것이 놀라워

11 Can you 동사 ~?: ~해 줄 수 있니? tell의 직접목적어 자리에 간접의문문(의문사+주어+동사)이 들어갔다. in the future: 미래에

12 (C) 새로운 전등을 보여 주면서, 전등을 켜고 끄기 위해 손을 사용할 필요가 없다고 말한다. (D) 전등을 켜고 끄는 방법을 말해 줄 수 있는지 물어보자 (B) "불 꺼" 또는 "불 켜"라고 말하면 된다고 답한다. (A) 말로 전등을 켜고 끄는 것이 간단하다고 말한다.

13 then은 과거의 특정 시점을 나타내는 부사이므로 현재완료와 함께 쓸 수 없다.

14 주어진 문장과 ③번은 '허가'의 의미로 쓰이고 있다. 나머지는 모두 '추측'을 나타낸다.

15 '추측'의 may를 이용한다.

16 (1) 과거 시제는 과거에 있었던 사실만을 나타낸다. (2) 현재완료는 과거의 어느 한 시점에 일어난 일이 현재까지 영향을 미칠 때 사용한다.

17 ⓐ와 ①, ④: 부사적 용법, ② 형용사적 용법 ③, ⑤: 명사적 용법

18 가게에서 상호가 '집는' 물건들은 자동으로 그의 스마트폰에 있는 가상 카드에 더해지고, 상호가 '되돌려 놓는' 물건들은 자동으로 그의 구매 목록에서 제거된다.

19 물건들을 자동으로 상호의 스마트폰에 있는 가상 카드에 더하기 위해 앱이 무슨 작동방식을 사용하는지는 대답할 수 없다. ① No. ② Yes. ④ Yes. ⑤ He doesn't need to wait in line to pay. His virtual card adds up all the prices and will charge him later.

20 자신의 몸과 취향에 맞는 옷을 디자인할 수 있다고 했기 때문에, '패션 디자이너'라고 하는 것이 적절하다. ① 건축가, ③ (기계·도로·교량 등을 설계·건축하는) 기사, 엔지니어 ⑤ 화가

21 ③ ~에도 불구하고

22 ⓑ와 ①번: 취향, ② <음식이> (~한) 맛이 나다, ③ 맛이 ~하다, ~한 맛이 나다, ④ 맛, ⑤ 맛을 보다, 시식[시음]하다

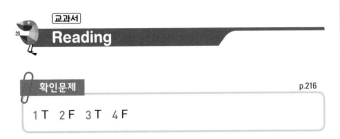

The 100th Customer

Reading

확인문제   p.216

1 T   2 F   3 T   4 F

확인문제   p.217

1 T   2 F   3 T   4 F

교과서 확인학습 A
p.218~219

01 100th	02 elderly
03 with her grandson	04 Quietly, the owner
05 How much	06 with a smile
07 too poor to pay	08 for her grandson
09 Are you sure	10 No
11 Don't worry	12 chewed on
13 eat, came over	
14 to give the boy a free meal	
15 was about to pay	16 the 100th customer
17 thanked Mr. Kang	
18 A month later, outside	19 was gathering
20 What	21 counting, who
22 Today is	23 treat, said to himself
24 looked down	25 the number, was
26 to help	27 went back into
28 bring everyone who	29 who needs
30 to arrive at	31 It's our turn
32 welcomed them, a free bowl of Gukbap	
33 Are you sure	34 with a smile
35 Don't worry	

교과서 확인학습 B
p.220~221

1 The 100th Customer

2 One day, an elderly woman walked into a restaurant.

3 She was with her grandson.

4 Quietly, the woman asked Mr. Kang, the owner of the restaurant.

5 "How much is a bowl of Gukbap?"

6 "It's 4,000 won, ma'am," Mr. Kang answered with a smile.

7 She was too poor to pay for two bowls.

8 She ordered a single bowl for her grandson.

9 "Are you sure you are not hungry, Grandma?" the boy asked, as he ate the hot soup.

10 "No, I'm not hungry.

11 Don't worry about me."

12 She picked up some Gimchi and chewed on it happily.

13 Mr. Kang watched them eat, and a warm feeling came over him.

14 He thought up a plan to give the boy a free meal.

15 When the woman was about to pay, Mr. Kang waved his hands and said, "No need, ma'am.

16 In my restaurant, you don't pay if you're the 100th customer of the day."

17 The woman and her grandson thanked Mr. Kang and left.

18 A month later, Mr. Kang saw the boy in the street outside the restaurant.

19 The boy was gathering stones.

20 "What are you doing?" asked Mr. Kang.

21 "I'm counting the number of customers who enter your restaurant.

22 Today is my grandma's birthday."

23 'He wants to be the 100th customer and treat his grandmother to a bowl of Gukbap!' Mr. Kang said to himself.

24 Mr. Kang looked down.

25 He could see that the number of stones was not yet even fifty.

26 He had to do something to help the boy gather 100 stones.

27 Mr. Kang went back into the restaurant and called his friends.

28 "Come to my restaurant now and bring everyone who works with you.

29 There is a boy who needs your help."

30 People began to arrive at the restaurant.

31 When the 99th customer arrived, Mr. Kang heard the boy say, "It's our turn, Grandma."

32 Mr. Kang welcomed them and served the woman a free bowl of Gukbap.

33 "Are you sure you're not hungry?" the woman

asked the boy.

34 The boy chewed loudly on some Gimchi and said with a smile, "No, I'm not hungry, Grandma.

35 Don't worry about me. Happy birthday!"

 서술형 실전문제 p.222~224

01 (1) (s)ingle (2) (t)reating (3) (e)lderly

02 (1) up (2) to

03 (1) raise (2) chew (3) Order (4) count

04 can't, to take

05 (1) even (2) meals (3) turn (4) yet

06 (c)hair / (c)hew

07 (1) I saw you enter(또는 entering) the museum.
 (2) I heard my friend laugh(또는 laughing) loudly in English class.
 (3) The kid is too short to reach that book.
 (4) I am so tired that I can't get up early.

08 (A) burning (B) to carry

09 (1) The shirt is too large to wear.
 (2) I heard Tom talk[talking] about me.
 (3) He is honest enough to tell the truth.

10 with

11 price

12 so, that, couldn't

13 (A) No (B) to pay (C) customer

14 to eat → eat 또는 eating

15 "자신의 식당에서는 그 날의 백 번째 손님이 되면 돈을 내지 않아도 된다."고 말하면서 돈을 받지 않는 것

16 that

17 그의 친구들에게 전화해서 함께 일하는 모든 사람들을 데리고 지금 자신의 식당으로 오라고 말하는 것

18 the 100th customer

19 say 또는 saying

20 get to 또는 reach

21 served a free bowl of Gukbap to the woman

01 (1) only: 유일한 single: 단 하나의, 단일의 / 이것은 이 지역의 유일한 은행이다. (2) deal with: (문제 등을) 다루다 treat: 다루다 / 비조직 범죄를 다룰 수 있는 새로운 방법들이 있다. (3) old: 나이든 elderly: 연세가 드신 / Sarah는 그녀의 나이 든 부모님을 돌본다.

02 (1) think up: ~을 생각해 내다 / 누가 새로운 상품의 이름을 생각해 냈니? pick up: 들어올리다, 집다 / 승객들이 가방을 집어 들고 있다. (2) treat A(사람) to B(사물): A에게 B를 대접하다 / 나는 그들에게 오늘 밤 저녁을 대접할 것이다. say to oneself: 혼잣말을 하다 / Johnson은 항상 혼잣말을 한다.

03 (1) raise: (자금 등을) 모으다 / 그들은 땅을 사기 위해 백만 달러를 모으기를 희망했다. (2) chew: (음식을) 씹다 / 나는 치통 때문에 음식을 잘 씹을 수가 없다. (3) order: (음식, 음료 등을) 주문하다 / 비용을 생각하지 말고 원하는 것을 무엇이든 주문하여라. regardless of: ~에 상관없이 (4) count: 수를 세다, 계산하다 / John은 동물들의 수를 세어야 했다.

04 can't wait to 동사원형: 빨리 ~하고 싶다, ~하는 것이 기다려지다 look forward to 동명사: ~하는 것을 기대하다

05 (1) even: (예상 밖의 놀라운 일을 나타내어) ~도, ~조차 (2) meal: 식사 (3) turn: (무엇을 할) 차례, 순번 (4) yet: (부정문, 의문문에서) 아직(안 했거나 못 했다는 뜻을 나타낼 때)

06 chair: 의자 / 한 사람이 앉기 위한, 등받이와 다리, 때때로 팔걸이가 있는 가구
 chew: (음식을) 씹다 / 음식을 삼키기 전에 이로 음식을 부수다

07 (1), (2) 지각동사의 목적어가 목적격보어의 행위의 주체가 될 경우 목적격보어로 원형부정사나 현재분사를 쓰는 것이 적절하다. (3), (4) 'too+형용사/부사+to+동사원형' 구문으로 '너무 ~해서 …할 수 없다, ~하기에는 너무 …하다'는 뜻을 나타내며, 'so+형용사/부사+that+주어+can't[couldn't]+동사원형'의 구문으로 바꾸어 쓸 수 있다.

08 (A) smell은 목적격보어로 현재분사가 적절하다. (B) '너무 ~해서 …할 수 없다, ~하기에는 너무 …하다'는 뜻을 나타내는 'too+형용사/부사+to+동사원형' 구문이다.

09 (1) 'too+형용사/부사+to+동사원형' 구문을 이용한다. (2) 지각동사의 목적격보어로 원형부정사나 현재분사를 쓴다. (3) '형용사/부사+enough+to부정사' 구문은 '~할 만큼 …하다, 충분히 ~해서 …할 수 있다'는 뜻이다.

10 ⓐ with her grandson: 손자와 함께, ⓒ with a smile: 미소 지으며

11 How much is ~? = What's the price of ~?

12 too ~ to = so ~ that 주어 can't

13 (A) '배고프지 않다'고 했으므로 No가 적절하다. (B) 돈을 '내려고 할 때'라고 해야 하므로 to pay가 적절하다. be about to: 막 ~하려는 참이다, (C) (상점의) 고객을 말하는 것이므로 customer가 적절하다. guest: 손님, 하객

14 지각동사는 목적격보어로 동사원형이나 현재분사가 온다.

15 다음에 이어지는 문장의 내용을 쓰면 된다.

16 ⓐ와 ⓓ에는 관계대명사 who나 that, ⓑ에는 접속사 that이 적절하다.

17 그의 친구들에게 전화해서 말한 내용을 쓰는 것이 적절하다.

18 그 소년을 그 날의 '백 번째 손님'이 되게 하고 싶었기 때문이다.

19 hear의 목적격보어로 동사원형이나 현재분사를 쓴다.

20 arrive at = get to = reach: ~에 도착하다

21 serve는 'to'를 사용하여 3형식으로 고친다.

01 ②   02 (1) (p)ick up   (2) (R)aise, (r)aise

03 (1) She treated him to lunch.

  (2) When he called me, I was about to leave.

  (3) The girl helped her sister make a cake.

  (4) I can't wait to watch it.

04 ③   05 ⑤   06 ③   07 ⑤

08 ③

09 (1) I felt something biting my leg.

  (2) We enjoyed listening to the bird sing.

  (3) Did you see the children playing soccer on the ground?

10 (1) Kate felt someone touch[touching] her bag.

  (2) I didn't hear you call[calling] me.

  (3) I watched the boy building a sandcastle at the beach.

  (4) I was so young that I couldn't watch the movie.

  (5) She got up early enough to catch the first train.

  (6) The tea is too hot to drink.

11 (1) She is so shy that she can't ask for help.

  (2) The stars in the sky are so many that we can't count them.

  (3) The problem is so easy that he can solve it.

12 ②, ⑤   13 ③

14 to give a free meal to the boy

15 할머니: 자신은 배고프지 않다고 말하며, 손자에게만 국밥을 사준 것.

  Mr. Kang : 할머니와 손자에게 '그 날의 백 번째 손님이 되면 돈을 내지 않아도 된다'고 말하며, 국밥 값을 받지 않은 것.

16 to   17 ⑤   18 ②   19 ③

20 served the woman a free bowl of Gukbap

21 ①   22 ⑤   23 ④

24 if you're the 100th customer of the day

25 ⑤

26 (A) himself (B) was (C) gather

27 ④   28 ②

29 the boy and his grandmother

30 free   31 ④   32 ③

33 touched   34 a free bowl of Gukbap

01 ② 접미사 -er을 붙여 '~하는 것'이라는 뜻의 명사가 되는 동사이다. dry: 건조하다 dryer: 건조기, 드라이어. 이외의 보기들은 접미사 -er을 붙여 '~하는 사람'이라는 뜻의 명사가 되는 동사들이다. ① own: 소유하다 owner: 주인, 소유주 ③ write: 쓰다, (작품·문서 등을) 저술하다 writer: 작가 ④ teach: 가르치다 teacher: 교사 ⑤ produce: 생산하다, 만들다 producer: 생산자, 제작자

02 (1) pick up: 들어올리다, 집다, ~을 (차에) 태우러 가다 / 나는 공항에 내 여동생을 태우러 갈 것이다. • 우리는 길거리의 쓰레기를 주워야 한다. (2) raise: (자금 등을) 모으다, 올리다 / • 정답을 안다면, 손을 올리세요. • 그들은 홍수 이재민을 돕기 위해서 자금을 모았다.

03 (1) treat A(사람) to B(사물): A에게 B를 대접하다 (2) be about to: 막 ~하려는 참이다 (3) help+목적어+동사원형: (목적어)가 ~하는 것을 돕다 (4) can't wait to 동사원형: 빨리 ~하고 싶다, ~하는 것이 기다려지다

04 ③ think up: ~을 생각해 내다 / 나는 더 나은 변명을 생각해 내야 했다.

05 be about to: 막 ~ 하려고 하다 What about ~ing?: ~하는 것이 어때?

06 raise: (자금 등을) 모으다 / 그는 자선기금 모금을 위한 연주회를 열었다.

07 ① It is too hot to go out today. ② He was so poor that he couldn't buy a car. ③ The problem is so easy that he can solve it. ④ Mike felt someone tap[tapping] him on the shoulder.

08 지각동사의 목적격보어로 원형부정사나 현재분사를 써야 한다. I felt the ground shake[shaking] once.

09 지각동사의 목적격보어로 원형부정사나 현재분사를 써야 한다. (1), (3)에는 진행형이 사용되고 있으므로 원형부정사보다는 현재분사가 적절하다.

10 (1)~(3) 지각동사의 목적격보어로 원형부정사나 현재분사를 쓴다. (4)~(6) too+형용사/부사+to+동사원형 = so+형용사/부사+that+주어+can't[couldn't]+동사원형, 형용사/부사+enough+to부정사 = so+형용사/부사+that+주어+can[could]+동사원형

11 too+형용사/부사+to+동사원형 = so+형용사/부사+that+주어+can't[couldn't]+동사원형, 형용사/부사+enough+to부정사 = so+형용사/부사+that+주어+can[could]+동사원형 (2), (3)번의 경우 to부정사의 목적어가 문장의 주어이므로 문제에서는 to부정사의 목적어를 쓰지 않았지만 that절로 바꿀 때는 써 주어야 함에 주의한다.

12 지각동사는 목적격보어로 동사원형이나 현재분사가 온다.

13 ⓐ와 ③번 [때] ~하고 있을 때, ~하면서(접속사), ① ~한 대로(접속사), ② ~로서(전치사), ④ ~라고(전치사), ⑤ [보통 as ... as로 형용사·부사 앞에서] ~와 같을 정도로, (앞의 as는 지시부사, 뒤의 as는 접속사)

14 give는 'to'를 사용하여 3형식으로 고친다.

15 할머니는 손자에게, Mr. Kang은 할머니와 손자에게 각각 배려하는 마음을 보였다.

16 ⓐ treat A(사람) to B(사물): A에게 B를 대접하다, ⓑ say to oneself: 혼잣말을 하다

17 주어진 문장의 do something에 주목한다. ⑤번 뒤 문장의 내용을 가리키므로 ⑤번이 적절하다.

18 ② 사려 깊은, (남을) 배려하는, ① 끈기 있는, ③ 재미있는, ④ 호기심 많은, ⑤ 외향적인

19 ⓐ와 ③번: 차례, ① 돌다(동사), ② (어떤 나이, 시기가) 되다(동사), ④ 돌리다(동사), ⑤ (방향) 전환

20 'free'를 보충하면 된다.

21 위 글은 배려와 사랑이 담긴 이야기이므로, 글의 분위기는 '감동적'이라고 하는 것이 적절하다. ① 가슴[마음]을 뭉클하게 하는, 감동적인, ② 우울하게 만드는, 우울한, ③ (특이해서) 웃기는[재미있는], ④ 비참한, ⑤ 지루한

22 ⑤ 감동한, ① 부끄러운, ② 흥분한, ③ 실망한, ④ 지루한

23 ⓑ와 ④번: 무료의, ① 자유로운, ② 다른 계획[약속]이 없는, ③ (갇히거나 걸린 데서) 풀어 주다[빼내다](동사), ⑤ (새장 등에) 갇혀 있지 않은

24 the 100th: 백 번째의

25 ⑤는 Mr. Kang을 가리키고, 나머지는 다 소년을 가리킨다.

26 (A) 주어와 목적어가 같으므로 재귀대명사 himself가 적절하다. (B) the number of는 단수 취급하므로 was가 적절하다. (C) 'help'는 동사원형과 to부정사를 목적격보어로 취하므로 gather가 적절하다.

27 ④ 강 씨가 아래를 내려다보았을 때 돌멩이의 개수가 아직 오십 개도 안 되는 것을 볼 수 있었다고 했기 때문에, 식당의 손님은 아직 오십 명을 넘지 않았다.

28 ⓐ와 ②, ⑤: 명사적 용법, ① 형용사적 용법, ③, ④: 부사적 용법

29 소년과 그의 할머니를 가리킨다.

30 free: 무료의, 비용이 들지 않는

31 위 글은 '일기'이다. ② (신문·잡지의) 글, 기사, ③ 수필, ⑤ (책·연극·영화 등에 대한) 논평[비평], 감상문

32 ③ 오늘 소년은 할머니께 공짜 국밥 한 그릇을 대접하고 싶어 했다.

33 moved = touched: 감동받은

34 free: 무료의, 비용이 들지 않는

교과서 파헤치기

단어 TEST Step 1   p.02

01 여행객	02 돌봄, 보살핌	03 외국으로(에서)
04 흔들다; 파도	05 ~을 용서하다, 너그러이 봐주다	
06 여행	07 전통적인	08 경험; 경험하다
09 역사적인, 역사상 중요한		10 기둥
11 섬	12 구르다, 굴리다	13 수도
14 전망, 경치	15 환호하다, 갈채하다; 환호	
16 일하다; 작품	17 언어	18 독특한
19 경기, 시합; 어울리다		20 빛나다
21 조심하는, 주의 깊은		22 선호하다
23 도움이 되는	24 경기장	25 동작
26 천장	27 미끄러지다, 활주하다	
28 보라색	29 베트남어; 베트남의	
30 설계하다, 디자인하다		31 근처에
32 극장	33 음식, 접시	34 도마뱀
35 ~으로 가득 차다	36 ~의 맞은편에	37 ~로 유명하다
38 입어 보다	39 ~로 알려져 있다	
40 (시간, 날짜를) 미루다, 연기하다		41 걸어서
42 ~을 응원하다	43 ~로부터 멀리	

단어 TEST Step 2   p.03

01 shine	02 historic	03 experience
04 island	05 traditional	06 roll
07 care	08 slide	09 near
10 helpful	11 excuse	12 purple
13 tourist	14 careful	15 wave
16 tour	17 view	18 cheer
19 dish	20 match	21 capital
22 design	23 movement	24 ceiling
25 lizard	26 column	27 prefer
28 work	29 language	30 abroad
31 unique	32 theater	33 stop
34 Vietnamese	35 across from	36 be full of
37 on top of	38 cheer for	39 put off
40 far from	41 be known for	42 try on
43 be famous for		

단어 TEST Step 3   p.04

1 shine, 빛나다   2 abroad, 외국으로(에서)
3 slide, 미끄러지다, 활주하다   4 ceiling, 천장
5 purple, 보라색   6 capital, 수도   7 lizard, 도마뱀
8 Spanish, 스페인의   9 cheer, 환호하다, 갈채하다

10 Vietnamese, 베트남의   11 theater, 극장
12 view, 전망, 경치   13 curry, 카레   14 prefer, 선호하다
15 tour, 여행   16 excuse, ~을 용서하다, 너그러이 봐주다

대화문 TEST Step 1   p.05~06

Listen & Speak 1 A

1 Excuse, Is, near / far from / How can, get there / Go straight, turn left, on your right
2 need to buy, Where can, buy / buy them at / Where is it / Go straight, blocks, across from the library

Listen & Speak 1 B

1 Excuse me, Where is / Go straight two blocks, on your right
2 Where is / straight one block, It's on, It's across from

Listen & Talk 2 A

1 It's, Let's go, have, fresh fruit juice / good, How, get there / on foot or by bus, Which do you prefer / prefer
2 What is, called / type, traditional clothing / try one on / Which do you prefer, yellow one / purple one

Listen & Talk 2 B

1 Which do you prefer / prefer hamburgers
2 Which do you prefer, or / prefer paella

Conversation A

Welcome to, we'll visit, see, on your right, near, view from, amazing, every year

Conversation B

How may, help / want to enjoy, view of / best place to go to / great places, on top of, Which do, prefer / prefer / Me, too / get, by bus / Where, nearest stop / straight one block, turn right, on your left / can see, There is / I think, Why don't we go, visit, later / sounds

대화문 TEST Step 2   p.07~08

Listen & Speak 1 A

1 B: Excuse me. Is the Picasso Museum near here?
  G: Yes. It's not far from here.
  B: How can I get there?
  G: Go straight one block and turn left. It's on your right.
2 B: Sally, I need to buy some candies for Halloween. Where can I buy them?
  G: You can buy them at Wendy's Candy Shop.
  B: Where is it?
  G: Go straight two blocks and turn right. It's across from the library.

Listen & Speak 1 B

1 A: Excuse me. Where is the park?

B: Go straight two blocks and turn left. It's on your right.

2 A: Excuse me. Where is the school?

B: Go straight one block and turn left. It's on your right. It's across from the restaurant.

Listen & Talk 2 A

1 B: It's really hot here in Thailand. Let's go to the night market and have some fresh fruit juice.

G: Sounds good. How do we get there?

B: We can go on foot or by bus. Which do you prefer?

G: I prefer the bus.

2 G: What is this long dress called?

M: It is an Ao dai, a type of traditional clothing from Vietnam.

G: Can I try one on?

M: Sure. Which do you prefer, the purple one or the yellow one?

G: The purple one, please.

Listen & Talk 2 B

1 A: Which do you prefer, hamburgers or spaghetti?

B: I prefer hamburgers.

2 A: Which do you prefer, curry or paella?

B: I prefer paella.

Conversation A

M: Welcome to London City Tour. Today, we'll visit famous places in London. Can you see the London Eye? It's on your right. It's a Ferris wheel near the River Thames. The view from the London Eye is amazing. Many people visit it every year.

Conversation B

Staff: How may I help you?

Hana's mom: We want to enjoy a good view of London.

Hana: Where is the best place to go to?

Staff: We have two great places. The London Eye is a Ferris wheel and the sky Garden is a glass garden on top of a tall building. Which do you prefer?

Hana's mom: Hmm... I prefer the London Eye.

Hana: Me, too.

Staff: Good choice. You can get there by bus.

Hana's mom: Where is the nearest stop?

Staff: Go straight one block and turn right. It's on your left. Have a good trip!

Hana: Wow, I can see all of London. Look! There is a big clock.

Hana's mom: I think that's Big Ben. Why don't we go and visit it later?

Hana: That sounds great.

본문 TEST Step 1　　　　　　　p.09~10

01 Happy Days, by　　02 traveled to, this

03 loved by, of　　04 visited, interesting places

05 Our trip, in　　06 capital, famous for

07 went, watch, match

08 excited, world's most famous

09 full of, fans　　10 by singing, waving, shouting

11 After, toured, went

12 While, walked around

13 visited, museum, watched

14 in, dancing, with, movements　　15 For, ate

16 traditional, dish with　　17 tasted like, in

18 so, that, all　　19 took, tour of

20 Both, designed by

21 creative, like, colorful　　22 After, visited

23 Work, going on

24 impressed, its, unique

25 ceiling, shone like, with

26 columns stood like

27 feel, creativity, love, nature

28 Traveling, wonderful experience 29 While, a lot

30 visit, country again

본문 TEST Step 2　　　　　　　p.11~12

01 Happy Days, by

02 traveled to Spain

03 is loved by lots of

04 visited, interesting places

05 Our trip started in

06 capital, is famous for

07 to watch, soccer match

08 were excited because, the world's most famous soccer players

09 was full of

10 cheered by singing, waving, shouting, other fans

11 After, toured, went to

12 While, walked around, many historic buildings

13 visited, watched

14 in a red dress was dancing, with wonderful movements

15 For dinner, ate

16 traditional Spanish dish with, meat, seafood

17 tasted like fried rice

18 so, that, all enjoyed　　19 took a tour of

20 were designed by

21 creative works like, colorful lizard

22 After, visited　　23 Work on, is still going on

24 was impressed by its size

25 shone like, with bright stars

26 stone columns stood like

27 could feel, creativity, his love of nature

28 Traveling, a wonderful experience

29 While, a lot   30 to visit

30 나는 그 나라를 다시 방문하고 싶다.

본문 TEST Step 3   p.13~14

1 스페인에서의 행복한 날들 – 박진우

2 나의 가족은 이번 여름에 스페인을 여행했다.

3 스페인은 수많은 관광객들에게 사랑받는다.

4 우리는 여러 흥미로운 장소를 방문했다.

5 우리의 여행은 마드리드에서 시작했다.

6 마드리드는 수도이며 축구로 유명하다.

7 우리는 축구 경기를 보기 위해서 경기장으로 갔다.

8 나의 여동생과 나는 세계에서 가장 유명한 축구 선수 몇몇을 볼 수 있었기 때문에 신이 났다.

9 경기장은 축구 팬들로 가득 차 있었다.

10 우리는 경기를 보는 동안 노래를 부르고, 손을 흔들고, 다른 팬들과 함께 소리를 치며 응원을 했다.

11 마드리드를 여행하고 난 후, 우리는 세비야로 갔다.

12 우리는 도시를 걸어다니는 동안, 역사상 중요한 많은 건물들을 보았다.

13 우리는 플라멩코 박물관을 방문해서 플라멩코 춤을 보았다.

14 빨간 드레스를 입은 여자가 멋진 동작으로 플라멩코를 추고 있었다.

15 저녁 식사로 우리는 파에야를 먹었다.

16 그것은 쌀과 채소, 고기, 해산물이 들어간 전통적인 스페인 요리이다.

17 그것은 한국의 볶음밥과 같은 맛이 났다.

18 너무 맛있어서 우리 모두는 그것을 즐겼다.

19 바르셀로나에서 우리는 구엘 공원과 사그라다 파밀리아를 둘러보았다.

20 두 곳 모두 Antoni Gaudi에 의해 설계되었다.

21 구엘 공원에서 우리는 형형색색의 도마뱀과 같은 몇몇 Gaudi 의 창의적인 작품들을 보았다.

22 구엘 공원을 본 다음, 우리는 사그라다 파밀리아를 방문했다.

23 건물 공사는 1883년에 시작되었고 오늘날까지도 여전히 진행 중이다.

24 나는 건물의 크기와 독특한 디자인에 감명 받았다.

25 사그라다 파밀리아 안의 천장은 밝은 별이 있는 밤하늘처럼 빛났다.

26 돌기둥은 큰 나무처럼 서 있었다.

27 구엘 공원과 사그라다 파밀리아에서 나는 Gaudi의 창의성과 자연에 대한 사랑을 느낄 수 있었다.

28 스페인 여행은 훌륭한 경험이었다.

29 나는 그곳에서 스페인에 대해 많은 것을 배웠다.

본문 TEST Step 4 - Step 5   p.15~18

1 My Happy Days in Spain – by Park Jinwoo

2 My family traveled to Spain this summer.

3 Spain is loved by lots of tourists.

4 We visited many interesting places.

5 Our trip started in Madrid.

6 Madrid is the capital and is famous for soccer.

7 We went to a stadium to watch a soccer match.

8 My sister and I were excited because we could watch some of the world's most famous soccer players.

9 The stadium was full of soccer fans.

10 As we watched the match, we cheered by singing songs, waving our hands, and shouting with the other fans.

11 After we toured Madrid, we went to Seville.

12 While we walked around the city, we saw many historic buildings.

13 We visited a flamenco museum and watched a flamenco dance.

14 A woman in a red dress was dancing the flamenco with wonderful movements.

15 For dinner, we ate paella.

16 It is a traditional Spanish dish with rice, vegetables, meat, and seafood.

17 It tasted like fried rice in Korea.

18 It was so delicious that we all enjoyed it.

19 In Barcelona, we took a tour of Park Guell and Sagrada Familia.

20 Both were designed by Antoni Gaudi.

21 In Park Guell, we saw some of Gaudi's creative works like a colorful lizard.

22 After Park Guell, we visited Sagrada Familia.

23 Work on the building started in 1883 and is still going on today.

24 I was impressed by its size and unique design.

25 The ceiling inside Sagrada Familia shone like the night sky with bright stars.

26 Its stone columns stood like big trees.

27 At Park Guell and Sagrada Familia I could feel Gaudi's creativity and his love of nature.

28 Traveling in Spain was a wonderful experience.

29 While I was there, I learned a lot about Spain.

30 I want to visit the country again.

Enjoy Writing

1. How much, know about
2. capital of Vietnam, is spoken
3. are popular dishes
4. Every year lots of
5. is well known for
6. so beautiful that, should

Project Step 3

1. chose, for a trip
2. is loved by, who, to do
3. have great experiences at

Wrap Up

1. was moved by
2. title of the book
3. was written by
4. so, that, many times

Enjoy Writing

1. How much do you know about Vietnam?
2. The capital of Vietnam is Hanoi. Vietnamese is spoken there.
3. Pho and banh mi are popular dishes in Vietnam.
4. Every year lots of tourists visit Halong Bay and Nha Trang.
5. Halong Bay has 1,969 islands and Nha Trang is well known for its beautiful beaches.
6. Vietnam is so beautiful that you should come someday.

Project Step 3

1. My group chose Hong Kong for a trip.
2. Hong Kong is loved by many people who want to do fun activities.
3. We'll have great experiences at Mong Kok Market, Victoria Peak, and Ocean Park.

Wrap Up

1. I was moved by a book.
2. The title of the book is *The Old Man and the Sea*.
3. It was written by Ernest Hemingway.
4. The story was so great that I read it many times .

11 muddy, 진흙투성이인, 진흙의   12 reed, 갈대
13 tide, 조수, 밀물과 썰물   14 filter, ~을 여과하다, 거르다
15 flow, 흐르다   16 provide, 제공하다, 주다

단어 TEST Step 1 p.21

01 (꽃이) 피다	02 갈대	03 피해
04 인사하다	05 절벽	06 산소
07 평원	08 게	09 쓰레기
10 생물, 생명체	11 진실, 사실	12 제거하다
13 표면	14 환경	15 각종의, 다양한
16 나타나다	17 이유	18 줄이다
19 홍수	20 생산하다, 만들다	21 관대한
22 규칙적으로	23 보호하다	24 엉망진창
25 폐	26 얼룩	27 정보

28 먹이를 주다, 먹이다
29 진흙투성이인, 진흙의, 질퍽한   30 필요한
31 일어나다, 발생하다   32 제공하다, 주다
33 조수, 밀물과 썰물 34 놀라움, 경이; ~을 궁금해 하다
35 운동하다   36 ~와 같은   37 ~에 좋다, 유익하다
38 A뿐만 아니라 B도   39 그런데
40 다수의, 많은 수의 41 (옷 등을) 벗다, 벗기다
42 ~로 유명하다   43 생계를 유지하다

단어 TEST Step 2 p.22

01 cave	02 appear	03 damage
04 cliff	05 environment	06 remove
07 bloom	08 filter	09 various
10 surface	11 creature	12 flow
13 regularly	14 generous	15 reason
16 flood	17 trash	18 produce
19 protect	20 wonder	21 oxygen
22 feed	23 truth	24 stain
25 reduce	26 greet	27 lung
28 mess	29 reed	30 muddy
31 necessary	32 occur	33 provide
34 greatly	35 by the way	36 make a living
37 be famous for	38 such as	39 be good for
40 a large number of		41 work out
42 take off	43 not only A but also B	

단어 TEST Step 3 p.23

1 mud, 진흙   2 plain, 평원   3 appear, 나타나다
4 information, 정보   5 surface, 표면   6 cliff, 절벽
7 land, 육지, 땅   8 creature, 생물, 생명체
9 generous, 관대한   10 lung, 폐

대화문 TEST Step 1 p.24~25

Listen & Speak 1 A
1. wonder what you did during / took, trip / By, plains / flat land
2. Look at, beautiful / lake / wonder how, are different / a long body of fresh, Unlike, flows toward / got it

Listen & Speak 1 B
1. what a mountain is / high
2. I wonder what, plain / large, flat, land

Listen & Speak 2 A
1. how many oceans there are / isn't it / There are, cover most / How much, cover / heard, cover about, surface
2. heard, rain forest is called, lungs / Lungs / Because, produces, oxygen / a lot

Listen & Speak 2 B
1. want / heard, lakes
2. want to go to / are famous caves

Conversation A
what, plant, looks like, grass, In, turns, wet, heard, is famous for

Conversation B
amazing place / let's get on / Look at, wonder what they are / reeds, reed / taller than / Let, take, of / reed field / heard, the largest one / Look at, turning / beautiful

Communication Task Step 1
place / special about / is light blue

대화문 TEST Step 2 p.26~27

Listen & Speak 1 A
1. G: I wonder what you did during the summer vacation.
   B: I took a trip to Kenya and saw many animals on the plains.
   G: Wonderful! By the way, what are the plains?
   B: They are large areas of flat land.
   G: I see.
2. G: Look at that lake! It's really beautiful.
   B: It's not a lake. It's a river.
   G: Is it? I wonder how a river and a lake are different.

B: A river is a long body of fresh water. Unlike a lake, a river flows toward the ocean.

G: I got it.

Listen & Speak 1 B

1. A: I wonder what a mountain is.

B: It is a very high area of land.

2. A: I wonder what a plain is.

B: It is a large, flat area of land.

Listen & Speak 2 A

1. B: Do you know how many oceans there are on the Earth?

G: The answer is four, isn't it?

B: No. There are five oceans on the Earth. They cover most of the Earth.

G: How much of the Earth do they cover?

B: I heard the oceans cover about 70% of the Earth's surface.

2. G: I heard the Amazon rain forest is called the lungs of the Earth.

B: Lungs? Why?

G: Because it produces about 20% of the Earth's oxygen.

B: Wow! That's a lot.

Listen & Speak 2 B

1. A: I want to go to Jecheon.

B: Why?

A: I heard there are beautiful lakes in Jecheon.

2. A: I want to go to Danyang.

B: Why?

A: I heard there are famous caves in Danyang.

Conversation A

M: Guess what this is! It's not a tree. It is a plant that looks like tall grass. In fall, it turns yellow. It grows well in wet lands. I heard Suncheon Bay is famous for this plant.

Conversation B

Dad: Do you want to see an amazing place?

Karl & Sister: Sure!

Dad: Then let's get on the train.

Sister: Look at the yellow plants! I wonder what they are.

Dad: They are reeds. Suncheon Bay has beautiful reed fields.

Karl: Wow, the reeds are even taller than you, Dad.

Sister: They really are. Let me take a picture of you.

Karl: This reed field is very large.

Dad: Yes. I heard it is the largest one in Korea.

Karl: Look at the sky. It's turning red.

Sister: Yes, it's beautiful.

Communication Task Step 1

A: What place do you have?

B: I have Moraine Lake. It's in Canada.

A: What is special about the place?

B: The color of the water is light blue.

본문 TEST Step 1   p.28~29

01 Nature's Gift 02 areas, muddy, seaside

03 appear, with, tide

04 show up, tides, covered

05 creatures, in, ways

06 important, roles, mudflats

07 Let's, what, do

08 home, living, seaside

09 Not only, but also

10 provide, types, for   11 Also, eat, there

12 my, sweet home   13 good for, too

14 mudflat, make, living, nearby

15 Thanks to, fresh

16 fun activities, such as

17 large number, feed on

18 nature's gift, living   19 help, greatly

20 hold, reduce damage, floods

21 filter, from, into

22 remove things, before

23 Thanks, reaches, clean   24 work as, lungs

25 huge, oxygen, necessary

26 keep, healthy, clean

27 Mudflats, aren't they

28 gift, nature, living

29 reasons, necessary, protect

본문 TEST Step 2   p.30~31

01 Nature's Gift 02 muddy land

03 disappear with every tide

04 During, show up, high tides, are covered by

05 sea creatures, in many ways

06 to understand the roles of mudflats

07 Let's, what they do

08 are home to, living things

09 Not only, but also

10 provide, types of, for   11 Also

12 home sweet home

13 are good for, too

14 make a living, by catching, nearby

15 Thanks to, fresh seafood

16 fun activities, such as, on mudflats

17 a large number of, feed on

18 nature's gift

19 help, environment greatly

20 hold, reduce damage from floods

21 filter, flows from, into

22 remove bad things, enters

23 Thanks to, that reaches the sea

24 as the Earth's lungs

25 a huge volume of, necessary

26 keep me healthy, clean

27 aren't they

28 from nature to living things

29 to protect mudflats

1 갯벌, 자연의 선물

2 갯벌은 바닷가의 진흙이 있는 넓은 지역이다.

3 갯벌은 조수와 함께 나타나고 사라진다.

4 썰물일 때 갯벌이 드러나고, 밀물일 때 바다에 덮인다.

5 갯벌은 바다 생물과 사람, 지구를 많은 방면에서 돕는다.

6 갯벌의 역할을 이해하는 것이 중요하다.

7 갯벌이 무엇을 하는지 살펴보자.

8 갯벌은 바닷가에 있는 많은 생물들에게 집이다.

9 플랑크톤처럼 작은 생명체뿐만 아니라 게와 물고기도 그곳에 산다.

10 갯벌은 그들에게 다양한 종류의 먹이를 제공한다.

11 또한, 많은 새들도 그곳에서 먹이를 먹는다.

12 게: 갯벌은 나의 단란한 집이에요.

13 갯벌은 사람들에게도 유익하다.

14 갯벌 지역 인근에 사는 사람들은 근처에서 물고기와 다른 바다 동물들을 잡아 생계를 꾸린다.

15 갯벌 덕분에 사람들은 신선한 해산물을 얻을 수 있다.

16 사람들은 갯벌에서 진흙 미끄럼 타기나 보디 페인팅과 같은 즐거운 활동을 즐길 수 있다.

17 그들은 또한 그곳에서 바다 동물들을 먹는 수많은 새를 관찰할 수도 있다.

18 남자아이: 갯벌은 생명체에게 주는 자연의 선물이에요!

19 갯벌은 환경에 크게 도움이 된다.

20 갯벌은 많은 양의 물을 수용해서 홍수의 피해를 줄여 준다.

21 또한, 갯벌은 땅에서 바다로 흘러가는 물을 걸러내 준다.

22 물이 바다로 들어가기 전에 물속에 있는 나쁜 물질을 갯벌이 제거한다.

23 갯벌 덕분에 바다에 도착한 물은 깨끗하다.

24 갯벌은 지구의 폐 역할을 한다.

25 그것들은 지구상의 생명에게 필요한 많은 양의 산소를 생산한다.

26 지구: 갯벌은 나를 건강하고 깨끗하게 지켜 줘요.

27 갯벌은 멋진 곳이다, 그렇지 않은가?

28 그곳은 자연이 지구상의 생물들에게 준 선물이다.

29 이러한 이유로, 갯벌을 보호하는것은 필수이다.

1 Mudflats, Nature's Gift

2 Mudflats are large areas of muddy land at the seaside.

3 They appear and disappear with every tide.

4 During low tides, they show up, and during high tides, they are covered by the sea.

5 Mudflats help sea creatures, people, and the Earth in many ways.

6 It is important to understand the roles of mudflats.

7 Let's see what they do.

8 Mudflats are home to a lot of living things at the seaside.

9 Not only very small living things like plankton but also crabs and fish live there.

10 Mudflats provide various types of food for them.

11 Also, many birds eat food there.

12 Crab: Mudflats are my home sweet home.

13 Mudflats are good for people, too.

14 People who live near mudflat areas make a living by catching fish and other sea animals nearby.

15 Thanks to mudflats, people can get fresh seafood.

16 People can enjoy fun activities, such as mud sliding and body painting on mudflats.

17 They can also watch a large number of birds that feed on the sea animals there.

18 Boy: Mudflats are nature's gift to living things!

19 Mudflats help the environment greatly.

20 Mudflats hold a lot of water, so they can reduce damage from floods.

21 Also, mudflats filter water that flows from the land into the sea.

22 They remove bad things in the water before it enters the sea.

23 Thanks to mudflats, the water that reaches the sea is clean.

24 Mudflats work as the Earth's lungs.

25 They produce a huge volume of oxygen that is necessary for life on the Earth.

26 Earth: Mudflats keep me healthy and clean.

27 Mudflats are wonderful places, aren't they?

28 They are a gift from nature to living things on the Earth.

29 For all these reasons, it is necessary to protect mudflats.

구석구석지문 TEST Step 1 p.38

Enjoy Writing B

1. with few, little
2. Not only, but also, such as
3. during the day
4. it, to wear, to block

Enjoy Writing B

1. about Mudflats
2. muddy land, seaside
3. Not only, but also, such as
4. show up, are covered by
5. to wear, to protect yourself, can bite

Wrap Up 1

1. finished making, want to hear
2. wonder what you will do
3. going, go fishing , climb a mountain
4. Is, all
5. On, going to go swimming
6. a lot of

구석구석지문 TEST Step 2 p.39

Enjoy Writing B

1. Deserts are dry land with few plants and little water.
2. Not only plants like elephant trees but also animals such as lizards and desert snakes live there.
3. It is hot during the day and cold at night.
4. If you go to a desert, it is important to wear a hat to block the sun.

Enjoy Writing B

1. All about Mudflats
2. Mudflats are muddy land at the seaside.
3. Not only plants like *hamcho* but also animals such as crabs and fish live there.
4. They show up during low tides and are covered by the sea during high tides.
5. If you go to mudflats, it is important to wear long clothes to protect yourself from animals that can bite you.

Wrap Up 1

1. B: I just finished making a plan for my trip. Do you want to hear it?
2. G: Sure. I wonder what you will do.

3. B: On the first day, I'm going to go fishing on a lake. The next day, I'm going to climb a mountain.
4. G: Is that all?
5. B: No. On the last day, I'm going to go swimming.
6. G: Wow. You will do a lot of activities.

단어 TEST Step 1 p.40

01 팀 동료	02 완벽한	03 침착한
04 이루다, 달성하다	05 어려움, 곤경, 장애	
06 직면하다, 직시하다		07 상
08 무서운	09 실패하다, ~하지 못하다	
10 마침내	11 긍정적인	12 점잖은
13 야구의 루	14 인정하다, 알아보다	
15 문장	16 비록 ~일지라도	17 재활용하다
18 극복하다	19 얻다, 획득하다	20 우수, 탁월, 뛰어남
21 아픔, 고통	22 주다, 수여하다, 증정하다	
23 노력	24 예우하다, ~을 공경하다	
25 빌려주다	26 주요한	27 뛰어난
28 존경	29 풀다, 해결하다	30 무례하게
31 지지	32 재능이 있는	33 구, 구절
34 인종 차별	35 마음속으로 생각하다	
36 더 이상 ~ 아닌	37 1등을 하다, 우승하다	
38 ~을 거절하다, 거부하다, 소리를 줄이다	39 포기하다	
40 반복해서	41 A에게 B를 수여하다, 증정하다	
42 타석에서	43 눈을 의심하다(놀람)	

단어 TEST Step 2 p.41

01 achieve	02 calm	03 recognize
04 difficulty	05 perfect	06 earn
07 although	08 excellence	09 pain
10 award	11 excellent	12 positive
13 face	14 recycle	15 respect
16 honor	17 fail	18 solve
19 talented	20 support	21 finally
22 gentle	23 present	24 rudely
25 teammate	26 sentence	27 bat
28 effort	29 lend	30 major
31 overcome	32 terrible	33 stadium
34 base	35 give up	36 think to oneself
37 no longer	38 thanks to	39 over and over
40 win first place	41 turn down	
42 present A with B		43 take a class

단어 TEST Step 3 p.42

1 excellent, 뛰어난 2 teammate, 팀 동료

3 baseman, (1, 2, 3) 루수 4 fail, 실패하다, ~하지 못하다

5 rudely, 무례하게 6 classical, (음악이) 클래식의

7 pain, 아픔, 고통 8 lend, 빌려주다

9 major, 주요한 10 overcome, 극복하다

11 bat, (공을) 치다 12 positive, 긍정적인

13 recognize, 인정하다, 알아보다

14 award, 상 15 calm, 침착한 16 support, 지지

대화문 TEST Step 1 p.43~44

Listen & Speak 1 A

1. find, math problem / too hard, I'm not good at math / Let, see, It's important that, to solve, use

2. looks great / finish yours / draw, How, good at drawing / takes, important, as often as you can / mean, keep practicing / right

Listen & Speak 1 B

1. hard to be, What / important, never give up / not forget

2. hard to, should / It's important that / will not forget

Listen & Speak 2 A

1. hard to do / matter / how to make / What do you mean by / mean, easy to do

2. have, want to win first place / crossed / What do you mean by / means, wish, good luck

Listen & Speak 2 B

1. are better than / What, mean by / mean, together, than working alone

2. Practice, perfect / mean by / mean, by doing, over and over

Conversation A

To achieve, failed, However, give up, took, classes, Finally, achieved, that, never give up

Conversation B

look, wrong / don't think, achieve / What do you mean by that / fail auditions, have to give up / actor / famous / failed more than / should keep trying, practice / It's important that you never give up

대화문 TEST Step 2 p.45~46

Listen & Speak 1 A

1. G: Hey, Minho. Did you find the answer to the math problem?

   B: No. It's too hard for me. I'm not good at math.

   G: Let me see. It's important that you use this math rule to solve the problem.

   B: Oh, I see. I'll use it.

2. G: Your poster looks great.

B: Thanks, Kate. Did you finish yours?

G: Not yet. I can't draw well. How can I become good at drawing?

B: It takes time. It's important that you draw as often as you can.

G: You mean I should keep practicing?

B: That's right.

Listen & Speak 1 B

1. A: It's hard to be a good dancer. What should I do?

B: It's important that you never give up.

A: Okay. I will not forget that.

2. A: It's hard to write a good story. What should I do?

B: It's important that you read many books.

A: Okay. I will not forget that.

Listen & Speak 2 A

1. G: Oh, this is hard to do.

B: What's the matter?

G: Can you teach me how to make cookies?

B: Sure. It's a walk in the park.

G: What do you mean by that?

B: I mean it's easy to do.

2. B: I have a singing contest tomorrow. I really want to win first place.

G: I'll keep my fingers crossed for you.

B: What do you mean by "keep my fingers crossed"?

G: It means I wish you good luck.

B: Thank you.

Listen & Speak 2 B

1. A: Two heads are better than one.

B: What do you mean by "Two heads are better than one"?

A: I mean working together is better than working alone.

2. A: Practice makes perfect.

B: What do you mean by "Practice makes perfect"?

A: I mean you learn something by doing it over and over.

Conversation A

M: To achieve my dream, I went to many auditions, but I often failed. However, I never gave up. I took acting and dancing classes. Finally, I achieved my goal. It's important that you never give up.

Conversation B

Hana: You look sad, Jiho. What's wrong?

Jiho: I don't think I can achieve my dream.

Amy: What do you mean by that?

Jiho: I want to be an actor, but I always fail auditions.

Maybe I have to give up.

Amy: Do you know this actor?

Jiho: Sure. He's a famous movie star.

Amy: He failed more than 100 auditions.

Jiho: Really? Maybe I should keep trying. I will practice more for my next audition.

Hana: That's right! It's important that you never give up.

본문 TEST Step 1 p.47~48

01 Breaks, Color Line 02 It, on April

03 went on, as, for

04 couldn't believe, eyes

05 first, American, player on

06 color line, broken

07 faced many difficulties

08 Although, talented, gentle, with

09 Every, turned, down because

10 bat, rudely, at

11 thought, himself, keep, focus

12 try, become, like

13 there, be more, league

14 put, energy into

15 With practice, batting, running

16 effort moved, teammates

17 one, up, tapped, on 18 Do, listen to

19 doing fine

20 support helped, to, harder

21 Finally, earned, respect, other

22 Thanks to, won, in

23 recognized, presented, with, same

24 other, asked, to join

25 uniform number

26 no longer, to honor

27 however, every, wears, wore 28 is called

본문 TEST Step 2 p.49~50

01 Breaks the Color Line

02 on April 15, 1947

03 African American, as, for

04 couldn't believe their eyes

05 the first African American player

06 the color line was broken

07 faced many difficulties

08 Although, talented player, to play with him

09 turned the team down

55

10 was at bat, rudely shouted at

11 thought to himself, keep calm, focus on

12 become, who people like

13 there will be more

14 put, into

15 With practice, at batting, base running

16 effort moved, teammates

17 shouted at, one of his teammates, up to, tapped him on the shoulder

18 Do not listen to   19 doing fine

20 helped, to play harder

21 earned the respect

22 Thanks to, won

23 recognized, presented, with, same year

24 other, asked, to join

25 uniform number

26 no longer wear, to honor him

27 Every, however, wears, wore   28 is called

---

1 Jackie Robinson 인종 차별을 깨다

2 1947년 4월 15일 뉴욕시에서였다.

3 아프리카계 미국인 Jackie Robinson은 브루클린 다저스의 2루수로 경기장에 나갔다.

4 사람들은 자신들의 눈을 의심했다.

5 그는 메이저리그 팀에서 경기한 최초의 아프리카계 미국인 선수였다.

6 그날 인종 차별이 깨졌다.

7 Robinson은 많은 어려움에 직면했다.

8 Robinson은 재능 있는 선수이고 온화한 사람이었지만 그의 팀원들은 그와 함께 경기하기를 원하지 않았다.

9 Robinson이 팀에 있었기 때문에 모든 호텔에서 그 팀을 거절했다.

10 그가 타석에 있을 때, 관중석에 있는 사람들이 그에게 무례하게 소리치기도 했다.

11 Robinson은 마음속으로 생각했다. '나는 평정심을 유지하고 야구에 집중해야 해.

12 나는 노력해서 사람들이 좋아하는 선수가 될 거야.

13 그러면 다음 시즌에는 아프리카계 미국인 선수가 리그에 더 많이 생길 거야.'

14 Robinson은 자신의 모든 시간과 에너지를 야구에 집중했다.

15 연습을 함으로써 그는 타격과 주루를 잘하게 되었다.

16 Robinson의 노력은 그의 팀원들을 감동시켰다.

17 사람들이 Robinson에게 소리쳤을 때, 그의 팀 동료 중 한 명이 Robinson에게 다가가 어깨를 두드렸다.

18 "그들 말을 듣지 마.

---

19 너는 잘하고 있어."라고 그가 말했다.

20 그의 지지는 Robinson이 더 열심히 경기하는 데 도움이 됐다.

21 마침내, Robinson은 다른 선수들과 팬들의 존경을 받았다.

22 Robinson 덕분에 다저스는 1947년에 내셔널리그 챔피언십에서 우승하게 되었다.

23 리그에서는 Robinson의 탁월함을 인정했고, 같은 해에 그에게 신인상을 수여했다.

24 그 시즌 이후, 다른 팀들은 아프리카계 미국인 선수들에게 자신들의 팀에 합류할 것을 요청했다.

25 Robinson의 등 번호는 42번이었다.

26 메이저리그 팀의 야구 선수들은 그에 대한 존경을 보여 주기 위해 더 이상 42번을 달지 않는다.

27 하지만 매년 4월 15일, 모든 선수들은 Robinson이 달았던 번호를 단다.

28 이 날을 '재키 로빈슨 데이'라고 부른다.

---

1 Jackie Robinson Breaks the Color Line

2 It was New York City on April 15, 1947.

3 Jackie Robinson, an African American, went on the field as second baseman for the Brooklyn Dodgers.

4 People couldn't believe their eyes.

5 He was the first African American player to play on a Major League team.

6 That day, the color line was broken.

7 Robinson faced many difficulties.

8 Although Robinson was a talented player and a gentle person, his teammates did not want to play with him.

9 Every hotel turned the team down because Robinson was on the team.

10 When he was at bat, people in the stands rudely shouted at him.

11 Robinson thought to himself, 'I need to keep calm and focus on baseball.

12 I will try and become a player who people like.

13 Then, next season, there will be more African American players in the league.'

14 Robinson put all his time and energy into baseball.

15 With practice, he became great at batting and base running.

16 Robinson's effort moved his teammates.

17 When people shouted at Robinson, one of his

teammates walked up to Robinson and tapped him on the shoulder.

18 "Do not listen to them.

19 You're doing fine," he said.

20 His support helped Robinson to play harder.

21 Finally, Robinson earned the respect of other players and fans.

22 Thanks to Robinson, the Dodgers won the National League Championship in 1947.

23 The league recognized Robinson's excellence and presented him with the Rookie of the Year Award in the same year.

24 After that season, other teams asked African American players to join them.

25 Robinson's uniform number was 42.

26 Baseball players in Major League teams no longer wear the number 42 to honor him.

27 Every year, however, on April 15, every player wears the number that Robinson wore.

28 The day is called "Jackie Robinson Day."

2. France was the first country which I visited.

3. Mary is the girl who I met in Paris.

4. The blue watch is the gift which I bought there for my brother.

Enjoy Writing B

1. How I Will Achieve My Dream

2. I want to be a designer.

3. There are three things that I need to do to achieve my dream.

4. I need to be healthy, be creative, and never give up.

5. Being healthy will help me keep going for my dream.

6. Being creative will help me do something different.

7. Plus, I will always tell myself never to give up because it will make me try harder.

Wrap Up 2

1. B: It's difficult to learn English.

2. G: Rome was not built in a day.

3. B: What do you mean by that?

4. G: I mean it takes time to achieve something.

5. B: I see .

구석구석지문 TEST Step 1 p.57

Language in Use

1. last year

2. the first country which, visited

3. who, met

4. gift which I bought, for

Enjoy Writing B

1. How, Achieve

2. want to be

3. that, need to, to achieve

4. healthy, creative, give up

5. Being, help, keep going

6. help me do

7. myself, to give up, make me try

Wrap Up 2

1. It's, to learn

2. was not built

3. What, mean by

4. takes, to achieve something

5. see

구석구석지문 TEST Step 2 p.58

Language in Use

1. I visited three countries last year.

9 decorate, 장식하다, 꾸미다   10 app, 애플리케이션
11 virtual, 가상의   12 station, 역, 정류장
13 advance, 발전   14 drone, (원격 조종의) 드론
15 law, 법칙, 법   16 charge, (지불, 대금 등을) 청구하다

단어 TEST Step 1　　　　　　　　p.59

01 계산대	02 자동적으로	03 상태, 조건
04 가격	05 ~을 추천하다	06 장식하다, 꾸미다
07 약	08 재료	09 사회
10 구조하다	11 과학 기술, 생산 기술	
12 (치수·모양 등이) 꼭 맞다		13 발전
14 온도	15 경험	
16 (지불, 대금 등을) 청구하다		
17 화려한, 공들인, 고급의		18 낮추다
19 기술	20 구입(품)	21 거대한
22 나중에, 후에	23 가상의	24 차이, 차이점
25 심하게, 아주 많이	26 법칙, 법	27 ~ 이후로
28 중력	29 배달하다	30 (돈을) 지불하다
31 방법, 방식	32 작동하다	33 환자
34 진짜의	35 ~할 것을 잊다	36 공중에
37 ~을 돌보다	38 ~할 준비가 되다	39 입다, 쓰다, 신다
40 돌아다니다	41 일어나다, 개최되다	
42 미래에	43 ~하고 싶다	

단어 TEST Step 2　　　　　　　　p.60

01 heavily	02 automatically	03 charge
04 librarian	05 condition	06 work
07 experience	08 save	09 advance
10 fit	11 gravity	12 huge
13 since	14 price	15 deliver
16 decorate	17 lower	18 rescue
19 skill	20 temperature	21 recommend
22 medicine	23 patient	24 difference
25 virtual	26 purchase	27 method
28 society	29 taste	30 material
31 offer	32 guess	33 pay
34 technology	35 take place	36 be ready for
37 put on	38 add up	39 take care of
40 don't have to 동사원형		41 move around
42 be worried about		43 in trouble

단어 TEST Step 3　　　　　　　　p.61

1 medicine, 약　2 rescue, 구조하다
3 automatically, 자동적으로　4 patient, 환자
5 material, 재료　6 recommend, ~을 추천하다
7 method, 방법, 방식　8 deliver, 배달하다

대화문 TEST Step 1　　　　　　　　p.62~63

Listen & Speak 1 A
1. forgot to turn off / need to return / turn, off / surprised that, off, with
2. Welcome to, like to visit / put, on / right, looks / isn't it / I'm surprised

Listen & Speak 1 B
1. there, surprises / surprised, walk
2. there anything, that surprises / I'm surprised that, itself automatically

Listen & Speak 2 A
1. help / looking for, show me one / Look at, for / Sounds / search for, by talking / will take
2. don't have to use, turn, on, off / tell, how to / on, out / on, simple

Listen & Speak 2 B
1. play, play . Sure
2. messy, clean
3. to go out, walk

Conversation A
work like, travel without, simple, by talking to, I'm surprised that, already living

Conversation B
are, books / Where can, gravity / librarian / looking for, gravity, recommend / fifty seven books / that you can recommend books / amazing / on, third floor

대화문 TEST Step 2　　　　　　　　p.64~65

Listen & Speak 1 A
1. G: Oh, I forgot to turn off the heater before I left home.
   B: Really? Then do you need to return home?
   G: No. I can turn it off with my smartphone.
   B: Wow, I'm surprised that you can turn off the heater with your smartphone.
2. W: Welcome to VR World. Would you like to visit Niagara Falls?
   B: Sure.
   W: Okay, put this on.

B: All right. Wow, it looks so real.

W: It is huge, isn't it?

B: Yes, and I'm surprised that I feel water on my face.

Listen & Speak 1 B

1. A: Is there anything in these pictures that surprises you?

   B: Yes. I'm surprised that this drone can walk a dog.

2. A: Is there anything in these pictures that surprises you?

   B: Yes. I'm surprised that this car can drive itself automatically.

Listen & Speak 2 A

1. W: May I help you?

   B: Hi, I'm looking for a smart watch. Can you show me one?

   W: Sure. Look at this one. It can play music for you.

   B: Sounds cool.

   W: Also, you can search for anything just by talking to it.

   B: That's great. I will take it.

2. M: Welcome. This is our new smart light. You don't have to use your hands to turn it on and off.

   W: Really? Then can you tell me how to do it?

   M: Just say, "Light on!" or "Light out!"

   W: Light on or light out? That's very simple.

Listen & Speak 2 B

1. A: I want to play go. Can you play go with me, please?

   B: Sure.

2. A: My room is messy. Can you clean it, please?

   B: Sure.

3. A: The dog wants to go out. Can you walk the dog, please?

   B: Sure.

Conversation A

M: These days, many things can work like humans. Some cars can travel without a human driver. We can make smartphones do simple work only by talking to them. I'm surprised that we're already living in the future.

Conversation B

Amy: Wow, there are so many books in this library.

Hana: You're right. Where can we find books about gravity?

Terry: Hi, I'm Terry, the AI librarian. Can I help you?

Amy: Hi. We're looking for books about gravity. Can you recommend one, please?

Terry: We have fifty seven books about gravity in this library. I think *The Law of Gravity* will be the best one for you.

Hana: I'm surprised that you can recommend books.

Amy: Right. That's amazing. Where is the book, Terry?

Terry: It's on the third floor. Come with me.

본문 TEST Step 1   p.66~67

01 Changing Society

02 Advances, caused, so far

03 future, make, changes

04 what, like, near

05 Shopping Center   06 much easier

07 There, lines, counters

08 enters, with, special, app

09 shop, takes, items

10 items, automatically added, virtual

11 puts, back, automatically removed

12 shopping, need, line, pay

13 adds up, charge, later   14 Isn't, fancy

15 Printed House, Clothes

16 lives, 3D printed

17 Building, cheaper, with, methods

18 looks fantastic, unique

19 produce, shapes, traditional, materials

20 also, clothes, by using

21 choose, fit, suit, tastes

22 fashion designer   23 in, Hospital

24 visiting, grandfather, hospital

25 AI nurse enters

26 moves around, checks, conditions

27 high temperature, medicine, lower

28 Have, thought, changes

29 take place, others, near

30 imagine other changes

31 Take, think about

본문 TEST Step 2   p.68~69

01 Changing

02 Advances, technology have caused, changes, so far

03 In the future, make more changes

04 Let's, may be like, near

05 Shopping Center

59

06 much easier　07 no lines, no counters

08 with, special shopping app

09 takes the items

10 are automatically added to, virtual

11 puts, back, is automatically removed from, list of purchases

12 shopping, does not need to, in line

13 adds up, prices, charge, later

14 Isn't, fancy　15 3D Printed, Clothes

16 lives, 3D printed

17 Building, faster and cheaper, with traditional methods

18 looks fantastic

19 house shapes, traditional building methods and materials

20 her clothes, by using

21 that fit, suit, tastes

22 fashion designer　23 in the Hospital

24 is visiting　25 An AI, enters

26 moves around, checks, conditions

27 high temperature, to lower his temperature

28 Have you ever thought

29 take place, others, in the near future

30 imagine other changes

31 Take some time to think

14 정말 멋지지 않은가?

15 수민이의 3D 프린터로 만든 집과 옷

16 수민이는 3D 프린터로 만든 집에 산다.

17 3D 프린터로 집을 짓는 것은 전통적인 방법으로 집을 짓는 것보다 더 빠르고 저렴하다.

18 수민이의 집은 독특한 디자인 때문에 멋져 보인다.

19 3D 프린터는 사람들이 전통 건축 방법과 재료들로 만들 수 없는 집 모양을 만들어 낼 수 있다.

20 수민이는 또한 집에서 3D 프린터를 사용해 옷을 만드는 것을 좋아한다.

21 그녀는 색깔과 재료를 고를 수 있고 자신의 몸과 취향에 맞는 옷을 디자인할 수 있다.

22 수민이는 이제 패션 디자이너이다!

23 병원에 있는 동민

24 동민이는 병원에 계시는 그의 할아버지를 방문하고 있다.

25 AI 간호사가 병실로 들어온다.

26 그것은 병실을 돌아다니고, 환자들의 상태를 확인한다.

27 AI 간호사가 동민이 할아버지가 열이 높다는 것을 알았을 때 그것은 그의 체온을 낮추기 위해 그에게 약을 준다.

28 여러분은 이러한 변화에 대해 생각해 본 적 있는가?

29 어떤 변화는 이미 일어나기 시작했고 반면 다른 것들은 가까운 미래에 일어날지도 모른다.

30 여러분은 다른 변화들을 상상할 수 있는가?

31 그것들에 대해 잠깐 생각해 보자.

1 변화하는 사회

2 과학과 기술의 발전은 지금까지 우리의 삶에 많은 변화를 초래해 왔다.

3 미래에 과학 기술은 더 많은 변화를 만들 것이다.

4 가까운 미래에 우리의 삶이 어떻게 될지 살펴보자.

5 쇼핑 센터에 있는 상호

6 쇼핑이 훨씬 쉽다.

7 줄도 없고 계산대도 없다.

8 상호는 특별한 쇼핑 앱이 있는 스마트폰을 가지고 가게로 들어간다.

9 가게에서 그는 그가 원하는 물건들을 집는다.

10 그 물건들은 자동으로 그의 스마트폰에 있는 가상 카드에 더해진다.

11 만약 상호가 물건을 되돌려 놓으면 그것은 자동으로 그의 구매 목록에서 제거된다.

12 쇼핑을 끝냈을 때 상호는 돈을 지불하기 위해 줄을 설 필요가 없다.

13 그의 가상 카드가 모든 가격을 더해서 나중에 그에게 청구할 것이다.

1 Changing Society

2 Advances in science and technology have caused many changes in our lives so far.

3 In the future, science and technology will make more changes.

4 Let's see what our lives may be like in the near future.

5 Sangho in the Shopping Center

6 Shopping is much easier.

7 There are no lines and no counters.

8 Sangho enters a shop with his smartphone which has a special shopping app.

9 In the shop, he takes the items he wants.

10 The items are automatically added to a virtual card on his smartphone.

11 If Sangho puts an item back, it is automatically removed from his list of purchases.

12 When he finishes shopping, Sangho does not need to wait in line to pay.

13 His virtual card adds up all the prices and will charge him later.

14 Isn't that fancy?

15 Sumin's 3D Printed House and Clothes

16 Sumin lives in a 3D printed house.

17 Building a 3D printed house is faster and cheaper than building a house with traditional methods.

18 Sumin's house looks fantastic because of its unique design.

19 A 3D printer can produce house shapes that people cannot make with traditional building methods and materials.

20 Sumin also likes to make her clothes at home by using a 3D printer.

21 She can choose colors and materials and can design clothes that fit her body and suit her tastes.

22 Sumin is now a fashion designer!

23 Dongmin in the Hospital

24 Dongmin is visiting his grandfather in the hospital.

25 An AI nurse enters the room.

26 It moves around the room and checks the patients' conditions.

27 When the AI nurse finds that Dongmin's grandfather has a high temperature, it gives him some medicine to lower his temperature.

28 Have you ever thought about these changes?

29 Some changes have already started to take place while others may start in the near future.

30 Can you imagine other changes?

31 Take some time to think about them.

4. show me one

5. shows you a map, pictures of streets

6. thanks

구석구석지문 TEST Step 2 p.77

Enjoy Writing B

1. Schools in 20 Years

2. Have you ever thought of how schools may change over the next 20 years?

3. Students may learn drone design.

4. Cleaning drones may help students at school.

5. There may be an AI teachers' room in every school.

6. Students may go to school only two or three times a week.

Project

1. Have you ever imagined life in the future?

2. People may use personal drones in their daily lives.

3. So there may be traffic lights for drones in the sky.

4. A lot of AI helpers may be created soon and they may help humans in lots of ways.

Wrap Up 1

1. G: Are you ready for your trip to London?

2. B: Yes, but I'm worried about getting lost. I'm not good at finding places.

3. G: Don't worry. There are many good smartphone apps you can use.

4. B: Can you show me one?

5. G: Sure. Use this one. It shows you a map of the city and pictures of streets.

6. B: Oh, thanks.

구석구석지문 TEST Step 1 p.76

Enjoy Writing B

1. in, Years

2. Have, thought, how schools may change

3. may learn

4. Cleaning, may help

5. There may be, in every school

6. may go, two or three times

Project

1. Have, imagined, in the future

2. may, in their daily lives

3. may be traffic lights

4. A lot of, may be created, in lots of ways

Wrap Up 1

1. Are, ready for

2. worried about getting lost, good at finding

3. Don't, There are, apps you can use

단어 TEST Step 1 p.78

01 단 하나의, 단일의 02 휴식, (학교의) 쉬는 시간
03 (가볍게) 톡톡 두드리다, 치다　　04 의자
05 생산자, 제작자　06 주인, 소유주
07 (무엇을 할) 차례, 순번
08 (부정문, 의문문에서) 아직
09 수를 세다, 계산하다
10 (음식, 음료 등을) 주문하다　　11 연세가 드신
12 손자　　13 (음식을) 씹다　14 만일 ~라면
15 ~도, ~조차　16 (지금 등을) 모으다
17 식사　　18 손님, 고객　　19 소설
20 침실　　21 참가자, 선수, 배우 22 계산대
23 대접하다, 다루다 24 (우묵한) 그릇, 통　25 ~해야 한다
26 막 ~하려는 참이다
27 A에게 B를 대접하다
28 빨리 ~하고 싶다, ~하는 것이 기다려지다
29 들어올리다, 집다, ~을 (차에) 태우러 가다
30 혼잣말을 하다　　31 (목적어)가 ~하는 것을 돕다
32 ~을 생각해 내다

단어 TEST Step 2 p.79

01 bedroom　02 counter　03 producer
04 chew　05 tap　06 turn
07 yet　08 order　09 player
10 chair　11 treat　12 elderly
13 count　14 bowl　15 raise
16 owner　17 break　18 grandson
19 if　20 meal　21 customer
22 novel　23 even　24 single
25 think up　26 have to 동사원형
27 pick up　28 treat A(사람) to B(사물)
29 help+목적어+동사원형
30 can't wait to 동사원형　31 be about to
32 say to oneself

단어 TEST Step 3 p.80

1 owner, 주인　2 single, 단 하나의　3 grandson, 손자
4 bedroom, 침실　5 novel, 소설　6 customer, 손님, 고객
7 treat, 대접하다　8 chew, (음식을) 씹다　9 meal, 식사
10 counter, 계산대　11 think up, ~을 생각해 내다
12 chair, 의자

본문 TEST Step 1 p.81~82

01 100th Customer　02 elderly, walked into
03 with her grandson　04 Quietly, asked, owner
05 How much, bowl　06 answered with, smile
07 poor, pay, bowls
08 ordered, single, grandson
09 sure, hungry, as, ate　10 No, hungry
11 Don't worry
12 picked up, chewed on
13 eat, feeling, over　14 thought up, free meal
15 about, pay, waved, need
16 pay if, 100th customer
17 woman, thanked, left
18 month later, saw, outside
19 was gathering stones
20 What, doing, asked
21 counting, number, who enter
22 Today is, grandma's
23 treat, to, bowl, himself
24 looked down　25 number, was, even
26 had, to help, gather　27 went back into, called
28 bring everyone, works with
29 There, needs, help
30 to arrive at　31 arrived, heard, turn
32 welcomed, served, free bowl
33 sure, hungry, asked
34 chewed loudly, with, smile
35 Don't worry, me

본문 TEST Step 2 p.83~84

01 100th Customer　02 elderly, walked into
03 with her grandson
04 Quietly, asked, the owner
05 How much, a bowl of　06 with a smile
07 too poor to pay
08 single, for her grandson 09 Are you sure, ate
10 No, not hungry　11 Don't worry about
12 chewed on, happily
13 watched, eat, came over
14 thought up, to give the boy a free meal
15 was about to pay, waved
16 pay, the 100th customer 17 thanked Mr. Kang
18 A month later, saw, outside
19 was gathering stones
20 What, doing　21 counting, who
22 Today is　23 treat, said to himself
24 looked down

25 the number, was, even fifty

26 to help

27 went back into, called

28 bring everyone who works with

29 who needs your help

30 began to arrive at   31 It's our turn

32 welcomed them, served, a free bowl of Gukbap

33 Are you sure

34 chewed loudly, with a smile

35 Don't worry

---

1 백 번째 손님

2 어느 날 한 할머니가 식당으로 걸어 들어왔다.

3 그녀는 손자와 함께 있었다.

4 그녀는 조용히 식당 주인인 강 씨에게 물었다.

5 "국밥 한 그릇이 얼마인가요?"

6 "4,000원입니다, 할머니." 강 씨는 미소 지으며 답했다.

7 그녀는 너무 가난해서 두 그릇 값을 지불할 수 없었다.

8 그녀는 손자를 위해 한 그릇을 주문했다.

9 "정말 배고프지 않으세요, 할머니?" 남자아이는 따뜻한 국물을 먹으며 물었다.

10 "응, 난 배고프지 않단다.

11 내 걱정하지 마라."

12 그녀는 행복하게 김치를 집어서 먹었다.

13 강 씨는 그들이 먹는 것을 지켜보았고, 따뜻한 감정이 밀려왔다.

14 그는 남자아이에게 무료로 식사를 주기 위해 계획을 생각해 냈다.

15 할머니가 돈을 내려고 할 때, 강 씨는 손을 흔들며 말했다. "필요 없습니다, 할머니.

16 저희 식당에서는 그 날의 백 번째 손님이 되면 돈을 내지 않아도 됩니다."

17 할머니와 손자는 강 씨에게 감사해 하며 떠났다.

18 한 달 후, 강 씨는 식당 밖 거리에서 그 남자아이를 보았다.

19 그 남자아이는 돌멩이를 모으고 있었다.

20 "너 뭐 하고 있니?" 강 씨가 물었다.

21 "저는 아저씨 식당에 들어가는 손님들의 수를 세고 있어요.

22 오늘이 우리 할머니 생신이거든요."

23 '저 아이는 백 번째 손님이 되어서 할머니께 공짜 국밥 한 그릇을 대접하고 싶어 하는구나.' 강 씨는 혼잣말을 했다.

24 강 씨는 아래를 내려다보았다.

25 그는 돌멩이의 개수가 아직 오십 개도 안 되는 것을 볼 수 있었다.

26 그는 남자아이가 돌멩이 백 개를 모으는 것을 돕기 위해 무언가를 해야 했다.

---

27 강 씨는 식당으로 되돌아가 그의 친구들에게 전화했다.

28 "지금 내 식당으로 오고, 자네와 함께 일하는 모든 사람들을 데려와 주게.

29 자네 도움이 필요한 남자아이가 있어."

30 사람들이 식당에 도착하기 시작했다.

31 아흔아홉 번째 손님이 도착했을 때 강 씨는 남자아이가 "우리 차례예요, 할머니."라고 말하는 것을 들었다.

32 강 씨는 그들을 반기며 할머니께 공짜 국밥 한 그릇을 제공했다.

33 "너 정말 배고프지 않니?" 할머니가 남자아이에게 물었다.

34 남자아이는 큰 소리로 김치를 씹고 미소 지으며 말했다. "네, 전 배고프지 않아요, 할머니.

35 제 걱정 마세요. 생신 축하드려요!"

---

1 The 100th Customer

2 One day, an elderly woman walked into a restaurant.

3 She was with her grandson.

4 Quietly, the woman asked Mr. Kang, the owner of the restaurant.

5 "How much is a bowl of Gukbap?"

6 "It's 4,000 won, ma'am," Mr. Kang answered with a smile.

7 She was too poor to pay for two bowls.

8 She ordered a single bowl for her grandson.

9 "Are you sure you are not hungry, Grandma?" the boy asked, as he ate the hot soup.

10 "No, I'm not hungry.

11 Don't worry about me."

12 She picked up some Gimchi and chewed on it happily.

13 Mr. Kang watched them eat, and a warm feeling came over him.

14 He thought up a plan to give the boy a free meal.

15 When the woman was about to pay, Mr. Kang waved his hands and said, "No need, ma'am.

16 In my restaurant, you don't pay if you're the 100th customer of the day."

17 The woman and her grandson thanked Mr. Kang and left.

18 A month later, Mr. Kang saw the boy in the street outside the restaurant.

19 The boy was gathering stones.

20 "What are you doing?" asked Mr. Kang.

21 "I'm counting the number of customers who enter your restaurant.

22 Today is my grandma's birthday."

23 'He wants to be the 100th customer and treat his grandmother to a bowl of Gukbap!' Mr. Kang said to himself.

24 Mr. Kang looked down.

25 He could see that the number of stones was not yet even fifty.

26 He had to do something to help the boy gather 100 stones.

27 Mr. Kang went back into the restaurant and called his friends.

28 "Come to my restaurant now and bring everyone who works with you.

29 There is a boy who needs your help."

30 People began to arrive at the restaurant.

31 When the 99th customer arrived, Mr. Kang heard the boy say, "It's our turn, Grandma."

32 Mr. Kang welcomed them and served the woman a free bowl of Gukbap.

33 "Are you sure you're not hungry?" the woman asked the boy.

34 The boy chewed loudly on some Gimchi and said with a smile, "No, I'm not hungry, Grandma.

35 Don't worry about me. Happy birthday!"

적중 100 + 특별부록

Plan B

우리학교 최신기출

시사 · 박준언 교과서를 배우는

학교 시험문제 분석 · 모음 · 해설집

전국단위 학교 시험문제 수집 및 분석
출제 빈도가 높은 문제 위주로 선별
문제 풀이에 필요한 상세한 해설

중2-2
영어

시사 · 박준언

적중 **100** + 특별부록

Plan B

우리학교
최신기출

중2-2
영어

시사 · 박준언

◎ 선택형 문항의 답안은 컴퓨터용 수정 싸인펜을 사용하여 OMR 답안지에 바르게 표기하시오.
◎ 서술형 문제는 답을 답안지에 반드시 검정 볼펜으로 쓰시오.
◎ 총 30문항 100점 만점입니다. 문항별 배점은 각 문항에 표시되어 있습니다.

[대전 ○○중]

01 다음 중 단어의 뜻이 <u>어색한</u> 것은?　　(3점)

① cheer – 응원하다
② movement – 움직임
③ creativity – 창의성
④ impress – 깊은 인상을 받은
⑤ historic – 역사적으로 중요한

[경기 ○○중]

02 다음 빈칸에 들어갈 말로 가장 적절한 것은?　　(3점)

When we take a _____, we go through a place (such as a building or city) in order to see and learn about the different parts of it.

① tour
② walk
③ class
④ shower
⑤ picture

[부산 ○○중]

03 다음 (A)~(C)에 들어갈 알맞은 단어를 바르게 나열한 것은?
　　(3점)

· We need to (A)_____ a closer look at that tree.
· The noise (B)_____ on 24 hours a day.
· Be (C)_____ when you drive on icy roads.

	(A)	(B)	(C)
①	have	tries	careless
②	take	goes	careful
③	make	goes	care
④	take	goes	careless
⑤	make	tries	careful

[서울 강남구 ○○중]

04 다음 단어의 영영 풀이가 올바른 것을 <u>모두</u> 고르면?　　(3점)

ⓐ plain: a large, flat area of land
ⓑ mountain: a very low area of land
ⓒ lake: a large area of water that is surrounded by land
ⓓ forest: land that is covered by plants and trees
ⓔ desert: land with many plants and enough water

① ⓐ, ⓑ, ⓒ
② ⓐ, ⓒ, ⓓ
③ ⓐ, ⓒ, ⓔ
④ ⓑ, ⓒ, ⓓ
⑤ ⓒ, ⓓ, ⓔ

05 다음 문장을 수동태로 바르게 고친 것은? (3점)

My grandma made this chair.

① This chair is made my grandma.

② This chair is made by my grandma.

③ This chair was made by my grandma.

④ This chair were made by my grandma.

⑤ This chair will be made by my grandma.

07 다음 문장을 수동태 문장으로 전환하시오. (4점)

He washes his car every day.

→ _____ every day.

08 다음 중 밑줄 친 부분이 어법상 어색한 것은? (3점)

① This book were written by him.

② This song was recorded by them.

③ The painting was stolen last week.

④ This window was broken by the flood.

⑤ Those pictures were painted by the artist.

06 다음 문장의 빈칸 ⓐ, ⓑ에 들어갈 말로 알맞은 것은? (4점)

• We ⓐ_____ the fence next week. • A new building ⓑ_____ over there next year.

	ⓐ	ⓑ
①	will paint	will build
②	will paint	will be built
③	will be painted	will built
④	are painted	will be built
⑤	will be painted	will be built

09 다음 문장 중 어법상 옳은 것은? (3점)

① The TV turned off by Mom.

② The painting is stolen last week.

③ English speaks all around the world.

④ The machine will be repaired by Mr. Kim.

⑤ My grandmother was made the sweater for me.

10 다음 표에서 주어진 정보를 가지고 베트남을 소개하는 글을 쓴 내용 중 표현이 맞지 <u>않는</u> 문장은? (4점)

Country	Vietnam
Capital	Hanoi
Language	Vietnamese
Dish	Pho, Bahn mi
Place	• Halong Bay has 1,969 islands • Nha Trang has beautiful beaches

① The capital of Vietnam is Hanoi.

② Vietnamese is spoken there.

③ Pho and banh mi are popular dishes in Vietnam.

④ Nha Trang has beautiful beaches.

⑤ Every year lots of tourists were visited by Halong Bay and Nha Trang.

11 다음 두 문장을 'so'와 'that'을 사용하여 한 문장으로 바꿔 쓰시오. (4점)

> It rained very hard. We put off the picnic.
> 비가 너무 많이 내려서 우리는 소풍을 연기했다.

→ _____

12 다음 지도를 보고 나눈 대화에서 (A)~(D)의 순서대로 알맞은 것은? (3점)

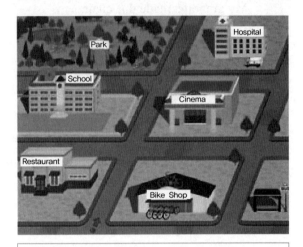

A: Excuse me. Where is the hospital?
B: Go straight (A)[one block / two blocks] and turn (B)[right / left]. It's on your (C)[right / left]. It's (D)[next to / across from] the cinema.

	(A)	(B)	(C)	(D)
①	two blocks	right	left	across from
②	one block	left	right	next to
③	two blocks	left	left	across from
④	one block	right	right	next to
⑤	one block	right	left	across from

13 Fill in the blank. (3점)

> A: Which do you prefer, spaghetti or pizza?
> B: _____ spaghetti.

① I wonder

② I heard

③ Where is

④ I prefer

⑤ I wonder how

14 다음 대화의 빈칸에 가장 적절한 표현은? (3점)

> B: Excuse me. _____
>   get to the Africa Museum?
> G: Sure. Go straight two blocks and turn right.
> B: Go straight and turn right. And then?
> G: It's on your left. It's across from the shoe store.
> B: I got it. Thank you very much.

① Where can I take a bus to
② How long do you walk to
③ Can you tell me how to
④ Where can you tell me
⑤ Which do you prefer to

[16~17] 다음 대화를 읽고 물음에 답하시오.

> Staff: How may I help you?
> Hana's mom: We want to enjoy a good view of London. (A)
> Hana: Where is the best place to go to?
> Staff: We have two great places. The London Eye is a Ferris wheel and the Sky Garden is a glass garden on top of a tall building. (B)
> Hana's mom: Hmm... I prefer the London Eye. (C)
> Hana: Me, too. (D)
> Staff: Good choice. You can get there by bus. Have a good trip!
> (.......)
> Hana: Wow, I can see all of London. Look! There is a big clock. (E)
> Hana's mom: I think that's Big Ben. Why don't we go and visit it later?
> Hana: That sounds great.

15 다음 중 짝지어진 대화가 <u>어색한</u> 것은? (3점)

① A: How can we get there?
   B: We can go there on foot or by bus.

② A: Excuse me. Is the Picasso Museum near here?
   B: Yes. It's not far from here.

③ A: Which do you prefer, the purple shirt or the yellow one?
   B: Yes. I like the red one.

④ A: Go straight and turn right. And then?
   B: It's on your left. It's across from the shoe store.

⑤ A: How about watching the movie *Best Friends* on Saturday?
   B: I'd love to. What time does it begin?

16 위 대화에서 주어진 표현이 들어가기에 알맞은 위치는? (3점)

> Which do you prefer?

① (A)   ② (B)   ③ (C)   ④ (D)   ⑤ (E)

17 위 대화를 읽은 후 질문에 대한 답을 찾을 수 <u>없는</u> 것은? (3점)

① Why do Hana and her mom visit this staff?

② What time do Hana and her mom get on the bus?

③ What are Hana and her mom going to do later?

④ How many places does this staff recommend?

⑤ Which place do the mom and her daughter like more, the Ferris wheel or the glass garden?

[19~22] 다음 글을 읽고 물음에 답하시오.

In Barcelona, we took a tour of Park Guell and Sagrada Familia. Both ⓐ<u>were designed</u> by Antoni Gaudi. In Park Guell, we saw some of Gaudi's ⓑ<u>creative</u> works like a colorful lizard.

After the Park Guell, we visited Sagrada Familia. Work on the building started in 1883 and ⓒ<u>is</u> still going on today. I ⓓ<u>impressed</u> by its size and unique design. The ceiling inside Sagrada Familia shone like the night sky with bright stars. Its stone columns stood like big trees. At Park Guell and Sagrada Familia I ⓔ<u>could feel</u> Gaudi's creativity and his love of nature.

Traveling in Spain was a wonderful experience. While I was there, I learned a lot about Spain. I want to visit the country again.

19 위 글의 밑줄 친 ⓐ~ⓔ 중 어법상 <u>어색한</u> 것은? (3점)

① ⓐ　② ⓑ　③ ⓒ　④ ⓓ　⑤ ⓔ

18 다음 글의 목적으로 알맞은 것은? (3점)

Man: Welcome to London City Tour. Today, we'll visit famous places in London. Can you see the London Eye? It's on your right. It's a Ferris wheel near the River Thames. The view from the London Eye is beautiful. Many people visit it every year.

① to share his travel experiences

② to tell tourists about the London Eye

③ to tell people things to do in London

④ to advise tourists on how to stay well in London

⑤ to tell everything tourists need to know before visiting London

20 위 글의 글쓴이가 여행에 대해 느끼는 감정은? (3점)

① sick

② tired

③ scared

④ gloomy

⑤ pleased

21 위 글의 'Sagrada Familia'에 대한 내용이 <u>아닌</u> 것은? (3점)

① It was designed by Antoni Gaudi.

② Work on the building started in 1883.

③ Work on the building is not finished yet.

④ We can see a colorful mosaic lizard in it.

⑤ Its ceiling looks like the night sky with bright stars.

[23~24] 다음 글을 읽고 물음에 답하시오.

Also, Spain is so famous for its foods that lots of people around the world enjoy them. Paella is a traditional Spanish dish from Valencia. It is a rice dish that can have meat, fish, seafood, and vegetables. Saffron is used to give it a yellow color and a unique taste. Jamón is dried Spanish ham that is served in thin slices. Jamón is named after the custom of drying the salted ham high on a mountain. Tapas are a great Spanish food tradition. They are small dishes of different types of foods like appetizers or snacks. The dishes may be cold or warm and can be served as snacks or a meal. Eating tapas is a great opportunity to taste as many different kinds of dishes as possible.

22 위 글에 나오는 단어의 영영 풀이에 해당되지 <u>않는</u> 것은? (3점)

① a shout of joy, *support or praise

② the skill and ability to produce something new, especially a work of art

③ go to certain places for sightseeing

④ all the plants, animals and things that *exist in the *universe

⑤ to produce light

*support 지지 *exist 존재하다 *universe 우주

23 위 글의 제목으로 알맞은 것은? (4점)

① 세계의 이름난 음식

② 스페인의 고유 음식

③ 다양한 디저트 음식

④ 푸드 트럭에서 파는 음식

⑤ 에피타이저로 알맞은 음식

24 위 글의 내용과 일치하지 <u>않는</u> 것은? (3점)

① Paella는 쌀로 만든 발렌시아 지방 음식이다.
② Jamón은 두껍게 자른 염장한 햄이다.
③ Saffron은 독특한 맛과 색을 제공한다.
④ Tapas는 차갑거나 따뜻하게 제공된다.
⑤ Tapas는 다양한 형태의 스낵과 같은 음식이다.

25 위 글을 읽고 답할 수 <u>없는</u> 질문은? (3점)

① Where did Jinwoo's family trip start?
② Who did Jinwoo shout with in a stadium?
③ Why did Jinwoo's family go to a stadium?
④ How many tourists visit Madrid every year?
⑤ Where did Jinwoo's family travel this summer?

26 위 글의 밑줄 친 단어 ⓐ~ⓔ와 <u>다른</u> 뜻으로 쓰인 것은? (4점)

① This story is very ⓐ<u>interesting</u>.
② What is the ⓑ<u>capital</u> of France?
③ We use a ⓒ<u>match</u> to light a fire.
④ All the parking spaces were ⓓ<u>full</u>.
⑤ Everybody ⓔ<u>cheered</u> when the firemen arrived.

[25~27] 다음 글을 읽고 물음에 답하시오.

> Jinwoo: My family traveled to Spain this summer. Lots of tourists love Spain. We visited many ⓐ<u>interesting</u> places.
> Our trip started in Madrid. Madrid is the ⓑ<u>capital</u> and ㉠<u>마드리드는 축구로 유명하다</u>. We went to a stadium to watch a soccer ⓒ<u>match</u>. My sister and I were excited because we could watch some of the world's most well-known soccer players. The stadium was ⓓ<u>full</u> of soccer fans. As we watched the match, we ⓔ<u>cheered</u> by singing songs, waving our hands, and shouting with other fans. After we toured Madrid, we went to Seville.

27 위 글의 밑줄 친 우리말 ㉠을 영어로 쓰시오. (4점)

㉠ 마드리드는 축구로 유명하다.

→ _____

After we toured Madrid, we went to Seville. ⓐ While we walked around the city, we saw many historic buildings. ⓑWe visited a flamenco museum and watched a flamenco dance. A woman (A)_____ a red dress was dancing the flamenco (B)_____ wonderful movements.

(C)_____ dinner, we ate paella. ⓒIt is a traditional Spanish dish with rice, vegetables, meat, and seafood. ⓓIt tasted like fried rice in Korea. ⓔFried rice is very popular in Korea. (가) 그것은 너무 맛있어서 우리 모두는 그것을 즐겼다.

29 위 글의 밑줄 친 ⓐ~ⓔ 중 흐름상 어색한 것은? (3점)

① ⓐ   ② ⓑ   ③ ⓒ   ④ ⓓ   ⑤ ⓔ

28 위 글의 빈칸 (A)~(C)에 들어갈 말이 바르게 짝지어진 것은? (4점)

	(A)	(B)	(C)
①	in	for	With
②	for	with	In
③	in	with	For
④	for	in	With
⑤	with	for	In

30 위 글의 밑줄 친 우리말 (가)와 의미가 일치하도록 주어진 단어들을 재배열하시오. (5점)

(가)그것은 너무 맛있어서 우리 모두는 그것을 즐겼다.

was / it / enjoyed / delicious / it / that / so / we all

→ _____

◎ 선택형 문항의 답안은 컴퓨터용 수정 싸인펜을 사용하여 OMR 답안지에 바르게 표기하시오.
◎ 서술형 문제는 답을 답안지에 반드시 검정 볼펜으로 쓰시오.
◎ 총 30문항 100점 만점입니다. 문항별 배점은 각 문항에 표시되어 있습니다.

[서울 강남구 ○○중]

01 다음 빈칸에 공통으로 들어갈 단어는? (3점)

• May I try _____ this shirt?
• Can I get there _____ foot?

① at   ② by   ③ in
④ on   ⑤ for

[경북 ○○중]

02 다음 빈칸에 들어갈 단어가 순서대로 바르게 짝지어진 것은? (3점)

• When you have a cold, drinking warm water can be _____.
• Drivers should be more _____ when they drive in a school zone.

① careful - thankful
② wonderful - careful
③ helpful - wonderful
④ useful - thankful
⑤ helpful - careful

[서울 강남구 ○○중]

03 다음 밑줄 친 단어의 쓰임이 잘못된 것은? (3점)

① We can learn from experience.
② The capital of Australia is Canberra.
③ His paintings are beautiful works of art.
④ Her pants match the blouse perfectly.
⑤ People should be more care when they cross the street.

[부산 ○○중]

04 다음 밑줄 친 표현 중 어색한 것은? (3점)

① My uncle makes a living as an engineer.
② Junsu is going to take a class to learn Spanish.
③ Amy has to take a choice between music and art.
④ I will make a phone call to Tom to tell him the truth.
⑤ After playing soccer, I used to take a shower with cold water.

[대전 ○○중]

05 다음 문장에서 어법상 어색한 부분을 바르게 고친 것은? (3점)

She swims too fast that I can't catch up with her.

① swims → swim
② too → so
③ that → what
④ can't → can
⑤ her → herself

[서울 강남구 ○○중]

06 다음 문장 중 어법상 옳은 것은? (3점)

① The picture were taken by Kevin.
② The first blue jeans made in 1932.
③ My sisters interested by Korean music.
④ Some flowers were given to me by him.
⑤ Did you satisfied with the trip to Sokcho?

07 다음 문장을 수동태 구문으로 바꾸어 표현할 때 빈칸에 들어갈 알맞은 단어를 쓰시오. (6점)

> • Shakespeare wrote "Romeo and Juliet."
> → "Romeo and Juliet" (A)_____ (B)_____ by Shakespeare.
>
> • Ms. Davis didn't take care of her dogs.
> → Her dogs (C)_____ (D)_____ care of by Ms. Davis.
>
> • They are building the bridge.
> → The bridge is (E)_____ (F)_____ by them.

(A): _____

(B): _____

(C): _____

(D): _____

(E): _____

(F): _____

08 다음 문장을 수동태 문장으로 전환하시오. (4점)

> Do you wear your mask?

→ _____ _____ _____ _____ _____ _____?

09 다음 중 어법상 옳은 문장은? (3점)

① We were catched in a heavy rain.

② The machine not was broken by him.

③ Will you let me know when it was did?

④ This is a song that will never be forgotten.

⑤ The traffic lights is controlled by a central computer.

10 다음 중 어법상 옳은 문장의 개수는? (3점)

> ⓐ The coffee is too hot to drink.
> ⓑ The tea is so hot that I can't drink it.
> ⓒ I was so sleepy that I couldn't stay awake.
> ⓓ I studied hard that so I could get better grades.
> ⓔ It was so a nice film that I watched it twice.
> ⓕ He got up so early that he could see the sunrise.

① 2개   ② 3개   ③ 4개

④ 5개   ⑤ 6개

11 다음 문장 중에서 영작이 바르지 <u>않은</u> 것은? (3점)

① 히터가 켜지지 않았다.

→ The heater was not turned on.

② 많은 집들이 홍수에 의해 훼손되었다.

→ Many houses were damaged by the flood.

③ 그 창문은 그에 의해 부서지지 않았다.

→ The window was not broken by his.

④ 그녀는 매우 아파서 움직일 수 없었다.

→ Because she was very sick, she couldn't move.

⑤ 어린이들이 너무 허약해서 움직이거나 심지어 울 수도 없다.

→ The children are too weak to move or even cry.

12 Fill in the blank. (3점)

> A: We want to enjoy a good view of London. Where is the best place to go?
> B: We have two great places! Which _____, The London Eye or the Sky Dome?
> A: I prefer the London Eye.

① I heard

② I wonder

③ will you

④ do you prefer

⑤ where the place

[13~14] 다음 대화를 읽고 물음에 답하시오.

> B: Jisu, why don't we watch the movie *Best Friends* on Saturday?
> G: Sounds good. What time does it begin?
> B: On Saturday there are two showings, one at five and the other at seven. (가)_____
> G: I prefer the seven showing.
> B: Okay. Then let's meet at six.
> G: Sounds good. See you then, Matt.
> *B: Matt, G: Jisu

13 위 대화의 빈칸 (가)에 들어갈 말을 〈조건〉에 맞게 서술하시오. (4점)

> **조건**
> 1. 완전한 영어 문장으로 완성할 것.
> 2. which를 반드시 사용할 것.
> 3. 4단어로 쓸 것.

→ _____

14 위 대화의 내용과 일치하는 것은? (3점)

① Jisu asks Matt to watch the movie together.

② Matt knows when the movie starts.

③ Matt likes the seven showing better.

④ Jisu likes the five showing more.

⑤ Jisu and Matt are going to watch the movie at six.

15 다음 ⓐ, ⓑ, ⓒ를 대화의 흐름에 맞게 배열한 것은? (3점)

A: What is this long dress called?

ⓐ Can I try this one on?
ⓑ It is an *Ao dai*, a type of traditional clothing from Vietnam.
ⓒ Sure. Which do you prefer, the purple one or the yellow one?

A: The purple one, please.

① ⓐ-ⓑ-ⓒ
② ⓐ-ⓒ-ⓑ
③ ⓑ-ⓐ-ⓒ
④ ⓑ-ⓒ-ⓐ
⑤ ⓒ-ⓑ-ⓐ

17 다음 짝지어진 대화가 <u>어색한</u> 것은? (3점)

① A: Is the Picasso Museum near here?
  B: Yes. It's not far from here.
② A: Which would you choose, curry or paella?
  B: Yes. I would choose some fruit juice.
③ A: How can we get to the hospital?
  B: Walk to the end of this block.
④ A: Where is the cinema?
  B: Go straight until you see a bank. It's next to the bank.
⑤ A: Which do you like better, the London Eye or the Sky Garden?
  B: I like the London Eye better.

16 다음 대화의 밑줄 친 우리말 ⓐ와 ⓑ를 〈보기〉의 어구를 이용하여 영어로 쓰시오. (6점)

A: Let's go on a trip abroad.
B: ⓐ<u>너는 도쿄와 런던 중에서 어느 도시를 선호하니?</u>
A: ⓑ<u>나는 런던을 선호해.</u> We should see the city's night view because it is very beautiful.
B: Okay. Let's go there.

보기
London / Tokyo / which city / prefer

→ ⓐ_____
  ⓑ_____

18 다음 대화의 흐름으로 보아 주어진 문장이 들어가기에 가장 알맞은 곳은? (3점)

I wonder how a river and a lake are different.

Hana: Look at that lake. It's really beautiful. (A)
Ben: It's not a lake. It's a river. (B)
Hana: Is it? (C)
Ben: A river is a long body of fresh water. Unlike a lake, a river flows toward the ocean. (D)
Hana: I got it. (E)

① (A)   ② (B)   ③ (C)
④ (D)   ⑤ (E)

19 다음 대화의 내용과 일치하지 <u>않는</u> 것은? (4점)

> A: How may I help you?
> B: We want to enjoy a good view of London.
> C: Where is the best place to go to?
> A: We have two great places. The London Eye is a Ferris wheel and the Sky Garden is a glass garden on top of a tall building. Which do you prefer?
> B: Hmm... I prefer the London Eye.
> C: Me, too.
> A: Good choice. You can get there by bus.
> B: Where is the nearest stop?
> A: Go straight one block and turn right. It's on your left. Have a good trip!
> ...
> C: Wow, I can see all of London. Look! There is a big clock.
> B: I think that's Big Ben. Why don't we go and visit it later?
> C: That sounds great.

① B and C will visit Big Ben, the big clock, later.

② B and C like the London Eye better than the Sky Garden.

③ They are talking about the places to get good views of London.

④ A is a tourist who is also asking for information about London.

⑤ The views from the London Eye and the Sky Garden are good.

[20~26] 다음 글을 읽고 물음에 답하시오.

After we toured Madrid, we went to Seville. While we walked around the city, we saw many historic buildings. We visited a flamenco museum and watched a flamenco dance. A woman in a red dress was dancing the flamenco with wonderful movements.

For dinner, we ate paella. It is a traditional Spanish dish with rice, vegetables, meat, and seafood. It tasted like fried rice in Korea. (가)<u>It was so delicious that we all enjoyed it.</u>

In Barcelona, we (나)_____ a tour of Park Guell and Sagrada Familia. (다)<u>Antoni Gaudi designed both.</u> In Park Guell, we saw some of Gaudi's creative works like a colorful lizard.

After Park Guell, we visited Sagrada Familia.
(A) Its stone columns stood like big trees. At Park Guell and Sagrada Familia I could feel Gaudi's creativity and his love of nature.
(B) Traveling in Spain was a wonderful experience. While I was there, I learned a lot about Spain. I want to visit the country again.
(C) Work on the building started in 1883 and is still going on today. I was impressed by its size and unique design. The ceiling inside Sagrada Familia shone like the night sky with bright stars.

20 위 글의 순서로 적절한 것은? (3점)

① (A)-(B)-(C)

② (A)-(C)-(B)

③ (B)-(A)-(C)

④ (B)-(C)-(A)

⑤ (C)-(A)-(B)

21 위 글의 밑줄 친 (가)에 대한 설명으로 옳지 <u>않은</u> 것은?　(3점)

① 'It'은 한국의 볶음밥을 가리킨다.
② 'so' 뒤에는 형용사나 부사를 쓴다.
③ 'that' 앞부분은 원인을 나타낸다.
④ 'that' 뒷부분은 결과를 나타낸다.
⑤ '그것이 너무 맛있어서 우리 모두 그것을 즐겼다.'
　라는 뜻이다.

24 위 글의 'I'가 여행 중 사진을 찍었다면 사진에서 찾아볼 수 <u>없</u>는 것은?　(3점)

① 밤하늘처럼 빛나는 천장
② 나무로 된 기둥
③ 공사 중인 건물
④ 역사적인 건물들
⑤ 빨간 드레스를 입은 댄서

22 위 글의 빈칸 (나)에 들어갈 단어로 적절한 것은?　(3점)

① did
② made
③ took
④ gave
⑤ got

25 위 글의 내용으로 알 수 <u>없는</u> 질문은?　(3점)

① How was traveling in Spain?
② When did work on Park Guell start?
③ Where did they visit after Park Guell?
④ What could the writer feel at Sagrada Familia?
⑤ Like what did the ceiling inside Sagrada Familia shine?

23 위 글의 밑줄 친 (다)와 같은 의미를 가진 문장은?　(3점)

① Both designed Antoni Gaudi.
② Both was designing by Antoni Gaudi.
③ Both was designed by Antoni Gaudi.
④ Both were designing by Antoni Gaudi.
⑤ Both were designed by Antoni Gaudi.

26 위 글의 Park Guell과 관련이 있는 것은?　(3점)

① 파에야
② 형형색색의 도마뱀
③ 독특한 디자인
④ 돌기둥
⑤ 빛나는 천장

My Happy Days in Spain
by Park Jinwoo

My family traveled to Spain this summer. Spain is (A)[loving / loved] by lots of tourists. We visited many interesting places.

Our trip started in Madrid. Madrid is the capital of Spain and is famous (B)[to / for] soccer. We went to a stadium to watch a soccer match. My sister and I were excited because we could watch some of the world's most famous soccer players.

The stadium was full of soccer fans. As we watched the match, we cheered by singing songs, waving our hands, and (C)[shouting / shouted] with the other fans.

[경기 ○○중]

28 위 글을 읽고 대답할 수 <u>없는</u> 질문은? (3점)

① Why were they excited?

② Where did their trip start?

③ What is the capital of Spain?

④ When did they travel to Spain?

⑤ Where did they get the tickets for the soccer match?

[충북 ○○중]

29 다음 중 위 글의 종류로 가장 적절한 것은? (3점)

① 소설

② 편지

③ 독후감

④ 논설문

⑤ 기행문

[부산 ○○중]

27 위 글의 (A)~(C)에서 가장 적절한 표현으로 짝지어진 것은? (4점)

	(A)	(B)	(C)
①	loving	to	shouting
②	loving	for	shouted
③	loved	for	shouting
④	loved	for	shouted
⑤	loved	to	shouting

[부산 ○○중]

30 위 글의 내용과 일치하지 <u>않는</u> 것은? (3점)

① Jinwoo는 이번 여름에 스페인에 갔다.

② Jinwoo는 스페인의 수도를 방문했다.

③ 축구 경기장은 팬들로 가득 차 있었다.

④ Jinwoo의 여동생은 유명한 축구 선수를 봤다.

⑤ Jinwoo는 춤을 추며 축구 경기를 응원했다.

2학년 영어 2학기 중간고사(6과) 1회

반		점수	
이름			

문항수 : 선택형(25문항) 서술형(5문항)	20 . . .

◎ 선택형 문항의 답안은 컴퓨터용 수정 싸인펜을 사용
하여 OMR 답안지에 바르게 표기하시오.
◎ 서술형 문제는 답을 답안지에 반드시 검정 볼펜으
로 쓰시오.
◎ 총 30문항 100점 만점입니다. 문항별 배점은 각
문항에 표시되어 있습니다.

[충북 ○○중]

01 다음 빈칸에 들어갈 수 <u>없는</u> 단어는?　　(3점)

> It is very _____ of him to say so.

① wise　　　　② foolish
③ generous　　④ necessary
⑤ kind

[경기 ○○중]

02 다음 밑줄 친 단어 중 <u>어색한</u> 것은?　　(3점)

① It was cold and <u>windy</u> yesterday.
② Jenny swims every day to stay <u>healthy</u>.
③ Take off your <u>mess</u> shoes before you enter here.
④ When I traveled in Italy, I had <u>wonderful</u> experience.
⑤ Drivers should be more <u>careful</u> when they drive on rainy days.

[대전 ○○중]

03 다음 정의에 해당하는 단어는?　　(3점)

> a large area of water that is surrounded by land

① lake　　　　② plain
③ desert　　　④ forest
⑤ mountain

[경기 ○○중]

04 다음 빈칸에 공통으로 들어갈 말로 적절한 것은?　　(3점)

> • Don't _____ a noise while you are in the library.
> • Amy has to _____ a choice between music and art.

① do
② get
③ make
④ take
⑤ have

[충북 ○○중]

05 다음 2개의 문장을 참고하여 not only ~ but also 구문을 사용하여 주어진 뜻의 문장을 완성하시오.　　(4점)

> (1) The girls like listening to music.
> (2) The girls like reading books, too.

> 그 소녀들은 음악을 듣는 것뿐만 아니라 책 읽는 것도 좋아합니다.

→ _____

[경기 ○○중]

06 다음 중 밑줄 친 부분이 어법상 <u>어색한</u> 것은?　　(3점)

① It was foolish <u>for him</u> to think so.
② It is not difficult <u>for her</u> to use this camera.
③ It is easy <u>for me</u> to understand this book.
④ It is necessary <u>for us</u> to turn off the lights.
⑤ It is dangerous <u>for you</u> to walk around at night.

07 다음 중 어법상 옳은 문장은? (3점)

① Not only you but also James play the piano.

② Her parents as well as Mina are healthy.

③ Both Jack and Sarah is coming.

④ Either you or he are wrong.

⑤ I like not only reading books but write them.

09 다음 빈칸에 〈보기〉의 ⓐ와 같은 단어가 들어가는 문장은 모두 몇 개인가? (3점)

> 보기
>
> It is dangerous ⓐ_____ us to walk around at night.

- It is kind _____ you to say so.
- It is foolish _____ him to give up.
- It is very rude _____ her to be late.
- It is easy _____ them to understand this book.
- It is important _____ you to be nice to your friends.

① 1개   ② 2개   ③ 3개

④ 4개   ⑤ 5개

08 다음 문법적으로 <u>어색한</u> 영어 문장을 바르게 고쳐 쓰고, 그 근거가 되는 가장 적절한 설명을 제시한 사람의 이름을 〈보기〉에서 골라 쓰시오. (6점)

> 보기
>
> - 가을: 영어에서는 'to+동사원형'으로 시작하는 to부정사구 형태의 긴 주어를 문장 뒷부분으로 보내.
> - 레이: 맞아. 그리고 비어 있는 원래 주어 자리엔 가주어 'It'을 써.
> - 리즈: 이 가주어 'It'은 의미가 없어.

> It is hard look right at you.

(1) 바르게 고친 영어 문장 전체

→ _____

(2) 근거를 제시한 사람 이름(1명)

→ _____

10 다음 우리말과 같은 뜻이 되도록 「가주어 it, 진주어 to부정사」 구문을 사용하여 영작하시오. (주어진 단어를 사용할 것) (6점)

> (1) 그들이 매일 운동하는 것은 중요하다.
> so / important / work out
>
> → _____

> (2) 어려움에 처한 사람들을 도와주다니 그녀는 참 친절하다.
> so / kind / people in need
>
> → _____

11 다음 두 문장을 「Not only A ~ but also B」구문을 사용하여 한 문장으로 연결하여 완성하시오. (4점)

Yumi speaks English very well.
+
Her sisters speak English very well, too.

→ _____

12 다음 대화의 흐름상 빈칸 (A)에 들어갈 말로 알맞은 것은? (3점)

G: I wonder what you did during the summer vacation.
B: I took a trip to Kenya and saw many animals on the plains.
G: Wonderful! By the way, what are the plains?
B: (A)_____
G: I see.

---

① They are large areas of flat land.

② They are very long bodies of fresh water.

③ They are water that has land all around it.

④ They are lands with few plants and little water.

⑤ They are very tall, natural places which are higher than the land around it.

[13~14] 다음 대화를 읽고 물음에 답하시오.

Dad: Do you ⓐwant to see an amazing place?
Karl & Sister: Sure!
Dad: Then let's ⓑget on the train.
Sister: Look at the yellow plants! What are they?
Dad: They are reeds. Suncheon Bay has beautiful reed fields.
Karl: Wow, the reeds are ⓒeven taller than you, Dad.
Sister: They really are. Let me ⓓtake a picture of you, Dad.
Karl: This reed field is very large.
Dad: Yes. I heard it is ⓔthe larger one in Korea.
Karl: Look at the sky. It's turning red.

---

13 위 대화의 ⓐ~ⓔ 중 어법상 어색한 것은? (3점)

① ⓐ   ② ⓑ   ③ ⓒ

④ ⓓ   ⑤ ⓔ

14 위 대화를 읽고 답을 할 수 없는 질문은? (3점)

① Who is taller, Karl or his dad?

② Who took a picture of Karl's dad?

③ What color is the sky turning?

④ How does Karl's family go to Suncheon Bay?

⑤ What did Karl's dad hear about the reed field?

15 Fill in the blank. (3점)

> A: _____
> B: I heard they are a popular Korean boy group.

① I wonder what you are.

② I wonder who BTS is.

③ I wonder what is in Jeju-do.

④ I wonder where Suncheon is.

⑤ I wonder what the capital of South Korea is.

16 다음 대화의 빈칸에 공통으로 들어가기에 가장 적절한 것은? (3점)

> G: What should I take to the desert?
> B1: You should take a hat. _____ the sun is strong during the day.
> G: Anything else?
> B2: You should take warm clothes. _____ it's very cold at night.

① I wonder

② I heard

③ I prefer

④ I don't know

⑤ Which do you prefer

17 다음 대화를 한 문단으로 요약할 때, 빈칸 ⓐ~ⓔ에 들어갈 단어가 바르게 짝지어진 것은? (4점)

> Tom: Do you know how many oceans there are on the Earth?
> Jane: The answer is four, isn't it?
> Tom: No. There are five oceans on the Earth. They cover most of the Earth.
> Jane: How much of the Earth do they cover?
> Tom: I head the oceans cover about 70% of the Earth's surface.
> Jane: Do you know the Amazon rain forest is called the lungs of the Earth?
> Tom: Lungs? Why?
> Jane: Because it produces about 20% of the Earth's oxygen.
> Tom: Wow! That's a lot.

> There are ⓐ_____ oceans on the Earth. The oceans cover about ⓑ_____ of the Earth's surface. The Amazon rain forest is called the ⓒ_____ of the Earth. It ⓓ_____ about 20% of the Earth's ⓔ_____.

① ⓐ-five

② ⓑ-60%

③ ⓒ-heart

④ ⓓ-reduces

⑤ ⓔ-trees

Mudflats help the environment greatly. (A) Mudflats hold a lot of water, so they can reduce damage from (가)_____. (B) Also, mudflats filter water that flows from the land into the sea. They remove bad things in the water before it enters the sea. (C) Mudflats work as the Earth's lungs. (D) They produce a huge volume of (나)_____ that is necessary for life on the Earth. (E)

Mudflats are wonderful places, aren't they? They are a gift from nature to living things on the Earth. For all these reasons, ⓐ갯벌을 보호하는 것이 필요하다.

[경북 ○○중]

18 위 글의 흐름으로 보아, 주어진 문장이 들어가기에 가장 적절한 곳은? (3점)

Thanks to mudflats, the water that reaches the sea is clean.

① (A)   ② (B)   ③ (C)
④ (D)   ⑤ (E)

[경북 ○○중]

19 위 글의 빈칸 (가), (나)에 들어갈 말이 바르게 짝지어진 것은? (3점)

(가)	(나)
① floods	oxygen
② floods	water
③ oxygen	floods
④ fire	oxygen
⑤ lightning	oxygen

[충북 ○○중]

20 위 글에서 갯벌이 환경에 미치는 영향으로 언급되지 않은 것은? (3점)

① reducing damage from floods
② keeping the temperature of water
③ producing a huge volume of oxygen
④ cleaning the water before reaching the sea
⑤ filtering water that flows from the land into the sea

[충북 ○○중]

21 위 글의 ⓐ와 같은 의미가 되도록 주어진 단어를 이용하여 문장을 완성하시오. (4점)

ⓐ갯벌을 보호하는 것이 필요하다

→ it _____

[22~25] 다음 글을 읽고 물음에 답하시오.

Mudflats are large areas of muddy land at the seaside. (가)They appear and disappear with every tide. During low tides, they show up, and during high tides, they (A)_____ by the sea. Mudflats help sea creatures, people, and the Earth in many ways. It is important (B)_____ the roles of mudflats. Let's see what they do.

22 위 글의 빈칸 (A), (B)에 들어갈 말이 바르게 짝지어진 것은?

(3점)

	(A)	(B)
①	cover	understands
②	covered	understood
③	are covered	understand
④	are covered	understanding
⑤	are covered	to understand

23 위 글의 밑줄 친 (가)가 가리키는 것으로 적절한 것은? (3점)

① mudflats
② low tides
③ creatures
④ crabs
⑤ fish

24 다음 중 위 글의 내용과 다른 것은? (3점)

① 플랑크톤은 갯벌을 오염시킨다.
② 갯벌의 중요성을 알 필요가 있다.
③ 갯벌은 지구와 생물들에게 도움을 준다.
④ 갯벌은 바닷가에 있다.
⑤ 갯벌은 밀물과 썰물에 나타나고 사라지고 한다.

25 위 글 뒤에 이어질 내용으로 가장 알맞은 것은? (3점)

① The various roles of mudflats
② The process of making mudflats
③ The activities that we can do at mudflats
④ The kinds of creature living at mudflats
⑤ The names of famous mudflats in Korea

[26~28] 다음 글을 읽고 물음에 답하시오.

Mudflats are important to the ecosystem. Mudflats attract a large number of seaside birds. These areas also house a number of crabs, fish, and clams which are food for the birds. (A)_____, mudflats are often good bird-watching places.

Mudflats also protect the land from sea waves. They act as a wall against waves. Mudflats across the world, however, are in danger. The first problem is developmental activities. Not only digging out mudflats for ships but also pollution is threatening mudflats. Also, the rising of sea levels due to global warming is (B)_____ large areas of mudflats. More than 65% of the mudflats around the Yellow Sea of Korea have been (C)_____ over the past 50 years.

26 위 글의 빈칸 (A)에 들어갈 가장 적절한 표현은? (3점)

① If
② Thus
③ Because
④ Though
⑤ Thanks to

Recently, mudflat hiking has been popular among tourists. Usually, shallow mudflat areas are chosen for mudflat hiking. This sport is already popular in northwest of Germany, Denmark, and the Netherlands. Tourists walk on the mudflat during low tide. The mudflats on the Wadden Sea areas in the North Sea are excellent for mudflat hiking. Mudflat hiking is not without its dangers. It is important to be careful of the dangers on mudflats. Small mistakes may lead to dangerous situations due to the rising water. Thus, mudflat hiking should be (A)_____ with a guide who knows the place well and can keep the hikers (B)_____.

27 위 글을 읽고, 바다의 수위가 상승하는 원인이 무엇인지 고르면? (3점)

① 지구 온난화
② 갯벌 개발
③ 방파제 설치
④ 탐조 여행객 수 증가
⑤ 플라스틱 쓰레기 증가

29 위 글의 빈칸 (A), (B)에 들어갈 알맞은 것은? (3점)

	(A)	(B)
①	do	save
②	did	sail
③	doing	same
④	done	danger
⑤	done	safe

28 위 글의 빈칸 (B), (C)에 들어갈 알맞은 것은? (3점)

	(B)	(C)
①	destroyed	produced
②	destroying	producing
③	producing	produced
④	destroying	destroyed
⑤	produced	producing

30 다음 중 위 글의 내용과 <u>다른</u> 것은? (3점)

① 관광객은 썰물 때 갯벌을 걷는다.
② 갯벌을 걷는 것은 위험할 수 있다.
③ 관광객들은 깊은 갯벌 걷기를 좋아한다.
④ 사소한 실수가 위험한 상황이 될 수 있다.
⑤ 독일 북서쪽 지역이 인기 있는 갯벌 걷기 장소이다.

◎ 선택형 문항의 답안은 컴퓨터용 수정 싸인펜을 사용하여 OMR 답안지에 바르게 표기하시오.
◎ 서술형 문제는 답을 답안지에 반드시 검정 볼펜으로 쓰시오.
◎ 총 30문항 100점 만점입니다. 문항별 배점은 각 문항에 표시되어 있습니다.

[경기 ㅇㅇ중]

01 다음 밑줄 친 "This"가 설명하는 것으로 가장 적절한 것은? (3점)

> This is the very small animal and plant life in an ocean, lake, etc.

① crab   ② worm
③ bird   ④ fish
⑤ plankton

[경북 ㅇㅇ중]

02 다음 중 밑줄 친 부분이 어색한 것은? (3점)

① It was cold and underlined windy yesterday.
② Tyler swims every day to stay healthy.
③ I feel so lucky to have such a good friend.
④ Take off your messy shoes before you enter here.
⑤ My pet cat is very friendy.

[충북 ㅇㅇ중]

03 다음 중 빈칸에 들어가는 단어가 다른 하나는? (4점)

① Don't _____ a noise in the library.
② Nancy will _____ a class to learn cooking.
③ They often _____ mistakes because they are stupid.
④ If you want to pass the test, you should _____ an effort.
⑤ Sally has to _____ a choice between math and science.

[충북 ㅇㅇ중]

04 다음 중 어법상 바르게 쓰인 것은? (3점)

① It's very kind for you to help the woman.
② Not only you but my cousin have a puppy.
③ The song is sung by Yumi at the party yesterday.
④ You should not only eat well but also work out regularly.
⑤ Jenny swims every day to stay health.

[경기 ㅇㅇ중]

05 다음 중 어법상 어색한 것은? (3점)

① My dog is not only cute but smart.
② I like not only English but also math.
③ It not only rained but snowed yesterday.
④ Not only you but also James play the piano.
⑤ She is good at not only singing but dancing.

[경북 ㅇㅇ중]

06 다음 중 to부정사의 쓰임이 나머지 넷과 다른 하나는? (3점)

① It is too cold to play outside.
② It is necessary to stay warm.
③ It is important to focus on the lecture.
④ It is good to learn foreign languages.
⑤ It is hard to get up early in the morning.

07 다음 우리말을 주어진 표현을 활용하여 알맞게 영작하시오. (not only ~ but also 구문을 활용하여 물음에 답하시오.) (4점)

나는 이야기를 읽는 것뿐만 아니라 그것들을 쓰는 것도 좋아한다.

→ I like _____.

   (reading stories, writing them)

→ _____

08 다음 〈조건〉에 따라 주어진 우리말을 영어로 쓰시오. (4점)

조건
- 가주어 'it'으로 시작하는 문장을 쓸 것.
- 제시어를 모두 활용하고, 필요시 단어의 모양을 바꾸거나 단어를 추가할 것.
- 제시어: every day, hard, work out

매일 운동하는 것은 어렵지 않았다.

→ _____

09 다음 문법적으로 어색한 영어 문장을 바르게 고쳐 쓰고, 그 근거가 되는 가장 적절한 설명을 제시한 사람의 이름을 〈보기〉에서 골라 쓰시오. (6점)

보기
- 원영: 'Not only A but also B' 구문은 as well as를 써서 바꿔 쓸 수 있다.
- 유진: 'also'는 생략할 수 있어.
- 이서: 이 구문을 주어 자리에 쓸 때, 동사의 수는 B에 일치시켜야 해.

Not only I but also my brother like chicken.

(1) 바르게 고친 영어 문장 전체

→ _____

(2) 근거를 제시한 사람 이름(1명)

→ _____

10 다음 중 어법상 옳은 문장을 고르면? (3점)

① Jihun not only dances but also sing well.
② I like not only reading stories but also write them.
③ Hana is good at not only math but also art.
④ Travis is not only smart but also generously.
⑤ You should not only sleep well but working out regularly.

11 Fill in the blank. (3점)

A: I want to go to Danyang.
B: _____ there are famous caves in Danyang.

① I heard
② I wonder
③ I see
④ You know
⑤ You don't hear

13 다음 대화의 내용과 일치하지 <u>않는</u> 것은? (3점)

Dad:	Do you want to see an amazing place?
Karl, Sister:	Sure!
Dad:	Then, let's get on the train.
Sister:	Look at the yellow plants! I wonder what they are.
Dad:	They are reeds. Suncheon Bay has beautiful reed fields.
Karl:	Wow, the reeds are even taller than you, Dad.
Sister:	They really are. Let me take a picture of you.
Karl:	This reed field is very large.
Dad:	Yes. It is the largest one in Korea.
Karl:	Look at the sky. It's turning red.
Sister:	Yes, it's beautiful.

① 하늘이 붉게 물들었다.
② 갈대가 Karl의 아버지보다 키가 크다.
③ 순천만의 갈대밭은 한국에서 가장 크다.
④ Karl의 여동생이 궁금해한 식물은 갈대이다.
⑤ Karl의 가족은 순천만에 버스를 타고 갔다.

12 다음 대화의 빈칸에 들어갈 말로 적절한 것은? (3점)

A: What should I take to the desert?
B: You should take a hat.
_____

① I feel it's very cold at night.
② I hope you enjoyed your trip.
③ I know it's very cloudy all day.
④ I think you don't understand me.
⑤ I heard the sun is strong during the day.

14 다음 대화가 자연스럽게 배열된 것은? (3점)

> G: I heard the Amazon rain forest is called the lungs of the Earth.
>
> (A) Lungs? Why?
> (B) Wow! That's a lot.
> (C) Because it produces about 20% of the Earth's oxygen.

① (A) - (B) - (C)
② (A) - (C) - (B)
③ (B) - (A) - (C)
④ (B) - (C) - (A)
⑤ (C) - (B) - (A)

16 다음 짝지어진 대화가 어색한 것은? (4점)

① A: I wonder how many caves there are in Korea.
  B: I do, too. Let me know when you find out.
② A: I heard that Iguazu Falls are the world's largest waterfalls.
  B: Really? I thought Niagara Falls are the largest ones.
③ A: Do you know where the White Cliffs of Dover are?
  B: They're in England. I'm aware that they formed up over millions of years.
④ A: I'm searching for information about whales. Can I ask where I can find some information?
  B: Sure, there are a lot of beaches in Jejudo.
⑤ A: I don't know what the Seven Wonders of the World are.
  B: As far as I know, Taj Mahal is one of them. Let's search for the others on the Internet.

15 다음 대화의 ⓐ~ⓔ 중 흐름상 어색한 문장은? (3점)

> G: Look at that lake! ⓐIt's really beautiful.
> B: ⓑIt's not a lake. It's a river.
> G: Is it? ⓒI wonder how a river and a lake are different.
> B: ⓓA river is a long body of fresh water. ⓔLike a lake, a river flows toward the ocean.
> G: I got it.

① ⓐ   ② ⓑ   ③ ⓒ
④ ⓓ   ⑤ ⓔ

All about _____

_____ are dry land with few plants and little water. Plants like elephant trees and animals such as lizards and desert snakes live there. It is hot during the day and cold at night. If you go to _____, it is important to wear a hat to block the sun.

[부산 ○○중]

17 위 글의 빈칸에 들어갈 가장 적절한 단어는? (대 · 소문자 무시)
(3점)

① Deserts
② Plains
③ Valleys
④ Hills
⑤ Mudflats

[충북 ○○중]

18 위 글을 읽고 답할 수 없는 것은? (3점)

① What are deserts?
② What plants live in deserts?
③ What animals live in deserts?
④ What is special about deserts?
⑤ What makes deserts' weather changeable?

Mudflats ⓐare good for people, too. People ⓑwho live near mudflat areas make a living ⓒby catching fish and other sea animals nearby. Thanks to mudflats, people can get fresh seafood. People can enjoy fun activities, ⓓsuch as mud sliding and body painting on mudflats. They can also watch a large number of birds ⓔthat feed on the sea animals there.

Mudflats help the environment greatly. (A) Mudflats hold a lot of water, so they can reduce damage from floods. (B) They (가)remove bad things in the water before ⓕit enters the sea. (C) Thanks to mudflats, the water that reaches the sea is clean. (D) Mudflats work ⓖas the Earth's lungs. (E) They produce a huge volume of oxygen that is necessary for life on the Earth.

Mudflats are wonderful places, aren't they? They are a gift from nature to living things on the Earth. For all these reasons, ⓗit is necessary to protect mudflats.

[부산 ○○중]

19 위 글의 흐름으로 보아, 주어진 문장이 들어가기에 가장 적절한 곳은? (3점)

Also, mudflats filter water that flows from the land into the sea.

① (A)   ② (B)   ③ (C)
④ (D)   ⑤ (E)

20 위 글의 밑줄 친 ⓐ~ⓗ 중, 옳은 설명을 있는 대로 고른 것은?

(4점)

> ⓐ are good for: '~에 유익하다'라는 뜻이다.
> ⓑ who: 'which'로 바꿔야 한다.
> ⓒ by catching: '잡자마자'라는 뜻이다.
> ⓓ such as: '~와 같은'이라는 뜻이다.
> ⓔ that: 'feed'를 꾸민다.
> ⓕ it: 'the water'를 가리킨다.
> ⓖ as: '~ 때문에'라는 뜻이다.
> ⓗ it: 'the Earth'를 가리킨다.

① ⓐ, ⓑ, ⓗ

② ⓐ, ⓓ, ⓕ

③ ⓑ, ⓒ, ⓖ

④ ⓒ, ⓔ, ⓗ

⑤ ⓓ, ⓔ, ⓕ

21 위 글의 제목으로 가장 어울리는 것을 고르면? (3점)

① Everybody will try to protect mudflats

② Mudflats show the history of the earth

③ People can make a friend in the mudflat

④ Mudflats are nature's gift to living things

⑤ Mudflats are easy places to find food for animals

22 위 글의 밑줄 친 (가)remove bad things in the water와 의미가 비슷한 한 단어를 본문에서 찾아 쓰시오. (4점)

→ _____

23 위 글을 읽고 갯벌의 장점으로 적당하지 <u>않은</u> 것은? (3점)

① 산소를 생산한다.

② 바닷물을 정화한다.

③ 홍수 피해를 감소시킨다.

④ 더러운 물질을 걸러낸다.

⑤ 환경에 전반적으로 도움을 준다.

24 위 글을 읽고 답할 수 <u>없는</u> 질문은? (3점)

① How can mudflats reduce damage from floods?

② What activities can people enjoy on mudflats?

③ What do mudflats produce for life on the Earth?

④ What kinds of seafood can people get on mudflats?

⑤ How do mudflats help people who live near mudflats?

Mudflats are large areas of muddy land at the seaside. They appear and disappear with every tide. During low tides, ⓐthey show up, and during high tides, (A)they are covered by the sea. Mudflats help sea creatures, people, and the Earth in many ways. It is important to understand the (가)_____ of mudflats. Let's see what ⓑthey do.

Mudflats are home to a lot of living things at the seaside. Not only very small living things like plankton but also crabs and fish live ⓒthere. Mudflats provide various types of food for ⓓthem. Also, many birds eat food ⓔthere.

[충북 ○○중]

25 위 글의 흐름상 빈칸 (가)에 들어갈 말로 가장 알맞은 것은? (3점)

① meanings ② origins
③ effects ④ roles
⑤ types

[대전 ○○중]

26 위 글의 제목으로 가장 적절한 것은? (3점)

① 갯벌의 역할 ② 갯벌의 보존
③ 갯벌의 위치 ④ 갯벌의 폐해
⑤ 갯벌의 생성

[부산 ○○중]

27 위 글의 밑줄 친 ⓐ~ⓔ 중 가리키는 대상이 나머지 넷과 다른 것은? (3점)

① ⓐ ② ⓑ ③ ⓒ
④ ⓓ ⑤ ⓔ

[충북 ○○중]

28 다음 중 위 글을 읽고 답할 수 없는 것은? (3점)

① What makes tides happen?
② When do mudflats show up?
③ When do mudflats disappear?
④ What do many birds do on mudflats?
⑤ What are mudflats?

[부산 ○○중]

29 다음 문장들은 위 글의 밑줄 친 (A)와 같은 수동태 문장들이다. 어법상 옳은 것은? (4점)

① The window was broken by he.
② Hangeul created by King Sejong.
③ Boram middle school was built in 1989.
④ Harry Potter was wrote by J.K.Rowling.
⑤ Was these pictures painted by the artist?

[부산 ○○중]

30 다음 중 위 글의 내용을 잘못 이해한 것은? (3점)

① 갯벌은 진흙으로 된 땅이다.
② 갯벌은 밀물일 때 사라진다.
③ 갯벌은 바다 생물들을 돕는다.
④ 대부분의 물고기들은 플랑크톤을 좋아한다.
⑤ 갯벌의 역할을 이해하는 것은 중요하다.

◎ 선택형 문항의 답안은 컴퓨터용 수정 싸인펜을 사용하여 OMR 답안지에 바르게 표기하시오.
◎ 서술형 문제는 답을 답안지에 반드시 검정 볼펜으로 쓰시오.
◎ 총 30문항 100점 만점입니다. 문항별 배점은 각 문항에 표시되어 있습니다.

[경기 ○○중]

01 다음 영영 풀이에 해당하는 낱말로 가장 적절한 것은? (3점)

> a player on the same team

① patient ② batter
③ teammate ④ customer
⑤ baseman

[서울 강남구 ○○중]

02 다음 중 영영 풀이가 알맞지 <u>않은</u> 것을 <u>모두</u> 고르면? (정답 2개) (3점)

① fail: to be able to do something
② award: a prize that is given to someone
③ shout: to say something in a loud voice
④ lend: to use something for a limited time
⑤ positive: believing that good things will happen rather than bad ones

[대전 ○○중]

03 다음 〈보기〉의 빈칸에 들어갈 알맞은 표현은? (3점)

보기
Gandhi lived his life for his country and _____ of others.

① kept calm
② turned down
③ thought to himself
④ earned the respect
⑤ saved many lives

[충북 ○○중]

04 다음 중 어법상 <u>어색한</u> 것은? (3점)

① Mr. Johnson told us to shake hands after the game.
② Mom asked me to return some books to the library.
③ I love the watch my uncle bought for me.
④ The teacher saw Mintae leaving the room.
⑤ I felt someone to tap me on the shoulder.

[서울 강남구 ○○중]

05 다음 문장을 어법상 적절하게 영작한 것은? (3점)

> 우리가 어제 본 영화는 재미있었다.

① The movie that we watch last night was fun.
② The movie was fun we watched last night.
③ The movie we watched last night was fun.
④ The movie which watched last night was fun.
⑤ The movie which we watching last night was fun.

06 다음 문장과 who의 쓰임이 같은 것은? (3점)

> He was a player <u>who</u> we wanted to scout.

① Kim is the student <u>who</u> studies hard.

② She had two sons <u>who</u> she loved very much.

③ We need a person <u>who</u> can speak French.

④ Ashley is the girl <u>who</u> is talking to my mom.

⑤ He is the man <u>who</u> understands different cultures.

07 다음 문장의 빈칸에 동일한 단어를 쓸 수 <u>없는</u> 것은? (3점)

① Mom wanted Lily _____ come to home by 8.

② My parents told me _____ become a doctor.

③ Sam asked her _____ be his date for the party.

④ I expected you _____ finish your homework by now.

⑤ She didn't let him _____ go out and play.

08 다음 우리말에 맞게 영작한 문장에 <u>어색한</u> 부분이 있다. <u>어색한</u> 부분을 찾아 기호를 쓰고, 〈조건〉에 맞게 바르게 고치시오. (5점)

> Mark는 내가 그에게 얼마의 돈을 빌려 주길 원했다.
> → Mark ⓐ<u>wanted</u> ⓑ<u>me</u> ⓒ<u>lending</u> ⓓ<u>him</u> some money.

> **조건**
> • (A)에는 기호만 적을 것.
> • (B)에는 완전한 문장을 다시 적을 것.

(A) 어색한 부분의 기호: _____

(B) 고쳐 쓰기: _____

09 다음 우리말을 목적격 관계대명사를 이용하여 〈보기〉의 어구를 모두 활용하여 배열하시오. (4점)

> 나는 삼촌이 나에게 사 주신 시계를 좋아한다.

> **보기**
> the watch / my uncle / me / bought / which

→ _____

10 다음 주어진 두 문장을 아래 조건을 참고하여 하나의 문장으로 다시 쓰시오. (4점)

> • The Brooklyn Dodgers was the team.
> • He wanted to join the team.

> **조건**
> • 관계대명사를 사용할 것.
> • 총 11글자로 쓸 것.

→ _____

> A: Oh, this is hard to do.
> B: What's the matter?
> A: Can you teach me how to make cookies?
> B: Sure. It's a walk in the park.
> A: ⓐ_____
> B: I mean ⓑ_____

12 위 대화의 ⓐ에 들어갈 말로 적절하지 <u>않은</u> 것은? (3점)

① What are you doing?

② What is that exactly?

③ What exactly do you mean?

④ What do you mean by that?

⑤ Could you explain about that?

11 다음 중 어법상 <u>틀린</u> 문장은? (3점)

① I can smell something burning!

② The man ordered us not to move.

③ I want my parents to spend time with me.

④ My father allowed me going to the concert.

⑤ Have you ever seen her singing?

13 위 대화의 ⓑ에 들어갈 말로 알맞은 것은? (3점)

① it's easy to do

② it's not easy to do

③ it's a terrible thing to do

④ it's not fun to walk in the park

⑤ it's good to go to the park sometimes

14 다음 대화에서 A의 마지막 질문에 대한 B의 응답으로 가장 적절한 것은? (3점)

A: Would you like to say something to the other skaters?
B: Yes, I want to say, "No pain, no gain."
A: What do you mean by that?
B: I mean _____.

① it's walk in a park
② we are always positive
③ we should read many books
④ I'll keep my fingers crossed for you
⑤ we can't achieve anything without hard work

16 Fill in the blank. (3점)

A: I have an important test tomorrow, so I'm going to _____ with my friend at the library.
B: What do you mean by that?
A: I mean I'm going to study hard with my friend at the library.

① eat some cake
② hit the books
③ be surprised
④ break a leg
⑤ be under the weather

15 다음 대화 중 <u>어색한</u> 것은? (3점)

① A: I want to go to Jejudo.
  B: Sounds good. I heard there are a lot of oreums in Jejudo.
② A: I wonder what a desert is.
  B: It is a land with few plants and little water.
③ A: I wonder what you did yesterday.
  B: I took a trip to Suncheon Bay and saw beautiful reed fields.
④ A: What should I take to the desert?
  B: I want to eat delicious dessert.
⑤ A: Why don't we go to Danyang?
  B: Okay. I heard there are famous caves.

17 다음 담임 선생님이 쓴 메모를 보고 주어진 단어를 이용하여 문장을 완성하시오. (6점)

To my students,
(A) Jina – open the windows for fresh air
(B) Chris – clean the board

(A): My teacher asked _____.
(B): My teacher wanted _____.

18 다음 두 문장을 관계대명사를 이용하여 한 문장으로 만드시오.

(6점)

> (1) That's the actor. I saw him in the magazine.
> (2) The store didn't have the jeans. I wanted to buy them.

조건

• 문장 전체를 완성할 것.

(1) _____

(2) _____

19 다음 글의 제목으로 가장 적절한 것은? (3점)

> I want to be a designer. There are three things that I need to do to achieve my dream. I need to be healthy, be creative, and never give up. Being healthy will help me keep going for my dream. Being creative will help me do something different. Plus, I will always tell myself never to give up because it will make me try harder.

① Dream Big

② Never Give Up

③ How I Will Achieve My Dream

④ Best Job I Chose for the Future

⑤ Three Steps to Find a Better Job

[20~25] 다음 글을 읽고 물음에 답하시오.

> Robinson's effort (가)moved ⓐhis teammates. When people shouted at Robinson, one of his teammates walked up to Robinson and tapped ⓑhim (A)[in / on] the shoulder. "Do not listen to them. You're doing fine," he said. ⓒHis support helped Robinson to play harder. Finally, Robinson earned the respect of other players and fans.
>
> Thanks to Robinson, the Dodgers won the National League Championship in 1947. The league recognized Robinson's excellence and presented ⓓhim (B)[to / with] the Rookie of the Year Award in the same year. After that season, other teams asked African American players to join them.
>
> Robinson's uniform number was 42. Baseball players in Major League teams no longer wear the number 42 to honor him. Every year, (C)[however / because], on April 15, every player wears the number that ⓔRobinson wore. The day (나)_____ "Jackie Robinson Day."

20 위 글의 밑줄 친 ⓐ~ⓔ 중 가리키는 대상이 나머지 넷과 <u>다른</u> 것은? (3점)

① ⓐ   ② ⓑ   ③ ⓒ

④ ⓓ   ⑤ ⓔ

21 위 글의 밑줄 친 (가)moved와 같은 의미로 쓰인 것은? (3점)

① Time is <u>moving</u> on.

② We <u>moved</u> house last week.

③ The movie was so <u>moving</u> that we all cried.

④ Let's <u>move</u> the group meeting to Wednesday.

⑤ The bus was already <u>moving</u> when I jumped on it.

22 위 글의 빈칸 (나)에 들어갈 call의 알맞은 형태는? (3점)

① was calling

② were called

③ is called

④ are called

⑤ called

23 위 글의 괄호 (A), (B), (C) 안에서 옳은 것끼리 짝지어진 것은? (3점)

	(A)	(B)	(C)
①	in	to	because
②	on	with	because
③	in	to	however
④	on	with	however
⑤	in	with	however

24 위 글의 내용과 일치하지 <u>않는</u> 것은? (3점)

① 마침내 Robinson은 다른 선수들과 팬들의 존경을 받는다.

② Robinson 덕분에 다저스는 1947년 내셔널리그 챔피언십에서 우승하게 되었다.

③ 리그에서는 1947년 Robinson에게 신인상을 수여했다.

④ Robinson의 등번호는 42번이었다.

⑤ 매년 Robinson의 생일에 모든 선수는 Robinson이 달았던 번호를 단다.

25 위 글의 내용을 바탕으로 영화를 제작하려고 할 때, 각 팀에서 준비해야 할 사항으로 <u>거리가 먼</u> 것은? (3점)

① 촬영팀: 사람들이 처음엔 Jackie Robinson을 응원하다가 나중엔 소리치고 야유하는 모습을 클로즈업해서 찍을 생각이야.

② 대본팀: 팀 동료 중 한 명이 Jackie Robinson의 어깨를 토닥이는 내용을 대본에 추가해야 해.

③ 소품팀: Jackie Robinson이 받은 올해의 신인상을 준비해야겠어.

④ 편집팀: Jackie Robinson Day를 나타내는 4월 15일이라는 날짜를 자막 효과로 편집해야 해.

⑤ 의상팀: Jackie Robinson Day에 모든 선수들이 입을 42번 번호가 적힌 유니폼을 준비해야겠어.

[26-30] 다음 글을 읽고 물음에 답하시오.

It was New York City (가)_____ April 15, 1947. Jackie Robinson, an African American, went on the field as second baseman for the Brooklyn Dodgers. People couldn't believe their eyes. He was the first African American player to play on a Major League team. That day, the color line was (A)_____.

Robinson faced many difficulties. ⓐ_____ Robinson was a talented player and a gentle person, his teammates did not want to play with him. Every hotel turned the team down ⓑ_____ Robinson was (나)_____ the team. ⓒ_____ he was at bat, people in the stands rudely (B)_____ at him.

Robinson thought to himself, 'I need to keep calm and focus on baseball. I will try and become a player (다)_____ people like. Then, next season, there will be more African American players in the league.' Robinson put all his time and energy into baseball. With practice, he became great at (C)_____ and base running.

27 위 글의 (가), (나)에 공통으로 들어가는 전치사는? (3점)

① on　　　　② of　　　　③ in
④ at　　　　⑤ by

28 위 글의 빈칸 (다)에 들어갈 알맞은 말은? (3점)

① what　　　　② which
③ whose　　　　④ who
⑤ when

29 위 글의 빈칸 ⓐ~ⓒ에 들어갈 접속사가 바르게 짝지어진 것은? (3점)

	ⓐ	ⓑ	ⓒ
①	Because	because	Before
②	Although	when	While
③	Because	because	When
④	Although	because	When
⑤	Because	when	Before

30 위 글을 읽고 답할 수 없는 것은? (3점)

① What position did Jackie Robinson play?
② On which team did Jackie Robinson play?
③ Why did every hotel turn the Dodgers down?
④ How many hours did Jackie Robinson practice?
⑤ When Robinson faced difficulties, what did he think to himself?

26 위 글의 빈칸 (A)~(C)에 들어갈 동사의 적절한 형태는? (3점)

	(A)	(B)	(C)
①	broke	shouted	bat
②	broke	shouting	batting
③	broken	shouted	bat
④	broken	shouting	batting
⑤	broken	shouted	batting

◎ 선택형 문항의 답안은 컴퓨터용 수정 싸인펜을 사용하여 OMR 답안지에 바르게 표기하시오.
◎ 서술형 문제는 답을 답안지에 반드시 검정 볼펜으로 쓰시오.
◎ 총 30문항 100점 만점입니다. 문항별 배점은 각 문항에 표시되어 있습니다.

[경기 ○○중]

01 다음 빈칸에 공통으로 들어갈 말로 가장 적절한 것은? (3점)

> • I wanted to _____ her offer, so I said to her, "No."
> • Will you _____ the volume? I can't focus.

① turn up
② calm down
③ think of
④ turn down
⑤ keep calm

[서울 강남구 ○○중]

02 다음 〈보기〉 중 어법상 빈칸에 사용될 수 있는 동사는 모두 몇 개인가? (3점)

> A: Honey, look at our son. He looks so tired.
> B: That's true. I think we should _____ him to take some rest.

보기
advise / allow / help / let / tell

① 1개   ② 2개   ③ 3개
④ 4개   ⑤ 5개

[부산 ○○중]

03 다음 중 밑줄 친 부분의 우리말 표현이 어색한 것은? (3점)

① People couldn't believe their eyes. (자신들의 눈을 의심하지 않았다)
② Classical music makes me keep calm. (평정을 유지하다)
③ Peter turned down dessert because he was too full. (거절했다)
④ Mr. Kim worked hard and earned the respect of his fiends. (존경을 받았다)
⑤ While Mary was looking at the sky, she thought to herself, "What a wonderful night!" (마음속으로 생각했다)

[경기 ○○중]

04 다음 빈칸에 공통으로 들어갈 수 있는 것은? (3점)

> • She is the girl _____ Sam likes.
> • Everything _____ I said was true.
> • This is the computer _____ I bought yesterday.

① who
② that
③ what
④ whom
⑤ which

05 다음 중 어법상 옳은 문장은? (3점)

① He told me go to the party.

② She encouraged me tried again.

③ My wife warned me not to be late.

④ I always want you to became happy.

⑤ The teacher made us left the classroom.

06 다음 중 생략할 수 있는 관계대명사는? (2개) (3점)

① This is the bike <u>that</u> she lost yesterday.

② This is the movie <u>which</u> was made in Korea.

③ I called my friends <u>who</u> didn't go to school.

④ I want to buy the newspaper <u>that</u> she is reading.

⑤ She saw the window <u>which</u> was broken by someone.

07 다음 문장을 〈조건〉에 맞게 영작하시오. (4점)

> Johnson 씨는 경기 후에 우리에게 악수하라고 말했다.

조건
• 〈보기〉의 어구를 모두 활용하되, 필요한 경우 단어의 형태를 바꿀 것.

보기
tell / shake / after the game

→ _____

08 다음 밑줄 친 부분 중, 어법상 <u>어색한</u> 것은? (3점)

① The phone <u>what</u> you picked up is mine.

② This is the bridge <u>which</u> my father built.

③ She is the scientist <u>whom</u> I want to meet.

④ The movie <u>which</u> I saw was interesting.

⑤ That is the computer <u>which</u> I bought last week.

09 다음 글의 (A), (B)를 목적격 관계대명사를 이용하여 〈조건〉에 맞게 채워 여행 기록을 완성하시오. (6점)

> I visited three countries last year. France was the first country that I visited.
> (A) Smith는 내가 Paris에서 만난 소년이다.
> (B) 그 파란 자전거는 내가 내 여동생을 위해 거기에서 산 선물이다.

조건
• 우리말에 맞게 영작할 것.
• 목적격 관계대명사를 생략하지 말고 반드시 포함하여 영작할 것.
• 목적격 관계대명사는 who, whom, which 중 하나를 사용할 것.

(A): _____

(B): _____

10 다음 두 문장을 관계대명사를 이용하여 한 문장으로 올바르게 만든 것은? (4점)

① This is the bag. I am carrying it.
  → This is the bag which I am carrying it.

② This is the dog. The lady is looking for it.
  → This is the dog which the lady is looking for it.

③ The teacher is Ms. Kim. I like her the most.
  → The teacher who I like the most is Ms. Kim.

④ The dictionary isn't good. I bought it yesterday.
  → The dictionary which I bought it yesterday isn't good.

⑤ You should see the girl. I met her in the contest.
  → You should see the girl who I met her in the contest.

11 다음 문장에서 선행사는 (A), 관계대명사는 (B)로 표시한 것 중 옳은 것은? (3점)

① I like the dress (B)which (A)Mary is wearing.

② (A)This is the guy (B)whom I was talking about.

③ Mina wants to be (A)a singer (B)whom everyone likes.

④ (A)Tom fell in love with the girl (B)who he met at the party.

⑤ The blue watch is the gift (B)which I bought for (A)my brother.

12 다음 우리말과 같은 뜻이 되도록 〈보기〉의 단어 중 일부를 사용하여 빈칸을 채우시오. (한 칸에 한 단어만 쓸 것) (6점)

(1) 나는 그녀에게 창문을 열어 달라고 말했다.
  = I _____ _____ _____ open the window.

(2) 그들은 그가 시험에 통과할 것이라고 예상했다.
  = They _____ _____ _____ _____ the test.

(3) 그녀는 우리에게 시끄럽게 굴지 말라고 충고했다.
  = She _____ _____ _____ _____ _____ a noise.

보기
(1) told / she / to / spoke / her
(2) pass / him / expected / to / passes / he / encouraged / passing / enabled / his
(3) made / to / allowed / us / advised / make / advise / didn't / making / allow / not / we

13 다음 문장을 괄호 안의 말을 재배열하여 완성하시오. (3점)

The boy (is / basketball / playing / outside / who) is my best friend.

→ The boy _____ is my best friend.

14 다음 질문에 대한 대답으로 알맞은 것은? (3점)

> Q: What does "keep my fingers crossed" mean?

① It means it's easy to do.

② It means I wish you good luck.

③ It means working together is better than alone.

④ It means you learn something by doing it over and over.

⑤ It means you can achieve your dream with a strong will.

[16~17] 다음 대화를 읽고 물음에 답하시오.

> Amy: You look sad, Jiho. What's wrong?
> Jiho: I don't think I can achieve my dream.
> Amy: What do you mean by that?
> Jiho: I want to be an actor, but I always fail auditions.
> Amy: Do you know this actor?
> Jiho: Sure. He's a famous movie star.
> Amy: He failed more than 100 auditions.
> Jiho: Really? Maybe I should keep trying. I will practice more for my next audition.

15 다음 대화의 빈칸에 들어갈 알맞은 말은? (3점)

> A: I want to play baduk.
>   Can you _____?
> B: Sure.

① clean it

② walk the dog

③ close the window

④ play it with me

⑤ get out of here

16 위 대화를 읽고 speaker가 Jiho에게 해줄 수 있는 조언을 〈조건〉에 맞추어 쓰시오. (4점)

> To achieve my dream, I went to many auditions, but I often failed. So, I took acting and dancing classes. Finally, I achieved my goal!

─ 조건 ─
• 주어진 우리말과 뜻이 통하도록 쓸 것.
• 「It's ~ that」 구문을 사용할 것.
• that 이하에는 주어와 동사를 반드시 쓸 것.

> 네가 절대 포기하지 않는 것이 중요하다.

→ It's _____ that _____ _____ _____
_____.

17 According to the conversation, which is NOT correct?

(3점)

① Jiho wants to be an actor.

② Jiho thinks he should keep trying.

③ Jiho will practice hard and prepare for the next audition.

④ Jiho is sad because he failed an audition for the first time.

⑤ Amy cheers up Jiho by telling the story about a famous movie star.

18 다음 대화의 (A)~(D)에 들어갈 말을 〈보기〉에서 골라 순서대로 바르게 나열한 것은?

(3점)

> Jiho: I don't think I can achieve my dream.
> Amy: (A) _____
> Jiho: (B) _____
> Amy: (C) _____
> Jiho: (D) _____
> Amy: He failed more than 100 auditions.
> Jiho: Really? Maybe I should keep trying. I will practice more for my next audition.

보기

ⓐ What do you mean by that?

ⓑ Do you know this actor?

ⓒ I want to be an actor, but I always fail auditions. Maybe I have to give up.

ⓓ Sure. He's a famous movie star.

  (A) (B) (C) (D)

① ⓐ ⓒ ⓑ ⓓ

② ⓐ ⓒ ⓓ ⓑ

③ ⓐ ⓑ ⓓ ⓒ

④ ⓒ ⓑ ⓐ ⓓ

⑤ ⓒ ⓑ ⓓ ⓐ

19 다음 중 대화의 흐름이 가장 어색한 것은?

(3점)

① A: How can I become good at drawing?

  B: It takes time. Just draw as often as you can.

② A: I have a singing contest tomorrow.

  B: I wish you good luck.

③ A: I want to write a good story.

  B: It's important that you read many books.

④ A: You look sad. What's wrong?

  B: I'll keep my fingers crossed.

⑤ A: Maybe you should keep trying.

  B: You're right. I'll practice more.

20 다음 대화의 빈칸에 들어갈 말로 가장 적절한 것은?

(3점)

> A: How can I become good at playing the guitar?
> B: It takes time. It's important that _____ _____.
> A: You mean I should keep practicing?
> B: That's right.

① you go to a concert

② you take a guitar class

③ you listen to a lot of music

④ you buy an expensive guitar

⑤ you play as often as you can

Robinson faced many difficulties. (A)[But / Although] Robinson was a talented player and a gentle person, his teammates did not want to play with him. Every hotel turned the team down because Robinson was on the team. When he was at bat, people in the stands rudely shouted at him.

Robinson thought to himself, 'I need to keep calm and focus on baseball. I will try and become a player who people like. Then, next season, there will be more African American players in the league.' Robinson put all his time and energy into baseball. With practice, he became great (B)[at / for] batting and base running.

Robinson's effort moved his teammates. (가) When people shouted at Robinson, one of his teammates walked up to Robinson and tapped him on the shoulder. (나) "Do not listen to them. You're doing fine," he said. His support helped Robinson (C)[played / to play] harder. (다)

Thanks to Robinson, the Dodgers won the National League Championship in 1947. (라) The league recognized Robinson's excellence and presented him with the Rookie of the Year Award in the same year. (마) After that season, other teams asked African American players to join them.

22 위 글의 내용에 알맞은 속담은? [경기 ○○중] (3점)

① Like father, like son.

② Practice makes perfect.

③ It's a walk in the park.

④ No news is good news.

⑤ A friend in need is a friend indeed.

21 위 글의 (가)~(마) 중 주어진 문장이 들어가기에 가장 적절한 곳은? [충북 ○○중] (3점)

Finally, Robinson earned the respect of other players and fans.

① (가) ② (나) ③ (다)

④ (라) ⑤ (마)

23 위 글의 괄호 (A), (B), (C) 안에서 문맥에 맞는 낱말로 가장 적절한 것은? [충북 ○○중] (3점)

	(A)	(B)	(C)
①	Although	at	to play
②	But	at	to play
③	Although	at	played
④	But	for	played
⑤	Although	for	played

24 What can be the best title of the story? (3점)

① The rookie of the year

② Robinson's uniform number

③ National League Championship

④ Robinson's kind teammates

⑤ Robinson, a player who broke the color line

[26~30] 다음 글을 읽고 물음에 답하시오.

It was New York City on April 15, 1947. Jackie Robinson, an African American, went on the field as second baseman for the Brooklyn Dodgers. People couldn't believe their eyes. He was the first African American player to play on a Major League team. That day, (가)the color line was broken.

Robinson faced many difficulties. (A)_____ Robinson was a talented player and a gentle person, his teammates did not want to play with him. Every hotel turned the team down (B)_____ Robinson was on the team. (C)_____ he was at bat, people in the stands rudely shouted at him.

Robinson thought to himself, 'I need to keep calm and focus on baseball. I will try and become a player ⓐ_____. Then, next season, there will be more African American players in the league.' Robinson put all his time and energy into baseball. With practice, he became great at batting and base running.

25 위 글의 내용과 일치하는 것은? (3점)

① Robinson은 많은 행운에 직면했다.

② Robinson은 온화한 사람이었지만 처음에는 팀원들이 함께 경기하기를 원하지 않았다.

③ 관중석에 있는 사람들은 늘 Robinson을 응원했다.

④ Robinson은 침착하게 야구에 집중해야 한다고 친구에게 말했다.

⑤ Robinson은 연습을 통해서 홈런을 칠 수 있었다.

26 위 글의 흐름상 (A)~(C)에 들어갈 말을 순서대로 나열한 것은? (3점)

	(A)	(B)	(C)
①	Because	although	Because
②	When	after	Although
③	After	although	When
④	While	after	Although
⑤	Although	because	When

27 위 글의 ⓐ에 들어갈 말로 적절하지 <u>않은</u> 것은?　(3점)

① people like
② who people like
③ that people like
④ which people like
⑤ whom people like

29 위 글의 내용과 <u>거리가 먼</u> 것은?　(3점)

① 모든 호텔은 Robinson의 팀을 거절했다.
② Jackie Robinson은 브루클린 다저스의 2루수로 경기장에 나갔다.
③ Jackie Robinson은 유능한 선수였기 때문에 동료들로부터 시기와 질투를 받았다.
④ Jackie Robinson이 타석에 있었을 때 관중들이 그를 향해 무례하게 소리쳤다.
⑤ Jackie Robinson은 메이저리그 팀에서 경기한 최초의 아프리카계 미국인 선수였다.

28 위 글의 밑줄 친 (가)color line의 뜻은?　(3점)

① 경계선
② 남녀 차별
③ 학력 차별
④ 지역 차별
⑤ 인종 차별

30 Why did Jackie Robinson have difficulties when he played baseball?　(4점)

→ Because _____.

◎ 선택형 문항의 답안은 컴퓨터용 수정 싸인펜을 사용하여 OMR 답안지에 바르게 표기하시오.

◎ 서술형 문제는 답을 답안지에 반드시 검정 볼펜으로 쓰시오.

◎ 총 30문항 100점 만점입니다. 문항별 배점은 각 문항에 표시되어 있습니다.

[대전 ○○중]

01 다음 동사들 중에서 과거분사가 <u>잘못된</u> 것은? (3점)

① cry → cryed
② cut → cut
③ lose → lost
④ read → read
⑤ teach → taught

[서울 강남구 ○○중]

02 다음 빈칸에 사용하기에 <u>어색한</u> 단어 하나는? (4점)

• Jegichagi is a _____ Korean game.
• The boy learned how to _____ up the numbers.
• The book was written from my _____ experience.
• We enjoyed the tomato festival that took _____ in Spain last month.

① add
② temperature
③ place
④ personal
⑤ traditional

[부산 ○○중]

03 다음 빈칸 (A), (B)에 들어갈 말이 순서대로 바르게 짝지어진 것은? (3점)

• They enjoyed the tomato festival that (A)_____ in Spain last month.
• My English teacher (B)_____ the classroom while we did our group work.

	(A)	(B)
①	took place	moved around
②	takes place	moving around
③	took place	move around
④	taking place	moving around
⑤	takes place	moved around

[충북 ○○중]

04 다음 중 문장의 표현 방식이 어색한 것 <u>두 개</u>를 고르면? (3점)

① Mary has good musical skills. She sings well.
② It's not easy to live in other countries because of cultural differences.
③ Everything in this story is about me. It was written from my person experience.
④ My younger sister learned how to add up the numbers one to ten.
⑤ I have lived in Busan a month ago.

05 다음 주어진 뜻이 되도록 빈칸에 들어갈 말로 가장 적절한 것은? (3점)

> 우리는 1999년부터 서로 알고 지냈다.
> We have _____ each other since 1999.

① know
② knew
③ known
④ be known
⑤ were known

07 다음 우리말을 조동사 may와 〈보기〉의 표현을 활용하여 알맞게 영작하시오. (4점)

> 나는 확신하지 못하지만 수민이가 나에게 약간의 도움을 줄지도 모른다.

보기
Sumin / offer

→ I'm not sure, but _____

08 다음 주어진 뜻이 모두 포함되도록 올바르게 영작한 것은? (3점)

> • I started to live in Korea in 2010.
> • I still live in Korea now.

① I live in Korea now.
② I lived in Korea in 2010.
③ I have been to Korea in 2010.
④ I have lived in Korea for 2010.
⑤ I have lived in Korea since 2010.

09 다음 문장을 〈조건〉에 맞게 현재완료가 포함된 문장으로 영작하시오. (4점)

> Andy는 그의 침실을 꾸미는 것을 막 끝냈다.

조건
• 〈보기〉의 단어를 모두 활용하되, 필요한 경우 단어의 형태를 바꿀 것.

보기
finish / decorate / just

→ Andy _____.

06 다음 우리말을 올바르게 영작한 것은? (3점)

> 오늘 오후에는 비가 오지 않을지도 모른다.

① It can rain this afternoon.
② It must not rain this afternoon.
③ It can't rain that afternoon.
④ It may not rain this afternoon.
⑤ It may not rain that afternoon.

10 다음 주어진 문장에서 어법상 <u>어색한</u> 부분을 모두 찾아 올바르게 고치시오. (5점)

> There may are some things who I needs to do to achieve my dreams.

→ _____

12 Fill in the blank. (3점)

> A: I want to make a webtoon but I can't draw well. What should I do?
> B: It takes time. _____ you draw as often as you can and never give up.

① What do you

② Can you do that

③ I'm surprised she

④ I'm surprised that

⑤ It's important that

13 다음 대화의 내용과 일치하는 것은? (3점)

> A: May I help you?
> B: Hi, I'm looking for a smart watch. Can you show me one?
> A: Sure. Look at this one. It can play music for you.
> B: Sounds cool.
> A: Also, you can search for anything just by talking to it.
> B: That's great. I will take it.

① A는 더 나은 제품을 인터넷으로 검색해 주었다.

② A가 추천해 준 제품에는 음성 인식 기능이 있다.

③ A는 음악을 작곡하는 기능이 있는 제품을 추천했다.

④ B는 사용하던 시계가 고장이 나서 새 시계를 구입하려고 한다.

⑤ B는 제품을 가져가서 체험을 해본 후에 구입 여부를 결정하기로 했다.

11 다음 대화의 밑줄 친 부분 중 어법상 <u>어색한</u> 것은? (3점)

> A: Oh, I forgot ⓐ<u>to turn off</u> the heater before I ⓑ<u>left</u> home.
> B: Really? Then do you need to return home?
> A: No, I can ⓒ<u>turn off it</u> with my smartphone.
> B: Wow, I'm ⓓ<u>surprised</u> that you can turn off the heater ⓔ<u>with</u> your smartphone.

① ⓐ   ② ⓑ   ③ ⓒ

④ ⓓ   ⑤ ⓔ

[14~16] 다음 대화를 읽고 물음에 답하시오.

Sena: Wow, there are so many books in this library.

Laura: You're right. Where can we find books about gravity?

Sena: Well... How about asking about it to a librarian?

Terry: Hi, I'm Terry, the AI librarian. Can I help you?

Sena: Hi. We're looking for books about gravity. Can you recommend one, please?

Terry: We have fifty seven books about gravity in this library. I think The Law of Gravity will be the best one for you.

Laura: (A)_____.

Sena: Right. (B)_____. Where is the book, Terry?

Terry: It's on the third floor. Come with me.

15 위 대화의 빈칸 (A)에 들어갈 적절한 말을 〈조건〉에 따라 서술하시오. (4점)

조건

- 단어 surprise를 활용하시오. (필요시 형태를 변형하시오.)
- 7단어 이상 10단어 이하의 완전한 문장으로 작성하시오.

→ _____

14 위 대화를 읽고 알 수 있는 것으로 적절하지 <u>않은</u> 것은? (3점)

① Sena and Laura were in the library which had an AI librarian.

② At first, Sena and Laura didn't know where the books which they're looking for were.

③ Sena and Laura were heard that there were many books about gravity.

④ Terry knew where the book he recommended was.

⑤ Terry would bring the book Sena and Laura want to them.

16 위 대화의 (B)에 들어갈 말로 알맞지 <u>않은</u> 것은? (3점)

① What a surprise!

② Can I help you?

③ I can't believe this.

④ I'm surprised.

⑤ That's amazing.

17 다음 중 대화의 흐름이 <u>어색한</u> 것은? (3점)

① A: May I have your last name, please?

B: Yes. It's Kim.

② A: I don't know why she is upset.

B: Well, she may have failed her test.

③ A: How may I help you?

B: I want to make a reservation for tonight.

④ A: May I sit here?

B: Yes, you may. This seat is taken.

⑤ A: What are you doing here? You may not come in without permission.

B: Sorry, I didn't know that.

19 다음 (A)~(C)를 자연스러운 대화가 되도록 바르게 배열한 것은? (3점)

A: Would you like to see our smart refrigerator?

(A) This button shows you the food items inside it and this one shows you recipes.

(B) I'm surprised that the refrigerator can do those things.

(C) Sure. What are these buttons for?

① (A) - (C) - (B)

② (B) - (A) - (C)

③ (B) - (C) - (A)

④ (C) - (A) - (B)

⑤ (C) - (B) - (A)

18 다음 대화의 내용과 일치하는 것은? (3점)

A: Are you ready for your trip to London?

B: Yes, but I'm worried about getting lost. I'm not good at finding places.

A: Don't worry. There are many good smartphone apps you can use.

B: Can you show me one?

A: Sure. Use this one. It shows you a map of the city and pictures of streets.

B: Oh, thanks.

① A is leaving for London.

② A does not use a smartphone.

③ B is very good at finding places.

④ B does not like the app that A recommends.

⑤ Users can see the pictures of streets on the smartphone app.

[20~27] 다음 글을 읽고 물음에 답하시오.

ⓐ<u>Advances in science and technology has caused many changes in our lives so far.</u> In the future, science and technology will make more changes. Let's see (A)<u>what our lives may be like in the future.</u>

<Sangho in the Shopping Center>

Shopping is much easier. There are no lines and no counters. ⓑ<u>Sangho enters a shop with his smartphone which has a special shopping app.</u> In the shop, he takes the items he wants. ⓒ<u>The items are automatically add to a virtual card on his smartphone.</u> (B)_____, it is automatically removed from his list of purchases. When he finishes shopping, Sangho does not need to wait in line to pay. His virtual card will (C)<u>charge</u> him later.

<Sumin's 3D Printed House and Clothes>
　Sumin lives in a 3D printed house. Building a 3D printed house is faster and cheaper than building a house with traditional methods. Sumin's house looks fantastic because of its unique design. ⓓA 3D printer can produce house shapes cannot make with traditional building methods and materials. Sumin also likes to make her clothes at home by using a 3D printer. ⓔShe can choose colors and materials and can design clothes that fit her body and suits her tastes. Sumin is now a (가)＿＿＿＿＿＿＿＿＿＿＿！

[서울 강남구 ○○중]

20 위 글의 밑줄 친 ⓐ~ⓔ 중 어법상 옳은 문장은? (4점)

① ⓐ　　　② ⓑ　　　③ ⓒ

④ ⓓ　　　⑤ ⓔ

[서울 강남구 ○○중]

22 위 글의 (A)를 어법에 맞게 직접의문문으로 바꾼 것은? (3점)

① What may our lives like in the future?

② What maybe our lives like in the future?

③ What may our lives be like in the future?

④ What our lives may like be in the future?

⑤ What maybe our lives likes in the future?

[경기 ○○중]

21 위 글의 의도로 가장 적절한 것은? (3점)

① to invite

② to inform

③ to thank

④ to persuade

⑤ to entertain

[서울 강남구 ○○중]

23 위 글의 내용상 (B)에 들어갈 말로 알맞은 것은? (3점)

① If he puts an item back

② If he takes another item

③ If he finds something to eat

④ If he wants to get out of the store

⑤ If someone wants to buy the same item

24 위 글의 (C)charge와 같은 뜻으로 사용된 것은?　　(3점)

① Actually, I am in <u>charge</u> of the office.

② There is no extra <u>charge</u> for breakfast.

③ They fixed my smartphone free of <u>charge</u>.

④ Would you like to put that on your <u>charge</u>?

⑤ The museum doesn't <u>charge</u> for admission.

26 위 글에 대해 일치하는 설명은 T, 일치하지 <u>않는</u> 설명은 F라 할 때 바르게 표시된 것은?　　(4점)

① Sangho doesn't use his smart phone for his shopping. (T)

② Sangho should wait in line for a long time to pay. (T)

③ Sangho goes into a shop without his smart phone. (T)

④ Sumin's house has a unique design. (F)

⑤ Sumin can make her own clothes with a 3D printer. (T)

27 위 글의 3D printer에 대한 설명으로 옳은 것은?　　(3점)

① It cannot make a huge thing like a house.

② Making something with a 3D printer costs more than making it with a traditional way.

③ People prefer to make a common shaped objects with 3D printers.

④ When you use a 3D printer, you can't choose the material which you want.

⑤ You can make 3D printed clothes that match you well.

25 위 글의 빈칸 (가)에 들어갈 적당한 표현은?　　(3점)

① scientist

② builder

③ teacher

④ store owner

⑤ fashion designer

[28~29] 다음 글을 읽고 물음에 답하시오.

Dongmin is visiting his grandfather in the hospital. An AI nurse enters the room. It moves around the room and checks the patients' conditions. When the AI nurse finds that Dongmin's grandfather has a high temperature, it gives him some medicine to lower his temperature.

Have you ever thought about these (A)_____? Some (A)_____ have already started to take place while others may start in the near future. Can you imagine other changes? Take some time to think about them.

[경기 ○○중]

28 위 글의 제목으로 가장 적절한 것은? (4점)

① AI의 장단점

② AI의 발달 과정

③ AI로 인한 부작용

④ AI는 어떻게 시작되었는가

⑤ AI가 가져올 수 있는 미래의 모습

[경기 ○○중]

29 위 글의 (A)에 공통으로 들어갈 낱말로 가장 적절한 것은? (3점)

① changes

② conditions

③ medicines

④ hospitals

⑤ temperatures

[충북 ○○중]

30 다음 글의 요지로 가장 적절한 것은? (4점)

Students are automatically checked for attendance as they pass through the school gate in the morning. There will be a smart wall in the classroom. It is a wall of screen that can use the whole wall as a digital blackboard. Students may learn 3D printing. AI teachers may help students at school. There may be a drone station in every school. Students may not carry paper textbooks anymore.

① Paper books will disappear in the future society.

② In the future, there will be several changes in the school.

③ A school becomes useless because of advances in technology.

④ There are some differences between the past school and the present school.

⑤ A drone and a 3d printer are the most important technologies in the future.

2학년 영어 2학기 기말고사(8과) 2회

문항수 : 선택형(24문항) 서술형(6문항)   20 . . .

◎ 선택형 문항의 답안은 컴퓨터용 수정 싸인펜을 사용하여 OMR 답안지에 바르게 표기하시오.
◎ 서술형 문제는 답을 답안지에 반드시 검정 볼펜으로 쓰시오.
◎ 총 30문항 100점 만점입니다. 문항별 배점은 각 문항에 표시되어 있습니다.

[대전 ○○중]

01 다음 중 〈보기〉와 같이 형용사로 바꿀 수 있는 것은? (3점)

> 보기
>
> tradition → traditional

① culture
② silence
③ importance
④ difference
⑤ excellence

[대전 ○○중]

02 다음 〈보기〉의 영영 풀이에 해당하는 단어는? (3점)

> 보기
>
> to ask someone to pay money

① charge   ② demand
③ method   ④ advance
⑤ purchase

[경기 ○○중]

03 다음은 동사의 3단 변화(원형-과거형-과거분사형)를 나타낸 것이다. 동사의 3단 변화가 <u>어색한</u> 것은? (3점)

① cut – cut – cut
② wear – wore – worn
③ find – found – found
④ mean – meant – meant
⑤ forget – forget – forgotten

[경기 ○○중]

04 다음 빈칸에 공통으로 들어갈 말로 가장 적절한 것은? (3점)

> • When the doctor left, the _____ looked at his wife.
> • You can't master math in a day. So be _____.

① patient
② charge
③ purchase
④ method
⑤ advance

[서울 강남구 ○○중]

05 다음 중 어법상 옳은 문장은 <u>모두</u> 몇 개인가? (3점)

> ⓐ I have swum in the river before.
> ⓑ Have you ever being to Europe?
> ⓒ They have never read a newspaper.
> ⓓ Sam have just drawn a beautiful picture.
> ⓔ We have been friends for a long time.

① 1개   ② 2개   ③ 3개
④ 4개   ⑤ 5개

[서울 강남구 ○○중]

06 다음 중 어법상 올바르지 <u>않은</u> 것은? (3점)

① May I try it on?
② Brian may not interested in math.
③ He may be tired after a long fight.
④ I'm not sure, but she may offer me some help.
⑤ Students may not carry paper textbooks anymore.

07 다음 문장을 어법에 맞지 않는 한 단어를 고쳐 올바른 문장으로 다시 쓰시오. (6점)

> (1) I have missing you so much.
> (2) Has you ever heard of this actor?
> (3) There may are other people that I don't know.

> **조건**
> • 문장 전체를 완성할 것.

(1) _____
(2) _____
(3) _____

09 다음 우리말을 조동사 may와 〈보기〉의 어구를 활용하여 알맞게 영작하시오. (4점)

> Chris는 답을 알지 못할지도 모른다.

> **보기**
> may / the answer

→ _____

10 다음 중 짝지어진 두 문장의 의미가 서로 <u>다른</u> 것은? (3점)

① She has gone to London.
  = She is planning to go to London.
② I was pleased with the gift.
  = I was pleased to receive the gift.
③ When did Columbus discover America?
  = When was America discovered by Columbus?
④ We call the day "Jackie Robinson Day."
  = The day is called "Jackie Robinson Day".
⑤ He lost his watch, so he doesn't have it now.
  = He has lost his watch.

08 다음 문장을 〈조건〉에 맞게 현재완료가 포함된 문장으로 영작하시오. (4점)

> Julie는 Brown씨를 10년 동안 알고 지냈다.

> **조건**
> • 〈보기〉의 단어를 모두 활용하되, 필요한 경우 단어의 형태를 바꿀 것.

> **보기**
> know / Mr. Brown / for

→ Julie _____.

11 다음 상황을 조건에 맞게 한 문장으로 작성하시오. (4점)

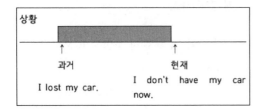

상황

과거   현재

I lost my car.   I don't have my car now.

조건

• 5단어로 된 현재완료 형태의 문장으로 작성할 것.

→ _____ _____ _____ _____

_____.

[13~15] 다음 대화를 읽고 물음에 답하시오.

A: Wow, there are so many books in this library.
H: You're right. Where can we find books about gravity?
T: Hi, I'm Terry, the AI librarian. How can I help you?
A: Hi. We're looking for books about gravity. (가)_____
T: We have fifty seven books about gravity in this library. I think The Law of Gravity will be the best one for you.
H: I'm surprised that ⓐ_____, Terry.
A: Right. That's amazing. Where is the book?
T: It's on the third floor. Come with me.

*A: Amy, H: Hana, T: Terry
*AI: Artificial Intelligence

12 다음 대화의 빈칸에 들어갈 말로 가장 적절한 것은? (3점)

A: I guess people may use a huge umbrella in the future.
B: _____
A: Sure. When it rains heavily, people may cover the city with the huge umbrella.
B: That's an interesting idea.
A: Maybe we can call it the 'Smart Umbrella.'

① May I borrow yours?
② Can you tell me more?
③ What is the price of that?
④ What do you think about that?
⑤ Can you recommend one, please?

13 위 대화의 내용과 일치하는 것은? (4점)

① Terry는 인간 사서이다.
② Amy는 도서관에서 57권의 책을 읽었다.
③ 책 The Law of Gravity는 도서관 5층에 있다.
④ Hana는 Terry의 추천을 마음에 들어하지 않는다.
⑤ Terry는 도서관에 있는 책들에 대한 정보를 가지고 있다.

14 위 대화의 내용상 ⓐ에 들어갈 말로 알맞은 것은? (3점)

① you can smell things on TV

② you can recommend books

③ you can work without gravity

④ you can feel water on your face

⑤ you can run 100 meters in 5 seconds

16 다음 대화의 흐름이 <u>어색한</u> 것은? (3점)

① A: Can you play baduk with me, please?

B: Sure. Let's play baduk.

② A: Please put these VR glasses on.

B: All right. Wow, it looks so real.

③ A: Oh, I forgot to turn off the heater.

B: I think we will drive cars in space.

④ A: Is there anything that surprises you?

B: I'm surprised that this car can drive itself automatically.

⑤ A: Hi, I'm looking for a smart watch.

B: Look at this one. It can play music for you.

17 다음 대화의 괄호 (A), (B), (C) 안에서 문맥에 맞는 것을 골라 순서대로 짝지은 것은? (3점)

M: Welcome. This is our new smartlight application. You don't have to use your (A)[hands / cellphone] to control the light.

W: Really? Then (B)[can / let] you tell me how to do it?

M: Just say, "Light on!" or "Light out!"

W: Light on or light out? That's very (C)[clear / difficult].

	(A)	(B)	(C)
①	hands	can	clear
②	hands	can	difficult
③	hands	let	clear
④	cellphone	can	clear
⑤	cellphone	let	difficult

15 위 대화의 (가)에 들어갈 말을 <조건>에 맞추어 완성하시오. (4점)

조건
• 주어진 우리말과 뜻이 통하도록 쓸 것.
• 조동사 can을 쓸 것.
• 주어를 반드시 쓸 것.

하나 추천해 줄 수 있나요?

→ _____ _____ _____ one, please?

These days, many things can work like humans. Some cars can travel without a human driver. We can make smartphones do simple work only by talking to them. I'm surprised that we're already living in the future.

[대전 ○○중]

18 위 글은 무엇에 대한 내용인가? (3점)

① 아동 학대
② 인공지능
③ 환경 오염
④ 특수 효과
⑤ 스마트폰 기술

[서울 강남구 ○○중]

19 위 글의 글쓴이의 심경으로 알맞은 것은? (3점)

① bored
② annoyed
③ surprised
④ disappointed
⑤ uninterested

Advances in science and technology have caused many changes in our lives so far. In the future, science and technology will make more changes. Let's see (라)(our, what, may, lives, be, like) in the near future.

(A) Sangho in the Shopping Center
(가) In the shop, he takes the items he wants. The items are automatically added to a virtual card on his smartphone. If Sangho puts an item back, it is automatically removed from his list of purchases. (나) When he finishes shopping, Sangho does not need to wait in line to pay. His virtual card adds up all the prices and will (바)charge him later. Isn't that fancy? (다) Shopping is _____ easier. There are no lines and no counters. Sangho enters a shop with his smartphone which has a special shopping app.

(B) Sumin's 3D Printed House and Clothes
(ㄱ) Sumin lives in a 3D printed house. Building a 3D printed house is faster and cheaper than building a house with traditional methods. (ㄴ) Sumin's house looks fantastic because of its unique design. (ㄷ) A 3D printer can produce house shapes that people cannot make with traditional building methods and materials. (ㄹ) She can choose colors and materials and can design clothes that fit her body and suit her tastes. (ㅁ) Sumin is now a fashion designer!

(C) Dongmin in the Hospital
Dongmin is visiting his grandfather in the hospital. An AI nurse ⓐenters the room. It moves around the room and ⓑchecks the patients' conditions. When the AI nurse ⓒfinds that Dongmin's grandfather has a high temperature, it ⓓgives him some medicine to ⓔincrease his temperature.

Have you ever thought about these changes? Some changes have already started to take place while others (마)may start in the near future. Can you imagine other changes? Take some time to think about them.

20 위 글 (A)의 (가)~(다)를 순서에 맞게 배열한 것으로 가장 적절한 것은? (3점)

① (가)-(다)-(나)

② (나)-(가)-(다)

③ (나)-(다)-(가)

④ (다)-(가)-(나)

⑤ (다)-(나)-(가)

21 위 글 (B)의 흐름으로 보아 주어진 문장이 들어가기에 가장 적절한 곳은? (3점)

> Sumin also likes to make her clothes at home by using a 3D printer.

① (ㄱ)　　　② (ㄴ)　　　③ (ㄷ)

④ (ㄹ)　　　⑤ (ㅁ)

22 위 글에서 (다) 문단의 빈칸에 들어갈 단어로 적절하지 <u>않은</u> 것은? (3점)

① very

② a lot

③ still

④ far

⑤ much

23 위 글의 밑줄 친 (라)의 괄호 안의 단어들을 내용에 맞게 순서대로 배열한 것은? (3점)

① what our lives may be like

② what our may be like lives

③ what like our lives may be

④ what may our lives be like

⑤ what be our lives may like

24 위 글의 (바)charge와 의미가 <u>다른</u> 것은? (3점)

① We <u>charge</u> ten dollars for this service.

② The government has <u>charged</u> with the development of sport in the city.

③ How much do you <u>charge</u> to dry-clean pants?

④ Please <u>charge</u> the dinner bill to my room.

⑤ If you do not return the book by December 14th, the library will <u>charge</u> you a late fee.

25 위 글의 밑줄 친 (마)may와 쓰임이 <u>다른</u> 것은? (3점)

① She <u>may</u> be American.

② It <u>may</u> rain in the evening.

③ You <u>may</u> come in if you wish.

④ Nelson <u>may</u> not want to go there.

⑤ Jack <u>may</u> go to the library tomorrow.

28 위 글에 쓰인 단어의 의미가 옳지 <u>않은</u> 것은? (3점)

단어	의미
① item	(A) 물건, 물품
② automatically	(A) 자동으로
③ charge	(A) 충전하다
④ with	(B) ~으로(수단, 방법)
⑤ conditions	(C) 상태, 상황

26 위 글 (C)의 밑줄 친 ⓐ~ⓔ 중 문맥상 낱말의 쓰임이 적절하지 <u>않은</u> 것은? (3점)

① ⓐ   ② ⓑ   ③ ⓒ

④ ⓓ   ⑤ ⓔ

29 위 글 (A)의 (나)단락에서 밑줄 친 that이 의미하는 바를 우리말로 서술하시오. (4점)

→ _____

27 위 글을 읽고 답할 수 <u>없는</u> 질문은? (4점)

① What can a 3D printer produce?

② What does Sangho enter a shop with?

③ What does an AI nurse do in the hospital?

④ If Sangho puts an item back, what happens?

⑤ What has made many difficulties in our lives so far?

30 위 글의 제목으로 가장 알맞은 것은? (3점)

① The Shopping Center in the Future

② Changing Society

③ Useful Inventions of the Past

④ Advances in Shopping

⑤ Information and Technology

정답 및 해설

Lesson 5 (중간)

01 ④	**02** ①	**03** ②	**04** ②	**05** ③	**06** ②

07 His car is washed by him　**08** ①　**09** ④　**10** ⑤

11 It rained so hard that we put off the picnic.　**12** ①　**13** ④

14 ③　**15** ③　**16** ②　**17** ②　**18** ②　**19** ④　**20** ⑤　**21** ④

22 ①　**23** ②　**24** ②　**25** ④　**26** ③

27 Madrid is famous for soccer.　　**28** ③　**29** ⑤

30 It was so delicious that we all enjoyed it.

01 ④ impress는 '깊은 인상을 주다'라는 뜻을 가진 동사이다.

02 어떤 장소의 여러 부분을 보기 위해 그 장소를 살펴보는 것은 ① tour(관광)이다.

03 (A) take a closer look at ~: ~를 자세히 살펴보다
(B) go on: 계속되다
(C) careful: 주의하는, 조심하는

04 ⓐ plain: 평원, 평지　ⓑ mountain: 산　ⓒ lake: 호수
ⓓ forest: 숲　ⓔ desert: 사막

05 수동태 문장을 만들 때는 본래의 동사를 be+p.p(과거분사형)로 고치는 것 뿐만 아니라 시제를 본래 문장과 일치시켜 표현해야 한다. 또한 본래 문장에서 주어 자리에 있던 행위의 주체는 by를 붙여 문장 뒤에 쓴다.

06 ⓐ 다음주에 울타리를 칠할 것이라는 내용이므로 미래 시제의 능동태인 will paint가 적절하다. / ⓑ 저곳에 내년에 새로운 건물이 지어질 것이라는 내용이다. 주어가 A new building이므로 미래 시제의 수동태인 will be built가 어법상 적절하다.

07 수동태 문장을 만들 때는 본래의 동사를 be+p.p(과거분사형)로 고치는 것 뿐만 아니라 시제를 본래 문장과 일치시켜 표현해야 한다. 또한 본래 문장에서 주어 자리에 있던 행위의 주체는 by를 붙여 문장 뒤에 쓴다. 따라서 his car가 주어가 되는 His car is washed by him으로 쓰는 것이 어법상 적절하다.

08 ① were written → was written으로 고쳐야 어법상 적절한 문장이 된다.

09 ① turned off → was turned off / ② is → was / ③ speaks → is spoken / ⑤ was made → made로 고쳐야 어법상 적절한 문장이 된다.

10 위 표에 따르면, Nha Trang은 아름다운 해변이 있고 Halong Bay에는 1969개의 섬이 있다고 한다. ⑤ Every year lots of tourists were visited by Halong Bay and Nha Trang.(매년 많은 관광객들이 Halong Bay와 Nha Trang에 의해 방문을 받

는다)는 언급은 어법상 잘못 되었으며 언급되어 있지도 않다.

11 'so ~ that 주어+동사' 구문은 '너무 ~해서 …하다'라는 의미로 인과 관계를 나타낸다.

12 위 대화에서 A는 병원 가는 길에 대해서 묻고 있다. 현재 위치에서 병원은 두 블록을 가서 우회전하면 왼쪽에 있는 건물이며 극장의 건너편에 있다. 따라서 (A) two blocks, (B) right, (C) left, (D) across from이 들어가는 것이 적절하다.

13 A가 "스파게티와 피자 중에 어느 것을 더 좋아하니?"라고 질문했으므로 이에 대한 B의 대답으로 가장 적절한 것은 ④ "I prefer ~.(난 ~을/를 선호해.)"이다.

14 B의 질문에 대한 G의 대답이 "두 블록을 직진해서 우회전하세요"이다. 따라서 빈칸에 들어갈 B의 말로 가장 적절한 것은 ③ Can you tell me how to(~하는 법을 말해주실 수 있나요?)이다.

15 "보라색 셔츠와 노란색 셔츠 중 어느 것을 좋아하니?"라는 A의 질문에 "응. 난 빨간색 셔츠를 좋아해."라는 B의 대답은 대화 흐름상 적절하지 않다.

16 "어느 것을 선호하세요?"라는 문장이 들어가기에 가장 적절한 곳은 하나의 엄마가 런던 아이가 더 마음에 든다고 말한 곳 앞인 (B)이다.

17 위 대화에서 ② What time do Hana and her mom get on the bus?(하나와 엄마는 버스를 몇 시에 타는가?)에 대해서는 언급된 바 없다.

18 위 글에서는 런던 도시 투어에 온 걸 환영한다고 말하면서 런던의 관광 명소인 런던 아이에 대해서 설명하고 있다. 따라서 위 글의 목적으로 가장 적절한 것은 ② to tell tourists about the London Eye(런던 아이에 대해서 관광객들에게 말해주기 위해)가 적절하다.

19 동사 impress는 '깊은 인상을 주다'라는 뜻을 갖는다.
ⓓ impressed → was impressed로 고쳐야 어법상 적절한 문장이 된다.

20 마지막 문단에서 글쓴이는 아주 멋진 경험을 했다고 말하면서 다시 방문하고 싶다고 말하고 있다. 따라서 글쓴이의 심정으로 가장 적절한 것은 ⑤ pleased(기쁜)이다.

21 위 글에 따르면, 형형색색의 도마뱀을 본 곳은 Sagrada Família가 아니라 Park Guell이다.

22 ① cheer: 응원하다　② creativity: 창조성, 창의성
③ travel: 여행하다　④ nature: 자연
⑤ shine(shone의 현재형): 빛나다

23 위 글에서는 스페인이 세계의 많은 사람들이 즐길 수 있는 음식들로 유명하다고 말하면서 스페인 음식들에 대해서 설명하고 있다. 따라서 위 글의 제목으로 가장 적절한 것은 ② '스페인의 고유 음식'이다.

24 위 글에서 'Jamón is dried Spanish ham that is served in

thin slices.(하몽은 얇게 자른 채로 제공되는 건조된 스페인 햄이다)'라고 언급되어 있다.

25 위 글에서는 ④ How many tourists visit Madrid every year?(매년 몇 명의 관광객들이 마드리드를 방문하는가?)에 대해서는 언급되어 있지 않다.

26 본문에 쓰인 match는 '경기, 시합'이라는 뜻으로 사용되었다. ③match는 '성냥'이라는 뜻을 가진 명사이다.

27 be famous for ~: ~로 유명하다

28 (A) in ~: ~를 입은 (B) with: ~를 써서
(C) for dinner: 저녁 식사로

29 위 글의 두 번째 문단에서는 스페인 음식인 파에야를 저녁식사로 먹으면서 한국의 볶음밥과 비슷하다고 짧게 언급했다. 따라서 ⑥ Fried rice is very popular in Korea.(볶음밥은 한국에서 매우 유명하다.)라는 문장은 흐름상 적절하지 않다.

30 'so+형용사/부사+that+주어+동사' 구문은 '너무 ~해서 …하다'라는 의미로 인과 관계를 나타낸다.

Lesson 5 (중간) 2회

```
01 ④  02 ⑤  03 ⑤  04 ③  05 ②  06 ④
07 (A) was (B) written (C) weren't (D) taken (E) being
    (E) built
08 Is your mask worn by you  09 ④  10 ③  11 ③  12 ④
13 Which do you prefer?     14 ②  15 ③
16 ⓐ Which city do you prefer, Tokyo or London?
    ⓑ I prefer London.
17 ②  18 ③  19 ④  20 ⑤  21 ①  22 ③  23 ⑤  24 ②
25 ②  26 ②  27 ③  28 ⑤  29 ⑤  30 ⑤
```

01 try on: ~을 입어보다 / on foot: 걸어서

02 첫 문장은 '감기에 걸렸을 때는, 따뜻한 물을 마시는 것이 도움이 된다'라는 의미이다. 두 번째는 '운전자들은 스쿨존에서 운전할 때 더 조심해야 한다'라는 의미의 문장이다. 따라서 빈칸에는 ⑤ helpful(도움이 되는) - careful(조심하는, 주의하는)이 가장 적절하다.

03 ⑤ '사람들이 길을 건널 때에는 더 조심해야 한다'라는 의미의 문장이다. 따라서 care는 '주의하는, 조심하는'이라는 뜻을 가진 형용사 careful로 고치는 것이 적절하다.

04 ③ take a choice → make a choice(선택하다)로 고쳐야 어법상 적절한 문장이 된다.

05 'so ~ that 주어+동사' 구문은 '너무 ~해서 …하다'라는 의미로 인과 관계를 나타낸다. 따라서 too를 so로 고치는 것이 어법상 적절하다.

06 ① were → was / ② made → were made / ③ interested by → are interested in / ⑤ Did → Were로 고쳐야 어법상 적절한 문장이 된다.

07 수동태는 '주어+be동사+동사의 과거분사+by+행위자'의 형식을 가지며 '…에 의해 ~되다[당하다]'라는 의미로 주어가 동사가 나타내는 행위를 당하거나 행동의 영향을 받는 것을 나타낸다. 수동태 문장의 주어 자리에는 능동태 문장의 목적어가 오고, by 다음에는 능동태 문장의 주어를 쓴다. 누가 그 동작을 했는지 중요하지 않거나 잘 모를 때, 수동태 문장으로 표현한다. 수동태는 현재, 과거, 미래 시제로 쓸 수 있고, 'be동사+동사의 과거분사'에서 be동사로 시제를 표현한다.

08 능동태 문장을 수동태 문장으로 바꿀 때, 수동태 문장의 주어 자리에는 능동태 문장의 목적어가 오고, by 다음에는 능동태 문장의 주어를 쓴다. 시제는 능동태 문장의 시제를 따른다. 따라서 your mask가 주어가 되는 의문문인 Is your mask worn by you로 쓰는 것이 어법상 적절하다.

09 ① catched → caught / ② not was broken → was not broken / ③ when it was did → when it was done / ⑤ is → are로 고쳐야 어법상 적절한 문장이 된다.

10 ⓓ hard that so → so hard that / ⓔ so a nice film → such a nice film로 고쳐야 어법상 적절한 문장이 된다.

11 전치사 by 뒤에는 목적격 대명사가 오는 것이 적절하다. 따라서 ③ by his → by him으로 고쳐야 어법상 적절한 문장이 된다.

12 "Which do you prefer, A or B?"는 "A와 B 중에 어떤 것을 더 선호하니?"라는 뜻으로 상대방의 선호를 묻는 표현이다.

13 남학생의 말에 대한 대답으로 여학생은 7시 상영하는 영화를 선호한다고 말하고 있다. 따라서 빈칸에 들어갈 말로 가장 적절한 것은 상대방의 선호를 묻는 표현인 "Which do you prefer, A or B?"이다. 'A or B'는 생략 가능하다.

14 Matt가 지수에게 영화를 보자고 제안하면서 5시 상영과 7시 상영하는 영화 중에 어느 것을 선호하는지 물어보고 있다.

15 A가 "이 긴 드레스는 뭐라고 불립니까?"라고 묻자, B가 그것은 아오자이이며, 베트남 전통 복식이라고 대답한다. A가 입어봐도 되냐고 묻자, B가 보라색과 노란색 중에 어떤 것이 더 마음에 드는지 묻고, A가 보라색이라고 말하는 순서로 이어지는 것이 흐름상 가장 자연스럽다.

16 "Which do you prefer, A or B?"는 "A와 B 중에 어느 것을 더 선호하니?"라는 뜻으로 상대방의 선호를 묻는 표현이다. 이에 대한 대답은 "I prefer A to B." 혹은 "I like A better than B." 등으로 할 수 있다.

17 "카레와 파에야 중에 어느 것을 고를 거니?"라는 A의 질문에 대해 "응. 난 과일 주스를 선택할래."라는 B의 대답은 흐름상 자연스럽지 않다.

18 "난 강과 호수가 어떻게 다른지 궁금해."라는 문장이 들어가기에 가장 적절한 곳은 Ben이 강과 호수의 차이점을 설명해주는 곳 앞인 (C)이다.

19 위 대화에 따르면, A는 B와 C에게 런던의 관광 명소에 대해서 설명해 주고 있다. 따라서 A가 런던 관광 정보를 묻고 있다는 설명은 적절하지 않다.

20 글쓴이가 Sagrada Familia를 방문했고, 1883년부터 공사를 시작했다고(C) 설명하면서 Sagrada Familia와 Park Guell에서 가우디의 창조성을 느낄 수 있다고 말한다(A). 이어서 스페인 여행이 매우 즐거웠고 다시 방문하고 싶다고(B) 말하는 순서로 이어지는 것이 흐름상 가장 자연스럽다.

21 'It'은 볶음밥이 아니라 문맥상 paella를 가리킨다.

22 관광을 했다는 내용이므로 take a tour라는 표현의 과거형인 took a tour가 되는 것이 적절하다.

23 (다)Antoni Gaudi designed both.는 '가우디가 두 개 다 디자인했다.'라는 의미의 문장이다. 따라서 목적어 both가 주어가 되는 수동태 문장으로 바꾸면 ⑤ Both were designed by Antoni Gaudi.로 쓸 수 있다.

24 마지막 문단에 따르면, 글쓴이가 Sagrada Familia에서 본 것은 나무로 된 기둥이 아니라 석조 기둥('Its stone columns stood like big trees.')이다.

25 위 글에서 ② When did work on Park Guell start?(구엘 공원 공사는 언제 시작했는가?)에 대해서는 언급된 바 없다.

26 세 번째 문단에 'In Park Guell, we saw some of Gaudi's creative works like a colorful lizard.(구엘 공원에서, 우리는 형형색색의 도마뱀과 같은 가우디의 창의적인 작품을 보았다.)'라고 언급되어 있다.

27 (A) 스페인이 많은 관광객들에 의해 사랑받는다는 의미이므로 수동태인 is loved가 되는 것이 어법상 적절하다. / (B) be famous for ~: ~로 유명하다 / (C) 다른 팬들과 함께 노래를 부르고 손을 흔들고 소리치면서 축구 팀을 응원했다는 내용이므로 by shouting이 되는 것이 적절하다.

28 위 글에서 ⑤ Where did they get the tickets for the soccer match?(그들은 축구 경기 티켓을 어디서 얻었는가?)에 대해서는 언급되어 있지 않다.

29 위 글에서는 글쓴이인 진우가 여름에 가족들과 스페인을 여행했던 경험에 대해서 이야기하고 있다. 따라서 위 글의 종류로 가장 적절한 것은 ⑤ '기행문'이다.

30 진우는 다른 팬들과 함께 노래를 부르고 손을 흔들고 소리치면서 축구 팀을 응원했다고 언급되어 있다.

Lesson 6 (중간)

01 ④ **02** ③ **03** ① **04** ③
05 The girls like not only listening to music but also reading books.
06 ① **07** ② **08** (1) It is hard to look right at you. (2) 가을
09 ②
10 (1) It is important for them to work out every day.
　 (2) It is so kind of her to help people in need.
11 Not only Yumi but also her sisters speak English very well.
12 ① **13** ⑤ **14** ① **15** ② **16** ② **17** ① **18** ③ **19** ①
20 ② **21** is necessary to protect mudflats **22** ⑤ **23** ①
24 ① **25** ① **26** ② **27** ① **28** ④ **29** ⑤ **30** ③

01 가주어 It - 진주어 to부정사 구문에서 의미상의 주어 'for+목적격'과 함께 사용되는 형용사에는 easy, difficult, hard, possible, impossible, important, dangerous 등이 있다. 사람의 성격이나 태도를 나타내는 형용사 뒤에는 'of+목적격' 형태로 의미상의 주어를 쓴다. 이러한 형용사에는 brave, kind, polite, generous, foolish, stupid, silly 등이 있다.

02 mess의 형용사형 messy(지저분한)가 올바르다.

03 '땅에 둘러싸여 있는 넓은 지역의 물'이라는 영영 풀이가 가리키는 것은 ① lake(호수)이다.

04 make a noise: 소란을 피우다, 부산하게 굴다
make a choice: 선택을 하다

05 상관접속사 'not only A but also B'는 'A 뿐만 아니라 B도 또한'이라는 뜻의 표현으로 A, B에는 문법상 대등한 어구가 온다.

06 ① for him → of him으로 고쳐야 어법상 적절한 문장이 된다.

07 ① play → plays / ③ is → are / ④ are → is / ⑤ write → writing으로 고쳐야 어법상 적절한 문장이 된다.

08 문장의 주어로 쓰인 to부정사가 수식어로 인해 길어진 경우, 보통 to부정사를 뒤로 보내고 대신 주어 자리에 가주어 it을 둔다. 이때 쓰인 it은 가주어이므로 구체적인 뜻이 없으며, '…하는 것은 ~하다'로 해석한다.

09 가주어 It - 진주어 to부정사 구문에서 의미상의 주어 'for+목적격'과 함께 사용되는 형용사에는 easy, difficult, hard, possible, impossible, important, dangerous 등이 있다. 사람의 성격이나 태도를 나타내는 형용사 뒤에는 'of+목적격' 형태로 의미상의 주어를 쓴다. 이러한 형용사에는 brave, kind, polite, generous, foolish, stupid, silly 등이 있다. 빈칸 ⓐ에는 for가 적절하다.

10 가주어 It - 진주어 to부정사 구문의 의미상 주어로 'for, of+목적격'의 형태로 쓸 수 있는데, for는 일반적인 상황에서, of는 사람의

성격이나 태도를 나타낼 때 쓴다.

11 상관접속사 'not only A but also B' 구문에서 A, B에는 문법상 대등한 어구가 온다. 또한 동사는 뒤에 오는 B에 일치시킨다.

12 A가 "평원이 무엇이냐?"라고 질문했으므로 이에 대한 B의 대답으로 가장 적절한 것은 ① They are large areas of flat land.(평평하고 넓은 대지)이다.

13 ⑤ the larger one → the largest one으로 고쳐야 어법상 적절한 문장이 된다.

14 위 글에서는 ① Who is taller, Karl or his dad?(Karl과 아버지 중에 누가 더 키가 큰가?)에 대해서는 언급된 바 없다.

15 A의 말에 대한 B의 대답이 "난 그들이 한국의 유명한 남자 아이돌이라는 걸 들었어."였다. 따라서 빈칸에 들어갈 A의 말로 가장 적절한 것은 ② I wonder who BTS is.(난 BTS가 누군지 궁금해.)이다.

16 위 대화에서 여학생은 사막에 무엇을 가져가야 하는지 물었고, 첫 번째 남학생은 낮 동안 해가 강하기 때문에 모자를 가져가야 한다고 충고한다. 두 번째 남학생은 사막은 밤에 매우 춥다고 들었기 때문에 따뜻한 옷을 챙겨 가야 한다고 충고한다. 따라서 빈칸에는 ② I heard(~라고 들었어.)가 가장 적절하다.

17 위 글에 따르면, ⓑ 60% → 70% / ⓒ heart → lungs / ⓓ reduces → produces / ⓔ trees → oxygen으로 고쳐야 문맥상 적절한 문장이 된다.

18 '갯벌 덕분에, 바다로 가는 물은 깨끗하다'라는 문장이 들어가기에 가장 적절한 곳은 갯벌이 바다로 가는 나쁜 것들을 제거해 준다고 말하는 곳 뒤인 (C)이다.

19 (가) 갯벌이 수분을 머금고 있으므로 홍수(floods)의 피해를 줄일 수 있다는 내용이 들어가는 것이 적절하다.
(나) 갯벌이 지구의 폐 역할을 하기 때문에 지구상의 생명체에게 필요한 산소(oxygen)를 제공한다는 내용이 들어가는 것이 적절하다.

20 위 글에서는 갯벌의 역할로 ② keeping the temperature of water(물의 온도를 유지)에 대해서는 언급된 바 없다.

21 문장의 주어로 쓰인 to부정사가 수식어로 인해 길어진 경우, 보통 to부정사를 뒤로 보내고 대신 주어 자리에 가주어 it을 둔다. 이때 쓰인 it은 가주어이므로 구체적인 뜻이 없으며, '…하는 것은 ~하다'로 해석한다.

22 (A) 갯벌은 바다에 의해 덮여 있다는 내용이므로 are covered가 적절하다.
(B) 갯벌이 지구와 사람, 생명체에게 도움을 주기 때문에 갯벌의 역할을 이해하는 것이 중요하다는 내용이다. 따라서 to부정사의 명사적 용법으로 쓰인 to understand가 적절하다.

23 (가)They는 앞서 언급된 복수 명사를 가리킨다. 따라서 (가)They가 가리키는 것으로 가장 적절한 것은 ① mudflats이

다.

24 위 글에서는 ① '플랑크톤은 갯벌을 오염시킨다.'에 대해서는 언급된 바 없다.

25 위 글의 후반부에 갯벌이 무슨 일을 하는지 알아보자고 말하고 있다. 따라서 바로 뒤에 이어질 내용으로 알맞은 것은 ① 'The various roles of mudflats' (갯벌의 다양한 역할)이다.

26 위 글에 따르면, 갯벌은 생태계에 중요한 역할을 한다. 특히 새의 먹이를 많이 제공한다고 한다고 말하면서 새를 관찰하기에 좋은 장소라고 말하고 있다. 따라서 빈칸에 들어갈 말로 가장 적절한 것은 ② Thus(그러므로)이다.

27 두 번째 문단에 따르면, 지구온난화로 인한 해수면 상승이 갯벌을 망가뜨리고 있다고('Also, the rising of sea levels due to global warming is destroying large areas of mudflats.') 말하고 있다.

28 두 번째 문단에서는 전세계의 갯벌이 위험에 처했다고 이야기하고 있다. 지구온난화로 인한 해수면 상승이 갯벌을 망가뜨리고 있으며, 지난 50년간 한국의 서해 갯벌의 65% 이상이 파괴되었다는 내용이다. 따라서 빈칸에는 각각 (B) destroying, (C) destroyed가 들어가는 것이 적절하다.

29 위 글의 후반부에, 갯벌 걷기를 할 때에는 주의해야 한다고 말하면서, 갯벌을 잘 알고 참여자들을 안전하게 할 수 있는 안내자가 동행해야 한다고 말하고 있다. 따라서 빈칸에는 각각 (A) done, (B) safe가 적절하다.

30 위 글에서 'Usually, shallow mudflat areas are chosen for mudflat hiking.(보통, 얕은 갯벌 지역이 갯벌 걷기를 위해 선택된다)'라고 언급되어 있다.

Lesson 6 (중간) 2회

01 ⑤ 02 ⑤ 03 ② 04 ④ 05 ④ 06 ①
07 I like not only reading stories but also writing them.
08 It was not hard to work out every day.
09 (1) Not only I but also my brother likes chicken. (2) 이서
10 ③ 11 ① 12 ⑤ 13 ⑤ 14 ② 15 ⑤ 16 ④ 17 ①
18 ⑤ 19 ② 20 ② 21 ④ 22 filter 23 ② 24 ④
25 ④ 26 ① 27 ④ 28 ① 29 ③ 30 ④

01 '바다나 호수 등에 있는 매우 작은 동식물'이라는 영영 풀이가 가리키는 것은 ⑤ plankton(플랑크톤)이다.

02 friendly: 친절한, 상냥한

03 ② take가 들어가는 것이 문맥상 적절하다. 나머지 빈칸에는 모두 make가 들어가는 것이 적절하다. / take a class: 수업을 듣다

04 ① for you → of you / ② have → has / ③ is sung → was

sung / ⑤ health → healthy로 고쳐야 어법상 적절한 문장이 된다.

05 ④ play → plays로 고쳐야 어법상 적절한 문장이 된다.

06 ① to play는 to부정사의 부사적 용법으로 사용되었다. 나머지는 모두 to부정사의 명사적 용법(~하는 것)으로 사용되었다.

07 상관접속사 'not only A but also B'는 'A 뿐만 아니라 B도 또한'이라는 뜻의 표현으로 A, B에는 문법상 대등한 어구가 온다.

08 문장의 주어로 쓰인 to부정사가 수식어로 인해 길어진 경우, 보통 to부정사를 뒤로 보내고 대신 주어 자리에 가주어 it을 둔다. 이때 쓰인 it은 가주어이므로 구체적인 뜻이 없으며, '…하는 것은 ~하다'로 해석한다.

09 상관접속사 'not only A but also B' 구문에서 A, B에는 문법상 대등한 어구가 온다. 또한 동사는 뒤에 오는 B에 일치시킨다.

10 ① sing → sings / ② write → writing / ④ generously → generous / ⑤ working → work로 고쳐야 어법상 적절한 문장이 된다.

11 A가 "단양에 가보고 싶어."라고 말했으므로 이에 대한 B의 대답으로 가장 적절한 것은 ① I heard there are famous caves in Danyang.(단양에 유명한 동굴들이 있다고 들었어.)이다.

12 A가 "사막에 무엇을 가져가야 하니?"라고 질문했고 이에 대해 B가 "모자를 가져가야 해."라고 대답했다. 따라서 빈칸에 들어갈 말로 가장 적절한 것은 ⑤ I heard the sun is strong during the day.(낮 동안 해가 강하다고 들었어.)이다.

13 위 대화에 따르면, Karl의 가족은 순천만에 기차를 타고 갔다("Then, let's get on the train.").

14 여학생이 "아마존 열대우림이 지구의 폐라고 들었다"고 말한다. 이에 상대방은 왜 그런지 이유를 물어보고(A), 여학생이 지구의 20%의 산소를 아마존 열대우림이 생산해 낸다고 말한다(C). 이에 상대방이 참 많은 양이라고(B) 말하는 순서로 이어지는 것이 흐름상 가장 자연스럽다.

15 ⓔLike(~와 같이)는 Unlike(~와 다르게)라고 고치는 것이 문맥상 적절하다.

16 "고래에 대해서 정보를 찾고 있어. 내가 어디서 정보를 찾을 수 있는지 알려줄래?"라는 A의 질문에 대해 "물론이지, 제주도에는 해변이 많아."라는 B의 대답은 흐름상 자연스럽지 않다.

17 위 글에 따르면, 빈칸은 물과 식물이 거의 없는 건조한 땅이라고 한다. 따라서 빈칸에 들어갈 말로 가장 적절한 것은 ① deserts(사막)이다.

18 위 글에서는 ⑤ What makes deserts' weather changeable?(무엇이 사막의 날씨를 변덕스럽게 만드는가?)에 대해서는 언급된 바 없다.

19 '또한, 갯벌은 육지에서 바다로 흘러가는 물을 여과한다.'라는 문장이 들어가기에 가장 적절한 곳은 갯벌이 물 속에 있는 나쁜 것들이 바다로 가기 전에 제거해 준다고 말하는 곳 앞인 (B)이다.

20 ⓑ 선행사가 people이므로 관계대명사는 who가 적절하다. / ⓒ by catching: 낚시를 해서 / ⓔ 관계대명사 that절은 a large number of birds를 수식한다. / ⓖ as는 '~로서'라는 뜻으로 사용되고 있다. / ⓗ it은 가주어로 to protect mudflats을 의미한다.

21 위 글에서는 갯벌에 대해서 소개하면서, 갯벌이 어떤 식으로 인간과 환경에 유익한지에 대해서 설명하고 있다. 따라서 위 글의 제목으로 가장 적절한 것은 ④ Mudflats are nature's gift to living things(갯벌은 생명체에게 주는 자연의 선물)이다.

22 filter: 여과하다, 거르다

23 위 글에 따르면, 갯벌은 바닷물을 정화하는 것이 아니라 바다로 흘러 들어가는 물을 정화시킨다('They remove bad things in the water before it enters the sea. Thanks to mudflats, the water that reaches the sea is clean.').

24 위 글에서는 ④ What kinds of seafood can people get on mudflats?(사람들은 어떤 종류의 해산물을 갯벌에서 얻을 수 있는가?)에 대해서는 언급된 바 없다.

25 첫 문단에서는 갯벌이 많은 방식으로 사람과 지구, 해양 생명체에 도움을 준다고 말하고 있다. 따라서 빈칸에 들어갈 말로 가장 적절한 것은 ④ roles(역할들)이다.

26 위 글에서는 갯벌은 해안가에 있는 넓은 진흙으로 된 지역이라고 정의를 내리면서 많은 방식으로 사람과 지구, 해양 생명체에 도움을 준다고 말하고 있다. 따라서 위 글의 제목으로 가장 적절한 것은 ① '갯벌의 역할'이다.

27 ④는 앞서 언급한 플랑크톤과 같은 물에 사는 작은 생명체, 게와 물고기를 가리킨다. 나머지는 모두 갯벌(mudflats)을 가리킨다.

28 위 글에서는 ① What makes tides happen?(무엇이 밀물과 썰물을 만드는가?)에 대해서는 언급된 바 없다.

29 ① by he → by him / ② created by → was created by / ④ was wrote → was written / ⑤ Was → Were로 고쳐야 어법상 적절한 문장이 된다.

30 두 번째 문단에서 'Not only very small living things like plankton but also crabs and fish live there. Mudflats provide various types of food for them.(플랑크톤과 같은 매우 작은 생명체 뿐만 아니라 게와 물고기가 갯벌에 산다. 갯벌은 그들을 위해 다양한 종류의 먹이를 제공한다.)라고 언급되어 있다. ④ '대부분의 물고기들은 플랑크톤을 좋아한다.'에 대해서는 언급된 바 없다.

Lesson 7 (기말)

> **01** ③ **02** ①, ④   **03** ④ **04** ⑤ **05** ③ **06** ② **07** ⑤
> **08** (A) ⓒ (B) Mark wanted me to lend him some money.
> **09** I like the watch which my uncle bought me.
> **10** The Brooklyn Dodgers was the team which[that] he wanted to join.
> **11** ④ **12** ① **13** ① **14** ⑤ **15** ④ **16** ②
> **17** (A) Jina to open the windows for fresh air
>   (B) Chris to clean the board
> **18** (1) That's the actor whom[who/that] I saw in the magazine.
>   (2) The store didn't have the jeans which[that] I wanted to buy.
> **19** ③ **20** ③ **21** ③ **22** ③ **23** ④ **24** ⑤ **25** ① **26** ⑤
> **27** ① **28** ④ **29** ④ **30** ④

01 '같은 팀에 있는 선수'라는 영영 풀이가 가리키는 것은 ③ teammate(팀의 동료)이다.

02 ① fail: 실패하다 ④ lend: 빌려주다

03 earn the respect of ~: ~의 존경을 받다

04 ⑤ to tap → tap 또는 tapping으로 고쳐야 어법상 적절한 문장이 된다.

05 두 문장을 연결할 때 겹치는 부분을 선행사로 만들고 관계대명사를 이용해 연결할 수 있다. 이때 관계대명사가 이끄는 절에서 관계대명사 who, which 또는 that이 주어 역할을 할 때 주격 관계대명사, 목적어 역할을 할 때는 목적격 관계대명사라고 한다. who는 선행사가 사람일 때, which는 선행사가 사물일 때, that은 두 경우 모두 쓸 수 있다. 목적격 관계대명사는 생략 가능하지만, 주격 관계대명사는 불가능하다.

06 <보기>와 ②who는 목적격 관계대명사로 선행사인 a player와 two sons를 수식하는 절을 이끈다. 나머지는 모두 관계대명사 who가 주격 관계대명사로 사용되었다.

07 5형식 문장에서 동사 allow, get, encourage, permit, force 등은 목적격보어로 to부정사를 쓴다. 동사 let은 목적격보어로 동사 원형을 쓴다.

08 5형식 문장에서 동사 want는 목적보어로 to부정사 형태를 취한다. 따라서 ⓒlending은 to lend로 고치는 것이 어법상 적절하다.

09 두 문장을 연결할 때 겹치는 부분을 선행사로 만들고 관계대명사를 이용해 연결할 수 있다. 이때 관계대명사가 이끄는 절에서 관계대명사 who, which 또는 that이 목적어 역할을 할 때 목적격 관계대명사라고 한다. who는 선행사가 사람일 때, which는 선행사가 사물일 때, that은 두 경우 모두 쓸 수 있다.

10 두 문장을 연결할 때 겹치는 부분을 선행사로 만들고 관계대명사를

이용해 연결할 수 있다. 이때 관계대명사가 이끄는 절에서 관계대 명사 who, which 또는 that이 목적어 역할을 할 때 목적격 관계 대명사라고 한다. who는 선행사가 사람일 때, which는 선행사가 사물일 때, that은 두 경우 모두 쓸 수 있다.

11 ④ going → to go로 고쳐야 어법상 적절한 문장이 된다.

12 대화 흐름상, A가 "a walk in the park"가 무슨 뜻이냐고 묻는 말이 들어가는 것이 적절하다.

13 대화 흐름상, A가 "a walk in the park"가 무슨 뜻이냐고 묻자 B 가 관용적 표현의 뜻인 "식은 죽 먹기"라고 알려주는 표현이 들어 가는 것이 자연스럽다.

14 A가 "그건 무슨 의미니?"라고 질문했으므로 이에 대한 B의 대답 으로 가장 적절한 것은 ⑤ we can't achieve anything without hard work(노력 없이는 어느 것도 이룰 수 없다)이다.

15 "사막에 무엇을 가져야 하니?"라는 A의 질문에 대해 "난 맛있 는 디저트가 먹고 싶어."라는 B의 대답은 흐름상 자연스럽지 않 다.

16 A의 말에 대해 B가 그것이 무슨 뜻이냐고 묻자, A는 도서관에서 "열심히 공부하는 것"이라고 대답하였다. 따라서 빈칸에 들어갈 A의 말로 가장 적절한 것은 ② hit the books(열심히 공부하다, 벼락치기 하다)이다.

17 동사 ask, allow, get, encourage, permit, force, want 등은 목적격보어로 to부정사를 쓴다. 따라서 위와 같은 동사를 쓸 경우, '주어+동사+목적어+to부정사'의 순서가 된다.

18 두 문장을 연결할 때 겹치는 부분을 선행사로 만들고 관계대명사를 이용해 연결할 수 있다. 이때 관계대명사가 이끄는 절에서 관계대 명사 who, which 또는 that이 목적어 역할을 할 때 목적격 관계 대명사라고 한다. who는 선행사가 사람일 때, which는 선행사가 사물일 때, that은 두 경우 모두 쓸 수 있다. 목적격 관계대명사는 생략 가능하다.

19 위 글에서는 디자이너라는 꿈을 이루기 위해 글쓴이가 생각하는 필 요한 일에 대해서 이야기하고 있다. 따라서 위 글의 제목으로 가장 적절한 것은 ③ How I Will Achieve My Dream(어떻게 내 꿈을 이룰 것인가)이다.

20 ⓒHis는 Robinson의 팀 동료를 의미한다. 나머지는 모두 Robinson을 가리키는 대명사이다.

21 (가)moved는 '감동시키다'라는 뜻의 동사로 사용되었다. / ① 흘 러가다, ② 이사하다, ④ (일정을) 옮기다, ⑤ 움직이다

22 매해 4월 15일은 Jackie Robinson을 기리는 날로 "Jackie Robinson의 날"로 불리고 있다고 한다. 따라서 빈칸 (나)에 들어 갈 말로 가장 적절한 것은 현재시제의 수동태인 ③ is called이다.

23 (A) on the shoulder: 어깨를, 어깨 위에 / (B) present A with B: A에게 B를 수여하다[주다] / (C) 42번이 Robinson에게 헌 정된 번호라서 아무도 그 번호를 등번호로 쓰지 않지만 매년 4월

15일에는 모든 선수들이 그 번호를 쓴다고 한다. 따라서 문맥상 however(그러나)가 적절하다. because는 접속사로서 주어와 동사를 이끈다.

24 마지막 문단에 따르면, 매년 Robinson의 생일이 아니라 Robinson을 기리는 날이기 때문에 모든 선수들이 Robinson의 등번호였던 42번이 쓰인 옷을 입는다고 언급되어 있다.

25 첫 문단에 따르면, 처음에는 사람들이 Robinson을 향해 야유했지만 나중에는 다른 선수들과 팬들의 존경을 받았다고 언급되어 있다.

26 (A) Robinson은 메이저리그에서 경기를 한 최초의 선수라고 언급되어 있다. 따라서 인종차별적인 구분선이 부숴졌다는 내용이므로 수동태 문장을 만드는 과거분사 broken이 적절하다.
(B) Robinson은 재능있는 선수였지만 다른 선수들이 그와 경기하고 싶어하지 않았고 사람들이 그를 향해 야유를 했다는 내용이다. 따라서 과거시제의 동사 shouted가 적절하다.
(C) 전치사 at이 쓰였기 때문에 동명사형인 batting이 들어가는 것이 적절하다.

27 날짜 앞에는 전치사 on을 쓰는 것이 적절하다. / on the team: 팀에 속해 있는

28 선행사가 a player이기 때문에 사람이 선행사일 경우 쓰는 목적격 관계대명사 that 또는 who를 쓰는 것이 어법상 적절하다.

29 ⓐ Robinson이 재능있는 선수였지만 그의 팀 선수들이 그와 경기하고 싶어하지 않았고 사람들이 그를 향해 야유를 했다는 내용이다. 따라서 Although(~에도 불구하고)가 들어가는 것이 적절하다.
ⓑ Robinson이 팀에 속해 있었기 때문에 호텔들이 그의 팀을 거절했다는 내용이다. 따라서 because가 적절하다.
ⓒ Robinson이 타석에 서 있을 때 사람들이 야유를 보냈다는 내용이다. 따라서 접속사 When이 적절하다.

30 위 글에서는 ④ How many hours did Jackie Robinson practice?(Robinson은 몇 시간을 연습했는가?)에 대해서는 언급된 바 없다.

Lesson 7 (기말) 2회

01 ④ 02 ④ 03 ① 04 ② 05 ③ 06 ①, ④
07 Mr. Johnson told us to shake hands after the game.
08 ①
09 (A) Smith is the boy who[whom] I met in Paris.
  (B) The blue bike is the gift[present] which I bought there for my sister.
10 ③ 11 ③

---

12 (1) told her to (2) expected him to pass
  (3) advised us not to make
13 who is playing basketball outside 14 ② 15 ④
16 important, you never give up (It's important that you never give up.)
17 ④ 18 ① 19 ④ 20 ⑤ 21 ③ 22 ② 23 ① 24 ⑤
25 ② 26 ⑤ 27 ④ 28 ⑤ 29 ③
30 he was the first African American player on a Major League team.

01 turn down: ~을 거절하다, (소리를) 낮추다

02 5형식 문장에서 advise와 allow, tell, help 등은 목적보어로 to부정사를 쓴다. let은 사역동사로 목적보어로 동사원형을 취한다.

03 'couldn't believe their eyes'는 '그들의 눈을 믿을 수 없었다'라는 뜻이다.

04 두 문장을 연결할 때 겹치는 부분을 선행사로 만들고 관계대명사를 이용해 연결할 수 있다. 이때 who는 선행사가 사람일 때, which는 선행사가 사물일 때, that은 두 경우 모두 쓸 수 있다.

05 ① go → to go / ② tried → to try / ④ became → become / ⑤ left → leave로 고쳐야 어법상 적절한 문장이 된다.

06 목적격 관계대명사는 생략 가능하지만 주격 관계대명사는 생략이 불가능하다.

07 5형식 문장에서 '~에게 …하라고 말하다'라는 뜻으로 쓰일 때 동사 tell은 목적보어로 to부정사를 쓴다.

08 ① what → that 또는 which로 고쳐야 어법상 적절한 문장이 된다.

09 두 문장을 연결할 때 겹치는 부분을 선행사로 만들고 관계대명사를 이용해 연결할 수 있다. 이때 관계대명사가 이끄는 절에서 관계대명사 who(whom), which 또는 that이 목적어 역할을 할 때 목적격 관계대명사라고 한다. who(whom)는 선행사가 사람일 때, which는 선행사가 사물일 때, that은 두 경우 모두 쓸 수 있다.

10 ① which I am carrying it → which I am carrying
② which the lady is looking for it → which the lady is looking for
④ which I bought it → which I bought
⑤ who I met her → who I met

11 ① 선행사는 the dress이다. ② 선행사는 the guy이다.
④ 선행사는 the girl이다. ⑤ 선행사는 the gift이다.

12 5형식 문장에서 동사 tell, expect, advise 등은 목적보어로 to부정사를 취한다. 따라서 위와 같은 동사를 쓸 경우, '주어+동사+목적어+to부정사'의 순서가 된다.

13 두 문장을 연결할 때 겹치는 부분을 선행사로 만들고 관계대명사를 이용해 연결할 수 있다. 이때 관계대명사가 이끄는 절에서 관계대

명사 who, which 또는 that이 주어 역할을 할 때 주격 관계대명사라고 한다. who는 선행사가 사람일 때 쓸 수 있다.

14 keep my fingers crossed는 직역하면 '손가락을 꼰 채로 있다'라는 뜻으로, '행운을 빌어주다'라는 관용적 의미로 사용된다.

15 A가 바둑을 두고 싶다고 말했고, 이에 대한 B의 대답이 "물론이지."였다. 따라서 빈칸에 들어갈 말로 가장 적절한 것은 ④ play baduk with me(나와 바둑을 둘래?)이다.

16 'It's important that 주어+동사 ~'는 '(주어)가 (동사)하는 것은 중요해.'라는 뜻으로 어떤 일을 강조하거나 조언할 때 쓸 수 있는 표현이다.

17 위 대화에 따르면, 지호는 오디션에서 처음으로 떨어진 것이 아니라 항상 오디션에서 떨어진다고("I always fail auditions.") 언급했다.

18 지호가 꿈을 이룰 수 없을 것 같다고 좌절하자, Amy는 무슨 뜻인지 묻는다(ⓐ). 이에 지호는 자신이 배우가 되고 싶은데 계속 오디션에서 떨어진다고 대답한다(ⓒ). 이에 Amy는 어떤 배우를 아는지 묻자(ⓑ), 지호는 그가 유명한 배우라고 대답하자(ⓓ) Amy가 그도 역시 수많은 오디션에서 떨어졌다고 위로하는 순서로 이어지는 것이 흐름상 가장 자연스럽다.

19 "슬퍼 보인다. 무슨 일이니?"라는 A의 말에 대해 "행운을 빌게."라는 B의 대답은 흐름상 자연스럽지 않다.

20 A는 기타를 잘 치고 싶어서 B에게 조언을 구하고 있다. B의 말에 대한 A의 반응이 "내가 계속 연습을 해야 한다는 말이니?"였다. 따라서 빈칸에 들어갈 B의 말로 가장 적절한 것은 ⑤ you play as often as you can(가능한 한 자주 기타 연주를 해.)이다.

21 '마침내, 로빈슨은 다른 선수들과 팬들의 존중을 얻었다.'라는 문장이 들어가기에 가장 적절한 곳은 한 동료가 그를 지지했고 그로 인해 그가 더 열심히 경기를 하게 되었으며 그의 팀이 상을 받았다고 이야기하고 있는 곳인 (다)이다.

22 위 글에서 Robinson은 재능있는 선수였지만 인종차별 때문에 재능을 펼치지 못하고 있었다. 그러나 야구에 시간과 에너지를 집중해서 그의 팀이 챔피언십 상을 수상하는 공로를 세웠다고 한다. 따라서 위 글의 내용에 맞는 속담으로 가장 적절한 것은 ② Practice makes perfect.(연습이 완벽을 만든다.)이다.

23 (A) Robinson이 재능있는 선수였지만 그의 팀 선수들이 그와 경기하고 싶어 하지 않았고 사람들이 그를 향해 야유를 했다는 내용이다. 따라서 Although(~에도 불구하고)가 들어가는 것이 적절하다. / (B) become great at: ~를 매우 잘하게 되다 (C) help는 5형식 문장에서 준사역동사로 쓰일 때 동사원형이나 to부정사를 목적보어로 취한다. 따라서 to play가 적절하다.

24 위 글에서 Robinson은 재능 있는 선수였지만 인종차별 때문에 재능을 펼치지 못하고 있었다. 그러나 야구에 시간과 에너지를 집중해서 그의 팀이 챔피언십 상을 수상하는 공로를 세웠다고 한다. 따

라서 위 글의 제목으로 가장 적절한 것은 ⑤ Robinson, a player who broke the color line(인종 차별을 깬 선수, Robinson)이 적절하다.

25 첫 문단에 'Although Robinson was a talented player and a gentle person, his teammates did not want to play with him.'라고 언급되어 있다.

26 (A) Robinson은 재능 있는 선수였지만 그의 팀 선수들은 그와 경기하고 싶어 하지 않았고 사람들이 그를 향해 야유를 했다는 내용이다. 따라서 Although(~에도 불구하고)가 들어가는 것이 적절하다.
(B) Robinson이 팀에 속해 있었기 때문에 호텔들이 그의 팀을 거절했다는 내용이다. 따라서 because가 적절하다.
(C) Robinson이 타석에 서 있을 때는 사람들이 야유를 보냈다는 내용이다. 따라서 접속사 When이 적절하다.

27 Robinson은 재능있는 선수였지만 그의 팀 선수들은 그와 경기하고 싶어하지 않았다. 그렇지만 Robinson은 노력해서 사람들이 좋아하는 선수가 되겠다고 다짐했고 실제로 그 꿈이 이루어졌다고 한다. 따라서 빈칸에 들어갈 말로 가장 적절하지 않은 것은 ④ which people like이다. 선행사가 사람일 경우 목적격 관계대명사로 which는 쓸 수 없다.

28 위 글에서 Robinson은 재능있는 선수였지만 인종 차별 때문에 재능을 펼치지 못하고 있었다. 따라서 (가)color line의 뜻은 ⑤ '인종 차별'이다.

29 위 글에 따르면, Jackie Robinson이 유능한 선수여서 동료들로부터 소외당한 것이 아니라 흑인이었기 때문에 소외당했다고 언급되어 있다.

30 위 글에 따르면, Jackie Robinson이 야구 선수로서 어려움을 겪은 이유는 그가 메이저리그 최초의 흑인 선수였기 때문이라고 언급되어 있다.

Lesson 8 (기말) 1회

01 ① **02** ② **03** ① **04** ③, ⑤ **05** ③ **06** ④
07 I'm not sure, but Sumin may offer me some help. **08** ⑤
09 Andy has just finished decorating his bedroom.
10 are → be / who → that[which] / needs → need **11** ③
12 ⑤ **13** ② **14** ⑤
15 I'm surprised that you can recommend books. **16** ②
17 ④ **18** ⑤ **19** ④ **20** ② **21** ② **22** ③ **23** ① **24** ⑤
25 ⑤ **26** ⑤ **27** ⑤ **28** ⑤ **29** ① **30** ②

01 cry의 변화형은 cry - cried - cried이다.

02 위에서부터 순서대로, traditional(전통적인), add up(합산하

다), personal(개인적인), take place(발생하다)가 들어가는 것이 문맥상 가장 자연스럽다.

03 (A) 전체 문장의 시제가 과거이므로 take place(발생하다)의 과거형인 took place가 적절하다.
(B) 전체 문장의 시제가 과거이므로 moved around(돌아다녔다)가 적절하다.

04 ③ my person experience는 my personal experience로, ⑤ I have lived in Busan a month ago.는 I lived in Busan a month ago.로 고치는 것이 어법상 적절하다.

05 과거의 어느 시점부터 현재까지 이어져 오고 있는 일을 표현할 때 현재완료시제(has/have+p.p.)를 이용해 나타낼 수 있다. 이때 전치사 since와 함께 쓰면 '~ 이후로'라는 뜻을 나타낸다.

06 조동사 may는 '~일지도 모른다'는 의미로는 추측을 나타내며, '~해도 된다'는 의미로 쓰일 땐 허락을 구하는 표현이 된다. 부정형은 may 뒤에 not을 붙여 'may+not+동사원형'의 형태로 쓴다.

07 조동사 may는 '~일지도 모른다'는 의미로 쓰일 때 추측을 나타내는 표현이 된다.

08 과거의 어느 시점부터 현재까지 이어져 오고 있는 일을 표현할 때 현재완료시제(has/have+p.p.)를 이용해 나타낼 수 있다. 이때 전치사 since와 함께 쓰면 '~ 이후로'라는 뜻을 나타낸다.

09 과거에 시작한 일이 현재에 막 끝났음을 의미할 때 현재완료시제(have p.p)를 이용할 수 있다. 이때 부사 just(막, 방금)를 사용할 수 있다.

10 (1) 조동사 뒤에는 동사원형을 쓴다. 따라서 may are는 may be로 쓰는 것이 어법상 적절하다.
(2) 선행사가 some things이므로 관계대명사는 who가 아니라 that이나 which를 쓰는 것이 적절하다.
(3) 주어가 1인칭 단수 I이므로 동사는 needs가 아니라 need가 적절하다.

11 이어동사는 대명사가 목적어로 쓰일 경우 두 단어 중간에 쓴다. 따라서 ⓒ turn off it → turn it off로 고쳐야 어법상 적절한 문장이 된다.

12 'It's important that 주어+동사 ~'는 '(주어)가 (동사)하는 것이 중요해.'라는 뜻으로 어떤 일을 강조하거나 조언할 때 쓸 수 있는 표현이다.

13 위 대화에 따르면, A는 스마트워치를 소개하면서 말만하면 검색이 된다고("Also, you can search for anything just by talking to it.") 말하고 있다.

14 위 대화에 따르면, 인공지능 사서인 Terry는 사람들이 원하는 책을 가져다줄 수 있는 것이 아니라 어디 있는지 알려줄 수 있다고 언급되어 있다.

15 위 대화에 따르면, 인공지능 사서인 Terry는 사람들이 원하는 책을 추천하고 어디 있는지 알려줄 수 있다고 한다. 따라서 빈칸 (A)

에 들어갈 반응으로 적절한 것은 "I'm surprised that you can recommend books.(네가 책을 추천할 수 있다니 놀랍다.)"이다.

16 위 대화에 따르면, 인공지능 사서인 Terry는 사람들이 원하는 책을 추천하고 어디 있는지 알려줄 수 있다고 한다. 따라서 빈칸 (B)에 들어갈 Sena의 반응으로 적절하지 않은 것은 ② Can I help you?(제가 도와드릴까요?)이다.

17 "제가 여기 앉아도 될까요?"라는 A의 질문에 대해 "네, 됩니다. 이 자리는 주인이 있어요."라는 B의 대답은 흐름상 자연스럽지 않다.

18 위 대화에 따르면, A가 언급한 어플리케이션은 도시의 지도와 거리 사진을 볼 수 있다고 한다.

19 A가 스마트 냉장고를 보고 싶냐고 묻자, B는 그렇다고 대답하면서 이 버튼들은 무엇이냐고 묻는다(C). A는 그 버튼은 냉장고 안에 들어있는 품목들을 보여주고 다른 버튼은 요리법을 보여준다고 (A) 대답한다. 이에 B가 냉장고가 그런 일을 할 수 있다니 놀랍다고(B) 말하는 순서로 이어지는 것이 흐름상 가장 자연스럽다.

20 ⓐ has caused → have caused ⓒ add → added
ⓓ cannot → which cannot ⓔ suits → suit

21 위 글에서는 과학과 기술의 진보가 사회를 변화시키고 있다고 이야기하면서 미래에 우리의 삶이 어떻게 변하게 될 것인지에 대해서 설명하고 있다. 따라서 위 글의 의도로 가장 적절한 것은 ② to inform(정보를 알려주기 위해)이다.

22 문장의 순서가 '의문사+주어+조동사+동사'인 간접의문문을 직접의문문으로 바꾸면, '의문사+조동사+주어+동사(원형)'이 된다.

23 어플리케이션으로 쇼핑할 때, 그것이 자동으로 품목을 더하고 뺄 수 있게 도와준다고 이야기하고 있다. 따라서 빈칸에 들어갈 말로 가장 적절한 것은 ① If he puts an item back(그가 물건을 제자리에 갖다놓으면)이다.

24 (C)charge는 '(돈을) 청구하다'라는 뜻의 동사로 사용되었다. /
①: 담당, 책임 ②, ③, ④: 요금

25 세 번째 문단에서 수민이는 3D 프린터를 이용해 원하는 옷을 디자인할 수 있다고 설명하고 있다. 따라서 빈칸에 들어갈 말로 가장 적절한 것은 ⑤ fashion designer(패션 디자이너)이다.

26 세 번째 문단에서 수민이는 3D 프린터를 이용해 원하는 옷을 디자인할 수 있다고 설명하고 있다.

27 세 번째 문단에서 수민이는 3D 프린터를 이용해 원하는 옷을 디자인할 수 있다고 말하면서 'She can choose colors and materials and can design clothes that fit her body and suit her tastes.'(그녀는 색과 재료를 고를 수 있고 자신의 몸에 어울리고 취향에 맞는 옷을 디자인할 수 있다)라고 설명하고 있다.

28 위 글에서는 인공지능 간호사가 하는 일에 대해서 설명하면서 그것

이 미래에 변화를 가져올 것이라고 말하고 있다. 따라서 위 글의 제목으로 가장 적절한 것은 ⑤ 'AI가 가져올 수 있는 미래의 모습'이다.

29 위 글에서는 인공지능 간호사가 하는 일에 대해서 설명하면서 그것이 미래에 변화를 가져올 것이라고 말하고 있다. 따라서 빈칸에 들어갈 말로 가장 적절한 것은 ① changes(변화들)이다.

30 위 글에서는 인공지능 기술을 이용해 학생들의 학교 생활이 어떻게 변화할 수 있는지에 대해서 설명하고 있다. 따라서 위 글의 요지로 가장 적절한 것은 ② In the future, there will be several changes in the school.(미래에, 학교에는 몇몇 변화가 생길 것이다.)이다.

Lesson 8 (기말)

01 ① 02 ① 03 ⑤ 04 ① 05 ③ 06 ②
07 (1) I have missed you so much.
　　(2) Have you ever heard of this actor?
　　(3) There may be other people that I don't know.
08 Julie has known Mr. Brown for ten years.
09 Chris may not know the answer.　　10 ①
11 I have lost my car.　12 ②　13 ⑤　14 ②
15 Can you recommend one, please?　16 ③
17 ①　18 ②　19 ③　20 ④　21 ④　22 ①　23 ①　24 ②
25 ③　26 ⑤　27 ⑤　28 ③
29 가상 카드가 물건의 가격을 모두 더하고, 나중에 청구하는 것
30 ②

01 silence - silent: 침묵하는
importance - important: 중요한
difference - different: 다른
excellence - excellent: 뛰어난, 탁월한

02 '누군가에게 돈을 내라고 요청하다'라는 영영 풀이가 가리키는 것은 ① charge(청구하다)이다.

03 동사 forget의 변화형은 forget - forgot - forgotten이다.

04 patient: 환자; 인내심 있는

05 ⓑ being → been
ⓓ have just drawn → has just drawn

06 ② may not interested → may not be interested로 고쳐야 어법상 적절한 문장이 된다.

07 (1), (2) 현재완료 시제는 과거부터 현재까지의 시점을 표현하는 시제로, 경험(~한 적 있다), 완료(막 ~를 끝마쳤다), 계속(~해 오고 있다), 결과(과거의 일이 원인이 되어 현재까지 영향을 미치는 경우)를 나타낼 때 쓸 수 있다.

(3) 조동사 may는 '~일지도 모른다'는 의미로 쓰일 때는 추측을 나타내는 표현이 된다.

08 과거의 어느 시점부터 현재까지 이어져 오고 있는 일을 표현할 때 현재완료 시제(has/have p.p)를 이용해 나타낼 수 있다. 이때 전치사 for와 함께 쓰면 '동안'이라는 뜻을 나타낸다.

09 조동사 may는 '~일지도 모른다'는 의미로는 추측을 나타내며, '~해도 된다'는 의미로 쓰일 때는 허락을 구하는 표현이 된다. 부정형은 may 뒤에 not을 붙여 'may+not+동사원형'의 형태로 쓴다.

10 ① 'She has gone to London.'은 '그녀는 런던으로 떠났다.'라는 의미로 현재까지 런던으로 떠나 있는 상태를 의미한다. 'She is planning to go to London.'은 '그녀는 런던에 갈 예정이다.'라는 의미의 문장이다.

11 현재완료 시제는 과거부터 현재까지의 시점을 표현하는 시제로, 경험(~한 적이 있다), 완료(막 ~를 끝마쳤다), 계속(~해 오고 있다), 결과(과거의 일이 원인이 되어 현재까지 영향을 미치는 경우)를 나타낼 때 쓸 수 있다. 위 경우에는 과거에 자동차를 잃어버렸고 현재까지 잃어버린 상태이므로 '결과'에 해당하는 현재완료 시제라고 할 수 있다.

12 B의 말을 듣고 A는 자신이 말한 거대한 우산에 대해서 더 자세히 설명하고 있다. 따라서 빈칸에 들어갈 말로 가장 적절한 것은 ② Can you tell me more?(더 자세히 말해줄 수 있니?)이다.

13 위 대화에 따르면, 인공지능 사서인 Terry는 사람들이 원하는 책을 도서관 책들 중에서 추천하고 어디 있는지 알려줄 수 있다.

14 위 대화에 따르면, 인공지능 사서인 Terry는 사람들이 원하는 책을 추천하고 어디 있는지 알려줄 수 있다고 한다. 따라서 빈칸 ⓐ에 들어갈 반응으로 적절한 것은 "I'm surprised that you can recommend books.(네가 책을 추천할 수 있다니 놀랍다.)"이다.

15 상대방에게 추천을 요청할 때, "Can you recommend ~?"(~를 추천해 주실 수 있나요?)와 같은 표현을 쓸 수 있다. "Could/Would you recommend ~ for me?"와 바꿔 쓸 수 있다.

16 "히터를 끄는 것을 잊어버렸어."라는 A의 말에 대해 "우리는 우주에서 자동차를 운전할 거야."라는 B의 대답은 흐름상 자연스럽지 않다.

17 (A) 불을 끄고 켜기 위해 손을 사용할 필요 없이 어플리케이션을 이용하면 된다고 이야기하고 있다. 따라서 hands가 적절하다.
(B) Can you tell me how to ~?: ~하는 방법을 말해줄 수 있니?
(C) 불을 끄고 켜기 위해 어플리케이션에 "불을 켜" 또는 "불을 꺼 줘"라고 말하면 된다고 말하고 있다. 따라서 빈칸에는 clear(알아듣기 쉬운)가 적절하다.

18 위 글에서는 많은 것들이 인간처럼 작동할 수 있다고 이야기하면서, 운전자가 없는 자율주행 자동차나 음성 인식 스마트폰을 예로

들고 있다. 따라서 위 글은 ② '인공지능'에 대한 글이다.

19 위 글의 후반부에 글쓴이는 우리가 이미 미래에 살고 있다는 것이 놀랍다고('I'm surprised that we're already living in the future.') 언급하고 있다.

20 첫 문단에서는 미래에는 쇼핑이 더욱 쉬워질 것이라고 말하면서, 줄 서는 일도 없고 카운터도 없으며 단지 특별한 쇼핑 어플리케이션만 있으면 된다고 말한다(다). 원하는 물건을 갖고 오면 어플이 자동으로 결제 목록에 물건을 추가하고, 다시 갖다 놓으면 자동으로 목록에서 뺀다고 한다(가). 쇼핑이 끝나면 돈을 내기 위해 줄을 설 필요 없이 나중에 지불할 돈을 청구한다고(나) 말하는 순서로 이어지는 것이 흐름상 가장 자연스럽다.

21 '수민이는 또한 3D프린터를 이용해 집에서 옷을 만드는 것을 좋아한다'라는 문장이 들어가기에 가장 적절한 곳은 색과 재료를 선택해 옷을 디자인할 수 있다는 곳인 (ㄹ)이다.

22 비교급을 강조할 때는 비교급 앞에 much, still, even, far, a lot 등의 부사(구)를 쓰며 '(...보다) 훨씬 더 ~한'이라는 의미를 갖는다. very는 원급의 형용사(또는 부사)를 수식하며, 비교급은 수식하지 않는다.

23 주어진 단어들은 문맥상 '우리의 미래가 어떤 모습일지'라는 뜻으로 사용되었다. 따라서 ① what our lives may be like가 적절하다.

24 (라)charge는 '(돈을) 청구하다'라는 뜻으로 사용되었다.
② charge는 '~를 담당하다, 책임지다'라는 뜻으로 사용되었다.

25 (마)may는 '~일지도 모른다'라는 뜻의 추측을 나타내는 표현으로 사용되었다. ③ may는 '~해도 된다'라는 뜻의 허락하는 표현이다.

26 병원에서 환자가 체온이 올라가면 인공지능 간호사 약을 처방해서 체온을 떨어뜨리게 도와준다는 내용이다. 따라서 ⓔincrease(증가시키다)는 lower(낮추다)로 고치는 것이 적절하다.

27 위 글에서는 ⑤ What has made many difficulties in our lives so far?(여태까지 우리의 삶에서 많은 어려움을 만든 것은 무엇인가?)에 대해서는 언급된 바 없다.

28 ③ charge는 '(돈을) 청구하다'라는 의미로 사용되었다.

29 (나) 문단에 따르면, AI 기술을 통해 쇼핑을 하고 줄을 서서 지불하지 않고, 가상의 카드가 가격을 모두 합산해 나중에 지불해야 하는 돈을 청구할 것이라고 말하고 있다. 따라서 지시대명사 that이 가리키는 것은 위의 내용이다.

30 위 글에서는 과학과 기술의 진보가 우리 삶에 많은 변화를 일으켰다고 말하면서 미래에는 더 많은 변화들이 생길 것이라고 말하고 있다. 따라서 위 글의 제목으로 가장 적절한 것은 ② Changing Society(변화하는 사회)이다.

MEMO

적중 100 + 특별부록

Plan B

우리학교
최신기출

시사 · 박준언 교과서를 배우는

학교 시험문제 분석 · 모음 · 해설집

전국단위 학교 시험문제 수집 및 분석
출제 빈도가 높은 문제 위주로 선별
문제 풀이에 필요한 상세한 해설

중2-2
영어

시사 · 박준언